# VOICES OF
# DISSENT

# VOICES OF DISSENT

## CRITICAL READINGS IN AMERICAN POLITICS

Seventh Edition

**William F. Grover**
*Saint Michael's College*

**Joseph G. Peschek**
*Hamline University*

PEARSON

Longman

New York  San Francisco  Boston
London  Toronto  Sydney  Tokyo  Singapore  Madrid
Mexico City  Munich  Paris  Cape Town  Hong Kong  Montreal

Editor-in-Chief: Eric Stano
Executive Marketing Manager: Ann Stypuloski
Production Manager: Denise Phillip
Project Coordination, Text Design, and Electronic Page Makeup: TexTech International
Cover Design Manager: Wendy Ann Fredericks
Cover Designer: Kay Petronio
Cover Photo: © Akhtar Soomro/epa/Corbis
Manufacturing Buyer: Roy Pickering
Printer and Binder: R.R. Donnelley & Sons/Crawfordsville
Cover Printer: R.R. Donnelley & Sons/Crawfordsville

Library of Congress Cataloging-in-Publication Data

Voices of dissent : critical readings in American politics / [edited by] William F. Grover,
Joseph G. Peschek. —7th ed.
    p. cm.
  Includes bibliographical references.
  ISBN-13: 978-0-205-56001-1
  ISBN-10:     0-205-56001-6
1. United States—Politics and government.   I. Grover, William F., 1956–
II. Peschek, Joseph G.
  JK21.V65 2008
  320.973—dc22

                                                        2007020914

Please visit us at www.ablongman.com

ISBN 13: 978-0-205-56001-1
ISBN 10:     0-205-56001-6

1 2 3 4 5 6 7 8 9 10—DOC—10 09 08 07

*For our students—May you build a world
more devoted to peace and justice.*

# CONTENTS

# Chapter 10: Visions of a New Democracy    315

# Resources for Further Study    340

# Appendix

# Credits    363

# PREFACE

## What's New About This New Edition?

In this seventh edition of *Voices of Dissent* more than a third of the articles are new, offering coverage of issues and topics that have become of pronounced importance since the sixth edition. We have also chosen fresh and stimulating readings that will widen and deepen students' understanding of contemporary American politics. Most fundamentally, we orient many of our revisions toward the context of the ongoing war in Iraq, with all the political, economic, social, and military implications and complications that come with war, particularly a highly unpopular one. Challenges to the democratic functioning of government institutions during the Bush years are explored by Matt Taibbi, Jennifer Van Bergen, and Mark Tushnet. Changes in electoral competition and voter identity are probed in a widely noted analysis by Thomas Frank as well as in a study by the reform group FairVote. As our first serious foray into the role of religion in American politics, we offer new selections by Michelle Goldberg and Brooke Allen. We include a notable address by Bill Moyers examing the many failings of the news media in providing citizens with an accurate account of the world in which we live. Susan George and Paul Krugman focus our attention on the myths and distortions of the ideology of unbridled capitalism, while Steven Hill and Jared Bernstein offer detailed suggestions for how we might extend real democratic governance both politically and economically. Finally, we have contributed our own studies of the iron triangle that shapes HIV/AIDS policy and the presidency of George W. Bush in light of the 2006 elections and the ongoing fiasco in Iraq.

## Approach

In our view, *Voices of Dissent* continues to be the only reader on the market that fundamentally challenges the political and economic status quo in America. It provides a systematic series of critical perspectives on American politics that goes beyond the range of debate between mainstream liberalism and conservatism. In developing this book, we drew on some of the best examples of a diverse and energizing body of critical scholarship that is all too often overlooked in government courses. Political economy, and the tension between capitalism and democracy, is a recurrent theme in the selections. Other articles explore the ideological effects of the mass media, the ecological results of uncontrolled economic growth, and the dynamics of class, race, gender, and religious divisions in the United States—issues central to our political life early in the twenty-first century. American governmental institutions and political processes are treated in five central chapters, but only after they are placed in the context of underlying economic and social structures, as well as the more apparent constitutional arrangements, that shape their design and impact.

## GOAL AND AUDIENCE

Our goal is to provide students with the intellectual tools to develop a sustained and integrated critique of the workings of U.S. democracy so that as citizens they can better contribute to a broader debate about the American future. We firmly believe that students today are open to a critical analysis of their political system and are eager to participate in a discussion about fresh alternatives. We also think that many instructors are interested in exposing their students and themselves to material that makes sense of the dissatisfaction with the status quo that registers daily in America today. Our book provides a set of readings to help accomplish these goals.

*Voices of Dissent* is designed for introductory college-level courses in American government. It could be used as a supplement to a variety of textbooks or in conjunction with several works that have a narrower focus. In our experience, some of the best opportunities for learning occur when alternative frameworks of analysis and explanation are matched against each other. For that reason, the pairing of our reader with a work that adopts a more conventional, or even sharply opposed, interpretation of American politics might prove quite stimulating.

## ORGANIZATION

We begin with a revised general introduction, "Why a *Critical* Reader?" Here we explain the intellectual and political orientation that shaped our selection of readings and contrast our outlook with what we call mainstream political science. The readings that follow are grouped into three sections. Part I looks at the broad structures that constrain and pattern American politics. The three chapters in this section look at democracy and political economy, ideology, and culture and the distinctive nature of the American state. Part II attends to the traditional subject matter of political processes and government institutions: the mass media, parties and elections, Congress, the presidency, and law and the courts. Many of the articles in this section are notable for relating familiar processes and institutions to the broader level of political analysis developed in Part I. Part III examines major political challenges facing the United States and explores visions for democratic revitalization in light of the critical analysis contained in the previous chapters.

## FEATURES

*Voices of Dissent* contains several features that make it an attractive and original resource. Our emphasis on the contextual centrality of corporate capitalism and individualist values should deepen students' understanding of the very meaning of politics. Article introductions relate selections to key political questions and overall themes of the book. Most chapters begin with a theoretical or conceptually oriented piece that identifies underlying issues relevant to the unconventional view of American politics this book has been designed to encourage. Our forty selections represent some of the best and most provocative writing on American politics, scholarly and journalistic, available today. Each article is followed by "Discussion Questions," which are meant to facilitate class dialog and debate. We have included a "Resources for Further Study" list to provide additional alternative information so that students can sustain this analytic framework beyond the classroom setting where they first may have encountered it. Finally, we have an appendix containing three classic political documents, whose importance must be considered in any critical analysis.

## ACKNOWLEDGMENTS

We wish to thank the following reviewers who made insightful comments and suggestions:

Brian Frederick, Northern Illinois University

Michael Givel, University of Oklahoma

Rob Mellen Jr., Washington State University

Mark O'Gorman, Maryville College

Greg Shaw, Illinois Wesleyan University

We also acknowledge the insight and encouragement of our editor at Pearson Longman, Eric Stano, and his staff. Finally, we thank Pat Troxell and Glenace Edwall for their continuing support and helpful suggestions.

WILLIAM F. GROVER
JOSEPH G. PESCHEK

# INTRODUCTION

# WHY A *CRITICAL* READER?

A long habit of not thinking a thing *wrong,* gives it a superficial appearance of being *right* . . .

—Thomas Paine, *Common Sense*

In January of 1776, Thomas Paine voiced Americans' growing aspirations for freedom and independence with his radical call for an end to the monarchical rule of the British Empire. His pamphlet *Common Sense* was a phenomenal success, with upwards of 150,000 copies printed, reaching an estimated one million people, unheard of numbers for his day. Paine's straightforward message found a receptive audience among ordinary people, whose often-inchoate opposition to the King was impeded by entrenched deference to royal authority. With fiery reasoning in support of dissent and republican government, he cut through the haze of "what was" and crystallized a vision of "what could be."

In January of 2000, the world entered a new millennium. If a contemporary Thomas Paine were to issue a radical call for "common sense" today, would the public even be able to hear it? We wonder. As introductory students of politics, the lessons of eighteenth-century America may seem like ancient history as you ponder political life in the twenty-first century. The revolutions in political thinking that punctuated the end of the last century occurred elsewhere. We are now more than fifteen years removed from such seismic shifts as the collapse of the Berlin Wall and the break-up of Eastern Europe as a Soviet satellite, the coordination into a single market of the economies of the European Community nations, and the demise of Communism in Russia and, albeit more slowly, in China. India, China, and some other Asian nations now stand poised to challenge the United States economically as they compete for a greater share of the world's resources and flourish as producers of jobs and investment opportunities. Religious fundamentalism is spreading at an alarming rate worldwide, with dramatic impacts on political structures. Historic world events have swept away the political, economic, military, and ideological basis of the Cold War, and with it much of what we knew as foreign affairs in the post–World War II period. Even in the face of such breathtakingly rapid transformations, we have been treated to a predictable chorus of political pundits and "experts" in the mass media reassuring us that recent

*End of History Thesis*

history confirms the universal appeal and unquestionable rightness of American versions of democracy and corporate capitalism. Despite everything, the tide of history still moves our way—we are told. Why swim against it?

## SHIFTING TIMES/ENDURING STRUCTURE

This seventh edition of *Voices of Dissent* carries on our call to you as students to swim against the tide and challenge the received wisdom of the day. The sentiments above speak of changes of historic magnitude. If anything, the changes we began to highlight in the first edition of our anthology have only accelerated since then. Thus, we continue to live in exciting yet crisis-filled times. As authors, we certainly don't write in a vacuum. Most fundamentally, the United States is a nation at war. For more than four years, President George W. Bush has kept the nation on a war footing in Iraq. His initial reasons for entering the war have long since evaporated, having been exposed as either miscalculations based on highly selective reading of intelligence or deliberate distortions. Growing legions of people of differing political persuasions acknowledge the unjustifiable nature of this war, while its continuation exerts tremendous pressure on our political system. As *The Nation*, the oldest weekly magazine in America, put it in its February 5, 2007, editorial criticizing President Bush's post-election decision to escalate the war in Iraq:

> World opinion is against it. The American people are against it. The Democratic Party is against it. The Congress of the United States is against it. The Iraq Study Group is against it. The Iraqi people are against it. The Iraqi *government* is against it. Many Republican law-makers are against it. The top brass are against it. But George W. Bush is going to do it: send 21,500 more troops into Iraq. Can a single man force a nation to fight a war it does not want to fight, expand a war it does not want to expand—possibly to other countries? If he can, is that nation any longer a democracy in any meaningful sense?

The stakes involved in this situation could not be more basic. We face the unilateral exercise of executive power that threatens the very nature of our democracy. The framing events for this challenge to democratic principles, of course, are the horrendous terrorist attacks of September 11, 2001, which precipitated the United States bombing of Afghanistan, the war in Iraq, and the larger ongoing "war on terror." As political analysts, we cannot escape the need to address myriad issues that flow out of circumstances that have seared themselves into the consciousness of the nation. The "war on terror" has been the ubiquitous theme of President Bush and the media. We are told on an almost daily basis that 9-11 "changed everything" in American politics. We are skeptical of that assertion. As renowned linguist and political analyst Noam Chomsky puts it in his controversial bestseller *9-11*:

> The horrifying atrocities of September 11 are something quite new in world affairs, not in their scale and character, but in the target. For the United States, this is the first time since the War of 1812 that the national territory has been under attack, or even threatened. . . . For the first time, the guns have been directed the other way. That is a dramatic change.

What hasn't changed, Chomsky reminds us, are the fundamental objectives of U.S. foreign policy. Supported as they always have been by massive use of state-sponsored violence and neglect of international law, these objectives reflect the structure of corporate, military, and political power in America. Indeed, the events of 9-11 and the "war on terror" have solidified that structure and obstructed potential challenges to it. Dissonant issues, which had begun to illuminate the dark side of U.S. power, seemingly disappeared overnight. Thus the remarkable rash of corporate abuses of power—from Enron and Arthur Anderson, to Global Crossing, Adelphia, ImClone, Tyco, Merrill Lynch, WorldCom, Dynergy, Qwest, and Martha Stewart Living Omnimedia—which had begun to receive media scrutiny, were shuffled off to the side after September 11. The sordid tale of corporate chief executive officers (CEOs) profiting while ordinary Americans watched their retirement savings disappear with the bursting of the 1990s dot-com bubble fell on deaf ears. All but forgotten was the widening gap between the rich and the poor in the United States, leaving the nation with class divisions based on income and wealth reminiscent of the late nineteenth century. In November of 2006, one successful Senate candidate from Virginia, James Webb, described the view from the top tier of the economic pyramid in stark terms: "It is not unfair to say that they are literally living in a different country." Overshadowing all of this and more—the intelligence ineptitude of the FBI and the CIA, inquiry into the Bush administration's own complacency about warnings of terrorist attacks in the summer prior to 9-11, environmental decay and alarming new evidence of global warming, scandals involving former House Majority Leader Tom De Lay (R-TX) and Republican superlobbyist Jack Abramoff—was the official story line: WAR! In these troubling times, we desperately need contemporary Thomas Paines to meet the challenges posed by these times of crisis. While dissenters risk being labeled "unpatriotic," it's a risk that must be taken in a true democracy. For structures of power endure.

## Democracy and its Discontents

As we prepared this new edition of *Voices of Dissent*, the American political landscape had changed in significant ways, after the relative stasis of the post-9/11 years. As a result of the 2006 congressional elections, divided government returned to Washington, as the Democrats regained control of both the Senate and the House of Representatives. This result stemmed above all from public disillusionment with the Iraq war, which by Election Day had lasted nearly as long as American involvement in World War II. Despite the growing opposition to the war, we are struck by the limitations on foreign policy discussion by most prominent political leaders, including many of those who are extremely critical of President Bush. In general, Democrats have been in lockstep with administration policy toward Iran and Israel. Moreover, few political leaders in the political mainstream—liberal or conservative—question the supposed need for American global dominance and the mission of the United States to spread "freedom" around the world. As historian Andrew J. Bacevich puts it, "When it comes to foreign policy, the fundamental divide in American politics today is not between left and right but between those who subscribe to the myth of the 'American Century' and those who do not."

Presidential elections can help bring the need for serious alternatives into sharper relief, and we ask you to observe the next presidential campaign from that perspective. More Americans have become aware of how our antiquated Electoral College devalues popular sovereignty. Had 60,000 Ohio voters in 2004 voted for John Kerry rather than George W. Bush, it would have been the second election in a row in which the candidate with the most popular votes had not been elected president. In Ohio and elsewhere serious questions have been raised about the fairness and security of our patchwork system of casting and counting votes. While campaign finance has been reformed through the 2002 McCain–Feingold law targeting soft money, the cash flow to campaigns has been rerouted and continues to grow. Indeed, the 2008 campaign may see the effective dismantlement of the system of partially publicly-financed presidential campaigns, as major candidates are poised to opt out in pursuit of larger sums of privately contributed dollars. Any serious approach to the revitalization of American democracy must make systematical electoral reform a priority.

Several potentially positive forms of political participation have emerged that draw on the Internet and other technologies. And in 2004 a rise in turnout among evangelical Christians and young first-time voters led to an improved turnout rate of about 59 percent. But in mid-term elections far fewer eligible voters cast ballots, as was again the case in 2006. Although America fancies itself as the greatest democracy on earth, in fact, the United States still remains mired at or near the bottom of all industrialized nations in terms of voter participation. Widespread popular disengagement from politics enables the influence of corporate business on government policy to grow, threatening to turn America into a plutocracy and make democracy an endangered species. As former presidential candidate Ralph Nader pointed out, "This control by the corporate government over our political government is creating a widening *democracy gap*. Active citizens are left shouting their concerns over a deep chasm between them and their government."

This chasm became apparent in the summer of 2005 when one of the worst natural disasters in American history occurred as Hurricane Katrina devastated New Orleans. Katrina's force was compounded by social and political disasters that lay bare the class and racial divisions of U.S. society. Americans were stunned by the lack of responsiveness by local, state, and national authorities. Many other domestic issues and trends are troubling as well, among them: the growing gap between the rich and the poor, with the top 1 percent of households now owning more wealth than the bottom 95 percent; an essentially stagnant standard of living for working and middle-class Americans over the last three decades; the soaring wage differential between CEOs and average factory workers, which resulted in CEOs earning over four hundred times what an average worker earned in 2006, up from 1980 when CEOs made forty-one times as much; the health care crunch that has left at least 45 million Americans without any medical coverage and an equal number with woefully inadequate coverage; the persistence of poverty (especially among children), with the poverty rate in 2006 remaining at 12.6 percent during the fourth year of an economic recovery; lingering racism and sexism as barriers to basic equality; and the crisis of environmental degradation, which is reaching potentially cataclysmic proportions globally.

Other, more hopeful signs of discontent have abounded in the last decade. In Seattle in November of 1999, and again in April of 2000 in Washington, D.C., tens of thousands of people from around the world came together to voice growing opposition to the World Trade Organization and other global financial institutions whose decisions set the rules of economic life far removed from citizen input. This nascent social movement—uniting students, environmentalists, working people, and other activists against the elite agenda of corporate capital—has shed light on the often secretive world of international economic decision making, raising deep doubts about the presumed wisdom of globalization. In February 2003, millions of people around the globe protested against the impending U.S. invasion of Iraq—the largest one-day protest in the history of the world. In January 2007 hundreds of thousands of citizens gathered on the National Mall in Washington to demand an end to ongoing Iraq war. We strongly believe that the American political system today has a superficial appearance of rightness, a veneer of public ritual and familiarity beneath which lies tremendous private (and increasingly public) discontent. Moreover, we sense students and teachers are interested in a challenging analysis of American politics that includes alternatives to conventional liberal and conservative approaches, which, we are all taught, mark the limits of "legitimate" debate. In our text, we ask you to move beyond these socialized limits in an attempt to span the "democracy gap."

## POSSIBLE RESPONSES

These and a host of other problems confront the student of politics. In the face of such formidable dilemmas, you are left with a few possible responses. One common response is *resignation*, expressed in such adages as "you can't fight city hall" and "don't rock the boat." Many students tell us they can see basic injustices but feel powerless to change anything. The continuing durability of this view is ironic, though, given the sweeping and rapid changes that have taken place elsewhere in the world in recent years. — *Where?*

Another response available to you is the *pluralist* interpretation of political life, which encourages piecemeal problem solving and an incremental view of change. Closely linked to *"Liberal" Pluralist* an inherited cultural assumption about politics and power, the pluralist model of politics dominates contemporary Political Science. Pluralism rests on the view of society as a collection of groups that compete over various policy areas. Through these groups, or acting as individuals through other democratic freedoms such as voting rights, representative institutions, and civil liberties, people can negotiate and compromise in an open political process. Group conflict is considered fair as long as the government serves as an unbiased umpire, maintaining a level-playing field for all groups. Power is said to be diffuse so that no one group has unfair advantages. When necessary, reforms occur as groups succeed (or fail) in having their ideas triumph over competing ideas. And the end result of this pluralist interaction is understood to reasonably approximate "the public interest." On a pluralist reading of politics, the system may have its flaws, but none are so fatal that the system itself is called into question. The pluralist understanding of American politics is a relatively comfortable one, for it allows students to retain the belief that the political process is open enough, and sufficiently fluid, to adapt to virtually any contingency without changing the basic power relations of the political economy. Moreover, pluralists define "politics" narrowly—as what *government* does—so that the model overlooks other arenas of power, among them corporate capital.

We contend that neither resignation nor pluralist incrementalism will help you make sense of the American political landscape. A third, more *critical* approach is warranted, one that challenges existing power relations. As currently practiced, politics speaks largely to the concerns of the already wealthy and influential. The political system does not offer the hope of a better life for most Americans, but rather leaves unquestioned a structure of power and privilege that endures regardless of which party controls Congress and the White House. In American political history, this kind of critical questioning often has been championed through the collective action of social movements, a point emphasized by many authors in this volume.

## A CRITICAL VIEW? BUT I'M NOT A "RADICAL!"

Our anthology seeks to contribute to the ongoing discussion about the need to rethink and broaden the range of political and economic options facing the country. For many of you this may be your first exposure to dissenting political orientations, which are marginalized, or rendered invisible, in the mass media and most college textbooks. Within Political Science, the field of American politics is awash in textbooks and readers that assume an orthodox pluralist perspective or provide a small sampling of differing viewpoints (though uniformly still heavily weighted toward the mainstream) on a series of issues of the day. Against this current, we adopt a critical stance, which challenges conventional self-congratulatory accounts of the American political system. We draw articles from the rich literature of radical scholarship, along with selected mainstream pieces, which add texture to the more critical interpretation.

While there are many ways to use our reader in introductory courses, we believe it may be most useful as an analytic complement to any of the myriad conventional textbooks on the market. It is through the competition of ideas that you will develop your capacity to think freely and critically. Our alternative perspective—which questions the very roots of political, economic, and ideological power in the United States—grows out of a positive belief that the current distribution of power and resources seriously impedes freedom, equality, and democracy, in the fullest sense of these terms. As proponents of real political participation and social justice, we critique the system in order to improve it when possible and change it when necessary.

With these thoughts in mind, we frankly hope our *reader* will make you feel uncomfortable, shake you up a bit, and ultimately stimulate you to ask deep questions about the American political and economic system. Our goal in this sense is a radical one, for we ask that in your study of American politics you "go to the root causes," the very definition of the word *radical*. A nation is not a healthy democracy simply because its politicians, corporate leaders, and the mass media constantly say it is or because other forms of more authoritarian control have tumbled down worldwide. And the democratic ideal is not close to being realized if the people continually are asked to settle for a political system that is merely "pretty good," or if at election time voters find themselves holding their noses and voting for the "lesser of two evils," or if the answers to our problems are assumed to lie in policies of a "moderate" direction. For, the legacy of Thomas Paine also reminds us:

> A thing moderately good is not so good as it ought to be. Moderation in temper is always a virtue; but moderation in principle is always a vice. (1792 Letter)

A truly healthy polity can thrive only when ordinary people have meaningful control over the decisions that directly affect their lives. Ralph Nader refers to such control as "deep democracy," which facilitates peoples' best efforts to achieve social justice and self-reliance. Democracy in the fullest sense should provide the societal context within which people's "instinct for freedom" can flourish, as Noam Chomsky has written in *Language and Politics*:

> I would like to believe that people have an instinct for freedom, that they really want to control their own affairs. They don't want to be pushed around, ordered, oppressed, etc., and they want a chance to do things that make sense, like constructive work in a way that they control, or maybe control together with others. I don't know any way to prove this. It's really a hope about what human beings are like—a hope that if social structures change sufficiently, those aspects of human nature will be realized.

We share the hope of these two modern-day Thomas Paines, a hope that is animated by a spirit Paine would have appreciated. Its realization—and the empowerment that would accompany it—is what informed, truly democratic citizenship is supposed to be about. We welcome feedback from students and teachers so we may learn whether this reader has helped you develop the analytic skills necessary to bring this hope closer to fruition.

# PART I

# STRUCTURE

If the foundation of your house is cracked and starting to weaken, it makes little sense to address the problem by applying a fresh coat of paint that would merely conceal the underlying reality of decay. In our view, the American political system is a lot like a house with an unstable foundation. Although the possibility of collapse certainly is not imminent, the structure of the American political economy, and the ideology that sustains it, is showing signs of severe stress. Moreover, this structure belies the cherished pluralist assumption (discussed in our Introduction) that our political system is one of open, fluid competition among groups. The inherent structural advantages, and disadvantages, accorded various groups significantly bias the political and economic system toward the interests of those who wield great power.

At the outset, we must acknowledge that the concept of *structure* is itself quite muddled. Mainstream political scientists often use the term "structure" in a shallow sense when discussing institutions of government, thus equating structure with the formal machinery of politics. This reduces structure to the institutional balance of power among the executive, legislative, and judicial branches of government. While these institutional interactions obviously merit our attention, the structure-as-institutions approach ignores the deeper structure of power within which institutions operate.

In Part I we explore this deep structure of American politics, with three chapters focusing on the primary structural components of political economy, ideology, and state-constitutional arrangements. Taken as a whole, they challenge you to consider whether tensions inherent in the relationship between democracy as a political concept and capitalism as a form of economic organization may in fact constitute a *problem* for the nation, not the solution to our problems, as we are socialized to believe. Are capitalism and a meaningful degree of democracy really compatible, or is capitalist democracy an oxymoron? Does our political culture enable us to consider carefully a wide range of alternative policy directions in the United States? If not, are we as "free" as we like to think? Why is the power of the state so closely connected to the private power of large economic entities? Does the U.S. Constitution strengthen this connection or provide ways to challenge it? To what extent have social movements been able to constrain and change this structure? These and many other troubling questions flow from a close reading of the selections in Part I.

Together, these three structural components form the basic context—the playing field—within which political institutions operate. Understanding this structure will help you make sense of what government institutions do and why problems so often seem to persist regardless of what policies are pursued in Washington. And it will help you come to grips with the pressures that impinge upon the foundations of American politics.

# CHAPTER 1

# DEMOCRACY AND POLITICAL ECONOMY

Politics is much more than government. Underlying this book of readings is the conviction that politics involves all relationships of power, whether they be economic, social, or cultural, as well as the interrelationship of government institutions. In their accounts of American politics, many political scientists focus on the Constitution and the three branches of government it established more than two hundred years ago. We include these traditional subjects but place them in a broader context that, in our view, will help you to understand better their actual workings and significance. Given our approach, it should not seem strange that we begin a book on American politics with what appears to be an economic focus.

Our first set of readings emphasizes the closely interwoven connection between democracy and political economy and the importance of understanding our capitalist system if we are to understand our politics. In the late eighteenth century, political economy was a commonsense way of thinking for Alexander Hamilton and other Founding Fathers, as we will see in Chapter 3. But in the twentieth century the study of economics and politics became institutionally separated in American colleges and in academic discourse, more generally. In recent years this conceptual chasm has been challenged from a variety of perspectives. The selections in Chapter 1 represent a revival of a broader, integrated analysis of American politics that challenges us to think critically about the relationship of capitalism and democracy. All of the authors in this chapter should help you to see politics as much broader than what goes on in government and as powerfully shaped and constrained by the dynamics of our economy. When this is understood it is difficult to be satisfied with a definition of democracy confined to the presence of elections and formal rights.

# 1 *Jim Hightower*

# THIS LAND IS YOUR LAND

*Jim Hightower is a best-selling author, radio commentator, public speaker, and former Texas agriculture commissioner whose populist humor sheds light on serious issues of political, economic, and social inequities. With a wit worthy of Will Rogers and an unquenchable fire in his belly, he delivers his politically subversive message to an audience increasingly fed up with a sham version of democracy in which politicians pretend to serve the interests of the people while really serving the interests of corporate America. In this selection from his book* If the Gods Had Meant for Us to Vote They Would Have Given Us Candidates, *Hightower deploys his humor to celebrate the revolutionary spirit of 1776, which he reminds us was at times quite anticorporate in character. Hightower traces the evolution of the corporation, an institution initially constrained by charters that regulated their behavior and which could be revoked by state legislatures and courts if the corporation failed to live up to charter conditions. In this manner the potential dangers of vast corporate power—dangers well known to the Framers—were kept in check. But as corporations and their wealthy benefactors fought back against charters after the Civil War, what emerged was the "runaway corporate autocracy" that is an affront to meaningful democratic authority. Hightower writes of efforts today to fight back against corporate power with campaigns mounted by citizens from Wayne, Pennsylvania, to Arcata, California. Such attempts to take back democracy from the clutches of corporation boardrooms are fueled by the "fire-breathing democratic passion" reminiscent of such cultural icons as Thomas Paine, Woody Guthrie, and Martin Luther King Jr. Ultimately, then, Hightower's message is full of hope—a hope whose realization requires the time, energy, vision, and humor of political mavericks animated by the promise of democracy.*

Woody Guthrie wrote "This Land" in 1940 while living in New York City, penning all six verses in one night while staying in a no-star hotel somewhere around Times Square. The song had been forming in his fertile mind for a long time as "he roamed and rambled" all around America, "walking that ribbon of highway." He wrote it not as a sweet sing-along glorifying the American landscape but as a proudly

---

*Source:* Jim Hightower, *If the Gods Had Meant for Us to Vote They Would Have Given Us Candidates,* New York: HarperCollins, 2000, pp. 307–324 and 337–339.

populist anthem for the hardscrabble people he traveled among. He had already written hundreds of songs that chronicled the lives and struggles of these workaday folks who are the strength of our great land, performing his songs for them on picket lines, in migrant camps, and at rallies, as well as performing on radio and at their dances. His music entertained, even as it encouraged people in their battles against the Pinkertons, politicians, and other authorities who fronted for the refined men with soft hands and hard eyes who ran things from afar.

When he wrote the words "*your* land," Woody was pointedly speaking to the steelworkers in Pittsburgh and dockworkers up and down the Pacific coast, the dust-bowl people (of whom he was one) who had lost their crops to drought and their farms to bankers, the workers who risked their lives to build the Grand Coulee and the itinerant harvesters who cut the wheat and stacked the hay, "trying to make about a dollar a day." Every schoolchild has sung "This Land's" gentle verses about the "endless skyway" and "diamond deserts," but the songbooks carefully excise Woody's verses that provoke ordinary citizens to rethink the established order, to realize their democratic strength, and to rebel against the structures of privilege that lock out the majority. Verses like:

> Was a big high wall there that tried to stop me
> A sign was painted said: "Private Property."
> But on the back side it didn't say nothing
> This side was made for you and me.[1]

Woody knew that this land is our land only if we make it so, only if we have the stomach to confront the elites and challenge the insidious forces of autocracy that are continually at work to make it exclusively their land, in the sense that they control the economic and political decisions that rule us. The essence of democracy is self-government. Anything less is a fraud. Being connected to the Internet is not democracy, having a choice between Gore and Bush is not democracy, receiving five hundred channels of digital television is not democracy, being awarded a slice of corporate-allocated prosperity is not democracy. Democracy is control. Whatever goals we strive for as a people—racial harmony, peace, economic fairness, privacy, clean water and air—all are dependent on our ability to control the decisions that affect these goals.

Pause for a moment to think of what an incredible treasure it is to have the right to govern ourselves. Precious few people in history have even had the possibility of asserting their common will over the will of the ruling powers, and the vast majority of earth's people today cannot even imagine such a right. But, in the Declaration of 1776, we have it in writing: ". . . governments are instituted among men, deriving their just powers from the *consent of the governed.*" We're in charge! Not kings of feudal barons, congresses or presidents, and damned sure not corporations or World Trade Organizations.

Having it on paper, though, doesn't make it so. Indeed when it was first written, it wasn't so for very many citizens at all. In the first presidential election, 1789, only 4 percent of the American people were allowed to vote. No women voted (they were chattel), no African Americans (they were slaves), no Native Americans (they were considered heathens), and no one who was without land (they were riffraff). A broader sense of self-rule came later, and only with great effort, pain, and suffering. From abolitionists to suffragists, from populists to Wobblies, from sit-down strikes to lunch-counter sit-ins, blood has flowed as generation after generation has battled the Powers That Be for a share of "Life, Liberty, and the Pursuit of Happiness." In the 224 years since Jefferson wrote of these "inalienable rights," thousands upon thousands of Americans have died in the ongoing struggle to democratize the Declaration, to extend the possibility of self-government to more citizens. What a debt we owe to those who have sacrificed so much to bring us this far, and what a gift this right to self-government is.

But will we hold on to it? Progress is never assured and democracy cannot be taken for granted,

---

[1]The excerpt used in this book was taken from Woody Guthrie's original manuscript and is different from the published words.

even in our country. There has been a radical back-sliding of democratic control in the past few years—a majority of Americans now find themselves effectively shut out of economic and political decision making, and even greater threats of our sovereignty loom in the ominous form of the WTO, NAFTA, and other antidemocratic creations of the global corporate powers. Democratic power is never given; it always has to be taken, then aggressively defended, and retaken when it slips from our hands, for the moneyed powers relentlessly press to gain supremacy and assert their private will over the majority. Today, our gift of democracy is endangered not by military might threatening a sudden, explosive coup but by the stealth of corporate lawyers and politicians, seizing a piece of self-government from us here, then another piece from over there, quietly installing an elitist regime issue by issue, law by law, place by place, with many citizens unaware that their people's authority is slipping away.

For the past couple of decades, this has been going on, greatly accelerating in the nineties, as corporate will has been enthroned, increasingly reigning supreme over every aspect of our lives—economics, politics, culture, and nature itself. We American people find ourselves, once again, at one of those "When in the course of human events" moments, when it is our time to face the reality that a despotic force is in our midst. In the name of all American rebels who have gone before, are we going to sit by, unwilling to confront the bully in front of us, which grows more powerful the longer we wait? You and I have the lofty responsibility to follow in the footsteps of those rebels, to oppose the corporate usurpers and fight for our nation's unique and hard-won right to self-government. Progress doesn't come by merely standing on guard but, as George Bernard Shaw said about a hundred years ago, "by attacking, and getting well-hammered yourself."

## WHAT THE HELL IS A CORPORATION?

This ubiquitous critter called the corporation—we're stuck with it, right? We've just got to learn to live with it, don't we, kind of like we live with

cockroaches? After all, a corporation has a kind of natural right to do business, doesn't it? No, no, and no. First of all, a corporation is not a business. It's nothing but a piece of paper, a bit of legalism that does not create a business but instead creates a protective association for individuals who want to do business yet want special protections for themselves against other people, against the public at large . . . against the very workings of democracy.

You can make widgets, you can farm, you can sell hardware or groceries, you can operate a hotel, you can provide banking services, or be in any other business without being a corporation. Most of the businesses in the world are *unincorporated* enterprises—individuals, sole proprietorships, partnerships, co-ops, or other forms of operation. Taking on corporations is not antibusiness at all—we must have businesses, but that does not mean we have to have corporations.

Where did we get the corporate structure? From the jolly Brits, who devised a devilish scheme called "joint stock companies" during their colonial phase. Empire and all that, eh what? The corporate entity was (and is) a legal fiction, first invented by the crown to assist the barons, merchant traders, and bankers of the day in plundering the wealth of the Empire's colonies, including those in our fair land. It was a way to amass the large sums of capital they needed to plunder faraway places, collecting money from investors to finance the plundering, then distributing the booty back to those investors. The corporate construct is dangerous not only because it can agglomerate an absolutely domineering amount of financial power but also because it allows the owners of the corporation (the shareholders) to profit from its business activities, yet accept *no responsibility* for any harm done by their company's business activities. All gain, no pain. The corporation is a legal shield, granting its owners an extraordinary protective privilege that no other business owners are allowed. Oh, did my company spill eleven million gallons of oil into Prince William Sound (Exxon), did it kill two thousand people in a chemical explosion in Bhopal, India (Union Carbide), did it defraud thousands of senior citizens who were persuaded to put money into bad securities (Prudential), did it dump cancer-causing PCBs into the Hudson River (General Electric)? So sorry, I'm sure, but that's none of my doing—the *corporation* did it. Yet, the corporation has no ass to be kicked, no scruff of the neck to be grabbed, no body to be tossed unceremoniously into the maximum security lockup, no conscience to make it contrite, and no soul that would allow the religious among us to believe that at least this wretched enterprise will be condemned to eternal hell.

To the built-in irresponsibility of the amorphous corporate entity, add the bottom-line imperative of the CEO and board of directors. Academicians, judges, and corporation executives themselves aver that the sole role of corporate management is to make as much money as possible for the shareholders (a group that prominently includes the managers). The managers have no responsibility—none—to workers, environment, consumers, community, flag, or anything else. To the contrary, the entire incentive is for management to cut corners, to shortchange, to exploit. It is not a matter of a CEO's good intentions or bad—it is the bottom line, and it must be served. Put away all hope, ye who go in asking corporations to be "good," "responsible," "accountable." It is not in their self-interest or in their nature—you might as well expect a Rott-weiler to meow.

As for corporations having natural rights, forget it. It's no longer taught in civics or history classes, and it's definitely not mentioned in today's politics or media, but corporations have no rights at all. Zero. Not even the right to exist. The state gives them the *privilege* to exist, but this existence can be narrowly defined and controlled by We the People. I realize this goes against the received wisdom, against the carefully nurtured assumption that corporations are somehow or other one of God's creatures with inherent powers that are larger and elevated above the powers of us common citizens. We can all be forgiven for assuming this, for that certainly is how it works in practice today. But it need not and should not work that way, nor was it meant to work that way when our country and most of our states were founded. Each corporation was and is the creature of the *citizenry,* allowed to exist only through receipt of a state charter. *We are the*

*sovereign,* not them. They are supposed to serve us, not vice versa.

Back to the future: the American Revolution. Jane Anne Morris, a thinker, digger, strategist, and agitator on the issue of corporate dominance, writes: "The people who founded this nation didn't fight a war so they could have a couple of 'citizen representatives' sitting in on meetings on the British East India Company. They carried out a revolution in order to be free of oppression: corporate, governmental, or otherwise; and to replace it with democratic self-government." Adams, Jefferson, Paine, and the rest had not had a happy experience with the corporations of the crown and were unabashedly anticorporate at the founding, with Jefferson even speaking of the need "to crush in its birth the aristocracy of our moneyed corporations."

The citizens of early America knew what they were up against: raw economic power. They were rightly wary of the corporate structure itself, knowing that it allowed a few individuals in the society to stockpile a massive amount of money and power, then use this and the corporate shield to pursue their private gain to the harm of the common good. Eighteenth- and nineteenth-century Americans were prescient when it came to these entities—citizens expressed concern that corporations would use their money as bribes to pervert democratic elections and buy both legislators and judges; farmers worried that corporations would use their muscle to monopolize markets and control crop prices; and industrial and craft workers were concerned that corporations would, as historian Louis Hartz has written, turn them into "a commodity," treating them "as much an article of commerce as woolens, cotton or yarn." They knew that the unbridled corporation was antithetical to the democratic principles they espoused and a threat to the very system of self-government they had established. So they made damned sure the corporation was securely bridled.

Anyone so timid as to think that it is radical for citizens today even to consider "interfering" with the private will of corporations is not made of the same stout stuff as the citizens who created our states and our country. In America's first hundred years, applicants could get a corporate charter only by approval of their state legislature, usually requiring a two-thirds vote to win one. Few charters were awarded, and those few corporations that got them were limited in their function, in how much money they could aggregate, in how long they could exist, and in how they could function. Citizens took their hard-won sovereignty seriously, adamantly defending it against the possibility of corporate usurpation. State after state imposed strict terms on the issuance of a charter, leaving no doubt about who was in charge. This is our hidden history of proud and aggressive citizenship, and you're likely to be amazed if you look into how the people of your state have stood up to corporate power in the not-so-distant past. Jane Anne Morris dug into the records of her state of Wisconsin and found that from 1848 to as recently as 1953, the legislature had imposed such charter conditions as these:

- Corporations had to have a clearly stated reason for existing, and if they failed to fulfill that purpose or went beyond it, their charter could be revoked.
- The legislature could revoke the charter for any particular reason or, as the Wisconsin attorney general ruled in 1913, "for no reason at all."
- Corporate management and stockholders could be held liable for corporate acts.
- Directors of the corporation were required to come from among the stockholders.
- If a corporation's principal place of business was Wisconsin, it had to have its headquarters and its meetings there.
- Charters were granted for a specific period of time, like twenty years, rather than "in perpetuity."
- Corporations could not own other corporations.
- Corporations could own real estate only if it was necessary to carry out their specific purpose.
- Corporations were flatly prohibited from making any political contribution, direct or indirect, and it was a felony crime if they did so.
- All corporate records and documents were open to the legislature and to the attorney general.

From Maine to California, Wisconsin to Texas, all states had similar stipulations on their books—and they were enforced! Especially important were the revocation clauses, which allowed state legislatures or courts to yank the operating licenses of corporations that behaved badly. Imagine. The people were in charge, the general welfare was paramount over corporate profit, civic authority prevailed over CEO whim. Richard Grossman and Ward Morehouse, two thoughtful activists who codirect POCLAD (the Program on Corporations, Laws and Democracy), have published an excellent pamphlet worthy of Thomas Paine, entitled "Taking Care of Business: Citizenship and the Charter of Incorporation." It notes that the corporate charter was a sacrosanct oath: "The penalty for abuse or misuse of the charter was not a fine or a slap on the wrist, but revocation of the charter and dissolution of the corporation. Citizens believed that it was society's inalienable right to abolish an evil." Charters were routinely revoked, including those of the most powerful—in 1894, the Central Labor Union of New York City cited a pattern of abuses against John D. Rockefeller's Standard Oil Trust of New York, asking the attorney general to request that the state supreme court revoke its charter. The AG did . . . and the court did.

After the Civil War, however, with the rise of the Robber Barons, a full-scale assault was begun by the moneyed interests against these inconvenient rules. Railroad baron Cornelius Vanderbilt issued the war cry of the antidemocratic elites when he thundered, "What do I care about the law? H'ain't I got the power?" For the next hundred years—stipulation by stipulation, state by state, bribe by bribe—the sovereign was steadily reduced to the subjugated. Corporate barons like Vanderbilt hauled sacks of money into state capitols to buy legislators and win charter changes favorable to them. The chief justice of Wisconsin's supreme court spoke as early as 1873 of "a new and dark power" that was looming, warning that "the enterprises of the country are aggregating vast corporate combinations of unexampled capital, marching, not for economical conquests only, but for political power. . . ." The Vanderbilts, Goulds, Rockefellers, and others had more money than hell has brimstone, and they used it to corrupt and dominate the same state legislatures that had been bulwarks of democratic resistance to the corporate empire builders. A Pennsylvania legislator is reported to have said, "Mr. Speaker, I move we adjourn, unless the Pennsylvania Railroad has some more business for us to transact."

Gradually, the bridle has been removed, resulting in what we have today—the runaway corporate autocracy that the founders predicted and feared. Shall we just accept it? Shall we timidly continue into another century with the status quo politics of the pathetic ClintonGoreBradley Democrats, who demand again and again that the people must adjust to the private agenda of a handful of corporate executives and investors?

"This is an exciting time to be an American," a Californian wrote to me several months ago. "We are in a crisis. We are on the brink of failure of our old democratic processes—swamped, subverted, perverted, and filibustered by the corporate feudal system and its totalitarian dominance of our lives. We have the opportunity and the duty to overcome all that," he wrote.

Bingo! In one succinct paragraph, this citizen has nailed it, and he is but one of a growing majority who know that "consent of the governed" is a mockery today, supplanted by a crude bribery system of corporate governance that is becoming as autocratic as anything imagined by King George III and his royally chartered British East India Company, Hudson's Bay Company, and the crown charters that ruled American colonies. Just a few examples: High-handed CEOs can, by fiat, off several thousand workers from the payroll, thereby jacking up the company's stock price and enriching themselves with tens of millions in stock gains, while the workers and their families are allowed no redress for their grievances; your bank, insurance company, credit-card firm, HMO, and other corporations can secretly collect the most intimate details of your private life, then use or sell this information in any way they see fit, without even informing you; imperious biotech corporations can mess dangerously with the very DNA of our food supply for no purpose except to enhance their profits, then force families to be the guinea pigs of their Frankenfood experiments, since there is no labeling of thousands of supermarket items (including baby food) already

containing these genetically altered organisms; conniving corporations routinely extract millions from townspeople as the price of building a factory or sports stadium in their town, then can renege on any pledge of job creation and, on whim, pull up stakes and abandon the town altogether; haughty HMOs can make decisions that kill you, yet Congress protects them from legal liability and punishment for your death; "speech" has been perverted to mean money, authorizing corporations and their executives to buy control of the entire political process; a chemical company can callously pollute our air, water, and food, leading to thousands of deaths, birth defects, and other horrors, yet continue doing business and continue polluting, with no punishment beyond, perhaps, a fine, which it easily absorbs and, in some cases, can deduct from its income taxes as a "cost of doing business"; a handful of media giants have attained absolute control over the content of news and the range of ideas that are broadcast on the *public's* airwaves, arbitrarily shrinking the democratic debate; the democratic decisions of a city council, state legislature, or other sovereign government can be arrogantly annulled by corporate action through antidemocratic entities established by NAFTA and the WTO.

Who the hell are these people? Who elected them to run our world? Why are we putting up with this crap? As the bumper sticker puts it: LEMMINGS OF THE WORLD UNITE! YOU HAVE NOTHING TO LOSE BUT YOUR PLACE IN LINE!

We need to crank up a political fight that has some guts to it, some fire-breathing democratic passion in it, some of the revolutionary spirit of 1776 behind it. This is not a fight about regulations or really even about corporations—it's about control, sovereignty, self-government, *democracy.* Let's force the issue and put it as starkly as it is: Are corporations going to rule, or are we? From time to time, I hear veterans of the civil rights and antiwar battles of the sixties bemoan the lack of a "Big Battle" today, one that can unite a majority across traditional political lines, one that is about justice for all, is loaded with citizen outrage, has the spark of genuine passion within it, and is worthy of bloody heads. Well, here it is: The self-evident battle of our era is to defeat corporate autocracy and establish citizen rule over our government, our economy, and our environment.

## WHEN YOU FIGHT THE DEVIL, FIGHT TO WIN

Practically every progressive struggle—campaign finance reform, rain forest destruction and global warming, sweatshops, family farms, fair trade, health care for all, unionization, military spending and arms sales, tax reform, alternative energy, healthy food, media access, hazardous waste dumps, redlining, alternative medicine, you name it—is being fought against one cluster of corporations or another. But it is not that corporation over there or this one over here that is the enemy, it is not one industry's contamination of our drinking water or another's perversion of the lawmaking process that is the problem—rather it is the corporation itself that must be addressed if we are to be a free people.

In his powerful pamphlet *Common Sense,* Thomas Paine touched the heart of the American Revolution when he wrote: "Ye that dare oppose not only tyranny but the tyrant, stand forth." We can all object to consequences and seek remedial action, but will we finally face the tyrant itself? That is the questions for progressives as we step into 2000. We can continue fighting the beast as we have been, through scattershot, uncoordinated efforts—a lawsuit here, an investigation there, some legislation, more regulations, prayer, and the always useful sacrificial goat. Occasionally, these approaches succeed. But, as Grossman and Morehouse have written, "Tactically, [this approach] means limiting ourselves to resisting harms one corporate site at a time, one corporate chemical or biotechnology product at a time; to correcting imperfections of the market; to working for yet more permitting and disclosure laws; to initiating procedural lawsuits and attempts to win compensation after corporate harm has been done; to battling regulatory and administrative agencies; to begging leaders of global corporations to please cause a little less harm."

In 1998, Britain's House of Lords dealt with the weighty matter of changing the official costume worn by the Lord Chancellor, that body's top official. The outfit included a long powdered wig, breeches, tights, buckled shoes, white gloves, and black stockings. The incumbent wanted very much not to look, as one reporter described him, like "the frog footman in 'Alice in Wonderland,'" so he proposed a switch to modern business attire. Traditionalists, however, opposed any change in the seventeenth-century garb. Lord Wattington put the case for tradition forcefully, summing up by declaring, "I can see no advantage to the Queen or the public if the Lord Chancellor removes his tights."

At the national level, inside the Beltway, too many of our progressive energies and resources are spent on fights that amount to removing the Lord Chancellor's tights. The piecemeal approach to fighting corporate abuses keeps us spread thin, separated from each other, on the defensive, riveted on the minutiae, and fighting on their terms (literally over the language of *their* laws and regulations, and in *their* courts and legislatures). More often than not, regulatory agencies are shams, working to sustain the business-as-usual tactics of corporations rather than to inhibit them, and the deck is stacked against the public interest anytime we find ourselves within these legalistic meat grinders. This is nothing new—historian Howard Zinn writes about the creation of the Interstate Commerce Commission in 1887, a "reform" pushed by President Grover Cleveland, ostensibly to regulate railroads. But railroad executives were told not to worry by Richard Olney, a railroad lawyer who was soon to be Cleveland's attorney general: "The Commission . . . is or can be made, of great use to the railroads. It satisfies the popular clamor for a government supervision of railroads, at the same time that its supervision is almost entirely nominal. . . . The part of wisdom is not to destroy the Commission, but to utilize it."

Piecemeal battles must certainly continue, but there is real and immediate corporate harm to be addressed for people and communities. But it's time for our strategic emphasis to shift to the offensive, raising what I believe to be the central political issues for the new century: *Who the hell is in charge here?*

It is an open question, despite the appearance that corporations have things pretty tightly locked down. Yes, they have the money, the media, the government, the two major parties, the police and military, and the deadening power of conventional wisdom. But so did King George III. We've been here before, we've done this, and we can do it again.

We've got a couple of things going for our side in this historic struggle. For one thing, our constitutional assertion of citizen control of corporations is still there, as is much of the language in the state codes that formally subjugates corporations to us. As Richard Grossman has found in his years of digging, "We still have the authority to *define* the corporations through their charters; we still have the authority to *amend* the charters; we still have the authority to *revoke* the charters—the language is still there. We still have the authority to *rewrite the state corporation codes* in order to *order* corporate executives to do what the sovereign people want to do." We have legal language and authority, a constitutional claim, a moral position firmly rooted in justice, and a powerful historic precedent that flows from the revolutionary patriots themselves.

We also have the common sense and revolutionary chutzpah of grassroots American agitators going for us. The commonsense side says: There are laws in our country that proclaim to human criminals "three strikes and you're out"—why not for corporations? Each year, hundreds of doctors, lawyers, accountants, and other professionals have their licenses to practice permanently revoked by the states—why not corporations? The Supreme Court has rules that the corporation is a "person" under the law; people who murder are removed from society—why not corporations?

The chutzpah side says: Let's go get 'em. And they are! The national media have been practically mum about it, but there already is an important movement among the citizenry to begin reestablishing citizen control over charters. In Wayne, Pennsylvania, the locals passed a 1998 ordinance that prohibits any corporation from doing business there if it has a history of consistently violating laws to protect workers, consumers, the environment, and so forth. In Jay, Maine, a town of paperworkers, the people were fed up with the repeated pollution of the water and air by the recalcitrant International Paper Company, so they enacted the "Jay Environmental and Improvement Ordinance," which gives the town of Jay the authority to monitor and regulate pollution by IPs Androscoggin paper mill—the townspeople have their own full-time environmental administrator with full authority to fine and shut down the mill for violations. In 1998, the people of South Dakota just said "no" to corporate hog factories in their state, voting by a sixty-to-forty margin for a constitutional amendment to prohibit corporations from owning livestock. Also in 1998, New York attorney general Dennis Vacco, a Republican, showed that the Council for Tobacco Research had acted fraudulently and illegally in pretending to do objective research when in fact it was nothing but a lobbyist and a front for the tobacco industry, leading to a settlement in which the council surrendered its corporate charter. The state's new attorney general, Democrat Elliott Spitzer, is expanding Vacco's initiative, considering all corporate charters fair game: "When a corporation is convicted of repeated felonies that harm or endanger the lives of human beings or destroy the environment, the corporation should be put to death, its corporate existence ended, and its assets taken and sold at public auction." He has hired a highly regarded public-interest attorney to oversee this effort.

Meanwhile, in the small coastal town of Arcata, California, there has been a remarkable two-year effort to put the issue of corporate usurpation of democratic authority into the public debate again. It began with Paul Cienfuegos, Gary Houser, and a few others, who organized Democracy Unlimited of Humboldt County, which in 1998 launched a citizens campaign to get on the ballot a local initiative called Measure F: Advisory Measure on Democracy and Corporations. After a few straightforward whereases about the sovereign power of people to govern themselves, the Measure resolved that "the people of Arcata support the amending of the California Constitution so as to clearly declare the authority of citizens over all corporations." The proposition then included a couple of practical steps that, very smartly, took a slow and minimalist approach toward advancing citizen sovereignty in Arcata, establishing a process for democratic discussion in town that could move people along, but not before they were ready to move. First was a simple provision that, if Measure F passed, the city council would sponsor two town hall meetings on this topic: "Can we have democracy when large corporations wield so much power and wealth under law?" Second was for the city government to create an official committee to develop policies and programs to assert democratic control over corporations doing business in Arcata.

The citizens campaign hit the streets, and in just twenty-six days got the signatures needed to put the measure on the ballot. They gained key endorsements from Arcata mayor Jim Test and groups like the central labor council and students at Humboldt State University, and they delivered materials to the doors of nearly every household and business in this town of about seventeen thousand people. In the November 1998 election, their effort paid off: Measure F passed with nearly 60 percent of the vote. Since then, this town has been having what every town, city, neighborhood, and village green needs—a heart-to-heart airing out of the basic question of "Who's in charge?" Ralph Nader visited in 1999 in support of citizen control, likening Arcata's democracy dialogue to the ride of Paul Revere. On the other side, Kenneth Fisher, a *Forbes* magazine columnist and a financial speculator, gave a lecture entitled "Societal Ethics Are Always Unethical," bemoaning Measure F as an example of the "tyranny of democracy." Then came the town hall meetings in April and May of 1999, which produced a turnout of more than six hundred people, far surpassing expectations. The opposition had been active, too, working hard to turn out a pro-corporatist crowd, led by a couple of very vocal officials with the Yakima Corporation, which is based in the area but manufactures at a Mexican border factory. The proceedings were structured so both sides made two presentations of eight minutes each—then the floor was open to the people. The freewheeling discussions went long past the set time, putting the lie to conventional wisdom that insists people are too busy, too satisfied, too uninformed, too unconcerned, too prosperous, too conservative, too short, too stupid, too whatever to get involved with something as "boring" as their own democracy. Overwhelmingly, participants favored Measure F, and the town's people are now at work

on developing the policies and programs for city hall that will put the well-being of the community above corporate whim on issues ranging from chain stores bankrupting local businesses to industry polluting the town's air and water.

Whatever the outcome at city hall, the effort already has accomplished something extraordinarily important: It has launched a citywide democratic conversation on a subject that hasn't been discussed in public for a century. Cienfuegos notes that thousands of local residents are now conversant with corporate rule and how it impacts their lives. It's a conversation that has become common in the cafés, Laundromats, in line at the post office, and elsewhere—literally taking root in the culture of the community. The groundbreaking work in Arcata continues, and it is spreading to other California towns, and to places like Olympia, Washington.

• • •

People are ready for politics that challenges the ongoing corporate grabfest. A recent series of focus-group sessions with middle-class folks (most of whom made in the range of $20,000–$60,000 a year) produced results that cannot be comforting to the Keepers of the Established Order:

- 68 percent of the people viewed corporate greed as an "equally important" or "more important" cause of working families' economic woes than big government—nearly half say corporations are the "more important" cause.
- 70 percent believe that such actions as massive downsizing, cutbacks on worker benefits, and sending U.S. jobs overseas are not motivated by the corporate need to be competitive and efficient, but by greed.
- 79 percent of Democrats in the groups, 67 percent of Republicans, and 74 percent of ticket splitters say the economic and human impacts of these corporate behaviors are serious enough to warrant purposeful government intervention.

I realize that this goes counter to the constant message from those on high who keep telling us that we Americans are a conservative people, but I find the regular folks of this country to be a gutsy bunch who, at their core, have an ingrained commitment to the ideal of democracy, a deep (and hardearned) distrust of concentrations of economic and political power, and a fighting spirit that doesn't need much kindling to flare. People are not "conservative," certainly not in the corporate sense, nor are they "liberal," in the sense of believing that more social programs and nitpicking regulations are going to clean up the messes that are being made by global corporate greed. People are antiestablishment mavericks, and they know (as any mother or kindergarten teacher can tell you) that the better plan is not to keep trying to clean up the messes but to get control over the brutes that are making the messes.

If the progressive movement is going to matter, going to make any difference at all in twenty-first-century politics, it has to understand and act on the latent radicalism (à la 1776) and maverick spirit of the true majority. The term "maverick" even has revolutionary roots—a member of the Maverick family was one of the five "liberty boys" killed at the "Boston Massacre" in 1770. But the term as we use it today actually came from another member of this same family. Samuel Maverick was his name, a pioneer Texas rancher who had fought in the 1836 revolution against the Mexican authorities. A thoroughly independent sort, Sam refused to brand his cattle. So, out on the range, any unbranded calf or steer one came across was said to be a maverick.

Go into the coffee shops and bars where middle-class workaday America hangs out, chat with the cab drivers and grocery clerks, visit working-class churches and neighborhood block parties, talk with nurses, janitors, mechanics, clerks, and restaurant workers while they're on break, shoot the breeze with the regulars at the barber shops or in the feed-and-seed stores. Here's where you'll find the maverick majority for the progressive politics I'm talking about, a constituency willing to run right at corporate power. This is where the progressive future is—not in Washington, fidgeting with policy on the fringes of power, quibbling over which of the namby-pamby corporate suck-ups running for president will do the most for "the cause."

Hey, let's gut it up, decamp from Washington, put our resources into the countryside, slug the corporate bastards right in the snout, and get it on with a grassroots politics that gives regular folks a reason to be excited and to get involved. Why not start the new century and millennium with a political crusade that is worthy of all of our energies and capabilities, a fight that is big enough, important enough, and bold enough to rally the workaday majority? It's the fight to take our government back, take our economy back, take our environment back by taking our sovereignty back—taking back our constitutional right as a people to *be in charge* of our own destinies.

"I may not get there with you," said a prophetic Martin Luther King Jr. in a sermon on the eve of his assassination, but "I've seen the promised land." The land that Reverend King saw is the same land that Woody Guthrie sang about in his cross-country rambles, and that I see today as I travel. It's *our* land, an extraordinary land where ordinary people are the strength, a place with awesome *possibility* to implement the democratic ideals of the people themselves. Through the generations, Americans have taken historic stands to hold on to and advance those ideals. Now is our time, our chance, and our duty to make real the promise of democracy—if not for ourselves, then for our grandchildren.

This *is* an exciting time to be an American.

---

## DISCUSSION QUESTIONS

1. Hightower states that "democracy is control." In what ways does corporate power interfere with popular sovereignty or control?
2. Interpret Hightower's remark that the corporate entity was and is a "legal fiction."
3. How does the case study of citizen action in Arcata, California, relate to Hightower's view of what form progressive politics should take?

**2** *Susan George*

# A SHORT HISTORY OF NEO-LIBERALISM

> *Over the past twenty five years, discussion of politics and public policy in the U.S. and other democratic capitalist countries has been shaped increasingly by the ideology of "neo-liberalism." As political economist Susan George explains, neo-liberalism advocates letting "the market" decide crucial social and political questions. Government social protections are to be slashed and corporations are to be empowered through greater freedom from regulation and taxation. In this article, which originated as a 1999 lecture in Thailand, George provides a brief history of neo-liberalism, noting that it represents a departure from the Keynesian and social democratic policy approaches that were dominant for several decades after World War II. One of George's key points is that neo-liberalism is not a "natural" or foreordained policy approach. It is a political and ideological perspective that has been promoted by a well-funded network of think tanks, research institutes, and publications. For George understanding neo-liberalism demands that we recognize clearly its winners and losers and its view of democracy as an "encumbrance."*

The Conference organizers have asked me for a brief history of neo-liberalism which they title "Twenty Years of Elite Economics." I'm sorry to tell you that in order to make any sense, I have to start even further back, some 50 years ago, just after the end of World War II.

In 1945 or 1950, if you had seriously proposed any of the ideas and policies in today's standard neo-liberal toolkit, you would have been laughed off the stage at or sent off to the insane asylum. At least in the Western countries, at that time, everyone was a Keynesian, a social democrat or a social-Christian democrat or some shade of Marxist. The idea that the market should be allowed to make major social and political decisions; the idea that the State should voluntarily reduce its role in the economy, or that corporations should be given total freedom, that trade unions should be curbed and citizens given much less rather than more social protection—such ideas were utterly foreign to the spirit of the time. Even if someone actually agreed with these ideas, he or she would have hesitated to take such a position in public and would have had a hard time finding an audience.

However incredible it may sound today, particularly to the younger members of the audience, the IMF and the World Bank were seen as progressive institutions. They were sometimes called Keynes's

*Source:* Lecture at the Conference on Economic Sovereignty in a Globalizing World, Bangkok, Thailand, March 24–26, 1999.

twins because they were the brain-children of Keynes and Harry Dexter White, one of Franklin Roosevelt's closest advisors. When these institutions were created at Bretton Woods in 1944, their mandate was to help prevent future conflicts by lending for reconstruction and development and by smoothing out temporary balance of payments problems. They had no control over individual government's economic decisions nor did their mandate include a license to intervene in national policy.

In the Western nations, the Welfare State and the New Deal had got underway in the 1930s but their spread had been interrupted by the war. The first order of business in the post-war world was to put them back in place. The other major item on the agenda was to get world trade moving—this was accomplished through the Marshall Plan which established Europe once again as the major trading partner for the U.S., the most powerful economy in the world. And it was at this time that the strong winds of decolonization also began to blow, whether freedom was obtained by grant as in India or through armed struggle as in Kenya, Vietnam and other nations.

On the whole, the world had signed on for an extremely progressive agenda. The great scholar Karl Polanyi published his masterwork, *The Great Transformation* in 1944, a fierce critique of nineteenth-century industrial, market-based society. Over 50 years ago Polanyi made this amazingly prophetic and modern statement: "To allow the market mechanism to be sole director of the fate of human beings and their natural environment . . . would result in the demolition of society." However, Polanyi was convinced that such a demolition could no longer happen in the post-war world because, as he said, "Within the nations we are witnessing a development under which the economic system ceases to lay down the law to society and the primacy of society over that system is secured."

Alas, Polanyi's optimism was misplaced—the whole point of neo-liberalism is that the market mechanism should be allowed to direct the fate of human beings. The economy should dictate its rules to society, not the other way around. And just as Polanyi foresaw, this doctrine is leading us directly towards the "demolition of society."

So what happened? Why have we reached this point half a century after the end of the Second World War? Or, as the organizers ask, "Why are we having this conference right now?" The short answer is "Because of the series of recent financial crises, especially in Asia". But this begs the question—the question they are really asking is "How did neo-liberalism ever emerge from its ultra-minoritarian ghetto to become the dominant doctrine in the world today?" Why can the IMF and the Bank intervene at will and force countries to participate in the world economy on basically unfavorable terms? Why is the Welfare State under threat in all the countries where it was established? Why is the environment on the edge of collapse and why are there so many poor people in both the rich and the poor countries at a time when there has never existed such great wealth? Those are the questions that need to be answered from an historical perspective.

As I've argued in detail in the U.S. quarterly journal *Dissent*, one explanation for this triumph of neo-liberalism and the economic, political, social and ecological disasters that go with it is that neo-liberals have bought and paid for their own vicious and regressive "Great Transformation". They have understood, as progressives have not, that ideas have consequences. Starting from a tiny embryo at the University of Chicago with the philosopher-economist Friedrich von Hayek and his students like Milton Friedman at its nucleus, the neo-liberals and their funders have created a huge international network of foundations, institutes, research centers, publications, scholars, writers and public relations hacks to develop, package and push their ideas and doctrine relentlessly.

They have built this highly efficient ideological cadre because they understand what the Italian Marxist thinker Antonio Gramsci was talking about when he developed the concept of cultural hegemony. If you can occupy peoples' heads, their hearts and their hands will follow. I do not have time to give you details here, but believe me, the ideological and promotional work of the right has been absolutely brilliant. They have spent hundreds of millions of dollars, but the result has been worth every penny to them because they have made neo-liberalism seem as if it were the natural and normal condition of humankind. No matter how many disasters of all kinds the neo-liberal system has visibly created, no matter what financial crises it may engender, no matter how many losers and outcasts it may create, it is still made to seem inevitable, like an act of God, the only possible economic and social order available to us.

Let me stress how important it is to understand that this vast neo-liberal experiment we are all being forced to live under has been created by people with a purpose. Once you grasp this, once you understand that neo-liberalism is not a force like gravity but a totally artificial construct, you can also understand that what some people have created, other people can change. But they cannot change it without recognizing the importance of ideas. I'm all for grassroots projects, but I also warn that these will collapse if the overall ideological climate is hostile to their goals.

So, from a small, unpopular sect with virtually no influence, neo-liberalism has become the major world religion with its dogmatic doctrine, its priesthood, its law-giving institutions and perhaps most important of all, its hell for heathen and sinners who dare to contest the revealed truth. Oskar Lafontaine, the ex-German Finance Minister whom the *Financial Times* called an "unreconstructed Keynesian" has just been consigned to that hell because he dared to propose higher taxes on corporations and tax cuts for ordinary and less well-off families.

Having set the ideological stage and the context, now let me fast-forward so that we are back in the twenty year time frame. That means 1979, the year Margaret Thatcher came to power and undertook the neo-liberal revolution in Britain. The Iron Lady was herself a disciple of Friedrich von Hayek, she was a social Darwinist and had no qualms about expressing her convictions. She was well known for justifying her program with the single word TINA, short for There Is No Alternative. The central value of Thatcher's doctrine and of neo-liberalism itself is the notion of competition—competition between nations, regions, firms and of course between individuals. Competition is central because it separates the sheep from the goats, the men from the boys, the fit from the unfit. It is supposed to allocate all resources, whether physical, natural, human or financial with the greatest possible efficiency.

In sharp contrast, the great Chinese philosopher Lao Tzu ended his *Tao-te Ching* with these words: "Above all, do not compete." The only actors in the neo-liberal world who seem to have taken his advice are the largest actors of all, the Transnational Corporations. The principle of competition scarcely applies to them; they prefer to practice what we could call Alliance Capitalism. It is no accident that, depending on the year, two-thirds to three-quarters of all the money labeled "Foreign Direct Investment" is not devoted to new, job-creating investment but to Mergers and Acquisitions which almost invariably result in job losses.

Because competition is always a virtue, its results cannot be bad. For the neo-liberal, the market is so wise and so good that like God, the Invisible Hand can bring good out of apparent evil. Thus Thatcher once said in a speech, "It is our job to glory in inequality and see that talents and abilities are given vent and expression for the benefit of us all." In other words, don't worry about those who might be left behind in the competitive struggle. People are unequal by nature, but this is good because the contributions of the well-born, the best-educated, the toughest, will eventually benefit everyone. Nothing in particular is owed to the weak, the poorly educated, what happens to them is their own fault, never the fault of society. If the competitive system is "given vent" as Margaret says, society will be the better for it. Unfortunately, the history of the past twenty years teaches us that exactly the opposite is the case.

In pre-Thatcher Britain, about one person in ten was classed as living below the poverty line, not a brilliant result but honorable as nations go and a lot better than in the pre-War period. Now one person in four, and one child in three is officially poor. This is the meaning of survival of the fittest: people who cannot heat their houses in winter, who must put a coin in the meter before they can have electricity or water, who do not own a warm waterproof coat, etc. I am taking these examples from the 1996 report of the British Child Poverty Action Group. I will illustrate the result of the Thatcher-Major "tax reforms" with a single example: During the 1980s, 1 percent of taxpayers received 29 percent of all the tax reduction benefits, such that a single person earning half the average salary found his or her taxes had gone up by 7 percent, whereas a single person earning 10 times the average salary got a reduction of 21 percent.

Another implication of competition as the central value of neo-liberalism is that the public sector must be brutally downsized because it does not and cannot obey the basic law of competing for profits or for market share. Privatization is one of the major economic transformations of the past twenty years. The trend began in Britain and has spread throughout the world.

Let me start by asking why capitalist countries, particularly in Europe, had public services to begin with, and why many still do. In reality, nearly all public services constitute what economists call "natural monopolies." A natural monopoly exists when the minimum size to guarantee maximum economic efficiency is equal to the actual size of the market. In other words, a company has to be a certain size to realize economies of scale and thus provide the best possible service at the lowest possible cost to the consumer. Public services also require very large investment outlays at the beginning—like railroad tracks or power grids—which does not encourage competition either. That's why public monopolies were the obvious optimum solution. But neo-liberals define anything public as ipso facto "inefficient".

So what happens when a natural monopoly is privatized? Quite normally and naturally, the new capitalist owners tend to impose monopoly prices on the public, while richly remunerating themselves. Classical economists call this outcome "structural market failure" because prices are higher than they ought to be and service to the consumer is not necessarily good. In order to prevent structural market failures, up to the mid-1980s, the capitalist countries of Europe almost universally entrusted the post office, telecoms, electricity, gas, railways, metros, air transport and usually other services like water, rubbish collection, etc. to state-owned monopolies. The U.S.A. is the big exception, perhaps because it is too huge geographically to favor natural monopolies.

In any event, Margaret Thatcher set out to change all that. As an added bonus, she could also use privatization to break the power of the trade unions. By destroying the public sector where unions were strongest, she was able to weaken them drastically. Thus between 1979 and 1994, the number of jobs in the public sector in Britain was reduced from over 7 million to 5 million, a drop of 29 percent. Virtually all the jobs eliminated were unionized jobs. Since private sector employment was stagnant during those fifteen years, the overall reduction in the number of British jobs came to 1.7 million, a drop of 7 percent compared to 1979. To neo-liberals, fewer workers is always better than more because workers impinge on shareholder value.

As for other effects of privatization, they were predictable and predicted. The managers of the newly privatized enterprises, often exactly the same people as before, doubled or tripled their own salaries. The government used taxpayer money to wipe out debts and recapitalize firms before putting them on the market—for example, the water authority got 5 billion pounds of debt relief plus 1.6 billion pounds called the "green dowry" to make the bride more attractive to prospective buyers. A lot of Public Relations fuss was made about how small stockholders would have a stake in these companies—and in fact 9 million Brits did buy shares—but half of them invested less than a thousand pounds and most of them sold their shares rather quickly, as soon as they could cash in on the instant profits.

From the results, one can easily see that the whole point of privatization is neither economic efficiency nor improved services to the consumer but simply to transfer wealth from the public purse—which could redistribute it to even out social inequalities—to private hands. In Britain and elsewhere, the overwhelming majority of privatized company shares are now in the hands of financial institutions and very large investors. The employees of British Telecom bought only 1 percent of the shares, those of British Aerospace 1.3 percent, etc. Prior to Ms Thatcher's onslaught, a lot of the public sector in Britain was profitable. Consequently, in 1984, public companies contributed over 7 billion pounds to the treasury. All that money is now going to private shareholders. Service in the privatized industries is now often disastrous—the *Financial*

*Times* reported an invasion of rats in the Yorkshire Water system and anyone who has survived taking Thames trains in Britain deserves a medal.

Exactly the same mechanisms have been at work throughout the world. In Britain, the Adam Smith Institute was the intellectual partner for creating the privatization ideology. USAID and the World Bank have also used Adam Smith experts and have pushed the privatization doctrine in the South. By 1991 the Bank had already made 114 loans to speed the process, and every year its Global Development Finance report lists hundreds of privatizations carried out in the Bank's borrowing countries.

I submit that we should stop talking about privatization and use words that tell the truth: we are talking about alienation and surrender of the product of decades of work by thousands of people to a tiny minority of large investors. This is one of the greatest hold-ups of ours or any generation.

Another structural feature of neo-liberalism consists in remunerating capital to the detriment of labor and thus moving wealth from the bottom of society to the top. If you are, roughly, in the top 20 percent of the income scale, you are likely to gain something from neo-liberalism and the higher you are up the ladder, the more you gain. Conversely, the bottom 80 percent all lose and the lower they are to begin with, the more they lose proportionally.

Lest you thought I had forgotten Ronald Reagan, let me illustrate this point with the observations of Kevin Phillips, a Republican analyst and former aid to President Nixon, who published a book in 1990 called *The Politics of Rich and Poor*. He charted the way Reagan's neo-liberal doctrine and policies had changed American income distribution between 1977 and 1988. These policies were largely elaborated by the conservative Heritage Foundation, the principle think-tank of the Reagan administration and still an important force in American politics. Over the decade of the 1980s, the top 10 percent of American families increased their average family income by 16 percent, the top 5 percent increased theirs by 23 percent, but the extremely lucky top 1 percent of American families could thank Reagan for a 50 percent increase. Their revenues went from

an affluent $270,000 to a heady $405,000. As for poorer Americans, the bottom 80 percent all lost something; true to the rule, the lower they were on the scale, the more they lost. The bottom 10 percent of Americans reached the nadir: according to Phillip's figures, they lost 15 percent of their already meager incomes: from an already rock-bottom average of $4,113 annually, they dropped to an inhuman $3,504. In 1977, the top 1 percent of American families had average incomes 65 times as great as those of the bottom 10 percent. A decade later, the top 1 percent was 115 times as well off as the bottom decile.

America is one of the most unequal societies on earth, but virtually all countries have seen inequalities increase over the past twenty years because of neo-liberal policies. UNCTAD published some damning evidence to this effect in its 1997 Trade and Development Report based on some 2600 separate studies of income inequalities, impoverishment and the hollowing out of the middle classes. The UNCTAD team documents these trends in dozens of widely differing societies, including China, Russia and the other former Socialist countries.

There is nothing mysterious about this trend towards greater inequality. Policies are specifically designed to give the already rich more disposable income, particularly through tax cuts and by pushing down wages. The theory and ideological justification for such measures is that higher incomes for the rich and higher profits will lead to more investment, better allocation of resources and therefore more jobs and welfare for everyone. In reality, as was perfectly predictable, moving money up the economic ladder has led to stock market bubbles, untold paper wealth for the few, and the kind of financial crises we shall be hearing a lot about in the course of this conference. If income is redistributed towards the bottom 80 percent of society, it will be used for consumption and consequently benefit employment. If wealth is redistributed towards the top, where people already have most of the things they need, it will go not into the local or national economy but to international stockmarkets.

As you are all aware, the same policies have been carried out throughout the South and East under the guise of structural adjustment, which is merely another name for neo-liberalism. I've used Thatcher and Reagan to illustrate the policies at the national level. At the international level, neo-liberals have concentrated all their efforts on three fundamental points:

- free trade in goods and services
- free circulation of capital
- freedom of investment

Over the past twenty years, the IMF has been strengthened enormously. Thanks to the debt crisis and the mechanism of conditionality, it has moved from balance of payments support to being quasi-universal dictator of so-called "sound" economic policies, meaning of course neo-liberal ones. The World Trade Organization was finally put in place in January 1995 after long and laborious negotiations, often rammed through parliaments which had little idea what they were ratifying. Thankfully, the most recent effort to make binding and universal neo-liberal rules, the Multilateral Agreement on Investment, has failed, at least temporarily. It would have given all rights to corporations, all obligations to governments and no rights at all to citizens.

The common denominator of these institutions is their lack of transparency and democratic accountability. This is the essence of neo-liberalism. It claims that the economy should dictate its rules to society, not the other way around. Democracy is an encumbrance, neo-liberalism is designed for winners, not for voters who, necessarily encompass the categories of both winners and losers.

I'd like to conclude by asking you to take very seriously indeed the neo-liberal definition of the loser, to whom nothing in particular is owed. Anyone can be ejected from the system at any time—because of illness, age, pregnancy, perceived failure, or simply because economic circumstances and the relentless transfer of wealth from top to bottom demand it. Shareholder value is all. Recently the *International Herald Tribune* reported that foreign investors are "snapping up" Thai and Korean companies and Banks. Not surprisingly, these purchases are expected to result in "heavy layoffs."

In other words, the results of years of work by thousands of Thais and Koreans is being transferred into foreign corporate hands. Many of those who labored to create that wealth have already been, or soon will be left on the pavement. Under the principles of competition and maximizing shareholder value, such behavior is seen not as criminally unjust but as normal and indeed virtuous.

I submit that neo-liberalism has changed the fundamental nature of politics. Politics used to be primarily about who ruled whom and who got what share of the pie. Aspects of both these central questions remain, of course, but the great new central question of politics is, in my view, "Who has a right to live and who does not." Radical exclusion is now the order of the day, I mean this deadly seriously.

I've given you rather a lot of bad news because the history of the past twenty years is full of it. But I don't want to end on such a depressing and pessimistic note. A lot is already happening to counter these life-threatening trends and there is enormous scope for further action.

This conference is going to help define much of that action which I believe must include an ideological offensive. It's time we set the agenda instead of letting the Masters of the Universe set it at Davos. I hope funders may also understand that they should not be funding just projects but also ideas. We can't count on the neo-liberals to do it, so we need to design workable and equitable international taxation systems, including a Tobin Tax on all monetary and financial market transactions and taxes on Transnational Corporation sales on a pro-rata basis. I expect we will go into detail on such questions in the workshops here. The proceeds of an international tax system should go to closing the North-South gap and to redistribution to all the people who have been robbed over the past twenty years.

Let me repeat what I said earlier: neo-liberalism is not the natural human condition, it is not supernatural, it can be challenged and replaced because its own failures will require this. We have to be ready with replacement policies which restore power to communities and democratic states while working to institute democracy, the rule of law and fair distribution at the international level. Business and the market have their place, but this place cannot occupy the entire sphere of human existence.

Further good news is that there is plenty of money sloshing around out there and a tiny fraction, a ridiculous, infinitesimal proportion of it would be enough to provide a decent life to every person on earth, to supply universal health and education, to clean up the environment and prevent further destruction to the planet, to close the North-South gap—at least according to the UNDP which calls for a paltry $40 billion a year. That, frankly, is peanuts.

Finally, please remember that neo-liberalism may be insatiable but it is not invulnerable. A coalition of international activists only yesterday obliged them to abandon, at least temporarily, their project to liberalize all investment through the MAI. The surprise victory of its opponents infuriated the supporters of corporate rule and demonstrates that well organized network guerillas can win battles. Now we have to regroup our forces and keep at them so that they cannot transfer the MAI to the WTO.

Look at it this way. We have the numbers on our side, because there are far more losers than winners in the neo-liberal game. We have the ideas, whereas theirs are finally coming into question because of repeated crisis. What we lack, so far, is the organization and the unity which in this age of advanced technology we can overcome. The threat is clearly transnational so the response must also be transnational. Solidarity no longer means aid, or not just aid, but finding the hidden synergies in each other's struggles so that our numerical force and the power of our ideas become overwhelming. I'm convinced this conference will contribute mightily to this goal and I thank you all for your kind attention.

---

## DISCUSSION QUESTIONS

1. According to George, in what ways does neo-liberalism amount to a kind of "elite economics"?
2. George says that "neo-liberalism is not the natural human condition." What is her explanation for how and why neo-liberal ideas became influential? In what ways might neo-liberalism be politically vulnerable?

**3** *Dan Clawson, Alan Neustadtl, and Mark Weller*

# WHY DOES THE AIR STINK? CORPORATE POWER AND PUBLIC POLICY

*How is economic power translated into political influence? Sociologists Dan Clawson, Alan Neustadtl, and Mark Weller examine the impact of corporate polit-ical action committees (PACs) on public policy. Uniquely drawing on interviews with PAC directors, they demonstrate how campaign contributions win "access" to members of Congress, resulting in loopholes and regulatory rules favorable to business. Clawson, Neustadtl, and Weller base their analysis of corporate PACs on a "field theory of power." Focus on this concept and consider its usefulness in understanding business "hegemony" in our political system. In a concluding sec-tion, the authors itemize the enormous public impact of private corporate power by providing a detailed list of decisions made by business companies in the United States. One implication of this analysis is that even if PACs were banned, business decisions would have a greater impact on our lives than most govern-ment decisions have, barring significant change in our economic system.*

Everybody wants clean air. Who could oppose it? "I spent seven years of my life trying to stop the Clean Air Act," explained the vice president of a major cor-poration that is a heavy-duty polluter. Nonetheless, he was perfectly willing to make campaign contribu-tions to members who voted for the act:

How a person votes on the final piece of leg-islation often is not representative of what they have done. Somebody will do a lot of things during the process. How many guys voted against the Clean Air Act? But during the process some of them were very sympa-thetic to some of our concerns.

In the world of Congress and political action committees things are not always what they seem. Members of Congress all want to vote for clean air, but they also want to get campaign contributions from corporations, and they want to pass a law that business will accept as "reasonable." The compro-mise solution is to gut the bill by crafting dozens of loopholes. These are inserted in private meetings or in subcommittee hearings that don't get much (if any) attention in the press. Then the public vote on the final bill can be nearly unanimous. Members of Congress can reassure their constituents and their corporate contributors: constituents, that they voted for the final bill; corporations, that they helped

*Source:* Dan Clawson, Alan Neustadtl, and Mark Weller, *Dollars and Votes: How Business Campaign Contributions Subvert Democracy,* Philadelphia: Temple University Press, 1998, pp. 6–12, 21–26, and 188–191.

weaken it in private. Clean air, and especially the Clean Air Act of 1990, can serve as an introduction to the kind of process we try to expose.

The public strongly supports clean air, and is unimpressed when corporate officials and apologists trot out their normal arguments—"corporations are already doing all they reasonably can to improve environmental quality," "we need to balance the costs against the benefits," "people will lose their jobs if we make controls any stricter." The original Clean Air Act was passed in 1970, revised in 1977, and not revised again until 1990. Although the initial goal was to have us breathing clean air by 1975, the deadline has been repeatedly extended—and the 1990 legislation provides a new set of deadlines to be reached sometime in the distant future.

Corporations control the production process unless the government specifically intervenes. Therefore, any delay in government action leaves corporations free to do as they choose; business often prefers a weak, ineffective, and unenforceable law. The laws have not only been slow to come, but corporations have also fought to delay or subvert implementation. The 1970 law ordered the Environmental Protection Agency (EPA) to regulate the hundreds of poisonous chemicals that are emitted by corporations, but, as William Greider notes, "In twenty years of stalling, dodging, and fighting off court orders, the EPA has managed to issue regulatory standards for a total of seven toxics."

Corporations have done exceptionally well politically, given the problem they face: The interests of business are diametrically opposed to those of the public. Clean air laws and amendments have been few and far between, enforcement is ineffective, and the penalties minimal. On the one hand, corporations *have* had to pay *billions for clean-ups;* on the other hand, the costs to date are a small fraction of what would be needed to actually clean up the environment.

This corporate struggle for the right to pollute takes place on many fronts. The most visible is public relations: the Chemical Manufacturers Association took out a two-page Earth Day ad in the *Washington Post* to demonstrate its concern; coincidentally, the names of many of the corporate signers

of this ad appear on the EPA's list of high-risk producers. Another front is expert studies that delay action while more information is gathered. The federally funded National Acid Precipitation Assessment Program took ten years and $600 million to figure out whether acid rain was in fact a problem. Both business and the Reagan administration argued that nothing should be done until the study was completed. Ultimately, the study was discredited: The "summary of findings" minimized the impact of acid rain, even though this did not accurately represent the expert research in the report. But the key site of struggle was Congress. For years, corporations successfully defeated legislation. In 1987 utility companies were offered a compromise bill on acid rain, but they "were very adamant that they had beat the thing since 1981 and they could always beat it," according to Representative Edward Madigan (Republican-Illinois). The utilities beat back all efforts at reform through the 1980s, but their intransigence probably hurt them when revisions finally came to be made.

The stage was set for a revision of the Clean Air Act when George Bush, "the environmental president," was elected, and George Mitchell, a strong supporter of environmentalism, became the Senate majority leader. But what sort of clean air bill would it be? "What we wanted," said Richard Ayres, head of the environmentalists' Clean Air Coalition, "is a health based standard—one-in-1-million cancer risk," a standard that would require corporations to clean up their plants until the cancer risk from their operations was reduced to one in a million. "The Senate bill still has the requirement," Ayres said, "but there are forty pages of extensions and exceptions and qualifications and loopholes that largely render the health standard a nullity." Greider reports, for example, "According to the EPA, there are now twenty-six coke ovens that pose a cancer risk greater than 1 in 1000 and six where the risk is greater than 1 in 100. Yet the new clean-air bill will give the steel industry another thirty years to deal with the problem."

This change from what the bill was supposed to do to what it did do came about through what corporate executives like to call the "access" process. The principal aim of most corporate campaign contributions is to help corporate executives gain "access" to key members of Congress and their staffs. In these meetings, corporate executives (and corporate PAC money) work to persuade the member of Congress to accept a predesigned loophole that will sound innocent but effectively undercut the stated intention of the bill. Representative John D. Dingell (Democrat-Michigan), who was chair of the House Committee, is a strong industry supporter; one of the people we interviewed called him "the point man for the Business Roundtable on clean air." Representative Henry A. Waxman (Democrat-California), chair of the subcommittee, is an environmentalist. Observers had expected a confrontation and contested votes on the floor of the Congress.

The problem for corporations was that, as one Republican staff aide said, "If any bill has the blessing of Waxman and the environmental groups, unless it is totally in outer space, who's going to vote against it?" But corporations successfully minimized public votes. Somehow, Waxman was persuaded to make behind-the-scenes compromises with Dingell so members, during an election year, didn't have to side publicly with business against the environment. Often the access process leads to loopholes that protect a single corporation, but for "clean" air most of the special deals targeted not specific companies but entire industries. The initial bill, for example, required cars to be able to use carefully specified, cleaner fuels. But the auto industry wanted the rules loosened, and Congress eventually incorporated a variant of a formula suggested by the head of General Motors' fuels and lubricants department.

Nor did corporations stop fighting even after they gutted the bill through amendments. Business pressed the EPA for favorable regulations to implement the law: "The cost of this legislation could vary dramatically, depending on how EPA interprets it," said William D. Fay, vice president of the National Coal Association, who headed the hilariously misnamed Clean Air Working Group, an industry coalition that fought to weaken the legislation. As one EPA aide working on acid rain regulations reported, "We're having a hard time getting our work done because of the number of phone calls we're getting" from corporations and their lawyers.

Corporations trying to get federal regulators to adopt the "right" regulations don't rely exclusively on the cogency of their arguments. They often exert pressure on a member of Congress to intervene for them at the EPA or other agency. Senators and representatives regularly intervene on behalf of constituents and contributors by doing everything from straightening out a social security problem to asking a regulatory agency to explain why it is pressuring a company. This process—like campaign finance—usually follows rules of etiquette. In addressing a regulatory agency, the senator does not say, "Lay off my campaign contributors or I'll cut your budget." One standard phrasing for letters asks regulators to resolve the problem "as quickly as possible within applicable rules and regulations." No matter how mild and careful the inquiry, the agency receiving the request is certain to give it extra attention; only after careful consideration will they refuse to make any accommodation.

Soft money—unregulated megabuck contributions—also shaped what happened to air quality. Archer Daniels Midland argued that increased use of ethanol would reduce pollution from gasoline; coincidentally, ADM controls a majority of the ethanol market. To reinforce its arguments, in the 1992 election ADM gave $90,000 to Democrats and $600,000 to Republicans, the latter supplemented with an additional $200,000 as an individual contribution from the company head, Dwayne Andreas. Many environmentalists were skeptical about ethanol's value in a clean air strategy, but President Bush issued regulations promoting wider use of ethanol; we presume he was impressed by the force of ADM's 800,000 Republican arguments. Bob Dole, the 1996 Republican presidential candidate, helped pass and defend special breaks for the ethanol industry; he not only appreciated ADM's Republican contributions, but presumably approved of the more than $1 million they gave to the American Red Cross during the period when it was headed by his wife, Elizabeth Dole. What about the post-1994 Republican-controlled Congress, defenders of the free market and opponents of government giveaways? Were they ready to end this subsidy program, cracking down on corporate welfare as they did on people welfare? Not a chance. In 1997, the Republican chair of the House Ways and Means Committee actually attempted to eliminate the special tax breaks for ethanol. Needless to say, he was immediately put in his place by other members of the Republican leadership, including Speaker Newt Gingrich and most of the Senate, with the subsidy locked in place for years to come, in spite of a General Accounting Office report that "found that the ethanol subsidy justifies none of its political boasts." The Center for Responsive Politics calculated that ADM, its executives and PAC, made more than $1 million in campaign contributions of various types; the only thing that had changed was that in 1996, with a Democratic president, this money was "divided more or less evenly between Republicans and Democrats."

The disparity in power between business and environmentalists looms large during the legislative process, but it is enormous afterward. When the Clean Air Act passed, corporations and industry groups offered positions, typically with large pay increases, to congressional staff members who wrote the law. The former congressional staff members who now work for corporations both know how to evade the law and can persuasively claim to EPA that they know what Congress intended. Environmental organizations pay substantially less than Congress and can't afford large staffs. They are seldom able to become involved in the details of the administrative process or to influence implementation and enforcement.

Having pushed Congress and the Environmental Protection Agency to allow as much pollution as possible, business then went to the Quayle council for rules allowing even more pollution. Vice President J. Danforth Quayle's council, technically known as the "Council on Competitiveness," was created by President Bush specifically to help reduce regulations on business. Quayle told the *Boston Globe* "that his council has an 'open door' to business groups and that he has a bias against regulations." During the Bush administration, this council reviewed, and could override, all regulations, including those by the EPA setting the limits at which a chemical was subject to regulation. The council also recommended that corporations be allowed to increase their polluting emissions if a state did not object within seven days of the proposed increase. Corporations thus have multiple opportunities to win. If they lose in Congress, they can win at the regulatory agency; if they lose there, they can try again at the Quayle Council (or later equivalent). If they lose there, they can try to reduce the money available to enforce regulations, or tie the issue up in the courts, or plan on accepting a minimal fine.

The operation of the Quayle council probably would have received little publicity, but reporters discovered that the executive director of the Council, Allan Hubbard, had a clear conflict of interest. Hubbard chaired the biweekly White House meetings on the Clean Air Act. He owned half of World Wide Chemical, received an average of more than $1 million a year in profits from it while directing the Quayle council, and continued to attend quarterly stockholder meetings. According to the *Boston Globe,* "Records on file with the Indianapolis Air Pollution Control Board show that World Wide Chemical emitted 17,000 to 19,000 pounds of chemicals into the air" in 1991. At that time the company did "not have the permit required to release the emissions," was "putting out nearly four times the allowable emissions without a permit, and could be subject to a $2,500-a-day penalty," according to David Jordan, director of the Indianapolis Air Pollution Board.

This does not, however, mean that business always gets exactly what it wants. In 1997, the Environmental Protection Agency proposed tough new rules for soot and smog. Business fought hard to weaken or eliminate the rules: hiring experts (from pro-business think tanks) to attack the scientific studies supporting the regulations and putting a raft of lobbyists ("many of them former congressional staffers," the *Washington Post* reported) to work securing the signatures of 250 members of Congress questioning the standards. But the late 1990s version of these industry mobilizations adds a new twist—creating a pseudo-grassroots campaign. For example, business, operating under a suitably disguised name (Foundation for Clean Air

Progress), paid for television ads telling farmers that the EPA rules would prohibit them from plowing on dry windy days, with other ads predicting the EPA rules "would lead to forced carpooling or bans on outdoor barbecues—claims the EPA dismisses as ridiculous." Along with the ads, industry worked to mobilize local politicians and business executives in what business groups called a "grass tops" campaign.

Despite a massive industry campaign, EPA head Carol Browner remained firm, and President Clinton was persuaded to go along. Of course, industry immediately began working on ways to undercut the regulations with congressional loopholes and exceptions—but business has suffered a defeat, and proponents of clean air (that is, most of the rest of us) had won at least a temporary and partial victory. And who leads the struggles to overturn or uphold these regulations? Just as before, Dingell and Waxman; Republicans "are skittish about challenging" the rules publicly, "so they gladly defer to Dingell as their surrogate." Dingell's forces have more than 130 cosponsors (about one-third of them Democrats) for a bill to, in effect, override the EPA standards.

In business-government relations most attention becomes focused on instances of scandal. The real issue, however, is not one or another scandal or conflict of interest, but rather the *system* of business-government relations, and especially of campaign finance, that offers business so many opportunities to craft loopholes, undermine regulations, and subvert enforcement. Still worse, many of these actions take place beyond public scrutiny.

·   ·   ·

## WHAT IS POWER?

Our analysis is based on an understanding of power that differs from that usually articulated by both business and politicians. The corporate PAC directors we interviewed insisted that they have no power.

If you were to ask me what kind of access and influence do we have, being roughly the 150th largest PAC, I would have to tell you that on the basis of our money we have zero. . . . If you look at the level of our contributions, we know we're not going to buy anybody's vote, we're not going to rent anybody, or whatever the clichés have been over the years. We know that.

The executives who expressed these views clearly meant these words sincerely. Their statements are based on roughly the same understanding of "power" that is current with political science, which is also the way the term was defined by Max Weber, the classical sociological theorist. Power, in this common conception, is the ability to make someone do something against their will. If that is what power means, then corporations rarely have any in relation to members of Congress, nor does soft money give the donor power over presidents. As one senior vice president said to us: "You certainly aren't going to be able to buy anybody for $500 or $1,000 or $10,000—it's a joke." Soft money donations of a million dollars might seem to change the equation, but we will argue they do not: Just as $10,000 won't buy a member of Congress, $1,000,000 won't buy a president. In this regard we agree with the corporate officials we interviewed: A corporation is not in a position to say to a member of Congress, "Either you vote for this bill, or we will defeat your bid for reelection." Rarely do they even say: "You vote for this bill or you won't get any money from us."

This definition of power as the ability to make someone do something against their will is what Steven Lukes calls a "one-dimensional" view of power. A two-dimensional view recognizes the existence of nondecisions: A potential issue never gets articulated or, if articulated by someone somewhere, never receives serious consideration. For example, in 1989 and 1990 one of the major political battles, and a focus of great effort by corporate PACs, was the Clean Air Act. Yet twenty or thirty years earlier, before the rise of the environmental movement, pollution was a nonissue: it simply was not considered, although its effects were, in retrospect, of great importance. In one of Sherlock Holmes stories, the key clue is that the dog didn't bark. A two-dimensional view of power makes the same point: The most important clue in some situation may be that no one noticed power was exercised—because there was no overt conflict.

Even this model of power is too restrictive, however, because it still focuses on discrete decisions and nondecisions. Tom Wartenberg calls these "interventional" models of power, and notes that, in such models "the primary locus of power . . . is a specific social interaction between two social agents." Such models do not recognize "the idea that the most fundamental use of power in society is its use in structuring the basic manner in which social agents interact with one another." Wartenberg argues, instead, for a "field theory" of power that analyzes social power as a force similar to a magnetic field. A magnetic field alters the motion of objects susceptible to magnetism. Similarly, the mere presence of a powerful social agent alters the social space for others and causes them to orient themselves toward the powerful agent. For example, one of the executives we interviewed took it for granted that "if we go see the congressman who represents [a city where the company has a major plant], where 10,000 of our employees are also his constituents, we don't need a PAC to go see him." The corporation is so important in that area that the member has to orient himself in relation to the corporation and its concerns. In a different sense, the very act of accepting a campaign contribution changes the way a member relates to a PAC, creating a sense of obligation, a need to reciprocate. The PAC contribution has altered the member's social space, his or her awareness of the company and wish to help it, even if no explicit commitments have been made.

## BUSINESS IS DIFFERENT

Power, we would argue, is not just the ability to force someone to do something against their will; it is most effective (and least recognized) when it shapes the field of action. Moreover, business's vast resources, influence on the economy, and general legitimacy place it on a different footing from other

campaign contributors. Every day a member of Congress accepts a $1,000 donation from a corporate PAC, goes to a committee hearing, proposes "minor" changes in a bill's wording, and has those changes accepted without discussion or examination. The changes "clarify" the language of the bill, legalizing higher levels of pollution for a specific pollutant, or exempting the company from some tax. The media do not report on this change, and no one speaks against it. On the other hand, if a PAC were formed by Drug Lords for Cocaine Legalization, no member would take their money. If a member introduced a "minor" wording change to make it easier to sell crack without bothersome police interference, the proposed change would attract massive attention, the campaign contribution would be labeled a scandal, the member's political career would be ruined, and the changed wording would not be incorporated into the bill. Drug Lords may make an extreme example, but approximately the same holds true for many groups: At present, equal rights for gays and lesbians could never be a minor and unnoticed addition to a bill with a different purpose.

Even groups with great social legitimacy encounter more opposition and controversy than business faces for proposals that are virtually without public support. One example is the contrast between the largely unopposed commitment of tens or hundreds of billions of dollars for the savings and loan bailout, compared to the sharp debate, close votes, and defeats for the rights of men and women to take *unpaid* parental leave. The classic term for something non-controversial that everyone must support is "a motherhood issue," and while it costs little to guarantee every woman the right to an *un*paid parental leave, this measure nonetheless generated intense scrutiny and controversy—going down to defeat under President Bush, passing under President Clinton, and then again becoming a focus of attack after the 1994 Republican takeover of Congress. Few indeed are the people publicly prepared to defend pollution or tax evasion. Nevertheless, business is routinely able to win pollution exemptions and tax loopholes. Although cumulatively some vague awareness of these provisions may trouble people, most are allowed individually to pass without scrutiny. *No* analysis of corporate political activity makes sense unless it begins with a recognition of this absolutely vital point. The PAC is a vital element of corporate power, but it does not operate by itself. The PAC donation is always backed by the wider power and influence of business.

Corporations are unlike other "special interest" groups not only because business has far more resources, but also because its acceptance and legitimacy. When people feel that "the system" is screwing them, they tend to blame politicians, the government, the media—but rarely business. In terms of campaign finance, while much of the public is outraged at the way money influences elections and public policy, the issue is almost always posed in terms of politicians, what they do or don't do. This is part of a pervasive double standard that largely exempts business from criticism. We, however, believe it is vital to scrutinize business as well.

We did two dozen radio call-in shows after the appearance of our last book, *Money Talks*. On almost every show, at least one call came from someone outraged that members of Congress had recently raised their pay to $125,100. (For 1998, it will be about $137,000.) Not a single person even mentioned corporate executives' pay. *Business Week* calculated that in 1996 corporate CEOs were paid an average of $5.8 million (counting salary, bonuses, and stock option grants), or more than 200 times the average worker's pay, and more than 40 times what members of Congress are paid. More anger is directed at Congress for delaying new environmental laws than at the companies who fight every step of the way to stall and subvert the legislation. When members of Congress do favors for large campaign contributors, anger is directed at the senators who went along, not at the business owner who paid the money (and usually initiated the pressure). The public focuses on the member's receipt of thousands of dollars, not on the business's receipt of millions (or hundreds of millions) in tax breaks or special treatment. It is a widely held belief that "politics is dirty." But little public comment and condemnation is generated when companies get away—quite literally—with murder. This disparity is evidence of business's success in shaping

public perceptions. Lee Atwater, George Bush's 1988 campaign manager, saw this as a key to Republican success:

> In the 1980 campaign, we were able to make the establishment, insofar as it is bad, the government. In other words, big government was the enemy, not big business. If the people think the problem is that taxes are too high, and the government interferes too much, then we are doing our job. But, if they get to the point where they say that the real problem is that rich people aren't paying taxes, . . . then the Democrats are going to be in good shape.

We argue that corporations are so different, and so dominant, that they exercise a special kind of power, what Antonio Gramsci called hegemony. Hegemony can be regarded as the ultimate example of a field of power that structures what people and groups do. It is sometimes referred to as a worldview, a way of thinking about the world that influences every action, and makes it difficult to even consider alternatives. But in Gramsci's analysis it is much more than this, it is a culture and set of institutions that structure life patterns and coerce a particular way of life. Susan Harding gives the example of relations between whites and blacks in the South prior to the 1960s. Black inferiority and subservience were not simply ideas articulated by white racists, they were incorporated into a set of social practices: segregated schools, restrooms, swimming pools, restaurants; the black obligation to refer to white men as "Mister"; the prohibition on referring to black men as "Mister"; the use of the term "boy" for black males of any age and social status; the white right to go to the front of any line or to take the seat of any African American, and so on. Most blacks recognized the injustice and absurdity of these rules, but this did not enable them to escape, much less defy, them. White hegemony could not be overthrown simply by recognizing its existence or articulating an ideal of equality; black people had to create a movement that transformed themselves, the South, and the nation as a whole.

Hegemony is most successful and most powerful, when it is unrecognized. White hegemony in the South was strong but never unrecognized and rarely uncontested. White southerners would have denied, probably in all sincerity, that they exercised power: "Why our nigras are perfectly happy that's the way they want to be treated." But many black southerners would have vigorously disputed this while talking to each other. In some sense, gender relations in the 1950s embodied a hegemony even more powerful than that of race relations. Betty Friedan titled the first chapter of *The Feminine Mystique* "The Problem That Has No Name," because women literally did not have a name for, did not recognize the existence of, their oppression. Women as well as men denied the existence of inequality or oppression, denied the systematic exercise of power to maintain unequal relations.

We argue that today business has enormous power and exercises effective hegemony, even though (perhaps because) this is largely undiscussed and unrecognized. *Politically,* business power today is similar to white treatment of blacks in 1959—business may sincerely deny its power, but many of the groups it exercises power over recognize it, feel dominated, resent this, and fight the power as best they can. At least until very recently, *economically,* business power was more like gender relations in 1959: Virtually no one saw this power as problematic. The revived labor movement is beginning to change this, and there are signs that a movement is beginning to contest corporate power. Nonetheless, if the issue is brought to people's attention, many still don't see a problem: "Well, so what? How else could it be? Maybe we don't like it, but that's just the way things are."

Hegemony is never absolute. African Americans and women both were (and are) forced to live in disadvantaged conditions, but simultaneously fought for dignity and respect. Unusual individuals always violated conventions and tested limits. A hegemonic power is usually opposed by a counterhegemony. Thus, while children in our society are taught to compete with each other to earn the praise of authority figures, and while most children

engage in this process much of the time, it is also true that the "teacher's pet" is likely to face ostracism. We hope this book makes a small contribution to weakening business hegemony and to developing a counterhegemony.

•   •   •

The primary power of the wealthy is not exercised by individuals or even by families. Power in our society is based in institutions, not individuals, and the power of wealth is channeled through corporations. There are more than 200,000 industrial corporations in the United States, but all companies are *not* created equal: The 500 largest industrials control three-quarters of the sales, assets, and profits of *all* industrial corporations. More than 250 of these companies had revenues of more than $5 billion. Similarly, in the service sector, 500 firms control a disproportionate share of the resources. The dominance of these corporations means that a handful of owners and top executives, perhaps one-hundredth of one percent of the U.S. population, or 25,000 individuals, have the power to make decisions that have a huge impact on all of our lives. Collectively these people exercise incalculable power, making decisions with more impact on most of our lives than those made by the entire elected government.

Consider for a moment those decisions that virtually everyone in our society agrees should be made by business. Consider, for this exercise, only those decisions on which there is broad bipartisan political agreement; exclude anything that would generally be considered ethically or legally dubious and anything where a significant fraction of elected officials dispute business's right. Exclude, as well, any actions that are taken only through business's influence on government, and confine your attention to the decisions made in operating businesses. Remember that any decision made by "business" is primarily determined by the 25,000 individuals at the top of the corporate ladder, since their companies control about three-quarters of *all* corporate sales, assets, employees, and profits.

## BUSINESS DECISIONS

What are some of these decisions? A brief and partial list indicates their scope:

### Decisions about Employment

- the number of people employed.
- when to have layoffs.
- the number of hours people work.
- when work begins in the morning and ends in the afternoon.
- whether to phase out full-time jobs and replace them with part-time, lower-wage, no-benefits jobs. In 1997, UPS workers and the Teamsters Union successfully contested the company's increasingly heavy reliance on part-timers, but it was big news that a union even attempted to raise the issue, much less that they were able to win.
- whether or not there is overtime, and whether it is compulsory.
- whether to allow flextime and job-sharing.
- the skill level of the jobs. Does the company make an effort to use lots of skilled workers paid good wages or is it always trying to de-skill positions and replace skilled workers with unskilled?
- the educational (and other) requirements for employment. Are certain educational levels *necessary* in order to be hired, or are they simply helpful? Are exconvicts or former mental patients eligible for all jobs or only some? What about the handicapped?
- whether the firm *de facto* discriminates in favor of men and whites or makes an active effort to recruit and promote minorities and women.
- workers' rights on the job. For example, do they have free speech? A worker at a Coca-Cola plant was given a three-day suspension (without pay) because his wife brought him a lunch with a soda from Burger King, at a time when Burger King sold Pepsi. It is totally legal to penalize an employee for this or many other such actions.
- job safety. In one of the most extreme examples, a worker was killed while performing a

dangerous task. Almost immediately thereafter another worker was ordered to do the same job and refused because he said conditions were unsafe and had not been remedied. The company fired him for this refusal, and the Supreme Court upheld the firing.
- (within limits) whether or not a union is recognized; whether the union and the workers are treated with dignity and respect; how bitterly and viciously the union is resisted.

### Investment Decisions

- decisions about whether to expand a plant, and if so, which plant to expand.
- whether to merge the corporation and "downsize" workers. Recently, a number of corporations have laid off thousands of employees, blighting communities and individual lives, at the same time giving huge bonuses to the top executives.
- whether to contract out jobs.
- whether to close down a plant; when and how to do so. Virtually no one questions a company's absolute right (in the United States, not in Europe) to shut down if it chooses to do so, no matter what the effect on the workers and communities.
- where to open new plants. The company has every right to bargain for the best deal it can get. Deals can include tax abatements and implicit agreements to ignore labor or pollution laws.

### Product and Marketing

- the products produced, including whether to introduce a new product and whether to discontinue an old stand-by.
- the design, both functional and aesthetic.
- the relative attention to different considerations: in a new car, how important is styling? sex appeal? fuel efficiency? safety? durability?
- the quality of the goods produced. Are they made to last, with high standards throughout, or are they just made to look good in the store and for the first month of use?

- the price for which goods are sold.
- the character of the advertising used to promote the product. Does it stress the significant features of the product, or distract through sex and extraneous symbols?
- the amount spent on advertising—90 percent of the commercials on prime time television are sponsored by the nation's 500 largest corporations.
- the places where ads appear—in left-wing journals? in right-wing journals? on television? on which programs?

## Community and Environment

- the level of pollution in the workplace: air, heat, noise, chemicals, and so on.
- the level of pollution in the outside environment. Beginning in the 1970s, for pollution both in the workplace and in the larger community, the government set maximum limits for a few items, but companies are completely free to do better than these standards. No government regulation prevents companies from setting and meeting tougher standards of their own devising. For example, in July 1991, a railroad tanker car derailed, tumbled into the Sacramento River, ruptured, and spilled pesticide. The pesticide was not listed as a regulated substance, and therefore the railroad was not required to carry it in a double-hulled tanker, though it could have chosen to do so. Though the pesticide was unregulated, it *was* strong enough to kill virtually all the fish in the river, formerly famous for its trout.
- the degree of consideration for the community: Does the company make an effort to be a good neighbor? Does it contribute to local charities? Support local initiatives?

This by no means exhausts the list of decisions that companies are allowed to make. Not only allowed to make, but expected and, in many cases, required to make. There is some regulation of business decisions at the margin, with possible regulation for issues such as: Can a company pull up stakes and leave town with no more than a day's notice? Can it dump raw wastes in the river? Can it make dubious claims in its advertising? For the most part, however, corporations are free to make decisions about their economic operations.

*If the government fails to act, big business can do as it wishes.*

---

## DISCUSSION QUESTIONS

1. Consider the discussion of hidden versus blatant power and relate this to the manner in which business exercised its privileged position through the Clean Air Act negotiations.
2. What comparisons may be drawn, if any, between white hegemony (prior to the 1960s) and corporate hegemony today?
3. If corporations that are so central to the structure of our economy do constitute a "field of power," can their hegemony be reconciled with our "democracy"?

# 4 *John Bellamy Foster*

# GLOBAL ECOLOGY
# AND THE COMMON GOOD

*Sociologist John Bellamy Foster questions the efficacy of much of contemporary environmentalism. He argues that proponents of a "new ecological morality" too often blame individual behavior for our environmental problems while downplaying or neglecting outright the root cause of global degradation: the "global treadmill of production." By focusing on individual consumer choices, or looking to socially responsible business people for leadership, conventional environmentalists offer a relatively comforting way out of our ecological crisis. Foster sees this as a dangerous false comfort. For the treadmill of production—which he likens to a giant squirrel cage—is driven by the six-point logic of our corporate capitalist economic structure, a structure which renowned sociologist C. Wright Mills considered to be the "structural immorality" embedded in our way of life. In short, we need to confront the paradox that our way of life undermines our way of life. Foster asks us to resist the treadmill of production through social movements aimed at creating a "true moral revolution," a revolution that transforms our thinking about the relationship between capitalist economic practices and the environment. Ponder the possibility that anything less than a new ethic of the common good, which inextricably connects environmental values to social justice, may well not be sufficient to save the earth from ecological calamity.*

Over the course of the twentieth century, human population has increased more than threefold and gross world product perhaps twentyfold. Such expansion has placed increasing pressure on the ecology of the planet. Everywhere we look—in the atmosphere, oceans, watersheds, forests, soil, etc.—it is now clear that rapid ecological decline is setting in.

Faced with the frightening reality of global ecological crisis, many are now calling for a moral revolution that would incorporate ecological values into our culture. This demand for a new ecological morality is, I believe, the essence of Green thinking. The kind of moral transformation envisaged is best captured by Aldo Leopold's land ethic, which says we abuse land because we regard it as a commodity belonging to us. When we begin to see land as a community to which we belong, we may begin to use it with love and respect.

*Source:* John Bellamy Foster, "Global Ecology and the Common Good," *Monthly Review,* Volume 46, Number 9, February 1995, pp. 1–10. Copyright © 1995 by *Monthly Review*. Reprinted by the author and *Monthly Review*.

Yet behind most appeals to ecological morality there lies the presumption that we live in a society where the morality of the individual is the key to the morality of society. If people as individuals could simply change their moral stance with respect to nature and alter their behavior in areas such as propagation, consumption, and the conduct of business, all would be well.

What is too often overlooked in such calls for moral transformation is the central institutional fact of our society: what might be called the global "treadmill of production." The logic of this treadmill can be broken down into six elements. First, built into this global system, and constituting its central rationale, is the increasing accumulation of wealth by a relatively small section of the population at the top of the social pyramid. Second, there is a long-term movement of workers away from self-employment and into wage jobs that are contingent on the continual expansion of production. Third, the competitive struggle between businesses necessitates on pain of extinction the allocation of accumulated wealth to new, revolutionary technologies that serve to expand production. Fourth, wants are manufactured in a manner that creates an insatiable hunger for more. Fifth, government becomes increasingly responsible for promoting national economic development, while ensuring some degree of "social security" for at least a portion of its citizens. Sixth, the dominant means of communication and education are part of the treadmill, serving to reinforce its priorities and values.

A defining trait of the system is that it is a kind of giant squirrel cage. Everyone, or nearly everyone, is part of this treadmill and is unable or unwilling to get off. Investors and managers are driven by the need to accumulate wealth and to expand the scale of their operations in order to prosper within a globally competitive milieu. For the vast majority, the commitment to the treadmill is more limited and indirect: they simply need to obtain jobs at liveable wages. But to retain those jobs and to maintain a given standard of living in these circumstances it is necessary, like the Red Queen in *Through the Looking Glass,* to run faster and faster in order to stay in the same place.

In such an environment, as the nineteenth-century German philosopher Arthur Schopenhauer once said, "A man can do what he wants. But he can't want what he wants." Our wants are conditioned by the kind of society in which we live. Looked at in this way, it is not individuals acting in accordance with their own innate desires, but rather the treadmill of production on which we are all placed that has become the main enemy of the environment.

Clearly, this treadmill leads in a direction that is incompatible with the basic ecological cycles of the planet. A continuous 3 percent average annual rate of growth in industrial production, such as obtained from 1970 to 1990, would mean that world industry would double in size every twenty-five years, grow sixteenfold approximately every century, increase by 250 times every two centuries, 4,000 times every three centuries, etc. Further, the tendency of the present treadmill of production is to expand the output of raw materials and energy because the greater this flow—from extraction through the delivery of final products to consumers—the more opportunity there is to realize profits. In order to generate profits, the treadmill relies heavily on energy-intensive, capital-intensive technology, which allows it to economize on labor inputs. Yet increased output and more substitution of energy and machines for labor mean a more rapid depletion of high-quality energy sources and other natural resources, and a larger amount of wastes dumped into the environment. It is unlikely therefore that the world could sustain many more doublings of industrial output under the present system without experiencing a complete ecological catastrophe. Indeed, we are already overshooting certain critical ecological thresholds.

Matters are made worse by the tendency in recent decades to move from "gross insults" to the environment to "microtoxicity." As synthetic products (like plastic) are substituted for natural ones (like wood and wool), the older pollutants associated with nineteenth-century industrialization are being replaced by more hazardous pollutants such as those resulting from chlorine-related (organochlorine) production—the source of DDT, dioxin, Agent Orange, PCBs, and CFCs. The degree of toxicity associated with a given level of output has thus risen fairly steadily over the last half century.

It would seem, then, that from an environmental perspective we have no choice but to resist the treadmill of production. This resistance must take the form of a far-reaching moral revolution. In order to carry out such a moral transformation we must confront what the great American sociologist C. Wright Mills called "the higher immorality." The "higher immorality" for Mills was a "structural immorality" built into the institutions of power in our society—in particular the treadmill of production. "In a civilization so thoroughly business-penetrated as America," he wrote, money becomes "the one unambiguous marker of success . . . the sovereign American value." Such a society, dominated by the corporate rich with the support of the political power elite, is a society of "organized irresponsibility," where moral virtue is divorced from success, and knowledge from power. Public communication, rather than constituting the basis for the exchange of ideas necessary for the conduct of a democracy, is largely given over to "an astounding volume of propaganda for commodities . . . addressed more often to the belly or to the groin than to the head or the heart." The corrupting influence that all of this has on the general public is visible in the loss of the capacity for moral indignation, the growth of cynicism, a drop in political participation, and the emergence of a passive, commercially centered existence. In short, the higher immorality spells the annihilation of a meaningful moral and political community.

Manifestations of this higher immorality—in which money divorced from all other considerations has become the supreme reality—are all around us. In 1992 alone U.S. business spent perhaps $1 trillion on marketing, simply convincing people to consume more and more goods. This exceeded by about $600 billion the amount spent on education—public and private—at all levels. Under these circumstances we can expect people to grow up with their heads full of information about saleable commodities, and empty of knowledge about human history, morality, culture, science and the environment. What is most valued in such a society is the latest style, the most expensive clothing, the finest car. Hence, it is not surprising that more than 93 percent of teenage girls questioned in a survey conducted in the late 1980s indicated that their favorite leisure activity was to go

shopping. Not long ago *Fortune* magazine quoted Dee Hock, former head of the Visa bank card operation, as saying, "It's not that people value money more but that they value everything else so much less—not that they are more greedy but that they have no other values to keep greed in check."

"Our social life is organized in such a way," German environmentalist Rudolf Bahro has observed, "that even people who work with their hands are more interested in a better car than in the single meal of the slum-dweller on the southern half of the earth or the need of the peasant there for water; or even a concern to expand their own consciousness, for their own self-realization."

Reflecting on the growing use of pesticides in our society, Rachel Carson wrote that this was indicative of "an era dominated by industry, in which the right to make money, at whatever cost to others, is seldom challenged."

Given the nature of the society in which we live, one must therefore be wary of solutions to environmental problems that place too much emphasis on the role of individuals, or too little emphasis on the treadmill of production and the higher immorality that it engenders. To be sure, it is necessary for individuals to struggle to organize their lives so that in their consumption they live more simply and ecologically. But to lay too much stress on this alone is to place too much onus on the individual, while ignoring institutional facts. Alan Durning of the Worldwatch Institute, for example, argues that "we consumers have an ethical obligation to curb our consumption, since it jeopardizes the chances for future generations. Unless we climb down the consumption ladder a few rungs, our grandchildren will inherit a planetary home impoverished by our affluence."

This may seem like simple common sense but it ignores the higher immorality of a society like the United States in which the dominant institutions treat the public as mere consumers to be targeted with all of the techniques of modern marketing. The average adult in the United States watches 21,000 television commercials a year, about 75 percent of which are paid for by the 100 largest corporations. It also ignores the fact that the treadmill of production is rooted not in consumption but in production. Within the context of this system it is therefore economically naive to think that the problem can be solved simply by getting consumers to refrain from consumption and instead to save and invest their income. To invest means to expand the scale of productive capacity, increasing the size of the treadmill.

Even more questionable are the underlying assumptions of those who seek to stop environmental degradation by appealing not to individuals in general but to the ethics of individuals at the top of the social pyramid and to corporations. Thus in his widely heralded book, *The Ecology of Commerce,* Paul Hawken argues for a new environmental ethic for businesspeople and corporations. After advocating an ambitious program for ecological change, Hawken states, "Nothing written, suggested, or proposed is possible unless business is willing to embrace the world we live within and lead the way." According to Hawken, "the ultimate purpose of business is not, or should not be, simply to make money. Nor is it merely a system of making and selling things. The promise of business is to increase the general well-being of humankind through service, a creative invention and ethical philosophy."

Thus he goes on to observe that, "If Dupont, Monsanto, and Dow believe they are in the synthetic chemical production business, and cannot change this belief, they and we are in trouble. If they believe they are in the business to serve people, to help solve problems, to use and employ the ingenuity of workers to improve the lives of people around them by learning from the nature that gives us life, we have a chance."

The central message here is that business people merely have to change the ethical bases of their conduct and all will be well with the environment. Such views underestimate the extent to which the treadmill of production and the higher immorality are built into our society. Ironically, Hawken's argument places too much responsibility and blame on the individual corporate manager—since he or she too is likely to be a mere cog in the wheel of the system. As the great linguistics theorist and media critic Noam Chomsky has explained, "The chairman of the board will always tell you that he spends his every waking hour laboring so that people will get the best possible products at the cheapest possible price and work in the best possible conditions. But it is an institutional

fact, independent of who the chairman of the board is, that he'd better be trying to maximize profit and market share, and if he doesn't do that, he's not going to be chairman of the board any more. If he were ever to succumb to the delusions that he expresses, he'd be out."

To be successful within any sphere in this society generally means that one has thoroughly internalized those values associated with the higher immorality. There is, as economist John Kenneth Galbraith has pointed out, a "culture of contentment" at the top of the social hierarchy; those who benefit most from the existing order have the least desire for change.

Resistance to the treadmill of production therefore has to come mainly from the lower echelons of society, and from social movements rather than individuals. This can only occur, to quote the late German Green Party leader Petra Kelly, if ecological concerns are "tied to issues of economic justice—the exploitation of the poor by the rich." Behind every environmental struggle of today there is a struggle over the expansion of the global treadmill—a case of landless workers or villagers who are compelled to destroy nature in order to survive, or of large corporations that seek to expand profits with little concern for the natural and social devastation that they leave in their wake. Ecological development is possible, but only if the economic as well as environmental injustices associated with the treadmill are addressed. An ecological approach to the economy is about having enough, not having more. It must have as its first priority people, particularly poor people, rather than production or even the environment, stressing the importance of meeting basic needs and long-term security. This is the common morality with which we must combat the higher immorality of the treadmill. Above all we must recognize the old truth, long understood by the romantic and socialist critics of capitalism, that increasing production does not eliminate poverty.

Indeed, the global treadmill is so designed that the poor countries of the world often help finance the rich ones. During the period from 1982 to 1990, the Third World was a "net exporter of hard currency to the developed countries, on average $30 billion per year." In this same period Third World debtors remitted to their creditors in the wealthy nations an average of almost $12.5 billion per month in payments on debt alone. This is equal to what the entire Third World spends each month on health and education. It is this system of global inequity that reinforces both overpopulation (since poverty spurs population growth) and the kind of rapacious development associated with the destruction of tropical rain forests in the Third World.

For those with a pragmatic bent, much of what I have said here may seem too global and too abstract. The essential point that I want to leave you with, however, is the notion that although we are all on the treadmill, we do not all relate to it in the same way and with the same degree of commitment. I have found in my research into the ancient forest struggle in the Northwest—and others have discovered the same thing in other settings—that ordinary workers have strong environmental values even though they may be at loggerheads with the environmental movement. In essence they are fighting for their lives and livelihoods at a fairly basic level.

We must find a way of putting people first in order to protect the environment. There are many ways of reducing the economic stakes in environmental destruction on the part of those who have little direct stake in the treadmill itself. But this means taking seriously issues of social and economic inequality as well as environmental destruction. Only by committing itself to what is now called "environmental justice" (combining environmental concerns and social justice) can the environmental movement avoid being cut off from those classes of individuals who are most resistant to the treadmill on social grounds. The alternative is to promote an environmental movement that is very successful in creating parks with Keep Out! signs, yet is complicit with the larger treadmill of production. By recognizing that it is not people (as individuals and in aggregate) that are enemies of the environment but the historically specific economic and social order in which we live, we can find sufficient common ground for a true moral revolution to save the earth.

---

## DISCUSSION QUESTIONS

1. Why does Foster believe that appealing generally to individual morality, or specifically to the ethics of business leaders, is an inadequate response to the global ecological crisis?
2. Why does Foster argue that environmental responses to the "treadmill of production" must be linked to issues of economic justice?
3. Reflecting on Foster's article, how might you be inspired to rethink the concept of "progress"? How does Foster analysis of the environmental crisis compare with that of Al Gore in the 2006 film 'An Inconvenient Truth'?

# CHAPTER 2

# IDEOLOGY AND POLITICAL CULTURE

Politics is "in here"—within ourselves—as well as "out there," inside of government institutions. Each of us perceives the world by way of an *ideology,* a socially produced and culturally reinforced mental map made up of values, beliefs, and assumptions about why the world is the way it is and what, if anything, should be done about it. Rooted in the history and culture of our society, political ideology has a taken-for-granted naturalness about it such that we are usually not conscious of its grip on us. When left unchallenged, our received ideology impedes our capacity for independent thought and serves as a power- ful force for social control. One of the goals of a liberal education should be to see our underlying beliefs and values for what they are and to understand the selectiveness of our ideology in what it discloses and affirms and in what it conceals and denies. The readings in this chapter address the nature and limitations of American political culture and ideology.

Any number of interpreters of U.S. history have identified *liberalism* as the dominant and unrivaled American ideology. Cut off from European brands of aristocratic conser- vatism on one hand, and working-class socialism on the other, Americans emphasized the values of individualism, private property, the free market, and limited government that had emerged in seventeenth- and eighteenth-century English thought, most notably in John Locke's *Second Treatise of Government* (1690). In this classical sense, liberalism is a broad set of ideas that encompasses both "liberal" and "conservative" positions today, a point that helps explain how limited our spectrum of political viewpoints actually is. As it developed out of the shadows of the feudal era, liberalism seemed to represent a great advance in human freedom. But given the interdependent nature of our increasingly multicultural world, how well do liberal individualism and the private market economy it legitimates pre- pare us for confronting the challenges of the twenty-first century?

*Handwritten margin notes:*

*Ideology As Natural*

*DQ*

*Liberalism*
*"Liberalism"   "Conservatism"*

*Explanation of Ideology*
- *Identify a Problem / Crisis*
- *Identify a Bad Guy*
- *Offer a Solution – An Alternative Vision*
- *Offer a Plan of Action*

41

**5** *Jennifer L. Hochschild*

# WHAT IS THE AMERICAN DREAM?

*In this selection, political scientist Jennifer Hochschild examines the four basic tenets of the American dream. The dream is rooted in a variation of philosopher John Locke's fantasy frontier, a state of nature where anyone is almost guaranteed to be able to achieve any success with enough personal determination. Hochschild discusses the myriad of ways American history and popular culture have portrayed the "almost-promise" of success, and the equally haunting power of the fear of failure. Having articulated the virtues of the American dream and its ascendance to the level of a seductive ideology, she then assesses the flaws inherent in the dream's four key tenets. Particularly troubling is the nightmarish quality of the dream for those who fail to achieve it, who are subsequently devalued by society and who, often, devalue themselves. Hochschild finds that the dream, taken as a whole, is overly (and unnecessarily) individualistic, fixated on an extremely narrow definition of "success," and analytically deceptive in that it encourages an emphasis on traits of individuals rather than political, economic, and social structures. Moreover, our political culture offers few alternative ideologies against which to evaluate the strengths and weakness of our own. Thus, the individually focused, nonstructural tendencies of the ideology of the American dream make it that much harder for U.S. citizens to fully understand themselves and the political world they inhabit.*

"In the beginning," wrote John Locke, "all the world was *America*." Locke was referring specifically to the absence of a cash nexus in primitive society. But the sentence evokes the unsullied newness, infinite possibility, limitless resources that are commonly understood to be the essence of the "American dream." The idea of the American dream has been attached to everything from religious freedom to a home in the suburbs, and it has inspired emotions ranging from deep satisfaction to disillusioned fury. Nevertheless, the phrase elicits for most Americans some variant of Locke's fantasy—a new world where anything can happen and good things might. . . .

## THE MEANING OF SUCCESS

The American dream consists of tenets about achieving success. Let us first explore the meaning of "success" and then consider the rules for achieving it.

People most often define success as the attainment of a high income, a prestigious job, economic security. My treatment is no exception. But *pace*

*Source:* Jennifer L. Hochschild, *Facing Up to the American Dream: Race, Class and the Soul of the Nation,* Princeton, NJ: Princeton University Press, 1995, pp. 15–38.

President Reagan, material well-being is only one form of accomplishment. People seek success from the pulpit to the stage of the Metropolitan Opera, from membership in the newest dance club to membership in the Senate. Success can be as amorphous and encompassing as "a right to say what they wanta say, do what they wanta do, and fashion a world into something that can be great for everyone."

Different kinds of success need not, but often do, conflict. A classic plot of American family sagas is the children's rejection of the parents' hard-won wealth and social standing in favor of some "deeper," more meaningful form of accomplishment. The rejection may be reversed, as Cotton Mather sadly reported:

> There have been very fine settlements in the north-east regions; but what is become of them? . . . One of our ministers once preaching to a congregation there, urged them to approve themselves a religious people from this consideration, "that otherwise they would contradict the main end of planting this wilderness"; whereupon a well-known person, then in the assembly, cryed out, "Sir, you are mistaken: you think you are preaching to the people at the [Plymouth] Bay; our main end was to catch fish."

Mather "wished that something more excellent had been the main end of the settlements in that brave country," but the ideology of the American dream itself remains agnostic as to the meaning of "something more excellent."

A definition of success involves measurement as well as content. Success can be measured in at least three ways, with important normative and behavioral consequences. First, it can be *absolute*. In this case, achieving the American dream implies reaching some threshold of well-being, higher than where one began but not necessarily dazzling. As Bruce Springsteen puts it, "I don't think the American dream was that everybody was going to make . . . a billion dollars, but it was that everybody was going to have an opportunity and the chance to live a life with some decency and some dignity and a chance for some self-respect."

Second, success can be *relative*. Here achieving the American dream consists in becoming better off than some comparison point, whether one's childhood, people in the old country, one's neighbors, a character from a book, another race or gender—anything or anyone that one measures oneself against. Relative success implies no threshold of well-being, and it may or may not entail continually changing the comparison group as one achieves a given level of accomplishment. A benign version of relative success is captured by James Comer's "kind of competition . . . we had . . . going on" with "the closest friends that we had":

> When we first met them, we had a dining room and they didn't. They went back and they turned one of their bedrooms into a dining room . . . After that we bought this big Buick car. And we came to their house and they had bought another car. She bought a fur coat one year and your dad bought me one the next. But it was a friendly thing, the way we raced. It gave you something to work for, to look forward to. Every year we tried to have something different to show them what we had done, and they would have something to show us.

William Byrd II articulated a more malign version in 1736: slaves "blow up the pride, and ruin the industry of our white people, who seeing a rank of poor creatures below them, detest work for fear it should make them look like slaves."

Success can, alternatively, be *competitive*—achieving victory over someone else. My success implies your failure. Competitors are usually people, whether known and concrete (opponents in a tennis match) or unknown and abstract (all other applicants for a job). *U.S. News and World Report,* in an article celebrating "SUCCESS! The Chase Is Back in Style Again," graphically illustrates the relationship among competitors in the business world. An opponent may, however, be entirely impersonal. John Henry, "the steel-drivin' man," is famed for beating a machine, and Paul Bunyan for taming the primeval forest.

# TENETS OF SUCCESS

> The American dream that we were all raised on is a simple but powerful one—if you work hard and play by the rules you should be given a chance to go as far as your God-given ability will take you.
>
> —President Bill Clinton, speech to Democratic Leadership Council, 1993

In one sentence, President Clinton has captured the bundle of shared, even unconsciously presumed, tenets about achieving success that make up the ideology of the American dream. Those tenets answer the questions: Who may pursue the American dream? In what does the pursuit consist? How does one successfully pursue the dream? Why is the pursuit worthy of our deepest commitment?

The answer to "who" in the standard ideology is "everyone, regardless of ascriptive traits, family background, or personal history." The answer to "what" is "the reasonable anticipation, though not the promise, of success, however it is defined." The answer to "how" is "through actions and traits under one's own control." The answer to "why" is "true success is associated with virtue." Let us consider each rule in turn.

## Who May Pursue Success?

The first tenet, that everyone may always pursue their dream, is the most direct connotation of Locke's "in the beginning. . . ." But the idea extends beyond the image of a pristine state of nature waiting for whoever "discovers" it. Even in the distinctly nonpristine, nonnatural world of Harlem or Harlan County, anyone can pursue a dream. A century ago, one moved to the frontier to hide a spotted past and begin afresh; Montana frontierswomen "never ask[ed] women where they come from or what they did before they came to live in our neck of the woods. If they wore a wedding band and were good wives, mothers, and neighbors that was enough for us to know."

But seldom, say Americans, does one need to take such dramatic steps; fewer than one-fifth see race, gender, religion, or class as very important for "getting ahead in life." Even two-thirds of the poor are certain that Americans like themselves "have a good chance of improving our standard of living," and up to three times as many Americans as Europeans make that claim. In effect, Americans believe that they can create a personal mini-state of nature that will allow them to slough off the past and invent a better future.

## What Does One Pursue?

The second tenet, that one may reasonably anticipate success, is less straightforward. "Reasonable anticipation" is far from a guarantee, as all children on the morning of their birthday know. But "reasonable anticipation" is also much more than simply longing; most children are fairly sure of getting at least some of what they wish for on their birthday. On a larger scale, from its inception America has been seen by many as an extravagant birthday party:

> Seagull: A whole countrie of English is there, man, . . . and . . . the Indians are so in love with 'hem that all the treasure they have they lay at their feete . . . Golde is more plentiful there than copper is with us. . . . Why, man, all their dripping pans and their chamberpots are pure golde; and all the chaines with which they chaine up their streets are massie golde; all the prisoners they take are fettered in golde; and for rubies and diamonds they goe forthe on holy dayes and gather 'hem by the sea shore to hang on their childrens coats.

Presumably few Britons even in 1605 took this message literally, but the hope of abundant riches—whether material, spiritual, or otherwise—persists.

Thus Americans are exhorted to "go for it" in their advertisements as well as their commencement addresses. And they do; three-quarters of Americans, compared with only one-third of Britons, West Germans, and Hungarians (and fewer Dutch), agree that they have a good chance of improving their standard of living. Twice as many Americans as Canadians or Japanese think future generations of their nationality will live better than the present generation.

## How Does One Pursue Success?

The third premise, for those who do not take Seagull literally, explains how one is to achieve the success that one anticipates. Ralph Waldo Emerson is uncharacteristically succinct on the point: "There is always a reason, *in the man,* for his good or bad fortune, and so in making money." Other nineteenth-century orators exhorted young men to

> Behold him [a statue of Benjamin Franklin], . . . holding out to you an example of diligence, economy and virtue, and personifying the triumphant success which may await those who follow it! Behold him, ye that are humblest and poorest . . . —lift up your heads and look at the image of a man who rose from nothing, who owed nothing to parentage or patronage, who enjoyed no advantages of early education, which are not open,—a hundredfold open,— to yourselves, who performed the most menial services in the business in which his early life was employed, but who lived to stand before Kings, and died to leave a name which the world will never forget.

Lest we smile at the quaint optimism (or crude propaganda) of our ancestors, consider a recent advertisement from Citicorp Bank. This carefully balanced group of shining faces—young and old, male and female, black, Latino, Nordic, and Asian—all gazing starry-eyed at the middle distance over the words "THE WILL TO SUCCEED IS PART OF THE AMERICAN SPIRIT" conveys the message of the third tenet in no uncertain terms.

This advertisement is well aimed; surveys unanimously show Americans' strong support for rewarding people in the marketplace according to their talents and accomplishments rather than their needs, efforts, or simple existence. And Americans mostly believe that people are in fact rewarded for their acts. In 1952 fully 88 percent of Americans agreed that "there is plenty of opportunity and

anyone who works hard can go as far as he wants"; in 1980, 70 percent concurred.

Comparisons across space yield the same results as comparisons across time. In a 1973 survey of youth in ten nations, only Swedes and British disagreed more than did Americans that a man's [*sic*] future is "virtually determined" by his family background. A decade later only 31 percent of Americans agreed that in their nation "what you achieve in life depends largely on your family background," compared with over 50 percent of Austrians and Britons, and over 60 percent of Italians. Most pointedly, half of American adolescents compared with one-fourth of British adolescents agreed in 1972 that "people get to be poor . . . [because] they don't work hard enough."

Americans also believe more than do Europeans that people ought not to be buffered from the consequences of their actions, so long as they have a fair start in life. Thus up to four times as many more Americans think college opportunities should be increased, but roughly half as many think the government should reduce the income disparity between high- and low-income citizens, or provide jobs or income support for the poor.

## Why is Success Worth Pursuing?

Implicit in the flows of oratory and survey responses is the fourth tenet of the American dream, that the pursuit of success warrants so much fervor because it is associated with virtue. "Associated with" means at least four things: virtue leads to success, success makes a person virtuous, success indicates virtue, or apparent success is not real success unless one is also virtuous.

That quintessential American, Benjamin Franklin, illustrates three of these associations: the *Autobiography* instructs us that "no Qualities were so likely to make a poor Man's Fortune as those of Probity & Integrity." Conversely, "Proverbial Sentences, chiefly such as inculcated Industry and Frugality," are included in *Poor Richard's Almanack* as "the Means of procuring Wealth and thereby securing Virtue, it being more difficult for a Man in Want to act always honestly, as . . . *it is hard for an empty*

Who deserves what?

*Sack to stand upright.*" Finally, mere wealth may actually impede true success, the attainment of which requires a long list of virtues: "Fond *Pride of Dress,* is sure a very Curse; E'er *Fancy* you consult, consult your Purse"; "A Ploughman on his Legs is higher than a Gentleman on his Knees"; and "Pride that dines on Vanity sups on Contempt."

Americans have learned Franklin's lessons well: they distinguish between the worthy and unworthy rich, as well as the deserving and undeserving poor. For example, most Americans characterize "yuppies" as people who "play fashionable games" and "eat in trendy restaurants," and on the whole they enjoy watching such forms of conspicuous consumption. But they also characterize yuppies as selfish, greedy, inclined to flaunt their wealth, and imbued with a false sense of superiority. These traits they mostly find unacceptable. Overall, Americans overwhelmingly deplore the 1980s sentiment of "making it fast while you can regardless of what happened to others." This is not simply a reaction against the Reagan years. In surveys throughout the 1970s, four in ten Americans deemed honesty to be the most important quality for a child to learn, compared with 2 percent proclaiming that a child should try hard to succeed. Virtually all Americans require that their friends be "honest" and "responsible"—core components of the third and fourth tenets.

Americans also focus more on virtue than do citizens of other nations, at least in their self-descriptions. A survey of youth in ten nations found that more Americans than people in any other country described their chief goal in life as "sincerity and love between myself and others," and in only one other nation (the Philippines) did more youth seek "salvation through faith." Conversely, only in Sweden did fewer youths seek "money and position," and only in three other countries did fewer seek "freedom from restrictions." More Americans than Europeans gain strength from religion, report prayer to be an important part of their daily life, and agree that there are universally applicable "clear guidelines about what is good or evil." In short, "this country succeeds in living a very sinful life without being deeply cynical. That is the difference between Europe and America, and it signifies that ethics *means* something here."

## The American Dream as Fantasy

We must beware reducing the dream to its components; as a whole it has an evocative resonance greater than the sum of its parts. The theme of most Walt Disney movies boil down to the lyrics in *Pinocchio:* "When you wish upon a star, makes no difference who you are, your dreams come true." It is no coincidence that Disney movies are so durable; they simply update Locke's fantasy. And the global, amorphous vision of establishing a city upon the hill, killing the great white whale, striking a vein of gold, making the world safe for democracy—or simply living a life of decency and dignity—underlies all analyses of what success means or what practices will attain it.

## VIRTUES OF THE AMERICAN DREAM

Combining the amorphous fantasy or the more precise tenets of the American dream with the various meanings of success shows the full richness—and seductiveness—of the ideology. If one measures success absolutely and accepts a wide array of indicators of success, the ideology portrays America as a land of plenty, and Americans as "people of plenty." This is the great theme of one of the most powerful children's sagas ever written in America, the *Little House in the Big Woods* series. Decades (and nine volumes) of grasshopper plagues, ferocious blizzards, cheating and cowardly railroad bosses, even hostile Indians cannot prevent Pa and his girls from eventually "winning their bet with Uncle Sam" and becoming prosperous homesteaders. In the words of one of Pa's songs:

> I am sure in this world there are plenty
> of good things enough for us all. . . .
> It's cowards alone that are crying
> And foolishly saying, "I can't."
> It is only by plodding and striving
> And laboring up the steep hill
> Of life, that you'll ever be thriving,
> Which you'll do if you've only the will.

If success is measured competitively and defined narrowly, however, the ideology portrays a different America. Hard work and virtue combined with scarce resources produce a few spectacular winners and many dismissible losers. This is the theme of John Rockefeller's turn-of-the-century Sunday school address:

> The growth of a large business is merely a survival of the fittest. ... The American Beauty rose can be produced in the splendor and fragrance which bring cheer to its beholder only by sacrificing the early buds which grow up around it. This is not an evil tendency in business. It is merely the working out of a law of nature and a law of God.

The *Little House* series has sold well over four million copies; Americans prefer the self-image of universal achievement to that of a few stalwarts triumphing over weaker contenders. What matters most, however, is not any single image but rather the elasticity and range of the ideology of the American dream. People can encourage themselves with soft versions, congratulate themselves with harder ones, and exult with the hardest, as their circumstances and characters warrant.

Thus the American dream is an impressive ideology. It has for centuries lured people to America and moved them around within it, and it has kept them striving in horrible conditions against impossible odds. Most Americans celebrate it unthinkingly, along with apple pie and motherhood; criticism typically is limited to imperfections in its application. But like apple pie and motherhood, the American dream turns out upon closer examination to be less than perfect. Let us look, then, at flaws intrinsic to the dream. *Dream itself is rarely doubted.*

# FLAWS IN THE TENETS OF THE AMERICAN DREAM

## The First Tenet

The first tenet, that everyone can participate equally and can always start over, is troubling to the degree that it is not true. It is, of course, never true in the strongest sense; people cannot shed their existing selves as snakes do their skin. So the myth of the individual mini-state of nature is just that—a fantasy to be sought but never achieved.

Fantasies are fine so long as people understand that that is what they are. For that reason, a weaker formulation of the first tenet—people start the pursuit of success with varying advantages, but no one is barred from the pursuit—is more troubling because the gap between ideological claim and actual fact is harder to recognize. As a factual claim, the first tenet is largely false; for most of American history, women of any race and men who were Native American, Asian, black, or poor were barred from all but a narrow range of "electable futures." Ascriptive constraints have arguably been weakened over time, but until recently no more than about a third of the population was able to take seriously the first premise of the American dream.

This flaw has implications beyond the evident ones of racism and sexism. The emotional potency of the American dream has made people who *were* able to identify with it the norm for everyone else. White men, especially European immigrants able to ride the wave of the Industrial Revolution (and to benefit from the absence of competition from the rest of the population) to comfort or even prosperity, are the epitomizing demonstration of America as the bountiful state of nature. Those who do not fit the model disappear from the collective self-portrait. Thus the irony is doubled; not only has the ideal of universal participation been denied to most Americans, but also the very fact of its denial has itself been denied in our national self-image.

This double irony creates deep misunderstandings and correspondingly deep political tensions. Whites increasingly believe that racial discrimination is slight and declining, and blacks increasingly believe the opposite. But this form of racial conflict is not unique. For example, surveys show that more women than men believe that women are discriminated against in employment and wages, in "being able to combine family and work," and in their overall chance to pursue their dreams. Similarly, regardless of when the survey was conducted, more men than women believe that women are better off now than a decade earlier with regard to these issues. Not surprisingly, bitter disagreements about the need for affirmative action, policies to stem sexual harassment, family leave policies, and the like ensue.

## The Second Tenet

The flaws of the second tenet of the American dream, the reasonable anticipation of success, stem from the close link between anticipation and expectation. That link presents little problem so long as there are enough resources and opportunities that everyone has a reasonable chance of having some expectations met. Indeed, panegyrics to the American dream always expound on the bounty and openness of the American continent. Governor James Glen typified eighteenth-century entrepreneurs of colonization by promising that

> Adventurers will be pleased to find a Change from Poverty and Distress to Ease and Plenty; they are invited to a Country not yet half settled, where the Rivers are crowded with Fish, and the Forests with Game; and no Game-Act to restrain them from enjoying those Bounties of Providence, no heavy Taxes to impoverish them, nor oppressive Landlords to snatch the hard-earned Morsel from the Mouth of Indigence, and where Industry will certainly inrich them.

Three centuries later, the message was unchanged:

> All my life I am thinking to come to this country. For what I read in the magazines, and the movies. . . . I would have a beautiful castle in the U.S. I will have a thousand servant. I will have five Rolls-Royces in my door. . . . We thinking everybody has this kind of life. . . . I have this kind of dream.

These fantasies are innocuous so long as resources roughly balance dreams for enough people enough of the time. But if they do not—worse yet, if they used to but do no longer—then the dream rapidly loses its appeal. The circumstances that cause resources no longer to balance dreams vary, from an economic downturn to a rapid increase in the number of dreamers to a narrowing of the grounds on which success is publicly recognized. The general point,

however, always holds: no one promises that dreams will be fulfilled, but the distinction between the right to dream and the right to succeed is psychologically hard to maintain and politically always blurred. It is especially hard to maintain because the dream sustains Americans against daily nightmares only if they believe that they have a significant likelihood, not just a formal chance, of reaching their goals.

In short, the right to aspire to success works as an ideological substitute for a guarantee of success only if it begins to approach it. When people recognize that chances for success are slim or getting slimmer, the whole tenor of the American dream changes dramatically for the worse.

The general problem of scarcity varies depending on how people measure success and how broadly they define possible goals. It is most obvious and acute for those focused on competitive success in only a few arenas; by definition resources and opportunities are insufficient to satisfy all dreamers in such a case. But it may be more problematic for those who measure success relatively or who admit a wide array of outcomes into their picture of success. After all, there are more such people and they have no a priori reason to assume that many will fail.

The problem of scarcity may be most devastating, however, for people anticipating absolute success or for people willing to see success almost anywhere. They, after all, have the least reason to expect failure. Losers of this type have an unmatched poignancy: "I don't dream any more like I used to. I believed that in this country, we would have all we needed for the decent life. I don't see that any more."

Conversely, the availability of resources and opportunities may shape the kind of success that Americans dream of. If resources are profoundly scarce (as in a famine) or inherently limited (as in election to the presidency), people almost certainly envision competitive success in that arena. If resources are moderately scarce, people will be concerned about their position relative to that of others, but will not necessarily see another's gain as their loss. When resources and opportunities seem wide open and broadly defined—anyone can achieve salvation, get an "A" on the exam, claim 160 acres of western prairie—people are most free to pursue their idiosyncratic dreams and to measure their achievement by their own absolute standard.

This logic suggests a dynamic: as resources become tighter or success is more narrowly defined, Americans are likely to shift their understanding of success from absolute to relative to competitive. Before the 1980s, claims one journalist, "there was always enough to go around, plenty of places in the sun. It didn't even matter much about the rich—so long as everyone was living better, it seemed the rich couldn't be denied their chance to get richer." But "today [in 1988] that wave [of prosperity] has crested. . . . Now when the rich get richer, the middle class stagnates—and the poor get decidedly poorer. If left unchecked, a polarization of income . . . is likely to provoke consequences that will affect America's politics and power, to say nothing of its psyche."

The risks of anticipating success do not stop with anticipation. Attaining one's dreams can be surprisingly problematic. From William Shakespeare to William Faulkner, writers have limned the loneliness of being at the top, the spiritual costs of cutthroat competition, the shallowness of a society that rewards achievement above all else. Alexis de Tocqueville characteristically provides one of the most eloquent of such admonitions:

> Every American is eaten up with longing to rise. . . . In America I have seen the freest and best educated of men in circumstances the happiest in the world; yet it seemed to me that a cloud habitually hung on their brow, and they seemed serious and almost sad even in their pleasures. The chief reason for this is that . . . [they] never stop thinking of the good things they have not got. . . . They clutch everything but hold nothing fast, and so lose grip as they hurry after some new delight.

The obsession with ever more material success threatens the body politic as well as the individual soul:

> When the taste for physical pleasures has grown more rapidly than either education or

experience of free institutions, the time comes when men are carried away and lose control of themselves at sight of the new good things they are ready to snatch. . . . There is no need to drag their rights away from citizens of this type; they themselves voluntarily let them go. . . . The role of government is left unfilled. If, at this critical moment, an able and ambitious man once gets power, he finds the way open for usurpations of every sort.

Not only nineteenth-century romantics cautioned against the failures of success. Today psychotherapists specialize in helping "troubled winners" or the "working wounded," for whom "a life too much devoted to pursuing money, power, position, and control over others ends up being emotionally impoverished." In short, material—and perhaps other forms of—success is not all it's cracked up to be, even (or especially) in a nation where it is the centerpiece of the pervasive ideology.

The problems of success, however, pale beside the problems of failure. Because success is so central to Americans' self-image, and because they expect as well as hope to achieve, Americans are not gracious about failure. Others' failure reminds them that the dream may be just that—a dream, to be distinguished from waking reality. Their own failure confirms that fear. As Zora Neale Hurston puts it, "there is something about poverty that smells like death."

Furthermore, the better the dream works for other people, the more devastating is failure for the smaller and smaller proportion of people left behind. In World War II, members of military units with a high probability of promotion were less satisfied with advancement opportunities than members of units with a much lower probability of promotion, because failure to be promoted in the former case was both more salient and more demonstrably a personal rather than a systemic flaw. The "tunnel effect" is a more nuanced depiction of this phenomenon of relative deprivation. The first stage is one of relative gratification, in which others' success enhances one's own well-being. After all, drivers in a traffic jam in a tunnel are initially pleased when cars in the adjacent lane begin to move "because advances of others supply information about a more benign external environment; receipt of this information produces gratification; and this gratification overcomes, or at least suspends, *envy.*" At some point, however, those left behind come to believe that their heightened expectations will not be met; not only are their hopes now dashed, but they are also worse off than when the upward mobility began. "Nonrealization of the expectation ['that my turn to move will soon come'] will at some point result in my 'becoming furious.'" And one is still stuck in the tunnel. In short, the ideology of the American dream includes no provision for failure; a failed dream denies the loser not only success but even a safe harbor within which to hide the loss.

*What would this provision look like?*

## 3 The Third Tenet

Failure is made more harsh by the third premise of the American dream—the belief that success results from actions and traits under one's own control. Logically, it does not follow that if success results from individual volition, then failure results from lack of volition. All one needs in order to see the logical flaw here is the distinction between necessary and sufficient. But that distinction is not obvious or intuitive, and in any case the psychologic of the American dream differs from strict logic. In the psychologic, if one may claim responsibility for success, one must accept responsibility for failure.

Americans who do everything they can and still fail may come to understand that effort and talent alone do not guarantee success. But they have a hard time persuading others. After all, they are losers— why listen to them? Will we not benefit more by listening to winners (who seldom challenge the premise that effort and talent breed success)?

## 4 The Fourth Tenet

Failure, then, is unseemly for two reasons: it challenges the blurring between anticipation and promise that is the emotional heart of the American dream, and people who fail are presumed to lack talent or will. The coup de grace comes from the fourth tenet of the dream, the association of success with virtue.

By the psychologic just described, if success implies virtue, failure implies sin.

American history and popular culture are replete with demonstrations of the connection between failure and sin. In the 1600s, indentured servants—kidnapped children, convicts, and struggling families alike—were described by earlier immigrants as "strong and idle beggars, vagabonds, egyptians, common and notorious whoores, theeves, and other dissolute and lousy persons." Nineteenth-century reformers concurred: fallen women are typically "the daughters of the ignorant, depraved, and vicious part of our population, trained up without culture of any kind, amidst the contagion of evil example, and enter upon a life of prostitution for the ratification of their unbridled passions, and become harlots altogether by choice."

Small wonder that in the late twentieth century even the poor blame the poor for their condition. Despite her vivid awareness of exploitation by the rich, an aging cleaning woman insists that many people are poor because they "make the money and drink it all up. They don't care about the kids or the clothes. Just have a bottle on that table all the time." Losers even blame themselves: an unemployed factory worker, handicapped by a childhood accident, "wish[es] to hell I could do it [save money for his children]. I always said for years, 'I wanna get rich, I wanna get rich.' But then, phew! My mind doesn't have the strong will. I say, 'Well, I'm *gonna* do it.' Only the next day's different." These people are typical. In 1985, over 60 percent of poor people but only 45 percent of the nonpoor agreed that "poor young women often have babies so they can collect welfare." Seven years later, the same proportions of poor and well-off agreed that welfare recipients "are taking advantage of the system."

The equation of failure with evil and success with virtue cannot be attributed to poor education or low status. College students "who learned that a fellow student had been awarded a cash prize as a result of a random drawing were likely to conclude that he had in fact worked especially hard." In another experiment, subjects rated a presumed victim of electric shocks who was randomly selected to receive compensation for her pain more favorably than a victim who would not be compensated.

"The sight of an innocent person suffering without possibility of reward or compensation motivated people to devalue the attractiveness of the victim in order to bring about a more appropriate fit between her fate and her character." Devaluing losers allows people to maintain their belief that the world is fundamentally just, even when it patently is not.

Losers are obviously harmed by the association of success with virtue. But the association creates equally important, if less obvious, problems for winners. Fitzwilliam Darcy, in Jane Austen's *Pride and Prejudice,* epitomizes the defect of pride: if I believe that virtue produced my success, or that success has made me even more virtuous, I am likely to become insufferably smug. That may not bother me much, but the fact that people around me feel the same way will. In addition, this equation raises the stakes very high for further rounds of endeavor. If I continue to win, all is well; if I falter, I lose my *amour propre* as well as my wealth or power. Alternatively, if I recognize that I partly owe my success to lying to a few clients, evading a few taxes, cheating a few employees, then I am likely to feel considerable guilt. This guilt might induce reform and recompense, but it may instead induce drinking to assuage the unease, persecuting other nonvirtuous winners, striving to show that losers are even more sinful, or simple hypocrisy.

These problems intensify when patterns of group success rather than the idiosyncrasies of individual success are at issue. When members of one group seem disproportionately successful, that group acquires a halo of ascribed virtue. Consider a 1907 article by Burton J. Hendrick on "The Great Jewish Invasion" in *McClure's Magazine.* The author's name, the publication, the date, and the title all lead one to expect an (at best, thinly veiled) anti-Semitic diatribe. The first few pages seem to confirm that expectation, with their claims that "the real modern Zion, greater in numbers and wealth and power than the old, steadily gathers on Manhattan Island," and that "the Jews are active, and invariably with success, in practically every business, professional, and intellectual field. The New Yorker constantly rubs shoulders with Israel." These feats are all the more "remarkable" because "the great mass of its [New York's] Jews are not what are commonly regarded as the most enlightened of their race" since they come from eastern Europe. After all, "no people have had a more inadequate preparation, educational and economic, for American citizenship."

Yet the article goes on to describe in careful and admiring detail how these dirt-poor, ignorant, orthodoxly non-Christian immigrants work, save, cooperate, sacrifice for their children—and end up wealthy beyond anyone's wildest imaginings. Nor are they merely money-grubbers; Russian Jews are "individualist[s]," the "city's largest productive force and the greatest contributor to its manufacturing wealth," demonstrating "intense ambition," abstinence, and foresight. In his highest accolade, Mr. Hendrick even insists that the Russian Jew's

> enthusiasm for America knows no bounds. He eagerly looks forward to the time when he can be naturalized. . . . The rapidity with which the New York Jew adopts the manners and trappings of Americans almost disproves his ancient heritage as a peculiar people. . . . Better than any other element, even the native stock, do they meet the two supreme tests of citizenship: they actually go to the polls, and when once there, vote independently.

In short, in one generation the east European Jewish immigrant has gone from an unassimilable, bovine drag on the American spirit to the epitome of all the American virtues. Nothing succeeds like success.

The contemporary equivalent of Mr. Hendrick's amazing Jews are Southeast Asians. A century ago, Chinese and Japanese immigrants could hardly be derogated enough. Now newspapers have a seemingly endless supply of rags-to-riches stories about destitute boat people whose daughter became the high school valedictorian a scant five years later and is now a pre-med student at Stanford. Such success is inevitably attributed to hard work, self-discipline, family support, and refusal to follow the bad example set by American-born peers. This portrayal is so ubiquitous that spokespeople for Asian immigrants feel impelled to insist publicly that not *all* Asians escape poverty, crime, and discrimination, and that even the successful pay a heavy emotional cost.

It would be churlish to argue that excessive praise is as bad as racism or ethnic slurs. But newly anointed groups are too often used to cast aspersions on some despised group that has not managed to fulfill the American dream. In Burton Hendrick's case, the main negative reference group is the Irish, who drink and gamble, yield their productive jobs to Jews, and—worst of all—band together in labor unions, in the "Irish vote," and in political party machines. In the case of immigrant Asians, the usual (if slightly more subtle) message is "Why can't African Americans do the same thing? At least they speak English when they start school." This dynamic adds yet another component to the nightmare of a failed American dream. Members of a denigrated group are disproportionately likely to fail to achieve their goals; they are blamed as individuals (and perhaps blame themselves) for their failure; and they carry a further stigma as members of a nonvirtuous (thus appropriately denigrated) group.

This effect of the fourth tenet can be taken a further, and most dangerous, step. For some Americans always, and for many Americans in some periods of our history, virtuous success has been defined as the dominance of some groups over others. This phenomenon extends the idea of competitive success from individual victories to collective hierarchies. If women are weak and emotional, it is *right* for men to control their bodies and wealth; if blacks are childlike pagans, it is *right* for whites to ensure their physical and spiritual survival through enslavement and conversion; if citizens of other nations refuse to recognize the value of capitalism and free elections, it is *right* for Americans to install a more enlightened government in their capitol. I find it hard to present these sentiments with a straight face, but they have arguably done almost as much as the American dream to shape Americans' beliefs, practices, and institutions.

## FLAWS IN THE AMERICAN DREAM TAKEN AS A WHOLE

### Atomistic Individualism

Not only each tenet, but also the ideology of the American dream as a whole, is flawed. One problem stems from the radical individualism often associated with the dream (although the ideology entails nothing that prohibits groups from pursuing collective success). Achievers mark their success by moving away from the tenement, ghetto, or holler of their impoverished and impotent youth, thus speeding the breakup of their ethnic community. This is a bittersweet phenomenon. The freedom to move up and out is desirable, or at least desired. But certainly those left behind, probably those who leave, and arguably the nation as a whole lose when groups of people with close cultural and personal ties break those ties in pursuit of or after attaining "the bitch-goddess, success." The line between autonomy and atomism is hard to draw.

American culture is full of stories about the mixed effects of success on communities and their residents. A Polish-American folk song tells of a man who emigrated to America, worked for three years in a foundry, returned home with "gold and silver," but found that "my children did not know me, for they fled from me, a stranger." The emancipated children may be as pained as the abandoned parents, as illustrated by the five brothers who complained to the *Jewish Daily Forward* in 1933:

> Imagine, even when we go with our father to buy something in a store on Fifth Avenue, New York, he insists on speaking Yiddish. We are not ashamed of our parents, God forbid, but they ought to know where it's proper and where it's not. If they talk Yiddish among themselves at home, or to us, it's bad enough, but among strangers and Christians? Is that nice?

Only irresponsible romanticism permits the wish that peasants and villagers would opt for tradition rather than opportunity. It is surely significant that across the world and throughout centuries, they almost never do. But one can still regret what is lost. And Thomas Hooker's warning cannot be shrugged off: "For if each man may do what is good in his owne eyes, proceed according to his own pleasure, so that none may crosse him or controll him by any power, there must of necessity follow the distraction and desolation of the whole."

## Narrowing "Success"

William James followed his comment on "the moral flabbiness born of the exclusive worship of the bitch-goddess, success" with the less well-known observation that "that—with the squalid cash interpretation put on the word success—is our national disease." It was at best indecorous for a man as wealthy and prestigious as William James to castigate others' pursuit of wealth or inattentiveness to philosophy. But his concern is warranted. The American dream is susceptible to having the open-ended definition of success, which can equally include salvation or writing the great American novel, narrowed to wealth, job status, or power. Well-educated women (not to speak of men) are embarrassed to admit that they would rather raise happy children than practice corporate law; environmentalists worry that the value of a beautiful forest cannot be monetized and therefore will not be considered in regulatory decisions. Even high school seniors, for whom "having lots of money" has become increasingly important over the past two decades, overwhelmingly and increasingly agree that "people are too much concerned with material things these days."

Sometimes market values colonize, rather than submerge, other values. Economists designing environmental regulations assign monetary value to a stand of redwood trees, thereby cheapening (note the metaphor) the meaning of the primeval forest in the eyes of environmentalists. Some feminists seek to enhance the status of women by calculating the wages due to housework and including them in the gross national product; other feminists see this move as turning loving wives and mothers into calculating *homo economici*. The problem in these and similar cases is not that the assignment of monetary worth is too high or low, but that the very process of assigning monetary worth reduces an array of values to a single thin one.

Only sentimentalism allows one to value the purity of artistic poverty over the sordidness of corporate wealth unless one made the choice after experiencing both states. But it is a serious flaw in the American dream if those who envision success in artistic or religious or altruistic terms must defend their vision as well as fight to achieve their chosen goals. Nothing in the ideology requires reducing success to money and power, but the ideology is so vulnerable to the reduction that that point must count as an internal flaw, not merely as grounds for an external attack.

## The Ideology as Deception

I have argued that the American dream need not be individualistic in the narrow sense, given that one can under its rubric pursue success for one's family or community as well as for oneself. But it is highly *individual,* in that it leads one to focus on people's behaviors rather than on economic processes, environmental constraints, or political structures as the causal explanation for social orderings. That focus is not itself a flaw; it is simply an epistemological choice with methodological implications for the study of American politics. But to the degree that the focus carries a moral message, it points to a weakness at the very heart of the dream.

The idea of the blank slate in the first tenet, the almost-promise of success of the second, the reliance on personal attributes in the third, the association of failure with sin in the fourth—all these elements of the dream make it extremely difficult for Americans to see that everyone cannot simultaneously attain more than absolute success. Capitalist markets require some firms to fail; elections require some candidates and policy preferences to lose; status hierarchies must have a bottom in order to have a top. But the optimistic language of and methodological individualism built into the American dream *necessarily* deceive people about these societal operations. We need not invoke hypocrites out of Mark Twain or "blue-eyed white devils" in order to understand why some people never attain success; hypocrisy or bias only enter the picture in determining *who* fails. But our basic institutions are designed to ensure that some fail, at least relatively, and a dream does nothing to help Americans cope with or even to recognize that fact.

*Explain*

## Few Alternative Visions

All ideologies are designed to put the best possible face on the social structure within which they operate, and all privilege some values over others. So all the flaws I have described, damning though they may seem, must themselves be judged in light of the comparable flaws of other ideological formations. That point is intended to soften slightly the critique of the American dream, but it also raises a final problem with it.

Americans have few alternative ideologies against which to measure the distinctive virtues and flaws of the American dream. Alternatives are not completely absent: Thoreau's *Walden* has long been recognized as a sharp political challenge couched in a literary classic. "Country-party" or labor republicanism, Protestant fundamentalism, and ascriptive Americanism similarly have deep roots and on occasion strong adherents and powerful institutional manifestations. But most Americans honor these alternative visions more in the breach than in the observance, if then. *Walden* is read by more students majoring in English than in political science. "Small is beautiful" and "social limits to growth" are slogans for a few, but warnings to many more. And

many possible visions—within-class solidarity and cross-class warfare, a military or theocratic polity pursuing collective glory, small cooperative enterprises living lightly on the land—are barely visible in the American political spectrum. In short, the political culture of the U.S. is largely shaped by a set of views in which the American dream is prominent, and by a set of institutions that make it even more prominent than views alone could do.

Tocqueville assured his readers that "up to now the Americans have happily avoided all the reefs I have just charted." Some Americans continue, 150 years later, to sail free, and perhaps they always will. But some have wrecked, and some have never gotten anywhere near the boat. For those afloat, the ideology of the American dream is a vindication, a goad to further efforts, a cause for celebration—and also grounds for anxiety, guilt and disillusionment. For the shipwrecked and drifters, the dream is a taunt, a condemnation, an object of fury—and also grounds for hope; renewed striving, and dreams for one's children.

---

## DISCUSSION QUESTIONS

1. According to Hochschild, what are the key tenets of success in the American dream, and in what ways might the American definition of success be considered narrow?
2. In what sense is the American dream a "fantasy?" How is this fantasy reinforced by American life and culture?
3. What does Hochschild mean by "atomistic individualism" and why does she consider it a flaw? Compare her argument on this point with the case made by Robert Bellah and his co-authors in the next selection.

**6** *Robert N. Bellah, Richard Madsen, William M. Sullivan, Ann Swidler, and Steven M. Tipton*

# LIBERAL INDIVIDUALISM AND THE CRISIS OF CITIZENSHIP

*Sociologist Robert Bellah and his four collaborators suggest that the exaggerated importance placed on individualism in America undermines citizenship and a strong sense of political community. Drawing on in-depth interviews with middle-class Americans for their much-discussed 1985 book* Habits of the Heart, *the authors contend that most of us are unable to find in political participation and public involvement elements of a good life. But this withdrawal into private pursuits leaves politics under the domination of those with the power and money to assert their organized interests. Writing more than a decade after the original publication of* Habits of the Heart, *Bellah draws on Robert Putnam's concept of "social capital" to argue that Americans face both a personal crisis and a social crisis that he calls a "crisis of civic membership." This crisis has been exacerbated by the success of "neocapitalism," an ideology that sees markets and privatization as the solutions to social problems. In contrast, Bellah calls for a revival of civic- and community-oriented discourses that historically have been subordinate to liberal-capitalist individualism and asks us to critically question the materialistic basis of our notion of a just society.*

How ought we to live? How do we think about how to live? Who are we, as Americans? What is our character? These are questions we have asked our fellow citizens in many parts of the country. We engaged them in conversations about their lives and about what matters most to them, talked about their families and communities, their doubts and uncertainties, and their hopes and fears with respect to the larger society. We found them eager to discuss the right way to live, what to teach our children, and what our public

and private responsibilities should be, but also a little dismayed by these subjects. These are important matters to those to whom we talked, and yet concern about moral questions is often relegated to the realm of private anxiety, as if it would be awkward or embarrassing to make it public. We hope this book will help transform this inner moral debate, often shared only with intimates, into public discourse. In these pages, Americans speak with us, and, indirectly, with one another, about issues that deeply concern us

*Source:* Robert N. Bellah, Richard Madsen, William M. Sullivan, Ann Swidler, and Steven M. Tipton, *Habits of the Heart: Individualism and Commitment in American Life,* Updated Edition, Berkeley and Los Angeles: University of California Press, 1996, pp. xli–xliii, xi, and xvi–xxvi.

all. As we will see, many doubt that we have enough in common to be able mutually to discuss our central aspirations and fears. It is one of our purposes to persuade them that we do.

The fundamental question we posed, and that was repeatedly posed to us, was how to preserve or create a morally coherent life. But the kind of life we want depends on the kind of people we are—on our character. Our inquiry can thus be located in a longstanding discussion of the relationship between character and society. In the eighth book of the *Republic,* Plato sketched a theory of the relationship between the moral character of a people and the nature of its political community, the way it organizes and governs itself. The founders of the American republic at the time of the Revolution adopted a much later version of the same theory. Since for them, as for the Americans with whom we talked, freedom was perhaps the most important value, they were particularly concerned with the qualities of character necessary for the creation of a free republic.

In the 1830s, the French social philosopher Alexis de Tocqueville offered the most comprehensive and penetrating analysis of the relationship between character and society in America that has ever been written. In his book *Democracy in America,* based on acute observation and wide conversation with Americans, Tocqueville described the mores—which he on occasion called "habits of the heart"—of the American people and showed how they helped to form American character. He singled out family life, our religious traditions, and our participation in local politics as helping to create the kind of person who could sustain a connection to a wider political community and thus ultimately support the maintenance of free institutions. He also warned that some aspects of our character—what he was one of the first to call "individualism"—might eventually isolate Americans one from another and thereby undermine the conditions of freedom.

The central problem of our book concerns the American individualism that Tocqueville described with a mixture of admiration and anxiety. It seems to us that it is individualism, and not equality, as Tocqueville thought, that has marched inexorably through our history. We are concerned that this individualism may have grown cancerous—that it

may be destroying those social integuments that Tocqueville saw as moderating its more destructive potentialities, that it may be threatening the survival of freedom itself. We want to know what individualism in America looks and feels like, and how the world appears in its light.

We are also interested in those cultural traditions and practices that, without destroying individuality, serve to limit and restrain the destructive side of individualism and provide alternative models for how Americans might live. We want to know how these have fared since Tocqueville's day, and how likely their renewal is.

While we focus on what people say, we are acutely aware that they often live in ways they cannot put into words. It is particularly here, in the tension between how we live and what our culture allows us to say, that we have found both some of our richest insights into the dilemmas our society faces and hope for the reappropriation of a common language in which those dilemmas can be discussed.

Taking our clue from Tocqueville, we believe that one of the keys to the survival of free institutions is the relationship between private and public life, the way in which citizens do, or do not, participate in the public sphere. We therefore decided to concentrate our research on how private and public life work in the United States: the extent to which private life either prepares people to take part in the public world or encourages them to find meaning exclusively in the private sphere, and the degree to which public life fulfills our private aspirations or discourages us so much that we withdraw from involvement in it.

•   •   •

## THE CRISIS OF CIVIC MEMBERSHIP

The consequences of radical individualism are more strikingly evident today than they were even a decade ago, when *Habits of the Heart* was published. In *Habits* we spoke of commitment, of community, and of citizenship as useful terms to contrast to an alienating individualism. Properly understood, these terms are still valuable for our current understanding. But today we think the phrase "civic membership" brings out something not quite captured by those other terms. While we criticized distorted forms of individualism, we never sought to neglect the central significance of the individual person or failed to sympathize with the difficulties faced by the individual self in our society. "Civic membership" points to that critical intersection of personal identity with social identity. If we face a crisis of civic identity, it is not just a social crisis, it is a personal crisis as well.

One way of characterizing the weakening of the practices of social life and civic engagement that we have called the crisis of civic membership is to speak of declining social capital. Robert Putnam, who has brought the term to public attention recently, defines social capital as follows: "By analogy with notions of physical capital and human capital—tools and training that enhance individual productivity—'social capital' refers to features of social organization, such as networks, norms, and trust, that facilitate coordination and cooperation for mutual benefits." There are a number of possible indices of social capital; the two that Putnam has used most extensively are associational membership and public trust.

Putnam has chosen a stunning image as the title of a recent article: "Bowling Alone: America's Declining Social Capital." He reports that between 1980 and 1993 the total number of bowlers in America increased by 10 percent, while league bowling decreased by 40 percent. Nor, he points out, is this a trivial example: nearly 80 million Americans went bowling at least once in 1993, nearly a third more than voted in the 1994 congressional elections and roughly the same as claim to attend church regularly. But Putnam uses bowling only as a symbol for the decline of American associational life, the vigor of which has been seen as the heart of our civic culture ever since Tocqueville visited the U.S. in the 1830s.

In the 1970s dramatic declines in membership began to hit organizations typically associated with women, such as the PTA and the League of Women Voters, in what has often been explained as the result of the massive entry of women into the workforce. In the 1980s falling membership struck traditionally male associations, such as the Lions, Elks, Masons, and Shriners, as well. Union membership has dropped by half since its peak in the middle 1950s. We all know of the continuing decline in the numbers of eligible voters who actually go the polls, but Putnam reminds us that the number of Americans who answer yes when asked whether they have attended a public meeting on town or school affairs in the last year has fallen by more than a third since 1973.

Almost the only groups that are growing are the support groups, such as twelve-step groups, that Robert Wuthnow has recently studied. These groups make minimal demands on their members and are oriented primarily to the needs of individuals: indeed, Wuthnow has characterized them as involving individuals who "focus on themselves in the presence of others," what we might call being alone together. Putnam argues that paper membership groups, such as the AARP (American Association of Retired Persons), which has grown to gargantuan proportions, have few or no civic consequences, because their members may have common interests but they have no meaningful interactions. Putnam also worries that the Internet, the electronic town meeting, and other much ballyhooed new technological devices are probably civically vacuous, because they do not sustain civic engagement. Talk radio, for instance, mobilizes private opinion, not public opinion, and trades on anxiety, anger, and distrust, all of which are deadly to civic culture. The one sphere that seems to be resisting the general trend is religion. Religious membership and church attendance have remained fairly constant after the decline from the religious boom of the 1950s, although membership in church-related groups has declined by about one-sixth since the 1960s.

What goes together with the decline of associational involvement is the decline of public trust. We are not surprised to hear that the proportion of Americans who reply that they trust the government in Washington only some of the time or almost never has risen steadily, from 30 percent in 1966 to 75 percent in 1992. But are we prepared to hear that the proportion of Americans who say that most people can be trusted fell by more than a third between 1960, when 58 percent chose that alternative, and 1993, when only 37 percent did?

The argument for decline in social capital is not one that we made in *Habits of the Heart. Habits* was essentially a cultural analysis more about language than about behavior. We worried that the language of individualism might undermine civic commitment, but we pointed to the historically high levels of associational membership in America and the relative strength of such memberships here compared with those in other advanced industrial nations. Whether there has really been such a decline is still controversial, but we are inclined to believe that tendencies that were not yet entirely clear in the early 1980s when *Habits* was written are now discernible and disconcerting.

We believe that the culture and language of individualism influence these trends but that there are also structural reasons for them, many of which stem from changes in the economy we have already mentioned. The decline in social capital is evident in different ways in different classes. For example, the decline in civic engagement in the overclass is indicated by their withdrawal into gated, guarded communities. It is also related to the constant movement of companies in the process of mergers and breakups. Rosabeth Kanter has recently suggested some of the consequences of this movement:

> For communities as well as employees this constant shuffling of company identities is confusing and its effects profound. Cities and towns rely on the private sector to augment public services and support community causes. There is a strong "headquarters bias" in this giving: companies based in a city tend to do more for it, contributing $75,000 a year on average more to the local United Way, than companies of similar size with headquarters elsewhere.

Kanter points out that the departure of a corporate headquarters from a middle-sized city can tear holes in the social fabric of that city. Not only are thousands of jobs lost but so is the civic leadership of the corporate executives. Local charities lose not only money but board members.

Corporate volatility can lead to a kind of placelessness at the top of the pyramid: "Cut loose from society the rich man can play his chosen role free of guilt and responsibility," observes Michael Lewis. "He becomes that great figure of American mythology—the roaming frontiersman. These days the man who has made a fortune is likely to spend more on his means of transportation than on his home: the private jet is the possession that most distinguishes him from the rest of us. . . . The old aristocratic conceit of place has given way to glorious placelessness." The mansions of the old rich were certainly expressions of conspicuous consumption, but they also encouraged a sense of responsibility for a particular place (city, state, region) where they were located. Wendell Berry has spoken of "itinerant professional vandals," who are perhaps not too different from Reich's "symbolic analysts," attached to no place at all and thus tempted to act more like an oligarchy than an establishment.

Moving to the opposite end of the income spectrum, Lee Rainwater, in his classic book *What Money Buys,* shows that poverty—income insufficient to maintain an acceptable level of living—operates to deprive the poor not only of material capital but of social capital as well. In traditional hierarchical societies, low levels of material well-being can be associated with established statuses that confer the benefits of clientship. In our kind of society, with its fundamentally egalitarian ideology and its emphasis on individual self-reliance, status—even personal identity—of those not-so-distant ancestors was one of vulnerable subordination, of being kicked around by people who told them what to do. Owning one's own home, taking vacations wherever one wants, being free to decide whom to see or what to buy once one has left the workplace—these are all freedoms that are especially cherished by those whose ancestors have never had them. The modest suburb is not the open frontier but it is, under the circumstances, a reasonable facsimile thereof.

Among the many ironies in the lives of at least a significant number of these middle Americans, however, is that labor union membership had much to do with their attainment of relative affluence and its attendant independence; yet for many of them the labor union has become one more alien institution from which they would like to be free. Middle Americans not only are suspicious of government, according to Gans, they don't like organizations of

*Shift to $$$ as Form of Participation*
*Economic Inequality → impact on Democracy*

any kind. Relative to the upper middle class (the lower echelons of what we have been calling the overclass), they are not joiners, belonging to only one or two associations at the most, the commonest being a church. While continuing to identify strongly with the nation, they are increasingly suspicious of politics, which they find confusing and dismaying. Their political participation declines steadily.

As a consequence of tendencies that Gans is probably right in asking us to understand, middle Americans are today losing the social capital that allowed them to attain their valued independence in the first place. Above all this is true of the decline of the labor movement. This decline stems from legislative changes in the last twenty years that have deprived unions of much of their power and influence, and from congressional refusal since 1991 to raise the minimum wage from $4.25 an hour. But, as we see in France and other European countries, where loyalty to labor unions has survived, such attacks can be turned back. In America, union meetings, even where there are unions, are attended by 5 percent of the members at most. Lacking the social capital that union membership would provide, anxious-class Americans are vulnerable in new ways to the arbitrary domination they thought they had escaped. One may lose even one's home and one's recreational vehicle if one's job is downsized and the only alternative employment is at the minimum wage.

The decline of social capital in America becomes particularly distressing if we consider what has happened to our political participation. In *Voice and Equality* Sydney Verba and his colleagues have recently given us a comprehensive review of political participation in the United States. Although the data concerning trends over time are not unambiguous, they do indicate certain tendencies. During the last thirty years the average level of education of the American public has risen steadily, but the level of political participation, which is usually associated with education, has not. This fact can be taken as an indication that, controlling for education, political participation has declined. Even more significant is the nature of the changes. Political party identification and membership have declined, while campaign

contributions and writing to congresspersons have increased. Both of these growing kinds of activities normally take place in the privacy of one's home as one writes a check or a letter. Verba and his associates note that neither generates the personal satisfactions associated with more social forms of political participation.

Further, making monetary contributions correlates highly with income and is the most unequal form of participation in our society. The increasing salience of monetary contributions as a form of political participation, as well as the general tendency for political participation to correlate with income, education, and occupation, leads to the summary conclusion of *Voice and Equality*:

Meaningful democratic participation requires that the voices of citizens in politics be clear, loud, and equal: clear so that public officials know what citizens want and need, loud so that officials have an incentive to pay attention to what they hear, and equal so that the democratic ideal of equal responsiveness to the preferences and interests of all is not violated. Our analysis of voluntary activity in American politics suggests that the public's voice is often loud, sometimes clear, but rarely equal.

Although unequal levels of education, occupation, and income favor the originally advantaged in securing the resources for political participation, there is one significant exception. Verba and his associates note that:

[o]nly religious institutions provide a counterbalance to this cumulative resource process. They play an unusual role in the American participatory system by providing opportunities for the development of civic skills to those who would otherwise be resource-poor. It is commonplace to ascribe the special character of American politics to the weakness of unions and the absence of class-based political parties that can mobilize the disadvantaged— in particular, the working class— to political activity. Another way that American society is exceptional is in how often Americans go

to church—with the result that the mobilizing function often performed elsewhere by unions and labor or social democratic parties is more likely to be performed by religious institutions.

To summarize the relationship of the decline of social capital to political participation we might consider how this relationship works out in the several social classes. Overall, with the exception of the activities centered in religious institutions, political participation has shifted away from those forms that require civic engagement to those that are essentially private, and above all to that of making monetary contributions. The unequal voice to which Verba and his associates point is an indication that the anxious class is seriously under-represented and the underclass scarcely represented at all. Even in the overclass, participation has shifted from more active forms of engagement to the more isolated forms of check- and letter-writing. Finally, Verba and his associates point out that the increasing importance of money in political life contributes to public cynicism: "In short, a participatory system in which money plays a more prominent role is one unlikely to leave either activists or the citizenry at large feeling better about politics."

## INDIVIDUALISM AND THE AMERICAN CRISIS

Most Americans agree that things are seriously amiss in our society—that we are not, as the poll questions often put it, "headed in the right direction"—but they differ over why this is so and what should be done about it. We have sought for answers in the structural problems that we have described under the rubrics of the crisis in civic membership and the decline of social capital. What are some of the other explanations? Perhaps the most widespread alternative explanation locates the source of our problems in a crisis of the family. The cry that what our society most needs is "family values" is not one to be dismissed lightly. Almost all the tendencies we have been describing threaten family life and are often experienced most acutely

within the family. Being unemployed and thus unable to get married or not having enough income to support an existing family due to downsizing or part-timing, along with the tensions caused by these conditions, can certainly be understood as family crisis. But why is the crisis expressed as a failure of family values?

It is unlikely that we will understand what is going on here unless we once again take into account the culture of individualism. If we see unemployment or reduced income because of downsizing as a purely individual problem rather than a structural problem of the economy, then we will seek to understand what is wrong with the unemployed or underemployed individual. If we also discern that such individuals are prone to have children out of wedlock, to divorce, or to fail to make child support payments, we may conclude that the cause is weakened family values. In *Habits of the Heart* we strongly affirmed the value of the family, and in both *Habits* and *The Good Society* we argued for renewed commitment to marriage and family responsibilities. But to imagine that problems arising from failures rooted in the structure of our economy and polity can primarily be traced to the failings of individuals with inadequate family values seems to us sadly mistaken. It not only increases the level of individual guilt, it also distracts attention from larger failures of collective responsibility.

The link between cultural individualism and the emphasis on family values has a further consequence. Families have traditionally been supported by the paid labor of men. Failure to support one's family may be taken as an indication of inadequate manhood. It is easy to draw the conclusion that if American men would only act like men, then family life would be improved and social problems solved. Some such way of thinking undoubtedly lies behind the movement known as Promise Keepers, as well as the Million Man March of 1995. While we share many of the values of these movements, we are skeptical that increased male responsibility will prove to be an adequate solution to our deep structural economic and political problems or even that it will do more than marginally diminish the severe strains on the American family. The notion that if men would only be men then all would be well in our society seems to us a sad cultural delusion.

Another common alternative explanation of our difficulties is to explain them as the failure of community. This is indeed valid, we believe, but only if our understanding of community is broad and deep enough. In many current usages of the term, however, community means face-to-face groups formed by the voluntary efforts of individuals. Used in this way, failure of community as the source of our problems can be interpreted to mean that if only more people would volunteer to help in soup kitchens or Habitat for Humanity or Meals on Wheels, then our social problems would be solved. As in the case of family values, *Habits of the Heart* strongly affirms face-to-face communities and the valuable contributions voluntary groups can make to society. But we do not believe that the deep structural problems that we face as a society can be effectively alleviated by an increase in devotion to community in this narrow sense. We would agree that an increase in the voluntary commitments of individuals can over the long haul increase our social capital and thus add to the resources we can bring to bear on our problems. But to get at the roots of our problems these resources must be used to overcome institutional difficulties that cannot be directly addressed by voluntary action alone.

We see another difficulty in emphasizing a small-scale and voluntaristic understanding of community as the solution to our problems. As we noted in discussing the work of Verba and his colleagues, voluntary activity tends to correlate with income, education, and occupation. "Joiners" are more apt to be found in the overclass than in the underclass or the anxious class, again with the significant exception of religious groups. This means that voluntary activities are less often designed to help the most deprived, though we don't want to overlook those that are, than to serve the interests of the affluent. This is particularly true of political voluntarism, as Verba and his associates have shown conclusively. Thus, dismantling structures of public provision for the most deprived in hopes that the voluntary sector will take over is misguided in three important respects. First, the voluntary sector has by no means the resources to take up the slack, as churches, charities, and foundations have been pointing out repeatedly in recent years. The second reason is that our more affluent citizens may feel they have fulfilled their obligation to society by giving time and money to "making a difference" through voluntary activity without taking into account that they have hardly made a dent in the real problems faced by most Americans. The third reason is that, as we noted, the voluntary sector is disproportionately run by our better-off citizens and a good many voluntary activities do more to protect the well-to-do than the needy.

There is another sense of community that also presents difficulties if we think the solution to our problems lies in reviving community, and that is the notion of community as neighborhood or locality. *Habits of the Heart* encourages strong neighborhoods and supports civic engagement in towns and cities. But residential segregation is a fact of life in contemporary America. Even leaving aside the hypersegregation of urban ghettos, segregation by class arising from differential housing costs is becoming increasingly evident in suburban America. Thus it is quite possible that in "getting involved" with one's neighborhood or even with one's suburban town one will never meet someone of a different race or class. One will not be exposed to the realities of life for people in circumstances different from one's own. One may even succumb to the natural human temptation to think that people who are different, particularly those lower in social status, are inferior. The anxious class does not want itself to be confused with the underclass. One of the least pleasant characteristics of the overclass, including its lower echelons in the educated upper middle class, is that they do not want to associate with middle Americans, with "Joe Six-Pack" and others who lack the proper cultural attributes. Even in the underclass, those who are not on welfare look down on those who are, and those who are on the dole briefly look down on those on it for a long time. Under such circumstances an exclusive emphasis on neighborhood solidarity could actually contribute to larger social problems rather than solving them.

What the explanations of our social problems that stress the failure of family values or the failure of community have in common is the notion that our problems are individual or in only a narrow sense social (that is, involving family and local community), rather than economic, political, and cultural. A related feature that these common explanations of our troubles share is hostility to the role of government or the state. If we can take care of ourselves, perhaps with a little help from our friends and family, who needs the state? Indeed, the state is often viewed as an interfering father who won't recognize that his children have grown up and don't need him anymore. He can't help solve our problems because it is in large measure he who created them.

In contrast, the market, in this mindset, seems benign, a mostly neutral theater for competition in which achievement is rewarded and incompetence punished. Some awareness exists, however, that markets are not neutral, that some people and organizations have enormous economic power and are capable of making decisions that adversely affect many citizens. From this point of view big business joins big government as the source of problems rather than their solution. Still, in America more than in most comparable societies, people are inclined to think that the market is fairer than the state.

## INDIVIDUALISM AND NEOCAPITALISM

The culture of individualism, then, has made no small contribution to the rise of the ideology we called neocapitalism in Chapter 10 of *Habits*. There we drew a picture of the American political situation that has turned out not to be entirely adequate. We suggested that the impasse between welfare liberalism and its counter-movement, neocapitalism, was coming to an end and that two alternatives, the administered society and economic democracy, were looming on the scene. As it turned out, this incipient pair of alternatives did not materialize, or at least they are enduring a long wait. Instead, neocapitalism has grown ever stronger ideologically and politically. Criticism of "big government" and "tax-and-spend liberalism" has mounted even as particular constituencies, which in the aggregate include most citizens, favor those forms of public provision that benefit them in particular, while opposing benefits they do not receive.

We do not believe we were wrong in seeing ten years ago the severe strains that the neocapitalist formula was creating for the nation. Today those strains are more obvious than ever. But we clearly underestimated the ideological fervor that the neocapitalist position was able to tap—ironically for us, because so much of that fervor derives from the very source we focused on in our book: individualism. The neocapitalist vision is viable only to the degree to which it can be seen as an expression—even a moral expression—of our dominant ideological individualism, with its compulsive stress on independence, its contempt for weakness, and its adulation of success.

---

## DISCUSSION QUESTIONS

1. Bellah and his coauthors contend that the ideology of individualism—the foundation of our political beliefs—may well have grown "cancerous." Explain this disease in our belief system. Do you agree that this may be a serious problem today?
2. What is "social capital" and how does its depletion contribute to the "crisis of civic membership"?
3. Why do authors believe that explanations of our social problems that stress the failure of family values or the failure of community are inadequate?

**7** *Michelle Goldberg*

# KINGDOM COMING: RESISTING THE POWER OF THE CHRISTIAN RIGHT

*The rise of religious fundamentalism is one of the key pivot points in twenty-first century world politics and culture. The American political scene has not escaped its growing impact as the evangelical right has flexed its political muscles at every level of government. Drawing on her 2006 book* Kingdom Coming: The Rise of Christian Nationalism, *in this article Michelle Goldberg, a senior contributing writer at* Salon.com, *assesses the threat posed to democracy by the rise of the ideology of Christian Nationalism. Goldberg views Christian Nationalism as a mass social movement aiming to "supplant Enlightenment rationalism with what it calls the 'Christian worldview.'" While both Christian nationalism and secularism are spreading, more moderate versions of Christianity are in decline, thus leaving a shrinking middle ground on which to debate the role of religion in our public lives. Within this polarized environment, Goldberg foresees the potential coarsening of politics in the U.S. as the absolutist perspective of the Christian right pressures government to respond to the publics' very real anxieties with public policies that threaten the civil liberties essential to a vibrant democracy. In opposition to the power of this rightward drift, she advocates that liberals and progressives undertake a three part approach that includes electoral reform, grassroots organizing and a media campaign—all measures designed to "make reality matter again."*

Whenever I talk about the growing power of the evangelical right with friends, they always ask the same question: What can we do? Usually I reply with a joke: Keep a bag packed and your passport current. I don't really mean it, but my anxiety is genuine. It's one thing to have a government that shows contempt for civil liberties; America has survived such men

before. It's quite another to have a mass movement—the largest and most powerful mass movement in the nation—rise up in opposition to the rights of its fellow citizens. The Constitution protects minorities, but that protection is not absolute; with a sufficiently sympathetic or apathetic majority, a tightly organized faction can get around it.

*Source:* Michelle Goldberg, "Saving Secular Society," *In These Times,* Volume 30, Number 6, May 16, 2006, pp. 32–35. Adapted from her book *Kingdom Coming: The Rise of Christian Nationalism,* New York: Norton, 2006.

The mass movement I've described aims to supplant Enlightenment rationalism with what it calls the "Christian worldview." The phrase is based on the conviction that true Christianity must govern every aspect of public and private life, and that all—government, science, history and culture—must be understood according to the dictates of scripture. There are biblically correct positions on every issue, from gay marriage to income tax rates, and only those with the right worldview can discern them. This is Christianity as a total ideology—I call it Christian nationalism. It's an ideology adhered to by millions of Americans, some of whom are very powerful. It's what drives a great many of the fights over religion, science, sex and pluralism now dividing communities all over the country.

I am not suggesting that religious tyranny is imminent in the United States. Our democracy is eroding and some of our rights are disappearing, but for most people, including those most opposed to the Christian nationalist agenda, life will most likely go on pretty much as normal for the foreseeable future. Thus for those who value secular society, apprehending the threat of Christian nationalism is tricky. It's like being a lobster in a pot, with the water heating up so slowly that you don't notice the moment at which it starts to kill you.

If current trends continue, we will see ever-increasing division and acrimony in our politics. That's partly because, as Christian nationalism spreads, secularism is spreading as well, while moderate Christianity is in decline. According to the City University of New York Graduate Center's comprehensive American religious identification survey, the percentage of Americans who identify as Christians has actually fallen in recent years, from 86 percent in 1990 to 77 percent in 2001. The survey found that the largest growth, in both absolute and percentage terms, was among those who don't subscribe to any religion. Their numbers more than doubled, from 14.3 million in 1990, when they constituted 8 percent of the population, to 29.4 million in 2001, when they made up 14 percent. "The top three 'gainers' in America's vast religious marketplace appear to be Evangelical Christians, those describing themselves as Non-Denominational Christians and those who profess no religion," the survey found. (The

percentage of other religious minorities remained small, totaling less than 4 percent of the population).

This is a recipe for polarization. As Christian nationalism becomes more militant, secularists and religious minorities will mobilize in opposition, ratcheting up the hostility. Thus we're likely to see a shrinking middle ground, with both camps increasingly viewing each other across a chasm of mutual incomprehension and contempt.

In the coming years, we will probably see the curtailment of the civil rights that gay people, women and religious minorities have won in the last few decades. With two Bush appointees on the Supreme Court, abortion rights will be narrowed; if the president gets a third, it could mean the end of *Roe v. Wade*. Expect increasing drives to ban gay people from being adoptive or foster parents, as well as attempts to fire gay schoolteachers. Evangelical leaders are encouraging their flocks to be alert to signs of homosexuality in their kids, which will lead to a growing number of gay teenagers forced into "reparative therapy" designed to turn them straight. (Focus on the Family urges parents to consider seeking help for boys as young as five if they show a "tendency to cry easily, be less athletic, and dislike the roughhousing that other boys enjoy.")

Christian nationalist symbolism and ideology will increasingly pervade public life. In addition to the war on evolution, there will be campaigns to teach Christian nationalist history in public schools. An elective course developed by the National Council on Bible Curriculum in Public Schools, a right-wing evangelical group, is already being offered by more than 300 school districts in 36 states. The influence of Christian nationalism in public schools, colleges, courts, social services and doctors' offices will deform American life, rendering it ever more pinched, mean, and divided.

There's still a long way, though, between this damaged version of democracy and real theocracy. Tremendous crises would have to shred what's left of the American consensus before religious fascism becomes a possibility. That means that secularists and liberals shouldn't get hysterical, but they also shouldn't be complacent.

Christian nationalism is still constrained by the Constitution, the courts, and by a passionate democratic (and occasionally Democratic) opposition. It's also limited by capitalism. Many corporations are happy to see their political allies harness the rage and passion of the Christian right's foot soldiers, but the culture industry is averse to government censorship. Nor is homophobia good for business, since many companies need to both recruit qualified gay employees and market to gay customers. Biotech firms are not going to want to hire graduates without a thorough understanding of evolution, so economic pressure will militate against creationism's invading a critical mass of the public schools.

It would take a national disaster, or several of them, for all these bulwarks to crumble and for Christian nationalists to truly "take the land," as Michael Farris, president of the evangelical Patrick Henry College, put it. Historically, totalitarian movements have been able to seize state power only when existing authorities prove unable to deal with catastrophic challenges—economic meltdown, security failures, military defeat—and people lose their faith in the legitimacy of the system.

Such calamities are certainly conceivable in America—Hurricane Katrina's aftermath offered a terrifying glimpse of how quickly order can collapse. If terrorists successfully strike again, we'd probably see significant curtailment of liberal dissenters' free speech rights, coupled with mounting right-wing belligerence, both religious and secular.

The breakdown in the system could also be subtler. Many experts have warned that America's debt is unsustainable and that economic crisis could be on the horizon. If there is a hard landing—due to an oil shock, a burst housing bubble, a sharp decline in the value of the dollar, or some other crisis—interest rates would shoot up, leaving many people unable to pay their floating-rate mortgages and credit card bills. Repossessions and bankruptcies would follow. The resulting anger could fuel radical populist movements of either the left or the right—more likely the right, since it has a far stronger ideological infrastructure in place in most of America.

Military disaster may also exacerbate such disaffection. America's war in Iraq seems nearly certain to come to an ignominious end. The real victims of failure there will be Iraqi, but many Americans will feel embittered, humiliated and sympathetic to the

stab-in-the-back rhetoric peddled by the right to explain how Bush's venture has gone so horribly wrong. It was the defeat in World War I, after all, that created the conditions for fascism to grow in Germany.

Perhaps America will be lucky, however, and muddle through its looming problems. In that case, Christian nationalism will continue to be a powerful and growing influence in American politics, although its expansion will happen more fitfully and gradually.

The country's demographics are on the movement's side. Megachurch culture is spreading. The exurbs where religious conservatism thrives are the fastest growing parts of America; in 2004, 97 of the country's 100 fastest-growing counties voted Republican. The disconnection of the exurbs is a large part of what makes the spread of Christian nationalism's fictitious reality possible, because there is very little to conflict with it.

A movement that constitutes its members' entire social world has a grip that's hard to break. In *The Origins of Totalitarianism,* Hannah Arendt put it this way: "Social atomization and extreme individualization preceded the mass movements which, much more easily and earlier than they did the sociable, non-individualistic members of the traditional parties, attracted the completely unorganized, the typical 'nonjoiners' who for individualistic reasons always had refused to recognize social links or obligations."

Those who want to fight Christian nationalism will need a long-term and multifaceted strategy. I see it as having three parts—electoral reform to give urban areas fair representation in the federal government, grassroots organizing to help people fight Christian nationalism on the ground and a media campaign to raise public awareness about the movement's real agenda.

My ideas are not about reconciliation or healing. It would be good if a leader stepped forward who could recognize the grievances of both sides, broker some sort of truce, and mend America's ragged divides. The anxieties that underlay Christian nationalism's appeal—fears about social breakdown, marital instability and cultural decline—are real. They should be acknowledged and, whenever possible, addressed. But as long as the movement aims at the destruction of secular society and the political enforcement of its theology, it has to be battled, not comforted and appeased.

And while I support liberal struggles for economic justice—higher wages, universal health care, affordable education, and retirement security—I don't think economic populism will do much to neutralize the religious right. Cultural interests are real interests, and many drives are stronger than material ones. As Arendt pointed out, totalitarian movements have always confounded observers who try to analyze them in terms of class.

Ultimately, a fight against Christian nationalist rule has to be a fight against the anti-urban bias built into the structure of our democracy. Because each state has two senators, the 7 percent of the population that live in the 17 least-populous states control more than a third of Congress's upper house. Conservative states are also overrepresented in the Electoral College. According to Steven Hill of the Center for Voting and Democracy, the combined populations of Montana, Wyoming, Nevada, North and South Dakota, Colorado, Nebraska, Kansas, Oklahoma, Arizona, and Alaska equal that of New York and Massachusetts, but the former states have a total of nine more votes in the Electoral College (as well as over five times the votes in the Senate). In America, conservatives literally count for more.

Liberals should work to abolish the Electoral College and to even out the composition of the Senate, perhaps by splitting some of the country's larger states. (A campaign for statehood for New York City might be a place to start.) It will be a grueling, Herculean job. With conservatives already indulging in fantasies of victimization at the hands of a maniacal Northeastern elite, it will take a monumental movement to wrest power away from them. Such a movement will come into being only when enough people in the blue states stop internalizing right-wing jeers about how out of touch they are with "real Americans" and start getting angry at being ruled by reactionaries who are out of touch with them.

After all, the heartland has no claim to moral authority. The states whose voters are most obsessed with "moral values" have the highest divorce and teen pregnancy rates. The country's highest murder rates are in the South and the lowest are in New England. The five states with the best-ranked public schools in the country—Massachusetts, Connecticut, Vermont, New Jersey and Wisconsin—are all progressive redoubts. The five states with the worst—New Mexico, Nevada, Arizona, Mississippi and Louisiana—all went for Bush.

The canard that the culture wars are a fight between "elites" versus "regular Americans" belies a profound split between different kinds of ordinary Americans, all feeling threatened by the others' baffling and alien values. Ironically, however, by buying into right-wing elite-baiting, liberals start thinking like out-of-touch elites. Rather than reflecting on what kind of policies would make their own lives better, what kind of country they want to live in, and who they want to represent them—and then figuring out how to win others to their vision—progressives flail about for ideas and symbols that they hope will appeal to some imaginary heartland rube. That is condescending.

One way for progressives to build a movement and fight Christian nationalism at the same time is to focus on local politics. For guidance, they need only look to the Christian Coalition: It wasn't until after Bill Clinton's election exiled the evangelical right from power in Washington that the Christian Coalition really developed its nationwide electoral apparatus.

The Christian right developed a talent for crafting state laws and amendments to serve as wedge issues, rallying their base, and forcing the other side to defend seemingly extreme positions. Campaigns to require parental consent for minors' abortions, for example, get overwhelming public support and put the pro-choice movement on the defensive while giving pro-lifers valuable political experience.

Liberals can use this strategy too. They can find issues to exploit the other side's radicalism, winning a few political victories and, just as important, marginalizing Christian nationalists in the eyes of their fellow citizens.

Progressives could work to pass local and state laws, by ballot initiative wherever possible, denying public funds to any organization that discriminates on the basis of religion. Because so much faith-based funding is distributed through the states, such laws could put an end to at least some of the taxpayer-funded bias practiced by the Salvation Army and other religious charities. Right now, very few people know that, thanks to Bush, a faith-based outfit can take tax dollars and then explicitly refuse to hire Jews, Hindus, Buddhists or Muslims. The issue needs far more publicity, and a political fight—or a series of them—would provide it. Better still, the campaign would contribute to the creation of a grassroots infrastructure—a network of people with political experience and a commitment to pluralism.

Progressives could also work on passing laws to mandate that pharmacists fill contraceptive prescriptions. (Such legislation has already been introduced in California, Missouri, New Jersey, Nevada, and West Virginia.) The commercials would practically write themselves. Imagine a harried couple talking with their doctor and deciding that they can't afford any more kids. The doctor writes a birth control prescription, the wife takes it to her pharmacist—and he sends her away with a religious lecture. The campaign could use one of the most successful slogans that abortion rights advocates ever devised: "Who decides—you or them?"

In conjunction with local initiatives, opponents of Christian nationalism need a new media strategy. Many people realize this. Fenton Communications, the agency that handles public relations for MoveOn, recently put together the Campaign to Defend the Constitution, a MoveOn-style grassroots group devoted to raising awareness about the religious right. With nearly 3.5 million members ready to be quickly mobilized to donate money, write letters or lobby politicians on behalf of progressive causes, MoveOn is the closest thing liberals have to the Christian Coalition, but its focus tends to be on economic justice, foreign policy and the environment rather than contentious social issues. The Campaign to Defend the Constitution intends to build a similar network to counter Christian nationalism wherever it appears.

Much of what media strategists need to do simply involves public education. Americans need to learn what Christian Reconstructionism means so that they can decide whether they approve of their congressmen consorting with theocrats. They need to realize that the Republican Party has become the stronghold of men who fundamentally oppose public education because they think women should school their kids themselves. (In *It Takes a Family,* Rick Santorum calls public education an "aberration" and predicts that home-schooling will flourish as "one viable option among many that will open up as we eliminate the heavy hand of the village elders' top-down control of education and allow a thousand parent-nurtured flowers to bloom.")

When it comes to the public relations fight against Christian nationalism, nothing is trickier than battles concerning public religious symbolism. Fights over crèches in public squares or Christmas hymns sung by school choirs are really about which aspects of the First Amendment should prevail—its protection of free speech or its ban on the establishment of religion. In general, I think it's best to err on the side of freedom of expression. As in most First Amendment disputes, the answer to speech (or, in this case, symbolism) that makes religious minorities feel excluded or alienated is more speech—menorahs, Buddhas, Diwali lights, symbols celebrating America's polyglot spiritualism.

There are no neat lines, no way to suck the venom out of these issues without capitulating completely. But one obvious step civil libertarians should take is a much more vocal stance in defense of evangelicals' free speech rights when they are unfairly curtailed. Although far less common than the Christian nationalists pretend, on a few occasions lawsuit-fearing officials have gone overboard in defending church/state separation, silencing religious speech that is protected by the First Amendment. (In one 2005 incident that got tremendous play in the right-wing press, a principal in Tennessee wouldn't allow a ten-year-old student to hold a Bible study during recess.) Such infringements should be fought for reasons both principled, because Christians have the same right to free speech as everyone else, and political, because these abuses generate a backlash that ultimately harms the cause of church/state separation.

The ACLU already does this, but few hear about it, because secularists lack the right's propaganda apparatus. Liberals need to create their own echo chamber to refute these kind of distortions while loudly supporting everyone's freedom of speech. Committed Christian nationalists won't be won over, but some of their would-be sympathizers might be inoculated against the claim that progressives want to extirpate their faith, making it harder for the right to frame every political dispute as part of a war against Jesus.

The challenge, finally, is to make reality matter again. If progressives can do that, perhaps America can be saved.

Writing just after 9/11, Salman Rushdie eviscerated those on the left who rationalized the terrorist attacks as a regrettable explosion of understandable third world rage: "The fundamentalist seeks to bring down a great deal more than buildings," he wrote. "Such people are against, to offer just a brief list,

freedom of speech, a multiparty political system, universal adult suffrage, accountable government, Jews, homosexuals, women's rights, pluralism, secularism, short skirts, dancing, beardlessness, evolution theory, sex." Christian nationalists have no problem with beardlessness, but except for that, Rushdie could have been describing them.

It makes no sense to fight religious authoritarianism abroad while letting it take over at home. The grinding, brutal war between modern and medieval values has spread chaos, fear, and misery across our poor planet. Far worse than the conflicts we're experiencing today, however, would be a world torn between competing fundamentalisms. Our side, America's side, must be the side of freedom and Enlightenment, of liberation from stale constricting dogmas. It must be the side that elevates reason above the commands of holy books and human solidarity above religious supremacism. Otherwise, God help us all.

---

## DISCUSSION QUESTIONS

1. Goldberg describes Christian nationalism as "a total ideology." Compare Christian nationalism to the ideology of classic liberalism. Discuss the strength and weaknesses of each.
2. According to Goldberg's analysis, Christian nationalism "will deform American life, rendering it ever more pinched, mean, and divided." Why is this form of religious fundamentalism likely to have such an impact? Do you think the three part strategy that Goldberg outlines to combat this impact is likely to succeed? Explain.

**8** *Robert Jensen*

# THE GREATEST NATION ON EARTH

*Since the terrorist attacks of September 11, 2001, journalism professor and political activist Robert Jensen has been the leading voice in the effort to rethink the notion of patriotism in the United States. His perspective begins with the simple and honest recognition of our place in the world: U.S. citizens are citizens of the empire. His book* Citizens of the Empire *lays bare the reality of global empire that underlies the pursuit of U.S. foreign policy regardless of which party occupies the White House, and regardless of the flowery principles offered in the name of justifying the exercise of power. The following selection addresses one of the three key political slogans that frame public discussion of the U.S. role in the world—the common invocation that the United States is the greatest nation on earth. Jensen contends that while this rhetorical principle permeates our political discourse, and appears as an unassailable truth because of its ubiquity, "any claim to being the greatest nation is depraved and dangerous, especially when made in the empire." He proceeds to unravel the many strands of this assertion of greatness, pointing out with clear examples the moral dangers of such claims. His argument will not be familiar to you and may, in fact, make you angry. Such a reaction underscores the power of ideology and cultural indoctrination that forms the analytic heart of Chapter 2. His call for us to imagine a political world where all people are valued equally presents us with a challenge—a challenge to take our professed values seriously enough to apply them uniformly in a balanced way, for "if we are to be a moral people, everything about the United States, like everything about any country, needs to be examined and assessed." In the post 9-11 world, such questioning is an essential prerequisite for the humility needed to begin the process of building a truly safe world, free from fear and terror. For this task, hollow sloganeering and "patriotic" sound bites will not do. Only a frank assessment of who we are and what we believe in offers the hope that we can move forward along with the rest of humanity.*

*Source:* Robert Jensen, *Citizens of the Empire: The Struggle To Claim Our Humanity,* San Francisco: City Lights Books, 2004, pp. 1–17.

In any debate, the person who has the power to set the framework and define the terms has an enormous advantage. Part of the struggle for the antiwar movement, and those taking critical positions more generally, is to avoid being trapped in the rhetoric of the dominant culture.

Especially since 9/11, through the wars in Afghanistan and Iraq, there have been three crucial rhetorical frameworks that have been difficult to challenge in public. All of them are related, but each has to be deconstructed separately. First is the assertion that the United States is the greatest nation on earth. Second is the claim that one must support the troops because they defend our freedom. Third is the assumption that patriotism is a positive value. Anyone who challenges any of these in public in the contemporary United States risks being labeled irrelevant, crazy, or both. But all three claims must be challenged if there is to be progressive political change.

My critique does not dictate a single political strategy for dealing with these rhetorical frameworks in public. With different audiences and in different situations, different strategies will be appropriate. But it is crucial to be clear about why these ideas are dangerous. Embedded in each are moral and political assertions and assumptions that have to be resisted, which should make progressive political people cautious about buying into the frameworks at all. I will suggest that it's important not just to criticize the dominant culture's version of each claim but to step back and critique the framework itself.

•    •    •

One of the requirements for being a mainstream American politician, Republican or Democrat, is the willingness to repeat constantly the assertion that the United States is "the greatest nation on earth," maybe even "the greatest nation in history." At hearings for the House Select Committee on Homeland Security on July 11, 2002, Texas Republican Dick Armey described the United States as "the greatest, most free nation the world has ever known." California Democrat Nancy Pelosi declared that America is "the greatest country that ever existed on the face of the earth." Even other nations that want to play ball with the United States have caught on. When George W. Bush visited our new favored ally in the Persian Gulf, Qatar, the *Al-Watan* newspaper described it as "A visit by the president of the greatest nation."

I want to offer a different assessment: Any claim to being the greatest nation is depraved and dangerous, especially when made in the empire.

## SIGN OF PATHOLOGY

Imagine your child, let's call him Joe, made the declaration, "I am the greatest ten-year-old on earth." If you were a loving parent, interested in helping your child develop into a decent person, what would you say? Let's assume you believe Joe to be a perfectly lovely boy, maybe even gifted in many ways. Would you indulge him in that fantasy? Most of us would not.

Instead, you would explain to Joe that however special he is, he is one of millions of ten-year-olds on the planet at that moment, and that—if there were a measure of greatness that could take into account all relevant attributes and abilities—the odds are against Joe coming out on top. But more important than that, you would explain to Joe that people are a wonderfully complex mix of many characteristics that are valued differently by different people, and that it would be impossible to make any sensible assessment of what makes one person the greatest. Even if you reduced it to a single item—let's say the ability to solve mathematical problems—there's no imaginable way to label one person the greatest. That's why people have so much fun arguing about, for example, who is the greatest hitter in baseball history. There's no way to answer the question definitively, and no one really expects to ever win; the fun is in the arguing.

Now, if Joe makes it to adulthood and continues to claim he is the greatest, we would come to one of two conclusions (assuming he's not saying it just to hype the sales of his book or sell tickets to some event): Either he is mentally unstable or he's an asshole. That is, either he believes it because there's something wrong with him cognitively and/or emotionally, or he believes it because he's an unpleasant person. It's painfully obvious that the best evidence that Joe is not the greatest is his claim to be that, for we can observe that throughout history people who have something in them that we might call "greatness" tend not to proclaim their own superiority.

So, we would want to put the brakes on young Joe's claim to greatness as soon as possible because of what tends to happen to people who believe they are the greatest: They lose perspective and tend to discount the feelings and legitimate claims of others. If I am so great, the reasoning goes, certainly my view of the world must be correct, and others who disagree with me—because they lack my greatness—must simply be wrong. And if they are wrong, well, I'm certainly within my rights as the greatest to make sure things turn out the way that I know (by virtue of my greatness) they should. The ability to force others to accept the decisions of those with greatness depends, of course, on power. If Joe takes positions in society that give him power, heaven help those below him.

All these observations are relevant to national assertions of greatness. Such claims ignore the complexity of societies and life within them. Even societies that do great things can have serious problems. We are all aware that a person with admirable qualities in one realm can have quite tragic flaws in another. The same is true of nations. Constant claims to being the greatest reveal a pathology in the national character. Crucially, that pathology is most dangerous in nations with great economic or military power (which tend to be the ones that most consistently make such claims). That is, the nations that claim to be great are usually the ones that can enforce their greatness through coercion and violence.

Nothing in this argument denies the ways that children or nations sometimes do great things. It is rather the claim to uniqueness in one's greatness that is at issue.

## WHAT IS GREATNESS

Let's assume, for the sake of discussion, that determining which nation on earth is the greatest would be a meaningful and useful enterprise. On what criteria would we base the evaluation? And how would the United States stack up? In other words, what is greatness?

We might start with history, where we would observe that the histories of nation-states typically are not pretty. At best, it's a mixed bag. The United States broke away from a colonial power ruled by a monarch, espousing the revolutionary political ideal of democratic rights for citizens. Even though the Founding Fathers' definition of "citizen" was narrow enough to exclude the vast majority of the population, that breakthrough was an inspirational moment in human history. That's why, when declaring an independent Vietnam in 1945, Ho Chi Minh borrowed language from the U.S. Declaration of Independence.

But from the beginning the new American experiment was also bathed in blood. The land base of the new nation was secured by a genocide that was almost successful. Depending on the estimate one uses for the precontact population of the continent (the number of people here before Columbus)—12 million is a conservative estimate—the extermination rate was from 95 to 99 percent. That is to say, by the end of the Indian wars at the close of the nineteenth century, the European invaders had successfully eliminated almost the entire indigenous population (or the "merciless Indian Savages" as they are labeled in the Declaration of Independence). Let's call that the first American holocaust.

The second American holocaust was African slavery, a crucial factor in the emergence of the textile industry and the industrial revolution in the United States. Historians still debate the number of Africans who worked as slaves in the New World and the number who died during the process of enslavement in Africa, during the Middle Passage, and in the New World. But it is safe to say that tens of millions of people were rounded up and that as many as half of them died in the process.

Some would say greatness is not perfection but the capacity for critical self-reflection, the ability to correct mistakes, the constant quest for progressive change. If that were the case, then a starting point would be honest acknowledgment of the way in which the land base and wealth of the nation had been acquired, leading to meaningful attempts at reparations for the harm caused along the way. Have the American people taken serious steps in that direction on these two fundamental questions regarding indigenous and African peoples? Is the privilege of running casinos on reservation land a just resolution of the first holocaust? Are the Voting Rights and Civil Rights Acts an adequate solution to the second? Can we see the many gains made on these fronts, yet still come to terms with lingering problems?

And what of the third American holocaust, the building of the American empire in the Third World? What did the nation that finally turned its back on slavery turn to?

—The Spanish-American War and the conquest of the Philippines, at a cost of at least 200,000 Filipino lives.

—The creation of a U.S.-dominated sphere in Central America backed by regular military incursions to make countries safe for U.S. investment, leading to twentieth-century support for local dictatorships that brutalized their populations, at a total cost of hundreds of thousands of dead and whole countries ruined.

—The economic and diplomatic support of French efforts to recolonize Vietnam after World War II and, after the failure of that effort, the U.S. invasion of South Vietnam and devastation of Laos and Cambodia, at a cost of 4 million Southeast Asians dead and a region destabilized.

We could list every immoral and illegal U.S. intervention into other nations, which often had the goal of destroying democratically elected governments, undermining attempts by people to throw off colonial rule, or ensuring that a government would follow orders from Washington. But the point is easily made: Subjecting claims of American greatness to historical review suggests a more complex story. The United States has made important strides in recent decades to shed a brutal racist history and create a fairer society at home, though still falling short of a truly honest accounting and often leaving the most vulnerable in seemingly perpetual poverty. At the same time, U.S. policy abroad has been relentlessly barbaric.

Such an examination would lead to some simple conclusions: The United States was founded on noble principles that it has advanced and, often at the same time, undermined. As the United States has emerged as a world power with imperial ambitions—and

we rest now at a place where commentators from all points on the political spectrum use the term "empire" to describe the United States, often in a celebratory fashion—we have much to answer for. Historically, empires are never benevolent, and nothing in history has changed that should lead to the conclusion that the United States will be the first benevolent empire. Unless, of course, one believes that God has a hand in all this.

## WHAT'S GOD GOT TO DO WITH IT?

During the 2000 presidential campaign, George W. Bush was trying to recover from his association with the painfully public bigotry of Bob Jones University. On matters of racism, it's impossible—even for politicians—to make claims about America's heroic history. But in remarks at the Simon Wiesenthal Center and the Museum of Tolerance, Bush said, "For all its flaws, I believe our nation is chosen by God and commissioned by history to be the model to the world of justice and inclusion and diversity without division."

This invocation of a direct connection to God and truth—what we might call the "pathology of the anointed"—is a peculiar and particularly dangerous feature of American history and the "greatest nation" claims. The story we tell ourselves goes something like this: Other nations throughout history have acted out of greed and self-interest, seeking territory, wealth, and power. They often did bad things in the world. Then came the United States, touched by God, a shining city on the hill, whose leaders created the first real democracy and went on to be the beacon of freedom for people around the world. Unlike the rest of the world, we act out of a cause nobler than greed; we are both the model of, and the vehicle for, peace, freedom, and democracy in the world.

That is a story that can be believed only in the United States by people sufficiently insulated from the reality of U.S. actions abroad to maintain such illusions. It is tempting to laugh at and dismiss these rhetorical flourishes of pandering politicians, but the commonness of the chosen-by-God assertions—and the lack of outrage or amusement at them—suggests that the claims are taken seriously both by significant segments of the public and the politicians. Just as it has been in the past, the consequences of this pathology of the anointed will be borne not by those chosen by God, but by those against whom God's-chosen decide to take aim.

What stance on these matters would leaders who took seriously their religious tradition take? Scripture, for those who believe it to be an authority, is—as is typical—mixed on these matters. But certainly one plausible reading of that text would lead one not to claims of greatness but of humility. As one of the Old Testament prophets, Micah, put it: "What does the Lord require of you but to do justice, and to love kindness, and to walk humbly with your God?" (Micah 6:8).

In the second presidential debate on October 11, 2000, Bush himself made this point. When asked how he would try to project the United States around the world, Bush used the word "humble" five times:

It really depends upon how our nation conducts itself in foreign policy. If we're an arrogant nation, they'll resent us, if we're a humble nation but strong, they'll welcome us. And our nation stands alone right now in the world in terms of power, and that's why we've got to be humble and yet project strength in a way that promotes freedom.

We're a freedom-loving nation. And if we're an arrogant nation, they'll view us that way, but if we're a humble nation, they'll respect us.

I think the United States must be humble and must be proud and confident of our values, but humble in how we treat nations that are figuring out how to chart their own course.

Although all available evidence suggests Bush and his advisers (or any other U.S. president, for that matter) were not serious about pursuing a foreign policy based in humility, his comments were sensible. Humility, it is important to remember, does not mean humiliation; it is a sign of strength, not weakness. It means recognizing that the United States is one nation among many; that the only way

to security is to work together democratically with other nations; and that multilateral institutions must be strengthened and we must be willing to accept the decisions of such bodies, even when they go against us.

In other words, the exact opposite of the path that the Bush administration has pursued.

## BLAME AMERICA FIRST?

When one points out these kinds of facts and analyses, which tend to get in the way of the "greatest nation" claims, a standard retort is, "Why do you blame America first?" Though it is a nonsensical question, the persistence and resonance of it in the culture requires a response.

First, it should not be controversial that when assessing the effects of actions, one is most clearly morally responsible for one's own actions. Depending on the circumstances, I may have obligations to act to curtail someone else's immoral behavior, but without question I have an obligation to curtail my own immoral behavior. In some circumstances, if someone else's immoral behavior is so egregious that the harm it does to others requires immediate intervention and such intervention is feasible in the real world, then there can be cases in which I have cause to temporarily put on hold an assessment of my own behavior to stop the greater evil. But such cases are rare, and the human tendency to rationalize our own bad behavior should give us pause whenever we claim that the greater good requires us to focus on the mistakes other people make before we tackle our own.

So, in place of the common phrase "judge not and ye shall not be judged," perhaps the rule should be "invite judgment of yourself by others, come to judgment about your behavior, commit to not repeating immoral behavior, repair to the degree possible the damage done by previous immoral acts, and keep an eye on others to help them in the same process."

There is no reason that the same logic that applies to us as individuals should not apply to us collectively as citizens of a nation. From such a vantage point, the emptiness of the accusation that one shouldn't "blame America first" becomes clear.

America should be blamed first, if and when America is blameworthy. If the United States has engaged in behavior that cannot be morally justified—such as the invasion of another country to overthrow its legally elected democratic government for the self-interested material gain of some segment of U.S. society—whom else should we blame? Because people often use the term "blame" in a way to redirect accountability (when Johnny blames Joey for breaking the toy, we suspect that Johnny actually had something to do with the accident himself), the phrase is designed to divert people from an honest assessment. A better formulation would be, "Why do you hold America accountable first?" In that case, the obvious answer—we should hold America accountable first when America is responsible—is somewhat easier for a reasonable person to see.

That does raise the question, of course, of who is a reasonable person. We might ask that question about, for example, George H. W. Bush, the father. In 1988, after the U.S. Navy warship *Vincennes* shot down an Iranian commercial airliner in a commercial corridor, killing 290 civilians, the then-vice president said, "I will never apologize for the United States of America. I don't care what the facts are."

Whether the firing was an understandable reaction to the misidentification of the Iranian aircraft (as apologists claim), a deliberate act to send Iran a message about U.S. intentions in the region (as some suspect), or the responsibility primarily of a hyperaggressive, trigger-happy commander (as others argue), Bush's declaration is an extraordinarily blunt admission that he does not adhere to even minimal moral standards. The grotesqueness of the episode was only compounded by the fact that Bush later awarded the ship's commander a Legion of Merit award for "exceptionally meritorious conduct in the performance of outstanding service." We could call it the "blame America never" approach.

## THE FACTS MATTER

My position does not lead to a blanket denunciation of the United States, our political institutions, or our culture. I simply put forward the proposition that facts matter. If we are to be moral people, everything about the United States, like everything about any country, needs to be examined and assessed. People often tell me, "You assume that everything about the United States is bad." But, of course, I do not assume that; it would be as absurd as the assumption that everything about the United States is good. After a lecture in which I outlined some of the important advances in the law of free speech in the United States but was also critical of contemporary U.S. foreign policy, someone in the audience asked, "Is there anything about America that you like?" Yes, I said, there is much I like—for example, the advances in the law of free speech that I just spent considerable time describing and celebrating. For some reason, honest assessments of both the successes and failures of the United States are seen as being hypercritical and negative.

The facts do matter, of course. And the "greatest nation on earth" mantra tends to lead us to get the facts wrong. Take the question of foreign aid. One would assume that the greatest nation on earth, which also happens to be the wealthiest nation on the planet with the largest economy, gives generously to nations less fortunate. And, in fact, many Americans do assume that. Unfortunately, it's wrong. Political journalist William Finnegan summarizes the polling data:

> Americans always overestimate the amount of foreign aid we give. In recent national polls, people have guessed, on average, that between 15 and 24 percent of the federal budget goes for foreign aid. In reality, it is less than 1 percent. The U.N. has set a foreign-aid goal for the rich countries of .7 percent of gross national product. *A few countries have attained that modest goal, all of them Scandinavian. The U.S. has never come close, indeed, it comes in dead last, consistently, in the yearly totals of rich-country foreign aid as a percentage of GNP.* In 2000, we gave .1 percent. President Bush's dramatic proposal, post-September 11, to increase foreign aid to $15 billion looks rather puny next to the $48 billion increase in this year's $379 billion military budget.

So, on this count, are the Scandinavian nations the greatest on earth? They also seem to have the edge on us in providing health care to their citizens. Here's the assessment of two prominent U.S. medical researchers:

> The absence of universal access in the United States is a global scandal. No other highly industrialized country has so many citizens totally without access to even the most rudimentary health care. Consider these facts: there are almost twice as many people in the U.S. without access to health care than the entire population of Scandinavia where access is a universal right.

One might think that the greatest nation on earth would not leave its most vulnerable citizens without reliable access to health care. There will be, of course, disagreement on how to best achieve that, but it seems not to be a serious goal among the dominant political players in the United States.

So, we score higher on legal guarantees of freedom of speech but lower on guarantees of health care compared with other developed countries. Our history and contemporary foreign policy suggest that self-interest and greed usually trump concern for human rights and democracy. Yet the existence of a democratic process at home—the product of much struggle by the forces interested in progressive

change—should leave us with hope that we can change the course of that policy through long-term, dedicated efforts. But to do that, honest reflection on the record is required. And it matters. It really matters. It is one thing for small and powerless nations to have delusions of grandeur; they can't do much damage outside their own borders. It is quite another thing for the nation with the most destructive military capacity in the history of the world—and a demonstrated willingness to use it to achieve self-interested goals—to play the "greatest nation on earth" game. To the degree that the game diminishes people's ability to assess facts, reach honest conclusions, and take moral action based on those conclusions, it increases the risk of people everywhere. It makes it easier for leaders to justify wars of conquest and mask the reasons for those wars. It's easy for a vice president to say, as Dick Cheney did in a speech in 2002:

> America is again called by history to use our overwhelming power in defense of our freedom. We've accepted that duty, certain of the justice of our cause and confident of the victory to come. For my part, I'm grateful for the opportunity to work with the president who is making us all proud upholding the cause of freedom and serving the greatest nation on Earth.

---

## DISCUSSION QUESTIONS

1. Discuss the ways in which you've been raised to buy in to the notion that we live in the greatest country in the world. How does this process work? Is it healthy for us as free thinkers?
2. Explain the many dangers that Jensen sees arising from the constant assertion of America's "greatness." How does Jensen respond to potential critics of his thesis?
3. Explain how a person in a foreign country might respond to Jensen's perspective about America's claims of greatness?

# CHAPTER 3

# CONSTITUTIONAL AND STATE STRUCTURES

Few, if any, American documents are worshiped as much as the Constitution. Political leaders across the ideological spectrum pay tribute to the 1787 parchment and its twenty-seven amendments as the bedrock of our political institutions and the sentry of our civil liberties. Not without reason, many Americans see more than two hundred years of constitutional government as a unique achievement in the modern world. Former president Ronald Reagan, for his part, discerned in the Founders' creation "a sureness and originality so great that I can't help but perceive the guiding hand of God, the first political system that insisted that power flows from the people to the state, not the other way around." But does the U.S. Constitution deserve such veneration?

Taken together, the articles in this chapter offer an analysis of the U.S. Constitution and the state it helped to establish that challenges this posture of self-congratulation. Familiar features like the separation of powers, checks and balances, and federalism are related to the Framers' concerns about democratic threats to property rights and to their vision of a new political economy energized by men of commerce and finance. These articles suggest that the Constitution has been irrelevant or even an obstacle to democratic advances and that, at the least, we should avoid making the document a patriotic fetish.

# 9 *Joshua Cohen and Joel Rogers*

# AMERICAN EXCEPTIONALISM AND THE POLITICS OF FRAGMENTATION

> *Joshua Cohen and Joel Rogers situate the Constitution within the broader context of the "exceptional" nature of the American state, which lacks the class-based politics that characterizes other advanced capitalist democracies. They argue that the basic structures of our polity, including its constitutional framework, encourage fragmentation among people of ordinary means and raise their costs of collective action. When this pattern becomes entrenched, popular control of public policy is constrained and the inequalities flowing from the economy are difficult to challenge. Students may want to focus on two aspects of Cohen and Rogers's piece. First, locate the six historical factors that, in their view, have contributed to the fragmentation of democratic politics. Second, consider their claim that the "essence of politics is collective action." Doesn't this cut across the grain of our "look out for number one" culture? Perhaps the ideology of liberal individualism, one of the focal points of articles in Chapter 2, is itself a factor that limits meaningful democratic action.*

The essence of politics is collective action—different people acting together for the achievement of common aims. There are many conditions for such action—including common interests, an awareness of those interests, a willingness to cooperate with one another, and the ability to sustain the costs of that cooperation.

On all these dimensions and others, the structure of the U.S. political system tends to constrain collective action by people of ordinary means. Most importantly, *American political conflict and bargaining is extremely fragmented.* Instead of bringing people together, the basic structures of American politics tend to keep them separate and divided, while encouraging the pursuit of narrower interests. This division raises the costs of coordination. Its effects are most sharply pronounced among those who have few resources to begin with—that is, among those whose "strength is in numbers," and not in their wallets.

Reflecting these tendencies to fragmentation, ordinary people in the U.S. are among the most politically disorganized in the world. Most strikingly, perhaps, the U.S. is virtually unique among advanced industrial capitalist democracies in never having had a labor party or socialist movement of significant

---

*Source:* Joshua Cohen and Joel Rogers, *Rules of the Game: American Politics and the Central America Movement,* Boston: South End Press, 1986, pp. 4–16.

strength and duration. To this day, conventional political debate here is not marked by the sort of class-based cleavages and terms ("workers" versus "capitalists") characteristic of the political systems of Italy, France, Germany, England, and indeed most of [the] advanced industrial world. This peculiar absence of class politics in the U.S.—one instance of the general fragmentation of the U.S. political system—is called "American exceptionalism."

. . . What generates these conditions in the first place? As might be expected, the answer is that over the course of U.S. history many factors have contributed, and that the importance of particular factors, and their interaction with others, has shifted over the course of U.S. history. Such historical variation and political complexity pose severe problems in providing an adequate rendering of American exceptionalism—problems which, we should emphasize, we do not pretend to solve here. These important complexities aside, however, there are six basic factors which can be identified as having contributed throughout *all* of U.S. history. Reinforcing one another, and given varied political expression, they have always been central to producing, and reproducing, the politics of fragmentation.

## CONSTITUTIONAL DESIGN

The basic founding document of the U.S., the Constitution, mandates a fragmented government structure. This has permitted, within a single nation, considerable political experimentation, particularly at the local level, and has helped ensure certain limits on the abuse of centralized powers. But the clear effect of constitutional fragmentation has also been to limit the potential for political cooperation among people of ordinary means, and this was something that the architects of the constitutional system, the "founding fathers," clearly recognized and desired.

In *The Federalist Papers,* for example, James Madison explained that a fragmented system would help cure "the mischiefs of faction," whose most common source was the distribution of property ownership:

Those who hold and those who are without property have ever formed distinct interests

in society. Those who are creditors, and those who are debtors, fall under a like discrimination. . . . The regulation of these various and interfering interests forms the principal task of modern legislation and involves the spirit of party and faction in the necessary and ordinary operations of government.

Madison was particularly concerned that a "majority faction" composed of those owning little property might come together to challenge inequalities in wealth and income. He saw two ways to prevent its formation:

Either the existence of the same passion or interest in a majority at the same time must be prevented, or the majority, having such coexistent passion or interest, must be rendered, by their number and local situation, unable to concert and carry into effect schemes of oppression.

In the constitutional scheme they eventually agreed upon, Madison and the other framers accordingly sought both to prevent majorities from forming common programs, and to impose barriers to the implementation of those programs, should they be formed. The most straightforward way this was done was by weakening and dividing the American state.

The Constitution, for example, mandates a *separation of powers* at the national level. The legislative, executive, and judicial functions are each assigned to distinct branches of government, and each branch is given powers to block the activities of the other two. While the power of the judiciary to curtail Congressional or Presidential action is great, probably the most important separation and source of blockage is that between executive and legislative authority. In contrast to parliamentary systems of representation, where the leader of the dominant party (or coalition of parties) in the legislature is also the chief executive of government, the U.S. Constitution mandates separate elections for Congress and the Presidency. This has commonly meant that the President comes from a party that does not command a majority within the legislature. Such differences between the executive and the legislature typically generate barriers to concerted national policy—except of course in those cases (foreign affairs being the source of most examples) where "bipartisan consensus" obtains between the major parties.

Additionally limiting the effectiveness of the national government, and limiting the potential for the emergence of majoritarian factions, is the principle of *federalism.* This means that public power is shared between the national government and the states. By contrast with "unified" governments, where subnational units are extensions of a central authority, the United States is a "divided" government, in which the states enjoy powers independent of the Federal government. Competing with the Federal government and one another, the fifty states produce wide variations in policy on basic issues, and reinforce political diversity and division. . . .

Even within national government, moreover, federalism shapes the perspective and interests of Congress. Candidates for Congress are not selected by national parties, but by state and local organizations. Members are then elected by local constituencies, and to stay in Congress they must satisfy the interests of those constituencies. Local interests are thus represented both in state governments and the national legislature. In fact, aside from the Presidency (and even there the case is ambiguous), there is no Federal office or body whose members are selected by exclusively national criteria. As House Speaker Tip O'Neill often points out, in the U.S. "*all* politics is local politics."

One effect of this is to immensely complicate the consideration of national issues, and to introduce yet additional barriers in generating coherent national policies. A closely related effect is the *discouragement* of attempts at such national coordination, and the *encouragement* of a local or regional orientation in political action. This orientation, in turn, tends to solidify differences and divisions among people located in different places.

## GEOGRAPHY AND NATURAL RESOURCES

In comparative terms, the United States has always been an enormous country, larger at its founding than all other countries of the time except Russia, and today, more than 200 years later, still larger than all countries but the Soviet Union, Canada, and China. Early on, the framers recognized that sheer size, like constitutional divisions, would tend to impose barriers to the existence and formation of mischievous majority factions. Rejecting the received wisdom in political theory, *The Federalist Papers* extolled the virtues of a "large commercial republic." Size would encourage a diversity of interests, and that diversity would in turn pose barriers to the existence and coordination of any stable popular majority.

In addition to encouraging diversity, the great size of the land, which for long periods had an open frontier, helped to provide a safety valve for social unrest. Those who did not like it in one place—and were not slaves—could simply leave. The widespread availability of free or very cheap land, moreover, facilitated widespread land *ownership*. This helped confirm Americans' status as a race of independent and free (white) men, and provided a ballast of popular support for a private property regime.

The repeated acquisition of new land helped prolong the period of an open frontier. Even after the rate of acquisition slowed, however, and even after the frontier was closed, the U.S. would also enjoy comparatively low population densities. Combined with the sheer size of the country, the sparse settlement of the land in turn meant that its different inhabitants could afford to operate in relative isolation from one another. This in turn encouraged extremely diverse, and largely uncoordinated, forms of political organization, giving further substance to the constitutional fragmentation of American politics.

Political fragmentation was also encouraged by America's strategic isolation. For most of its history—at least from the peace with Britain that concluded the War of 1812 to the Japanese attack on Pearl Harbor in 1941—the U.S. enjoyed a long unbroken period of strategic isolation, during which thousands of miles of ocean provided a bar to credible attack from abroad. It could thus develop without much concern for the activities of other nations, and could afford the highly decentralized political system that more threatened nations could not.

Finally, in addition to being big and isolated, the U.S. enjoyed (and continues to enjoy) tremendous advantages of climate and natural resources.

Even leaving aside the productive activities of men and women, it is truly the richest nation on earth. Virtually all of the country is located in the temperate zone, which is ideal for agriculture and industry. Early settlers found vast deposits of timber and basic minerals, some of the best farmland on earth, apparently limitless water resources for farming and industry, and extended systems of lakes and rivers that eased the flow of trade. Once these resources were taken from their Native American owners, this was an almost perfect setting for economic development, which proceeded quickly.

By providing the basis for a comparatively high standard of living, these natural endowments tended to discourage efforts at collective organization along class lines. Throughout almost all of American history, and even after they had changed from a race of independent farmers to a population of wage and salary workers, ordinary people in the U.S. were paid more, and lived far better, than their counterparts in Western Europe and the rest of the developed world. In this relatively affluent environment, and especially given all the other social and political incentives to seek private gains, the appeal of collective organization was diminished. As the German economist Werner Sombart once overstated the point, "Socialist utopias came to nothing on roast beef and apple pie."

# UNEVEN ECONOMIC DEVELOPMENT

The very rapid emergence of the U.S. as a major economic power concealed tremendous differences within the U.S. in the level and scope of economic activity. It was only after the Civil War that capitalism was firmly established as the exclusive mode of economic production in the U.S., and only after World War II, with the industrial development of the South, that it was possible to speak of a truly national industrial economy. This unevenness, combined with the tremendous diversity of American economic activity, encouraged different and competing interests in different regions of the country. An incalculably large part of American politics—from immigration to energy policy—is and always has been concerned with managing these differences.

Like so many other dynamics of American politics, this phenomenon of regional diversity was most dramatically highlighted by the Civil War. In that effort, infant industry and finance in the Northeast and Midwest joined with independent farming interests to crush the plantation South, initiating a period of economic and political subordination that would last well into the twentieth century. The long deflation that followed the war (like most major wars, it had been paid for by printing money) eventually ignited the great agrarian protest movement of the Populists, which drew particular strength from independent farmers in the South, Midwest, and West. But within a generation of the close of the war predominantly Northeastern industrial and financial interests had crushed the Populists as well, and were busy rolling back political organization, and even electoral participation, among the dependent classes.

Such dramatic events aside, and even after the great levelling of regional differences that has occurred over the past forty years, uneven and diverse economic development tends to fragment U.S. politics. Among elites, the enduring vitality of regional splits is evident in phenomena like the "Sagebrush Rebellion," which pits Western business interests against the Northeast in a battle over environmental regulation and Federal land management in the West. Among nonelites, it is evident in the difficulties northern workers have encountered from their southern counterparts in responding to "runaway" shops down South. Regional economic differences continue to slow concerted national responses to problems, and to divide ordinary people with potentially shared interests from one another.

# RACISM

The first black slaves were brought to America in the early 1600s. By the time of the Declaration of Independence in 1776, slavery was established in all thirteen colonies. Oppressive relations between whites and blacks in America are as old as the country itself.

The history since is familiar, or should be. Shortly after the Revolution, the "First Emancipation" began in New England, as state after state abolished slavery, or phased it out. The most substantial black populations, however, were located in the South, and this "emancipation" stopped at Virginia. Growing tensions between the slave and non-slave states, which were importantly tensions between a precapitalist plantation economy and the imperatives of free capitalist development, eventually erupted in the Civil War. Ostensibly the war freed the slaves, but with the collapse of "radical" efforts to reconstruct the South in the postwar period, an elaborate system of oppressive and segregationist race relations was soon reestablished.

It would not be until well into the twentieth century—when the combined push of the mechanization of southern agriculture, and the pull of labor-starved northern industry in World War II, brought millions of blacks north—that racism began to be seriously addressed on a national scale. And it would not be until the 1960s, and only then under the pressures of massive protest and civil disobedience, that the major legal components of discrimination would be broken down. The fight over *de facto* discrimination—in housing, education, employment, and other essentials—continues, and blacks and whites in this country continue to live very different sorts of lives.

Volumes have been written on American racism. Suffice it to say here that there is no more persistent form of division in American politics, and none more debilitating to popular democratic politics. In the pre-Civil War period, the small number of "freemen" who trickled North were almost universally excluded from early worker organizations. In the late nineteenth century, each of the great attempts at forging classwide ties in labor failed to confront the race question, giving force to endless employer strategies of "divide and conquer" between antagonistic racial groups. In the twentieth century, at the peak of worker organization immediately after World War II, the failure to press the issue of racial equality by organizing the South defined the limits of labor's national power for a

generation, and hastened its decline. And even today, 120 years after the close of the Civil War, racial animosity and fear, and the forms and habits of political association based on them, continue to impede the construction of a truly popular democratic coalition. The racial and ethnic tensions which marked the Rainbow Coalition's effort in 1984 provide ample evidence on this point.

## 5  ETHNIC AND RELIGIOUS DIVISIONS

At least until the turn of the twentieth century, the great natural wealth of the U.S., along with its rapid economic development and low population density, produced chronic labor shortages. The solution to this problem was provided by immigrant labor.

Over 1820–1830 only a little over 150,000 immigrants came to the U.S. Three decades later, over 1851–1860, the inflow had risen to 2.6 million. By 1881–1890, as the U.S. entered a peak phase in industrialization, the number doubled to 5.2 million. And at its high point, over 1901–1910, it rose to 8.7 million, or better than 10 percent of the resident population. In today's terms, that would amount to roughly 25 million new workers over the course of the 1980s.

Given all the other constraints on popular action, the fact that the population of the U.S. was comprised of people from diverse cultural backgrounds—while surely one of the appealing features of American society—contributed to the general fragmentation of U.S. politics and the weakness of worker organization within it. Coming to a vast land, with a decentralized political structure, successive waves of immigrants took up residence in communities that were often isolated from one another, and developed political commitments and organizations peculiar to individual locales. The deeply ethnic character of much local American politics—Slavs in the Midwest, Irish in Boston, Jews in New York—can be traced to this experience. The fact that the system was sufficiently porous and diffuse to permit such localized expressions, in turn, tended to consolidate patterns of organizational isolation along ethnic grounds. The myth of the American "melting pot" was only that—a myth. In all sorts of ways, immigrants found that they could preserve ethnic identities in the new land. But the maintenance of these diverse identities also tended to undermine attempts to forge alliances among workers that cut across ethnic differences.

Complementing the barriers of language and custom, and immensely important throughout American politics, were the deep religious splits with which ethnic divisions were commonly associated. In part because Americans never had to struggle for land or political rights against an entrenched church, the U.S. has always been a deeply religious country, and throughout its history religion has often served as an organizing metaphor for political action. Popular support for the Revolutionary War, for example, was fueled by the "First Great Awakening" of Protestant religious fervor; and black churches have long supplied the backbone of struggles for civil rights.

Even more often, however, religious differences have served to undermine or distort popular democratic politics. The arrival of waves of Irish Catholic immigrants in the 1850s, for example, led to the nativist backlash of the "Know Nothing" movement, and helped trigger the realignment of political parties that issued in the modern Republican and Democratic parties. This divided workers along Protestant/Catholic lines, reflected not only in the parties but in all manner of popular organizations. And just as the U.S. was entering the second great phase of industrialization in the late nineteenth century, a tidal wave of new immigrants from southern and eastern Europe introduced yet additional divisions into emergent worker organizations. Ably exploited by employers, ethnic and religious cleavages repeatedly wrecked efforts at working class solidarity.

## STATE REPRESSION

Despite the many structural barriers to their coordination, ordinary Americans have often banded together to attempt to improve their condition. With some rare and notable exceptions, these efforts have met with physical violence, imprisonment, brutally applied court sanctions, or more subtle forms of harassment and intimidation sponsored by the state. Such state repression makes for a long history, coextensive with the history of the United States. It runs roughly from the 1786 suppression of the protests of indebted farmers in Massachusetts (Shays's Rebellion), through the labor injunctions that helped wreck worker organizations in the late nineteenth century, to the Reagan administration's surveillance of Central America activists, and prosecution of church groups offering sanctuary to refugees from U.S. policies in that region.

Over the last 200 years, there have been too many government sponsored shootings, beatings, lynchings, police spies, agents provocateurs, goons, scabs, rigged trials, imprisonments, burglaries, and illegal wiretaps to permit easy summary here. Once again we only note the obvious. By raising the costs of political action to individuals—in money, physical pain, imprisonment, or the destruction of their personal lives—repression makes it less likely that individuals will be willing to engage in collective political activity at all. And this is especially true for those individuals, comprising the most obvious mischievous faction, who can least afford those costs, since they have little "property" or other resources of their own.

Over the course of U.S. history, these six basic factors—constitutional design, geography and natural resources, uneven economic development, racism, ethnic and religious divisions, and state repression—have repeatedly constrained popular democratic action in the U.S. As indicated earlier, appreciating the interaction of these different factors at different times would require discussion of the peculiarities of particular circumstances and periods, and of the ways in which these divisions were themselves institutionalized and given political expression. This, again, we cannot do here. What is important to recognize, however, is that these sources of divisions are enduring and ongoing features of U.S. politics, and not merely of historical interest. They operate now, as well as having operated in the past.

## DISCUSSION QUESTIONS

1. Cohen and Rogers state that "ordinary people in the United States are among the most politically disorganized in the world." What evidence of this do the authors provide and how does that relate to the issue of "American exceptionalism"?
2. Have the six basic factors contributing to American exceptionalism been equally important in U.S. history? Which are most important today?

**10** *Kenneth M. Dolbeare and Linda Medcalf*

# THE DARK SIDE OF THE CONSTITUTION

*In a wide-ranging essay, written for the constitutional bicentennial in 1987, Kenneth Dolbeare and Linda Medcalf explore what they call the "dark side" of the Constitution, critically examining its meaning and values while relating them to contemporary political ills. Writing in the spirit of historian Charles Beard, whose 1913 book* An Economic Interpretation of the Constitution *was a path-breaking critical study, they detail the Framers' concern for the protection of property, placing their fear of democracy in the context of such threatening events as Shays's Rebellion among farmers in western Massachusetts. The Constitution is read in light of the top-down model of political economy espoused by Alexander Hamilton and initially implemented during his tenure as Treasury Secretary in the 1790s. Dolbeare and Medcalf argue that current problems like policy gridlock, low voter turnout, and the general lack of political responsiveness are direct results of the hegemony of Hamiltonian principles in the twentieth century, and outline measures that might help to reverse the de-democratization of American politics.*

The golden glow of the Constitution's bicentennial celebration—already well launched—threatens to blind us all at a time when Americans most need to see clearly. We do not refer to the harmless factual errors and the merely misleading exaggerations that accompany this latest patriotic spectacular. Our national myopia is far more serious. In the midst of institutional paralysis, an urgent but unaddressed policy agenda, and the protracted withdrawal of the American public from "public" affairs, we continue to celebrate the Constitution as an unrivaled political achievement. When we most need to critically examine our fundamental structures, we embark on a laudatory extravaganza—and do so with full scholarly support.

But, from its inception, there has been a dark side to the United States Constitution that accounts in part for many of the acknowledged ills of contemporary American politics. Low voter turnout, lack of confidence in government, the decline of the political parties, institutional deadlock and indecisiveness, the pervasiveness of protest, frustration, and resentment—all these can be traced to the deliberate anti-democratic design of our founding document and the way it was completed by Alexander Hamilton's nation-building program.

*Source:* Kenneth M. Dolbeare and Linda Medcalf, "The Dark Side of the Constitution." *The Case Against the Constitution: From the Antifederalists to the Present,* Kenneth M. Dolbeare and John F. Manley, eds., Armonk, NY: M.E. Sharpe, 1987, pp. 120–124, 126–133, and 136–141.

In effect, the Framers, and Alexander Hamilton in particular, wrought too well. Their chief ambition—a strong and stable political economy insulated from popular control—is now threatened by the consequences of the very methods chosen to achieve that goal 200 years ago.

There is no news in the point that the men of 1787 sought to protect property and contain democracy. They have more than amply testified to this themselves. It is only later celebrants who have sought to make the Framers into "realistic" architects of a neutral political system; the Framers, and their opponents, knew better. But the celebrants have written history, and held office, in a country where democracy became a vital symbol. It became increasingly necessary to change the definition of democracy, in order to fit the reality of the limitations on popular impact that the Framers so artfully designed. Just as the proponents of the Constitution preempted the label "Federalist," turning it into its opposite, the celebrants of the Constitution worked similar magic with the word "democracy."

Alexander Hamilton's vital contributions to the development of a strong central government have been noted often, although by a minority of commentators. The crucial contract clause, several key Federalist essays, ratification in New York, and the various programs on credit, funding, the bank, and manufacturing are all recognized as major contributions to the development of the new nation. However, these are usually seen episodically, as independent events or specific isolated achievements in a context evolving in response to many other initiatives. Few have adequately appreciated Hamilton's grand design in its entirety, understood it as an agenda partially completed by the convention and partially by Hamilton later, or recognized its full realization in our twentieth-century history and contemporary situation. Instead, the utterly unrealized Jeffersonian image, more consistent with our attachment to "democracy," has dominated our national self-conception and our national rhetoric.

Inherent in Hamilton's grand design is a set of political implications with profound importance. He created an intricate central government machine that encouraged and rewarded behavior appropriate to his

*Capitalist Vision*

vision of a national commercial-financial-industrial economy—the entrepreneurial, productive, growth-oriented behavior that was to define our economic, political, and cultural life and identity for centuries. It was our first "industrial policy," incubating capitalism as a crucial by-product. *Insulated from Politics*

Hamilton also insulated the machine against the possibility that popular majorities or political chicanery might alter the outcomes he deemed essential to the creation of a great nation. In the process, by building upon the dark side of the Constitution, the Framers' property-protecting provisions and fear of democracy, Hamilton succeeded in almost completely removing the *substance* of public policy from popular hands. We live amidst the consequences today.

*Aims*

(1)

In this paper, we first review briefly the Framers' intentions and actions regarding the protection of property, both absolutely and from the interference of popular majorities. We shall see, as have many historians and political scientists before us, that the Framers were both class conscious and thorough in their efforts.

Then we explore Hamilton's grand design, its political implications, and the protection he added to assure that his system would be insulated in multiple ways against popular impact. Hamilton wove a web that deliberately deflected popular preferences away from the most sensitive and crucial areas of public policy—financial affairs, and the nature and distribution of wealth in the country. More specifically, he developed major expansive constitutional doctrines and set up the power of judicial review. One of the most important and intended results was the ensuing heavy reliance upon the law and the courts as decision makers, and a governing role for the legal profession. This erected an ostensibly neutral and objective shield that first obscured what was happening and then made it seem natural and inevitable.

(2)

Finally, we show how this system, in its twentieth-century maturity, has come to threaten the very political stability and productive national economy that were the Framers' and Hamilton's goals. What the more knowingly purposeful defenders of this system did when faced with the inescapable prospect of popular participation was *first* to build a maze of

(3)

multiple limits on the effects of that participation, and *second,* to remove the substance of key policies into another, more remote, decision-making system. What its subsequent defenders have done is to triumphantly label the result "democracy."

Ironically, the great republican experiment has been converted into something like what the Framers feared almost as much as democracy—an absolutist monarchy complete with ongoing baronial struggles for court power and privilege, subject only to the occasional disturbance of crowds running in the streets. In the discouraging character and prospects of our contemporary politics, therefore, we have not experienced the *perversion* of the Framers' intent so much as we have seen the *fulfillment* of the dark side of the Constitution.

# I. The Framers' Constitution

## The Framers' Attitudes :   *Fear Anarchy / Contain Democracy*

As is well known, only a few of the delegates to the convention of 1787 were distinguished by concern for the rights and goals of popular majorities. Most of these dropped out or ended up among the Antifederalists in opposition to ratification. The general attitude of the main body of Framers can be summarized in the phrase "too much democracy." As James Madison put it in *Federalist No. 10:*

> Complaints are everywhere heard from our most considerate and virtuous citizens, equally the friends of public and private faith and of public and personal liberty, that our governments are too unstable, that the public good is disregarded in the conflicts of rival parties, and that measures are too often decided, not according to the rules of justice and the rights of the minor party, but by the superior force of an interested and overbearing majority.

Or, as Hamilton wrote in *Federalist No. 15:* "There are material imperfections in our national system and . . . something is necessary to be done to rescue us from impending anarchy."

Concerns focused on "a rage for paper money, for an abolition of debts, for an equal division of property, or for any other improper or wicked

project." All these improper projects and unjust legislation, of course, sprang from the state legislatures, where "men of more humble, more rural origins, less educated, and with more parochial interests" held sway. Even Jefferson could not support such an excess: "173 despots would surely be as oppressive as one," he wrote. "An *elective despotism* was not the government we fought for." Shays's Rebellion was much on the delegates' minds, and for many, provided the final straw. As Gordon Wood points out:

> Finally, when even Massachusetts with its supposedly model constitution [one of the less democratic of the states] experienced popular excesses, including Shays' Rebellion and the subsequent legislative "tyranny" of Shaysite sympathizers, many leaders were ready to shift the arena of constitutional change from the states to the nation.

The Framers' contemporaries were well aware of the backgrounds and biases of those who drafted our founding document. The Antifederalist writings of the period are full of accusations on this count. According to Jackson Turner Main, "the criticism that the Constitution favored the few at the expense of the many was almost universal." In the words of one prominent Antifederalist: "It changes, totally changes, the form of your present government. From a well-digested, well-formed democratic, you are at once rushing into an aristocratic government." The late Herbert Storing, who collected and edited the Antifederalist writings, called this "the underlying theme of a vast quantity of the specific criticism by the Anti-Federalists of the proposed Constitution."

"The Federal Farmer," a prominent opponent of the Constitution, argued that the state conventions should revise and amend the proposed Constitution as needed, before ratification. Otherwise, the liberty of free men will be lost to those who "avariciously grasp at all power and property." An aristocratic group had

> taken the political field, and with its fashionable dependents, and the tongue and the pen, is endeavouring to establish in great haste, a politer kind of government. . . . The fact is, these aristocrats support and hasten the

adoption of the proposed constitution, merely because they think it is a stepping stone to their favorite object. I think I am well founded in this idea; I think the general politics of these men support it, as well as the common observation among them.

In addition, the Federal Farmer asserted,

This system promises a large field of employment to military gentlemen, and gentlemen of the law; and . . . it will afford security to creditors, to the clergy, salary-men and others depending on money payments.

[Once] power is transferred from the many to the few, all changes become extremely difficult; the government, in this case, being beneficial to the few, they will be exceedingly artful and adroit in preventing any measures which may lead to a change.

"Centinel," in his letters in opposition, was even more forceful, terming the effort to foist the Constitution on unsuspecting citizens "a most daring attempt to establish a despotic aristocracy among freemen, that the world has ever witnessed." He added:

From this investigation into the organization of this government, it appears that it is devoid of all responsibility or accountability to the great body of the people, and that so far from being a regular balanced government, it would be in practice a *permanent ARISTOCRACY*.

Why Contain Democracy — Positive Vision

## The Lure of the New Economy

As early as 1785, Hamilton and others had more in mind than merely the containment of democracy. They began to envision a new kind of commercial economy that would replace production for one's own use with production for sale elsewhere. Trade, transportation, and accompanying financial opportunities would be vastly expanded on a national scale. Eventually, such a national market and exchange system would penetrate parochial communities and replace the almost subsistence-level agricultural economies characteristic of all but the seacoast towns and cosmopolitan centers of the time.

But there would be no national commercial economy unless the Articles of Confederation could be replaced by some more powerful central government. That central government would not only put the brakes on the pernicious projects of the local majorities, but would protect the "property"—the contracts, bonds, paper, credit, etc.—essential to a commercial economy. Such a government would defend the hard money that made for a sound economy, promote the national market through uniform laws and otherwise overcome state protectionism, use import regulations both for taxes and to protect American goods against British competition, and establish sound credit in the international commercial community.

There were two prospective opponents whose interests would be directly damaged by such a new government. One was the mass of heavily indebted back-country farmers still stirred by the Revolutionary dream of equality and individual rights. The other was the state legislatures whose support the farmers sought in their struggle against their creditors and others of the "better people," and which would have had ample institutional reasons to be opposed to any strengthening of the center. An adequate new government would have to control both these threats.

The public campaign for the new government began with the call to the Annapolis Convention in 1786, though its origins are visible much earlier in the correspondence and speeches of advocates. A rather full reform proposal came from Hamilton as early as September 3, 1780, in his letter to James Duane, in which he stated that "The first step must be to give Congress powers competent to the public exigencies." In its call for the Annapolis Convention, the Virginia Legislature was more specific:

To take into consideration the *trade* and *commerce* of the United States; to consider how far an uniform system, in their commercial intercourse and regulations, might be necessary to their common interest and permanent harmony, and to report to the several States such an act relative to this great object, as when unanimously ratified by them, would enable the United States, in Congress assembled, effectually to provide for the same.

As is well known, the Annapolis Convention was attended by only twelve delegates from five states. Among them was Alexander Hamilton, who seized the opportunity to issue the call for the constitutional convention, as follows:

> Your Commissioners cannot forbear to indulge an expression of their earnest and unanimous wish, that speedy measures may be taken, to effect a general meeting of the States, in a future Convention, for the same and such other purposes, as the situation of public affairs, may be found to require. . . .
>
> In this persuasion your Commissioners submit an opinion, that the Idea of extending the powers of their Deputies, to other objects, than those of Commerce . . . will deserve to be incorporated into that of a future Convention. . . .
>
> That there are important defects in the system of the Federal Government is acknowledged by the Acts of all those States, which have concurred in the present Meeting; That the defects, upon a closer examination, may be found greater and more numerous, than even these acts imply, is at least so far probable . . . as may reasonably be supposed to merit a deliberate and candid discussion. . . .
>
> Your Commissioners . . . beg leave to suggest their unanimous conviction, that it may essentially tend to advance the interests of the union, if the States, by whom they have been respectively delegated, would themselves concur, and use their endeavours to procure the concurrence of the other States, in the appointment of Commissioners, to meet at Philadelphia on the second Monday in May next, to take into consideration the situation of the United States, to devise such further provisions as shall appear to them necessary to render the constitution of the Federal Government adequate to the exigencies of the Union. . . .

Shays's Rebellion, that heroic and desperate act by a handful of farmers, is surely the dominant symbol of the period and in many ways the real source of the Constitution. It was the frightening, triggering event that caused a particular selection of delegates to be appointed by their legislatures, induced them to spend a hot summer at an uncertain task in Philadelphia, and provided the context for their work and its later reception. For Hamilton and his cause, it was a godsend. For the convention, it was the ever present threat that led to acceptance of several of the preventive provisions of the Constitution.

For us, Shays's Rebellion may serve to synthesize and express the two streams of thinking that led to the Constitution. The need to protect property and contain democracy could hardly be made more compelling. The need for a powerful central government that could protect commercial interests against citizens, if necessary, is indelibly clear. The basic principles that would have to be enforced in order to prevent such incidents were precisely those that would help to build the new national commercial economy.

The Framers' Constitution responds to both of these concerns, but leaves a substantial part of the second less explicit, and thus subject to Hamilton's later completion in the first administration. While there was little or no disagreement about the need to protect property and contain democracy, some delegates (particularly from the South) certainly would have had reservations about the new national economy and its implications for central government power if they had fully realized what was happening. The convention avoided potential conflict by leaving some provisions incomplete or undefined, in effect passing the responsibility to the first Congress.

In effect, several Framers (Hamilton central among them) were calling for the country—or at least its decisive elites—to make a crucial choice. The choice they advocated was to move from the current mostly agricultural economy (large plantations in the South, and small farms throughout the country) to a national commercial economy in which trade and finance would be dominant. They did not make this call openly, of course, and perhaps some of them did not grasp its totality or significance. Small wonder that their opponents did not see and oppose their design in explicit ways.

## The Constitution as Synthesis

The Constitution's many provisions limiting the potential impact of popular majorities are too well known to require extensive comment. They range broadly from the design of basic structures, to methods of constituting the government, to limits on its powers. Examples in each category are separation of powers and checks and balances, the various forms of insulating elections, and prohibitions against specific acts that might impinge upon property rights. *Empowered to Protect Nat'l Gov't*

More interesting and perhaps less familiar—at least in their totality as a means of instituting a new economy—are the several provisions that create and defend the new national commercial economy through central government power. Many of these provisions were unselfconsciously promoted under the rubric of "protection of property." They were meant to insure that "the rules of justice and the rights of the minor party," as Madison said, would be maintained, even in the face of the "superior force of an interested and overbearing majority." Many do double duty as limits on popular majorities, *but that is exactly the point.* The new economy *necessitated* a national political system in which commercial and financial interests were assured that new and potentially unpopular rules and practices would nevertheless be enforced reliably and consistently—and, it was hoped, be accepted under the more widespread acceptance of the necessity of protection for property rights.

The powers granted to the Congress in Article I, Section 8 and denied to the states in Section 10 amount to the framework for a new fiscal and commercial public policy. Congress gains the power to declare what shall constitute money and to control its value, while the states are forbidden to coin money, emit bills of credit, or allow anything but gold and silver coin in payment of debts. As a result, the states (and their "too democratic" legislatures) were prevented from issuing paper money or defining what might serve as legal tender for the payment of debts, and the gold and silver preferred by bankers and creditors would continue as the basis of the economy.

The Congress also acquired effective taxing powers, and with them the potential to become a creditworthy engine of economic development. Paying existing debts would make it possible to borrow more, to stabilize the currency, and to encourage investment and expansion in various ways. Vital among these tax powers was the power to impose duties and imposts. These are not only the easiest way to collect taxes, but also a means to manage access to the American market—whether to protect infant American industries or to open up other nations' markets. By contrast with the new powers of Congress and the past practice of the states alike, the states were firmly and completely excluded from all such powers (except for the strictly limited purposes of inspections).

The centrality of the famous "commerce clause" to the creation of the new national economy can hardly be debated, even if the question of exclusivity remains at issue today. Hamilton and some of the Framers would undoubtedly have preferred that the mere presence of this provision be understood to preclude the states from acting in the field of interstate commerce at all. But it is not a serious obstacle to their ends that the states be allowed to employ their police or regulatory powers in this area when the Congress has not fully occupied the field or acted in ways that conflict with such state legislation. More important to the creation of the new economy were the requirements for uniformity on the part of national laws pertaining to commerce.

Finally, the contract clause must be appreciated as something more than a prohibition that would assure creditors against any future Shays-type rebellions. Article I, Section 10 includes the prohibition against state laws impairing the obligations of contract as one of a long series of limitations starting with "No states shall. . . ." Clearly, this would render unconstitutional and void any state law that changed the terms of repayment of any existing private contract. By making such contracts into fixed "givens" of economic life, it also tended to discourage popular majorities from seeking redress of economic grievances from their state legislatures.

In Hamilton's hands, the clause applied equally to *public* contracts, so that state legislatures would lose the long-standing sovereign privilege of changing or withdrawing prior grants or franchises. Stability and predictability would be assured, but at the cost of legislative responsiveness to shifting popular preferences.

As Forrest McDonald has shown, this clause may also be distinguished as having been inserted in the Constitution through something like a Hamiltonian coup. At least we know that the convention had twice rejected the principle, and that it was re-inserted by the five-member Committee of Style at the last moment and (apparently) accepted without argument by a weary convention. McDonald makes the case that Hamilton was the only one of the five to grasp the potential in such a clause and therefore must have brought about its last-minute inclusion almost single-handedly.

These primarily economic provisions only sketch the outline of the Framers' intent. They do not by any means constitute the Constitution's entire commitment to the support of the new commercial economy. There are many other provisions that, when taken together, add up to some extensive buttressing of that economy. These include the privileges and immunities of state citizens (to do business in other states), full faith and credit requirements (so that contracts could be enforced and debtors pursued), authorization for a federal court system (for some of the same purposes), and the guarantee and supremacy clauses.

In the United States of the 1780s, it would have been politically difficult, if not impossible, to devise a government that was not, at the least, republican. The Framers had to devise a document with at least the appearance of some democracy, and which could be defended as "republican." Thus, the Constitution does have "democratical" features. However, between the fear of the majority and the desire to protect the newly developing property of the commercial classes, the Framers found it necessary to create a document with a darker side, as we have outlined.

The spare and often ambiguous language of the Constitution was ideally suited to Hamilton's interpretation and expansion. It is Hamilton's interpretations, such as that involving the necessary and proper clause and the creation of the bank, and his expansions, such as in the development of the power of judicial review, that really brought the new national commercial economy into life in the Constitution.

The Framers sketched an outline, but Hamilton made it real. Commercial property and its developing economic relations were protected, and, by the completion of Hamilton's program, removed from the public policy agenda. The ability to change the economy, to deal with substantive public policy issues such as the distribution of wealth and fiscal and monetary measures, was effectively removed from popular control. The "majority" was now contained.

## II. Hamilton's Grand Design and Legislative Programs

As a constitutional architect of vision and purpose, no American compares with Alexander Hamilton. From his earliest critiques of the Articles to the legal cases he argued after leaving the Cabinet, Hamilton pursued a single comprehensive image of a future economy and a government that would promote and defend it. If one person can be singled out, surely Hamilton—not Madison—was the primary driving force behind the origin, character, and ultimate meaning of the American Constitution.

Hamilton's Federalist essays are widely known for their emphasis on the weakness of the Articles and the contrasting need for energy in government, taxing powers to maintain that government's creditworthiness, a strong executive, direct application of national laws to individuals, and the like. All of these reflect characteristic Hamiltonian principles, and together they indicate a direction for the new system.

But the Hamiltonian design comes into its clearest focus from two other major sources which represent the main thrust of his efforts to complete the work of the convention. The first of these is the set of Reports and accompanying legislation and opinions that Hamilton authored as Secretary of the Treasury. The other is Federalist No. 78 and its argument for the power of judicial review, a bold and in many respects original expansion of central government power which helped to raise the courts, the law, and the legal profession to a governing role unprecedented then and unequaled elsewhere today.

•   •   •

What Hamilton demonstrated in these Reports was a clear conception of the national government's capacity to serve as the manipulator of an array of carrots and sticks that would move the economy in desirable directions. Hamilton was also clear about who should determine what those desirable directions might be, and who should benefit from such purposeful action. Men of commercial foresight and experience, and probably of property, should hold such powers, and use them for mutual—and hence national—benefit. Most of all, no such system could tolerate significant popular involvement or impact.

Hamilton's design, let us acknowledge, was intended to build national strength and grandeur, on the model of the British Empire he so much admired. In practical terms, it added up to a new set of legal concepts, new financial principles and methods at the national level, and a new overall developmental role for the national government. His incipient commercial-financial economy (soon to emerge, with industrialization, as capitalism) required changing a number of key legal principles long established in the pre-commercial common law. It required creative use of the national debt, deliberate management of the currency, purposeful industrial policy, and conscious inducements in the form of grants of rights to the vast lands inexpensively acquired by the national government through treaties and conquest.

Most of all, Hamilton's design required insulation against reactions from all sides, and particularly against popular efforts to change the patterns of wealth distribution that this design would accomplish. Hamilton's answer to this compelling need was twofold.

*First,* as we have just seen, he placed the reins of power as far from the people as he could—in a centrally guided financial and development system that would be as hard to identify as it would be to reach and change. Hamilton's system had an early demonstration while he was Secretary of the Treasury, and was legitimated by Jefferson's failure to demolish it while in office. But it was visible only in isolated pieces—growing, merging, self-validating pieces like the restoration and refinement of the Bank, the development of the tariff and internal improvements

and the income tax, the vigorous use of judicial review, the triumph of the legal profession—until its full flowering in the Progressive-New Deal Era.

Hamilton stood for an economy that would be dynamic, responsive to opportunities, and oriented to long-term growth. That economy required farsighted elites to assure that the government would offer incentives for development, stabilize its context, and control its excesses. Government could also serve by providing a means of deflecting or absorbing popular complaints. For all of these goals, the government had to be big, powerful, highly centralized, and removed from the people—but apparently highly responsive to them. Herbert Croly aptly named the twentieth-century version of Hamilton's design "a Hamiltonian government for Jeffersonian ends." Thus the two ever-contending strands of American political thought—our two major images of the desirable American political economy—came to an ultimate merger. Together, they gave credence to labeling Hamilton's national government with the venerable Jeffersonian symbol of "democracy."

The *second* means by which Hamilton sought insulation from popular impact was through transferring as much policymaking as possible into the far less visible and apparently neutral and mechanical hands of courts and lawyers. This strategy encompassed not only the usual and often discretionary law-enforcing role of courts, but more significantly a deliberate lawchanging function and—most important of all—a major policymaking role for the Supreme Court at least equal to that of the other branches.

The effect of Hamilton's various efforts in this area was to raise courts, the law, and the legal profession into a covert policy-making system representing his best hope of protecting the national economy from popular interference. He was apparently willing to pay the price of the law's rigidities and tendency toward backward-looking in order to insulate the economy and its distribution patterns in this way. But the price paid by the people—and ultimately by the constitutional system itself—has yet to be calculated.

# III. THE CONSEQUENCES OF THE DARK SIDE

Any list of the basic problems of current American politics would surely include institutional deadlock, the decline of the political parties, domination by special interests, the multiplicity and complexity of issues, television's role in diverting attention away from public policy, and the deplorable levels of knowledge and interest on the part of most citizens. For each problem, there are one or more standard explanations.

Most of the explanations (and prescriptions for improvement when the situation is not deemed totally hopeless) take one of two forms. The first involves a focus on specific causal factors, i.e., the effects of incumbency, patterns of campaign contributions, the candidate focus of the media, and so forth. The second is more or less an inventory of the incurable failures of the American people: low and declining turnout at elections, ignorance and self-interestedness, an enduring spectator orientation, apparent manipulability by money and media, and an inability to grasp and act on issues.

These standard explanations amount to a massive exercise in blaming the victim. More important, the situation is actually *worse,* and much more fundamental, than generally suggested. We have no quarrel with the list of problems. If anything, we would lengthen and deepen any such list, and would predict that many others will soon be doing so. The United States is already beginning to emerge from the self-congratulatory stupor of the early 1980s. Realism will be in vogue again by the next recession.

Many of the problems of our politics have their origins in the deliberate design of the Constitution, particularly as it was developed by Hamilton. The problems are *real*. The people's response to them is *rational*. What is missing is recognition that the roots of the problem lie in Hamilton's very success.

Today's national government is highly centralized, a huge and distant bureaucracy related in a merely episodic manner to gridlocked and unresponsive policy-making institutions. The web of special interests is a pragmatic answer, albeit one

that represents only the most powerful few. Media and money call the tune for parties and candidates. People may quite rationally decide not to study issues or to participate in such a system.

What has brought about this set of problems and popular response? One absolutely fundamental cause is Hamilton's successful removal of the substance of policy from popular reach. The major pieces of Hamilton's design—the financial system and the legal system—were put in place in the late 1700s and early 1800s by Hamilton and his followers. They became fully integrated and coherently employed in the Progressive Era, from which the rise of the truly centralized Hamiltonian state can be dated.

These two major pieces of Hamilton's design, however, had more than proved their value in the nineteenth century. Each served effectively to obscure unpopular basic national policies from visibility, displace and eventually absorb popular complaints within apparently neutral and objective machines, and frustrate even quite determined popular movements. As Morton Horwitz has shown, the legal system took on its economic role as covert redistributor and allocator of financial burdens as early as the 1820s and 1830s. As opponents of the Bank alleged from the start, and as Goodwyn, Sharkey and others have shown with respect to the financing of the Civil War, the financial system effectively enriched the wealthy while putting the burden on the working and later the middle classes.

When the high point of judicial review was reached in the early 1890s and successfully defended in the election of 1896, the full Hamiltonian legal system was in place. The Supreme Court's power was confirmed; the multitude of state courts were encouraged; and the governing role of an increasingly elite and corporate-oriented Bar was further legitimated. Passage of the Federal Reserve Act offered a final financial link and means of leverage for the same corporate banking-legal community.

Once this system was consolidated in the First World War, participation could actually be encouraged because there was little chance that popular majorities could do much damage. If the basic defenses erected by the Framers did not work, then surely Hamilton's system would divert and absorb popular efforts until they were harmless. Nevertheless, the "better people" were still fearful, not just because of the near-success of labor and the Populists in the 1890s, but also because of the growing ranks of immigrants. Thus, deliberate repression sought to discourage lower-class opposition and electoral participation for a decade or more, just as Hamilton's system was crystallizing. A newly refurbished ("democratic") rationalizing ideology was soon bolstered by powerful new means of communication and indoctrination.

The net result of all these efforts was dramatic decline in electoral turnout in the twentieth century.

Women were added to the eligible electorate in 1920, and blacks and many immigrants had been effectively subtracted in the previous decades, so that turnout percentages are not strictly comparable. However, it is still a shock to realize that elections in the 1880s and 1890s generally had turnout levels over 70 percent and often exceeding 80 percent. Today, when women have had 60 years of experience with the franchise and a whole new generation of black voters has entered the active electorate, we count ourselves lucky to attract more than half of the eligible electorate to the polls.

Where have all the voters gone? They have caught on that the system is rigged. Popular majorities' efforts to change either the distribution of wealth and power or the basic policies that seem necessary to maintain that structure of wealth and power simply don't seem possible. To be sure, decades of accomplishment by the ideological defenders and celebrants of this system have encouraged Americans to accept it as "democracy." Americans learn to want or, more likely, consider inevitable whatever is produced, to settle for various diversionary satisfactions, and/or to fear change and even suspect that those who do seek change must have self-interested and unpatriotic motives. These are ideological rationalizations for the central fact that the Hamiltonian Constitution excludes people from directly affecting important public policy outcomes.

This is not to say that there is no history of popular impact on government, or that the Supreme

Court is merely a tool of the corporations. Either such caricature of our argument would be silly. What is important is that popular impact, such as it is, can be made effective only in very limited ways through the electoral process. For the most part, it must come through disruption—riots, massive strikes, demonstrations involving the threat of violence, and other attacks on the social order itself. What does it mean for a popular government that its people are politically effective only when they threaten to destroy it?

The Supreme Court has made many decisions, particularly in the middle years of this century, that advanced basic democratic rights. But that was a result of judicial appointments, not an attribute of the institution. The Supreme Court has, and can, and may well again, make precisely the opposite kinds of decisions. What does it mean for a popular government that its basic policies can be set by a transitory majority drawn from a body of nine life-appointed lawyers?

What we are saying is that the Framers' two major goals are threatened today by the success with which Hamilton and his followers implemented those goals. We do not have a stable political economic system, and we do not have the capacity to make the choices necessary to assure a strong and successful American political economy.

Our political system works by fits and starts. It is neither responsive nor accountable and it lacks solid grounding in the body of its people. It sits and waits for the next crisis. Unfortunately, to solve that crisis, it may have to transform itself into something that will be *very* difficult to rationalize as "democracy."

We have not addressed the great issues of nuclear war, planetary survival, or even American economic viability in a drastically changing world economy—not because the people don't care, but because there is no linkage between the people's felt needs and their policymakers. No such basic policies can be implemented, even if policymakers were to concur, without the sustained support of some major portion of the people.

To solve our problems, or merely to fulfill the Framers' goals in the wholly different conditions of our times, we will have to come to terms with Hamilton's Constitution in a realistic manner. Perhaps the best way to honor the Framers' work is not to join in obfuscating celebrations, but to act as they did under like circumstances.

We might start by critically exploring the ways in which today's analogue of the Articles of Confederation is defective in achieving goals that are necessary and desirable for the *future*. Obviously, like the Framers, we would have to address basic principles of social order and purpose—if we have not completely forgotten how to do so. (That we *have* forgotten is strongly suggested by the nature of the proposals currently offered for constitutional "reform.")

Curing the defects of Hamilton's Constitution may not be possible, for many reasons. It may be that patterns of material advantage, or the depth of the problems we face, or the sheer size of the country, make it practically impossible. Or our situation may be even worse: perhaps generations of structural deflection—of elites as well as of the general public—from considering the Constitution in a realistic manner has made it impossible for us to do so now. Decades of cultural lowering of the criteria of democracy may have made it impossible for us to recapture its fuller definition and potential.

If there is a route out of our crisis, it lies in deliberately reversing Hamilton's strategy. That is, we must seek to re-engage the people in their government, and particularly in ways that enable them to have direct impact on the substance of important public policies. Without regard to what might be "realistic" or "practical" in light of today's power distribution, or to questions of strategy, the kinds of measures to which consideration might be given are of the following order:

a. Radical decentralization, perhaps to some regional system, reserving only a few global functions for the national government, to put government within reach of the people;

b. Removing the incumbent character of the national government by putting limits on the number of terms that Representatives and Senators can serve;

c. Reducing the role of money by requiring free television time for public affairs issues, party deliberations and arguments, and candidates' presentations;

d. Sharply contracting the policy-making role of courts and lawyers by transferring jurisdiction of constitutional and major policy issues to openly political forums;

e. Instituting mechanisms for direct action—the old initiative and referendum in modern form, with encouragement and provision of educational opportunities and some screen for levels of information;

f. Making registration immediate and eligibility for voting open to all, if necessary by decentralized computer access;

g. Reviving the parties by starting at the local and state levels and providing a series of thresholds through which, by showing increasing levels of popular participation, parties might increasingly acquire control over campaign funding and nominations;

h. Overhauling the public education system to make public affairs a vital and exciting part of the curriculum, welcome controversy, and set future-oriented public service once again at the center of the aspirations of all citizens.

These suggestions are only a start, intended to illustrate the combined fundamental-and-electoral level at which rethinking must begin. They are easily caricatured, and of course they are not "realistic." The point is that institutional tinkering will not suffice.

When problems such as we have described are real, remedies must be radical; that is the lesson the Framers taught in 1787. Only when the people are re-engaged in a government within their reach will Hamilton's damage be undone. At that point, we can proceed to build upon his successes, and seek to truly achieve the stable political system and productive economy that were his vision for the new nation. Only the bright hope of a new twenty-first-century vision can finally transcend the dark side of our much-celebrated eighteenth-century Constitution.

## DISCUSSION QUESTIONS

1. According to Dolbeare and Medcalf, how is the dark side of the constitution related to Alexander Hamilton's model of political economy?
2. To what extent are the current problems of American politics rooted in the design of our Constitution and to what extent do they have other causes?

**11** *Brooke Allen*

# OUR GODLESS CONSTITUTION

*One of the axioms of American political culture is that our eighteenth-century Founding Fathers were deeply religious, weaving Christian principles into the political fabric of the nation. In this brief historical survey, scholar and literary critic Brooke Allen debunks this assumption as myth. Rather than god-fearing Christians fashioning the nation in the image of God, Allen depicts many of our key Founders—George Washington, Thomas Jefferson, John Adams, Thomas Paine, Benjamin Franklin, James Madison—as at best religious skeptics, more deeply wed to Enlightenment rationality than any religious dogma. Our Constitution, The Federalist Papers and other founding documents make scant reference to God and virtually none to Jesus. Widespread fear of the of the oppressive potential of what we today would call religious fundamentalism relegated theological pronouncements to a mostly minor, mostly rhetorical role in our constitutional framework and early political discourse as a nation. Understanding why religion was viewed so skeptically—and why that skepticism ordinarily is not part of our national story—sheds light on our constitutional background and on the ideological conditioning we receive as part of our political culture.*

Our Constitution makes no mention whatever of God. Our nation was founded not on Christian principles but on Enlightenment ones. God only entered the picture as a very minor player, and Jesus Christ was conspicuously absent. The omission was too obvious to have been anything but deliberate, in spite of Alexander Hamilton's flippant responses when asked about it: According to one account, he said that the new nation was not in need of "foreign aid"; according to another, he simply said "we forgot." But as Hamilton's biographer Ron Chernow points out, Hamilton never forgot anything important.

In the eighty-five essays that make up *The Federalist,* God is mentioned only twice (both times by Madison, who uses the word, as Gore Vidal has remarked, in the "only Heaven knows" sense). In the Declaration of Independence, He gets two brief nods: a reference to "the Laws of Nature and Nature's God," and the famous line about men being "endowed by their Creator with certain inalienable rights." More blatant official references to a deity date from long after the founding period: "In God We Trust" did not appear on our coinage until the Civil War, and "under God" was introduced into the

*Source:* Brooke Allen, "Our Godless Constitution," *The Nation,* Volume 280, Number 7, February 21, 2005, pp. 15–20.

Pledge of Allegiance during the McCarthy hysteria in 1954.

In 1797 our government concluded a "Treaty of Peace and Friendship between the United States of America and the Bey and Subjects of Tripoli, or Barbary," now known simply as the Treaty of Tripoli. Article 11 of the treaty contains these words:

As the Government of the United States . . . is not in any sense founded on the Christian religion—as it has in itself no character of enmity against the laws, religion, or tranquillity of Musselmen—and as the said States never have entered into any war or act of hostility against any Mehomitan nation, it is declared by the parties that no pretext arising from religious opinions shall ever produce an interruption of the harmony existing between the two countries.

This document was endorsed by Secretary of State Timothy Pickering and President John Adams. It was then sent to the Senate for ratification; the vote was unanimous. It is worth pointing out that although this was the 339th time a recorded vote had been required by the Senate, it was only the third unanimous vote in the Senate's history. There is no record of debate or dissent. The text of the treaty was printed in full in the Philadelphia Gazette and in two New York papers, but there were no screams of outrage, as one might expect today.

The Founding Fathers were not religious men, and they fought hard to erect, in Thomas Jefferson's words, "a wall of separation between church and state." John Adams opined that if they were not restrained by legal measures, Puritans—the fundamentalists of their day—would "whip and crop, and pillory and roast." The historical epoch had afforded these men ample opportunity to observe the corruption to which established priesthoods were liable, as well as "the impious presumption of legislators and rulers," as Jefferson wrote, "civil as well as ecclesiastical, who, being themselves but fallible and uninspired men, have assumed dominion over the faith of others, setting up their own opinions and modes of thinking as the only true and infallible, and as such endeavoring to impose them on others, hath established and maintained false religions over the greatest part of the world and through all time."

If we define a Christian as a person who believes in the divinity of Jesus Christ, then it is safe to say that some of the key Founding Fathers were not Christians at all. Benjamin Franklin, Thomas Jefferson and Tom Paine were deists—that is, they believed in one Supreme Being but rejected revelation and all the supernatural elements of the Christian Church; the word of the Creator, they believed, could best be read in Nature. John Adams was a professed liberal Unitarian, but he, too, in his private correspondence seems more deist than Christian.

George Washington and James Madison also leaned toward deism, although neither took much interest in religious matters. Madison believed that "religious bondage shackles and debilitates the mind and unfits it for every noble enterprize." He spoke of the "almost fifteen centuries" during which Christianity had been on trial: "What have been its fruits? More or less in all places, pride and indolence in the Clergy, ignorance and servility in the laity, in both, superstition, bigotry, and persecution." If Washington mentioned the Almighty in a public address, as he occasionally did, he was careful to refer to Him not as "God" but with some nondenominational moniker like "Great Author" or "Almighty Being." It is interesting to note that the Father of our Country spoke no words of a religious nature on his deathbed, although fully aware that he was dying, and did not ask for a man of God to be present; his last act was to take his own pulse, the consummate gesture of a creature of the age of scientific rationalism.

Tom Paine, a polemicist rather than a politician, could afford to be perfectly honest about his religious beliefs, which were baldly deist in the tradition of Voltaire: "I believe in one God, and no more; and I hope for happiness beyond this life. . . . I do not believe in the creed professed by the Jewish church, by the Roman church, by the Greek church, by the Turkish church, by the Protestant church, nor by any church that I know of. My own mind is my own church." This is how he opened *The Age of Reason*, his virulent attack on Christianity. In it he railed against the "obscene stories, the voluptuous debaucheries, the cruel and torturous executions, the unrelenting vindictiveness" of the Old Testament, "a history of wickedness, that has served to corrupt and brutalize mankind." The New Testament is less brutalizing but more absurd, the story of Christ's divine genesis a "fable, which for absurdity and extravagance is not exceeded by any thing that is to be found in the mythology of the ancients." He held the idea of the Resurrection in especial ridicule: Indeed, "the wretched contrivance with which this latter part is told, exceeds every thing that went before it." Paine was careful to contrast the tortuous twists of theology with the pure clarity of deism. "The true deist has but one Deity; and his religion consists in contemplating the power, wisdom, and benignity of the Deity in his works, and in endeavoring to imitate him in every thing moral, scientifical, and mechanical."

Paine's rhetoric was so fervent that he was inevitably branded an atheist. Men like Franklin, Adams and Jefferson could not risk being tarred with that brush, and in fact Jefferson got into a good deal of trouble for continuing his friendship with Paine and entertaining him at Monticello. These statesmen had to be far more circumspect than the turbulent Paine, yet if we examine their beliefs it is all but impossible to see just how theirs differed from his.

Franklin was the oldest of the Founding Fathers. He was also the most worldly and sophisticated, and was well aware of the Machiavellian principle that if one aspires to influence the masses, one must at least profess religious sentiments. By his own definition he was a deist, although one French acquaintance claimed that "our free-thinkers have adroitly sounded him on his religion, and they maintain that they have discovered he is one of their own, that is that he has none at all." If he did have a religion, it was strictly utilitarian: As his biographer Gordon Wood has said, "He praised religion for whatever moral effects it had, but for little else." Divine revelation, Franklin freely admitted, had "no weight with me," and the covenant of grace seemed "unintelligible" and "not beneficial." As for the pious hypocrites who have ever controlled nations, "A man compounded of law and gospel is able to cheat a whole country with his religion and then destroy them under color of law"—a comment we should carefully consider at this turning point in the history of our Republic.

Here is Franklin's considered summary of his own beliefs, in response to a query by Ezra Stiles, the president of Yale. He wrote it just six weeks before his death at the age of 84:

> Here is my creed. I believe in one God, Creator of the universe. That he governs it by his providence. That he ought to be worshipped. That the most acceptable service we render to him is doing good to his other children. That the soul of Man is immortal, and will be treated with justice in another life respecting its conduct in this. These I take to be the fundamental points in all sound religion, and I regard them as you do in whatever sect I meet with them.
>
> As for Jesus of Nazareth, my opinion of whom you particularly desire, I think his system of morals and his religion, as he left them to us, the best the world ever saw or is likely to see; but I apprehend it has received various corrupting changes, and I have, with most of the present dissenters in England, some doubts as to his divinity; though it is a question I do not dogmatize upon, having never studied it, and think it needless to busy myself with now, when I expect soon an opportunity of knowing the truth with less trouble. I see no harm, however, in its being believed, if that belief has the good consequence, as it probably has, of making his doctrines more respected and better observed, especially as I do not perceive that the Supreme takes it amiss, by distinguishing the unbelievers in his government of the world with any particular marks of his displeasure.

Jefferson thoroughly agreed with Franklin on the corruptions the teachings of Jesus had undergone. "The metaphysical abstractions of Athanasius, and the maniacal ravings of Calvin, tinctured plentifully with the foggy dreams of Plato, have so loaded [Christianity] with absurdities and incomprehensibilities" that it was almost impossible to recapture "its native simplicity and purity." Like Paine, Jefferson felt that the miracles claimed by the New Testament put an intolerable strain on credulity. "The day will come," he predicted (wrongly, so far), "when the mystical generation of Jesus, by the supreme being as his father in the womb of a virgin, will be classed with the fable of the generation of Minerva in the brain of Jupiter." The Revelation of St. John he dismissed as "the ravings of a maniac."

Jefferson edited his own version of the New Testament, "The Life and Morals of Jesus of Nazareth," in which he carefully deleted all the miraculous passages from the works of the Evangelists. He intended it, he said, as "a document in proof that I am a real Christian, that is to say, a disciple of the doctrines of Jesus." This was clearly a defense against his many enemies, who hoped to blacken his reputation by comparing him with the vile atheist Paine. His biographer Joseph Ellis is undoubtedly correct, though, in seeing disingenuousness here: "If [Jefferson] had been completely scrupulous, he would have described himself as a deist who admired the ethical teachings of Jesus as a man rather than as the son of God. (In modern-day parlance, he was a secular humanist.)" In short, not a Christian at all.

The three accomplishments Jefferson was proudest of—those that he requested be put on his tombstone—were the founding of the University of Virginia and the authorship of the Declaration of Independence and the Virginia Statute for Religious Freedom. The latter was a truly radical document that would eventually influence the separation of church and state in the U.S. Constitution; when it was passed by the Virginia legislature in 1786, Jefferson rejoiced that there was finally "freedom for the Jew and the Gentile, the Christian and the Mohammeden, the Hindu and infidel of every denomination"—note his respect, still unusual today, for the sensibilities of the "infidel." The University of Virginia was notable among early-American seats of higher education in that it had no religious affiliation whatever. Jefferson even banned the teaching of theology at the school.

If we were to speak of Jefferson in modern political categories, we would have to admit that he was a pure libertarian, in religious as in other matters. His real commitment (or lack thereof) to the teachings of Jesus Christ is plain from a famous throwaway comment he made: "It does me no injury for my neighbor to say there are twenty gods or no god. It neither

picks my pocket nor breaks my leg." This raised plenty of hackles when it got about, and Jefferson had to go to some pains to restore his reputation as a good Christian. But one can only conclude, with Ellis, that he was no Christian at all.

John Adams, though no more religious than Jefferson, had inherited the fatalistic mindset of the Puritan culture in which he had grown up. He personally endorsed the Enlightenment commitment to Reason but did not share Jefferson's optimism about its future, writing to him, "I wish that Superstition in Religion exciting Superstition in Polliticks . . . may never blow up all your benevolent and phylanthropic Lucubrations," but that "the History of all Ages is against you." As an old man he observed, "Twenty times in the course of my late reading have I been upon the point of breaking out, 'This would be the best of all possible worlds, if there were no religion in it!'" Speaking ex cathedra, as a relic of the founding generation, he expressed his admiration for the Roman system whereby every man could worship whom, what and how he pleased. When his young listeners objected that this was paganism, Adams replied that it was indeed, and laughed.

In their fascinating and eloquent valetudinarian correspondence, Adams and Jefferson had a great deal to say about religion. Pressed by Jefferson to define his personal creed, Adams replied that it was "contained in four short words, 'Be just and good.'" Jefferson replied, "The result of our fifty or sixty years of religious reading, in the four words, 'Be just and good,' is that in which all our inquiries must end; as the riddles of all priesthoods end in four more, 'ubi panis, ibi deus.' What all agree in, is probably right. What no two agree in, most probably wrong."

This was a clear reference to Voltaire's *Reflections on Religion*. As Voltaire put it:

There are no sects in geometry. One does not speak of a Euclidean, an Archimedean. When the truth is evident, it is impossible for parties and factions to arise. . . . Well, to what dogma do all minds agree? To the worship of a God, and to honesty. All the philosophers of the world who have had a religion have said in all ages: "There is a God, and one must be just." There, then, is the universal religion established in all ages and throughout mankind. The point in which they all agree is therefore true, and the systems through which they differ are therefore false.

Of course all these men knew, as all modern presidential candidates know, that to admit to theological skepticism is political suicide. During Jefferson's presidency a friend observed him on his way to church, carrying a large prayer book. "You going to church, Mr. J," remarked the friend. "You do not believe a word in it." Jefferson didn't exactly deny the charge. "Sir," he replied, "no nation has ever yet existed or been governed without religion. Nor can be. The Christian religion is the best religion that has been given to man and I as chief Magistrate of this nation am bound to give it the sanction of my example. Good morning Sir."

Like Jefferson, every recent President has understood the necessity of at least paying lip service to the piety of most American voters. All of our leaders, Democrat and Republican, have attended church, and have made very sure they are seen to do so. But there is a difference between offering this gesture of respect for majority beliefs and manipulating and pandering to the bigotry, prejudice and millennial fantasies of Christian extremists. Though for public consumption the Founding Fathers identified themselves as Christians, they were, at least by today's standards, remarkably honest about their misgivings when it came to theological doctrine, and religion in general came very low on the list of their concerns and priorities— always excepting, that is, their determination to keep the new nation free from bondage to its rule.

---

## DISCUSSION QUESTIONS

1. Focusing on a few of our more famous Founding Fathers, identify their major objections to the intersection of religion and political life. How would you describe them religiously?
2. In the penultimate paragraph, Allen points out that politicians—then and now—know that to acknowledge any personal skepticism about religion amounts to "political suicide." Given how untethered our Founding Fathers were to theological precepts, speculate about why being skeptical about religion—or being non-religious—is political suicide.

## 12 *Howard Zinn*

# SOME TRUTHS ARE NOT SELF-EVIDENT

*Writing during the bicentennial celebrations of 1987, historian and political scientist Howard Zinn makes a case that the Constitution is of minor importance in determining the degree of justice, liberty, and democracy in our society. While not denying the symbolic and moral weight of the Constitution, Zinn contends that social movements and citizen action have been far more significant in the realization of democratic values over the course of American history. He provides examples from the areas of racial equality, freedom of speech, economic justice, sexual equality, and questions of war and peace to support his claim that a "mere document" like the Constitution "is no substitute for the energy, boldness, and concerted action of the citizens."*

This year [1987] Americans are talking about the Constitution but asking the wrong questions, such as, Could the Founding Fathers have done better? That concern is pointless, 200 years after the fact. Or, Does the Constitution provide the framework for a just and democratic society today? That question is also misplaced, because the Constitution, whatever its language and however interpreted by the Supreme Court, does not determine the degree of justice, liberty or democracy in our society.

The proper question, I believe, is not how good a document is or was the Constitution but, What effect does it have on the quality of our lives? And the answer to that, it seems to me, is, Very little. The Constitution makes promises it cannot by itself keep, and therefore deludes us into complacency about the rights we have. It is conspicuously silent on certain other rights that all human beings deserve. And it

pretends to set limits on governmental powers, when in fact those limits are easily ignored.

I am not arguing that the Constitution has no importance; words have moral power and principles can be useful even when ambiguous. But, like other historic documents, the Constitution is of minor importance compared with the actions that citizens take, especially when those actions are joined in social movements. Such movements have worked, historically, to secure the rights our human sensibilities tell us are self-evidently ours, whether or not those rights are "granted" by the Constitution.

Let me illustrate my point with five issues of liberty and justice:

First is the matter of racial equality. When slavery was abolished, it was not by constitutional fiat but by the joining of military necessity with the moral force of a great antislavery movement, acting

---

*Source:* Howard Zinn, "Some Truths Are Not Self-Evident." *The Nation,* Volume 245, Number 3, August 18, 1987, pp. 87–88.

outside the Constitution and often against the law. The Thirteenth, Fourteenth and Fifteenth Amendments wrote into the Constitution rights that extra-legal action had already won. But the Fourteenth and Fifteenth Amendments were ignored for almost a hundred years. The right to equal protection of the law and the right to vote, even the Supreme Court decision in *Brown v. Board of Education* in 1954 underlining the meaning of the equal protection clause, did not become operative until blacks, in the fifteen years following the Montgomery bus boycott, shook up the nation by tumultuous actions inside and outside the law.

The Constitution played a helpful but marginal role in all that. Black people, in the political context of the 1960s, would have demanded equality whether or not the Constitution called for it, just as the antislavery movement demanded abolition even in the absence of constitutional support.

What about the most vaunted of constitutional rights, free speech? Historically, the Supreme Court has given the right to free speech only shaky support, seesawing erratically by sometimes affirming and sometimes overriding restrictions. Whatever a distant Court decided, the real right of citizens to free expression has been determined by the immediate power of the local police on the street, by the employer in the workplace and by the financial limits on the ability to use the mass media.

The existence of a First Amendment has been inspirational but its protection elusive. Its reality has depended on the willingness of citizens, whether labor organizers, socialists or Jehovah's Witnesses, to insist on their right to speak and write. Liberties have not been given; they have been taken. And whether in the future we have a right to say what we want, or air what we say, will be determined not by the existence of the First Amendment or the latest Supreme Court decision but by whether we are courageous enough to speak up at the risk of being jailed or fired, organized enough to defend our speech against official interference and can command resources enough to get our ideas before a reasonably large public.

What of economic justice? The Constitution is silent on the right to earn a moderate income, silent on the rights to medical care and decent housing as legitimate claims of every human being from infancy to old age. Whatever degree of economic justice has been attained in this country (impressive compared with others, shameful compared with our resources) cannot be attributed to something in the Constitution. It is the result of the concerted action of laborers and farmers over the centuries, using strikes, boycotts and minor rebellions of all sorts, to get redress of grievances directly from employers and indirectly from legislators. In the future, as in the past, the Constitution will sleep as citizens battle over the distribution of the nation's wealth, and will be awakened only to mark the score.

On sexual equality the Constitution is also silent. What women have achieved thus far is the result of their own determination, in the feminist upsurge of the nineteenth and early twentieth centuries, and the more recent women's liberation movement. Women have accomplished this outside the Constitution, by raising female and male consciousness and inducing courts and legislators to recognize what the Constitution ignores.

Finally, in an age in which war approaches genocide, the irrelevance of the Constitution is especially striking. Long, ravaging conflicts in Korea and Vietnam were waged without following Constitutional procedures, and if there is a nuclear exchange, the decision to launch U.S. missiles will be made, as it was in those cases, by the President and a few advisers. The public will be shut out of the process and deliberately kept uninformed by an intricate web of secrecy and deceit. The current Iran/*contra* scandal hearings before Congressional select committees should be understood as exposing not an aberration but a steady state of foreign policy.

It was not constitutional checks and balances but an aroused populace that prodded Lyndon Johnson and then Richard Nixon into deciding to extricate the United States from Vietnam. In the immediate future, our lives will depend not on the existence of the Constitution but on the power of an aroused citizenry demanding that we not go to war, and on Americans refusing, as did so many G.I.s and civilians in the Vietnam era, to cooperate in the conduct of a war.

The Constitution, like the Bible, has some good words. It is also, like the Bible, easily manipulated, distorted, ignored and used to make us feel comfortable and protected. But we risk the loss of our lives and liberties if we depend on a mere document to defend them. A constitution is a fine adornment for a democratic society, but it is no substitute for the energy, boldness and concerted action of the citizens.

---

## DISCUSSION QUESTIONS

1. What is Zinn's main point about the relationship of the Constitution to political change and the expansion of democracy?
2. Identify the five issues of justice and liberty discussed by Zinn and explain how each relates to his main point about the Constitution.

# PART **II**

# POLITICS AND INSTITUTIONS

The formal institutions of the U.S. government exercise considerable influence over all of us. They touch our lives in many ways, quite independently of whether or not we want them to. Americans remain uneasy about the impact of government institutions. Surveys conducted since the 1960s reveal an erosion of trust in all government institutions. Americans generally do not trust the federal government to "do the right thing." One survey found that "an environment in which a majority of Americans believe that most people can't be trusted breeds attitudes that hold all politicians as corrupt, venal, and self-serving, and government action as doomed to failure."

While recognizing widespread public distrust, government nonetheless does matter. Congress, for example, has the authority to spend nearly $3.0 trillion in fiscal year 2008. This is a staggering sum of money. And it undoubtedly is the case that the expenditure of those funds, not to mention the taxes levied to create the budget in the first place, will have an impact on us, whether we drive on federally subsidized roads, work in federally regulated workplaces, receive Social Security payments, or, perhaps in your case, receive federal loans to attend college. Notwithstanding debates over the social and moral implications of the nation's budgetary priorities, and recognizing the often exaggerated nature of protests from conservatives against the alleged evils of "big government," the fact remains that we *have* a large and active national government. It makes good sense to try to understand it.

The five chapters in Part II examine key political institutions and processes and the three branches of the federal government: the mass media, political parties and elections, as well as Congress, the presidency, and the courts—the three cornerstones of the Constitutional separation of powers. Although conventional political science texts include discussions of these institutional "nuts and bolts," we locate them against the backdrop of the structure of power analyzed in Part I. Thus we are stressing that political processes and government institutions do not make decisions in a vacuum; policymakers operate within the confines of economic and ideological boundaries that sharply limit the range of the possible.

We contend that your capacity to see the system clearly depends on your willingness to focus *first* on the structure and *second* on the processes and institutions. That is why we have organized the book this way. This distinction between primary focus and secondary focus may seem like hairsplitting, but actually it is crucial. Mainstream accounts of American politics downplay or ignore outright the deeper structural concerns, thus amplifying the institutions. To do so is to give analytic priority to the parts of government that are most directly accountable to the public, which in turn makes the system appear fairer and more democratic than it really is. Such a conventional focus on institutions also offers hope that if we can just elect the candidate with the best personality or the right party affiliation, our political problems can be effectively addressed with minimal, if any, changes.

While relatively comforting, this hope is not warranted. Significant progress in meeting the needs of the people requires questioning the structure itself. This obviously confronts you with a less comfortable and more daunting task, but it rests on an honest admission of what lies ahead for the student who seeks to interpret, and perhaps change, the political world we inhabit. In the final analysis, then, do our political institutions and the policy process deserve careful scrutiny? Absolutely. Part II will help you in this regard, but always be critically aware of the playing field where the clash of institutions takes place.

# CHAPTER 4

# MASS MEDIA AND POLITICS

As a looming presence in contemporary America, the mass media are inescapable. Indeed, Americans are eager consumers of media products and spend countless hours in contact with some form of media. Enhanced by technological breakthroughs of the late twentieth century, cable TV and the Internet allow access to more sources of information than ever before. Certainly the media have the potential to serve democratic ends by providing citizens with high-quality electoral and policy information as well as by acting as a watchdog over government and other powerful institutions. In practice, however, the mass media, driven by corporate profit imperatives, all too often contribute to cynicism, depoliticization, and a truncated and illusory view of the way the world works. The result, in the words of communications scholar Robert W. McChesney, is a "rich media" and a "poor democracy." Articles in this chapter provide the analytical tools to critically dissect the role of the mass media in politics today.

**13** *Robert W. McChesney and John Nichols*

# IT'S THE MEDIA, STUPID

*During the 1992 presidential election, candidate Bill Clinton's campaign team hung a now-famous sign in their headquarters that read "It's the economy, stupid." The sign served as a reminder to link all discussions of policy issues to the faltering economy, thereby constantly connecting issues to a central critique of President George Bush's handling of the economy. In this article, Robert McChesney, a media scholar and activist, and John Nichols, a journalist, similarly seek to draw constant attention to the central importance of connecting all discussions about reforming American democracy to the need for media reform. They begin by emphasizing the important connection between the free flow of information and a healthy democratic society. Then they outline the problem in straightforward terms: by 2000, fewer than ten giant media conglomerates dominated the mass media of the United States, with firms like Disney, AOL-Time Warner, SONY, and GE leading the way. This level of corporate control over what we see and hear as "news" guarantees that the values of profit-maximizing and commercialism will guide the U.S. media system, to the detriment of news that truly informs the public on the crucial issues of the day. The result is news that does not challenge the world-view of elite interests, nor offer a broad range of competing perspectives, thus greatly diminishing the quality of democracy. Or as the authors put it, corporate media has fanned the flames of a "crisis for democracy." To address this crisis, McChesney and Nichols offer an ambitious agenda for media reform aimed at strengthening democratic participation and citizenship. For the authors contend that what is needed in the twenty-first century is nothing short of a "broad crusade for democratic renewal in America."*

Participatory self-government, or democracy, works best when at least three criteria are met. First, it helps when there are not significant disparities in economic wealth and property ownership across the society. Such disparities undermine the ability of citizens to act as equals. Second, it helps when there is a sense of community and a notion that an individual's well-being is determined to no small extent by the community's well-being. This provides democratic political culture with a substance that cannot exist if

*Source:* Robert W. McChesney, *Corporate Media and the Threat to Democracy,* New York: Seven Stories Press, 1997, pp. 5–7; Robert W. McChesney and John Nichols, *It's the Media, Stupid,* New York: Seven Stories Press, 2000, pp. 21–25, 27–39, 110–115, and 119–120.

everyone is simply out to advance narrowly defined self-interests, even if those interests might be harmful to the community as a whole. Third, democracy requires that there be an effective system of political communication, broadly construed, that informs and engages the citizenry, drawing people meaningfully into the polity. This becomes especially important as societies grow larger and more complex, but has been true for all societies dedicated toward self-government. While democracies by definition must respect individual freedoms, these freedoms can only be exercised in a meaningful sense when the citizenry is informed, engaged, and participating. Moreover, without this, political debate can scarcely address the central issues of power and resource allocation that must be at the heart of public deliberation in a democracy. As James Madison noted, "A popular government without popular information, or the means of acquiring it, is but a prologue to a farce or a tragedy, or perhaps both."

These three criteria are related. In nondemocratic societies those in power invariably dominate the communication systems to maintain their rule. In democratic societies the manner by which the media system is structured, controlled and subsidized is of central political importance. Control over the means of communication is an integral aspect of political and economic power. In many nations, to their credit, media policy debates have been and are important political issues. In the U.S., to the contrary, private commercial control over communication is often regarded as innately democratic and benevolent, and therefore not subject to political discussion. Government involvement with media or communication is almost universally denigrated in the U.S. as a direct invitation to tyranny, no matter how well intended. The preponderance of U.S. mass communications is controlled by less than two dozen enormous profit-maximizing corporations, which receive much of their income from advertising placed largely by other huge corporations. But the extent of this media ownership and control goes generally unremarked in the media and intellectual culture, and there appears to be little sense of concern about its dimensions among citizenry as a whole.

•  •  •

It was the rainiest, wettest, coldest April morning Washington had seen in a long time. And still they came—thousands of mostly young activists determined to mount a nonviolent but noisy protest outside the spring 2000 meetings of the World Bank and the International Monetary Fund (IMF). As they reached a key intersection near the World Bank building, they were blocked by armed battalions of riot police and National Guardsmen. The authorities stood their ground, but the Mobilization for Global Justice activists refused to back down.

This was the sort of standoff to which even the most jaded television assignment editors dispatched their crews—despite the fact that the weather made for some fogged-up camera lenses. On the street, a reporter for one Washington television station pulled aside a young woman who was soaking wet, and announced to the cameraman that it was time to do a live shot. When the signal came that they were on air, the reporter started to make small talk with the activist about the miserable weather. "I really want to talk about the policies of the World Bank and the IMF," the young woman said. "Their structural adjustment policies are causing real harm in specific countries around the world. . . ." The reporter pulled the microphone back, looked to the camera and said, "Well, everybody has an opinion. Let's go back to the anchor desk."

That same afternoon, as young people who had attended teach-ins, listened to debates and read literature and books in preparation for the demonstration continued to face down the police in the streets, conservative commentator Tony Snow was attacking the protestors on Washington radio as ignorant and uninformed. The next morning, *The Wall Street Journal* referred to them as "Global Village Idiots." The supposedly liberal *Washington Post* and *New York Times* editorial pages both dismissed the protests as not much more than a waste of police resources and everyone else's time. And, despite the fact that at least 150 activists were still in jail, and that people in Washington, across the nation and indeed, around the world, were buzzing about a new era of activism, television news programs went back to broadcasting the usual mix of commercials and vapid "news you can use."

Molly Ivins put it rather succinctly when she observed, a few days later, that "for reasons unclear to me, the mainstream media seem to have decided that anyone who questions any aspect of globalization is an extremist nut, despite the rather obvious fact that global poverty is growing under the kind auspices of the World Bank, the International Monetary Fund, and the World Trade Organization."

In our view, the reasons for this are clear. The closer a story gets to examining corporate power the less reliable our corporate media system is as a source of information that is useful to the citizens of a democracy. And on issues like the global capitalist economy, the corporate media are doubly unreliable, because they rank as perhaps the foremost beneficiaries of Wall Street-designed trade deals like NAFTA, and of the machinations of the three multilateral agencies developed to shape the global economy to serve corporate interests: the World Bank, the IMF and the World Trade Organization (WTO). Moreover, almost all the favored mainstream sources for coverage of global economic affairs are strident advocates for a corporate-driven vision of globalization. Thus, corporate journalists—even those low enough on the pecking order to be dispatched to stand in the rain on a Washington street corner—generally will find arguments against the status quo incomprehensible.

Just as the media dropped the ball in Washington in April 2000, it blew a chance to cover an even more dramatic story of citizens speaking truth to power in the fall of 1999, when the WTO met in Seattle. As one of the most significant challenges to global economics in decades was playing out—a challenge so powerful that the WTO meetings were actually shut down for a time and ultimately failed to launch a new round of trade liberalization, a challenge so intense that President Clinton felt compelled to assert his agreement on a variety of issues with those protesting in the streets—the broadcast media treated the story as an event of secondary importance. There was no round-the-clock coverage, as was seen only four months earlier when John F. Kennedy Jr.'s fatal plane crash reshaped the broadcast schedules of CNN, the Fox News Channel, and every other cable TV news service for two full weeks. During the WTO meetings and demonstrations—which dealt with

arguably the most important political issues of our age—no attempt was made to provide comprehensive coverage. One night, as demonstrators filled the streets of Seattle and ministers of finance battled through the night over the most fundamental questions of how the global economy would be structured, as the President of the U.S. hunkered down in a hotel surrounded by armed troops, the Fox News Channel interrupted its scheduled programming for a live special report . . . not from Seattle, but from the scene of the latest doings of the parents of JonBenet Ramsey.

What happened in Seattle sums up the crisis for democracy that occurs when the media system is set up primarily to maximize profit for a handful of enormous self-interested corporations. An Orwellian disconnect is created. The news required for a functional democracy—the news that empowers citizens to act in their own interest and for the good of society—is discarded to make way for the trivial, sensational, and salacious. How many Americans have come home from a school board meeting, a city council session, a local demonstration or a mass national rally to discover the vital issues they had just addressed are being ignored or distorted? The flow of information that is the lifeblood of democracy is being choked by a media system that every day ignores a world of injustice and inequality, and the growing resistance to it. . . .

Back in 1992, Bill Clinton's campaign strategists hung a sign in the war room of their Little Rock headquarters that read, "It's the economy, stupid." The point of the sign was to remind campaign workers to circle every discussion of election issues around to the subject of the sagging economy. In many senses, this book is like that sign. We are here to argue that it's time to point out the connections between media reform and democratic renewal. To sound a wake up call reminding us that access to communications is a nonnegotiable demand in a democratic society, and that scoring real victories for labor, the environment, and social justice will be made all the more possible by opening up the democratizing the media. Meanwhile, when the corporate press comes looking for a soundbite on what the ruckus is all about, tell them, "It's the media, stupid."

•       •       •

Americans devour media at a staggering rate; in 1999 the average American spent almost twelve hours per day with some form of media. We are also in the midst of an unprecedented technological revolution—based around digital technologies, typified by the Internet—that looks to weave media and electronic communication into nearly every waking moment of our lives. In conventional parlance, these developments are presented as benign; they are all about liberating individuals, investors, and consumers from the constraints of time and space while offering a cornucopia of exciting new options and possibilities. This, however, is a superficial and misleading perspective on what is happening. Indeed, when one lifts the hood, so to speak, to see what is driving the media revolution, a very different picture emerges. It is instead a world where highly concentrated corporate power is pulling the strings to dominate our existence so as to maximize return to shareholders, and to protect the corporation's role—and corporate power in general—from being subjected to the public scrutiny and political debate it so richly deserves. It is a poison pill for democracy.

Yet in our American democracy the issue of media barely registers. The structures of our media, the concentration of its ownership, the role that it plays in shaping the lives of our children, in commercializing our culture, and in warping our elections, has been off-limits. When we examine the reality of media in the year 2000, however, it becomes clear that this circumstance must shift. The case for making media an issue is made, above all, by a survey of the contemporary media landscape.

In 2000, the U.S. media system is dominated by fewer than ten transnational conglomerates: Disney, AOL-Time Warner, News Corporation, Viacom, Seagram (Universal), Sony, Liberty (AT&T), Bertelsmann, and General Electric (NBC). Their media revenues range from roughly $8 billion to $30 billion per year. These firms tend to have holdings in numerous media sectors. AOL-Time Warner, for example, ranks among the largest players in film production, recorded music, TV show production, cable TV channels, cable TV systems, book publishing, magazine publishing, and Internet service provision. The great profit in media today comes from taking a

movie or TV show and milking it for maximum return through spin-off books, CDs, video games, and merchandise. Another twelve to fifteen firms, which do from $2 or $3 billion to $8 billion per year in business, round out the system. These firms—like Comcast, Hearst, New York Times, Washington Post, Cox, Advance, Tribune Company, Gannett—tend to be less developed conglomerates, focusing on only two or three media sectors. All in all, these two dozen or so firms control the overwhelming percentage of movies, TV shows, cable systems, cable channels, TV stations, radio stations, books, magazines, newspapers, billboards, music, and TV networks that constitute the media culture that occupies one-half of the average American's life. It is an extraordinary degree of economic and social power located in very few hands.

It has not always been this way. Much of this concentration has taken place in the past few decades, as technology and market imperatives made concentration and conglomeration far more attractive and necessary. Today it is impossible for the small, independent firm to be anything but a marginal player in the industries mentioned above. Most important, the flames of media concentration were fanned by a collapsing commitment on the part of the federal government to serious antitrust prosecution, a diminution of the federal standards regarding fairness, and government "deregulation," most notably the 1996 Telecommunications Act. Congressional approval of the Telecommunications Act, after only a stilted and disengaged debate, was a historic turning point in media policy making in the United States, as it permitted a consolidation of media and communication ownership that had previously been unthinkable.

A surface survey of the statistics regarding media ownership, while deeply disturbing in what it reveals, fails to convey the full depth of the concentration of media ownership. Not only are media markets dominated by a handful of conglomerates with "barriers to entry," making it nearly impossible for newcomers to challenge their dominance, but they are also closely linked to each other in a manner that suggests almost a cartel-like arrangement. Some of the largest media firms own parts of the other giants; Liberty, for example, is the second largest shareholder in News Corporation and among the largest shareholders in AOL-Time Warner. Moreover, the media giants employ equity joint ventures—where two competing firms share ownership in a single venture—to an extent unknown almost anywhere else in the economy. These joint ventures work to reduce competition, lower risk, and increase profits. By 1999 the nine largest media giants had an equity join venture with six, on average, of the other eight giants; often a media giant would have multiple joint ventures with another firm. In sum, this is a tightly knit community of owners, dominated by some of the wealthiest individuals in the world. Indeed, thirteen of the hundred wealthiest individuals in the world—all of whom are worth over $4 billion—are media magnates.

Such concentration of media ownership is clearly negative by any standard that cherishes free speech and diversity in the marketplace of ideas. But concentration in media ownership is not the sole cause of the problems with the media, and in some cases it is not a significant factor at all. Concentration is important to a large extent because it magnifies the limitations of a commercial media system, and makes those limitations less susceptible to redress by the market. But this sounds very abstract, so let's cut to the bone: the problem with concentrated media is that it accentuates the two main problems of commercial media, hypercommercialism and denigration of public service. These are really two sides of the same coin. As massive media corporations are better able to commercially carpet bomb society, their ability or willingness to provide material with editorial and creative integrity declines. It is not that the individuals who run these firms are bad people; the problem is that they do destructive things by rationally following the market cues they are given. We have a media system set up to serve private investors first and foremost, not public citizens.

No better example of how this process works can be found than in the U.S. radio industry. Since deregulation of ownership in 1996, some one-half of U.S. stations have been sold. A few massive giants, owning hundreds of stations—as many as eight in each market—have come to dominate the industry. As profits shoot through the roof, low-budget standardized fare has nearly eliminated the local content, character, and creativity that were once features of this relatively inexpensive electronic medium. "A huge wave of consolidation has turned music stations into cash cows that focus on narrow playlists aimed at squeezing the most revenue from the richest demographics," the trade publication *Variety* observed in 1999. "Truth be told, in this era of megamergers, there has never been a greater need for a little diversity on the dial."

The radio example points to the one other crucial group, aside from media owners, that gets treated with love and affection by corporate media executives: the corporate advertising community. Businesses spent some $214 billion in the U.S. on advertising in 1999—some 2.4 percent of the GDP—and almost all of this money ended up in the hands of some media firm. Though journalists and civics teachers bristle at the notion, those media that depend upon advertising for the lion's share of their income—radio, TV, newspapers, magazines—are, in effect, part of the advertising industry. Throughout the 1990s the media giants used their market power to pummel their customers with ads and to bend over backward to make their media attractive to Madison Avenue. By 1999 the four major TV networks, for example, were providing nearly sixteen minutes per hour of commercials during prime time, an enormous increase from just a decade earlier. A conglomerate like Time Warner was able to sign a $200 million advertising deal with General Motors that "crosses most of the entertainment company's divisions," so that "GM will have a first-look option on all automobile marketing opportunities within Warner Bros. operations." Not content with traditional advertising, media firms are now working on "virtual ads," whereby "a marketer's product can be seamlessly inserted into live or taped broadcasts." With ads so inserted during actual programs, viewers will be unable to avoid the commercials through zapping. Advertising has also been plugged into new venues, such as video games. But this does not capture the full spread of commercialism. In television, for example, the new growth area for revenues is selling merchandise that is shown on its programs. It barely caused a ripple when Tommy Hilfiger hired the Viacom-owned cable channel VH1, rather than an ad agency, to produce a series of TV ads, because VH1 is so effective at selling. In sum, the entire U.S. media experience increasingly resembles an infomercial.

Nowhere is the commercial marination of the American mind more apparent than in the case of children, where the advertising assault was increased exponentially in the 1990s. There are now four full-time cable channels (owned by the four largest U.S. media firms) bombarding children with commercial programming twenty-four hours per day. Advertisers have targeted the youth market as arguably the most important in the nation. Girls between the ages of seven and fourteen spend some $24 billion per year and influence parental decisions worth another $66 billion. Commercial indoctrination of children is crucial to corporate America. One study revealed that when eight-year-olds were shown two pictures of identical shoes, one with the Nike logo and the other with the Kmart logo, they liked both equally. The response of twelve-year-olds was "Kmart, are you kidding me?" This desire to indoctrinate fuels the commercial drive into education and suggests that the moral foundation for coming generations may be resting on a dubious base. Nobody knows what the exact consequence of this commercial blitzkrieg upon children will be, but the range of debate extends from "pretty bad" to "absolutely terrible." The only thing we know for certain is that the media giants and advertisers who prosper from it do not care and cannot care. It is outside their frame of reference.

In this light, it is worth considering the status of the long-standing conflict between "church and state" in media; this refers to the ability of journalists and creative workers to conduct their affairs without having output determined by what serves the immediate interests of advertisers, or owners for that matter. In conventional wisdom, the U.S. media system has been at its best when the divider between "church and state"—especially though not exclusively in journalism—has been pronounced and respected. That way media users can regard the articles and news and entertainment programs they read, see, and hear in the media as reflecting the best judgment of media workers, not the surreptitious bribe of a commercial interest. Nowhere has the collapse of editorial integrity been more pronounced than in magazine publishing. As the late Alexander Liberman, legendary editorial director of Condé Nast, noted in 1999, advertisers "have too much power. They determine, if not specifically, then generally what magazines are now." A series of scandals in the late 1990s affirmed what has been suspected: Advertisers have tremendous control over the editorial copy in U.S. magazines, and editors who are discomfited by this had best find employment elsewhere. "They're glitz bags," Norman Mailer said of magazines in 1999. "They are so obviously driven by the ads that the ads take prominence over the stories."

Hollywood films have so thoroughly embraced commercial values that *Variety* now writes of the "burgeoning subfield of Product Placement Cinema." Conglomerate control of films and music and television (all of the TV networks, all of the main studios but the floundering MGM, and all four of the firms that dominate the U.S. music scene are owned by the eight largest media firms) has opened the floodgates to commercialism and has proven deadly for creativity. "A movie studio is part of this huge corporate cocoon," Peter Bart, editor of *Variety* and former head of Paramount, writes, "and therefore, theoretically, a studio should be willing to take bigger risks because one bad movie . . . won't erode the value of the [parent company's] shares. But the way it works out, the studios are if anything more risk averse. They are desperate to hedge their bets. It's the nature of bureaucratic self-protection. . . . The pressure is reflected in the sort of movies that get made . . . the sort of pablum that studios chewed on for ten years, that's gone through endless rewrites, has been pretested by endless focus groups, and is successful—if insipid." Or as an executive at Time Warner's "independent" studio New Line Pictures puts it, "We're very marketing-driven as a company. I'm instructed not to greenlight a project if I can't articulate how to sell it." As Bart concludes, this is "not exactly a recipe for art."

This said, we are not attempting to make a blanket indictment of everything produced by the corporate media system. We are not suggesting that every article or broadcast segment is foul, nor that they are all tainted, nor even that some material that is tainted cannot also be good. There are extremely talented people employed in the commercial media system, and the pressure to satisfy audiences does indeed sometimes promote excellent fare. But corporate and commercial pressures greatly undermine the overall quality of the system and skew it in ways that are not at all the result of audience demand. In the world of corporate media, the key is to attract the preferred target audience while spending as little money as possible. In the battle for consumer attention, this strongly promotes a rehashing of tried-and-true formulae, as well as the use of sex, violence, and what is termed "shock" or "gross-out" fare. In a world where people are surrounded by innumerable media options (albeit owned by numerable firms), sex and violence are proven attention getters.

Corporate control and hypercommercialism are having what may be their most devastating effects in the real of journalism. There is no need to romanticize the nature of U.S. professional journalism from the middle of the century into the 1980s; in many respects it was deeply flawed. Yet whatever autonomy and integrity journalism enjoyed during that time of Bob Woodward, Carl Bernstein, and *Lou Grant* is now under sustained and unyielding attack by corporate owners in the hunt for profit. No more striking evidence for this exists than the results of a 1999 Pew Research Center poll of journalists concerning their profession. Until the 1990s, journalists tended to be stalwart defenders of the media system, and most scholarship emphasized journalists' hypersensitivity to criticism of their field. No more. The Pew poll found that "at both the local and national level, majorities of working journalists say the increased bottom-line pressure is hurting the quality of coverage." "This past year," David Halberstam wrote in 1999, "has been, I think, the worst year for American journalism since I entered the profession forty-four years ago." Bob Woodward, the Watergate investigator who has enjoyed one of the most successful and prestigious media careers of the era, says that in these days of hypercommercialism and

hypercompetition, "No one is the keeper of the conscience of journalism."

The brave new world of corporate journalism manifests itself in many ways. The primary effects of tightened corporate control are a serious reduction in staff, combined with pressure to do vastly less expensive and less controversial lifestyle and feature stories. Where there is "news," it often takes the form of canned crime reports that foster unrealistic and unnecessary fears. This is the magic elixir for the bottom line. Sometimes the new world of corporate journalism is typified by blatant corporate censorship of stories that might hurt the image of the media owner. But the maniacal media baron as portrayed in James Bond films or profiles of Rupert Murdoch is far less a danger than the cautious and compromised editor who seeks to "balance" a responsibility to readers or viewers with a duty to serve his boss and the advertisers. In media today, even among journalists who entered the field for the noblest of reasons, there is an internalized bias to simply shy away from controversial journalism that might enmesh a media firm in a battle with powerful corporations or government agencies. True, such conflicts have always been the stuff of great journalism, but they can make for very bad business, and in the current climate business trumps journalism just about every time.

The most common and noticeable effect of the corporate noose on journalism is that it simply allows commercial values to redirect journalism to its most profitable position. So it is that relatively vast resources are deployed for news pitched at a narrow business class, and suited to their needs and prejudices; it is predominant in newspapers, magazines, and television. Likewise, news for the masses increasingly consists of stories about celebrities, royal families, athletes, natural disasters, plane crashes, and train wrecks. Political coverage is limited to regurgitating what some politician says, and "good" journalism is practiced when a politician from the other side of the aisle is given a chance to respond. But that is not journalism; it is stenography. Perhaps the strongest indictment of corporate journalism is that the preponderance of it would be compatible with an authoritarian political regime. So it is that China has few qualms about letting most commercial news from the U.S. inside its borders; it can see that this low caliber of journalism is hardly a threat to its rule. It is the BBC, with its regrettable penchant for covering politics seriously, that draws the commissar's ire.

There is also intense pressure for journalism to contribute immediately and directly to the bottom line. One Tennessee TV station received adverse publicity for offering to do TV news "puff pieces" on local businesses in exchange for $15,000 payments. It is important to note, however, that the mistake made by that Tennessee station was not the spirit of the offer—it well reflects the pattern across the news media—but, rather, the baldness of it. Firms also use the news to hype their other programming, as in 1996 when NBC *Nightly News* made the Summer Olympics its most covered news story that year, even though none of the other networks had the Olympics ranked on their top-ten lists. Why? Because NBC was airing the Olympics that summer—and reaping the attendant financial rewards. The fall of 1999 saw a huge debate erupt in newspaper circles after the *Los Angeles Times* devoted the entire editorial space in an edition of its 164-page Sunday magazine to articles, photos and graphics describing downtown Los Angeles' new Staples Center sports arena. The newspaper did not reveal at the time of the magazine's publication, however, that it would be dividing the $2 million in revenues generated by the section with the owners of the arena. So dark was the scenario that the former publisher of the *L.A. Times,* Otis Chandler, sent a letter to the staff describing the new management's move as "unbelievably stupid and unprofessional."

Above all, however, the *L.A. Times* was blatant. It allowed the corrupting linkage between advertisers and the media to be clearly identified. More often than not, a measure of subtlety keeps controversies under wraps.

In addition to triviality and craven commercialism, the willingness or capacity of U.S. journalism to challenge elite assumptions or to question the status quo—never especially great in the best of times—has shriveled. So it was, for example, that the preponderance of media coverage of the 1999 war in Kosovo lamely reflected elite opinion in the U.S., when even the rudimentary application of traditional journalism standards would point to severe discrepancies in the official story line.

All told, this creates a crisis for democracy. Alexis de Tocqueville rightly celebrated the role that a free and diverse media plays not only in greasing the wheels of electoral systems but in maintaining the very structures of civil society. The nineteenth-century surveyor of the American public landscape went so far as to say of news organizations, "They maintain civilization." Who would seriously attempt to make such a statement about today's media?

•　　•　　•

What is necessary, in the end, is for media reform to be advanced as part of a progressive platform for democratic reform across society. The foundation of a broader progressive platform will be the demand for social justice and an attack upon social inequality and the moral stench of a society operated purely along commercial lines. In the U.S. today, the richest one percent of the population has as much money to spend as the poorest 100 million Americans, double the ratio for just twenty years earlier. The political system reinforces this inequality by being, as is now roundly acknowledged, a plaything for big business where the interests of the balance of society have been pushed to the margins if not forgotten. The corporate media system reinforces this inequality and rule of the market and limits the possibility of democratic reform. In sum, media reform is inexorably intertwined with broader democratic reform; they rise and fall together.

Hence we return to the point that emerged forcefully in the analysis of media reform around the world: the importance of political parties to provide necessary leadership and to force the issue into the political arena. In the U.S., both the Republican and Democratic Parties, with only a few prominent exceptions, have been and are in the pay of the corporate media and communication giants. It is unlikely that any breakthroughs can be expected there until much spadework is done. The logical place to begin that spadework ought to be the small parties and factions of the left in America, the New

Party, the Greens, the Labor Party, Democratic Socialists of America, Americans for Democratic Action, and U.S. Action. In our view, all of these groups need to incorporate media reform issues into their platforms and their visions. Ideally, these organizations, which have remarkably similar stances on a host of issues, might adopt a shared vision—perhaps as a step toward building the sort of labor, left, green, feminist, people of color coalitions seen in New Zealand's Alliance Party, Iceland's Alliance, and other Third Left groupings. In Wisconsin, already, the Greens and New Party activists are working together on joint projects. In Washington, D.C., the Greens have merged with the D.C. Statehood Party.

Sadly, however, these new left parties have dropped the ball concerning media so far, with only one or two exceptions. As U.S. Rep. Bernie Sanders, the Vermont independent who is the only socialist member of the U.S. House of Representatives, and who has made media reform a central issue for over a decade has noted: "This is an issue that is absolutely vital to democracy, and that only the left can address. The New Party, the Green Party, the Labor Party, progressive Democrats should be all over this issue. But, for most of the left, it's not even on the agenda." This has to change, and change soon, both for the sake of media reform and for the sake of these parties and progressive politics in the United States. It is difficult for us to imagine a better place to build trust and cooperation across these left groupings than with a shared response to media, which has been so devastatingly dismissive of third-party initiatives, save those of billionaire hot dogs Ross Perot and Donald Trump.

Who would contribute to the shaping of a progressive media reform platform. Ideally, it would be shaped as similar platforms in Sweden, Finland, Canada, and other lands have been. Local and national groups working on media reform would participate. There would also be significant input from media unions, such as the Newspaper Guild, the National Writers Union, and the American Federation of Television and Radio Artists. We believe these groups could get the ball rolling by coming together in support of a set of basic principles not unlike those advanced by Britain's Campaign for Press and Broadcast Freedom.

There is every reason to believe that these groups could ultimately agree on an agenda that calls for basic reforms, such as:

- Expansion of funding for traditional public-service broadcasting with an eye toward making it fully noncommercial and democratically accountable. In particular, substantial new funding should be provided for the development of news and public affairs programming that will fill the gap created by the collapse of serious newsgathering by the networks and their local affiliates.

- Development of noncommercial, community-run, public-access television and radio systems that are distinct from public-service broadcasting and that are deeply rooted in local communities. As part of this initiative, the federal government should remove barriers to the development of microradio initiatives. Seed money, similar to that provided by government and foundations for economic development in low-income and minority communities, should be targeted toward groups seeking to develop microradio.

- Setting far stricter standards for commercial broadcasters in exchange for granting them broadcast licenses. For example, why not ban or strictly limit advertising on childrens' programs and on news broadcasts? Why not take a percentage of the broadcasters' revenues and set it aside for creative people and journalists to control time set aside for children's shows and newscasts? Why not make a condition of receiving a broadcast license that the broadcaster will not carry any paid political advertising during electoral campaigns? And that they will provide free time to all, liberally defined, viable candidates?

- Creation of a broad initiative to limit advertising in general, using regulation and taxation to prevent commercial saturation.

- Reassertion of anti-trust protections in order to limit the amount of media that can be owned by one firm. Why not, for example, limit radio stations to one per owner? The benefits of concentrated ownership accrue entirely to owners, not to the public. Make it government policy to encourage diversity of ownership and diversity of editorial opinions, as was intended by the First Amendment. There should, as well, be a reassertion of traditional restrictions on cross-ownership of media within particular communities.
- Renewing the commitment of the U.S. government to develop incentives aimed at encouraging and protecting minority ownership of broadcast and cable outlets.
- Promotion of newspaper and magazine competition through the use of tax deductions or subsidies. One approach might allow taxpayers to deduct the cost of a limited number of newspaper and magazine subscriptions—as some professionals and academics now do. Such an initiative would boost the circulations of publications from across the ideological spectrum, but would be particularly helpful to publications that target low-income, working-class, and elderly citizens, as well as students. Significantly lowered postal fees for nonprofit publications that have minimal advertising might also be appropriate.
- Strengthen the position of media unions by encouraging the development of a stronger role for workers in determining the editorial content of news publications and broadcast news. As in European countries, union protections in the U.S. should be strengthened in order to assure that working journalists are free to perform their duties with an eye toward serving the public interest.
- Develop a new national program of subsidies for film and cultural production, particularly by members of ethnic and racial minority groups, women, low-income citizens, and others who frequently have a hard time finding market support for their artistic expressions.
- Use tax breaks and subsidies to promote creation of publishing and production cooperatives and other arts and culture vehicles designed to provide noncommercial outlets for writers and artists to bring meaningful, controversial, and substantive work to mass audiences. One proposal put forth by economist Dean Baker would let any American redirect $150 from their tax payments to any nonprofit medium of their choice. This could funnel as much as $25 billion into nonprofit media and create a very healthy competition among new and revitalized outlets for democratic and cultural expression. All this could be done without any government official gumming up the works.

In combination, these proposals would go a long way toward creating a strong democratic sector on the rapidly commercializing Internet, as every medium today has a web component almost by definition. By the same token, media reformers must demand that there be formal hearings and public deliberations on the future of digital communication systems. At present the crucial technical decisions are being made quietly behind closed doors to the benefit of the corporate community. That has to be stopped.

·       ·       ·

We believe that a media reform movement with clear goals and a clear strategy for achieving them will be a fundamental building block of a broad crusade for democratic renewal in America—a bold, powerful and ultimately successful initiative that has the potential to make this nation's promise for democracy real. It will be a movement that takes an issue too long neglected and pushes that concern to the center of the national debate. It will be a movement that gives us an answer to the powers-that-be who seek constantly to divert us from issues of consequence. It will be a movement that empowers us to respond to their distractions and deceits by laughing in their faces and saying: "It's the media, stupid."

## DISCUSSION QUESTIONS

1. Identify and reflect on McChesney and Nichols's three criteria of participatory self-government.
2. In what ways do the consolidation of corporate control over the media and growing media commercialism represent a threat both to democracy and to journalism?
3. Identify the key elements of McChesney and Nichols's progressive media reform agenda. How might support for this agenda be built?

# 14 W. Lance Bennett

# NEWS CONTENT AND ILLUSION: FOUR INFORMATION BIASES THAT MATTER

*Debates about the quality of news coverage in the United States often revolve around assertions that the mass media are either too liberal or too conservative, depending on the politics of the critic. In this article, taken from his popular book* News: The Politics of Illusion, *political scientist W. Lance Bennett argues that this liberal versus conservative controversy about journalistic bias is a "dead-end debate." Rather than focusing on the ideological slant of the news, Bennett asks us to consider "universal information problems", that lead journalists to frame stories in such a way that familiar political narratives come to replace hard-hitting investigative coverage. These "information biases" transcend ideology, debasing the quality of public information while contributing to the transformation of news into a "mass-produced consumer product." The four characteristics of the news include personalization, dramatization, fragmentation, and the authority-disorder bias. They developed as an outgrowth of the connection between evolving communications technologies and the profit motive that drives the corporate media. Taken together, while these four traits heighten the dramatic tension of news reports, they also feed the public's disenchantment with the news, accentuating already rampant public cynicism and furthering the distance between citizens and their leaders. Ultimately, Bennett contends, democracy is weakened by the way news stories are presented—the information biases inherent in the dominant news format—regardless of any ideological tilt that may or may not actually exist. Coupled with the forgoing analysis of McChesney and Nichols, the troubling issue we are left to ponder is whether our cherished notion of the "free press" retains any semblance of reality in the twenty-first century.*

It is a writer's obligation to impose narrative. Everyone does this. Every time you take a lump of material and turn it into something you are imposing a narrative. It's a writer's obligation to do this. And, by the same token, it is apparently a journalist's obligation to

*Source:* W. Lance Bennett, *News: The Politics of Illusion,* 5th edition. New York: Longman, 2003, pp. 41–50 and 75–76.

pretend that he never does anything of the sort. The journalist claims to believe that the narrative emerges from the lump of material, rises up and smacks you in the face like marsh gas.

—Nora Ephron

When George W. Bush announced his presidential candidacy a breathtaking seventeen months before the 2000 presidential election, he did so on a movie-set stage in Iowa, surrounded by bales of hay and a shiny red forklift behind him. The day's news coverage anointed him the front-runner. As if to prove their point, reporters noted that Bush attracted by far the greatest press entourage, even though three other prominent candidates were also campaigning in the state that day. Mr. Bush wittily acknowledged that news organizations have choices about where they assign reporters, as he took the microphone on his campaign plane shortly after it took off for Iowa that morning. He quipped to the crowd of reporters on board: "Thanks for coming. We know you have a choice of candidates when you fly, and we appreciate you choosing Great Expectations." Great Expectations was the nickname he gave the plane as part of a larger spin effort to defuse the typical pattern of news building up expectations about candidates only to dramatize their next fall. Mr. Bush again played flight attendant when he asked the reporters to "Please stow your expectations securely in your overhead bins, as they may shift during the trip and can fall and hurt someone—especially me."

This campaign 2000 story was written more in an entertainment format than as a means to deliver serious political information; it was personality-centered, well-scripted, and set as a comedy scene in which Mr. Bush played a flight attendant doing the pre-takeoff announcement. The story was also artificial in the sense of being disconnected from larger questions about the race, the issues, or Mr. Bush's qualifications for being president. Most importantly, there was no clear basis on which the Washington press had decreed him the front-runner. True, the ability to deliver clever lines may be some qualification for being president, but the readers of the news story would be unable to know if Mr. Bush uttered that monologue spontaneously or if it was scripted as

part his advisors' communication strategy to win over a skeptical press pack. Perhaps, in the mediated reality of contemporary politics, the distinction between an innate ability to think on one's feet and learning to deliver a scripted performance no longer matters.

A closer look at this front-runner story and the campaign news that surrounded it reveals one tangible political condition mentioned in passing that might explain why journalists granted Mr. Bush the early lead: money. Mr. Bush had already set a record for early campaign fund-raising. Raising the largest amount of money makes a candidate front-runner in the eyes of political insiders, as well as in the story lines of the prominent national journalists who cover politics from the perspectives of insiders. Pegging the political fortunes of candidates to the sizes of their war chests is not an idle measure of potential electoral success. It is money, after all, that indicates the strength of business and interest group belief that a candidate will support their political goals. And it takes money to bring a candidate's political messages to voters who are more expensive to reach than ever before. Yet one of the reasons that people are hard to reach is that they tend not to trust politicians or the journalists who cover them. And one of the reasons that people mistrust the political establishment is money. Both polls and public interest groups often identify money as one of the ills of politics.

The insider view that politics is bitter, partisan, personalized, manipulative and money-driven may be a defensible perspective (it is the inside view, after all), but this does not make it the only choice that news organizations have about how to cover government. This is not to argue that topics such as money should be ignored in campaign coverage. To the contrary, the question is how news organizations decide to play those topics in their stories.

Consider the choices that news organizations have in how to frame a campaign story in which money is a potential plot element. *Framing involves choosing a broad organizing theme for selecting, emphasizing, and linking the elements of a story such as the scenes, the characters, their actions, and supporting documentation.* For example the framing of the previous story might have been shifted from the *horse race* to the *money chase,* with a serious investigation of the interests to which Mr. Bush and the other candidates might be indebted. Yet the above story and hundreds more that followed it throughout the campaign told the tale of the horse race one more time. In the horse race plot, money is generally left poorly developed in the background, requiring us to decode the reasons why George W. Bush may be the leading candidate. Also typical of many political stories, this dramatized news fragment was implicitly negative. Money has become a code for what ails our public life, a disruptive or disordering principle in the democratic order of things.

The opening of the Bush presidential campaign thus displayed the information biases of many political news stories: (1) it was personality oriented, (2) with dramatic staging and scripting, (3) that left it fragmented or disconnected from underlying political issues and realities (such as Mr. Bush's issue positions or other qualifications for being named the leading candidate), and (4) its implicit message (about money in this case) is typically negative, suggesting threats to the normal order of things. The result is that while people may tune in to news for its entertainment value, they also find reason in many stories to doubt or dismiss politics in general.

This communication system appears to contribute to a public that is increasingly cynical and disillusioned with politics and government. The paradox is that journalists complain about the over-scripted campaigns, and, more generally, the staged events they cover, but they seem unable to find other ways to write stories or to replace the cynical tone with perspectives that might help citizens become more engaged. As a result of these and other factors, large numbers of people actively avoid politics, while watching the media spectacle with a mixture of disbelief and disapproval. Meanwhile more people escape from public affairs and political participation into ever more personalized media worlds that one observer has likened to the gated communities and suburban enclaves into which many people have physically migrated in society.

Let's move from the opening story of the 2000 election to the dramatic conclusion. To make a long story short, the *Bush as front-runner* story (with minor variations) swept through the news media for

a time until it was replaced by other campaign *horse race* dramas, often with Mr. Gore as front-runner, each creating an episode to advance a long running story that must (if we are to call it news) continue to develop. Thus Mr. Bush and Democratic front-runner Al Gore jockeyed through the primaries, walked through heavily-scripted conventions, see-sawed through the debates, and finally headed to the finish line in one of the closest contests in American history. In an unexpected twist, the story was jarred from its predictable ending (an election night winner) because the electoral vote count was so close that it did not decide the result. The dispute over a handful of votes in Florida was eventually ended by a Supreme Court ruling that left many on both sides angry at the process that determined the result.

Did this photo finish in the presidential horse race of 2000 draw a large crowd of excited spectators? Hardly. The voter turnout reached a new modern era low beneath 50 percent. Continuous weekly polling of voters by *The Vanishing Voter,* a Harvard project led by Thomas Patterson and Marvin Kalb, revealed that a majority of voters did not become interested in the election until after it was over and the dispute in Florida broke out.

The point here is not to place the blame for civic disengagement on the news media. Journalists complained throughout the campaign that they had little to work with. How much more could they say about Al Gore's woodenness or George Bush's feeble grasp of foreign policy? Yet this begs the question: Why were journalists acting like movie critics giving barely passing reviews to all those poorly-scripted and repetitively-acted political performances? Why was there so little innovative coverage that might stimulate citizen engagement with the election either on the level of the candidates (for example, the political and economic interests that they represented) or on the level of stirring involvement beyond the momentary act of voting in the most important democratic ritual in the civic culture?

It is remarkable that the leading news organizations not only converged in their horse race and campaign strategy coverage, but they stuck with those narrative choices in the face of clear voter disinterest. Even in the final weeks of the contest, stories with standardized dramatized framings such as the *horse race,* the *war room,* and other military metaphors out-numbered stories on all the issues in the race, combined, by a wide margin. For example, a study of *The Washington Post* and *The New York Times* in the final two weeks of the campaign showed that dramatized framings of the race or the strategic conflict outnumbered all policy issue stories by a margin of 69 to 45 in the *Post,* while the *Times'* melodrama-to-issue gap was even greater at 93 to 63. *Consider the possibility that the choices of such narrative framings of politics contain information biases that are far more serious and at the same time more difficult for the average person to detect than ideological biases.*

## A DIFFERENT KIND OF BIAS

This [article] takes a close look at news content. The concern is with information biases that make news hard to use as a guide to citizen action because they obscure the big picture in which daily events take place, and, in addition, they often convey a negative or cynical tone about politics that undermines citizen motivation for digging deeper to learn more or to become engaged. . . . Most debates about journalistic bias are concerned with the question of ideology. For example, does the news have a liberal or conservative, a Democratic or Republican, drift? To briefly review the argument, some variations in news content or political emphasis may occur, but they can seldom be explained as the result of journalists routinely injecting their partisan views into the news. To the contrary, the avoidance of political partisanship by journalists is reinforced, among other means, by the professional ethics codes of journalists, by the editors who monitor their work, and by the business values of the companies they work for.

Another important point to recall is that people who see a consistent ideological press bias (that is, across most stories or over extended periods of time) are seeing it with the help of their own ideology. This generalization is supported by opinion research showing that people in the middle see the press as generally neutral, whereas those on the left complain that the news is too conservative, and those on the right think the news has a left-leaning bias. There are at least two ironies in this ongoing and inherently

unresolvable debate about ideological bias. First, even if neutrality or objectivity could be achieved, citizens with strong views on particular issues would not recognize it. Second, even if the news contained strong ideological or issue biases, people with a point of view (who are most likely to detect bias in the first place) would be well equipped to defend themselves against such biases. Indeed many nations favor a partisan press system as the best way to conduct public debates and to explore issues. . . .

So, many Americans are caught up in dead-end debates about a kind of news bias that is at once far less systematic and much less dangerous than commonly assumed. In the meantime, and this may be the greatest irony of all, these preoccupations with the politics of journalists detract attention from other information bias that really are worth worrying about. A more sensible approach to news bias is to look for those universal information problems that hinder the efforts of citizens, whatever their ideology, to take part in political life.

The task [of this article] is to understand the U.S. public information system at a deeper level than the endless debates over ideological bias. Fortunately most of the pieces to the news puzzle are right in front of us. For all of its defects, the news continues to be largely a public production, with government press offices, media organizations, and popular tastes all available for inspection. . . .

In turning to the workings of this system, it is important to understand that the news biases examined here have evolved over a long period of time. Their roots can be traced to the transition from a partisan to a commercial press in the 1800s. . . . It is thus helpful to think of the biases that we see at any point in time as historical products of the changing system of relations between people, press, and politicians. These relations continually shape and construct news and contribute to its evolving forms.

## FOUR INFORMATION BIASES THAT MATTER: AN OVERVIEW

Our expectations about the quality of public information are rather high. Most of us grew up with history books full of journalistic heroism exercised in the name of truth and free speech. We learned that the American Revolution was inspired by the political rhetoric of the underground press and by printers' effective opposition to the British Stamp Act. The lesson from the trial of Peter Zenger has endured through time: *the truth is not libelous.* The goal of the history book journalists was as unswerving as it was noble: to guarantee for the American people the most accurate, critical, coherent, illuminating, and independent reporting of political events. Yet Peter Zenger would probably not recognize, much less feel comfortable working in, a modern news organization.

Like it or not, the news has become a mass-produced consumer product, bearing little resemblance to history book images. Communication technologies, beginning with the wire services and progressing to satellite feeds and digital video, interact with corporate profit motives to create generic, "lowest-common-denominator" information formats. Those news story formulas often lack critical perspectives and coherent or useful organizing principles. . . . The illusions of coherence, diversity, and relevance have been achieved through packaging the news to suit the psychological tastes of different segments of the market audience. It is necessary to look beyond ideology and the packaging of our favorite news source in order to see the remarkable similarities that run through most mainstream news content. In particular, there are four characteristics of news that stand out as reasons why public information in the United States does not do as much as it could to advance the cause of democracy: *personalization, dramatization, fragmentation,* and the *authority-disorder bias.*

## PERSONALIZATION

If there is a single most important flaw in the American news style, it is the overwhelming tendency to downplay the big social, economic, or political picture in favor of the human trials, tragedies, and triumphs that sit at the surface of events. For example, instead of focusing on power and process, the media concentrate on the people engaged in political combat over the issues. The reasons for this are numerous, from the journalist's fear that probing

analysis will turn off audiences to the relative ease of telling the human-interest side of a story as opposed to explaining deeper causes and effects.

It is easy for the news audience to react for or against the actors in these personalized human-interest stories. When people are invited to take the news personally, they can find a wide range of private, emotional meanings in it, however, the meanings inspired by personalized news may not add up to the shared critical and analytical meanings on which a healthy democracy thrives. Personalized news encourages people to take an egocentric rather than a socially concerned view of political problems. The focus on personalities encourages a passive spectator attitude among the public. Moreover, the common media focus on flawed political personalities at the center of mistakes and scandals invites people to project their general anger and frustration at society or in their private lives onto the distant symbolic targets of politics. Either way, whether the focus is on sympathetic heroes and victims or hateful scoundrels and culprits, the media preference for personalized human-interest news creates a "can't-see-the-forest-for-the-trees" information bias that makes it difficult to see the big (institutional) picture that lies beyond the many actors crowding center stage who are caught in the eye of the news camera.

The tendency to personalize the news would be less worrisome if human-interest angles were used to hook audiences into more serious analysis of issues and problems. Almost all great literature and theater, from the Greek dramas to the modern day, use strong characters to promote audience identifications and reactions in order to draw people into thinking about larger moral and social issues. American news often stops at the character development stage, however, and leaves the larger lessons and social significance, if there is any, to the imagination of the audience. As a result, the main problem with personalized news is that the focus on personal concerns is seldom linked to more in-depth analysis. What often passes for analysis are opaque news formulas such as "he/she was a reflection of us," a line that was used in the media frenzies that followed the deaths of Britain's Princess Diana and America's John Kennedy, Jr.

Even when large portions of the public reject personalized news formulas, as in the case of the year-long journalistic preoccupation with whether President Clinton's personal sexual behavior undermined his leadership, the personalization never stops. This systematic tendency to personalize situations is one of the defining biases of news.

# DRAMATIZATION

Compounding the information bias of personalization is a second news property in which the aspects of events that are reported tend to be the ones most easily dramatized in simple "stories." As noted above, American journalism has settled overwhelmingly on the reporting form of stories or narratives, as contrasted, for example, to analytical essays, political polemics, or more scientific-style problem reports. Stories invite dramatization, particularly with sharply drawn actors at their center.

News dramas emphasize crisis over continuity, the present over the past or future, conflicts and relationship problems between the personalities at their center, and the impact of scandals on personal political careers. News dramas downplay complex policy information, the workings of government institutions, and the bases of power behind the central characters. Lost in the news drama (*melodrama* is often the more appropriate term) are sustained analyses of the persistent problems of our time, such as inequality, hunger, resource depletion, population pressures, environmental collapse, toxic waste, and political oppression. Serious though such human problems are, they just are not dramatic enough on a day-to-day level to make the news.

Important topics do come up, of course, such as when natural disasters strike, nuclear waste contaminates air or water supplies, or genocide breaks out in a distant land. Chronic conditions generally become news only when they reach astounding levels that threaten large-scale cataclysm through famine, depression, war, or revolution. But then the stories go away, again leaving the origins of and the solutions for those problems little-discussed in all but the biggest of stories. Most of these seemingly sudden "crises" are years in the making: deforestation that

worsens flooding, neglected nuclear dumps festering in the Arctic or in Washington State, or bandit governments in African nations undermining the hope for civil society. With a steady flow of information provided by experts and issue advocacy organizations, these stories could be kept in the news as reminders to publics and politicians that there may be more important things than the glitzy media event of the day or the routine political skirmishing in Washington.

Crises, not the slow buildups to them, are the perfect news material, meaning that they fit neatly into the dramatization bias. The "crisis cycle" portrayed in the news is classic dramatic fare, with rising action, falling action, sharply drawn characters, and, of course, plot resolutions. By its very definition, a crisis is something that will subside on its own or reach dramatic closure through clean-up efforts or humanitarian relief operations. Unfortunately the crisis cycles that characterize our news system only reinforce the popular impression that high levels of human difficulty are inevitable and therefore acceptable. Crises are resolved when situations return to "manageable" levels of difficulty. Seldom are underlying problems treated and eliminated at their source. The news is certainly not the cause of these problems, but it could become part of the solution if it substituted illumination of causes for dramatic coverage of symptoms.

As in the case of personalization, dramatization would not be a problem if it were used mainly as an attention-focusing device to introduce more background and context surrounding events. Drama can help us engage with the great forces of history, science, politics, or human relations. When drama is used to bring analysis into mind, it is a good thing. When drama is employed as a cheap emotional device to focus on human conflict and travail, or farce and frailty, the larger significance of events becomes easily lost in waves of immediate emotion. The potential advantages of drama to enlighten and explain are sacrificed to the lesser tendencies of melodrama to excite, anger, and further personalize events. Thus the news often resembles real-life soap operas, only with far more important consequences than the ones on entertainment TV.

One of the things that makes the news dramatic—indeed, that may even drive news drama—is the use of visuals: photos, graphics, and live-action video. These elements of stories not only make the distant world seem more real, they make the news more believable. In many ways, particularly for television, the pictures may not only tell the stories but help editors and reporters decide which stories to tell and how to tell them.

In principle, there is nothing wrong with the emphasis on sights in news production. In fact one might argue that thinking visually is the best way to engage the senses more fully in communicating about society and politics. Yet there is often a tension between not reporting important stories that are hard to picture and reporting possibly unimportant stories simply because they offer great visual images. . . . The economics of audience attention often shade editorial decisions in the direction of starting with the pictures and then adding the words.

It is important to worry about the bases of such editorial decisions because in many ways they distinguish between good and bad uses of news drama. When stories are selected more for visuals than for larger political significance and context, the scripting of the story may bend information rather badly to suggest that the pictures do, in fact, reflect the larger situation. And since there is more than a grain of truth to the old adage that "seeing is believing," people may be compelled to see aspects of society that simply are not there or that are not there in the ways they are dramatically portrayed in the news. The visually graphic coverage of crime on TV is an example of this. . . . At the very least, the selection of news stories primarily because they offer dramatic images is one of several important reasons why the news is often so fragmented or disconnected from larger political or economic contexts that would provide other ways to tell the story.

## FRAGMENTATION

The emphasis on personal and dramatic qualities of events feeds into a third information characteristic of the news: the isolation of stories from each other and from their larger contexts so that information in the news becomes fragmented and hard to assemble into a big picture. The fragmentation of information begins by emphasizing individual actors over the political contexts in which they operate. Fragmentation is then heightened by the use of dramatic formats that turn events into self-contained, isolated happenings. The fragmentation of information is further exaggerated by the severe space limits nearly all media impose for fear of boring readers and viewers with too much information.

Thus the news comes to us in sketchy dramatic capsules that make it difficult to see the causes of problems, their historical significance, or the connections across issues. It can even be difficult to follow the development of a particular issue over time as stories rise and fall more in response to the actions and reactions of prominent public figures than to independent reporting based on investigation of events. In addition, because it is difficult to bring historical background into the news, the impression is created of a world of chaotic events and crises that appear and disappear because the news picture offers little explanation of their origins.

## THE AUTHORITY-DISORDER BIAS

Passing for depth and coherence in this system of personalized, dramatized, and fragmented information is a fourth news tendency in which the authoritative voices of officials take center stage in many political news dramas to interpret the threatening and confusing events that threaten the order of social life. There is bias in placing so much news focus on the largely emotional questions of Who's in charge? and Will order be restored? (As opposed, for example, to What is the problem?, Why is it a problem?, What are the alternative explanations beyond the official ones?, and What can citizens do to make the situation better?)

It may be tempting to say that government, after all, is centrally about authority and order, so why shouldn't these concerns be central preoccupations of the news? The problem comes when journalists build themes about authority and order into the news as core dramatic emotional plot elements, rather than letting them pass through the news gates more formally when they arise in public debate, much the way partisan political views are generally reported. Instead, the focus on authority and order is often driven by considerations of what makes for bigger, more dramatic, more emotional stories.

Whether the world is returned to a safe, normal place, or the very idea of a normal world is called in question, the news is preoccupied with order, along with related questions of whether authorities are capable of establishing or restoring it. It is easy to see why these generic plot elements are so central to news: They are versatile and tireless themes that can be combined endlessly within personalized, dramatized, and fragmented news episodes. When the dramatic balance between order and disorder is not a plausible focus for an event, the news quickly turns the plot pair around and challenges authority itself, perhaps by publicizing the latest scandal charge against a leader or by opening the news gates to one politician willing to attack another.

In the past, it could be argued that the news more often resolved the authority-order balance in favor of official pronouncements aimed at "normalizing" conflicted situations by creating the appearance of order and control. A classic scenario of politics, according to political scientist Murray Edelman, is for authorities to take central stage to respond to crises (sometimes after having stirred them up in the first place) with emotionally reassuring promises that they will be handled effectively. Today's authorities still play out their parts, but the news increasingly finds ways to challenge either the pronouncements of officials or the presumption of order in society, or both. In short, the biggest change in portrayals of authority and order in the news . . . is that the dominant news focus has shifted away from trusted authorities providing reassuring promises to restore chaotic situations to a state of order or normalcy. Such stories continue to appear, of course, but the growing news trend is to portray unsympathetic, scheming politicians who often fail to solve problems, leaving disorder in their wake.

What is the evidence for the proposition that news is more negative and less likely to paint reassuring pictures of the return to normalcy following dramatic crises and scandals? . . . For reasons having

more to do with the news business than with external realities, the following changes have been charted in news content in recent years:

- increased levels of mayhem (crime, violence, accidents, health threats, freeway chases, and other images of social chaos)
- greater volume of criticism of government, politicians, and their policies, and less focus on the substance of policies
- higher journalistic tone of cynicism and negativity.

Many of these order-challenging news patterns are relatively subtle, reflecting the "hidden hand" of economic decisions within news organizations. For example, . . . the news recorded great increases in crime stories in the 1990s during a period in which officially reported rates of most violent crimes actually declined. This suggests that images of social disorder may be based on little more than choosing stories for their attention-getting effects. Images of disorder can be further amplified through subtle emphases in news writing. For example, is the traditional American family *threatened* by the increase in single-parent and two-working-parent households, or is the family in America simply *changing* in these ways as part of the normal course of social change?

The reason for thinking about authority and order as separable but related aspects of many news stories is that they are often set at odds with each other to create the dramatic tension in stories. Thus it would be too simple to say that authorities are almost always challenged and that disorder most often prevails. As news organizations take greater dramatic license with news plots, the two elements are mixed to achieve the greatest dramatic effect. A classic news plot represents authorities such as police, fire, and health officials as forces of good battling to restore order against social evils such as crime, violence, or disease. In one variation on this formula, crime or the latest health threat may seem to be running out of control, but officials appear in the news to tell us how we can be safe. Given the levels of mayhem and disorder in much of the news, the presence of at least some reassuring line of authority is a necessary dramatic counterpoint.

Moreover, the question of what actually happened in a particular incident is often unclear at the time that news teams arrive. So we encounter the familiar news formula that goes: "The police aren't exactly sure what happened here yet, but their investigation is in progress, and we expect a report soon."

When authorities are anchoring a scene, dramatic speculation about levels of disorder may soar in news scripts. A typical example comes from a local newscast in Orlando, Florida, where Channel 6 announced an "exclusive" and promised a report from their "live truck" at the scene. The newscast opened with the anchor describing "A shocking scene in a Lake Mary neighborhood tonight. A home surrounded by crime-scene tape. A death police are calling 'suspicious.'" As the anchor spoke, the screen flashed the words "Neighborhood Shocker." Cut to the reporter live from the scene who further dramatized the death of a sixty-six-year-old woman by saying that police did not know what happened. As if to document this claim, the reporter interviewed a police officer who said that there were no signs of violence, forced entry, or robbery. Although this statement could easily have supported either an order or a disorder plot for the story, the local news format clearly favored playing the murder mystery/shocker plot. The reporter announced that the police planned an autopsy the next day and did not know what they would find. The live feed ended with the reporter saying that, in the mean time, they "want to keep a very tight lid on what happened. ... Live in Lake Mary, Nicole Smith, Channel 6 News." The next day, it turned out that the woman had died naturally of a heart attack. So much for the "Neighborhood Shocker." As one observer noted, "Journalism Shocker" would have been a more appropriate on-screen warning.

By contrast, other dramatic plot formulas challenge authority either by focusing on alleged personal failings of politicians or by finding examples of government failures. The political poster story of the 1990s was about wasteful government spending. Many news organizations, both local and national, have run prominent features on "How government is wasting your tax dollars." The lure of such dramatic accounts over more representative news descriptions is illustrated in a *Los Angeles Times* investigative series on government spending on computers in different agencies. Even though the investigation turned up many positive examples of taxpayer dollars well spent, here is how the story opened:

WASHINGTON—After pumping $300 billion into computer systems in the last two decades, the federal government has compiled a record of failure that has jeopardized the nation's welfare, eroded public safety and squandered untold billions of dollars.

Whether or not most events fit the authority-disorder plot, it is easy enough to make them fit. A news show with a regular feature on government waste will, of course, find some alleged example of waste every time the feature is scheduled. Also, since there are few features on good things the government is doing, examples of government thrift (other than those forced by budget cuts) are less likely to be news.

•     •     •

Consider the picture so far: Each day news consumers are bombarded by dozens of compartmentalized, unrelated dramatic capsules. Some emotional satisfaction can be derived from forming strong identifications with or against the actors who star in these mini-dramas. But what about facts? What about knowledge and practical information? Unless the consumer has an existing interest or perspective on the subject, recalling facts from the news resembles a trivia game played alone. Most people cannot remember three-fourths of the stories in a TV news broadcast immediately after watching it, and information recall about the remembered quarter is sketchy at best.

Communication scholars have developed considerable empirical support for these four information biases in the news. There is now a sizable literature that reads like an inventory of these problems. The tendencies toward personalization, dramatization, and fragmentation have all been remarkably enduring over time, although they may have become more exaggerated with the economic pressures of the business. . . . While the focus on authority and order is also an enduring defining feature of the news, the shifting balance from order to mayhem and the unreflectively negative tone toward officials has left many observers puzzled and concerned. Indeed many politicians say they have left government because of the relentlessly negative media scrutiny, while others have surrounded themselves by legions of media consultants and handlers. At the same time that many journalists criticize their own product in these terms, they confess being helpless to change it under the current system of profit- and ratings-driven business values.

## DISCUSSION QUESTIONS

1. Identify and explain the four information biases that Bennett explores. How do these biases affect what we see and hear as news? Can you think of ways any recent news stories have been influenced by these four biases?
2. In what way(s) is the quality of democracy imperiled by the continued consumption of news framed by information biases? Do you think that citizens would feel a stronger attachment to the political world if the news they received delved more honestly, analytically, and historically into the problems we face as a society?

**15** *Norman Solomon*

# THE MILITARY-INDUSTRIAL-MEDIA COMPLEX

*In his 1961 farewell address President Dwight D. Eisenhower, a former general, warned of the influence of a growing "military-industrial complex." In this article, media critic Norman Solomon extends Eisenhower's concept to include the role of the corporate media in promoting militarism and a rosy colored view of U.S. military intervention. Corporate conglomerates that own the major media have close social and financial connections with the military and the foreign policy elite. Solomon contends that the major media, especially television, frame military conflicts from a pro-U.S. perspective that downplays the extent and significance of civilian casualties. Solomon provides examples from three major military actions: the Gulf War of 1991, the bombing of Serbia in 1999, and the invasion of Iraq in 2003. He finds that on-camera sources for television network newscasts were overwhelmingly pro-war in the Iraq case, with anti-war or opposition voices barely audible. Note that these trends involve all the major networks, including CNN, and not just on the openly right-wing Fox News Network.*

After eight years in the White House, Dwight Eisenhower delivered his farewell address on January 17, 1961. The former general warned of "an immense military establishment and a large arms industry." He added that "we must guard against the acquisition of unwarranted influence, whether sought or unsought, by the military-industrial complex."

One way or another, a military-industrial complex now extends to much of corporate media. In the process, firms with military ties routinely advertise in news outlets. Often, media magnates and people on the boards of large media-related corporations enjoy close links—financial and social—with the military industry and Washington's foreign-policy establishment.

Sometimes a media-owning corporation is itself a significant weapons merchant. In 1991, when my colleague Martin A. Lee and I looked into the stake that one major media-invested company had in the latest war, what we found was sobering: NBC's owner General Electric designed, manufactured or supplied parts or maintenance for nearly every major weapon system used by the U.S. during the Gulf War—including the Patriot and Tomahawk Cruise

*Source:* Norman Solomon, "The Military-Industrial Media Complex," *Extra!*, July–August 2005. Excerpted from Norman Solomon's book, *War Made Easy: How Presidents and Pundits Keep Spinning Us to Death,* Hoboken, NJ: John Wiley & Sons, 2005.

missiles, the Stealth bomber, the B-52 bomber, the AWACS plane, and the NAVSTAR spy satellite system. "In other words," we wrote in *Unreliable Sources*, "when correspondents and paid consultants on NBC television praised the performance of U.S. weapons, they were extolling equipment made by GE, the corporation that pays their salaries."

During just one year, 1989, General Electric had received close to $2 billion in military contracts related to systems that ended up being utilized for the Gulf War. Fifteen years later, the company still had a big stake in military spending. In 2004, when the Pentagon released its list of top military contractors for the latest fiscal year, General Electric ranked eighth with $2.8 billion in contracts.

Given the extent of shared sensibilities and financial synergies within what amounts to a huge military-industrial-media complex, it shouldn't be surprising that—whether in the prelude to the Gulf War of 1991 or the Iraq invasion of 2003—the U.S.'s biggest media institutions did little to illuminate how Washington and business interests had combined to strengthen and arm Saddam Hussein during many of his worst crimes.

"In the 1980s and afterward, the United States underwrote 24 American corporations so they could sell to Saddam Hussein weapons of mass destruction, which he used against Iran, at that time the prime Middle Eastern enemy of the United States," Ben Bagdikian wrote in *The New Media Monopoly,* the 2004 edition of his landmark book on the news business. "Hussein used U.S.-supplied poison gas" against Iranians and Kurds "while the United States looked the other way. This was the same Saddam Hussein who then, as in 2000, was a tyrant subjecting dissenters in his regime to unspeakable tortures and committing genocide against his Kurdish minorities." In corporate medialand, history could be supremely relevant when it focused on Hussein's torture and genocide, but the historic assistance he got from the U.S. government and American firms was apt to be off the subject and beside the point.

## SPINNING CIVILIAN DEATHS

By the time of the 1991 Gulf War, retired colonels, generals and admirals had become mainstays in network TV studios during wartime. Language such as "collateral damage" flowed effortlessly between journalists and military men, who shared perspectives on the occasionally mentioned and even more rarely seen civilians killed by U.S. firepower.

At the outset of the Gulf War, NBC's Tom Brokaw echoed the White House and a frequent chorus from U.S. journalists by telling viewers: "We must point out again and again that it is Saddam Hussein who put these innocents in harm's way." When those innocents got a mention, the U.S. government was often depicted as anxious to avoid hurting them. A couple of days into the war, Ted Koppel told ABC viewers that "great effort is taken, sometimes at great personal cost to American pilots, that civilian targets are not hit." Two weeks later, Brokaw was offering assurances that "the U.S. has fought this war at arm's length with long-range missiles, high-tech weapons . . . to keep casualties down."

With such nifty phrasing, no matter how many civilians might die as a result of American bombardment, the U.S. government—and by implication, its taxpayers—could always deny the slightest responsibility. And a frequent U.S. media message was that Saddam Hussein would use civilian casualties for propaganda purposes, as though that diminished the importance of those deaths. With the Gulf War in its fourth week, Bruce Morton of CBS provided this news analysis: "If Saddam Hussein can turn the world against the effort, convince the world that women and children are the targets of the air campaign, then he will have won a battle, his only one so far."

In American televisionland, when Iraqi civilians weren't being discounted or dismissed as Saddam's propaganda fodder, they were liable to be rendered nonpersons by omission. On the same day that 2,000 bombing runs occurred over Baghdad, anchor Ted Koppel reported: "Aside from the Scud missile that landed in Tel Aviv earlier, it's been a quiet night in the Middle East."

News coverage of the Gulf War in U.S. media was sufficiently laudatory to the war-makers in Washington that a former assistant secretary of state, Hodding Carter, remarked: "If I were the government, I'd be paying the press for the kind of coverage it is getting right now." A former media strategy ace for President Reagan put a finer point on the matter. "If you were going to hire a public relations firm to do the media relations for an international event," said Michael Deaver, "it couldn't be done any better than this is being done."

## "THROUGH THE SAME LENS"

When the media watch group FAIR conducted a survey of network news sources during the Gulf War's first two weeks, the most frequent repeat analyst was ABC's Anthony Cordesman. Not surprisingly, the former high-ranking official at the Defense Department and National Security Council gave the warmakers high marks for being trustworthy. "I think the Pentagon is giving it to you absolutely straight," Cordesman said.

The standard media coverage boosted the war. "Usually missing from the news was analysis from a perspective critical of U.S. policy," FAIR reported. "The media's rule of thumb seemed to be that to support the war was to be objective, while to be anti-war was to carry a bias." Eased along by that media rule of thumb was the sanitized language of Pentagonspeak as mediaspeak: "Again and again, the mantra of 'surgical strikes against military targets' was repeated by journalists, even though Pentagon briefers acknowledged that they were aiming at civilian roads, bridges and public utilities vital to the survival of the civilian population."

As the Gulf War came to an end, people watching CBS saw Dan Rather close an interview with the 1st Marine Division commander by shaking his hand and exclaiming: "Again, general, congratulations on a job wonderfully done!"

Chris Hedges covered the Gulf War for the *New York Times*. More than a decade later, he wrote in a book (*War Is a Force That Gives Us Meaning*): "The notion that the press was used in the war is incorrect. The press wanted to be used. It saw itself as part of the war effort." Truth-seeking independence was far from the media agenda. "The press was as eager to be of service to the state during the war as most everyone else. Such docility on the part of the press made it easier to do what governments do in wartime, indeed what governments do much of the time, and that is lie."

Variations in news coverage did not change the overwhelming sameness of outlook: "I boycotted the pool system, but my reports did not puncture the myth or question the grand crusade to free Kuwait. I allowed soldiers to grumble. I shed a little light on the lies spread to make the war look like a coalition, but I did not challenge in any real way the patriotism and jingoism that enthused the crowds back home. We all used the same phrases. We all looked at Iraq through the same lens."

## LEGITIMATING TARGETS

In late April 1999, with the bombing of Yugoslavia in its fifth week, many prominent American journalists gathered at a posh Manhattan hotel for the annual awards dinner of the prestigious Overseas Press Club. They heard a very complimentary speech by Richard Holbrooke, one of the key U.S. diplomats behind recent policies in the Balkans. "The kind of coverage we're seeing from the *New York Times,* the *Washington Post*, NBC, CBS, ABC, CNN and the newsmagazines lately on Kosovo," he told the assembled media professionals, "has been extraordinary and exemplary." Holbrooke had good reasons to praise the nation's leading journalists. That spring, when the Kosovo crisis exploded into a U.S.-led air war, news organizations functioned more like a fourth branch of government than a Fourth Estate. The pattern was familiar.

Instead of challenging Orwellian techniques, media outlets did much to foist them on the public. Journalists relied on official sources—with non-stop interviews, behind-the-scenes backgrounders, televised briefings and grainy bomb-site videos. Newspeak routinely sanitized NATO's bombardment of populated areas. Correspondents went through linguistic contortions that preserved favorite fictions of Washington policymakers.

"NATO began its second month of bombing against Yugoslavia today with new strikes against military targets that disrupted civilian electrical and water supplies . . ." The first words of the lead article on the *New York Times* front page the last Sunday in April 1999 accepted and propagated a remarkable concept, widely promoted by U.S. officials: The bombing disrupted "civilian" electricity and water, yet the targets were "military." Never mind that such destruction of infrastructure would predictably lead to outbreaks of disease and civilian deaths.

On the newspaper's op-ed page, columnist Thomas Friedman made explicit his enthusiasm for destroying civilian necessities: "It should be lights out in Belgrade: Every power grid, water pipe, bridge, road and war-related factory has to be targeted."

American TV networks didn't hesitate to show footage of U.S. bombers and missiles in flight—but rarely showed what really happened to people at the receiving end. Echoing Pentagon hype about the wondrous performances of Uncle Sam's weaponry, U.S. journalists did not often provide unflinching accounts of the results in human terms. Yet reporter Robert Fisk of London's *Independent* managed to do so:

> Deep inside the tangle of cement and plastic and iron, in what had once been the make-up room next to the broadcasting studio of Serb Television, was all that was left of a young woman, burnt alive when NATO's missile exploded in the radio control room. Within six hours, the [British] Secretary of State for International Development, Clare Short, declared the place a "legitimate target." It wasn't an argument worth debating with the wounded— one of them a young technician who could only be extracted from the hundreds of tons of concrete in which he was encased by amputating both his legs. ... By dusk last night, 10 crushed bodies—two of them women—had been tugged from beneath the concrete, another man had died in hospital and 15 other technicians and secretaries still lay buried.

In the spring of 1999, as usual, selected images and skewed facts on television made it easier for Americans to accept—or even applaud—the exploding bombs funded by their tax dollars and dropped in their names. "The citizens of the NATO alliance cannot see the Serbs that their aircraft have killed," the *Financial Times* noted. On American television,

the warfare appeared to be wondrous and fairly bloodless.

When the *New York Times'* Friedman reflected on the first dozen days of what he called NATO's "surgical bombing," he engaged in easy punditry. "Let's see what 12 weeks of less than surgical bombing does," he wrote.

> Sleek B-2 Stealth bombers and F-117A jets kept appearing in file footage on TV networks. Journalists talked with keen anticipation about Apache AH-64 attack helicopters on the way; military analysts told of the great things such aircraft could do. Reverence for the latest weaponry was acute.

## "WE GOT A BIG THUMBS-UP"

Mostly, the American television coverage of the Iraq invasion in spring 2003 was akin to scripted "reality TV," starting with careful screening of participants. CNN was so worried about staying within proper bounds that it cleared on-air talent with the Defense Department, as CNN executive Eason Jordan later acknowledged: "I went to the Pentagon myself several times before the war started and met with important people there and said, for instance— 'At CNN, here are the generals we're thinking of retaining to advise us on the air and off about the war'—and we got a big thumbs-up on all of them. That was important."

During the war that followed, the "embedding" of about 700 reporters in spring 2003 was hailed as a breakthrough. Those war correspondents stayed close to the troops invading Iraq, and news reports conveyed some vivid frontline visuals along with compelling personal immediacy. But with the context usually confined to the warriors' frame of reference, a kind of reciprocal bonding quickly set in. "I'm with the U.S. 7th Cavalry along the northern Kuwaiti border," said CNN's embedded Walter Rodgers during a typical report, using the word "we" to refer interchangeably to his network, the U.S. military or both:

> We are in what the army calls its attack position. We have not yet crossed into Iraq at this

point. At that point, we will tell you, when we do, of course, that we will cross the line of departure. What we are in is essentially a formation, much the way you would have seen with the U.S. Cavalry in the nineteenth-century American frontier. The Bradley tanks, the Bradley fighting vehicles are behind me. Beyond that perimeter, we've got dozens more Bradleys and M1A1 main battle tanks. . . .

With American troops moving into action, CNN's Aaron Brown emphasized that he and his colleagues "wish them nothing but safety." He did not express any such wish for the Iraqi people in harm's way.

## SELF-IMPOSED CONSTRAINTS

The launch of a war is always accompanied by tremendous media excitement, especially on television. A strong adrenaline rush pervades the coverage. Even formerly reserved journalists tend to embrace the spectacle providing a proud military narrative familiar to Americans, who have seen thousands of movies and TV shows conveying such storylines. War preparations may have proceeded amid public controversy, but White House strategists are keenly aware that a powerful wave of "support our troops" sentiment will kick in for news coverage as soon as the war starts. In media debate, from the outset of war, predictable imbalances boost pro-war sentiment.

This is not a matter of government censorship or even restrictions. Serving as bookends for U.S.-led wars in the 1990s, a pair of studies by FAIR marked the more narrow discourse once the U.S. military went on the attack. Whether the year was '91 or '99, whether the country under the U.S. warplanes was Iraq or Yugoslavia, major U.S. media outlets facilitated Washington's efforts to whip up support for the new war. The constraints on mainstream news organizations were, in customary fashion, largely self-imposed.

During the first two weeks of the Gulf War, voices of domestic opposition were all but excluded from the nightly news programs on TV networks. (The few strong denunciations of the war that made

it onto the air were usually from Iraqis.) In total, FAIR found, only 1.5 percent of the sources were identified as American anti-war demonstrators; out of 878 sources cited on the newscasts, just one was a leader of a U.S. peace organization.

Eight years later, the pattern was similar: In the spring of 1999, FAIR studied coverage during the first two weeks of the bombing of Yugoslavia and found "a strong imbalance toward supporters of NATO air strikes." Examining the transcripts of two influential TV programs, ABC's *Nightline* and the PBS *NewsHour with Jim Lehrer,* FAIR documented that only 8 percent of the 291 sources were critics of NATO's U.S.-led bombing. Forty-five percent of sources were current or former U.S. government and military officials, NATO representatives or NATO troops. On *Nightline,* the study found, no U.S. sources other than Serbian-Americans were given air time to voice opposition.

Summarizing FAIR's research over a 15-year period, sociologist Michael Dolny underscored the news media's chronic "over-reliance on official sources," and he also emphasized that "opponents of war are under-represented compared to the percentage of citizens opposed to military conflict."

## "WAVING THE FLAG"

Those patterns were on display in 2003 with the Iraq invasion, when FAIR conducted a study of the 1,617 on-camera sources who appeared on the evening newscasts of six U.S. television networks during the three weeks beginning with the start of the war:

Nearly two-thirds of all sources, 64 percent, were pro-war, while 71 percent of U.S. guests favored the war. Anti-war voices were 10 percent of all sources, but just 6 percent of non-Iraqi sources and only 3 percent of U.S. sources. Thus viewers were more than six times as likely to see a pro-war source as one who was anti-war; counting only U.S. guests, the ratio increases to 25 to 1.

Less than 1 percent of the U.S. sources were anti-war on the CBS *Evening News* during the Iraq war's first three weeks. Meanwhile, as FAIR's researchers commented wryly, public television's PBS *NewsHour* program hosted by Jim Lehrer "also had a relatively low percentage of U.S. anti-war voices—perhaps because the show less frequently features on-the-street interviews, to which critics of the war were usually relegated." During the invasion, the major network studios were virtually off-limits to vehement American opponents of the war.

For the most part, U.S. networks sanitized their war coverage, which was wall-to-wall on cable. As usual, the enthusiasm for war was extreme on Fox News Channel. After a pre-invasion make-over, the fashion was similar for MSNBC. (In a timely manner, that cable network had canceled the nightly *Donahue* program three weeks before the invasion began. A leaked in-house report—*AllYourTV.com,*—said

that Phil Donahue's show would present a "difficult public face for NBC in a time of war. . . . He seems to delight in presenting guests who are anti-war, anti-Bush and skeptical of the administration's motives." The danger, quickly averted, was that the show could become "a home for the liberal anti-war agenda at the same time that our competitors are waving the flag at every opportunity.")

At the other end of the narrow cable-news spectrum, CNN cranked up its own pro-war fervor. Those perspectives deserved to be heard. But on the large TV networks, such voices were so dominant that they amounted to a virtual monopoly in the "marketplace of ideas."

---

## DISCUSSION QUESTIONS

1. What similarities does Solomon see in the network coverage of the conflicts in the Gulf, Serbia, and Iraq?
2. In your view, what effect does the pattern of news coverage of foreign conflicts have on public opinion?

# 16 *Bill Moyers*

# *TAKE PUBLIC BROADCASTING BACK*

*Following the attacks of September 11, 2001, the Public Broadcasting Service (PBS) asked veteran broadcast journalist Bill Moyers to come up with a new weekly TV show that would air a wider range of voices and perspectives than commonly heard on either public or commercial television. The result was Moyers's popular PBS weekly news series NOW. In this article, Moyers recounts the story of the conservative attack against his show and, indeed, the attack on all of public broadcasting, with Moyers as public enemy #1. Delivered as the closing address before the National Conference on Media Reform in 2005, Moyers explains the rightwing assault on his show, a show which was designed to allow anti-establishment voices to offer their insights along with the more typical array of Democrats and Republicans. Moyers did not want the program to mimic what he saw as the "conventional rules of beltway journalism"—where Democratic and Republican power holders are allowed to frame debates as they see fit, with viewers left merely to conclude that the truth lies in between these two ends of the spectrum. He contends that in a healthy democracy, the media should allow for a broader array of perspectives, moving beyond the limits of conventional debate. The show was investigative. The show was hard-hitting. And the show's popularity angered some powerful public officials, private funders and the Chair of the Corporation for Public Broadcasting (CPB), Kenneth Tomlinson. Along with member stations, the CPB funds PBS, so Tomlinson's anger at Moyers led to an intense partisan battle and a level of intimidation that threatened the heart of public television. Moyers's story sheds light on the importance for democracy of a truly free and open media system. It also offers a warning about the forces that threaten the free flow of information and analysis in a world increasingly controlled by an amalgam of public and private interests hostile to the diversity of ideas. Without such diversity, orthodoxy "can kill a democracy."*

*Source:* Bill Moyers, "Take Public Broadcasting Back," Closing Address, National Conference on Media Reform, May 15, 2005.

I can't imagine better company on this beautiful Sunday morning in St. Louis. You're church for me today, and there's no congregation in the country where I would be more likely to find more kindred souls than are gathered here.

There are so many different vocations and callings in this room—so many different interests and aspirations of people who want to reform the media or produce for the media—that only a presiding bishop like Bob McChesney with his great ecumenical heart could bring us together for a weekend like this.

What joins us all under Bob's embracing welcome is our commitment to public media. Pat Aufderheide got it right, I think, in the recent issue of *In These Times* when she wrote: "This is a moment when public media outlets can make a powerful case for themselves. Public radio, public TV, cable access, public DBS channels, media arts centers, youth media projects, nonprofit Internet news services . . . low-power radio and webcasting are all part of a nearly-invisible feature of today's media map: the public media sector. They exist not to make a profit, not to push an ideology, not to serve customers, but to create a public—a group of people who can talk productively with those who don't share their views, and defend the interests of the people who have to live with the consequences of corporate and governmental power."

She gives examples of the possibilities. "Look at what happened," she said, "when thousands of people who watched Stanley Nelson's 'The Murder of Emmett Till' on their public television channels joined a postcard campaign that re-opened the murder case after more than half a century. Look at NPR's courageous coverage of the Iraq war, an expensive endeavor that wins no points from this Administration. Look at Chicago Access Network's Community Forum, where nonprofits throughout the region can showcase their issues and find volunteers."

For all our flaws, Pat argues that the public media are a very important resource in a noisy and polluted information environment.

You can also take wings reading Jason Miller's May 4th article on *ZNet* about the mainstream media. While it is true that much of it is corrupted by the influence of government and corporate interests, Miller writes, there are still men and women in the mainstream who practice a high degree of journalistic integrity and who do challenge us with their stories and analysis. But the real hope "lies within the internet with its two billion or more web sites providing a wealth of information drawn from almost unlimited resources that span the globe. . . . If knowledge is power, one's capacity to increase that power increases exponentially through navigation of the Internet for news and information."

Surely this is one issue that unites us as we leave here today. The fight to preserve the web from corporate gatekeepers joins media reformers, producers and educators—and it's a fight that has only just begun.

I want to tell you about another fight we're in today. The story I've come to share with you goes to the core of our belief that the quality of democracy and the quality of journalism are deeply entwined. I can tell this story because I've been living it. It's been in the news this week, including reports of more attacks on a single journalist—yours truly—by the right-wing media and their allies at the Corporation for Public Broadcasting.

As some of you know, CPB was established almost forty years ago to set broad policy for public broadcasting and to be a firewall between political influence and program content. What some on this board are now doing today, led by its chairman, Kenneth Tomlinson, is too important, too disturbing and yes, even too dangerous for a gathering like this not to address.

We're seeing unfold a contemporary example of the age-old ambition of power and ideology to squelch and punish journalists who tell the stories that make princes and priests uncomfortable.

Let me assure you that I take in stride attacks by the radical right-wingers who have not given up demonizing me although I retired over six months ago. They've been after me for years now and I suspect they will be stomping on my grave to make sure I don't come back from the dead. I should remind them, however, that one of our boys pulled it off some two thousand years ago—after the Pharisees, Sadducees and Caesar's surrogates thought they had shut him up for good. Of course I won't be expecting that kind of miracle, but I should put my detractors on notice: They might just compel me out of the rocking chair and back into the anchor chair.

Who are they? I mean the people obsessed with control, using the government to threaten and intimidate. I mean the people who are hollowing out middle-class security even as they enlist the sons and daughters of the working class in a war to make sure Ahmed Chalabi winds up controlling Iraq's oil. I mean the people who turn faith based initiatives into a slush fund and who encourage the pious to look heavenward and pray so as not to see the long arm of privilege and power picking their pockets. I mean the people who squelch free speech in an effort to obliterate dissent and consolidate their orthodoxy into the official view of reality from which any deviation becomes unpatriotic heresy.

That's who I mean. And if that's editorializing, so be it. A free press is one where it's okay to state the conclusion you're led to by the evidence.

One reason I'm in hot water is because my colleagues and I at *NOW* didn't play by the conventional rules of beltway journalism. Those rules divide the world into Democrats and Republicans, liberals and conservatives, and allow journalists to pretend they have done their job if, instead of reporting the truth behind the news, they merely give each side an opportunity to spin the news.

Jonathan Mermin writes about this in a recent essay in *World Policy Journal*. Mermin quotes David Ignatius of the *Washington Post* on why the deep interests of the American public are so poorly served by beltway journalism. The "rules of our game," says Ignatius, "make it hard for us to tee up an issue . . . without a news peg." He offers a case in point: the debacle of America's occupation of Iraq. "If Senator so and so hasn't criticized post-war planning for Iraq," says Ignatius, "then it's hard for a reporter to write a story about that."

Mermin also quotes public television's Jim Lehrer acknowledging that unless an official says something is so, it isn't news. Why were journalists not discussing the occupation of Iraq? Because, says Lehrer, "the word occupation . . . was never mentioned in the run-up to the war." Washington talked about the invasion as "a war of liberation, not a war of occupation, so as a consequence, "those of

us in journalism never even looked at the issue of occupation."

"In other words," says Jonathan Mermin, "if the government isn't talking about it, we don't report it." He concludes, "[Lehrer's] somewhat jarring declaration, one of many recent admissions by journalists that their reporting failed to prepare the public for the calamitous occupation that has followed the 'liberation' of Iraq, reveals just how far the actual practice of American journalism has deviated from the First Amendment ideal of a press that is independent of the government."

Take the example (also cited by Mermin) of Charles J. Hanley. Hanley is a Pulitzer Prize winning reporter for the Associated Press, whose fall 2003 story on the torture of Iraqis in American prisons— before a U.S. Army report and photographs documenting the abuse surfaced—was ignored by major American newspapers. Hanley attributes this lack of interest to the fact that "It was not an officially sanctioned story that begins with a handout from an official source." Furthermore, Iraqis recounting their own personal experience of Abu Ghraib simply did not have the credibility with beltway journalists of American officials denying that such things happened. Judith Miller of *The New York Times*, among others, relied on the credibility of official but unnamed sources when she served essentially as the government stenographer for claims that Iraq possessed weapons of mass destruction.

These "rules of the game" permit Washington officials to set the agenda for journalism, leaving the press all too often simply to recount what officials say instead of subjecting their words and deeds to critical scrutiny. Instead of acting as filters for readers and viewers, sifting the truth from the propaganda, reporters and anchors attentively transcribe both sides of the spin invariably failing to provide context, background or any sense of which claims hold up and which are misleading.

I decided long ago that this wasn't healthy for democracy. I came to see that "news is what people want to keep hidden and everything else is publicity." In my documentaries–whether on the Watergate scandals thirty years ago or the Iran Contra conspiracy twenty years ago or Bill Clinton's fund raising scandals ten years ago or, five years ago, the chemical industry's long and despicable cover up of its cynical and unspeakable withholding of critical data about its toxic products from its workers, I realized that investigative journalism could not be a collaboration between the journalist and the subject. Objectivity is not satisfied by two opposing people offering competing opinions, leaving the viewer to split the difference.

I came to believe that objective journalism means describing the object being reported on, including the little fibs and fantasies as well as the Big Lie of the people in power. In no way does this permit journalists to make accusations and allegations. It means, instead, making sure that your reporting and your conclusions can be nailed to the post with confirming evidence.

This is always hard to do, but it has never been harder than today. Without a trace of irony, the powers-that-be have appropriated the newspeak vernacular of George Orwell's *1984*. They give us a program vowing "No Child Left Behind" while cutting funds for educating disadvantaged kids. They give us legislation cheerily calling for "Clear Skies" and "Healthy Forests" that give us neither. And that's just for starters.

In Orwell's *1984,* the character Syme, one of the writers of that totalitarian society's dictionary, explains to the protagonist Winston, "Don't you see that the whole aim of Newspeak is to narrow the range of thought?" "Has it ever occurred to you, Winston, that by the year 2050, at the very latest, not a single human being will be alive who could understand such a conversation as we are having now? The whole climate of thought," he said, "will be different. In fact there will be no thought, as we understand it now. Orthodoxy means not thinking—not needing to think. Orthodoxy is unconsciousness."

An unconscious people, an indoctrinated people, a people fed only on partisan information and opinion that confirm their own bias, a people made morbidly obese in mind and spirit by the junk food of propaganda, is less inclined to put up a fight, to ask questions and be skeptical. That kind of orthodoxy can kill a democracy–or worse.

I learned about this the hard way. I grew up in the South where the truth about slavery, race, and segregation had been driven from the pulpits, driven from the classrooms and driven from the newsrooms. It took a bloody Civil War to bring the truth home and then it took another hundred years for the truth to make us free.

Then I served in the Johnson administration. Imbued with cold war orthodoxy and confident that "might makes right," we circled the wagons, listened only to each other, and pursued policies the evidence couldn't carry. The results were devastating for Vietnamese and Americans.

I brought all of this to the task when PBS asked me after 9/11 to start a new weekly broadcast. They wanted us to make it different from anything else on the air—commercial or public broadcasting. They asked us to tell stories no one else was reporting and to offer a venue to people who might not otherwise be heard. That wasn't a hard sell. I had been deeply impressed by studies published in leading peer-reviewed scholarly journals by a team of researchers led by Vassar College sociologist William Hoynes. Extensive research on the content of public television over a decade found that political discussions on our public affairs programs generally included a limited set of voices that offer a narrow range of perspectives on current issues and events. Instead of far-ranging discussions and debates, the kind that might engage viewers as citizens, not simply as audiences, this research found that public affairs programs on PBS stations were populated by the standard set of elite news sources. Whether government officials and Washington journalists (talking about political strategy) or corporate sources (talking about stock prices or the economy from the investor's viewpoint), public television, unfortunately, all too often was offering the same kind of discussions, and a similar brand of insider discourse, that is featured regularly on commercial television.

Who didn't appear was also revealing. Hoynes and his team found that in contrast to the conservative mantra that public television routinely featured the voices of anti-establishment critics, "alternative perspectives were rare on public television and were effectively drowned out by the stream of government and corporate views that represented the vast majority of sources on our broadcasts." The so-called 'experts' who got most of the face time came primarily from mainstream news organizations and Washington think tanks rather than diverse interests. Economic news, for example, was almost entirely refracted through the views of business people, investors and business journalists. Voices outside the corporate/Wall Street universe—nonprofessional workers, labor representatives, consumer advocates and the general public were rarely heard. In sum, these two studies concluded, the economic coverage was so narrow that the views and the activities of most citizens became irrelevant.

All this went against the Public Broadcasting Act of 1967 that created the Corporation for Public Broadcasting. I know. I was there. As a young policy assistant to President Johnson, I attended my first meeting to discuss the future of public broadcasting in 1964 in the office of the Commissioner of Education. I know firsthand that the Public Broadcasting Act was meant to provide an alternative to commercial television and to reflect the diversity of the American people.

This, too, was on my mind when we assembled the team for *NOW*. It was just after the terrorist attacks of 9/11. We agreed on two priorities. First, we wanted to do our part to keep the conversation of democracy going. That meant talking to a wide range of people across the spectrum—left, right and center. It meant poets, philosophers, politicians, scientists, sages and scribblers. It meant Isabel Allende, the novelist, and Amity Shlaes, the columnist for the *Financial Times*. It meant the former nun and best-selling author Karen Armstrong, and it meant the right-wing evangelical columnist, Cal Thomas. It meant Arundhati Roy from India, Doris Lessing from London, David Suzuki from Canada, and Bernard Henry-Levi from Paris. It also meant two successive editors of the *Wall Street Journal*, Robert Bartley and Paul Gigot, the editor of *The Economist*, Bill Emmott, the *Nation*'s Katrina vanden Heuvel and the *Los Angeles Weekly*'s John Powers. It means liberals like Frank Wu, Ossie Davis and Gregory Nava, and conservatives like Frank Gaffney, Grover Norquist, and Richard Viguerie. It meant Archbishop Desmond Tutu and Bishop Wilton Gregory of the Catholic Bishops conference in this country. It meant

the conservative Christian activist and lobbyist, Ralph Reed, and the dissident Catholic Sister Joan Chittister. We threw the conversation of democracy open to all comers. Most of those who came responded the same way that Ron Paul, Republican and Libertarian congressman from Texas did when he wrote me after his appearance, "I have received hundreds of positive e-mails from your viewers. I appreciate the format of your program which allows time for a full discussion of ideas . . . I'm tired of political shows featuring two guests shouting over each other and offering the same arguments . . . *NOW* was truly refreshing."

Hold your applause because that's not the point of the story.

We had a second priority. We intended to do strong, honest and accurate reporting, telling stories we knew people in high places wouldn't like.

I told our producers and correspondents that in our field reporting our job was to get as close as possible to the verifiable truth. This was all the more imperative in the aftermath of the terrorist attacks. America could be entering a long war against an elusive and stateless enemy with no definable measure of victory and no limit to its duration, cost or foreboding fear. The rise of a homeland security state meant government could justify extraordinary measures in exchange for protecting citizens against unnamed, even unproven, threats.

Furthermore, increased spending during a national emergency can produce a spectacle of corruption behind a smokescreen of secrecy. I reminded our team of the words of the news photographer in Tom Stoppard's play who said, "People do terrible things to each other, but it's worse when everyone is kept in the dark."

I also reminded them of how the correspondent and historian, Richard Reeves, answered a student who asked him to define real news. "Real news," Reeves responded, "is the news you and I need to keep our freedoms."

For these reasons and in that spirit we went about reporting on Washington as no one else in broadcasting—except occasionally *60 Minutes*—was doing. We reported on the expansion of the Justice Department's power of surveillance. We reported on the escalating Pentagon budget and expensive weapons that didn't work. We reported on how campaign contributions influenced legislation and policy to skew resources to the comfortable and well-connected while our troops were fighting in Afghanistan and Iraq with inadequate training and armor. We reported on how the Bush administration was shredding the Freedom of Information Act. We went around the country to report on how closed door, back room deals in Washington were costing ordinary workers and tax payers their livelihood and security. We reported on offshore tax havens that enable wealthy and powerful Americans to avoid their fair share of national security and the social contract.

And always—because what people know depends on who owns the press—we kept coming back to the media business itself—to how mega media corporations were pushing journalism further and further down the hierarchy of values, how giant radio cartels were silencing critics while shutting communities off from essential information, and how the mega media companies were lobbying the FCC for the right to grow ever more powerful.

The broadcast caught on. Our ratings grew every year. There was even a spell when we were the only public affairs broadcast on PBS whose audience was going up instead of down.

Our journalistic peers took notice. *The Los Angeles Times* said, "*NOW*'s team of reporters has regularly put the rest of the media to shame, pursuing stories few others bother to touch."

The *Philadelphia Inquirer* said our segments on the sciences, the arts, politics and the economy were "provocative public television at its best."

The *Austin American Statesman* called *NOW* "the perfect antidote to today's high pitched decibel level-a smart, calm, timely news program."

Frazier Moore of the Associated Press said we were "hard-edged when appropriate but never Hardball. Don't expect combat. Civility reigns."

And the *Baton Rouge Advocate* said "*NOW* invites viewers to consider the deeper implication of the daily headlines," drawing on "a wide range of viewpoints which transcend the typical labels of the political left or right."

Let me repeat that: *NOW* draws on "a wide range of viewpoints which transcend the typical labels of the political left or right."

The Public Broadcasting Act of 1967 had been prophetic. Open public television to the American people—offer diverse interests, ideas and voices . . . be fearless in your belief in democracy—and they will come.

Hold your applause–that's not the point of the story.

The point of the story is something only a handful of our team, including my wife and partner Judith Davidson Moyers, and I knew at the time—that the success of *NOW*'s journalism was creating a backlash in Washington.

The more compelling our journalism, the angrier the radical right of the Republican party became. That's because the one thing they loathe more than liberals is the truth. And the quickest way to be damned by them as liberal is to tell the truth.

This is the point of my story: Ideologues don't want you to go beyond the typical labels of left and right. They embrace a world view that can't be proven wrong because they will admit no evidence to the contrary. They want your reporting to validate their belief system and when it doesn't, God forbid. Never mind that their own stars were getting a fair shake on *NOW*: Gigot, Viguerie, David Keene of the American Conservative Union, Stephen Moore of the Club for Growth, and others. No, our reporting was giving the radical right fits because it wasn't the party line. It wasn't that we were getting it wrong. Only three times in three years did we err factually, and in each case we corrected those errors as soon as we confirmed their inaccuracy. The problem was that we were getting it right, not right-wing—telling stories that partisans in power didn't want told.

I've always thought the American eagle needed a left wing and a right wing. The right wing would see to it that economic interests had their legitimate concerns addressed. The left wing would see to it that ordinary people were included in the bargain. Both would keep the great bird on course. But with two right wings or two left wings, it's no longer an eagle and it's going to crash.

My occasional commentaries got to them as well. Although apparently he never watched the broadcast (I guess he couldn't take the diversity) Senator Trent Lott came out squealing like a stuck pig when after the mid-term elections in 2002 I described what was likely to happen now that all three branches of government were about to be controlled by one party dominated by the religious, corporate and political right. Instead of congratulating the winners for their election victory as some network broadcasters had done—or celebrating their victory as Fox, *The Washington Times, The Weekly Standard, Talk Radio* and other partisan Republican journalists had done—I provided a little independent analysis of what the victory meant. And I did it the old fashioned way: I looked at the record, took the winners at their word, and drew the logical conclusion that they would use power as they always said they would. And I set forth this conclusion in my usual modest Texas way.

Events since then have confirmed the accuracy of what I said, but, to repeat, being right is exactly what the right doesn't want journalists to be.

Strange things began to happen. Friends in Washington called to say that they had heard of muttered threats that the PBS reauthorization would be held off "unless Moyers is dealt with." The Chairman of the Corporation for Public Broadcasting, Kenneth Tomlinson, was said to be quite agitated. Apparently there was apoplexy in the right wing aerie when I closed the broadcast one Friday night by putting an American flag in my lapel and said–well, here's exactly what I said.

"I wore my flag tonight. First time. Until now I haven't thought it necessary to display a little metallic icon of patriotism for everyone to see. It was enough to vote, pay my taxes, perform my civic duties, speak my mind, and do my best to raise our kids to be good Americans.

Sometimes I would offer a small prayer of gratitude that I had been born in a country whose institutions sustained me, whose armed forces protected me, and whose ideals inspired me; I offered my heart's affections in return. It no more occurred to me to flaunt the flag on my chest than it did to pin my mother's picture on my lapel to prove her son's love. Mother knew where I stood; so does my country. I even tuck a valentine in my tax returns on April 15.

So what's this doing here? Well, I put it on to take it back. The flag's been hijacked and turned into a logo—the trademark of a monopoly on patriotism. On those Sunday morning talk shows, official chests appear adorned with the flag as if it is the good housekeeping seal of approval. During the State of the Union, did you notice Bush and Cheney wearing the flag? How come? No administration's patriotism is ever in doubt, only its policies. And the flag bestows no immunity from error. When I see flags sprouting on official lapels, I think of the time in China when I saw Mao's little red book on every official's desk, omnipresent and unread.

But more galling than anything are all those moralistic ideologues in Washington sporting the flag in their lapels while writing books and running Web sites and publishing magazines attacking dissenters as un-American. They are people whose ardor for war grows disproportionately to their distance from the fighting. They're in the same league as those swarms of corporate lobbyists wearing flags and prowling Capitol Hill for tax breaks even as they call for more spending on war.

So I put this on as a modest riposte to men with flags in their lapels who shoot missiles from the safety of Washington think tanks, or argue that sacrifice is good as long as they don't have to make it, or approve of bribing governments to join the coalition of the willing (after they first stash the cash.) I put it on to remind myself that not every patriot thinks we should do to the people of Baghdad what Bin Laden did to us. The flag belongs to the country, not to the government. And it reminds me that it's not un-American to think that war—except in self-defense—is a failure of moral imagination, political nerve, and diplomacy. Come to think of it, standing up to your government can mean standing up for your country."

That did it. That—and our continuing reporting on overpricing at Halliburton, chicanery on K-Street, and the heavy, if divinely guided, hand of Tom DeLay.

When Senator Lott protested that the Corporation for Public Broadcasting "has not seemed willing to deal with Bill Moyers," a new member of the board, a Republican fundraiser named Cheryl Halperin, who had been appointed by President Bush, agreed that CPB needed more power to do just that sort of thing. She left no doubt about the kind of penalty she would like to see imposed on malefactors like Moyers.

As rumors circulated about all this, I asked to meet with the CPB board to hear for myself what was being said. I thought it would be helpful for someone like me, who had been present at the creation and part of the system for almost 40 years, to talk about how CPB had been intended to be a heat shield to protect public broadcasters from exactly this kind of intimidation. After all, I'd been there at the time of Richard Nixon's attempted coup. In those days, public television had been really feisty and independent, and often targeted for attacks. A Woody Allen special that poked fun at Henry Kissinger in the Nixon administration had actually been cancelled. The White House had been so outraged over a documentary called the "Banks and the Poor" that PBS was driven to adopt new guidelines. That didn't satisfy Nixon, and when public television hired two NBC reporters—Robert McNeil and Sander Vanocur—to co-anchor some new broadcasts, it was, for Nixon, the last straw. According to White House memos at the time, he was determined to "get the left wing commentators who are cutting us up off public television at once—indeed, yesterday if possible."

Sound familiar?

Nixon vetoed the authorization for CPB with a message written in part by his sidekick Pat Buchanan who in a private memo had castigated Vanocur, MacNeil, *Washington Week in Review, Black Journal* and Bill Moyers as "unbalanced against the administration."

It does sound familiar.

I always knew Nixon would be back. I just didn't know this time he would be the Chairman of the Corporation for Public Broadcasting.

Buchanan and Nixon succeeded in cutting CPB funding for all public affairs programming except for Black Journal. They knocked out multiyear funding for the National Public Affairs Center for Television, otherwise known as NPACT. And they voted to take away from the PBS staff the ultimate responsibility for the production of programming.

But in those days—and this is what I wanted to share with Kenneth Tomlinson and his colleagues on the CPB board-there were still Republicans in America who did not march in ideological lockstep and who stood on principle against politicizing public television. The chairman of the public station in Dallas was an industrialist named Ralph Rogers, a Republican but no party hack, who saw the White House intimidation as an assault on freedom of the press and led a nationwide effort to stop it. The chairman of CPB was former Republican congressman Thomas Curtis, who was also a principled man. He resigned, claiming White House interference. Within a few months, the crisis was over. CPB maintained its independence, PBS grew in strength, and Richard Nixon would soon face impeachment and resign for violating the public trust, not just public broadcasting. Paradoxically, the very Public Affairs Center for Television that Nixon had tried to kill—NPACT—put PBS on the map by rebroadcasting in prime time each day's Watergate hearings, drawing huge ratings night after night and establishing PBS as an ally of democracy. We should still be doing that sort of thing.

That was 33 years ago. I thought the current CPB board would like to hear and talk about the importance of standing up to political interference. I was wrong. They wouldn't meet with me. I tried three times. And it was all downhill after that.

I was naïve, I guess. I simply never imagined that any CPB chairman, Democrat or Republican, would cross the line from resisting White House pressure to carrying it out for the White House. But that's what Kenneth Tomlinson has done. On Fox News this week he denied that he's carrying out a White House mandate or that he's ever had any conversations with any Bush administration official about PBS. But *The New York Times* reported that he enlisted Karl Rove to help kill a proposal that would have put on the CPB board people with experience in local radio and television. *The Times* also reported that "on the recommendation of administration officials" Tomlinson hired a White House flack (I know the genre) named Mary Catherine Andrews as a senior CPB staff member. While she was still reporting to Karl Rove at the White House, Andrews set up CPB's new ombudsman's office and had a hand in hiring the two people who will fill it, one of whom once worked for . . . you guessed it . . . Kenneth Tomlinson.

I would like to give Mr. Tomlinson the benefit of the doubt, but I can't. According to a book written about the *Reader's Digest* when he was its Editor-in-Chief, he surrounded himself with other right-wingers—a pattern he's now following at the Corporation for Public Broadcasting. There is Ms. Andrews from the White House. For Acting President he hired Ken Ferree from the FCC, who was Michael Powell's enforcer when Powell was deciding how to go about allowing the big media companies to get even bigger. According to a forthcoming book, one of Ferree's jobs was to engage in tactics designed to dismiss any serious objection to media monopolies. And, according to Eric Alterman, Ferree was even more contemptuous than Michael Powell of public participation in the process of determining media ownership. Alterman identifies Ferree as the FCC staffer who decided to issue a 'protective order' designed to keep secret the market research on which the Republican majority on the commission based their vote to permit greater media consolidation.

It's not likely that with guys like this running the CPB some public television producer is going to say, "Hey, let's do something on how big media is affecting democracy."

Call it preventive capitulation.

As everyone knows, Mr. Tomlinson also put up a considerable sum of money, reportedly over five million dollars, for a new weekly broadcast featuring Paul Gigot and the editorial board of the *Wall Street Journal*. Gigot is a smart journalist, a sharp editor, and a fine fellow. I had him on *NOW* several times and even proposed that he become a regular contributor. The conversation of democracy—remember? All stripes.

But I confess to some puzzlement that the *Wall Street Journal*, which in the past editorialized to cut PBS off the public tap, is now being subsidized by American taxpayers although its parent company, Dow Jones, had revenues in just the first quarter of this year of 400 million dollars.

I thought public television was supposed to be an alternative to commercial media, not a funder of it.

But in this weird deal, you get a glimpse of the kind of programming Mr. Tomlinson apparently seems to prefer. Alone of the big major newspapers, the *Wall Street Journal*, has no op-ed page where different opinions can compete with its right-wing editorials. The Journal's PBS broadcast is just as homogenous–right-wingers talking to each other. Why not $5 million to put the editors of *The Nation* on PBS? Or Amy Goodman's *Democracy Now*! You balance right-wing talk with left-wing talk.

There's more. Only two weeks ago did we learn that Mr. Tomlinson had spent $10,000 last year to hire a contractor who would watch my show and report on political bias. That's right. Kenneth Y. Tomlinson spent $10,000 of your money to hire a guy to watch *NOW* to find out who my guests were and what my stories were.

Ten thousand dollars.

Gee, Ken, for $2.50 a week, you could pick up a copy of *TV Guide* on the newsstand. A subscription is even cheaper, and I would have sent you a coupon that can save you up to 62%.

For that matter, Ken, all you had to do was watch the show yourself. You could have made it easier with a double Jim Bean, your favorite. Or you could have gone on line where the listings are posted. Hell, you could have called me—collect—and I would have told you what was on the broadcast that night.

Ten thousand dollars. That would have bought five tables at Thursday night's Conservative Salute for Tom DeLay. Better yet, that ten grand would pay for the books in an elementary school classroom or an upgrade of its computer lab.

But having sent that cash, what did he find? Only Mr. Tomlinson knows. He apparently decided not to share the results with his staff or his board or leak it to Robert Novak. The public paid for it–but Ken Tomlinson acts as if he owns it.

In a May 10th op-ed piece, in Reverend Moon's conservative *Washington Times*, Mr. Tomlinson maintained he had not released the findings because public broadcasting is such a delicate institution he did not want to "damage public broadcasting's image with controversy." Where I come from in Texas, we shovel that kind of stuff every day.

As we learned only this week, that's not the only news Mr. Tomlinson tried to keep to himself. As reported by Jeff Chester's Center for Digital Democracy of which I am a supporter, there were two public opinion surveys commissioned by CPB but not released to the media–not even to PBS and NPR! According to a source who talked to *Salon.com*, "the first results were too good and [Tomlinson] didn't believe them. After the Iraq war, the board commissioned another round of polling and they thought they'd get worse results."

But they didn't.

The data revealed that, in reality, public broadcasting has an 80% favorable rating and that "the majority of the U.S. adult population does not believe that the news and information programming on public broadcasting is biased."

In fact, more than half believed PBS provided more in-depth and trustworthy news and information than the networks and 55% said PBS was "fair and balanced."

I repeat: I would like to have given Mr. Tomlinson the benefit of the doubt. But this is the man who was running The Voice of America back in 1984 when a partisan named Charlie Wick was politicizing the United States Information Agency of which Voice of America was a part. It turned out there was a blacklist of people who had been removed from the list of prominent Americans sent abroad to lecture on behalf of America and the USIA. What's more, it was discovered that evidence as to how those people were chosen to be on the blacklist— more than 700 documents—had been shredded. Among those on the lists of journalists, writers, scholars and politicians were dangerous left wing subversives like Walter Cronkite, James Baldwin, Gary Hart, Ralph Nader, Ben Bradley, Coretta Scott King and David Brinkley.

The person who took the fall for the black list was another right-winger. He resigned. Shortly thereafter, so did Kenneth Tomlinson, who had been one of the people in the agency with the authority to see the lists of potential speakers and allowed to strike people's names.

Let me be clear about this: there is no record, apparently, of what Ken Tomlinson did. We don't know whether he supported or protested the blacklisting of so many American liberals. Or what he thinks of it now.

But I had hoped Bill O'Reilly would have asked him about it when he appeared on *The O'Reilly Factor* this week. He didn't. Instead, Tomlinson went on attacking me with O'Reilly egging him on, and he went on denying he was carrying out a partisan mandate despite published reports to the contrary. The only time you could be sure he was telling the truth was at the end of the broadcast when he said to O'Reilly, "We love your show."

*We love your show.*

I wrote Kenneth Tomlinson on Friday and asked him to sit down with me for one hour on PBS and talk about all this. I suggested that he choose the moderator and the guidelines.

There is one other thing in particular I would like to ask him about. In his op-ed essay this week in *The Washington Times*, Ken Tomlinson tells of a phone call from an old friend complaining about my bias. Wrote Mr. Tomlinson: "The friend explained that the foundation he heads made a six-figure contribution to his local television station for digital conversion. But he declared there would be no more contributions until something was done about the network's bias."

Apparently that's Kenneth Tomlinson's method of governance. Money talks and buys the influence it wants.

I would like to ask him to listen to a different voice.

This letter came to me last year from a woman in New York, five pages of handwriting. She said, among other things, that "After the worst sneak attack in our history, there's not been a moment to reflect, a moment to let the horror resonate, a moment to feel the pain and regroup as humans. No, since I lost my husband on 9/11, not only our family's world, but the whole world seems to have gotten even worse than that tragic day." She wanted me to know that on 9/11 her husband was not on duty.

"He was home with me having coffee. My daughter and grandson, living only five blocks from the Towers, had to be evacuated with masks—terror all around . . . my other daughter, near the Brooklyn Bridge . . . my son in high school. But my Charlie took off like a lightening bolt to be with his men from the Special Operations Command. 'Bring my gear to the plaza,' he told his aide immediately after the first plane struck the North Tower. . . . He took action based on the responsibility he felt for his job and his men and for those Towers that he loved."

In the FDNY, she continued, chain-of-command rules extend to every captain of every fire house in the city. "If anything happens in the firehouse—at any time—even if the Captain isn't on duty or on vacation—that Captain is responsible for everything that goes on there 24/7." So she asked: "Why is this Administration responsible for nothing? All that they do is pass the blame. This is not leadership. . . . Watch everyone pass the blame again in this recent torture case [Abu Ghraib] of Iraqi prisons. . . ."

She told me that she and her husband had watched my series on "Joseph Campbell and the Power of Myth" together and that now she was a faithful fan of NOW. She wrote: "We need more programs like yours to wake America up. . . . Such programs must continue amidst the sea of false images and name calling that divide America now. . . . Such programs give us hope that search will continue to get this imperfect human condition on to a higher plane. So thank you and all of those who work with you. Without public broadcasting, all we would call news would be merely carefully controlled propaganda."

Enclosed with the letter was a check made out to "Channel 13–*NOW*" for $500.

I keep a copy of that check above my desk to remind me of what journalism is about.

Kenneth Tomlinson has his demanding donors. I'll take the widow's mite any day.

Someone has said recently that the great raucous mob that is democracy is rarely heard and that it's not just the fault of the current residents of the White House and the capital. There's too great a chasm between those of us in this business and those who depend on TV and radio as their window to the world. We treat them too much as an audience and not enough as citizens. They're invited to look through the window but too infrequently to come through the door and to participate, to make public broadcasting truly public.

To that end, five public interests groups including Common Cause and Consumers Union will be holding informational sessions around the country to "take public broadcasting back"—to take it back from threats, from interference, from those who would tell us we can only think what they command us to think.

It's a worthy goal.

We're big kids; we can handle controversy and diversity, whether it's political or religious points of view or two loving lesbian moms and their kids, visited by a cartoon rabbit. We are not too fragile or insecure to see America and the world entire for all their magnificent and sometimes violent confusion. There used to be a thing or a commodity we put great store by," John Steinbeck wrote. "It was called the people."

---

## DISCUSSION QUESTIONS

1. Characterize Moyers's view of democracy. Characterize his view of what journalism ideally should be. Explain why from his perspective, public media are so important to the functioning of a healthy democracy.

2. We all know that given the explosion of cable television, there are hundreds of stations to choose from. Thus, don't we already have a diverse range of choices? Is Moyers's call for a strengthening of public broadcasting really necessary? Explain.

# CHAPTER 5

# PARTIES AND ELECTIONS

Elections and voting in America today reveal a wide gap between democratic ideals of citizen participation in the substantive discussion of issues and the realities of low voter turnout, the ascendancy of image and emotional manipulation in campaigns, and the distorting impact of big money. In principle, a broad franchise and regular elections (in which competing parties offer distinct approaches to important problems) should provide citizens with a link to government officials. This link should ensure responsiveness to public concerns and a measure of control over public policy. Indeed, many Americans have seen the very existence of elections and the right to vote as proof of the democratic nature of our political system. But many others are aware of the discrepancy between ideals and reality. This gap was underscored by the disputed presidential election of 2000. Readings in this chapter will help you understand this gap and what might be done to bridge it.

# 17 *Thomas Frank*

# WHAT'S THE MATTER WITH AMERICA?

*In this selection from his best selling book* What's the Matter with Kansas? *author Thomas Frank explores what he considers the "preeminent question of our times," namely why ever-increasing numbers of working class and average income Americans vote for conservative politicians whose policies intensify the economic hardships faced by those very same Americans. Frank attributes this "derangement" to the "Great Backlash," a cultural anger that emerged in the 1960s to be harnessed by Republican politicians who appeal to socially and culturally conservative issues in the service of economic ends that advance the fortunes of corporations and the wealthy. Or as Frank characterizes it, "The leaders of the backlash may talk Christ, but they walk corporate." The result has been a boon to the Republican party. As they attract more angry, disaffected former Democrats with anti-abortion, anti-gay, anti-Hollywood and other appeals central to the culture wars of our era, their economic agenda worsens the plight of those voters, whose anger intensifies even more, enhancing the power of Republicans in a kind of self-fulfilling spiral. While Frank views this political transformation through its impact on his home state of Kansas, this same "panorama of madness" pervades the entire nation. Indeed, it is the hallmark of party politics in the U.S. today.*

The poorest county in America isn't in Appalachia or the Deep South. It is on the Great Plains, a region of struggling ranchers and dying farm towns, and in the election of 2000 the Republican candidate for president, George W. Bush, carried it by a majority of greater than 80 percent.

This puzzled me when I first read about it, as it puzzles many of the people I know. For us it is the Democrats that are the party of workers, of the poor, of the weak and the victimized. Understanding this, we think, is basic; it is part of the ABCs of adulthood. When I told a friend of mine about that impoverished High Plains county so enamored of President Bush, she was perplexed. "How can anyone who has ever worked for someone else vote Republican?" she asked. How could so many people get it so wrong?

Her question is apt; it is, in many ways, the preeminent question of our times. People getting their fundamental interests wrong is what American

*Source:* Thomas Frank, *What's the Matter with Kansas?* New York: Henry Holt, 2004, pp. 1–10.

political life is all about. This species of derangement is the bedrock of our civic order; it is the foundation on which all else rests. This derangement has put the Republicans in charge of all three branches of government; it has elected presidents, senators, governors; it shifts the Democrats to the right and then impeaches Bill Clinton just for fun.

If you earn over $300,000 a year, you owe a great deal to this derangement. Raise a glass sometime to those indigent High Plains Republicans as you contemplate your good fortune: It is thanks to their self-denying votes that you are no longer burdened by the estate tax, or troublesome labor unions, or meddling banking regulators. Thanks to the allegiance of these sons and daughters of toil, you have escaped what your affluent forebears used to call "confiscatory" income tax levels. It is thanks to them that you were able to buy two Rolexes this year instead of one and get that Segway with the special gold trim.

Or perhaps you are one of those many, many millions of average-income. Americans who see nothing deranged about this at all. For you this picture of hard-times conservatism makes perfect sense, and it is the opposite phenomenon—working-class people who insist on voting for liberals—that strikes you as an indecipherable puzzlement. Maybe you see it the way the bumper sticker I spotted at a Kansas City gun show puts it: "A working person that *supports* Democrats is like a chicken that *supports* Col. Sanders!"

Maybe you were one of those who stood up for America way back in 1968, sick of hearing those rich kids in beads bad-mouth the country every night on TV. Maybe you knew exactly what Richard Nixon meant when he talked about the "silent majority," the people whose hard work was rewarded with constant insults from the network news, the Hollywood movies, and the know-it-all college professors, none of them interested in anything you had to say. Or maybe it was the liberal judges who got you mad as hell, casually rewriting the laws of your state according to some daft idea they had picked up at a cocktail party, or ordering your town to shoulder some billion-dollar desegregation scheme that they had dreamed up on their own, or turning criminals loose to prey on the hardworking and the industrious. Or

perhaps it was the drive for gun control, which was obviously directed toward the same end of disarming and ultimately disempowering people like you.

Maybe Ronald Reagan pulled you into the conservative swirl, the way he talked about that sunshiny, Glenn Miller America you remembered from the time before the world went to hell. Or maybe Rush Limbaugh won you over, with his daily beatdown of the arrogant and the self-important. Or maybe you were pushed; maybe Bill Clinton made a Republican out of you with his patently phony "compassion" and his obvious contempt for average, non-Ivy Americans, the ones he had the nerve to order into combat even though he himself took the coward's way out when his turn came.

Nearly everyone has a conversion story they can tell: how their dad had been a union steelworker and a stalwart Democrat, but how all their brothers and sisters started voting Republican; or how their cousin gave up on Methodism and started going to the Pentecostal church out on the edge of town; or how they themselves just got so sick of being scolded for eating meat or for wearing clothes emblazoned with the State U's Indian mascot that one day Fox News started to seem "fair and balanced" to them after all.

Take the family of a friend of mine, a guy who came from one of those midwestern cities that sociologists used to descend upon periodically because it was supposed to be so "typical." It was a middling-sized industrial burg where they made machine tools, auto parts, and so forth. When Reagan took office in 1981, more than half the working population of the city was employed in factories, and most of them were union members. The ethos of the place was working-class, and the city was prosperous, tidy, and liberal, in the old sense of the word.

My friend's dad was a teacher in the local public schools, a loyal member of the teachers' union, and a more dedicated liberal than most: not only had he been a staunch supporter of George McGovern, but in the 1980 Democratic primary he had voted for Barbara Jordan, the black U.S. Representative from Texas. My friend, meanwhile, was in those days a high school Republican, a Reagan youth who fancied Adam Smith ties and savored the writing of William F. Buckley. The dad would listen to the son spout off about Milton Friedman and the godliness of free-market capitalism, and he would just shake his head. *Someday, kid, you'll know what a jerk you are.*

It was the dad, though, who was eventually converted. These days he votes for the farthest-right Republicans he can find on the ballot. The particular issue that brought him over was abortion. A devout Catholic, my friend's dad was persuaded in the early nineties that the sanctity of the fetus outweighed all of his other concerns, and from there he gradually accepted the whole pantheon of conservative devil-figures: the elite media and the American Civil Liberties Union, contemptuous of our values; the la-di-da feminists; the idea that Christians are vilely persecuted—right here in the U.S. of A. It doesn't even bother him, really, when his new hero Bill O'Reilly blasts the teachers' union as a group that "does not love America."

His superaverage midwestern town, meanwhile, has followed the same trajectory. Even as Republican economic policy laid waste to the city's industries, unions, and neighborhoods, the townsfolk responded by lashing out on cultural issues, eventually winding up with a hard-right Republican congressman, a born-again Christian who campaigned largely on an anti-abortion platform. Today the city looks like a miniature Detroit. And with every bit of economic bad news it seems to get more bitter, more cynical, and more conservative still.

This derangement is the signature expression of the Great Backlash, a style of conservatism that first came snarling onto the national stage in response to the partying and protests of the late sixties. While earlier forms of conservatism emphasized fiscal sobriety, the backlash mobilizes voters with explosive social issues—summoning public outrage over everything from busing to un-Christian art—which it then marries to pro-business economic policies. Cultural anger is marshaled to achieve economic ends. And it is these economic achievements—not the forgettable skirmishes of the never-ending culture wars—that are the movement's greatest monuments. The backlash is what has made possible the international free-market consensus of recent years, with all the privatization, deregulation, and deunionization that are its components. Backlash ensures that Republicans will continue to be returned to office even when their free-market miracles fail and their libertarian schemes don't deliver and their "New Economy" collapses. It makes possible the policy pushers' fantasies of "globalization" and a free-trade empire that are foisted upon the rest of the world with such self-assurance. Because some artist decides to shock the hicks by dunking Jesus in urine, the entire planet must remake itself along the lines preferred by the Republican Party, U.S.A.

The Great Backlash has made the laissez-faire revival possible, but this does not mean that it speaks to us in the manner of the capitalists of old, invoking the divine right of money or demanding that the lowly learn their place in the great chain of being. On the contrary; the backlash imagines itself as a foe of the elite, as the voice of the unfairly persecuted, as a righteous protest of the people on history's receiving end. That its champions today control all three branches of government matters not a whit. That its greatest beneficiaries are the wealthiest people on the planet does not give it pause.

In fact, backlash leaders systematically downplay the politics of economics. The movement's basic premise is that culture outweighs economics as a matter of public concern—that *Values Matter Most*, as one backlash title has it. On those grounds it rallies citizens who would once have been reliable partisans of the New Deal to the standard of conservatism. Old-fashioned values may count when conservatives appear on the stump, but once conservatives are in office the only old-fashioned situation they care to revive is an economic regimen of low wages and lax regulations. Over the last three decades they have smashed the welfare state, reduced the tax burden on corporations and the wealthy, and generally facilitated the country's return to a nineteenth-century pattern of wealth distribution. Thus the primary contradiction of the backlash: it is a working-class movement that has done incalculable, historic harm to working-class people.

The leaders of the backlash may talk Christ, but they walk corporate. Values may "matter most" to voters, but they always take a backseat to the needs of money once the elections are won. This is a basic earmark of the phenomenon, absolutely consistent across its decades-long history. Abortion is never halted. Affirmative action is never abolished. The culture industry is never forced to clean up its act. Even the greatest culture warrior of them all was a notorious cop-out once it came time to deliver, "Reagan made himself the champion of 'traditional values,' but there is no evidence he regarded their restoration as a high priority," wrote Christopher Lasch, one of the most astute analysts of the backlash sensibility. "What he really cared about was the revival of the unregulated capitalism of the twenties: the repeal of the New Deal."

This is vexing for observers, and one might expect it to vex the movement's true believers even more. Their grandstanding leaders never deliver, their fury mounts and mounts, and nevertheless they turn out every two years to return their right-wing heroes to office for a second, a third, a twentieth try. The trick never ages; the illusion never wears off. *Vote* to stop abortion; *receive* a rollback in capital gains taxes. *Vote* to make our country strong again; *receive* deindustrialization. *Vote* to screw those politically correct college professors; *receive* electricity deregulation. *Vote* to get government off our backs; *receive* conglomeration and monopoly everywhere from media to meatpacking. *Vote* to stand tall against terrorists; *receive* Social Security privatization. *Vote* to strike a blow against elitism; *receive* a social order in which wealth is more concentrated than ever before in our lifetimes, in which workers have been stripped of power and CEOs are rewarded in a manner beyond imagining.

Backlash theorists, as we shall see, imagine countless conspiracies in which the wealthy, powerful, and well connected—the liberal media, the atheistic scientists, the obnoxious eastern elite—pull the strings and make the puppets dance. And yet the backlash itself has been a political trap so devastating to the interests of Middle America that even the most diabolical of string-pullers would have had trouble dreaming it up. Here, after all, is a rebellion against "the establishment" that has wound up abolishing the tax on inherited estates. Here is a movement whose response to the power structure is to make the rich even richer; whose answer to the inexorable degradation of working-class life is to lash out angrily at labor unions and liberal workplace-safety programs; whose solution to the rise of ignorance in America is to pull the rug out from under public education.

Like a French Revolution in reverse—one in which the sans-culottes pour down the streets demanding more power for the aristocracy—the backlash pushes the spectrum of the acceptable to the right, to the right, farther to the right. It may never bring prayer back to the schools, but it has rescued all manner of right-wing economic nostrums from history's dustbin. Having rolled back the landmark economic reforms of the sixties (the war on poverty) and those of the thirties (labor law, agricultural price supports, banking regulation), its leaders now turn their guns on the accomplishments of the earliest years of progressivism (Woodrow Wilson's estate tax; Theodore Roosevelt's antitrust measures). With a little more effort, the backlash may well repeal the entire twentieth century.

As a formula for holding together a dominant political coalition, the backlash seems so improbable and so self-contradictory that liberal observers often have trouble believing it is actually happening. By all rights, they figure, these two groups—business and blue-collar—should be at each other's throats. For the Republican Party to present itself as the champion of working-class America strikes liberals as such an egregious denial of political reality that they dismiss the whole phenomenon, refusing to take it seriously. The Great Backlash, they believe, is nothing but crypto-racism, or a disease of the elderly, or the random gripings of religious rednecks, or the protests of "angry white men" feeling left behind by history.

But to understand the backlash in this way is to miss its power as an idea and its broad popular vitality. It keeps coming despite everything, a plague of bitterness capable of spreading from the old to the young, from Protestant fundamentalists to Catholics and Jews, and from the angry white man to every demographic shading imaginable.

It matters not at all that the forces that triggered the original "silent majority" back in Nixon's day have long since disappeared; the backlash roars on undiminished, its rage carrying easily across the decades. The confident liberals who led America in those days are a dying species. The New Left, with its gleeful obscenities and contempt for the flag, is extinct altogether. The whole "affluent society," with its paternalistic corporations and powerful labor unions, fades farther into the ether with each passing year. But the backlash endures. It continues to dream its terrifying dreams of national decline, epic lawlessness, and betrayal at the top regardless of what is actually going on in the world.

Along the way what was once genuine and grassroots and even "populist" about the backlash phenomenon has been transformed into a stimulus-response melodrama with a plot as formulaic as an episode of *The O'Reilly Factor* and with results as predictable—and as profitable—as Coca-Cola advertising. In one end you feed an item about, say, the menace of gay marriage, and at the other end you generate, almost mechanically, an uptick of middle-American indignation, angry letters to the editor an electoral harvest of the most gratifying sort.

From the air-conditioned heights of a suburban office complex this may look like a new age of reason, with the Web sites singing each to each, with a mall down the way that every week has miraculously anticipated our subtly shifting tastes, with a global economy whose rich rewards just keep flowing, and with a long parade of rust-free Infinitis purring down the streets of beautifully manicured planned communities. But on closer inspection the country seems more like a panorama of madness and delusion worthy of Hieronymous Bosch: of sturdy blue-collar patriots reciting the Pledge while they strangle their own life chances; of small farmers proudly voting themselves off the land; of devoted family men carefully seeing to it that their children will never be able to afford college or proper health care; of working-class guys in midwestern cities cheering as they deliver up a landslide for a candidate whose policies will end their way of life, will transform their region into a "rust belt," will strike people like them blows from which they will never recover.

---

## DISCUSSION QUESTIONS

1. Frank argues that the backlash conservatism creates numerous contradictions. Explore some of the contradictions. Why does he view them as "self-damaging"?
2. At one point Frank offers the following semi-humorous contention: "With a little more effort, the backlash may well repeal the entire twentieth century." Explain what he means by that?
3. The thrust of Frank's argument rests on the belief that while backlash conservatism offers cultural issues to motivate voters, subsequent economic policy ruins the livelihoods of those same voters. In essence, he thinks economics should be more fundamental than social issues. Do you agree? Is it "deranged" for voters to allow concern for divisive social/cultural issues to trump economic concerns?

# 18 *FairVote*

# THE SHRINKING ELECTORAL BATTLEGROUND

*In the presidential election of 2004, the campaigns concentrated on a handful of "swing" or "battleground" states. George W. Bush and John F. Kerry concentrated their resources and personal appearances in these contested states, neglecting to a large extent much of the rest of the country. In this study by the electoral reform research and advocacy group FairVote, a model of "state partisanship" is used to explain why the United States has experienced a decrease in the number of competitive battleground states in presidential elections, For example in 1960, 24 states with a total of 327 electoral votes were battlegrounds. In 2004, only 13 states with 159 electoral votes were similarly competitive. The study explains why these partisan divisions are hardening and what impact they have on American democracy. The fundamental reality, according to the study, is that fewer and fewer Americans play a meaningful role in electing the president—and that the major party campaigns act on that understanding with utter disregard for the interests and views of most voters outside of swing states. The result is a two-tiered system for voters, with damaging impact on voter turnout, racial fairness, political equality and the future of American democracy. The evidence presented by the FairVote authors leads them to propose that the Electoral College be abolished and replaced by the direct election of the president so that all votes count equally and the principles of majority rule and one person, one vote are respected.*

*Suggests Abolition of the Electoral College*

## [OVERVIEW]

No elected office in the United States captures the public's imagination like the presidency. The White House represents this nation's elected royalty, providing a human face to our government and the inspiration for one key element of the American dream: belief that any young person, anywhere in the nation, can proudly announce to their friends, "Someday I will be president." The vast majority of Americans with that dream must settle for other opportunities in life, but in a nation founded on the principle that all men and women are created equal, all Americans should have the right to a meaningful vote in presidential elections. *— Spirit of this Essay*

*Source:* FairVote, "The Shrinking Battleground: The 2008 Presidential Elections and Beyond," 2005. Available online at: www.fairvote.org/presidential.

This principle, however, is violated by our use of the Electoral College, a convoluted and capricious electoral process that weights Americans' votes differently based on where they live and allows a candidate to win election despite receiving fewer votes than another candidate—a perverse result that happened in 2000 and would have happened again in 2004 if George Bush had won the popular vote by less than 425,000 votes.

Inequality in our presidential election system is taking on disturbing new dimensions. The combination of the Electoral College, hardening partisan voting patterns, sophisticated campaign techniques and high-tech tools are creating a two-tier class structure in our democracy: second class citizens disregarded as irrelevant in presidential elections and the fortunate few who receive increasing care and attention by virtue of living in one of the dwindling number of competitive battleground states like Florida and Ohio.

In 1960, for example, when John Kennedy narrowly defeated Richard Nixon, two-thirds of states were competitive. Fully 24 states in 1960 were genuine political battlegrounds, together representing 327 electoral votes. Fast forward to 2004. The number of competitive races plunged to barely a third of the states, and the number of comparable battlegrounds dwindled to only 13, representing just 159 electoral votes. At the same time, the number of completely non-competitive states (those where one party would win by more than 16% in a nationally even race) increased from nine states representing 64 electoral votes in 1960 to 20 states with 163 electoral votes in 2004.

These changes have a direct impact on candidate behavior and voter participation, particularly with the modern era's precise methods of polling and marketing that allow campaigns to focus on narrow slices of the electorate. In August 2004, President George W. Bush's campaign strategist Matthew Dowd remarked that President Bush's campaign had not polled outside of the 18 closest states in more than two years. Despite having more resources than any campaign in history, Dowd knew his candidate didn't need to waste a dime on learning the views of most Americans. A cursory look at John Kerry's campaign itinerary during the general election suggests that his campaign also focused exclusively on the same battleground states. As a result, the interests and opinions of the bulk of "second-class" Americans living in what this report terms "spectator states" were only addressed if they happened to coincide with those of the "first-class" Americans living in the states where their participation might affect the outcome of the election.

The trends behind this two-tier democracy show every indication of continuing to exacerbate these divisions. Many Americans would like to see the parties break out of their narrow focus on a handful of swing states and instead build national unity by seeking votes around the nation, in "red" and "blue" states alike. But unless we establish a national vote for president, those hopes are in vain. The partisan realignment responsible for increasing the division between first-class Americans in battleground states and second-class Americans in spectator states shows few signs of changing any time soon, and the stakes in winning the presidency are too high for major party candidates to "waste" resources on states that are simply not going to matter in a competitive election.

Indeed voting patterns across the country show less variation from election to election today than just twenty years ago, and majorities in most states are growing more solidly partisan. In a competitive election in 2008, therefore, the percentage of Americans likely to gain attention from presidential candidates in the general election almost certainly will be the lowest in the modern era.

As disturbing as this conclusion is in the short-term, there are even more serious long-term implications of our nation's hardening partisan patterns and decreasing numbers of competitive states over time. New voter turnout analyses by scholars like Trinity College's Mark Franklin provide convincing evidence that the voting behavior of most citizens is established for life during their first three or four elections when eligible to vote.

With hundreds of millions of dollars for voter registration and mobilization now targeted on battleground states and virtually nothing on spectator states, a sharp difference in turnout based on where one lives all too easily could continue for the rest of this young generation's lives. Improving turnout in presidential elections is like changing the direction of the Titanic—it happens all too slowly. A clear rift is already evident in the voting patterns of citizens in battleground and spectator states, with those in spectator states being much less likely to go to the polls. Without changes in this division of battleground and spectator states, the principle of equality will be undercut for decades. Second-class status will become entrenched for millions of young Americans who have the misfortune to live in one of the two-thirds of states that aren't battlegrounds in presidential elections.

## THE 2004 PRESIDENTIAL ELECTIONS: ACCURACY, TRENDS AND PARTISAN IMPLICATIONS.

*The Shrinking Battleground* provides a valuable means to better understand the 2004 presidential election. Nationally Republican George W. Bush won 50.73% of the nationwide popular vote to Democrat John Kerry's 48.27%. After losing the popular vote by more a half-million votes in 2000 with 47.87%, Bush raised his vote share by nearly three percent in 2004 and defeated Kerry by more than three million votes in an election with the highest national election turnout since the 1960s.

But just because the 2004 elections escaped sustained national attention on a state's controversial ballot count on the order of Florida in the 2000 elections should not disguise the fact that this election again was historically close, that the Ohio election process caused partisan bitterness and that the narrow national division that has existed between the major parties since the end of the Cold War shows every indication of continuing. One measure of current partisan consistency was how closely the partisanship of states in 2000 tracked state partisanship in 2004. Of the presidential contests in the 50 states and the District of Columbia, only two states (the low-population states of Vermont and Alaska) changed their partisanship by more than 3.9%. Partisanship in 32 states stayed nearly the same, changing by 2% or less.

The summary charts on the 2000 and 2004 presidential elections and partisanship trends by state from 1960 to 2004 are important building blocks for our analysis. They reveal that the generally modest changes in partisanship (Democratic gains in 29 contests, Republicans in 22) had little impact on the results.

Of those changes affecting which states are or might become battlegrounds, most moved the affected state in the direction of being less competitive, rather than more. For example, tables 1 and 2 list the ten states where partisanship shifted the

## Table 1   Biggest Pro-Republican Partisan Shifts in 2004 Election

| STATE | 2000 | 2004 | GAIN | ANALYSIS |
|-------|------|------|------|----------|
| Alabama | 57.72% | 61.58% | 3.86% | Shift from comfortable R to landslide R |
| Tennessee | 52.19% | 55.91% | 3.71% | Shift from lean R to comfortable R |
| Hawaii | 41.10% | 44.40% | 3.30% | Remains comfortable D |
| Oklahoma | 61.20% | 64.34% | 3.14% | Remains landslide R |
| New Jersey | 42.34% | 45.43% | 3.08% | Remains comfortable D |
| Rhode Island | 35.72% | 38.39% | 2.67% | Remains landslide D |
| Connecticut | 41.53% | 43.59% | 2.06% | Remain comfortable D |
| Louisiana | 54.10% | 56.02% | 1.93% | Secures state as comfortable R |
| New York | 37.77% | 39.63% | 1.86% | Remains landslide D |
| West Virginia | 53.42% | 55.20% | 1.78% | Secures state as comfortable R |

**Table 2   Biggest Pro-Democratic Partisan Shifts in 2004 Election**

| STATE | 2000 | 2004 | GAIN | ANALYSIS |
|-------|------|------|------|----------|
| Vermont | 45.29% | 38.70% | 6.59% | Shifts from comfortable D to landslide D |
| Alaska | 65.74% | 61.54% | 4.19% | Remains landslide R |
| Montana | 62.80% | 59.02% | 3.78% | Remains comfortable R |
| Maine | 47.70% | 44.27% | 3.43% | Shift from lean D to comfortable D |
| Oregon | 50.04% | 46.69% | 3.35% | Shift from tossup to comfortable D |
| Colorado | 54.44% | 51.11% | 3.33% | Shift from comfortable D to tossup R |
| District of Columbia | 12.16% | 8.85% | 3.31% | Exaggerates existing landslide D |
| New Hampshire | 50.89% | 48.09% | 2.81% | Remains tossup, now favoring D |
| Idaho | 70.03% | 67.83% | 2.20% | Remains landslide R |
| Ohio | 52.01% | 49.82% | 2.19% | Remains tossup, now favoring D |

most for each party. Of those changes that had any impact on battleground status, five states (Louisiana, Maine, Oregon Tennessee, West Virginia) became notably less competitive. Only Colorado grew more competitive.

In partisan terms, a close inspection of the 2004 elections provides one conclusion that may be counter-intuitive given the national results. In the most hotly contested battleground states, John Kerry's campaign in fact did relatively well. While George Bush won the presidency in 2000 even as he lost the national popular vote by more than 500,000, our analysis suggests that he would have lost the 2004 election even if winning the national popular vote by as many as 425,000 votes. A reduction in Bush's national victory margin from 2.46% to 0.35% likely would have tipped Ohio toward John Kerry, along with Iowa and New Mexico, giving Kerry a 284 to 254 electoral vote victory. Table 3 is an analysis of the 13 closest states in 2004 and their partisan shifts.

**Table 3   Shifts in GOP Partisanship in 2004 Election's 13 Closest States (within 47–53%)**

| STATE | 2000 | 2004 | CHANGE | DEMOCRATIC GAINS | REPUBLIC GAINS |
|-------|------|------|--------|------------------|----------------|
| Colorado | 54.44% | 51.11% | −3.33% | 3.33% | |
| Florida | 50.26% | 51.27% | 1.01% | | 1.01% |
| Iowa | 50.10% | 49.10% | −1.00% | 1.00% | |
| Michigan | 47.69% | 47.06% | −0.63% | 0.63% | |
| Minnesota | 49.06% | 47.03% | −2.03% | 2.03% | |
| Missouri | 51.93% | 52.37% | 0.44% | | 0.44% |
| Nevada | 52.03% | 50.07% | −1.97% | 1.97% | |
| New Hampshire | 50.89% | 48.09% | −2.81% | 2.81% | |
| New Mexico | 50.23% | 49.17% | −1.06% | 1.06% | |
| Ohio | 52.01% | 49.82% | −2.19% | 2.19% | |
| Pennsylvania | 48.18% | 47.52% | −0.66% | 0.66% | |
| Virginia | 54.28% | 52.87% | −1.41% | 1.41% | |
| Wisconsin | 50.15% | 48.58% | −1.57% | 1.57% | |
| Average | 50.87% | 49.54% | −1.33% | | |

In these battlegrounds, Democrats on a per-state average improved their performance by 1.33% percent, with gains in 11 of 13 states. This slight shift toward Democrats could have an impact on the 2008 elections. George Bush would have won 10 of these 13 hotly contested states in 2000 had the election been tied in the national popular vote, but in 2004 he would have won only five of these states in a nationally even election. The fact that Democrats did relatively better in battlegrounds than in the rest of the country suggests that the Democrats' campaign efforts centered on swing states were slightly more effective than those of the Republicans. It was George Bush's national advantage in voter preference that carried him to victory.

The Kerry campaign's relative success in battlegrounds thus helps explains why there were so few shifts in the Electoral College map. Indeed 47 of the 50 states and the District of Columbia awarded their electoral votes to parties exactly as they had done in 2000. The three states that shifted—New Hampshire (to Democrat), Iowa and New Mexico (to Republican)—were among the five most closely contested elections in the 2000 election. A shift of just 18,774 votes in those states would have meant an exact repeat of the 2000 state-by-state election results. A shift of just 20,417 votes in Iowa, New Mexico and Nevada would have given the country an Electoral College tie and thrown the outcome of the race to the U.S. House of Representatives.

## Shrinking Battlegrounds and the Hardening of the Partisan Divide: Elections 1960–2004

On average the last five electoral cycles have seen a deepening schism between Democratic and Republican states. This schism can be measured both by the number of states that have shifted from being relatively competitive to safe for one party and by the number of highly partisan states that have now become extremely different from the national average.

For the past four and a half decades the difference in partisanship between the ten most Republican and the ten most Democratic states ranged between 18% and 22%. As recently as 1988 this disparity was only 16%. The past two elections, however, have seen an average spread of 27.5% in 2000, and 26.6% in 2004.

The rise in partisanship has been particularly pronounced for Republican states. In 1988, the ten most Republican states had an average partisan bias of 58.2%. By 2004, the ten most Republican states had average partisanship of 64.5%, with all ten of these states having partisanship scores over 60% (Figure 1).

The result of this growing division is that less and less of the population lives in competitive states in a nationally competitive election. While at least half the states were within five percent of even

**Table 4    Number of States within Partisanship Brackets, 1960–2004 (Note Steady Decline in Competitive Bracket 45–55)**

| Partisanship scores | 1960 | 1964 | 1968 | 1972 | 1976 | 1980 | 1984 | 1988 | 1992 | 1996 | 2000 | 2004 | Average |
|---|---|---|---|---|---|---|---|---|---|---|---|---|---|
| 60+ | 2 | 8 | 2 | 5 | 5 | 7 | 4 | 1 | 2 | 6 | 11 | 10 | 5 |
| 55–60 | 9 | 9 | 11 | 11 | 4 | 7 | 9 | 14 | 9 | 11 | 7 | 10 | 9 |
| 55–50 | **16** | **9** | **20** | **16** | **21** | **10** | **21** | **15** | **17** | **11** | **16** | **8** | **15** |
| 50–45 | **17** | **15** | **11** | **12** | **12** | **20** | **9** | **11** | **17** | **16** | **6** | **11** | **13** |
| 45–40 | 2 | 6 | 3 | 5 | 6 | 4 | 7 | 9 | 5 | 3 | 7 | 7 | 5 |
| 40–0 | 4 | 4 | 4 | 2 | 3 | 3 | 1 | 1 | 1 | 4 | 4 | 5 | 3 |

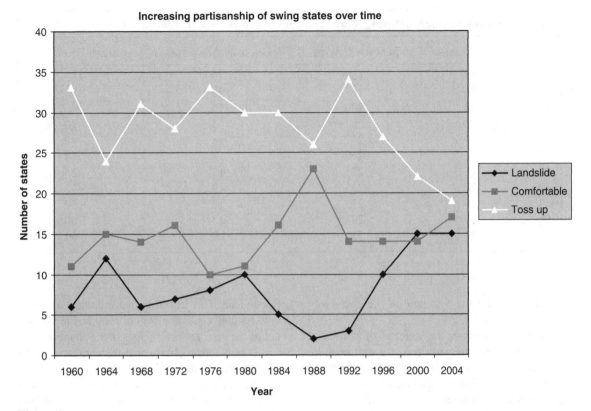

**Figure 1**

partisanship in every election between 1960 and 1996, this number of potentially competitive states dropped to 22 states in 2000 and to only 19 states in 2004 (Table 4).

Between 1960 and 1992 an average of 20 states could be fairly classified as likely to have been highly competitive in a nationally close election (meaning that a candidate from either major party could expect to win between 47% and 53%). Among these states typically were almost all of the nation's most populous states and enough total states to represent a majority of American citizens.

In the last three elections cycles, however, there was a marked reduction in the number of competitive states, even as the national electorate as a whole has become more evenly divided. Whereas 22 states were competitive in the 1992 election,

only 13 states were up for grabs when Clinton ran against Bob Dole in 1996. The number of contested states rebounded somewhat to 16 states in 2000— still well below the number common in previous close elections without an incumbent candidate— then plunged back to 13 in 2004.

This represents the smallest number of battleground states in the entire course of our analysis since 1960. While no fewer than 319 electoral votes were located in battleground states in 1960 (more than enough to elect a President), only 159 electoral votes could reasonably be considered up for grabs in 2004. While a majority of electoral votes were located in swing states as recently as 1988, the total number of competitive electoral votes began to drop in 1992 to the point where the elections in 2000 and 2004 saw the number of competitive electoral votes

| Year | Swing states | Electoral votes | Uncompetitive states | Electoral votes |
|------|------|------|------|------|
| **Table 5** Shifts in Numbers of Swing States and Uncompetitive States, 1960–2004 | | | | |
| 2004 | 13 | 159 | 20 | 163 |
| 2000 | 16 | 167 | 20 | 166 |
| 1996 | 13 | 206 | 13 | 90 |
| 1992 | 22 | 207 | 5 | 20 |
| 1988 | 21 | 272 | 8 | 40 |
| 1984 | 21 | 260 | 9 | 44 |
| 1980 | 15 | 221 | 13 | 58 |
| 1972 | 22 | 235 | 9 | 46 |
| 1968 | 19 | 273 | 11 | 57 |
| 1964 | 17 | 204 | 13 | 100 |
| 1960 | 23 | 319 | 9 | 64 |

fall below 200 for the first time in the post-1960 period of our analysis.

At the same time, the number of spectator states (ones where one party enjoys a partisanship advantage of at least 58%) has risen to unprecedented levels. Just five states with a total of 20 electoral votes were completely out of reach in 1992. The number of uncontestable electoral votes skyrocketed to 20 states with 166 electoral votes in 2000 and 163 electoral votes in 2004. From 1960 to 1996, the total number of uncompetitive electoral votes had never exceeded 100. In 2004, for the first time, the number of completely uncompetitive electoral votes exceeded the number of electoral votes in competitive states.

Swing states are within 3.0% of a 50% partisanship; uncompetitive states are more than 8.0% from a 50% partisanship.

What's behind this growth in the number of spectator states? Our research supports the common perception that our country is becoming more starkly divided along "red" and "blue" political lines, with Democrats becoming more clearly a party of the coasts and big cities and with Republicans dominating the interior. As these battle lines become increasingly well defined, the populations of rural states become less likely to vote Democrat while urban dwellers become equally less likely to vote

Republican. This leaves a small minority of states, with roughly equal numbers of rural and urban voters, as the true "tossup" regions of the country.

It also appears likely that the number of competitive states will stabilize at present levels for the next several electoral cycles. While the exact number of battleground and spectator states varies from election to election, it typically takes a significant change in partisan makeup of a state's population to have a substantial impact on its partisanship. Major changes can happen, but almost always over time— the South, for example, has nearly completely shifted from Democratic majorities to Republican majorities over the past forty years—but there is no indication of comparable shifts currently underway. Over the coming years, we are likely to continue to see a fairly deep, regional-based partisan schism between the major parties in which few states will be truly up for grabs in any election that is close nationally.

## PARTISAN IMPLICATIONS FOR THE 2008 ELECTIONS

Looking toward the 2008 presidential election, FairVote's electoral model allows us to broadly project state-by-state voting outcomes based on historic voter behavior and the nationwide appeal of the major party candidates. While it is impossible to guess the exact popular vote total in the next election, we can build scenarios based on theoretical vote outcomes.

We base our 2008 election analysis on state partisanship and trends in the 2004 election. If John Kerry had captured exactly half of the popular vote in 2004 he would likely have become president. With three million more votes, Kerry would have slightly improved his performance in all the states, allowing him to narrowly carry Iowa, New Mexico, and Ohio, in addition to the states he already won. This would have given Democrats a 284–254 victory in the Electoral College. Under this scenario, Ohio would have remained the critical race of the election, with Kerry likely winning the statewide vote by 0.36 percentage points, slightly more than 20,000 votes.

We recognize that factors beyond party control have the capacity to move the electorate away from a 50%-50% division. But using our partisanship model and applying it to likely outcomes of the popular vote demonstrates a slight Electoral College bias to Democrats in tight elections while Republicans gain a larger Electoral College majority in comfortable wins.

Assuming another close presidential contest in 2008—a plausible assumption, but one that our analytical model of partisanship does not address—our analysis suggests that the "big three states" of 2004 may well be reduced to "the big two": Ohio and

| REPUBLICAN WINS 52% OF THE POPULAR VOTE | REPUBLICAN WINS 55% OF THE POPULAR VOTE |
|---|---|
| Wins Electoral College 300–238 | Wins Electoral College 384–154 |
| DEMOCRAT WINS 52% OF THE POPULAR VOTE | DEMOCRAT WINS 55% OF THE POPULAR VOTE |
| Wins Electoral College 321–217 | Wins Electoral College 376–162 |

Florida. Pennsylvania might stay highly competitive, but no other big state appears likely to have a chance to be in play, and far more 2004 battleground states moved away from being toss-ups than toward them. If a Republican carries both Ohio and Florida, therefore, that candidate almost certainly will win. If a Democrat wins just one of these two states, that Democrat likely will win. Given that the major parties almost certainly have come to this same conclusion, how they position themselves to win those two states may well determine the presidency in 2008.

There are a handful of other states that will matter, although there likely will be fewer than ten true battlegrounds in 2008. More than ever, the vast majority of Americans will be reduced to spectator status in the next election, looking on as candidates shower all their attention and money on a narrow slice of the American public.

## REFORM IMPLICATIONS OF THE SHRINKING BATTLEGROUND: VOTER TURNOUT, ELECTION ADMINISTRATION, CIVIL RIGHTS AND THE ELECTORAL COLLEGE

The implications of our analysis of the shrinking battleground in American presidential elections go beyond which party might win the 2008 election: they go to the heart of American democracy. Consider its impact in four areas: voter participation, controversies over election administration, racial fairness and the Electoral College.

### Voter Turnout Now and Over Time

The current two-tier system of electing the president is creating a culture of political haves and have-nots that will likely affect voter participation rates in battleground states and spectator states for generations to come. With only a small number of battleground states, and a closely divided electorate, it becomes increasingly likely that future elections will be decided by some combination of the same states that decided the 2004 election.

Thus, meaningful suffrage—the ability to go to a poll and cast a vote for a candidate without effective foreknowledge of the electoral outcome in that state—will be restricted to citizens in a small number of highly contentious states that represent perhaps a quarter of the nation's electorate. The parties and their backers will spend hundreds of millions of dollars to register and mobilize these voters. The rest of the nation will be spectators to the election, ignored by the campaigns.

The impact on voter turnout is already pronounced. In the 12 most competitive states in 2004, turnout was 63%, up from 54% in 2000. In the 12 most lopsided states, turnout was 53%, up from 51% in 2000. The gap in turnout between these two state groupings soared from 3% to 10%. Given the financial resources certain to be targeted on mobilization in 2008 battlegrounds, expect this gap to widen.

Indeed the effect on turnout will likely go beyond just one or two elections. Young Americans becoming eligible to vote will be treated quite differently based on where they live, with far more intense efforts to register and mobilize newly eligible voters in battleground states. Mark Franklin's recent seminal work on voter participation (Voter Turnout and the Dynamics of Electoral Competition in Established Democracies Since 1945) provides an analysis of voter turnout and factors affecting it in more than two dozen nations over several generations. One of his findings is that voting behavior is often established by what a person does in the first elections after becoming eligible to vote. The "imprint" of whether one votes in these elections typically lasts a lifetime.

We already can see dramatic evidence of the impact of our two-tiered system in youth participation rates. According to the University of Maryland-based organization CIRCLE, in 2000 a slim majority (51%) of young voters (age 18–29) turned out in battleground states, while only 38% of young voters in the rest of the country went to the polls. In 2004 the gap between youth turnout in battleground and non-competitive states widened. CIRCLE found that 64.4% of young people voted in ten battleground states. Their turnout was only slightly less than the average swing state turnout of 66.1%, showing that young adults were mobilized

to vote where their votes clearly mattered. (Note that CIRCLE's numbers are based on survey data. Surveys slightly inflate turnout numbers for all groups.)

The story was very different in the rest of the country. Only 47.6% of 18–29 year olds voted in the other forty states and the District of Columbia. This is fully 17% below the turnout rates of youth voters in battleground states and much farther below the average turnout for older voters (58.9%) in these non-battleground states. Another election or two with this disparity will make it very likely that turnout in current non-battleground states will stay below turnout in current battleground states for decades even if by 2016 we were to get rid of the Electoral College and provide a fair, one-person, one-vote presidential election (Figure 2).

## Election Administration Controversies

The 2000 presidential elections exposed just how antiquated and underfunded our system of registering voters, counting ballots and running elections had become in most states. In our dangerously decentralized system of protecting the right to vote, states typically delegate the conduct of elections to localities—meaning most important decisions about presidential elections are made separately by more than 13,000 local governments. In the wake of Florida's election fiasco, Congress for the first time in history helped fund elections and established a national commission to set some national standards. But the United States still falls short of establishing the kind of predictable election administration found in most democracies.

In an era of close presidential elections with continued use of the Electoral College, this kind of election administration is highly problematic. A national election would almost never be so close that the results wouldn't be definitive. But with 51 separate contests deciding the presidency, the odds are increased that in every close election there will be narrow votes in enough states that the conduct of election will be controversial—and end up in courts. Even in 2004, in an election where George

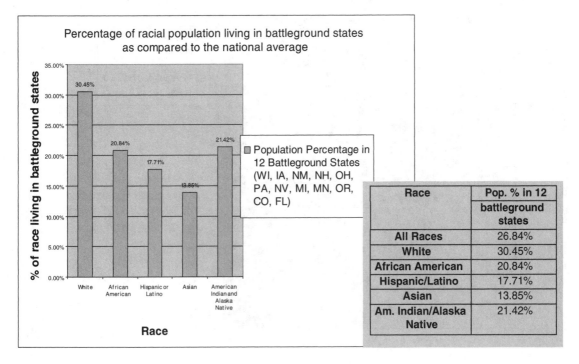

**Figure 2**

Bush won the popular vote by more than three million votes, the serious problems with Ohio's elections—featuring battles over voter registration, provisional ballots, partisan observers in polling places and the shockingly long lines experienced by many voters—led to expensive litigation and suspicions that the election was not decided fairly. Given today's hardening partisan divisions, expect even more controversy and litigation in our elections until we take the right to vote more seriously, increase funding for elections and establish stronger national standards and clearer pre-election and post-election accountability.

## Racial Fairness

The United States has a disturbing history of policy on race relations, from slavery to Jim Crow laws to having an Electoral College in the first place. Race remains a powder keg, regularly ignited in political battles and policy debates. With that history, it is essential we have a presidential election system that encourages fairness and does away with discrimination at the polls.

The current breakdown of battlegrounds and spectator states does the opposite. Consider that 27% of the nation's population lives in the twelve closest battleground states in the 2004 elections. If all racial groups were distributed evenly throughout the country, therefore, 27% of each of the nation's racial and ethnic groups would live in these states.

The reality is far different. Racial minorities are far more likely to live in spectator states than white voters. While more than 30% of the nation's white population lives in the battleground states, just 21% of African Americans and Native Americans, 18% of Latinos and 14% of Asian Americans live in these states. In other words, three out of every 10 white Americans live in a battleground state, but less than two of every ten people of color share this opportunity (Figure 3).

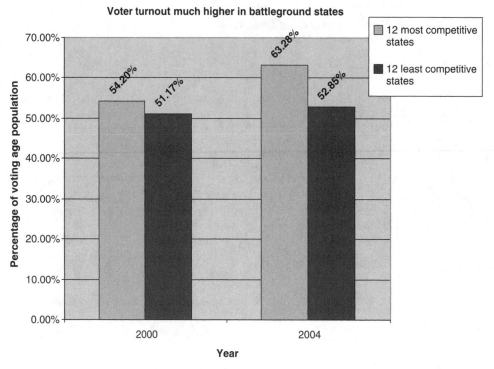

Figure 3

## Electoral College Reform

FairVote is unambiguous in its support for abolishing the Electoral College and establishing direct election of the president by majority vote, with elections decided according to the fundamental democratic principles of majority rule and of one person, one vote.

But direct election isn't the only constitutional amendment that a responsible Congress would be debating. Even Electoral College defenders have little excuse to maintain certain elements within the current structure that have every chance of causing major problems in the years ahead. Consider two examples that demand attention all the more in this time of close national elections.

Faithless Electors: Voters have every right to expect electors in their state to represent their state's popular will. However, there remains no federal law preventing electors from voting for someone other

than a state's popular choice, and laws in some states that seek to shield voters against such "faithless electors" may not be constitutional.

On a regular basis, some electors indeed disregard the will of their state's voters. In 2000, an elector from Washington, D.C. refused to vote for Al Gore. In 2004, an elector in Minnesota mistakenly voted for John Edwards instead of John Kerry, and a West Virginian Republican elector publicly considered not voting for George Bush. In the modern era, it's hard to imagine why we should risk the possibility that one elector could unilaterally reverse the outcome of a Presidential election. In this era of close elections, backers of the Electoral College are flirting with disaster if they do not pursue constitutional change to either bind electors or eliminate the office of electors and have electoral votes awarded automatically according to a state's rules.

The method of choosing the president when the Electoral College deadlocks: As long as the U.S.

House of Representatives has an uneven number of Representatives or does not give the citizens of Washington, D.C. representation in the House, the total number of electoral votes will be even. An even number of electoral votes makes a tie in the Electoral College possible. When no candidate wins an Electoral College majority, the election is decided by the U.S. House of Representatives, with each state's delegation casting one vote.

Indeed we narrowly missed ties in the Electoral College in our two most recent elections. In 2004, a change of 18,776 votes (just 0.015% of national total) in Iowa, New Mexico and Nevada would have resulted in a tie. In 2000, a change of 5,381 votes (0.0051% of national total) in four states (Florida, New Mexico, Wisconsin and Iowa) would have resulted in a tie.

Third party and independent candidates also periodically tend to run well in the United States. In 2008, it will have been 16 years since Ross Perot won nearly a fifth of the national vote and 40 years since George Wallace won several southern states. In this era of tightly contested elections, comparable success by a third party or independent candidate in winning just a handful of electoral votes could deny any candidate an Electoral College majority.

Having an election decided in the House would likely be fiercely contested by whichever party lost, particularly if its candidate won the popular vote. There is simply no twenty-first-century justification for the Constitution's provision that each state's House delegation casts one vote regardless of population. Thus, when Congress picks the president, 36 million Californians and 22 million Texans would have no more voice in the selection of the President than less than half a million people of Wyoming. States with evenly divided partisan delegation would somehow need to pick a winner. Consider what might have happened in 2000, when Al Gore won the popular vote, but Republicans controlled a majority of state delegations. Partisan bitterness in the wake of such a vote would likely dwarf anything this nation has experienced since the Civil War.

This rule for picking presidential winners is even harder to defend than faithless electors, yet may well come into play in upcoming elections given our state of partisan division and potential third party candidacies. Electoral College defenders have every reason to develop a more equitable process to prevent such a constitutional crisis.

## A NATIONAL POPULAR VOTE

FairVote's analysis in *The Shrinking Battleground* provides powerful evidence that the time has come for a renewal of the movement for direct popular election of the president that came so close to success in Congress in the late 1960s. In every election in this country we adhere to the principle of one person, one vote, except when it comes to the presidency. The Electoral College already has seated four second-place winners, and a shift of less than 1% of the vote in several additional elections would have handed the presidency to candidates losing the popular vote.

The United States calls for spreading democracy throughout the world, yet our presidential system at home is terribly flawed. It undercuts basic democratic principles and entrenches a two-tier democracy with a minority of first-class citizens and a majority of second-class citizens. It leaves a majority of our young adults and a disproportionate share of our people of color shut out of opportunities to meaningfully engage in electing their national leader—a dangerous and divisive precedent for the future.

For more than fifty years the Gallup poll has shown that a large majority of Americans wants to abolish the Electoral College and adopt a straight, one-person, one-vote system of electing the president. A national popular vote for president, particularly one held under Australian-style instant runoff voting rules that ensure a majority winner in every election [see Article 20], would ensure that every vote is equally important, that candidates address regional issues everywhere, that campaigns reach for support into every corner of this vast country and that winners reflect the will of the people.

We call on Congress to address this report's disturbing findings and to prove that basic principles of democracy like equality, majority rule and one-person, one-vote are as important to Americans as they should be to emerging democracies. Abolishing the Electoral College will help make the United States a modern democracy ready for today's complex times. The integrity and health of our democracy depend upon it.

---

## DISCUSSION QUESTIONS

1. How do the authors define "battleground states?" In what ways are the racial characteristics of these states different from those of other states?
2. What are the major flaws in the current system of selecting the president? Do you agree that the Electoral College should be abolished?

**19** *Arlie Hochschild*

# LET THEM EAT WAR

*In the past decade political commentators have often identified upscale "wired workers" or suburban "soccer moms" as the key swing group in the electorate. In this article, sociologist Arlie Hochschild examines white, blue-collar men as a key voting bloc. Following up on the analysis of Joel Rogers and Ruy Teixeira in their much-discussed book* America's Forgotten Majority *(2000), Hochschild looks at the political identity of the so-called "Nascar Dads" in the Bush years. She searches for explanations of higher than average support for President Bush among this group, despite concerns over job security, wages, health, and safety. She argues that Bush has carried on a long-standing Republican politics of dispacement, whereby blue-collar fears of economic decline come to focus on an assortment of convenient enemies, in this case "evildoers" abroad. Hochschild's provocative analysis was written in the fall of 2003. We ask you to consider its validity in light of the presidential election of 2004, and what we learned about the voting choices of white, blue-collar men.*

[In late 2003] George W. Bush was sinking in the polls, but a few beats on the war drum could reverse that trend and re-elect him in 2004. Ironically, the sector of American society now poised to keep him in the White House is the one which stands to lose the most from virtually all of his policies—blue-collar men. A full 49% of them and 38% percent of blue-collar women told a January 2003 Roper poll they would vote for Bush in 2004.

In fact, blue-collar workers were more pro-Bush than professionals and managers among whom only 40% of men and 32% of women, when polled, favor him; that is, people who reported to Roper such occupations as painter, furniture mover, waitress, and sewer repairman were more likely to be for our pro-big business president than people with occupations like doctor, attorney, CPA or property manager. High-school graduates and dropouts were more pro-Bush (41%) than people with graduate degrees (36%). And people with family incomes of $30,000 or less were no more opposed to Bush than those with incomes of $75,000 or more.

We should think about this. The blue-collar vote is huge. Skilled and semi-skilled manual jobs are on the decline, of course, but if we count as blue-collar those workers without a college degree, as Ruy Teixeira and Joel Rogers do in their book *Why the White Working Class Still Matters,* then

*Source:* Arlie Hochschild, "Let Them Eat War," *TomDispatch.com,* 2 October 2003. Available online at: http://www.tomdispatch.com/index.mhtml?pid=986

blue-collar voters represent 55% of all voters. They are, the authors note, the real swing vote in America. "Their loyalties shift the most from election to election and in so doing determine the winners in American politics."

This fact has not been lost on Republican strategists who are now targeting right-leaning blue-collar men, or as they call them, "Nascar Dads." These are, reporter Liz Clarke of the *Washington Post* tells us, "lower or middle-class men who once voted Democratic but who now favor Republicans." Nascar Dads, commentator Bill Decker adds, are likely to be racing-car fans, live in rural areas, and have voted for Bush in 2000. Bush is giving special attention to steelworkers, autoworkers, carpenters and other building-trades workers, according to Richard Dunham and Aaron Bernstein of *Business Week,* and finding common cause on such issues as placing tariffs on imported steel and offering tax breaks on pensions.

We can certainly understand why Bush wants blue-collar voters. But why would a near majority of blue-collar voters still want Bush? Millionaires, billionaires for Bush, well, sure; he's their man. But why pipe fitters and cafeteria workers? Some are drawn to his pro-marriage, pro-church, pro-gun stands, but could those issues override a voter's economic self-interest?

Let's consider the situation. Since Bush took office in 2000, the U.S. has lost 4.9 million jobs (2.5 million net), the vast majority of them in manufacturing. While this cannot be blamed entirely on Bush, his bleed-'em-dry approach to the non-Pentagon parts of the government has led him to do nothing to help blue-collar workers learn new trades, find affordable housing, or help their children go to college. The loosening of Occupational Health and Safety Administration regulations has made plants less safe. Bush's agricultural policies favor agribusiness and have put many small and medium-sized farms into bankruptcy. His tax cuts are creating state budget shortfalls, which will hit the public schools blue-collar children go to, and erode what services they now get. He has put industrialists in his environmental posts, so that the air and water will grow dirtier. His administration's disregard for the severe understaffing of America's

nursing homes means worse care for the elderly parents of the Nascar Dad as they live out their last days. His invasion of Iraq has sent blue-collar children and relatives to the front. Indeed, his entire tap-the-hornets'-nest foreign policy has made the U.S. arguably less secure than it was before he took office. Indeed, a recent series of polls revealed that most people around the world believe him to be a greater danger than Osama bin Laden. Many blue-collar voters know at least some of this already. So why are so many of them pro-Bush anyway?

## WONDERING ABOUT THE NASCAR DAD

Among blue-collar voters, more men than women favor Bush, so we can ask what's going on with the men. It might seem that their pocketbooks say one thing, their votes another, but could it be that, by some good fortune, blue-collar men are actually better off than we imagine? No, that can't be it. About a fifth of them had household incomes of $30,000 or less; 4 in 10 between $30,000 and $75,000; and 4 in 10 $75,000 or more. Among the poorest blue-collar families (with household incomes of $30,000 or less) a full 44% were pro-Bush. Perhaps even more strikingly, $75,000-plus Nascar Dads are more likely to favor Bush than their income-counterparts who hold professional and managerial jobs.

Even if poor blue-collar men were pro-Bush in general, we might at least assume that they would oppose Bush's massive program of tax cuts if they thought it favored the rich? If we did, then we'd be wrong again. "Do you think this tax plan benefits mainly the rich or benefits everyone?" Roper interviewers asked. Among blue-collar men who answered, "Yes, it benefits mainly the rich," 56% percent nonetheless favored the plan. Among blue-collar men with $30,000 or less who answered "yes" and who believed that yes, this tax cut "benefits mainly the rich," a full 53% favored it. This far exceeds the 35% of people who make $75,000 or more, knew the tax cut favored the rich, and still supported it.

So, what's going on? Should we throw out the classic Clinton-era explanation for how we all vote: "It's the economy, stupid?" Not right away. Maybe the blue-collar man who favors that tax cut is thinking "the economy stupid" but only in the short term. He badly needs even the small amounts of money he'll get from a tax cut to repair his car or contribute to the rent. But then many working-class men labor decade after decade at difficult jobs to secure a future for their children. So if they think long term as a way of life, why are they thinking short-term when it comes to their vote?

One possibility is that the Nascar Dad is not well informed; that indeed, like the rest of us, he's been duped. For example, he may have fallen for the Karl Rove-inspired bandwagon effect. "Bush is unbeatable," he hears, or "Bush has a $200,000,000 re-election fund. Get with the winner." It makes you a winner too, he feels. This might account for some blue-collar Bush support, but it doesn't explain why the Nascar Dad would be more likely to be taken in by the bandwagon effect than the professional or managerial dad. Anyway, most blue-collar men would seem to be no less likely than anyone else to vote their conscience, regardless of whom they think will win, and that's not even counting those who root for the underdog as a matter of principle.

But another kind of manipulation could be going on. A certain amount of crucial information has gone missing in the Bush years. As has recently become clear, information that would be of great interest to the Nascar Dad has been withheld. With jobs disappearing at a staggering rate, the Bureau of Labor Statistics ended its Mass Layoff Tracking Study on Christmas Eve of 2002, thanks to this administration. And although Congressional Democrats managed to get funding for the study restored in February of 2003, the loss of 614,167 jobs in those two months was unannounced.

Conveying the truth in a misleading manner is, of course, another way of manipulating people. As the linguist George Lakoff astutely observes, the term "tax relief" slyly invites us to imagine taxes as an affliction and those who propose them as villains. If we add in such distortions to the suppression of vital information, the Nascar Dad who listens to Rush Limbaugh on the commute home, turns on *Fox News* at dinner, and is too tired after working overtime to catch more than the headlines is perhaps

a man being exposed to only one side of the political story.

But then Nascar Dad could always turn the radio dial. He could do a google search on job loss on his kid's computer. He could talk to his union buddies—if he's one of the 12% who are still unionized—or to his slightly more liberal wife. It could be he knows perfectly well that he's being lied to, but believes people are usually being lied to, and that Bush is, in this respect, still the better of two evils. But how could that be?

Maybe it's because Bush fits an underlying recipe for the kind of confident, authoritative father figure such dads believe should run the ship of state as they believe a man should run a family. Republican rhetoric may appeal to the blue-collar man, Lakoff suggests, because we tend to match our view of good politics with our image of a good family. The appeal of any political leader, he believes, lies in the way he matches our images of the father in the ideal family. There are two main pictures of such an ideal American family, Lakoff argues. According to a "strict father family" model, dad should provide for the family, control mom, and use discipline to teach his children how to survive in a competitive and hostile world. Those who advocate the strict father model, Lakoff reasons, favor a "strict father" kind of government. If an administration fits this model, it supports the family (by maximizing overall wealth). It protects the family from harm (by building up the military). It raises the children to be self-reliant and obedient (by fostering citizens who ask for little and speak when spoken to). The match-up here is, of course, to Bush Republicans.

Then there is the "nurturing parent family" model in which parents don't simply control their children but encourage their development. The government equivalent would be offering services to the citizenry, funding education, health, and welfare, and emphasizing diplomacy on a global stage. The core values here are empathy and responsibility, not control and discipline and the match up is to the pro-public sector Dean/Kucinich Democrats. Studies have shown that blue-collar ideals are closer to the strict father than to the nurturing parent model. But that's been true for a very long time, while the blue-collar vote sometimes goes left as in the 1930s, and sometimes goes right as it's doing now. So we can't simply pin the pro-Bush Nascar Dad vote on a sudden change in blue-collar family ideals.

## APPEALING TO THE "FORGOTTEN AMERICAN"

Maybe, however, something deeper is going on, which has so far permitted Bush's flag-waving and cowboy-boot-strutting to trump issues of job security, wages, safety, and health—and even, in the case of Bush's threats of further war—life itself. In an essay, "The White Man Unburdened," in a recent *New York Review of Books,* Norman Mailer recently argued that the war in Iraq returned to white males a lost sense of mastery, offering them a feeling of revenge for imagined wrongs, and a sense of psychic rejuvenation. In the last thirty years, white men have taken a drubbing, he notes, especially the three quarters of them who lack college degrees. Between 1979 and 1999, for example, real wages for male high-school graduates dropped 24%. In addition, Mailer notes, white working class men have lost white champs in football, basketball and boxing. (A lot of white men cheer black athletes, of course, whomever they vote for.) But the war in Iraq, Mailer notes, gave white men white heroes. By climbing into his jumpsuit, stepping out of an S–3B Viking jet onto the aircraft carrier *USS Abraham Lincoln,* Bush posed as—one could say impersonated—such a hero.

Mailer is talking here about white men and support for the war in Iraq. But we're talking about something that cuts deeper into emotional life, and stretches further back into the twin histories of American labor and Republican presidencies. For Republicans have been capturing blue-collar hearts for some time now. In the summer of 1971, Jefferson Cowie tells us in a recent essay, Richard Nixon worked out a semi-clandestine "blue-collar strategy." Nixon instructed Jerome Rosow of the Department of Labor to draw up a confidential report, only 25 copies of which were circulated. One of them got into the hands of a *Wall Street Journal* reporter who exposed it under the banner, "Secret Report Tells Nixon How to Help White Workingmen and Win Their Votes."

As the article noted, "President Nixon has before him a confidential blueprint designed to help him capture the hearts and votes of the nation's white working men—the traditionally Democratic 'forgotten Americans' that the Administration believes are ripe for political plucking." According to close advisor, H.R. Haldeman, Nixon's plan was to maintain an image as "a tough, courageous, masculine leader." The never-ending Nixon tapes actually catch Nixon talking with aides Haldeman and Ehlichman about an episode in the popular television show "All in the Family" in which the working-class Archie Bunker confronts an old buddy, a former football player who has just come out of the closet as gay. Nixon then recounts on tape how civilizations decline when homosexuality rises, and concludes, "We have to stand up to this." Nixon sought to appeal to the blue-collar man's straightness (at least he still had that), his superiority over women (that, too), and his native-born whiteness (and that). As Cowie sums it up, "It was neither the entire working class nor its material grievances on which the administration would focus; rather it was the 'feeling of being forgotten' among white male workers that Nixon and his advisors would seek to tap."

Until Nixon, Republicans had for a century written off the blue-collar voter. But turning Marx on his head, Nixon appealed not to a desire for real economic change but to the distress caused by the absence of it. And it worked as it's doing again now. In the 1972 contest between Nixon and McGovern, 57% of the manual worker vote and 54% of the union vote went to Nixon. (This meant 22- and 25-point gains for Nixon over his 1968 presidential run.) After Nixon, other Republican presidents—Ford, Reagan, and Bush Sr.—followed in the same footsteps, although not always so cleverly.

Now George Bush Jr. is pursuing a sequel strategy by again appealing to the emotions of male blue-collar voters. Only he's added a new element to the mix. Instead of appealing, as Nixon did, to anger at economic decline, Bush is appealing to fear of economic displacement, and offering the

Nascar Dad a set of villains to blame, and a hero to thank—George W. Bush.

Let's begin by re-imagining the blue-collar man, for we do not normally think of him as a fearful man. The very term "Nascar Dad" like the earlier term "Joe Six Pack" suggests, somewhat dismissively, an "I'm-alright-Jack" kind of guy. We imagine him with his son, some money in his pocket, in the stands with the other guys rooting for his favorite driver and car. The term doesn't call to mind a restless house-husband or a despondent divorcee living back in his parents' house and seeing his kids every other weekend. In other words, the very image we start with may lead us away from clues to his worldview, his feelings, his politics and the links between these.

Since the 1970s, the blue-collar man has taken a lot of economic hits. The buying power of his paycheck, the size of his benefits, the security of his job—all these have diminished. As Ed Landry, a 62-year-old-machinist interviewed by Paul Solman on the *Lehrer News Hour* said, "We went to lunch and our jobs went to China." He searched for another job and couldn't find one. He was even turned down for a job as a grocery bagger. "I was told that we'd get back to you. Did they?" Solman asked. "No. I couldn't believe it myself. I couldn't get the job." In today's jobless recovery, the average jobless stint for a man like Landry is now 19 weeks, the longest since 1983. Jobs that don't even exist at present may eventually open up, experts reassure us, but they aren't opening up yet. In the meantime, three out of every four available jobs are low-level service jobs. A lot of workers like Ed Landry, cast out of one economic sector, have been unable to land a job even at the bottom of another.

For anyone who stakes his pride on earning an honest day's pay, this economic fall is, unsurprisingly enough, hard to bear. How, then, do these blue-collar men feel about it? Ed Landry said he felt "numb." Others are anxious, humiliated and, as who wouldn't be, fearful. But in cultural terms, Nascar Dad isn't supposed to feel afraid. What he can feel though is angry. As Susan Faludi has described so well in her book *Stiffed,* that is what many such men feel. As a friend who works in a

Maine lumber mill among blue-collar Republicans explained about his co-workers, "They felt that everyone else—women, kids, minorities—were all moving up, and they felt like they were moving down. Even the spotted owl seemed like it was on its way up, while he and his job, were on the way down. And he's angry."

## STRUTTING THE POLITICAL FLIGHT DECK

But is that anger directed downward—at "welfare cheats," women, gays, blacks, and immigrants—or is it aimed up at job exporters and rich tax dodgers? Or out at alien enemies? The answer is likely to depend on the political turn of the screw. The Republicans are clearly doing all they can to aim that anger down or out, but in any case away from the rich beneficiaries of Bush's tax cut. Unhinging the personal from the political, playing on identity politics, Republican strategists have offered the blue-collar voter a Faustian bargain: We'll lift your self-respect by putting down women, minorities, immigrants, even those spotted owls. We'll honor the manly fortitude you've shown in taking bad news. But (and this is implicit) don't ask us to do anything to change that bad news. Instead of Marie Antoinette's "let them eat cake," we have—and this is Bush's twist on the old Nixonian strategy—"let them eat war."

Paired with this is an aggressive right-wing attempt to mobilize blue-collar fear, resentment and a sense of being lost—and attach it to the fear of American vulnerability, American loss. By doing so, Bush aims to win the blue-collar man's identification with big business, empire, and himself. The resentment anyone might feel at the personnel officer who didn't have the courtesy to call him back and tell him he didn't have the job, Bush now redirects toward the target of Osama bin Laden, and when we can't find him, Saddam Hussein and when we can't find him . . . And these enemies are now so intimate that we see them close up on the small screen in our bedrooms and call them by their first names.

Whether strutting across a flight deck or mocking the enemy, Bush with his seemingly fearless bravado—ironically born of class entitlement—offers an aura of confidence. And this confidence dampens, even if temporarily, the feelings of insecurity and fear exacerbated by virtually every major domestic and foreign policy initiative of the Bush administration. Maybe it comes down to this: George W. Bush is deregulating American global capitalism with one hand while regulating the feelings it produces with the other. Or, to put it another way, he is doing nothing to change the causes of fear and everything to channel the feeling and expression of it. He speaks to a working man's lost pride and his fear of the future by offering an image of fearlessness. He poses here in his union jacket, there in his pilot's jumpsuit, taunting the Iraqis to "bring 'em on"—all of it meant to feed something in the heart of a frightened man. In this light, even Bush's "bad boy" past is a plus. He steals a wreath off a Macy's door for his Yale fraternity and careens around drunk in Daddy's car. But in the politics of anger and fear, the Republican politics of feelings, this is a plus.

There is a paradox here. While Nixon was born into a lower-middle-class family, his distrustful personality ensured that his embrace of the blue-collar voter would prove to be wary and distrustful. Paradoxically, Bush, who was born to wealth, seems really to like being the top gun talking to "regular guys." In this way, Bush adds to Nixon's strategy his lone-ranger machismo.

More important, Nixon came into power already saddled with an unpopular war. Bush has taken a single horrific set of attacks on September 11, 2001, and mobilized his supporters and their feelings around them. Unlike Nixon, Bush created his own war, declared it ongoing but triumphant, and fed it to his potential supporters. His policy—and this his political advisor Karl Rove has carefully calibrated—is something like the old bait- and-switch. He continues to take the steaks out of the blue-collar refrig- erator and to declare instead, "let them eat war." He has been, in effect, strip-mining the emotional responses of blue-collar men to the problems his own administration is so intent on causing.

But there is a chance this won't work. For one thing, the war may turn out to have been a bad idea, Bush's equivalent of a runaway plant. For another thing, working men may smell a skunk. Many of them may resent those they think have emerged from the pack behind them and are now getting ahead, and they may fear for their future. But they may also come to question whether they've been offered Osama bin Laden as a stand-in for the many unfixed problems they face. They may wonder whether their own emotions aren't just one more natural resource the Republicans are exploiting for their profit. What we urgently need now, of course, is a presidential candidate who addresses the root causes of blue-collar anger and fear and who actually tackles the problems before us all, instead of pandering to the emotions bad times evoke.

---

## DISCUSSION QUESTIONS

1. Identify key facts about the economic and demographic profile of blue-collar workers, as presented by Hochschild. In what ways have their living conditions become more strained in recent years?
2. According to Hochschild, in what ways does Bush's "war on terrorism" provide the "Nascar Dads" with a positive sense of identity? Why would Hochschild regard this identity as based on a process of "displacement"?

## 20 *Lani Guinier*

# AFTER THE DELUGE: ELECTORAL REFORM IN THE WAKE OF THE ELECTION OF 2000

*In the wake of the historic presidential election of 2000—with the outcome hanging in the balance for well over a month after election day, rampant charges of fraud and disenfranchisement, a national split between the popular vote winner and the Electoral College winner, and the ultimately decisive role played by the U.S. Supreme Court in stopping the Florida recount—a cry has gone up for all manner of election law reform. In this post-election analysis, Harvard law professor and long-time electoral reform advocate Lani Guinier weighs in on the side of a major overhaul of the electoral system. Guinier urges Americans to seize this rare opportunity to see the nation's electoral flaws under the glaring media spotlight and address many basic questions about how we vote. She examines the nation's extremely low voter turnout rate, the class and race-based nature of who votes, the often antiquated mechanics of voting procedures, the equally antiquated Electoral College, and the winner-take-all system of allocating electoral votes. In each area she identifies the need for major changes if we are to seriously strive to be a nation that fulfills the still-elusive promise of democracy—a promise that declares that every vote, and every voter, counts. Moreover, she sees a role for an active and engaged citizenry to call for substantial reform and to monitor the electoral process at the grassroots level, thus helping to reinvigorate civic life. Guinier's perspective suggests that there are many lessons to be learned from the controversy that has raged over the first U.S. presidential election of the twenty-first century. It remains to be seen how attentive we are as students of democracy.*

For years many of us have called for a national conversation about what it means to be a multiracial democracy. We have enumerated the glaring flaws inherent in our winner-take-all form of voting, which has produced a steady decline in voter participation, underrepresentation of racial minorities in office, lack of meaningful competition and choice in most elections, and the general failure of politics to mobilize, inform and inspire half the eligible electorate. But nothing changed. Democracy

*Source:* Lani Guinier, "Making Every Vote Count." *The Nation,* Volume 271, Number 18, December 4, 2000, pp. 5–7.

*Get Numbers*

was an asterisk in political debate, typically encompassed in a vague reference to "campaign finance reform." Enter Florida.

The fiasco there provides a rare opportunity to rethink and improve our voting practices in a way that reflects our professed desire to have "every vote count." This conversation has already begun, as several highly educated communities in Palm Beach experienced the same sense of systematic disfranchisement that beset the area's poorer and less-educated communities of color. "It felt like Birmingham last night," Mari Castellanos, a Latina activist in Miami, wrote in an e-mail describing a mammoth rally at the 14,000-member New Birth Baptist Church, a primarily African-American congregation in Miami. "The sanctuary was standing room only. So were the overflow rooms and the school hall, where congregants connected via large TV screens. The people sang and prayed and listened. Story after story was told of voters being turned away at the polls, of ballots being destroyed, of NAACP election literature being discarded at the main post office, of Spanish-speaking poll workers being sent to Creole precincts and vice-versa. . . . Union leaders, civil rights activists, Black elected officials, ministers, rabbis and an incredibly passionate and inspiring Marlene Bastiene—president of the Haitian women's organization—spoke for two or three minutes each, reminding the assembly of the price their communities had paid for the right to vote and vowing not to be disfranchised ever again."

We must not let this once-in-a-generation moment pass without addressing the basic questions these impassioned citizens are raising: Who votes, how do they vote, whom do they vote for, how are their votes counted and what happens after the voting? These questions go to the very legitimacy of our democratic procedures, not just in Florida but nationwide—and the answers could lead to profound but eminently achievable reforms.

*Who votes—and doesn't?* As with the rest of the nation, in Florida only about half of all adults vote, about the same as the national average. Even more disturbing, nonvoters are increasingly low-income, young and less educated. This trend persists despite the Voting Rights Act, which since 1970 has banned literacy tests nationwide as prerequisites for voting—a ban enacted by Congress and unanimously upheld by the Supreme Court.

We are a democracy that supposedly believes in universal suffrage, and yet the differential turnout between high-income and low-income voters is far greater than in Europe, where it ranges from 5 to 10 percent. More than two-thirds of people in America with incomes greater than $50,000 vote, compared with one-third of those with income under $10,000. Those convicted of a felony are permanently banned from voting in Florida and twelve other states. In Florida alone, this year more than 40,000 ex-felons, about half of them black, were denied the opportunity to vote. Canada, on the other hand, takes special steps to register former prisoners and bring them into full citizenship.

*How do they vote?* Florida now abounds with stories of long poll lines, confusing ballots and strict limitations on how long voters could spend in the voting booth. The shocking number of invalid ballots—more ballots were "spoiled" in the presidential race than were cast for "spoiler" Ralph Nader—are a direct result of antiquated voting mechanics that would shame any nation, let alone one of the world's oldest democracies. Even the better-educated older voters of Palm Beach found, to their surprise, how much they had in common with more frequently disfranchised populations. Given how many decisions voters are expected to make in less than five minutes in the polling booth, it is common sense that the polls should be open over a weekend, or at least for twenty-four hours, and that Election Day should be a national holiday. By highlighting our wretched record on voting practices, Florida raises the obvious question: Do we really want large voter participation?

*Whom do they vote for?* Obviously, Florida voters chose among Al Gore, George Bush and a handful of minor-party candidates who, given their status as unlikely to win, were generally ignored and at best chastised as spoilers. But as many voters are now realizing, in the presidential race they were voting not for the candidates whose name they selected (or attempted to select) but for "electors" to that opaque institution, the Electoral College.

Our constitutional framers did some things well—chiefly dulling the edge of winner-take-all elections through institutions that demand coalition-building, compromise and recognition of certain minority voices—but the Electoral College was created on illegitimate grounds and has no place in a modern democracy.

As Yale law professor Akhil Reed Amar argues, the Electoral College was established as a device to boost the power of Southern states in the election of the President. The same "compromise" that gave Southern states more House members by counting slaves as three-fifths of a person for purposes of apportioning representation (while giving them none of the privileges of citizenship) gave those states Electoral College votes in proportion to their Congressional delegation. This hypocrisy enhanced the Southern states' Electoral College percentage, and as a result, Virginia slaveowners controlled the presidency for thirty-two of our first thirty-six years.

Its immoral origins notwithstanding, the Electoral College was soon justified as a deliberative body that would choose among several candidates and assure the voice of small geographic areas. But under the Electoral College, voters in small states have more than just a voice; indeed their say often exceeds that of voters in big states. In Wyoming one vote in the Electoral College corresponds to 71,000 voters; in Florida, one electoral vote corresponds to 238,000 voters. At minimum we should eliminate the extra bias that adding electors for each of two senators gives our smallest states. As Robert Naiman of the Center for Economic and Policy Research reports, allowing each state only as many electors as it has members in the House of Representatives would mean, for example, that even if Bush won Oregon and Florida, he would have 216 and Gore would have 220 electoral votes.

Today its backers still argue that the Electoral College is necessary to insure that small states are not ignored by the presidential candidates. Yet the many states—including the small ones—that weren't close in this election were neglected by both campaigns. Some of the nation's biggest states, with the most people of color, saw very little presidential campaigning and get-out-the-vote activity. Given their lopsided results this year, we can expect California, Illinois, New York, Texas and nearly all Southern states to be shunned in the 2004 campaign.

How are their votes counted? The presidency rests on a handful of votes in Florida because allocation of electoral votes is winner-take-all—if Gore wins by ten votes out of 6 million, he will win 100 percent of the state's twenty-five electoral votes. The ballots cast for a losing candidate are always "invalid" for the purposes of representation; only those cast for the winner actually "count." Thus winner-take-all elections underrepresent the voice of the minority and exaggerate the power of one state's razor-thin majority. Winner-take-all is the great barrier to representation of political and racial minorities at both the federal and the state level. No blacks or Latinos serve in the U.S. Senate or in any governor's mansion. Third-party candidates did not win a single state legislature race except for a handful in Vermont.

Given the national questioning of the Electoral College sparked by the anomalous gap between the popular vote and the college's vote in the presidential election, those committed to real representative democracy now have a chance to shine a spotlight on the glaring flaws and disenfranchisement inherent in winner-take-all practices and to propose important reforms.

What we need are election rules that encourage voter turnout rather than suppress it. A system of proportional representation—which would allocate seats to parties based on their proportion of the total vote—would more fairly reflect intense feeling within the electorate, mobilize more people to participate and even encourage those who do participate to do so beyond just the single act of voting on Election Day. Most democracies around the world have some form of proportional voting and manage to engage a much greater percentage of their citizens in elections. Proportional representation in South Africa, for example, allows the white Afrikaner parties and the ANC to gain seats in the national legislature commensurate with the total number of votes cast for each party. Under this system, third parties are a plausible alternative. Moreover, to allow third parties to run presidential candidates without being "spoilers," some advocate instant-runoff elections in which voters would rank their choices for President (see box on next page). That way, even voters whose top choice loses the election could influence the race among the other candidates.

Winner-take-all elections, by contrast, encourage the two major parties to concentrate primarily on the "undecideds" and to take tens of millions of dollars of corporate and special-interest contributions to broadcast ads on the public airwaves appealing to the center of the political spectrum. Winner-take-all incentives discourage either of the two major parties from trying to learn, through organizing and door-knocking, how to mobilize the vast numbers of disengaged poor and working-class voters. Rather than develop a vision, they produce a product and fail to build political capacity from the ground up.

*What happens after the voting?* Our nation is more focused on elections now than it has been for decades; yet on any given Sunday, more people will watch professional football than voted this November. What democracy demands is a system of elections that enables minor parties to gain a voice in the legislature and encourages the development of local political organizations that educate and mobilize voters.

Between elections, grassroots organizations could play an important monitoring role now unfulfilled by the two major parties. If the Bush campaign is right that large numbers of ballots using the same butterfly format were thrown out in previous elections in Palm Beach, then something is wrong with more than the ballot. For those Democratic senior citizens in Palm Beach, it was not enough that their election supervisor was a Democrat. They needed a vibrant local organization that could have served as a watchdog, alerting voters and election officials that there were problems with the ballot. No one should inadvertently vote for two candidates; the same watchdog organizations should require ballot-counting machines like those in some states that notify the voter of such problems before he or she leaves the booth. Voters should be asked, as on the popular TV quiz show, "Is that your final answer?" And surely we cannot claim to be a functioning democracy when voters are turned away from the polls or denied assistance in violation of both state and federal law.

Before the lessons of Florida are forgotten, let us use this window of opportunity to forge a strong pro-democracy coalition to rally around "one vote, one value." The value of a vote depends on it being fairly counted but also on its counting toward the election of the person the voter chose as her representative. This can happen only if we recognize the excesses of winner-take-all voting and stop exaggerating the power of the winner by denying the loser any voice at all.

---

## DISCUSSION QUESTIONS

1. In what ways does Lani Guinier see democracy being compromised by current electoral laws and practices in the United States?
2. How did the communities affected by the electoral fiasco in Florida react to the situation following the 2000 presidential election? What role does Guinier see communities potentially playing in the fight to reform electoral law?
3. What is your reaction to Guinier's proposals, especially with regard to the Electoral College?

## WHAT IS INSTANT RUNOFF VOTING?

IRV is a ranked ballot method of voting that results in a winner chosen by a majority of the voters. The voters rank the candidates in order of preference. Each voter has one vote which counts for the highest preferred candidate that can use it. The term "Instant Runoff Voting" was coined because the method of transferring votes from defeated candidates to continuing candidates is just like a runoff election except that it is accomplished on one ballot. It is also known as Single Transferable Vote (single winner version), Alternative Vote, and Majority Preferential Vote.

### Rank the candidates in order of preference—your first choice and your runoff choices

|       | 1st choice | 2nd choice | 3rd choice |
|-------|------------|------------|------------|
| John  | ☑          | ☐          | ☐          |
| Bill  | ☐          | ☑          | ☐          |
| Frank | ☐          | ☐          | ☑          |

### How are the votes counted in IRV?

First choices are counted. If no candidate receives a majority, the candidate with the fewest votes is defeated, and those votes are transferred to the next ranked candidate on each ballot. The votes are recounted. The process continues until one candidate has a majority of the votes and is declared the winner.

|                                  | 1st Choices | Instant Runoff | Final Results |
|----------------------------------|-------------|----------------|---------------|
| John                             | 35          | +16            | 51 winner     |
| Bill                             | 20          | −16            |               |
| Frank                            | 45          | +4             | 49            |
| Total                            | 100         |                |               |
| Winning Threshold<br>50% + 1 =   | 51          |                |               |

Instant Runoff Example

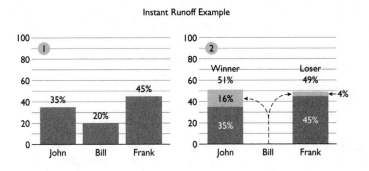

# CHAPTER 6

# CONGRESS

Congress has frequently been described as the world's foremost legislative body, but its performance often disappoints Americans. Polls show consistently that we have less confidence in the legislative branch than in either the presidency or the judiciary. Ironically, the legislature is the first branch of government discussed in the Constitution, and there is no doubt that most of the Framers intended Congress to be the primary policy-making institution. In the nineteenth century, with the exception of several periods of strong presidential leadership, the Congress did in fact exert this kind of primacy in our political system. But in the twentieth century, and particularly since the 1930s, increased assertion of presidential power has left the Congress as a reactive and fragmented body, though still with the power to block presidential initiatives.

Former Speaker of the House of Representatives Thomas P. "Tip" O'Neill used to say that all politics is local. Part of the problem with Congress is the mismatch between its local orientation and the increasingly national and international imperatives placed on the U.S. state to secure the domestic health and worldwide expansion of corporate capitalism. Members of Congress, especially in the House, are elected to represent states and districts with specific social needs, economic characteristics, and local power structures. Overlaying this local orientation and contributing to congressional indecision are weak party structures, the impact of campaign contributions, the typically great advantages for incumbents seeking reelection, and the ubiquitous impact of interest groups on policy-making. All of these pressures make it difficult for Congress to set an independent agenda for attaining the public good through taking on the myriad social and economic problems facing America. And these pressures are exacerbated by the bitter partisan divide in Congress evident in recent years.

# 21 *John C. Berg*

# CONGRESS AND BIG BUSINESS

*Political scientist John Berg frames this chapter with an article that places Congress within the context of a theory of society that views class structure, the needs of corporate capitalism, and our dominant liberal ideology as basic structural determinants that set the boundaries of debate on policy issues. Following in the tradition of Philip Brenner's pathbreaking 1983 book* The Limits and Possibilities of Congress, *Berg analyzes how congressional politics can be seen as part of the larger ongoing social conflict in America. Contrary to the principles of pluralist theory (see our Introduction), this conflict privileges the interests of one key participant—giant multinational corporations—who exercise dominating class power, or "hegemony." Berg uses several examples to illustrate how and why Congress protects corporate interests with a swiftness and effectiveness that other classes and groups do not enjoy. He then details three ways in which corporate hegemony is built into the structure of Congress: through the legal system of the country, governmental separation of powers, and the power of specific congressional committees. Big business certainly does not win all the time, but the rules of the game are skewed so that their overall interests dominate policy debates and outcomes regardless of the party and personalities of congressional leaders.*

Money talks. Everyone knows that. It talks a lot to Congress. Well-heeled lobbyists, political action committees (PACs), expense-paid junkets, multimillion-dollar campaigns, and juicy honoraria are abiding elements of American political lore. Everyone knows, too, that the rich do better than other people at getting their opinions heard and their interests accommodated by legislators. Average citizens, political scientists, and the members of Congress themselves join in bewailing the excessive importance of money in politics.

Congressional politics is part of the fundamental social conflict in America. Congress is one arena in which this conflict takes place, but it is not an independent arena. Forces outside Congress influence what goes on inside it; in particular, if the Marxist theory is correct, Congress is influenced heavily by the economic structure of our society. Those who dominate the American economy dominate Congress as well. But Congress is also the most democratic part of our national government. Thus, oppressed social groups have found it the

*Economic ⟷ Political*

*Source:* John C. Berg, *Unequal Struggle: Class, Gender, Race, and Power in the U.S. Congress,* Boulder, CO: Westview Press, 1994, pp. 31–34 and 37–44.

most permeable part of the state, often seeking to use congressional politics to advance their cause. . . .

We can see the effect of economic structure when we compare the way Congress handles different issues. In 1977, with the nation suffering from an energy shortage that restricted economic growth, hurt the balance of trade, inflated the cost of living, and forced many poor people to go without heat in winter, President Jimmy Carter presented a comprehensive national energy plan to Congress. After two years of hearings, backroom negotiations, and public debate, Congress managed to pass only one part of the plan: It removed price controls from natural gas, thus making energy even more expensive.

In 1989 the wreck of the oil tanker Exxon *Valdez* killed thousands of waterfowl, fish, marine mammals, and plants, threatened the ecological balance of Prince William Sound, and infuriated the public. Individual members of Congress responded with thousands of dramatic public speeches; but it was sixteen months before Congress as a legislative body managed to pass a bill raising the limits on liability of negligent oil shippers from $150 to $1,200 per ton of oil. Although the final bill was considered a victory by environmental lobbyists, several concessions had to be made to the oil industry before it could be passed. Double-hull requirements for oil tankers were deferred until 2010 (and to 2015 for most barges and for ships unloading offshore to lighters), oil companies shipping oil in tankers owned by others were exempted, and state governors lost any power to determine when a cleanup was complete.

In the early 1980s a large number of savings and loan associations—known as thrift institutions, or simply "thrifts"—began to lose money; by 1987 many were in danger of failing. The Federal Savings and Loan Insurance Corporation (FSLIC), which insured thrift deposits of $100,000 or less, warned that it might not be able to pay all the claims. Congress gave the FSLIC another $10 billion in 1987, but otherwise did nothing until after the 1988 election. Then, in early 1989, Congress moved with remarkable speed to enact a complicated—and expensive—reorganization plan for the thrift industry. President George Bush proposed a plan on February 6 and signed a new law on August 9. The S&L Bailout—as it became known—would cost $50 billion by the end of 1991, and at least $110 billion by 1999; some of the money would be paid to the holders of insured accounts, but much of it would be used to subsidize healthier, more profitable banks and thrifts in taking over unhealthy ones.

In this case Congress acted not only quickly but ingeniously. Since the passage of the Gramm-Rudman-Hollings Deficit Reduction Act (GRH) in 1985, new spending programs had been difficult to create. The bill deftly evaded this problem. It simply labeled $30 billion "off-budget" and assigned the remaining $20 billion to a fiscal year that had already begun—and which therefore had already passed the GRH test.

One could argue that Congress acted so quickly and smoothly in the savings and loan case because it simply had to. The nation faced a crisis, and failure to act would have had unthinkable consequences. However, this line of thought leads to further questions. What is a crisis? What sort of consequences are unthinkable? In 1991 a cholera epidemic broke out in Peru, threatening to spread throughout South and Central America; it was expected to be hard to stop because the projected cost of the necessary sanitary improvements was prohibitive—$200 billion over twelve years, or about the same as the savings and loan bailout.

Closer to home, it has been argued that American public education is in crisis. Millions of young people fail to complete high school; millions more graduate unable to read, to multiply fractions, or to understand the basic nature of atoms and molecules. These consequences are unthinkably tragic, but they are happening, and Congress has not found the will to prevent them.

Marxists use the concept of *hegemony* to explain the differences between these two crises. Hegemony refers to the dominating power of a social class (or part of one) whose class interests have come to be widely accepted as equivalent to the interests of society as a whole. The United States today is dominated in this way by the giant multinational corporations.

•    •    •

*The Hegemonic Force in American Politics*

The American economy is not just capitalist; it is dominated by a small number of gigantic capitalist corporations. In 1988, the 500 largest industrial corporations in the United States—the so-called Fortune 500—had total sales of over $2 trillion. One-fifth of this amount, $402,183,000,000, was produced by just five companies: General Motors (GM), Ford, Exxon, International Business Machines (IBM), and General Electric (GE). In the same year, there were about 3.5 million corporations, and 14 million non-farm proprietorships and partnerships, in the United States. The three major automobile makers alone employed 1,270,000 people, had assets of $356 billion, and earned profits of $11.2 billion. The ten largest commercial banks—all but one of them located in New York City—had assets of $860 billion, with nearly one-quarter of that, $207 billion, held by one bank, New York's Citicorp.

These giants are so big that the rest of the country needs them to be healthy. When Chrysler Corporation, only the third largest automobile maker, faced possible bankruptcy, the federal government stepped in to save it. It stepped in again to avert the failure of Chicago-based Continental Bank Corporation, the fourteenth largest commercial bank. As this practice has become more common, it has acquired a name, the "too big to fail" doctrine. It is one example of *hegemony*.

When Charles E. ("Engine Charlie") Wilson went from president of General Motors to secretary of defense in the Eisenhower administration, he told a Senate committee that he was not worried about any possible conflict of interest because he had always believed that "what was good for our country was good for General Motors, and vice versa. The difference did not exist. Our company is too big. It goes with the welfare of the country."

In the largest sense, Wilson was dead wrong. GM has been a cumbersome, inefficient enterprise that has contributed greatly to a whole range of national problems, from low productivity to air pollution to worker alienation. But in the short run—that is, given that GM already existed—Wilson was right. GM's huge labor force, its annual sales, and its impact as a customer on other major industries were so great that a failure of GM—or of another

giant corporation—might well have plunged the whole economy into recession.

## CORPORATE HEGEMONY

Until sometime in the early 1970s the giant financial and industrial corporations were able to dominate America and much of the rest of the world. This domination gave them a sense of security and led some to conclude that they were more interested in stability than in profits. Since that time, however, their dominance has been threatened by growing international competition. The best-known example is the auto industry, in which the big three U.S. automakers have lost market share to Japanese and European competitors both at home and abroad; but the same thing has occurred in many other industries as well.

This new global competition has changed both the composition and the interests of the hegemonic bloc. By reviving the emphasis on profits it has reinforced the dominance of finance capital over industrial corporations. Such once-mighty giants as IBM have learned that Wall Street would rather shift its investments to other companies and industries than support them in fighting to preserve their corporate position. The willingness of many corporations to accept high wages and benefits and a certain amount of government regulation is likewise falling before international competitive pressure. These changes in the economic position of U.S. big business have had important political results; but the basic division between hegemonic and non-hegemonic sectors of the capitalist class remains.

Politics and ideology tend to reflect economics. Thus, the state (including Congress) tends to further the interests of the giant corporations; and public debate tends to be carried on in terms that incorporate those interests—as in 1990, when President Bush referred to protection of Exxon's oil supplies in the Persian Gulf as a defense of "our way of life." This is not automatically so. The non-hegemonic classes can and do organize themselves to contend for political power, and to change the terms of public discourse. But they find it harder to win; and unless they succeed in changing the economic structure as well, such political and ideological reforms are likely to be only temporary. Let us look at some concrete examples.

The crisis in the savings and loan industry threatened to destabilize the whole financial system, endangering giant banks along with small thrift institutions. It thus struck at the heart of corporate hegemony. The nature of this hegemony is missed by much left rhetoric. For example, Manning Marable has written recently:

> Is it right for a government to spend billions and billions for bailing out fat cats who profited from the savings and loan scam while millions of jobless Americans stand in unemployment lines desperate for work? Is it fair that billions of our dollars are allocated for the Pentagon's permanent war economy to obliterate the lives of millions of poor people from Panama to Iraq to Grenada to Vietnam, while two million Americans sleep in the streets and 37 million Americans lack any form of medical coverage?

The policies Marable decries are indeed neither right nor fair; but even those members of Congress who agree with this characterization fear that allowing the savings and loan industry to collapse, or (more debatably) cutting the military budget, would send even more millions to the unemployment lines or into the streets. For this reason, debate within Congress about the savings and loan crisis has centered on who should take the blame, not on whether to act.

By contrast, the crisis in education strikes at the U.S. working class, and cholera threatens workers and peasants in other countries. Millions of lives may be blighted, neighborhoods destabilized, and great human suffering caused, but most members of Congress still see a solution as optional—something we certainly ought to do if we can just find the money. Even the advocates of school reform find it useful to base their arguments on the need of capitalism for a more skilled labor force.

This is the theory of hegemony in its bare bones. Hegemonic interests are privileged in that Congress and the state act quickly and effectively to protect them; they find it more difficult to promote other interests that are equally vital in human terms. But students of politics must ask how this privilege is maintained. What is it about our political system—what is it about Congress—that makes it more responsive to hegemonic interests than to others?

In fact, the interests of the great corporations are well entrenched in the structure of American government. This structure is itself the product of past political struggles, dating back at least to the drafting of the Constitution. Some of these struggles have been won by the working class, farmers, and petty bourgeoisie; by women; by racial minorities; and by other democratizing forces. But on the whole, the trend has been toward the kind of state envisioned by Alexander Hamilton, a state dedicated to furthering business interests.

Corporate hegemony is built into the structure of Congress on at least three levels. First, it has become part of our basic legal order. Second, it is built into the separation of powers, which places the most crucial decisions outside of Congress's reach. Finally, it is part of the internal structure of Congress itself. The end result of decades of conflict is that Congress finds it easy to act on behalf of corporate interests and difficult to act against them. These structural features are reinforced by the nature of the American electoral system, and by the weakness of anticapitalist ideology.

Americans think of our legal order as founded on individual rights. However, the meaning of these rights has been transformed since the U.S. Constitution was first written. On the one hand, rights have been broadened and extended in such a way that the universalistic language of the Declaration of Independence is now applied to the propertyless, to women, and to the descendants of slaves, none of whom had been included at first. On the other hand, the language of rights has been applied to big business, becoming a fundamental restraint on the power of Congress and other democratic institutions to regulate business in the public interest.

Perhaps the most important business victory was the extension of individual civil rights to corporations. Today this extension has become such a basic feature of our legal system that we tend not to notice it, but it came about only in the latter half of the nineteenth century. Through a combination of state and federal legislation and Supreme Court decisions, two legal doctrines became firmly established. First, corporations—which had been conceived of originally as quasi-state agencies chartered by the state in order to achieve an important public purpose, such as building a bridge or a canal, settling Massachusetts Bay, or conquering India—were transformed into a means of concentrating capital without exposing its individual owners to excessive risk, for the sole purpose of making money.

Second, these corporations gained the status of *persons* under the law, and as such won the legal rights granted to persons by the Fourteenth Amendment. This amendment had been designed to give federal protection to the freed slaves; but the Supreme Court ignored this purpose for seventy years, while using the amendment to protect corporations from government regulation. The Court has since backed away from some of its more extreme interpretations, but the basic legal structure of corporate rights continues to place many possible policies beyond the bounds of congressional or state legislative action.

Most recently, the Supreme Court has extended freedom of expression to corporate persons. The Court ruled in 1975 that the First Amendment applied to commercial advertising and, in 1980, extended it to cover political advocacy by businesses. A constitutional provision intended to protect human democracy and individualism thereby became a barrier to attempts to protect democratic discourse from the domination of capital.

The interests of giant corporations are also built into the operation of the constitutional separation of powers. Those who study the making of public policy know that the balance of power between Congress and the president varies with the issue at hand. The executive branch has the largest role in foreign policy, military action, and the regulation of the national economy. The president can order military action, recognize foreign governments, or sign Executive Agreements without congressional approval. Even when funds must be appropriated by Congress, he has considerable discretion to

divert them to other purposes—and, as the Iran-*contra* case showed, he also has the *de facto* ability to exceed that discretion. He and his appointees also play the major role in attempts to regulate the national economy.

Congress, for its part, wields more detailed control over such issues as aid to education, environmental protection, housing, health, and welfare. In these areas, presidentially appointed officials must work with specific mandates and finite appropriations from Congress, and important issues are often decided by Congress, in committees or by floor amendments.

Some of these differences are rooted in the Constitution, whereas others have emerged since—as with the creation of the Federal Reserve System; but in general, those policy areas that are more vital to the interests of the great corporations are further removed from the influence of Congress.

Nonhegemonic classes and groups have better access to Congress than to the president and his inner cabinet, but this access does not give them proportional influence over those matters most important to the hegemonic fraction. The president can invade Grenada or Panama, go to war with Iraq, or sponsor terrorist attacks in Nicaragua, and Congress finds it hard to restrain him. The Federal Reserve system sets the nation's monetary policy, a key determinant of the fate of our economy, with little accountability to Congress or even to the president. In the case of foreign affairs, Congress's power is limited by the Constitution, which makes the president commander in chief of the armed forces; but it has been unable to resist the erosion of its own power to declare war. The United States fought both the Korean and Vietnam wars without formal declarations of war by Congress, and in the case of Vietnam the fighting continued long after Congress had turned against it. Finding itself unable to stop a war that was under way, Congress passed the War Powers Act of 1974; but this act has proved ineffective, having often been ignored by the president. However, the regulation of banking and currency are powers assigned to Congress; its loss of influence in these areas is the result of its own past decisions to create and maintain the Federal Reserve

System. As a result, Congress must try to manage the economy—if it wishes to try at all—by raising or lowering federal taxes and spending, tools that are difficult to wield and uncertain in their effect. The powers to regulate interest rates and the money supply have proven more effective, but they have been removed from Congress and given to the Federal Reserve Board and the Federal Open Market Committee. In both cases, political struggles of the past have helped form structures that bias the political struggles of today.

The class basis of the separation of powers, and its changes over time, merit further study. As a simple approximation we could say that hegemonic interests dominate the presidency, whereas the influence of other social forces is confined to Congress. But hegemony operates within Congress as well. Congress has been unable to stop presidents from encroaching on its traditional powers partly because the interests that dominate the presidency also control the main levers of power within Congress.

Decisionmaking in each house of Congress is formally democratic, usually by majority vote. Yet small groups of members have always possessed the greatest share of power over decisions. Such power can come from control over the flow of bills to the floor, as with the party leaderships and the House Rules Committee; or from control over important legislative subject matter, as with the appropriations, tax-writing, and budget committees. The Appropriations, Rules, and Ways and Means committees in the House are called "exclusive committees"—because they are so important that their members are not supposed to serve on other standing committees at the same time (a rule often broken, as it happens). The House Budget Committee is a special case; it is formed of selected representatives from other committees, and its chair, rather than being chosen by seniority, is elected by the House and considered a member of the House leadership. The Senate also recognizes certain committees as having extra importance: Appropriations, Budget, Finance (the Senate equivalent of House Ways and Means), and Foreign Relations (given special importance in the Senate because of that body's treaty ratification power).

For ease of reference, all of these will be referred to from now on as *hegemonic committees*.

Both party leadership and hegemonic committee positions are almost always held by members who have incorporated the hegemonic ideology into their own outlooks. Several studies have shown that positions of power go to those members who have a "responsible legislative style," one of the essential elements of which is a willingness to put what is conceived of as the national interest ahead of narrow constituency interests.

For hegemonic committees, congressional leaders also prefer to pick members who come from seats that are relatively safe, so that they will be less subject to popular pressure on controversial decisions. There is also some self-selection of members. Richard Fenno, in a famous study of House committees, found that representatives were most likely to seek seats on the Ways and Means or Appropriations committees if they were more interested in achieving power as an end in itself than in promoting specific policies. Given the structure of American society, such power can best be pursued by choosing to side with big business.

These selection procedures do not work perfectly. However, potentially dissident committee members find themselves outnumbered and face strong pressure not to rock the boat. If they cooperate with hegemonic interests, they can use their committee positions to win significant benefits for their districts or for other interests they support; but if they come to be seen as troublemakers, such benefits are much harder to come by. Generally such pressures are enough to keep potential dissidents in line.

The hegemonic faction does not dominate Congress through sheer force; its power is maintained only by the tacit, and sometimes open, support of a majority of the members, who could vote to change the structure at any time. One of the strengths of Congress is that its leaders understand this contingency and act consciously to maintain their support. "Responsibility" includes "reciprocity" and "accommodation"—the willingness of a member of Ways and Means, for example, to serve as a voice for interests in his or her region that want particular concessions in the tax code, and to cooperate with members from other regions with like interests. The willingness to grant such concessions from time to time provides the solid foundation for the Ways and Means Committee's ability at other times to gain acceptance of an omnibus tax bill under a closed rule.

As Fenno observes, the power of the hegemonic committees is reinforced by institutional pride. House members want the Ways and Means Committee to be strong, because its power is, to some extent, theirs as well.

In addition to a generalized willingness to be accommodating, hegemony within Congress can involve specific accommodations of particular groups. For example, the Rayburn-McCormack leadership of the House Democrats—whose successors, known as the Austin-Boston Axis, remained in control of the House Democratic leadership through the 1980s—won and maintained power on the basis both of a moderate New Deal ideology and of a very specific agreement that amendments to the tax code that were regarded unfavorably by Southwestern oil interests would not be allowed on the floor. The oil industry has since been forced to fight harder for its interests, but it continues to be well represented in the House and Senate tax-writing committees, and still receives tax treatment more favorable than that accorded to most other industries. This arrangement is a reflection of the central position of the oil companies in the American economy—their inclusion in the hegemonic bloc—but it is not an automatic result of that economic importance. Rather, it is the consequence of a series of political victories by which the representatives of the oil companies have gained control of some of the levers of congressional power.

These three structural factors—the basic legal order, the division of powers among the branches of government, and the power of the hegemonic committees within Congress—provide the terrain on which pluralist conflict takes place. This conflict is fought out with the usual weapons of democratic politics—namely, votes and money; but the giant corporations enter the battle already in possession of the commanding heights and are therefore much more likely to win.

---

## DISCUSSION QUESTIONS

1. What situations constitute a crisis to the U.S. Congress? According to what interests are crisis situations determined?
2. What evidence does Berg provide that corporations use our political system to exercise their hegemony? Relate this argument to Article 3 by Clawson, Neustadtl, and Weller by comparing the authors' perspectives on corporate hegemony.

# DEMOCRACY ON DRUGS: HOW A BILL REALLY BECOMES A LAW

*There's an old adage in politics that goes like this: The two things you shouldn't see in the process of being made are sausage and legislation. The following selection is a report from Common Cause, a Washington-based nonpartisan citizens' lobbying organization that offers a window into the legislative process. It does not present us with a sanitized picture; it shows us the dirt and the blood. In late November of 2003 the House and Senate handed President Bush a huge legislative victory by passing a bill establishing a voluntary prescription drug program under Medicare, one of the centerpieces of the President's domestic agenda. The bill passed 220–215 in the House and 54–44 in the Senate. The Common Cause study chronicles a tale of deceit, manipulation, strong arm tactics, procedural violations, secrecy and favoritism toward the pharmaceutical industry—all undertaken by the Republican leadership of Congress in the pursuit of private corporate profit under the guise of the public interest of the 40 million Medicare beneficiaries. So heavy-handed were the Republican tactics that in the fall of 2004 House Majority Leader Tom Delay (R-TX) was officially admonished by the House Ethics Committee for his efforts to strong arm Rep. Nick Smith (R-MI) into changing his vote against the bill. The Medicare prescription drug saga belies the neat and tidy legislative flow charts that grace standard high school and college American government textbooks. And as Common Cause points out, the sum total of irregularities and shenanigans involved in this story raises troubling questions about the democratic process and its promise of fairness and accountability. "From start to finish, the $535 billion Medicare bill . . . has been a study in shutting out opposing voices and suppressing the flow of vital information." The result was a giveaway to pharmaceutical companies with negligible, if any benefits for the elderly. Students of government might be left wondering: is this any way to run a legislature?*

*Source:* Common Cause, *Democracy on Drugs. The Medicare/Prescription Drug Bill: A Study in How Government Shouldn't Work,* Washington, DC: Common Cause, May 18, 2004.

## INTRODUCTION

Our Constitution reflects the over-arching concern of the Founding Fathers that the rights of the minority be jealously preserved and protected, even in the presence of a strong majority. From start to finish, the $535 billion Medicare bill passed by Congress and signed by President Bush late in 2003 has been a study in shutting out opposing voices and suppressing the flow of vital information.

This Common Cause report chronicles a series of incidents, large and small, that add up to a consistent effort by the Administration and Congressional leadership to bypass or undermine the rules and laws that are in place to ensure that our government works in an open and accountable manner and that all voices are heard on critical public policy issues.

The Medicare bill is the product of a process that included:

- Charges of bribery, delayed votes, inappropriate cabinet member lobbying and censoring of C-SPAN cameras.
- The Administration misleading Congress by withholding its own cost estimates for the prescription drug legislation—estimates that greatly exceeded what the President was telling the public. A career civil servant being threatened with his job if he told Congress the truth.
- Congressional Members excluded from the House-Senate conference committee that finalized the bill. Only a "coalition of the willing" was invited to participate.
- A principal author of the bill was forced to step down as head of a powerful House committee after it was reported that he was negotiating a $2 million a year lobbying job with the drug industry while he was moving the proposal through his committee. And a key Administration official involved in pushing the legislation was also offered lucrative private sector health-care jobs.
- The drug industry showered Congress with campaign contributions and spent millions of dollars on highly paid lobbyists who swarmed Capitol Hill while the bill was being considered.

- A propaganda campaign waged by the Department of Health and Human Services. The Administration paid people to pose as journalists in television segments that praised the benefits of the new Medicare law, and spent tens of millions of dollars on a campaign promoting the new program.

## CHARGES OF BRIBERY ON THE HOUSE FLOOR

"directly or indirectly, corruptly gives, offers or promises anything of value to any public official . . . with intent to influence any official act."

—U.S. Code. Title 18 Sec. 201. "Bribery of public officials"

At the break of dawn on Nov. 22, 2003, Representative Nick Smith (R-MI) was about to cast his vote against a Medicare/prescription drug bill so flawed and controversial that the Republican House leadership held the vote open for three hours while they pressured their own Republican colleagues to vote for the bill. Votes in the House typically are open for 15 minutes.

Strong-arming Members of the House to vote with the leadership is routine business, but what went on in those early morning hours appears to have slid over the line from political pressure to outright bribery.

A Nov. 23, 2003 column written by Rep. Smith appearing on his website reads:

I was targeted by lobbyists and the congressional leadership to change my vote, being a fiscal conservative and being on record as a no vote. Secretary of Health and Human Services Tommy Thompson and Speaker of the House Dennis Hastert talked to me for a long time about the bill and about why I should vote yes. Other members and groups made offers of extensive financial campaign support and endorsements for my son Brad who is running for my seat. They also made threats of working against Brad if I voted no.

On Dec. 1, 2003, in a radio interview with Kevin Vandenbroek of WKZO in Kalamazoo, Mich., Rep. Smith said:

> They started out by offering the carrot, and they know what's important to every member, and what's important to me is my family and my kids. And I've term-limited myself, and so Bradley my son is running for [my congressional seat] and so the first offer was to give him $100,000-plus for his campaign and endorsement by national leadership. And I said No, I'm gonna stick to my guns on what I think is right for the constituents in my district.

Since Rep. Smith went public with his allegations, he has made several attempts to modify his original statement. Speaking to David Frownfelder of the *Daily Telegram* in Adrian, Mich. Rep. Smith said:

> I was told there would be aggressive, substantial support for my son, Brad [in his race for Congress] if I could vote yes on the bill. There were offers of endorsements and so maybe a member [of Congress] sitting close by said, 'Boy that really could be big money.' Tens of thousands or hundreds of thousands. But never was I offered any exact amount of money in exchange for my vote. Technically, in the legal description that I later reviewed on what a bribe is, probably it didn't meet the legal description of a bribe.

## CENSORING C-SPAN

C-SPAN cameras perched above the House floor have for 25 years allowed the public to see for themselves how their representatives are carrying on the public's business. But the night of the vote on the prescription drug bill, the House leadership censored the public's view of the chamber.

In an interview on the 25th anniversary of C-SPAN's television coverage of Congress, the head of C-SPAN, Brian Lamb, noted that the congressional leadership has always controlled the cameras in the House and Senate chambers, generally focused on whoever is speaking, but also panning across the chamber to show activity on the floor. Lamb pointed out how the leadership's control of the cameras can subvert C-SPAN's studiously nonpartisan, objective coverage of Congress. Lamb said:

> You saw what happened in the middle of the night over the vote on Medicare on the floor of the House of Representatives, when they controlled the cameras. And I noticed that the camera wasn't moving from—it usually moves constantly from side to side. For almost the entire two or three hours that they had it open, the camera was showing the Democratic side. And that's where people don't get a fair shot.

In other words, the Republican leadership of the House intentionally diverted the C-SPAN cameras away from the Republican side of the House floor. Consequently, there is no visual record of who was talking to who that night while votes were sought by the leadership.

## HHS SECRETARY ON THE HOUSE FLOOR

Rep. Smith said he was pressured during the three-hour vote by his own House leadership, but also, to his surprise, by the Department of Health and Human Services (HHS) Secretary Tommy Thompson, who made an unusual appearance on the House floor that night.

While House rules allow federal department heads to be in the House chamber, it is rare for such an official to be lobbying for legislation being considered by the House. According to *National Journal's CongressDaily*, Secretary Thompson defended the fact that he had broken House customs by lobbying members on the House floor during the final, three-hour roll call vote on the Medicare reform bill. "I spent five months working on this bill. I think it was only proper my being on the floor," Thompson said. But it appears Thompson's activities that night were a sharp departure from House customs.

# MISLEADING CONGRESS AND WITHHOLDING PIVOTAL INFORMATION

"No government official should ever be muzzled from providing critical information to Congress."

—Senator Chuck Grassley (R-IA)
Senate Finance Committee Chairman

In 1997, Rep. Bill Thomas (R-CA) added language to the Balanced Budget Act conference report citing the importance of access by Congress to the estimates of HHS chief actuary (then, as now, Richard Foster). Some of that language in the conference report reads as follows:

It is important to emphasize that the Senate Committee on Finance, the House Committee on Ways and Means, and the House Committee on Commerce all rely on their ability to seek estimates and other technical assistance from the Chief Actuary, especially when developing new legislation. ... The process of monitoring, updating and reforming the Medicare and Medicaid programs is greatly enhanced by the free flow of actuarial information from the Office of the Actuary to the committees of jurisdiction in the Congress. ... When information is delayed or circumscribed by the operation of an internal Administration clearance process or the inadequacy of actuarial resources, the Committees' ability to make informed decisions based on the best available information is compromised.

Flying in the face of this statement, Foster, who has been the chief auditor in HHS for several years, said that he was threatened with dismissal if he released his official estimate of the cost of the prescription drug bill. His estimate added $156.5 billion to the estimated cost and likely would have led to several conservative Republicans voting against the bill.

In a public statement, Foster said:

For many years my office has provided technical assistance to the administration and Congress on a nonpartisan basis. But in June 2003, the Medicare administrator, Tom Scully, decided to restrict the practice of our responding directly to Congressional requests and ordered us to provide responses to him so he could decide what to do with them. There was a pattern of withholding information for what I perceived to be political purposes, which I thought was inappropriate.

Foster has said that he gave analyses in June 2003 to the White House and the Office of Management and Budget—which were not shared with Congress—predicting that prescription drug benefits being drafted on Capitol Hill would cost about $156 billion more than President Bush said he wanted to spend. Since Congress passed the Medicare bill, the Administration has revised its estimated 10-year cost of the program to $534 billion. Its original estimate was $395 billion.

Foster, the government's chief analyst of Medicare costs, says that he was warned repeatedly by his former boss, Thomas A. Scully, the Medicare administrator for three years, that he would be dismissed if he replied directly to legislative requests for information about prescription drug bills pending in Congress. In an email released by Foster, Scully's assistant, Jeffrey Flick, instructed the actuary to answer Republican queries regarding provisions in the Medicare bill but was warned—in bold font—not to provide information for Democratic requests "with anyone else until Tom Scully explicitly talks with you—authorizing release of information. The consequences for insubordination are extremely severe," Flick wrote in bold type. Interviews with federal officials, including Foster and Scully, make clear that the actuary's numbers were circulating within the Administration, and possibly among some Republican supporters of the bill on Capitol Hill, throughout the second half of last year, as Congress voted on the prescription drug bill, first in June and again in November.

At a hearing on Feb. 10, Secretary Thompson told lawmakers as much. Thompson said, "we knew all along" that the administration's cost estimates would be higher, but said he did not have a final figure until Dec. 24, 2003, after the bill was already signed into law.

On April 26, the Congressional Research Service issued a letter on the legality of Scully's decision to withhold information from Congress. Its conclusions read in part as follows:

> . . . actions which purposefully result in the transmission of knowingly false information to the United States Congress, and actions that involving the intentional and active prevention of the communication of accurate information to Congress in derogation of Federal law or responsibilities, might in certain circumstances involve activities which constitute violations of federal criminal provisions. . . . The issuance by an officer or employee in a department or agency of the Federal Government of a "gag order" on subordinate employees, to expressly prevent and prohibit those employees from communicating directly with Members or committees of Congress, would appear to violate a specific and express prohibition of federal law.

## Conference Committee Lockout

"This meeting is only open to the coalition of the willing."

—Rep. Bill Thomas (R-CA)
Chairman of the House Ways and Means
Committee

When the House and Senate each passed their own version of the Medicare bill, the Republican leadership at first followed routine procedure by appointing a 17-member conference committee to work out the differences between the two pieces of legislation. Seven Democrats were appointed to the committee. However, only two of those Democrats, Senators Max Baucus (MT) and John Breaux (LA),

were included in the closed-door meetings that had actually produced the final legislation. Why? Because they were among the few Democrats who would not raise significant objections to the bill. According to conference members from both parties, when the bill was made available to the rest of the committee, they were given just one hour to review the 678-page document before they voted.

The ranking Democrat on the Ways and Means Committee, Rep. Charles Rangel (NY), was among the members of the original conference committee. However, he was excluded from the closed-door meetings. He arrived uninvited to one meeting, and Rep. Thomas, the conference chairman, stopped substantive discussion of the legislation until Rep. Rangel left.

Democrats and others have complained the tactics like those employed during the conference on the Medicare bill are becoming more common. Similar lockouts were staged during crucial conference committee meetings on huge energy and transportation bills. More and more the role of the full conference committee is perfunctory while the details of the legislation are hammered out in closed meetings that include only a small coterie handpicked by the party leadership.

## Scully Cashes In

In December 2003, as the ink of the President's signature was drying on the Medicare bill, Thomas A. Scully, the government official responsible for Medicare, announced that he was leaving the government for lucrative health care jobs in the private sector. He joined Alston & Bird, a law firm that represents hospitals, drug manufacturers and other companies in the health care industry. Scully also accepted a job with Welsh, Carson, Anderson & Stowe, a New York investment firm specializing in telecommunications and health care.

Surprisingly, even though federal law generally bars presidential appointees such as Scully from discussing possible employment with firms involved in matters handled by those officials, Scully obtained a waiver from the HHS ethics officer so that he could negotiate with potential employers while he helped write the Medicare law. These jobs did not just drop into his lap in December. He had apparently been negotiating with healthcare-related firms at the same time he was helping the Administration push the controversial prescription drug legislation through Congress, which directly affected those industries.

Apparently in response to criticism of Scully's waiver, the White house ordered federal agencies to cease issuing ethics waivers for senior Administration appointees that would allow them to pursue jobs with private companies while influencing federal policies that could affect those companies. A memo issued on Jan. 6, 2004 by the White House Chief of Staff stated that, effective immediately, such waivers could only be approved by the White House.

## Tauzin Negotiates Phrma Job While Negotiating Prescription Drug Bill

As Medicare chief Scully was job searching while also helping pass the drug legislation, a powerful Member of Congress was also looking for a new job.

The Pharmaceutical Research and Manufacturers Association (PhRMA), the trade group for name-brand drug producers, reportedly offered Representative Billy Tauzin (R-LA) the top position at PhRMA and a compensation package that "would be the biggest deal given to anyone at a trade association," around $2 million a year, according to *The Washington Post*. The offer came just two months after Rep. Tauzin helped negotiate a $534 billion Medicare prescription drug bill widely viewed as a boon to pharmaceutical companies, which stand to make billions in profits while avoiding government price restrictions.

In February 2004, Common Cause called on Tauzin to resign his chairmanship of the powerful House Energy and Commerce Committee, saying "Even if your job negotiations with PhRMA began after your work on the Medicare bill was over, as you have reportedly said, it leaves one wondering whether you were trying to please PhRMA and what PhRMA may have promised you in return."

Tauzin denied there were any dealings with industry in exchange for his work on the bill, but he

stepped down from the chairmanship of the House Energy and Commerce Committee in early February, while negotiations over the PhRMA lobbying post continued. The job remains open and Tauzin may still be eligible if it remains open at the end of his term.

## Drug Industry Money Undermined The Process

As the Congressional fight on prescription drugs loomed, the drug industry drew up plans for raising millions of dollars to defeat efforts to reduce drug prices. The financial stakes were huge and the industry began to spend enormous amounts of money on campaign spending, lobbying, and advertising to influence the outcome of the legislation.

No group epitomized this more than PhRMA. PhRMA not only had a tremendous stake in the bill, but also turned out to be a major winner. The law prohibits the federal government from negotiating for lower drug prices and prohibits the reimportation of prescription drugs that are produced in the U.S. but sold for significantly less in other countries, which would also bring down the price of drugs.

PhRMA increased its yearly budget 23 percent to $150 million in anticipation of the upcoming Medicare fight. While PhRMA's interests range from international policy to local initiatives, industry protection in the Medicare reform bill was its top priority. According to published reports, PhRMA planned to spend $1 million for an "intellectual echo chamber of economists—a standing network of economists and thought leaders to speak against federal price control regulations through articles and testimony, and to serve as a rapid response team." Says one PhRMA document, "Unless we achieve enactment this year of market-based Medicare drug coverage for seniors, the industry's vulnerability will increase in the remainder of 2003 and in the 2004 election year."

PhRMA is well known as one of Washington's most powerful lobbying forces. The trade group alone spent $16 million on lobbying in 2003, according to federal lobby disclosure reports filed with the Senate Office of Public Records. Including lobbying spent by all of PhRMA's companies, the group spent at least $72.6 million lobbying in 2003—or roughly $135,701 per member of Congress.

PhRMA has capitalized on hiring former Members of Congress and their staffs as part of its lobbying army. According to reports, PhRMA lobbyists include former Reps. Vic Fazio (D-CA), Vin Weber (R-MN) and Bill Paxon (R-NY). Other drug industry lobbyists include David W. Beier, former domestic policy advisor for Vice President Al Gore; Dave Larson, former health policy advisor to Senator Bill First (R-TN); and Edwin A. Buckham, former chief of staff to Rep. Tom DeLay.

The industry maintains a constant presence among policymakers. For example, in the weeks following the House and Senate's passage of their respective Medicare bills in June, pharmaceutical companies organized parties for congressional staffers that worked on the legislation. According to *The Washington Post*, the drug company Johnson & Johnson planned a cocktail party near the Capitol. The invitations read, "In recognition of your part in the historic passage of Medicare drug bills by both houses of Congress . . ." After Common Cause sent letters to Senate conferees and House leaders stating that attendance by staff members to the party could violate congressional ethics rules, the leadership discouraged their staff from going and the party was later cancelled. Congressional staff still had the opportunity, however, to attend a "Rooftop Rendezvous" thrown by PhRMA and hospital trade groups.

## HHS PROPAGANDA CAMPAIGN

Once legislation passes Congress and is signed into law by the President, it is the job of the executive branch to implement the new law, including informing the public of the effect or the benefits of the new law. HHS, charged with implementing the new prescription drug law, immediately launched a multi-million dollar campaign promoting the new prescription drug benefit under the guise of public service advertising.

Early this year, HHS created a TV ad designed to educate the public on the new drug benefits, but

many criticized the ads as being political advertisements for the Administration that mislead the public about the facts of the new program. Adding to the concern about politicization of the prescription drug program was a contract for $9.5 million for producing and distributing the ads that went to a partisan media company, National Media, Inc.

HHS has also produced videos that were sent to broadcasters around the country touting the new program. The videos feature hired "reporters" who appear to be delivering straight news stories, but do not identify the government as the producer. Two videos end with the voice of a woman who says, "In Washington, I'm Karen Ryan reporting." The "reporter" in the commercial is reading from a script written by HHS.

The General Accounting Office (GAO) is now investigating these "fake video news" clips. The GAO will determine if they constitute illegal "covert propaganda." Federal law prohibits the use of federal money for "publicity or propaganda purposes" not authorized by Congress.

## CONCLUSION

Posted on Congressional websites is a document called "How Our Laws Are Made." [http://thomas.loc.gov/home/lawsmade.toc.html]. No one really believes the process meticulously detailed in the document is followed exactly—legislating is a messy process. But the laws, rules and procedures cited in the document are there to ensure that democratic principles are not empty words in the Constitution, but inform the way our government operates on a daily basis.

This report has told a tale of the rush to pass a thinly supported prescription drug bill that was a prime political goal of the Administration. In that rush, supporters showed disregard for the law, congressional rules, and other procedures and customs. We must reform and strengthen some of those laws and rules and, perhaps more importantly, those public officials must be held accountable. Americans must be assured that democracy is not just another word, but an integral part of how our government operates.

## DISCUSSION QUESTIONS

1. What are the various ways the Republican leadership of Congress and the executive branch undermined the legislative process in pursuit of a Medicare and prescription drug reform bill? How is democracy threatened by such tactics?
2. Why do you think there is such a gulf between the appearance and reality of how a bill becomes a law within the U.S. Congress? Would the quality of citizenship be improved if the truth were more widely known? Explain.

# 23 *Matt Taibbi*

# FOUR AMENDMENTS AND A FUNERAL: THE HOUSE OF HORRORS THAT IS CONGRESS

*In the summer of 2005,* Rolling Stone *reporter Matt Taibbi spent a month shadowing Vermont's lone congressman, Rep. Bernie Sanders, around the corridors of the House of Representatives. Sanders is the longest-serving Independent in the history of the U.S. Congress. He served eight terms in the House of Representatives before winning election to the Senate in 2006. As Taibbi's "tour guide," Sanders afforded him the opportunity to watch the legislative process from the trenches. What Taibbi witnessed actually was a series of victories for Sanders—some called it "the best winning streak of his career"—as four of his role call amendments fared well in the House, in the process challenging several powerful business interests as well as the Bush administration. Two of the amendments attempted to curb the scope of the Patriot Act, one sought to block a $5 billion loan to Westinghouse to build nuclear power plant in China, and a fourth would have cancelled a $1.9 billion contract to corporate giant Lockheed Martin. In the end, though, the power wielded by Republican congressional leaders trumped Sanders's carefully crafted legislative coalitions, and he ultimately came away empty handed. None of the insider details Taibbi reveals are particularly unusual. Indeed, they were business as usual, as private power overcame public purpose. But the public seldom has this clear a glimpse into the inner workings of congressional battles. When paired with the battle over Medicare prescription drug program in Article 22, the picture that emerges raises serious questions about the nature of our representative democracy.*

*Source:* Matt Taibbi, "Four Amendments and a Funeral," *Rolling Stone Magazine,* Issue 981, August 25, 2005, pp. 79–90.

It was a fairy-tale political season for George W. Bush, and it seemed like no one in the world noticed. Amid bombs in London, bloodshed in Iraq, a missing blonde in Aruba and a scandal curling up on the doorstep of Karl Rove, Bush's Republican Party quietly celebrated a massacre on Capitol Hill. Two of the most long-awaited legislative wet dreams of the Washington Insiders Club—an energy bill and a much-delayed highway bill—breezed into law. One mildly nervous evening was all it took to pass through the House the Central American Free Trade Agreement (CAFTA), for years now a primary strategic focus of the battle-in-Seattle activist scene. And accompanied by scarcely a whimper from the Democratic opposition, a second version of the notorious USA Patriot Act passed triumphantly through both houses of Congress, with most of the law being made permanent this time.

Bush's summer bills [in 2005] were extraordinary pieces of legislation, broad in scope, transparently brazen and audaciously indulgent. They gave an energy industry drowning in the most obscene profits in its history billions of dollars in subsidies and tax breaks, including $2.9 billion for the coal industry. The highway bill set new standards for monstrous and indefensibly wasteful spending, with Congress allocating $100,000 for a single traffic light in Canoga Park, California, and $223 million for the construction of a bridge linking the mainland an Alaskan island with a population of just fifty.

It was a veritable bonfire of public money, and it raged with all the brilliance of an Alabama book-burning. And what fueled it all were the little details you never heard about. The energy bill alone was 1,724 pages long. By the time the newspapers reduced this Tolstoyan monster to the size of a single headline announcing its passage, only a very few Americans understood that it was an ambitious giveaway to energy interests. But the drama of the legislative process is never in the broad strokes but in the bloody skirmishes and power plays that happen behind the scenes.

To understand the breadth of Bush's summer sweep, you had to watch the hand-fighting at close range. You had to watch opposition gambits die slow deaths in afternoon committee hearings, listen as members fell on their swords in exchange for favors and be there to see hordes of lobbyists rush in to reverse key votes at the last minute. All of these things I did—with the help of a tour guide.

Nobody knows how this place is run," says Rep. Bernie Sanders. "If they did, they'd go nuts."

Sanders is a tall, angular man with a messy head of gull-white hair and a circa-1977 set of big-framed eyeglasses. Minus the austere congressional office, you might mistake him for a physics professor or a journalist of the Jimmy Breslin school.

Vermont's sole representative in the House, Sanders is expected to become the first Independent ever elected to the U.S. Senate next year. He is something of a cause celebre on both the left and right these days, with each side overreacting to varying degrees to the idea of a self-described "democratic socialist" coming so near to a seat in the upper house.

Some months before, a Sanders aide had tried to sell me on a story about his boss, but over lunch we ended up talking about Congress itself. Like a lot of people who have worked on the Hill a little too long, the aide had a strange look in his eyes—the desperate look of a man who's been marooned on a remote island, subsisting on bugs and abalone for years on end. You worry that he might grab your lapel in frustration at any moment. "It's unbelievable," he said. "Worse than you can possibly imagine. The things that go on . . ."

Some time later I came back to the aide and told him that a standard campaign-season political profile was something I probably couldn't do, but if Sanders would be willing to give me an insider's guided tour of the horrors of Congress, I'd be interested.

"Like an evil, adult version of *Schoolhouse Rock*," I said.

The aide laughed and explained that the best time for me to go would be just before the summer recess, a period when Congress rushes to pass a number of appropriations bills. "It's like orgy season," he said. "You won't want to miss that."

I thought Sanders would be an ideal subject for a variety of reasons, but mainly for his Independent status. For all the fuss over his "socialist" tag, Sanders is really a classic populist outsider. The mere fact that Sanders signed off on the idea of serving as my guide says a lot about his attitude toward government in general: He wants people to see exactly what he's up against.

I had no way of knowing that Sanders would be a perfect subject for another, more compelling reason. In the first few weeks of my stay in Washington, Sanders introduced and passed, against very long odds, three important amendments. A fourth very nearly made it and would have passed had it gone to a vote. During this time, Sanders took on powerful adversaries, including Lockheed Martin, Westinghouse, the Export-Import Bank and the Bush administration. And by using the basic tools of democracy—floor votes on clearly posed questions, with the aid of painstakingly built coalitions of allies from both sides of the aisle—he, a lone Independent, beat them all.

It was an impressive run, with some in his office calling it the best winning streak of his career. Except for one thing.

By my last week in Washington, all of his victories had been rolled back, each carefully nurtured amendment perishing in the grossly corrupt and absurd vortex of political dysfunction that is today's U.S. Congress. What began as a tale of political valor ended as a grotesque object lesson in the ugly realities of American politics—the pitfalls of digging for hope in a shit mountain.

Sanders, to his credit, was still glad that I had come. "It's good that you saw this," he said. "People need to know."

## AMENDMENT 1

At 2 p.m. on Wednesday, July 20th, Sanders leaves his office in the Rayburn Building and heads down a tunnel passageway to the Capitol, en route to a Rules Committee hearing. "People have this impression that you can raise any amendment you want," he says. "They say, 'Why aren't you doing something about this?' That's not the way the system works."

Amendments occupy a great deal of most legislators' time, particularly those lawmakers in the minority. Members of Congress do author major bills, but more commonly they make minor adjustments to the bigger bills. Rather than write their own anti-terrorism bill, for instance, lawmakers will try to amend the Patriot Act, either by creating a new clause in the law or expanding or limiting some existing provision. The bill that ultimately becomes law is an aggregate of the original legislation and all the amendments offered and passed by all the different congresspersons along the way.

Sanders is the amendment king of the current House of Representatives. Since the Republicans took over Congress in 1995, no other lawmaker—not Tom DeLay, not Nancy Pelosi—has passed more roll-call amendments (amendments that actually went to a vote on the floor) than Bernie Sanders. He accomplishes this on the one hand by being relentlessly active, and on the other by using his status as an Independent to form left-right coalitions.

On this particular day, Sanders carries with him an amendment to Section 215 of the second version of the Patriot Act, which is due to go to the House floor for a reauthorization vote the next day. Unlike many such measures, which are often arcane and shrouded in minutiae, the Sanders amendment is simple, a proposed rollback of one of the Patriot Act's most egregious powers: Section 215 allows law enforcement to conduct broad searches of ordinary citizens—even those not suspected of ties to terrorism—without any judicial oversight at all. To a civil libertarian like Sanders, it is probably a gross insult that at as late a date as the year 2005 he still has to spend his time defending a concept like probable cause before an ostensibly enlightened legislature. But the legislation itself will prove not half as insulting as the roadblocks he must overcome to force a vote on the issue.

The House Rules Committee is perhaps the free world's outstanding bureaucratic abomination—a tiny, airless closet deep in the labyrinth of the Capitol where some of the very meanest people on earth spend their days cleaning democracy like a fish. The official function of the committee is to decide which bills and amendments will be voted on by Congress and also to schedule the parameters of debate. If Rules votes against your amendment, your amendment dies. If you control the Rules Committee, you control Congress.

The committee has nine majority members and four minority members. But in fact, only one of those thirteen people matters. Unlike on most committees, whose chairmen are usually chosen on the basis of seniority, the Rules chairman is the appointee of the Speaker of the House.

The current chairman, David Dreier, is a pencil-necked Christian Scientist from Southern California, with exquisite hygiene and a passion for brightly colored ties. While a dependable enough yes man to have remained Rules chairman for six years now, he is basically a human appendage, a prosthetic attachment on the person of the House majority leader, Tom DeLay. "David carries out the wishes of the Republican leadership right down the line," said former Texas Congressman Martin Frost, until last year the committee's ranking Democrat.

There is no proven method of influencing the Rules Committee. In fact, in taking on the committee, Democrats and Independents like Sanders normally have only one weapon at their disposal.

"Shame," says James McGovern, a Massachusetts Democrat and one of the minority members on the committee. "Once in a great while we can shame them into allowing a vote on something or other."

The Rules Committee meets in a squalid little space the size of a high school classroom, with poor lighting and nothing on the walls but lifeless landscapes and portraits of stern-looking congressmen of yore. The grim setting is an important part of the committee's character. In the vast, majestic complex that is the U.S. Capitol—an awesome structure where every chance turn leads to architectural wonderment—the room where perhaps the most crucial decisions of all are made is a dark, seldom-visited hole in the shadow of the press gallery.

The committee is the last stop on the legislative express, a kind of border outpost where bills are held up before they are allowed to pass into law. It meets sporadically, convening when a bill is ready to be sent to the floor for a vote.

Around 3 p.m., Sanders emerges from this hole into the hallway. For the last hour or so, he has been sitting with his hands folded on his lap in a corner of the cramped committee room, listening as a parade of witnesses and committee members babbled on in stream-of-consciousness fashion about the vagaries of the Patriot Act. He heard, for instance, Texas Republican Pete Sessions explain his "philosophy" of how to deal with terrorists, which includes, he said, "killing them or removing them from the country."

Tom Cole of Oklahoma, another Republican committee member, breathlessly congratulated witnesses who had helped prepare the act. "This is a very important piece of legislation," he drawled. "Y'all have done a really good job."

Nodding bashfully in agreement with Cole's words was Wisconsin Republican James Sensenbrenner Jr. As chairman of the Judiciary Committee, Sensenbrenner is the majority lawmaker in whose scaly womb the Patriot Act gestated until its recent delivery to Rules. Though he was here as a witness, his obvious purpose was to bare his fangs in the direction of anyone or anything who would threaten his offspring.

Sensenbrenner is your basic Fat Evil Prick, perfectly cast as a dictatorial committee chairman: He has the requisite moist-with-sweat pink neck, the dour expression, the penchant for pointless bile and vengefulness. Only a month before, on June 10th, Sensenbrenner suddenly decided he'd heard enough during a Judiciary Committee hearing on the Patriot Act and went completely Tasmanian devil on a group of Democratic witnesses who had come to share stories of abuses at places like Guantanamo Bay. Apparently not wanting to hear any of that stuff, Sensenbrenner got up midmeeting and killed the lights, turned off the microphones and shut down the C-Span feed, before marching his fellow Republicans out of the room—leaving the Democrats and their witnesses in the dark.

This lights-out technique was actually pioneered by another Republican, former Commerce Committee chairman Thomas Bliley, who in 1995 hit the lights on a roomful of senior citizens who had come to protest Newt Gingrich's Medicare plan. Bliley, however, went one step further than Sensenbrenner, ordering Capitol police to arrest the old folks when they refused to move. Sensenbrenner might have tried the same thing in his outburst, except that his party had just voted to underfund the Capitol police.

Thus it is strange now, in the Rules Committee hearing, to see the legendarily impatient Sensenbrenner lounging happily in his witness chair like a giant toad sunning on nature's perfect rock. He speaks at length about the efficacy of the Patriot Act in combating the certain evils of the free-library system ("I don't think we want to turn libraries into sanctuaries") and responds to questions about the removal of an expiration date on the new bill ("We don't have sunsets on Amtrak or Social Security, either").

Such pronouncements provoke strident responses from the four Democratic members of the committee—Doris Matsui of California, Alcee Hastings of Florida, Louise Slaughter of upstate New York and McGovern of Massachusetts—who until now have scarcely stirred throughout the hearing. The Democrats generally occupy a four-seat row on the far left end of the panel table, and during hearings they tend to sit there in mute, impotent rage, looking like the unhappiest four heads of lettuce to ever come out of the ground. The one thing they are allowed to do is argue. Sensenbrenner gives them just such an opportunity, and soon he and McGovern fall into a row about gag orders.

In the middle of the exchange, Sanders gets up and, looking like a film lover leaving in the middle of a bad movie, motions for me to join him in the hallway. He gestures at the committee room. "It's cramped, it's uncomfortable, there isn't enough room for the public or press," he says. "That's intentional. If they wanted people to see this, they'd pick a better hall."

Sanders then asks me if I noticed anything unusual about the squabbling between Sensenbrenner and McGovern. "Think about it," he says, checking his watch. "How hard is it to say, 'Mr. Sanders, be here at 4:30 p.m.'? Answer: not hard at all. You see, a lot of the things we do around here are structured. On the floor, in other committees, it's like that. But in the Rules Committee, they just go on forever. You see what I'm getting at?"

I shrug.

"It has the effect of discouraging people from offering amendments," he says. "Members know that they're going to have to sit for a long time. Eventually they have to choose between coming here and conducting other business. And a lot of them choose other business . . . That's what that show in there was about."

## AMENDMENT 2

As he waits for his chance to address the Rules Committee, Sanders is actually armed with not one but two amendments. The measures are essentially the same, both using identical language to prohibit warrantless searches of libraries and bookstores. The only difference is, the amendment Sanders is trying to get past the committee would permanently outlaw such searches under the Patriot Act. The second amendment takes a more temporary approach, denying the Justice Department funding in next year's budget to conduct those types of searches.

This kind of creative measure—so-called limitation amendments—are often the best chance for a minority member like Sanders to influence legislation. For one thing, it's easier to offer such amendments to appropriations bills than it is to amend bills like the Patriot Act. Therefore, Sanders often brings issues to a vote by attempting to limit the funds for certain government programs—targeting a federal loan here, a bloated contract there. "It's just another way of getting at an issue," says Sanders.

In this case, the tactic worked. A month earlier, on June 15th, the House passed Sanders' amendment to limit funding for library and bookstore searches by a vote of 238-187, with thirty-eight Republicans joining 199 Democrats.

The move wasn't a cure-all; it was just a short-term fix. But it enabled Sanders to approach the Rules Committee holding more than his hat in his hand. With the June vote, he had concrete evidence to show the committee that if his amendment to permanently alter the Patriot Act were allowed to reach the floor, it would pass. Now, if Tom DeLay & Co. were going to disallow Sanders' amendment, they were going to have to openly defy a majority vote of the U.S. Congress to do so.

Which, it turns out, isn't much of a stumbling block.

While Sanders was facing the Rules Committee, House leaders were openly threatening their fellow members about the upcoming vote on CAFTA. "We will twist their arms until they break" was the Stalin-esque announcement of Arizona Republican Jim Kolbe. The hard-ass, horse-head-in-the-bed threat is a defining characteristic of this current set of House leaders, whose willingness to go to extreme lengths to get their way has become legend. In 2003, Nick Smith, a Michigan legislator nearing retirement, was told by Republican leadership that if he didn't vote for the GOP's Medicare bill, the party would put forward a primary challenger against his son Brad, who was planning to run for his seat.

Members who cross DeLay & Co. invariably find themselves stripped of influence and/or important committee positions. When Rep. Chris Smith complained about Bush's policy toward veterans, he was relieved of his seat as the Veterans' Committee chairman. When Joel Hefley locked horns with Dennis Hastert during the Tom DeLay ethics flap, Hefley lost his spot as the House Ethics Committee chairman.

In other words, these leaders don't mind screwing even their friends any chance they get. Take the kneecapping of Arizona Republican Jeff Flake, whose surrender on the Patriot Act issue paved the way for the trashing of the Sanders amendment.

Flake, who sits on Sensenbrenner's Judiciary Committee, had been one of the leading Republican critics of the Patriot Act. He was particularly explicit in his support for sunset provisions in the law, which would prevent it from being made permanent. In April, for instance, a Flake spokesman told the *Los Angeles Times*, "Law enforcement officials would be more circumspect if they were faced with the prospect of having to come to Congress every couple of years and justify the provisions."

When Sanders offered his amendment to deny funding for warrantless searches, Flake was right there by his side. But now, only a few weeks later, Flake suddenly offers his own amendment, aimed at the same provision of the Patriot Act as Sanders', but with one big difference: It surrenders on the issue of probable cause. The Flake amendment would require only that the FBI director approve any library and bookstore searches.

It is hard to imagine a more toothless, panty-waist piece of legislation than Flake's measure. In essence, it is a decree from the legislative branch righteously demanding that the executive branch authorize its own behavior—exactly the kind of comical "compromise" measure one would expect the leadership to propose as a replacement for the Sanders plan.

Flake clearly had made a deal with the House leadership. It is not known what he got in return, but it appears that his overlords made him pay for it. Before the final vote on any bill, the opposition party has a chance to offer what is called a "motion to recommit," which gives Congress a last chance to re-examine a bill before voting on it. When the Democrats introduced this motion before the final vote, the House Republican leadership had to ask someone to stand up against it. They, naturally, turned to Flake, the chastened dissenter, to run the errand.

Flake is a sunny-looking sort of guy with a slim build and blow-dried blond hair. He looks like a surfer or maybe the manager of a Guitar Center in Ventura or El Segundo: outwardly cheerful, happy and ill-suited, facially anyway, for the real nut-cutting politics of this sort. When it comes time for him to give his speech, Flake meanders to the podium like a man who has just had his head clanged between a pair of cymbals. The lump in his throat is the size of a casaba melon. He begins, "Mr. Speaker, I am probably the last person expected to speak on behalf of the committee or the leadership in genera . . ."

When Flake mentions his own amendments, his voice drops as he tries to sound proud of them—but the most he can say is, "They are good." Then he becomes downright philosophical: "Sometimes as my hero in politics said once . . . Barry Goldwater said, 'Politics is nothing more than public business . . . You don't always get everything you want.'"

It is a painful performance. Later, commenting on the Flake speech, Sanders shakes his head. "They made him walk the plank there," he says.

Flake denies he cut a deal to sell out on the Patriot Act. But his cave-in effectively spelled the end of the Sanders amendment. The Republicans point to the Flake amendment to show that they addressed concerns about library and bookstore searches. Essentially, the House leaders have taken the Sanders measure, cut all the guts out of it, bullied one of their own into offering it in the form of a separate amendment and sent it sailing through the House, leaving Sanders—and probable cause—to suck eggs.

## AMENDMENT 1 REDUX

Late in the afternoon, after waiting several hours for his turn, Sanders finally gets a chance to address the Rules Committee. His remarks are short but violent. He angrily demands that the committee let Congress vote on his amendment, noting that the appropriations version of it had already passed the House by fifty-one votes. "I would regard it as an outrageous abuse of power to deny this amendment the opportunity to be part of this bill," he shouts. "We had this debate already—and our side won."

In response, Republicans on the committee cast a collective "whatever, dude" gaze. "Sometimes, you can engage them a little," Sanders says later. But most of the time it works out like this.

Shortly after Sanders finishes his remarks, the Rules Committee members scurry to begin what will be a very long night of work. To most everyone outside those nine majority members, what transpires in the committee the night before a floor vote is a mystery on the order of the identity of Jack the Ripper or the nature of human afterlife. Even the Democrats who sit on the committee have only a vague awareness of what goes on. "They can completely rewrite bills," says McGovern. "Then they take it to the floor an hour later. Nobody knows what's in those bills."

One singular example of this came four years ago, when the Judiciary Committee delivered the first Patriot Act to the Rules Committee for its consideration. Dreier trashed that version of the act, which had been put together by the bipartisan committee, and replaced it with a completely different bill that had been written by John Ashcroft's Justice Department.

The bill went to the floor a few hours later, where it passed into law. The Rules Committee is supposed to wait out a three-day period before sending the bill to the House, ostensibly in order to give the members a chance to read the bill. The three-day period is only supposed to be waived in case of emergency. However, the Rules Committee of DeLay and Dreier waives the three-day period as a matter of routine. This forces members of Congress to essentially cast blind yes-or-no votes to bills whose contents are likely to be an absolute mystery to them.

There is therefore an element of Christmas morning in each decision of the committee. On the day of a floor vote, you look under the tree (i.e., the Rules Committee Web site) and check to see if your amendment survived. And so, on the morning of July 21st, Sanders' staff goes online and clicks on a link H.R. 3199—USA PATRIOT AND TERRORISM PREVENTION REAUTHORIZATION ACT OF 2005. Twenty of sixty-three amendments have survived, most of them inconsequential. The Sanders amendment isn't one of them.

On a sweltering Tuesday morning in the Rayburn Building, a bookend location in the multibuilding home of the House of Representatives, a very long line has formed in the first-floor corridor, outside the Financial Services Committee. In the ongoing orgy of greed that is the U.S. Congress, the Financial Services Committee is the hottest spot. Joel Barkin, a former press aide to Sanders, calls Financial Services the "job committee," because staffers who work for members on that committee move into high-paying jobs on Wall Street or in the credit-card industry with ridiculous ease.

"It seems like once a week, I'd get an e-mail from some staffer involved with that committee," he says, shaking his head. "They'd be announcing their new jobs with MBNA or MasterCard or whatever. I mean, to send that over an e-mail all over Congress—at least try to hide it, you know?"

On this particular morning, about half of the people in the line to get into the committee appear to be congressional staffers, mostly young men in ties and dress shirts. The rest are disheveled, beaten-down- looking men, most of them black, leaning against the walls.

These conspicuous characters are called "linestanders." A lot of them are homeless. This is their job: They wait in line all morning so some lobbyist for Akin, Gump or any one of a thousand other firms doesn't have to. "Three days a week," says William McCall (who has a home), holding up three fingers. "Come in Tuesday, Wednesday and Thursday. Get between twelve and forty dollars."

When a photographer approaches to take a picture of the line, all the line-standers but McCall refuse to be photo-graphed and cover their faces with newspapers. I smile at this: Only the homeless have enough sense to be ashamed of being seen in Congress.

In reality, everybody in Congress is a stand-in for some kind of lobbyist. In many cases it's difficult to tell whether it's the companies that are lobbying the legislators or whether it's the other way around.

# AMENDMENT 3

Across the Rayburn building on the second floor, a two-page memo rolls over the fax machine in Sanders' office. Warren Gunnels, the congressman's legislative director, has been working the phones all day long, monitoring the Capitol Hill gossip around a vote that is to take place in the Senate later that afternoon. Now a contact of his has sent him a fax copy of an item making its way around the senatorial offices that day. Gunnels looks at the paper and laughs.

The memo appears to be printed on the official stationery of the Export-Import Bank, a federally subsidized institution whose official purpose is to lend money to overseas business ventures as a means of creating a market for U.S. exports. That's the official mission. A less full-of-shit description of Ex-Im might describe it as a federal slush fund that gives away massive low-interest loans to companies that a) don't need the money and b) have recently made gigantic contributions to the right people.

The afternoon Senate vote is the next act in a genuinely thrilling drama that Sanders himself started in the House a few weeks before. On June 28th, Sanders scored a stunning victory when the House voted 313-114 to approve his amendment to block a $5 billion loan by the Ex-Im Bank to West-inghouse to build four nuclear power plants in China.

The Ex-Im loan was a policy so dumb and violently opposed to American interests that lawmakers who voted for it had serious trouble coming up with a plausible excuse for approving it. In essence, the U.S. was giving $5 billion to a state-subsidized British utility (Westinghouse is a subsidiary of British Nuclear Fuels) to build up the infrastructure of our biggest trade competitor, along the way sharing advanced nuclear technology with a Chinese conglomerate that had, in the past, shared nuclear know-how with Iran and Pakistan.

John Hart, a spokesman for Oklahoma Republican Sen. Tom Coburn (who would later sponsor the Senate version of the Sanders amendment), laughs when asked what his opponents were using as an excuse for the bill. "One reason I got," Hart says, "was that if we build nuclear power plants in China, then China would be less dependent on foreign oil, and they would consume less foreign oil, and so as a result our oil prices would go down." He laughs again. "You'd think there would be more direct ways of lowering gas prices," he says.

Oddly enough, Coburn, a hard-line pro-war, pro-life conservative who once advocated the death penalty for abortion doctors, is a natural ally for the "socialist" Sanders on an issue like this one. Sanders frequently looks for co-sponsors among what he and his staff call "honest conservatives," people like California's Dana Rohrabacher and Texas libertarian Ron Paul, with whom Sanders frequently works on trade issues. "A lot of times, guys like my boss will have a lot in common with someone like Sanders," says Jeff Deist, an aide to Rep. Paul. "We're frustrated by the same obstacles in the system."

In the case of Westinghouse, the bill's real interest for the Senate had little to do with gas prices and a lot to do with protecting a party member in trouble. Many of the 5,000 jobs the loan was supposed to create were in Pennsylvania, where Rick Santorum, the GOP incumbent, was struggling to hold off a challenger. "Five billion for 5,000 jobs," Sanders says, shaking his head in disbelief. "That's $1 million per job. And they say I'm crazy."

This morning, with the Senate vote only a few hours away, the lobbying has kicked into very high gear. That lobbyists for Westinghouse are phone-blitzing senatorial offices is no surprise. Somewhat more surprising are reports that the Ex-Im Bank itself is hustling the senatorial staff.

"Technically speaking, government agencies aren't allowed to lobby," says Gunnels. "But they sure do a lot of informing just before big votes."

The document that has just spilled over the Sanders fax line is printed with a cover sheet from the Ex-Im Bank. It looks like an internal memo, sent by Ex-Im's "Senior Legislative Analyst," Beverley Thompson.

The document contains a series of cheery talking points about the Ex-Im loan to China, which taken together seem to indicate that the loan is a darn good idea. Nowhere does the document simply come out and say, "We recommend that the Sanders amendment against this loan be defeated." But the meaning is fairly clear.

One odd feature of the document is a notation at the top of the page that reads, "FYI—this info has not been cleared." In government offices, documents must be cleared for public consumption before they can be distributed outside the agency. What this memo seems to suggest, then, is that the recipient was being given choice inside info from the Ex-Im Bank, a strange thing for the bank to be doing out in the open.

The Sanders office has seen this kind of thing before. In the summer of 2003, it received a very similar kind of document purportedly from the Treasury. Printed on Treasury stationery, the document contained, like the Ex-Im memo, a list of talking points that seemed to argue against a Sanders amendment. The issue in that case involved a set of new Treasury regulations that would have made it easier for companies to convert their employees' traditional pension plans into a new type of plan called a cash-balance pension plan.

Among the companies that would have been affected by the regulations was IBM, which stood to save billions by converting to this new system. And guess who turned out to have written the "Treasury Department Memo" that was circulated to members of Congress, on the eve of the vote?

That's right: IBM.

"It was hilarious," recalls Gunnels. "The Treasury Department logo was even kind of tilted, like it had been pasted on. It looked like a third-grader had done it."

Persistent questioning by Sanders' staff led to an admission by the Treasury Department that the document had indeed been doctored by IBM. The company, in turn, issued a utterly nonsensical mea culpa ("We believed that we were redistributing a public document that we had understood was widely distributed by the Treasury") that has to rank as one of the lamer corporate non-apologies in recent years.

It seemed obvious that the company had acted in conjunction with one or more Treasury employees to create the phony document. But no Treasury employee has ever been exposed, nor has IBM ever been sanctioned. "They turned the case over to the Inspector General's Office," says Gunnels. Jeff Weaver, Sanders' chief of staff, adds, "And they've done absolutely nothing."

So long as the investigation is still open, Gunnels explains, there is no way to request documents pertaining to the case through the Freedom of Information Act. "That investigation will probably stay open a long time," he says.

Every time Congress is ordered to clean up its lobbyist culture, its responses come off like leprechaun tricks. For instance, when the Lobby Disclosure Act of 1995 ordered the House and the Senate to create an electronic lobbyist registry system, so that the public could use the latest technology to keep track of Washington's 34,000-plus lobbyists and whom they work for, the two houses only half-complied.

The secretary of the Senate created an electronic database, all right, but what a database: The system was little more than a giant computerized pile of downloadable scanned images of all the individual registration forms and semiannual reports. The Senate system, however, was a significant improvement over the House system. The House responded to the 1995 law by entirely ignoring it.

All of Washington seems to be in on the lobbyist leprechaun game. News even leaked that corporations had managed to convince the local sports teams, the Wizards and the Capitals, to create special courtside and/or rinkside tickets. The tickets would not be available to the general public but would have an official list price of $49.50 and could be purchased by corporate customers. Why the low list price? Because congressional rules prohibit gifts to congressmen with a cost above fifty dollars.

## AMENDMENT 4

The Ex-Im amendment was not the only victory Sanders had scored on the government-waste front that month. In fact, just two days after he passed the Ex-Im amendment, Sanders secured another apparent major victory against a formidable corporate opponent. By a vote of 238-177, the House passed a Sanders amendment to cancel a $1.9 billion contract that the Federal Aviation Administration had awarded to Lockheed Martin to privatize a series of regional Flight Service Stations.

Several factors went into the drafting of this amendment. For one thing, the FAA-Lockheed deal would have resulted in the loss of about 1,000 jobs around the country from the closure of thirty-eight Flight Service Stations, which are basically small regional centers that give out weather information and provide some basic air-traffic assistance. Thirty-five of those projected job losses would have come from a station in Burlington, Vermont, so in opposing the deal, Sanders was behaving like a traditional congressman, protecting his home turf.

But there were other concerns. The FAA deal was an early test run for a Bush policy idea called "competitive sourcing," which is just a clunky euphemism for the privatization of traditionally governmental services. Sanders is generally opposed to competitive sourcing, mainly on cost and quality grounds.

Beyond that, Sanders sees in issues like the Westinghouse deal and the Lockheed Martin deal a consistent pattern of surrender to business interests by Congress. Too often, he says, Congress fails to tie government assistance to the company's record in preserving American jobs.

"I have no problem with the argument that we should help businesses out," Sanders says. "But if you go to these hearings, no one ever asks the question 'How many jobs have you exported over the years? If we give you money, will you promise not to export any more jobs?' "

He laughs. "It's funny. Some of these companies, they'll be straight with you. General Electric, for instance. They come right out and say, 'We're moving to China.' And if you ask them why, in that case, you should subsidize them, they say, 'If you don't help us, we'll move to China faster.' "

Given how powerful Lockheed Martin is on Capitol Hill—the company even has the contract to maintain the server for the computers in Congress—the Lockheed vote was surprisingly easy. Maybe too easy. On the surface, it looked like traditional politics all the way, with Sanders applying his usual formula of securing as many Democratic votes as possible, then working to pry loose enough Republicans to get the vote through. In this case, the latter task proved not all that difficult, as Sanders had natural allies in each of those Republican representatives with targeted flight stations in their districts.

But when the vote sailed through by a comfortable margin, Sanders didn't celebrate. Sometimes, he says, a vote like this one will pass easily in the House precisely because the leadership knows it will be able to kill it down the line.

"I don't want to accuse my fellow members of cynicism," he says, "but sometimes they'll vote for an amendment just so they can go back home and say they fought for this or that. In reality, they've been assured by the leadership that the measure will never make it through."

And if an offending bill somehow makes it through the House and the Senate, there's always the next and last step: the conference committee. Comprising bipartisan groups of "conferees" from the relevant House and Senate authorizing committees, these committees negotiate the final version of a bill. Like the Rules Committee, it has absolute power to make wholesale changes—which it usually does, safely out of the public's view.

With a measure like Sanders' Lockheed amendment, the chances were always going to be very slim that it would survive the whole process. Among other things, President Bush responded to the passage of the anti-Lockheed amendment by immediately threatening to veto the entire Transportation budget to which it was attached. (Bush made the same threat, incidentally, in response to the Ex-Im amendment, which was attached to the Foreign Operations budget.)

"Now the conference committee has political cover," Sanders says. "It's either take them out and restore that loan and that contract or the president vetoes an entire appropriations bill—and there's no funding for Foreign Operations or Transportation. There's really no choice."

In the case of the Lockheed amendment, however, things never get that far. Despite the amendment's comfortable victory in the House, weeks pass, and the Sanders staff cannot find a senator to sponsor the measure in the upper house. Though the staff still has hopes that a sponsor will be found, it's not always that easy to arrange. Especially when the president threatens a veto over the matter.

As for the Ex-Im amendment, the Sanders gambit against it perishes on that Tuesday afternoon, July 19th, as the Senate wallops the Coburn version of the amendment, 62-37. According to Gunnels, the key vote ends up being cast by Democrat Harry Reid of Nevada.

"It was still close, around 24-23 or so, before Reid voted," he says. "It looked like a lot of Democrats were waiting to see which way he would go, him being the minority leader and all. As soon as he voted no, a whole slew of Democrats followed him, and the amendment was dead."

Reid's predecessor as minority leader, Tom Daschle, was a marionette of the banking and credit-card industries whose public persona recalled a hopped-up suburban vacuum-cleaner salesman. In the wake of the Daschle experiment, Reid is the perfect inheritor of the Democratic leadership mantle: a dour, pro-life Mormon with a campaign chest full of casino money. Trying to figure out his motives on this vote proved no less difficult than figuring out what the Democratic Party stands for in general.

When I call Reid's office, spokesman Jim Manley initially refuses to offer an explanation for the senator's vote. He seems weirdly defensive about the issue, and we go back and forth on the matter for a while before he finally reads a statement explaining—or purporting to, anyway—his boss's vote on the China loan.

"As with questions raised about other transactions involving China, legitimate concerns are at issue," he reads. "But rather than Congress intervening in one transaction after another, what we really need is a coherent and comprehensive policy to address the emergence of China as an economic threat. This administration has failed to develop a China policy . . . and this utter failure has fueled congressional and public unease . . . Got that?"

"Um," I say, copying it down. "Sure. Wait—if the problem is that there's no comprehensive policy for China, why give them $5 billion to build nuclear plants? Why not give them, say, nothing at all?"

Silence on the other end of the line. Finally, Manley speaks.

"This administration has failed to develop a China policy," he repeats coldly. "And this utter failure has fueled congressional and public unease . . ."

In the end, after just a few weeks, every one of Sanders' victories was transformed into a defeat. He had won three major amendments and would likely have won a fourth, if the Rules Committee had permitted a vote on his Patriot Act measure. In each case, Sanders proved that his positions held wide support—even among a population as timid and corrupt as the U.S. Congress. Yet even after passing his amendments by wide margins, he never really came close to converting popular will into law.

Sanders seem to take it strangely in stride. After a month of watching him and other members, I get the strong impression that even the idealists in Congress have learned to accept the body on its own terms. Congress isn't the steady assembly line of consensus policy ideas it's sold as, but a kind of permanent emergency in which a majority of members work day and night to burgle the national treasure and burn the Constitution. A largely castrated minority tries, Alamo-style, to slow them down—but in the end spends most of its time beating calculated retreats and making loose plans to fight another day.

Taken all together, the whole thing is an ingenious system for inhibiting progress and the popular will. The deck is stacked just enough to make sure that nothing ever changes. But just enough is left to chance to make sure that hope never completely dies out. And who knows, maybe it evolved that way for a reason.

"It's funny," Sanders says. "When I first came to Congress, I'd been mayor of Burlington, Vermont—a professional politician. And I didn't know any of this. I assumed that if you get majorities in both houses, you win. I figured, it's democracy, right?"

Well, that's what they call it, anyway.

---

## DISCUSSION QUESTIONS

1. Reflecting on life on Capitol Hill, Rep. Sanders tells Taibbi: "Nobody knows how this place is run. If they did, they'd go nuts." Why do you think the legislative process is so unknown to the American people? Do you agree that people would "go nuts" if they were aware of what happens within Congress?

2. With each of Sanders's legislative initiatives, a victory seemingly was won, only to be reversed and turned into a defeat at the last minute. What were the obstacles he encountered with his amendments? Comment on the quality of representative democracy in light of Taibbi's account of his time as an observer of the public policy process.

# CONGRESSIONAL INERTIA: IRON TRIANGLES OLD AND NEW

*American citizens often complain about the performance of Congress. They are generally unhappy with the lack of cooperation between the two political parties in Congress and how little actually gets done in Washington. And when Congress does act, citizens seldom view that action as benefiting the average middle-class and working-class American. In this article, political scientists Patricia Siplon and William Grover draw upon the time-tested concept of the "iron triangle" to explain the causes of congressional inertia. They trace the history of iron triangles to the earlier notion of the "military–industrial complex," which was articulated most notably by President Dwight Eisenhower in his 1961 Farewell Address, and later expanded into a full-blown analysis of defense contracting by political scientist Gordon Adams. Adams defined the iron triangle as a symbiotic relationship among three sets of political actors: congressional committees and subcommittees, executive branch agencies, and private interest groups, particularly corporations. He was troubled by ever-rising defense budgets and how in the process of forming U.S. defense policy, private corporate interests regularly came to be equated with the public interest. Congress too willingly abandoned its oversight function in favor of promoting, seemingly at any cost, the smooth advancement of Pentagon plans and defense contractor profits. Moving beyond the classic example of military budgets, Siplon and Grover turn their attention to the role of iron triangles in human immunodeficiency virus (HIV)/acquired immunodeficiency syndrome (AIDS) policy. Since the early 1980s, the pharmaceutical industry has vigorously lobbied Congress, and worked closely with the Food and Drug Administration, to shape the nation's approach to the development, regulation, and pricing of drugs to fight the AIDS pandemic. The resulting pharmaceutical iron triangle dramatically impacted the development, pricing, and availability of the drugs azidothymidine (AZT) and Norvir. In the face of the deaths of millions suffering from AIDS worldwide over more than two decades, the fight to*

*Source:* The authors have written this article specifically for the seventh edition of *Voices of Dissent.*

*provide widespread access to cheap generic AIDS drugs continues, with occasional victories for social groups challenging this particular iron triangle. As with the classic example of defense contracting, when it comes to the life and death circumstances with HIV/AIDS policy, Congress far too often plays the role of a lapdog for corporate and executive branch policymakers, instead of acting as a watchdog for the interests of American citizens.*

What Congress does matters. As the new 110th Congress convened in January of 2007, it began the process of constructing the fiscal year 2008 budget, authorizing spending in the vicinity of $2.8 trillion when the new fiscal year begins October 1. This is an incomprehensibly large amount of money—a sum that represents many things.[1] Most notably, it is a numerical statement about priorities; what we value as a society is indicated in how we allocate our budgetary resources. What do U.S. citizens think of those who allocate our budgetary resources? If we follow poll data, the answer clearly is: "not much." It has long been noted that while citizens routinely rate their own Senators and Representatives favorably, Congress as an institution gets very low marks. A *New York Times*/CBS news poll released in late September 2006 showed the approval rating for Congress at barely 25 percent, a dozen points below President George W. Bush's own anemic approval rating. The accompanying story observed that public "disdain for Congress is as intense as it has been since 1994," when Republicans captured both the House and Senate for the first time in decades. A full 77 percent of respondents in the *Times*/CBS poll said the 109th Congress had not done a good enough job to merit being reelected. Accordingly, voters expressed their displeasure with Republican control of Congress in November 2006, returning Democrats to power in the House and, more narrowly, in the Senate.

Clearly something is afoot here. Opposition to the Bush administration's debacle in Iraq surely soured voters, as did corruption scandals involving some leading officials. But beneath those immediate issues lies a deeper sense that Congress does not deliver the goods—at least for ordinary Americans. As an institution, Congress is widely perceived to suffer from entrenched inertia that leaves it unable to change course. Why is it so difficult for our legislative branch to change direction to respond to shifting priorities?

## A BRIEF HISTORY OF A METAPHOR

Political science is awash in metaphors. The intent of a well-constructed metaphor is to capture some complex aspect of politics with an easily understood example. The opening paragraph above involves the most important and complicated function performed by Congress—readily conceptualized as controlling the national "purse strings." A multitude of metaphors winds its way through our political landscape: "horse races," "landslides," "pork," "log rolling," "hawks and doves," "quagmires"—these barely scratch the surface. Indeed, Sociologist Max Weber once famously argued that a combination of passion and perspective is needed to succeed in politics, characterizing politics itself as, metaphorically, "a strong and slow boring of

[1]Tellingly, among the things that figure does *not* include, however, is spending for the wars in Iraq and Afghanistan, to date upwards of $500 billion, most of which the House and Senate have taken "off the books" with special emergency bills.

hard boards." Understanding the difficulty in getting Congress to change course, to address policy issues in a fresh way with the public interest at heart, involves one of the most apt metaphors used in congressional studies, the "iron triangle."

The origins of the iron triangle metaphor are rooted in the development of a closely related concept known as the "military–industrial complex." Although references to the military–industrial complex go back at least to the early part of the twentieth century, the most well-known usage came in President Dwight Eisenhower's Farewell Address on January 17, 1961. Eisenhower was a moderate Republican with vast military experience, having served as Supreme Commander of allied forces in World War II. He used his Farewell Address to issue a prescient warning about the combined power of the military bureaucracy of the executive branch (particularly the Defense Department) and the arms industry:

> This conjunction of an immense military establishment and a large arms industry is new in the American experience. The total influence—economic, political even spiritual—is felt in every city, every statehouse, every office of the federal government. We recognize the imperative need for this development. Yet we must not fail to comprehend its grave implications. Our toil, resources and livelihood are all involved; so is the very structure of our society. In the councils of government, we must guard against the acquisition of unwarranted influence, whether sought or unsought, by the *military–industrial complex*. The potential for the disastrous rise of misplaced power exists and will persist.

From President Eisenhower's perspective, the stakes involved could not have been higher. He went on to characterize the "huge industrial and military machinery of defense" as a potential threat to our liberties and to democracy itself. In a draft of his address, Eisenhower had referred to the "military–industrial–congressional complex," dropping the word "congressional" in deference to the

sensitivities of members of Congress. But it was clear that he was concerned about the role Congress played in perpetuating the power of this alliance of the Pentagon and private corporate defense contractors.

It fell to Gordon Adams, a defense analyst and professor of international affairs, to more fully flesh out the political and economic implications of the iron triangle in his 1981 book *The Politics of Defense Contracting: The Iron Triangle*. Adams defined the iron triangle as a political relationship among three sets of participants in a specific policy area. This symbiotic relationship involves congressional committees and subcommittees, agencies within the executive branch bureaucracy, and private interest groups. In the case of defense policy, the relevant policy actors are the House and Senate Armed Services Committees, as well as the House and Senate Defense Appropriations Subcommittees; for the executive branch the chief player is the Defense Department, although the Department of Energy and National Aeronautics and Space Administration (NASA) also might be involved; and the key interest groups are corporate defense contractors, their trade associations, and policy research institutions. In his study, Adams focused particularly on defense contractors such as Boeing, General Dynamics, Grumman, Lockheed, McDonnell Douglas, Northrop, several of which have long since merged. Working together to pursue a common set of interests, these three points of the triangle form a policy "subgovernment" whose political and economic power is exceptionally hard to challenge. Through lobbying and entertainment, campaign contributions, congressional hearings, shared personnel, and public policy articulation, these three sets of institutional actors develop a high level of expertise in the area of defense policy and a shared outlook on what constitutes "acceptable" debate on defense spending. From the perspective of those participating in the triangle, it looks as though the vital area of national defense policy is capably handled by this alliance of Congress, bureaucratic agencies, and interest groups. What could be wrong with a system that promotes shared knowledge and broadened expertise?

## FROM WATCHDOG TO LAPDOG

As these triangular interactions grow, a set of mutually beneficial "sweetheart" relationships develop. Members of congressional committees and subcommittees constantly need campaign contributions and continually seek the perspective of Pentagon and corporate players for the latest information. Representatives and Senators from the defense-related committees protect their expertise and specialization, becoming insulated from views outside the triangle that might question their priorities and their definitions of national security. The Pentagon always seeks new weapons systems and more funding for troops to support the administration's defense strategy and fosters a particular outlook on foreign and military policy through research institutions that share a pro-military perspective. For their part, defense contractors want to market new and improved weapons systems, which are central to their pursuit of profit and the provision of millions of jobs. So all three sets of participants have a vested interest in the perpetuation of the triangle.

As Adams pointed out, the normal operation of the iron triangle has troubling implications for democracy, blurring if not eliminating the distinction between the public interest and private interests. Corporate views of "national security" merge with governmental views, as Congress and the Defense Department come to equate the private interests of contractors with the pubic interest. With the growing role of high-tech weapons systems in the U.S. economy, what emerges is, something critics of the military have long called, a "permanent war economy," wherein the nation's economic health requires actual war and the continual threat of future wars—a situation that raises grave moral concerns and confirms one of President Eisenhower's worst fears. It is in the area of congressional politics, though, where we find perhaps the most unsettling impact, involving the interconnected role of money, people, and oversight.

The House and Senate are the governing institutions most closely aligned with the people. It is here that citizens have their most direct contact with national policy. The strength of the iron triangle can erode that contact. Earlier we mentioned that the most important function Congress performs is control of the nation's "purse strings." Each year Congress raises (through taxation) and spends (through appropriations) our hard-earned money. Money is the conduit for much of our politics. Campaign contributions from individuals and political action committees are the lifeblood of incumbent reelection campaigns. The Pentagon wants a larger portion of the budget each year from committees that authorize and spend money on national defense. Defense contractors spend millions of dollars lobbying Congress for contracts that can run into the billions. By one estimate, there are some 35,000 registered lobbyists in Washington, DC, and collectively all types of interest groups spend upwards of $200 million per month to sway the opinions of federal policymakers. And who does the swaying? In addition to money, this is where personnel come in to play.

The iron triangle fosters close personal relations among people who sit at all three points of the triangle. It is common for, say, a Senator who serves on the Armed Services Committee to retire and go to work as a lobbyist for a defense contractor with whom he has worked on military policy for years. Thus he will be paid handsomely to lobby his former colleagues on the relevant Senate committee. Likewise, senior Pentagon officials are often drawn from the ranks of defense corporations, or from corporately funded policy research institutes with a shared, friendly view of military strategy. The degree to which personnel are interlocked is quite high. This revolving-door situation leads to the phenomenon of "recycled elites," people who move around to various points of the triangle, further insulating policymakers from outsider influences. The examples are many.

One especially clear current illustration of recycled elites within the iron triangle is Vice President Dick Cheney. Cheney worked in the administrations of both Presidents Nixon and Ford. In 1978, he was elected to Congress where he served as Wyoming's lone Representative for six terms, developing a reputation as an extremely pro-defense Congressman. He served as Secretary of Defense for President George H. W. Bush from 1989 to 1993 and joined a conservative think tank, the American Enterprise Institute, in 1993. From 1995 to 2000, he was Chair and CEO of Halliburton Energy Services. Halliburton is an oil services corporation that has been lavished with military contracts worth tens of millions of dollars to help rebuild Iraq during the war and is now charged with defrauding the federal government for its work on many of those contracts. During his Halliburton days, he also was a member of the conservative "Project for a New American Century," along with Donald Rumsfeld and several other future architects of President George W. Bush's foreign and defense policy. And of course, he has been vice president in President Bush's administration since 2001. Cheney thus has held positions on all three points of the iron triangle. He is a prime example of how a community of interests, a way of looking at the world, is forged within the triangle. Such a worldview insulates the players from dissenting perspectives. While expertise surely is gathered over time, discussion of military policy is confined to a stiflingly narrow range of debate over the means of achieving a shared set of perspectives. Those perspectives themselves—the ends of policy—are not on the table. As a result, while policymakers may come and go, weapons systems are built, soldiers fight and die, and roots of U.S. foreign and military policy—the basic political and economic interests that underlie them—remain essentially unchanged.

In addition to money and personnel, a third factor to consider in exploring the impact of the iron triangle on congressional relations is oversight. If the most fundamental role of Congress is to control the nation's "purse strings," oversight is its second most pressing job. Oversight means that the House and Senate are charged with looking out for the public interest by overseeing the conduct of executive branch agencies that implement the policies Congress passes into law. Congress performs this role in many ways, for example, by holding congressional committee hearings and by conducting studies (armed with subpoena power) to investigate various agencies of the executive branch. The average citizen would have difficulty finding the time to single-handedly monitor the details of policy making and policy implementation. Congress is supposed to do

that for us. In a sense, our elected representatives serve as our eyes and ears in Washington. It is this oversight role—the role of a "watchdog"—that is so valuable to a healthy democracy. But if Congress has been captured by the industry it is supposed to oversee and regulate—in the classic iron triangle case, the defense industry—then the watchdog becomes a mere lapdog of industry, tethered to a set of interests from which it is ideally supposed to maintain some critical distance. When that critical distance has been lost, and the watchdog is tamed and transformed into a lapdog, the foundation of representative democracy is weakened.

The iron triangle began as a way to understand the intractability of an insulated way of approaching military budgets and national security policy. Yet the concept can be applied to virtually any policy area, as this case study demonstrates with regard to human immunodeficiency virus (HIV)/acquired immunodeficiency syndrome (AIDS)—another public policy issue where life and death literally hang in the balance.

## New Policy, New Triangles

In 1981, scientists at the government agency in charge of monitoring the nation's health, the Centers for Disease Control and Prevention (CDC), realized that they were tracking a new and deadly disease. No one knew what caused it or how to treat it. They only knew that it seemed to be attacking people in the prime of their lives, whose condition then quickly deteriorated and who died of diseases such as rare types of pneumonia seldom seen among healthy populations. From people experiencing the new illness in themselves or a loved one, there was an urgent call for new drugs to fight the causative agent—which we now know as the HIV—or at least the diseases and infections that HIV was facilitating. For ill and at-risk populations, new treatments were literally a matter of life and death. For drug companies, they were an opportunity to market an array of new products at the high prices that desperate people are willing to pay.

As a corporate interest group, it is hard to imagine one more well situated to achieve its aims in

Washington than the pharmaceutical lobby. Although iron triangles work by making sure that members of key congressional committees and subcommittees are deeply beholden to the industry at hand, the pharmaceutical industry has hedged its bets by spreading its largess more widely. A 2005 report for the Center for Public Integrity found that it has spent more than $800 million in state and federal lobbying and campaign donations in the preceding seven years, making it second only to the insurance industry in combined expenditures (and first, when looking at lobbying only). The report also noted that most of this lobbying money was spent on the salaries of the three-thousand-strong lobbying force it has assembled, more than a third of which comes from the ranks of Congress and federal bureaucracies.

During the early 1980s, private and public laboratories raced to identify the new disease agent and find and mass-produce both treatments for infections caused by HIV and medicines designed to combat the virus itself. The pharmaceutical industry was already well placed to take advantage of the output of these laboratories. As the outlines of the AIDS pandemic began to take shape, a preexisting iron triangle, or more accurately, several iron triangles, anchored by the pharmaceutical industry absorbed this new policy area. The iron triangle most directly involved with the drug-related aspects of AIDS policy is the same iron triangle that operates around the development, regulation, and pricing of drugs generally. Like other iron triangles, it consists of a congressional committee or subcommittee, executive branch agencies, and private interests. On the House side, the congressional committee that most directly oversees the pharmaceutical industry is the House Energy and Commerce Committee, which is divided into six subcommittees, of which the Subcommittee on Health has most direct oversight of both public health and food and drugs. Of the executive branch agencies, the Food and Drug Administration (FDA), the organization charged with making sure that medicines are both safe and effective, has direct regulatory power over the pharmaceutical industry, although others, including the National Institutes of Health (NIH), also work very closely with the industry. The FDA also oversees the approval process of

new drugs, a task that would prove extremely important as new drugs emerged in the early years after the discovery of HIV. Finally, the pharmaceutical industry is well represented by a host of lobbyists and industry representatives: the two largest are Pharmaceutical Research and Manufacturers of America (PhRMA) and the Biotechnology Industry Organization. To say that these triangle elements are closely connected is a gross understatement: one telling indication of just how close is the fact that PhRMA's president is the former Chair of the Energy and Commerce Committee, twenty-four-year House veteran Billy Tauzin. This fact is all the more remarkable when one considers that Tauzin began negotiating the terms of his new employment with PhRMA (reported to include an annual salary in excess of $2 million dollars) only weeks after he had achieved the passage of a Medicare reform bill he had helped to write (see Article 22). That bill had many provisions straight out of the PhRMA playbook, including prohibitions of government negotiations with pharmaceutical companies for lower prices and refusal to allow lower-cost imports from Canada. The cozy relationship was reinforced when Tauzin's successor as chair of the committee, fellow Republican James Greenwood, was snapped up for a similar position (and a high six-figure salary) by the pharmaceutical industry's other main lobbying group, the Biotechnology Industry Organization.

## GOVERNMENT GIVEAWAYS AND THE FIRST AIDS DRUG

The first drug approved to combat HIV—azidothymidine (AZT), otherwise known as Retrovir—was licensed to the drug company Burroughs Wellcome (now two mergers later the international giant GlaxoSmithKline) in 1987. Although Burroughs Wellcome claimed the right to price the new drug—at the hefty price tag of $10,000 for a year's supply—the company had not actually discovered it. That distinction belonged to a researcher, Jerome Horwitz, who developed the compound as an anticancer drug in 1964, with funding from the National Cancer Institute (NCI). Nor did they conduct the original laboratory research that determined that AZT worked in a test tube against HIV. That was done by government-funded laboratories at Duke University and the NCI.

After Burroughs Wellcome got the good news from Duke and the NCI, the company quickly found a way to put its close relationship with the FDA to its advantage. David Barry, a virologist at Wellcome and a former researcher at the FDA, called Ellen Cooper, head of the Division of Antiviral Drug Products at the FDA, to see about expediting AZT's classification as an Investigational New Drug, the next stage in its approval process. Cooper suggested that preliminary data be sent as they were completed; when the final full application was sent, Cooper took less than a week to approve it. Burroughs Wellcome then put the drug through two of the three phases that the FDA traditionally requires for drug approval. Phase I ran for six weeks with nineteen subjects at the NCI and Duke University. Phase II followed, also at Duke and NCI, with 282 subjects, although only 27 participated in the full twenty-four weeks of the trial. Phase III trials were then waived, and the drug was approved on a 10–1 vote by an FDA advisory committee on January 16, 1987. By drug research standards, this one had been a relatively straightforward undertaking. It was formulated in a laboratory supported by a government grant and researched by two other publicly funded entities in small trials with few subjects, with steps explicitly expedited or waived along the way.

So why the $10,000 price tag? That question was asked, but not answered, during hearings of the House Subcommittee on Health and Environment (predecessor to the current Health Subcommittee) in March 1987. After pointing vaguely to the expenses that generally go into the development of any new drug, T. E. Haigler, the then CEO of Burroughs Wellcome, refused to divulge numbers to the more pointed questions of Democratic Congressman Ron Wyden, who asked for actual research and development costs. Though Wyden showed his exasperation (asking "why didn't you just set the price at $100,000 per patient?"), the direction of the power in this relationship was clearly displayed. The government might finance the discovery of the drug and the research that went

into it, but to question the price set for this publicly financed medication by a private company was clearly not within its power.

Eventually the price of AZT came down, though not through pressure from either the FDA or Congress. Rather, it was the work of enraged activists, banding together in a new group, the AIDS Coalition to Unleash Power (ACT UP), that forced the drop. Two weeks after Congress' ill-fated hearing, ACT UP staged the first protest of its existence on Wall Street, garnering headlines in major newspapers, and forcing Burroughs Wellcome to drop their prices by 20 percent to stem the tide of negative publicity. Two years later, with AZT still the only approved antiretroviral on the market and in the face of findings that AZT was helpful for those not yet suffering from full-blown AIDS, Burroughs Wellcome saw a ten-fold increase in its potential market, but once again resisted demands to lower its price. AIDS activists fought back, this time with an imaginative action within and outside the New York Stock Exchange that noisily shut down transactions for five minutes. Four days later, Burroughs Wellcome announced a second 20 percent price cut.

## THE MORE THINGS CHANGE, THE MORE THEY STAY THE SAME

Two decades and millions of AIDS deaths later, the power of the pharmaceutical iron triangle appears to have remained intact. One thing that has changed is that, at least in wealthy countries, AIDS has moved from being a fatal disease to a chronic condition, manageable through a combination of drug therapies, often referred to as the "cocktail." Protease inhibitors are one type of drugs within the cocktail, and one of these is the drug ritonavir, more commonly known by its trade name, Norvir. The patent for Norvir is held by Abbott Laboratories, which now markets the drug not as a protease inhibitor but as a booster to be taken with the cocktail to heighten the effects of other protease inhibitors. But Abbott never actually developed Norvir. That was done with federal money in the form of a multimillion-dollar government grant from the NIH. The public interest group Consumer Project on Technology has estimated that, in all, Abbott's investment in clinical trials to test the drug it did not pay to develop was under $15 million, yet during its first five years on the market (1996–2001), Abbott's sales of Norvir totaled $1 billion. Yet despite these very healthy sales, none of which need to go to recoup costs of research and development (a common drug company justification for high prices), Abbott chose to raise its price again in 2003 by a whopping 400 percent. The price of the most common booster dose went from $1,600 to $7,800 per year. This price increase was particularly galling to AIDS activists in light of the fact that even before the increase, Norvir was selling in other wealthy countries for less than half the price, and the price increase meant that U.S. citizens were paying five to ten times more for a drug developed with their tax dollars than people in other wealthy countries.

Early attempts to sway Abbott were of the less confrontational variety: AIDS doctors around the country signed petitions asking Abbott to reexamine its pricing policies, and advocacy organizations organized similar petition drives on the same topic. When these failed, HIV-infected people and activists decided to use Norvir as a worst-case example for calling in a never-used power referred to as "march in" authority. This authority came from a piece of legislation passed in 1980 known as the Bayh–Dole Act, which gives the Secretary of Health and Human Services the power to open competition on a patent that was developed with federal funding (as Norvir was with an NIH grant) but is not available at a reasonable price to the public. Jamie Love, president of the nonprofit group Essential Inventions, made the formal petition to the government in January 2004. The NIH responded in May by holding a hearing, for which there is no official written record. Among those invited to testify was Birch Bayh, who had been one of the Senators who had drafted the original law. As the national press noted, he testified *against* the march-in provision he had drafted, arguing that march-in could only be used if it were proven that the drug was not reaching the people who needed it. In his early August ruling, NIH Director Elias Zerhouni concurred, finding that Norvir was being made available to patients "on reasonable terms."

In the same year that the NIH was doing the bidding of the pharmaceutical industry at home, a newer government bureaucracy, the Office of the Global AIDS Coordinator, was serving it abroad. In 2003, President Bush had shocked many by announcing in his State of the Union a new global AIDS initiative, the President's Emergency Plan for AIDS Relief (PEPFAR), as a new five-year multibillion-dollar program to address the AIDS pandemic in some of the worst-affected countries on the planet. Equally surprising was his mention in the speech of the possibility of treating people for under $300 a year—a possibility that could only happen through the purchase of generic drugs adamantly opposed by the pharmaceutical lobby in the United States. Activists were cautiously optimistic, thinking the speech signaled that the Administration might be coming around to accept the use of these generic medicines being used by private humanitarian pilot programs in Africa. But these hopes were dashed when the Administration announced that it was opposed to using these products and called for a meeting in the African country of Botswana. At the meeting, the Office of the Global AIDS Coordinator argued that these generic drugs, some of which were four times cheaper than the most deeply discounted drugs offered by the U.S.-based companies, should not be given to sub-Saharan Africans because, though they had been through the World Health Organization's approval process, they had not been approved by the FDA. In the face of pressure from activist and humanitarian groups, the government eventually allowed some of the drugs to go through the FDA process, but in the months between the meeting and approval, they were not made available to the tens of thousands under treatment. During the interim, the shadow cast by the American iron triangle controlled by the pharmaceutical industry extended all the way to remote villages in Africa.

## Prospects and Conclusions: Even Iron Melts

Although iron triangles are incredibly strong, there is evidence to suggest that they are not indestructible. Secrecy, citizen ignorance and indifference, and the absence of countervailing forces all foster their development and maintenance. But conversely, public education, citizen monitoring, and mass mobilization are valuable tools in weakening these structures. President Eisenhower acknowledged as much in his aforementioned Farewell Address, noting that "an alert and knowledgeable citizenry" was needed to serve as a check on military-industrial ambitions. More specifically, two aspects of politics can weaken the solidity of iron triangles. First, budgetary restrictions can diminish the financial resources available to fund projects favored by corporate interests. In conditions of huge budget deficits or economic crisis, even privileged business groups can come up empty-handed. But this potential impediment to iron triangles tends to be transitory. When the financial cloud lifts, the priorities of private interests are quickly reasserted. And as we have learned in the aftermath of 9/11, even in situations of massive budgetary red ink, with deficits as far as the eye can see, certain corporate interests still can get what they want if their specific interest in profits comes to be tied directly to the general "national interest," as with private defense contractors like Halliburton and it subsidiaries, who continue to flourish while most competing domestic interests languish in Congress.

Beyond such budgetary considerations, though, lies a second, more long-term avenue for weakening iron triangles. Pressure from social movements can serve to challenge our legislators and the private interest groups whose priorities Congress too often serves. As the drug company Burroughs Wellcome discovered in our AIDS case study, it was easier to flout the authority of nominal holders of power—members of the Congressional subcommittee tasked to oversee their pricing policies—than it was to maintain their pricing in the face of an implacable social movement willing to take to the streets and colorfully demonstrate in front of television cameras that profits were taking precedence over access to life-saving medicines. If pressure such as this from democratic grassroots movements can be sustained over time by committed activists, it can have a lasting impact on our national priorities. In sum, at high enough temperatures (1,535°C, to be exact) even iron melts. And when it comes to iron triangles, "street heat" can be the catalyst.

---

## DISCUSSION QUESTIONS

1. Identify the three components of the "iron triangle." Siplon and Grover list budgeting and oversight as two important powers that Congress could use to provide for the public interest. Why is it so difficult to use them to weaken iron triangles?

2. To what extent do you believe that the AIDS activist movement that has challenged the iron triangles related to pharmaceutical policy can be a model for others seeking to weaken iron triangles? Do you believe there were factors specific to AIDS that might not be replicable to other social movements, and if so, what are they?

3. If President Eisenhower was right in viewing an "alert and knowledgeable citizenry" as an effective check on the military–industrial complex (and by extension, other iron triangles), how might public education of the citizenry occur?

# CHAPTER 7

# THE PRESIDENCY

The presidency has come to occupy the center stage of American government. Anyone who hopes to understand the American political system, especially as it has developed since the 1930s, must come to terms with the nature of the presidency. After World War II, the expansion of presidential power that began under President Franklin D. Roosevelt continued, and this growth was generally celebrated by scholars and other observers of the office, who saw in the president a personification of the American system of government. But in the 1960s and 1970s, abuses symbolized by Vietnam and Watergate and the downfalls of Lyndon Johnson and Richard Nixon led to a more critical view of the "imperial presidency." Despite an upward trend in public trust in the presidency in the 1980s, the Iran-contra affair of 1986–1987, the impeachment and trial of President Bill Clinton in the late 1990s, and the hotly contested presidential election of 2000 call into question the ability of the presidency to resolve policy conflicts in an equitable and responsible way. This presidential challenge persists even after the post–9/11 "rally-'round-the-flag" response, which boosted George W. Bush's approval ratings to record levels.

As president during the Great Depression and World War II, Franklin D. Roosevelt established the model of strong executive leadership that was venerated in postwar America. Indeed, even Ronald Reagan expressed his admiration for Roosevelt's leadership style at the very time he was attempting to reverse the liberal turn in public policy inaugurated by the New Deal. Still, given the recurrent crises that have beset the presidency in the past thirty years, many recent explanations of the presidency emphasize that the chief executive is, or should be, limited in powers by the constitutional structure and is not the free agent in policy decisions that the FDR model of presidential power suggested. In our view, it is no doubt important to put the president in the context of other government actors, but it is even more important to understand the interaction between the president and forces outside of government, such as the economy and the business community, social and political movements, and the role of the United States in the international political economy. The readings in this chapter should help you to put the presidency into context, as the tenure of George W. Bush nears its conclusion.

**25** *Michael A. Genovese*

# THE LIMITS OF PRESIDENTIAL POWER

*Political observers have commented frequently on the modern gulf between high public expectations of the American presidency and disappointing presidential performance. Michael Genovese, a scholar of the presidency, provides a deeper explanation of this gap by identifying two structural constraints that shape and limit presidential action. The first constraint is the economic framework of corporate capitalism. Drawing on the work of Charles Lindblom, whose analysis of the privileged position of business is featured in Chapter 1, Genovese notes that presidents who pursue reform agendas run the risk of losing business confidence. The need for business confidence has become an unexamined assumption of the modern presidency, an assumption with conservative implications for public policy and political change. Genovese also shows how the nature of the contemporary international economic system shapes presidential policy. Presidents operate in the context of global capitalism or "globalization," which involves powerful pressures towards market economies, open markets, free trade, and economic interdependence. Genovese contends that despite the superpower status of the United States and the benefits that derive from this status, economic globalism "takes power out of the hands of nations and places it in the hands of markets and corporations." Presidents are less free to pursue policies that do not succumb to the demands of the market.*

Presidential politics operates within an economic framework of corporate capitalism. How does this reality shape and influence presidential behavior?

Two major functions of the modern capitalist state are (1) the stimulation of material accumulation and (2) the legitimization of the social order. The first function derives from the fact that the state is ultimately held responsible for meeting the material needs of the society; thus, at least in some minimal terms, economic deterioration is blamed on presidents. But in this regard the capitalist state is "weak," in that it does not own the means of production; they are privately held and will not be put in operation unless a return (profit) on investment is foreseen. Thus, the capitalist state must use the carrot more than the stick, by helping the owning class in the accumulation of profit in order to promote production. Conversely, the owning class is in a strong position with presidents, who face the likelihood of an "investment strike" if policy is seen

*Source:* Michael Genovese, *The Presidential Dilemma: Leadership in the American System,* 2nd edition. New York: Longman, 2003, pp. 73–79.

to hurt profits. This gives business a privileged position and places the president in a position of some dependency on what is referred to as "business confidence." In order to govern effectively, presidents must please the business community, lest they face a decline in business confidence and a deterioration of the overall economy, thus leading to a decline in presidential popularity and power.

It is just this situation that Charles Lindblom—though not referring specifically to the presidency—discusses in his article "The Market as Prison." Lindblom argues that political regimes with market systems have built-in defense systems that automatically trigger punishment whenever there is an attempt to tamper with or alter the basic structures of such systems. This built-in punishing mechanism makes market systems resilient and highly resistant to change because attempts at change bring quick and sure punishment. As Lindblom writes, "Many kinds of market reform automatically trigger punishments in the form of unemployment or a sluggish economy." This punishment is not the result of any conspiracy on the part of business; it is simply a built-in by-product of market oriented systems. Lindblom writes:

Business people do not have to debate whether or not to impose the penalty. They need do no more ... than tend to their own business, which means that, without thought of effecting a punishment on us, they restrict investment and jobs simply in the course of being prudent managers of their enterprises.

While Lindblom does not focus on the presidency in this context, he does discuss the notion that the economic system is highly resistant to change by political leaders. He describes the situation thus:

What about government officials? It is critical to the efficiency of automatic punishment that it be visited on them. For it is they who immediately or proximately decide to persist in policy changes or to withdraw from such initiatives. The penalty visited on them by business disincentives caused by proposed policies is that declining business activity is a threat to the party and the officials in power. When a decline in prosperity and employment is brought about by decisions of corporate and other business executives, it is not they but government officials who consequently are retired from their offices.

That result, then, is why the market might be characterized as a prison. For a broad category of political/economic affairs, it imprisons policy making, and imprisons our attempts to improve our institutions. It greatly cripples our attempts to improve the social world because it afflicts us with sluggish economic performance and unemployment simply because we begin to debate or undertake reform.

Thus, with policy making being "imprisoned" in market-oriented systems, the leverage of presidents for reform is severely restricted by this self-regulating, self-punishing mechanism built into the system.

The other function, legitimization of the social order, derives from the need for the state to be seen as ruling in the interest of all, not in the interest of a dominant class. Welfare programs for the nonowning classes and entitlement programs for the middle class are examples of policies to satisfy this task. But when profits are squeezed, the revenues to support such programs become tight, and a crisis for the state can occur because it cannot reach an adequate balance between these contradictory goals.

Edward S. Greenberg develops the notion of the privileged position of business in policy making in these words:

Presidents must act in such a way that they maintain the confidence of business leaders and ensure an economic environment conducive to profitable investment. The president's popularity and thus much of his ability to effect a domestic program and foreign policy objectives is dependent on the state of the economy and the sense of well-being felt by the American people.

Since business people cannot be forced to make productive, job-creating investments in the American economy, government must induce them to do so. They are induced, in the main, by public policies that encourage and ensure profitability, especially among the most powerful economic actors and enterprises in the system. Thus, while no president can afford to respond to every whim of important business leaders, all his actions are bounded by the need to maintain "business confidence."

There is no active conspiracy on the part of business to "capture" the presidency. Rather, presidential success is intimately connected with business success. As presidential popularity rises and falls, in part due to economic conditions, presidents quickly learn that what is good for business is usually good for presidential popularity. When corporate capitalism gains, the president usually gains. Conversely, a sluggish economy is blamed on an administration's activities or lack thereof. Thus, the fate of the president is closely connected to fluctuations in the economy. Presidents help themselves by helping business.

In this way, presidents who do not have the confidence of business find themselves at a distinct political and economic disadvantage. As John Kennedy noted:

I understand better every day why Roosevelt, who started out such a mild fellow, ended up so ferociously antibusiness. It is hard as hell to be friendly with people who keep trying to cut your legs off . . . There are about ten thousand people in this country involved in this—bankers, industrialists, lawyers, publishers, politicians—a small group, but doing everything they can to say we are going into a depression because business has no confidence in the administration. They are starting to call me the Democratic Hoover. Well, we're not going to take that.

But Kennedy recognized the other side of the business confidence coin as well, as he attempted to act as economic cheerleader:

This country cannot prosper unless business prospers. This country cannot meet its obligations and tax obligations and all the rest

unless business is doing well. Business will not do well and we will not have full employment unless there is a chance to make a profit. So there is no long-run hostility between business and government. There cannot be. We cannot succeed unless they succeed.

Similarly, presidents who wish to pursue a reform agenda find themselves in a bind: "Do I sacrifice economic reforms for economic performance and personal popularity, or, do I play it safe and hope for incremental changes?" Which president would want to stir the embers of the market's self-punishing mechanism? Shortly after his election, Bill Clinton met with his top economic advisors to devise an economic stimulus package. After a lengthy discussion, a consensus was reluctantly arrived at that determined the first priority of the president: to rescue the bond market. Angry and frustrated that his reform agenda was being hijacked by the bond market, an exasperated Clinton threw his arms up in the air and said, "We've all become Eisenhower Republicans!" Which president could afford to stir the beast that will likely produce a sluggish economy and lower presidential popularity? Thus, presidential leverage in economic reform is severely limited by the invisible prison of the market.

Thomas Cronin, probably the most highly regarded of today's presidential scholars, begins to suggest a structural impediment in presidential choice vis-à-vis the business community when, in a lengthy reexamination of Richard Neustadt's *Presidential Power,* he chides Neustadt for failing "to take into account the degree to which presidents are almost invariably stabilizers or protectors of the status quo rather than agents of redistribution or progressive change." Cronin adds that "all our presidents have had to prove their political orthodoxy and their acceptability to a wide array of established powers, especially to corporate leaders."

Political scientist Bruce Miroff notes that presidential scholars remain firmly committed to a "progressive" interpretation of the presidency. But as Miroff writes, "The Presidency, even (perhaps especially) in liberal hands, is best understood as the chief stabilizer—and not the leading force for change—in American politics." No president has "sought to question, much less assault, corporate power and its extraordinary skewing of resources and rewards. The present structure of the American economy has been accepted by modern Presidents as a given of American life."

In line with Charles Lindblom's concerns, Miroff writes:

Because of their acceptance of the prevailing social and economic order, even the more liberal of recent Presidents have had little novel or profound that they really wanted to achieve in domestic affairs. Their most controversial domestic proposals have envisioned only modest reforms. Basically, these Presidents have sought to patch up remaining holes in the New Deal, and to stabilize and rationalize the corporate economy. None have acknowledged more fundamental problems in American society; none have proposed anything that resembles a program of social and economic reconstruction. Contrary to the conventional view, it has not been an obstructionist Congress or an apathetic public that has kept Presidents since FDR from major domestic accomplishments as much as it has been the orthodoxy of their own domestic vision.

Presidents are thus constrained by the needs of corporate capitalism. They are in part imprisoned, limited in what they can do, by the requirements of accumulation and legitimization.

The United States is the world's only superpower. In fact, it is a hyper-power. With military might second to none, a massive economy, and cultural penetration to all parts of the globe (I defy you to go to any large city in any country in the world and not find a McDonalds, Starbucks, or a local kid wearing a New York Yankee baseball cap or a "23" basketball jersey), the United States is the hegemonic power, or "big kid on the block." But if we are so strong, why do we seem so weak? Why, at a time when there are no rivals to power, is our grip on international events so fragile and tenuous?

When the Soviet Union imploded—marking the end of the Cold War—analysts wondered what international regime would replace the old order. For a time policymakers groped for an answer. George Bush (the first), in response to the invasion of Kuwait by Iraq, developed a multinationalist coalition based on a "new world order." But as the Gulf War ended, Bush abandoned this promising approach to international order and stability.

It was not until the Clinton years that the parameters of the new regime would come into view. Called "globalization," it encompassed an international acceptance of global capitalism—market economies, open markets, free trade, and integration and interdependence. Building on the institutions designed to oversee, coordinate, and stabilize the international economy—the International Monetary Fund (IMF), the World Bank, and the General Agreement on Tariffs and Trade (GATT), now the World Trade Organization (WTO)—these institutions have helped create a more integrated international economy.

The promise of globalism is political (countries that are connected by common bonds will better cooperate) and economic (a rising tide lifts all boats, although critics might argue that the rising tide lifts all yachts!) Those opposing the rise of globalism fear the widening gap between rich and poor nations, environmental degradation, and a decline in worker's rights.

In this age of globalization, what role and power would be assumed by the United States? And what role and power would be assumed by the presidency? Globalism takes power out of the hands of nations and places it in the hands of the market and corporations. National sovereignty is diminished as the requirements of the global economy drive policy. Globalism demands that market forces shape policy. Thus governments must please the international market or decline.

The United States is the most powerful actor in this system, and draws benefits from its leadership position. But this new system inhibits the freedom of a president to choose. Bound by the demands of a global economy, and the need to develop multinational responses to a variety of problems, the president is less free to pursue policies he chooses and increasingly compelled to succumb to the demands of the market.

Globalism is a two-edged sword. It brings some economic benefits but imposes further limits on choice. Non-Governmental Organizations (NGOs), international institutions, central banks, and market forces gain in power. Nations—and the U.S. president—lose power.

---

## DISCUSSION QUESTIONS

1. How does Genovese use the theories of "accumulation" and "legitimization" to explain how the structure of our political economy imposes a squeeze on the office of president?
2. In what way does economic "globalization" place new limitations on the president's power? Has the international power of the American president changed as a result of the September 11, 2001, terrorist attacks?

# 26 *Bruce Miroff*

# THE PRESIDENTIAL SPECTACLE

*Public support has always been important to presidential governance, but modern presidents have "gone public" to an unprecedented degree in an attempt to shape public perceptions. Bruce Miroff, a political scientist who has written important books on the Kennedy presidency and on styles of presidential leadership, analyzes the relationship between the presidency and the public in a mass media age in which the presidency has assumed primacy in the political system. Drawing on cultural theory, Miroff argues that presidents actively shape public perceptions through the creation of images and the presentation of symbolic "spectacles." Miroff develops the notion of the presidency as spectacle through innovative case studies of Ronald Reagan, George H. W. Bush, Bill Clinton, and George W. Bush. Miroff's analysis of the "spectacular" nature of the presidency raises disturbing questions about American democracy. Popular sovereignty requires an accurate public understanding of the course and consequences of presidential action. But the presidential spectacle helps to obscure our understanding of actual presidential performance and relegates citizens to spectators at a performance.*

One of the most distinctive features of the modern presidency is its constant cultivation of popular support. The Framers of the Constitution envisioned a president substantially insulated from the demands and passions of the people by the long term and dignity of the office. The modern president, in contrast, not only responds to popular demands and passions but also actively reaches out to shape them. The possibilities opened up by modern technology and the problems presented by the increased fragility of institutional coalitions lead presidents to turn to the public for support and strength. If popular backing

is to be maintained, however, the public must believe in the president's leadership qualities.

Observers of presidential politics have come to recognize the centrality of the president's relationship with the American public. George Edwards has written of "the public presidency" and argued that the "greatest source of influence for the president is public approval." Samuel Kernell has suggested that presidential appeals for popular support now overshadow more traditional methods of seeking influence, especially bargaining. Presidents today, Kernell argues, are "going public," and he demonstrates

*Source:* Bruce Miroff, "The Presidential Spectacle." *The Presidency and the Political System*, 7th edition, edited by Michael Nelson, Washington, DC: CQ Press, 2006, pp. 255–282.

their propensity to cultivate popular support by recording the mounting frequency of their public addresses, public appearances, and political travel. These constitute, he claims, "the repertoire of modern leadership."

This new understanding of presidential leadership can be carried further. A president's approach to, and impact on, public perceptions are not limited to overt appeals in speeches and appearances. Much of what the modern presidency does, in fact, involves the projection of images whose purpose is to shape public understanding and gain popular support. A significant—and growing—part of the presidency revolves around the enactment of leadership as a spectacle.

To examine the presidency as a spectacle is to ask not only how a president seeks to appear but also what the public sees. We are accustomed to gauging the public's responses to a president with polls that measure approval and disapproval of overall performance in office and effectiveness in managing the economy and foreign policy. Yet these evaluative categories may say more about the kind of information that politicians or academic researchers want than about the terms in which most members of a president's audience actually view the president. A public that responds mainly to presidential spectacles will not ignore the president's performance, but its understanding of that performance, as well as its sense of the overarching and intangible strengths and weaknesses of the administration, will be colored by the terms of the spectacle.

## The Presidency as Spectacle

A spectacle is a kind of symbolic event, one in which particular details stand for broader and deeper meanings. What differentiates a spectacle from other kinds of symbolic events is the centrality of character and action. A spectacle presents intriguing and often dominating characters not in static poses but through actions that establish their public identities.

*Spectacle* implies a clear division between actors and spectators. As Daniel Dayan and Elihu Katz have noted, a spectacle possesses "a narrowness of focus, a limited set of appropriate responses,

and . . . a minimal level of interaction. What there is to see is very clearly exhibited; spectacle implies a distinction between the roles of performers and audience." A spectacle does not permit the audience to interrupt the action and redirect its meaning. Spectators can become absorbed in a spectacle or can find it unconvincing, but they cannot become performers. A spectacle is not designed for mass participation; it is not a democratic event.

Perhaps the most distinctive characteristic of a spectacle is that the actions that constitute it are meaningful not for what they achieve but for what they signify. Actions in a spectacle are gestures rather than means to an end. What is important is that they be understandable and impressive to the spectators. Roland Barthes illustrates this distinction between gestures and means in his classic discussion of professional wrestling as a spectacle. Barthes shows that professional wrestling is completely unlike professional boxing. Boxing is a form of competition, a contest of skill in a situation of uncertainty. What matters is the outcome, and because that is in doubt, we can wager on it. But in professional wrestling, the outcome is preordained; it would be senseless to bet on who is going to win. What matters in professional wrestling is the gestures made during the match, gestures by performers portraying distinctive characters, gestures that carry moral significance. In a typical match, an evil character threatens a good character, knocks him down on the canvas, abuses him with dirty tricks, but ultimately loses when the good character rises up to exact a just revenge.

It may seem odd to approach the presidency through an analogy with boxing and wrestling—but let us pursue it for a moment. Much of what presidents do is analogous to what boxers do: they engage in contests of power and policy with other political actors, contests in which the outcomes are uncertain. But a growing amount of presidential activity is akin to pro wrestling. The contemporary presidency is presented by the White House (with the collaboration of the media) as a series of spectacles in which a larger-than-life main character and a supporting team engage in emblematic bouts with immoral or dangerous adversaries.

A number of contemporary developments have converged to foster the rise of spectacle in the modern presidency. The mass media have become its principal vehicle. Focusing more of their coverage on presidents than on any other person or institution in American life, the media keep them constantly before the public and give them unmatched opportunities to display their leadership qualities. Television provides the view most amenable to spectacle; by favoring the visual and the dramatic, it promotes stories with simple plotlines over complex analyses of causes and consequences. But other media are not fundamentally different. As David Paletz and Robert Entman have shown, nearly all American journalists "define events from a short-term, antihistorical perspective; see individual or group action, not structural or other impersonal long run forces, at the root of most occurrences; and simplify and reduce stories to conventional symbols for easy assimilation by audiences."

The mass media are not, to be sure, always reliable vehicles for presidential spectacles. Reporters may frame their stories in terms that undermine the meanings the White House intends to convey. Their desire for controversy can feed off presidential spectacles, but it also can destroy them. The media can contribute to spectacular failures in the presidency as well as to successful spectacles.

Spectacle has also been fostered by the president's rise to primacy in the American political system. A political order originally centered on institutions has given way, especially in the public mind, to a political order that centers on the person of the president. Theodore Lowi wrote, "Since the president has become the embodiment of government, it seems perfectly normal for millions upon millions of Americans to concentrate their hopes and fears directly and personally upon him." The "personal president" that Lowi described is the object of popular expectations; those expectations, Stephen Wayne and Thomas Cronin have shown, are both excessive and contradictory. The president must attempt to satisfy the public by delivering tangible benefits, such as economic growth, but these will almost never be enough. Not surprisingly, then, presidents turn to the gestures of the spectacle to satisfy their audience.

To understand the modern presidency as a form of spectacle, we must consider the presentation of presidents as spectacular characters, the role of their teams as supporting performers, and the arrangement of gestures that convey the meaning of their actions to the audience.

A contemporary president is, to borrow a phrase from Guy Debord, "the spectacular representation of a living human being." An enormous amount of attention is paid to the president as a public character; every deed, quality, and even foible is regarded as fascinating and important. The American public may not learn the details of policy formulation, but they know that Gerald Ford bumps his head on helicopter door frames, that Ronald Reagan likes jellybeans, and that Bill Clinton enjoys hanging out with Hollywood celebrities. In a spectacle, a president's character possesses intrinsic as well as symbolic value; it is to be appreciated for its own sake. The spectators do not press presidents to specify what economic or social benefits they are providing; nor do they closely inquire into the truthfulness of the claims presidents make. (To the extent that they do evaluate the president in such terms, they step outside the terms of the spectacle.) The president's featured qualities are presented as benefits in themselves. Thus John F. Kennedy's glamour casts his whole era in a romanticized glow, Ronald Reagan's amiability relieves the grim national mood that had developed under his predecessors, and George W. Bush's traditional marriage rebukes the cultural decay associated with Bill Clinton's sex scandals.

The president's character must be not only appealing in itself but also magnified by the spectacle. The spectacle makes the president appear exceptionally decisive, tough, courageous, prescient, or prudent. Whether the president is in fact all or any of these things is obscured. What matters is that he or she is presented as having these qualities, in magnitudes far beyond what ordinary citizens can imagine themselves to possess. The president must appear confident and masterful before spectators whose very position, as onlookers, denies them the possibility of mastery.

The presidential qualities most likely to be magnified will be those that contrast dramatically with the attributes that drew criticism to the previous president. Reagan, following a president perceived as weak, was featured in spectacles that highlighted his potency. The elder Bush, succeeding a president notorious for his disengagement from the workings of his own administration, was featured in spectacles of hands-on management. Clinton, supplanting a president who seemed disengaged from the economic problems of ordinary Americans, began his administration with spectacles of populist intimacy. The younger Bush, replacing a president notorious for personal indiscipline and staff disorder, presents a corporate-style White House where meetings run on time and proper business attire is required in the Oval Office.

Presidents are the principal figures in presidential spectacles, but they have the help of aides and advisers. The star performer is surrounded by a team. Members of the president's team can, through the supporting parts they play, enhance or detract from the spectacle's effect on the audience. For a president's team to enhance the spectacles, its members should project attractive qualities that either resemble the featured attributes of the president or make up for the president's perceived deficiencies. A team will diminish presidential spectacles if its members project qualities that underscore the president's weaknesses.

A performance team, Erving Goffman has shown, contains "a set of individuals whose intimate cooperation is required if a given projected definition of the situation is to be maintained." There are a number of ways the team can disrupt presidential spectacles. A member of the team can call too much attention to himself or herself, partially upstaging the president. This was one of the disruptive practices that made the Reagan White House eager to be rid of Secretary of State Alexander Haig. A team member can give away important secrets to the audience; Budget Director David Stockman's famous confessions about supply-side economics to a reporter for the Atlantic jeopardized the mystique of economic innovation that the Reagan administration had created in 1981. Worst of all, a member of the team can, perhaps inadvertently, discredit the central meanings that a presidential spectacle has

been designed to establish. The revelations of Budget Director Bert Lance's questionable banking practices deflated the lofty moral tone established at the beginning of the Carter presidency.

The audience watching a presidential spectacle, the White House hopes, is as impressed by gestures as by results. Indeed, the gestures are sometimes preferable to the results. Thus, a "show" of force by the president is preferable to the death and destruction that are the results of force. The ways in which the invasion of Grenada in 1983, the bombing of Libya in 1986, and the seizing of the Panamanian dictator Manuel Noriega in 1990 were portrayed to the American public suggest an eagerness in the White House to present the image of military toughness but not the casualties from military conflict—even when they are the enemy's casualties.

Gestures overshadow results in a presidential spectacle. They also overshadow facts. But facts are not obliterated. They remain present; they are needed, in a sense, to nurture the gestures. Without real events, presidential spectacles would not be impressive; they would seem contrived, mere pseudoevents. Some of the facts that emerge in the course of an event, however, might discredit its presentation as spectacle. Therefore, a successful spectacle, such as Reagan's "liberation" of Grenada, must be more powerful than any of the facts on which it draws. Rising above contradictory or disconfirming details, the spectacle must transfigure the more pliant facts and make them carriers of its most spectacular gestures.

Presidential spectacles are seldom pure spectacles in the sense that a wrestling match can be a pure spectacle. Although they may involve a good deal of advance planning and careful calculation of gestures, they cannot be completely scripted in advance. Unexpected and unpredictable events will occur during a presidential spectacle. If the White House is fortunate and skillful, it can capitalize on some of those events by using them to enhance the spectacle. If the White House is not so lucky or talented, such events can detract from, or even undermine, the spectacle.

Also unlike wrestling or other pure spectacles, the presidential variety often has more than one audience. Its primary purpose is to construct meanings for the American public. But it also can direct messages to those whom the White House has identified as its foes or the sources of its problems. In 1981, when Reagan fired the air traffic controllers of the Professional Air Traffic Controllers' Organization (PATCO) because they engaged in an illegal strike, he presented to the public the spectacle of a tough, determined president who would uphold the law and, unlike his predecessor, would not be pushed around by grasping interest groups. The spectacle also conveyed to organized labor that the White House knew how to feed popular skepticism about unions and could make things difficult for a labor movement that became too assertive.

As the PATCO firing shows, some presidential spectacles retain important policy dimensions. One could imagine a continuum in which one end represents pure policy and the other pure spectacle. Toward the policy end one would find behind-the-scenes presidential actions, including quiet bargaining over domestic policies (such as Lyndon Johnson's lining up of Republican support for civil rights legislation) and covert actions in foreign affairs (such as the Nixon administration's use of the CIA to "destabilize" a socialist regime in Chile). Toward the spectacle end would be presidential posturing at home (law and order and drugs have been handy topics) and dramatic foreign travel (from 1972 until the 1989 massacre in Tiananmen Square, China was a particular presidential favorite). Most of the president's actions are a mix of policy and spectacle.

## THE TRIUMPH OF SPECTACLE: RONALD REAGAN

The Reagan presidency was a triumph of spectacle. In the realm of substantive policy, it was marked by striking failures as well as significant successes. But even the most egregious of the failures—public exposure of the disastrous covert policy of selling arms to Iran and diverting some of the profits to the Nicaraguan contras—proved to be only a temporary blow to the political fortunes of the most spectacular president in decades. With the help of two heart-warming summits with Soviet leader Mikhail Gorbachev, Reagan recovered from the Iran-contra debacle and left office near the peak of his popularity. His presidency, for the most part, floated above its flawed processes and failed policies, secure in the brilliant glow of its successful spectacles.

The basis of this success was the character of Ronald Reagan. His previous career in movies and television made him comfortable with and adept at spectacles; he moved easily from one kind to another. Reagan presented to his audience a multifaceted character, funny yet powerful, ordinary yet heroic, individual yet representative. His was a character richer even than Kennedy's in mythic resonance.

Coming into office after Jimmy Carter, a president who was widely perceived as weak, Reagan as a spectacle character projected potency. His administration featured a number of spectacles in which Reagan displayed his decisiveness, forcefulness, and will to prevail. The image of masculine toughness was played up repeatedly. The American people saw a president who, even though in his seventies, rode horses and exercised vigorously, a president who liked to quote (and thereby identify himself with) movie tough guys such as Clint Eastwood and Sylvester Stallone. Yet Reagan's strength was nicely balanced by his amiability; his aggressiveness was rendered benign by his characteristic one-line quips. The warm grin took the edge off the toughness, removed any intimations of callousness or violence.

Quickly dubbed "the Great Communicator," Reagan presented his character not through eloquent rhetoric but through storytelling. As Paul Erickson has demonstrated, Reagan liked to tell tales of "stock symbolic characters," figures whose values and behavior were "heavily colored with Reagan's ideological and emotional principles." Although the villains in these tales ranged from Washington bureaucrats to Marxist dictators, the heroes, whether ordinary people or inspirational figures like Knute Rockne, shared a belief in America. Examined more closely, these heroes turned out to resemble Reagan himself. Praising the heroism of Americans, Reagan, as the representative American, praised himself.

The power of Reagan's character rested not only on its intrinsic attractiveness but also on its symbolic appeal. The spectacle specialists who worked for Reagan seized on the idea of making him an emblem for the American identity. In a June 1984 memo, White House aide Richard Darman sketched a reelection strategy that revolved around the president's mythic role: "Paint RR as the personification of all that is right with or heroized by America. Leave Mondale in a position where an attack on Reagan is tantamount to an attack on America's idealized image of itself." Having come into office at a time of considerable anxiety, with many Americans uncertain about the economy, their future, and the country itself, Reagan was an immensely reassuring character. He had not been marked by the shocks of recent U.S. history—and he denied that those shocks had meaning. He told Americans that the Vietnam War was noble rather than appalling, that Watergate was forgotten, that racial conflict was a thing of the distant past, and that the U.S. economy still offered the American dream to any aspiring individual. Reagan (the character) and America (the country) were presented in the spectacles of the Reagan presidency as timeless, above the decay of aging and the difficulties of history.

The Reagan team assumed special importance because Reagan ran what Lou Cannon has called "the delegated presidency." As the public knew, his team members carried on most of the business of the executive branch; Reagan's own work habits were decidedly relaxed. Reagan's team did not contain many performers who reinforced the president's character, as Kennedy's youthful, energetic New Frontiersmen had. But it featured several figures whose spectacle role was to compensate for Reagan's deficiencies or to carry on his mission with a greater air of vigor than the amiable president usually conveyed. The Reagan presidency was not free of disruptive characters—Alexander Haig's and James Watt's unattractive qualities and gestures called the president's spectacle into question. But Reagan removed these characters before too much damage had been done.

David Stockman was the most publicized supporting player in the first months of 1981. His image in the media was formidable. Newsweek, for example, marveled at how "his buzz-saw intellect has helped him stage a series of bravura performances before Congress" and acclaimed him "the

Reagan Administration's boy wonder." There was spectacle appeal in the sight of the nation's youngest budget director serving as the right arm of the nation's oldest chief executive. More important, Stockman's appearance as the master of budget numbers compensated for a president who was notoriously uninterested in data. Stockman faded in spectacle value after his disastrous confession in fall 1981 that budget numbers had been doctored to show the results the administration wanted.

As Reagan's longtime aide, Edwin Meese III was one of the most prominent members of the president's team. Meese's principal spectacle role was not as a White House manager but as a cop. Even before he moved from the White House to the Justice Department, Meese became the voice and the symbol of the administration's tough stance on law-and-order issues. Although the president sometimes spoke about law and order, Meese took on the issue with a vigor that his more benign boss could not convey.

In foreign affairs, the Reagan administration developed an effective balance of images in the persons of Secretary of Defense Caspar Weinberger and Secretary of State George Shultz. Weinberger quickly became the administration's most visible cold war hard-liner. As the tireless spokesperson and unbudging champion of a soaring defense budget, he was a handy symbol for the Reagan military buildup. Nicholas Lemann noted that although "Weinberger's predecessor, Harold Brown, devoted himself almost completely to management, Weinberger . . . operated more and more on the theatrical side." His grim, hawk-like visage was as much a reminder of the Soviet threat as the alarming, book-length reports on the Russian behemoth that his Defense Department issued every year. Yet Weinberger sometimes could seem too alarming, feeding the fears of those who worried about Reagan's warmaking proclivities.

Once Haig was pushed out as secretary of state, however, the Reagan administration found the ideal counterpoint to Weinberger in George Shultz. In contrast to both Haig and Weinberger, Shultz was a reassuring figure. He was portrayed in the media in soothing terms: low-key, quiet, conciliatory. In form and demeanor he came across, in the words of Time, "as a good gray diplomat." Shultz was taken to be the voice of foreign policy moderation in an administration otherwise dominated by hard-liners. Actually, Shultz had better cold war credentials than Weinberger, having been a founding member of the hard-line Committee on the Present Danger in 1976. And he was more inclined to support the use of military force than was the secretary of defense, who reflected the caution of a Pentagon gun-shy after the Vietnam experience. But Shultz's real views were less evident than his spectacle role as the gentle diplomat.

The Reagan presidency benefited not only from a spectacular main character and a useful team but also from talent and good fortune in enacting spectacle gestures. The Reagan years were sprinkled with events—the PATCO strike, the Geneva summit, the Libyan bombing, and others—whose significance primarily lay in their spectacle value. The most striking Reagan spectacle of all was the invasion of Grenada. As the archetypal presidential spectacle, Grenada deserves a close look.

Reagan ordered American forces to invade the island of Grenada in October 1983. Relations had become tense between the Reagan administration and the Marxist regime of Grenada's Maurice Bishop. When Bishop was overthrown and murdered by a clique of more militant Marxists, the Reagan administration began to consider military action. It was urged to invade by the Organization of Eastern Caribbean States, composed of Grenada's island neighbors. And it had a pretext for action in ensuring the safety of the Americans—most of them medical students—on the island. Once the decision to invade was made, U.S. troops landed in force, evacuated most of the students, and seized the island after encountering brief but unexpectedly stiff resistance. Reagan administration officials announced that in the course of securing the island U.S. forces had discovered large caches of military supplies and documents indicating that Cuba planned to turn Grenada into a base for the export of communist revolution and terror.

The details that eventually came to light cast doubt on the Reagan administration's claims of a threat to the American students and a buildup of "sophisticated" Cuban weaponry in Grenada. Beyond such details, there was the sheer incongruity

between the importance bestowed on Grenada by the Reagan administration and the insignificance of the danger it posed. Grenada is a tiny island, with a population of 100,000, a land area of 133 square miles, and an economy whose exports totaled $19 million in 1981. That U.S. troops could secure it was never in question; as Richard Gabriel has noted. "In terms of actual combat forces, the U.S. outnumbered the island's defenders approximately ten to one." Grenada's importance did not derive from the military, political, and economic implications of America's actions, but from its value as a spectacle.

What was this spectacle about? Its meaning was articulated by a triumphant President Reagan: "Our days of weakness are over. Our military forces are back on their feet and standing tall." Reagan, even more than the American military, came across in the media as "standing tall" in Grenada.

The spectacle actually began with the president on a weekend golfing vacation in Augusta, Georgia. His vacation was interrupted first by planning for an invasion of Grenada and then by news that the U.S. Marine barracks in Beirut had been bombed. Once the news of the Grenada landings replaced the tragedy in Beirut on the front page and television screen, the golfing angle proved to be an apt beginning for a spectacle. It was used to dramatize the ability of a relaxed and genial president to rise to a grave challenge. And it supplied the White House with an unusual backdrop to present the president in charge, with members of his team by his side. As Francis X. Clines reported in the *New York Times:*

> The White House offered the public some graphic tableaux, snapped by the White House photographer over the weekend, depicting the President at the center of various conferences. He is seen in bathrobe and slippers being briefed by Mr. Shultz and Mr. McFarlane, then out on the Augusta fairway, pausing at the wheel of his golf cart as he receives another dispatch. Mr. Shultz is getting the latest word in another, holding the special security phone with a golf glove on.

Pictures of the president as decision maker were particularly effective because pictures from Grenada itself were lacking; the Reagan administration had barred the American press from covering the invasion. This move outraged the press but was extremely useful to the spectacle, which would have been subverted by pictures of dead bodies or civilian casualties or by independent sources of information with which congressional critics could raise unpleasant questions.

The initial meaning of the Grenada spectacle was established by Reagan in his announcement of the invasion. The enemy was suitably evil: "a brutal group of leftist thugs." America's objectives were purely moral—to protect the lives of innocent people on the island, namely American medical students, and to restore democracy to the people of Grenada. And the actions taken were unmistakably forceful: "The United States had no choice but to act strongly and decisively."

But the spectacle of Grenada soon expanded beyond this initial definition. The evacuation of the medical students provided one of those unanticipated occurrences that heighten the power of spectacle. When several of the students kissed the airport tarmac to express their relief and joy at returning to American soil, the resulting pictures on television and in the newspapers were better than anything the administration could have orchestrated. They provided the spectacle with historical as well as emotional resonance. Here was a second hostage crisis—but where Carter had been helpless to release captive Americans from Iran, Reagan had swiftly come to the rescue.

Rescue of the students quickly took second place, however, to a new theme: the claim that U.S. forces had uncovered and uprooted a hidden Soviet-Cuban base for adventurism and terrorism. In his nationally televised address, Reagan did not ignore the Iran analogy: "The nightmare of our hostages in Iran must never be repeated." But he stressed the greater drama of defeating a sinister communist plot. "Grenada, we were told, was a friendly island paradise for tourism. Well, it wasn't. It was a Soviet-Cuban colony being readied as a major military bastion to export terror and undermine democracy. We got there just in time." Grenada was turning out to be an even better spectacle for Reagan: He had rescued not only the students but the people of all the Americas as well.

As the spectacle expanded and grew more heroic, public approval increased. The president's standing in the polls went up. Time reported that "a post-invasion poll taken by the Washington Post and ABC News showed that 63% of Americans approve the way Reagan is handling the presidency, the highest level in two years, and attributed his gain largely to the Grenada intervention." Congressional critics, although skeptical of many of the claims the administration made, began to stifle their doubts and chime in with endorsements in accordance with the polls. An unnamed White House aide, quoted in Newsweek, drew the obvious lesson: "You can scream and shout and gnash your teeth all you want, but the folks out there like it. It was done right and done with dispatch."

In its final gestures, the Grenada spectacle actually commemorated itself. Reagan invited the medical students to the White House and, predictably, basked in their praise and cheers. The Pentagon contributed its symbolic share, awarding some eight thousand medals for the Grenada operation—more than the number of American troops that had set foot on the island. In actuality, Gabriel has shown, "the operation was marred by a number of military failures." Yet these were obscured by the triumphant appearances of the spectacle.

That the spectacle of Grenada was more potent and would prove more lasting in its effects than any disconfirming facts was observed at the time by Anthony Lewis. Reagan "knew the facts would come out eventually," wrote Lewis. "But if that day could be postponed, it might make a great political difference. People would be left with their first impression that this was a decisive President fighting communism." Grenada became for most Americans a highlight of Reagan's first term. Insignificant in military or diplomatic terms, as spectacle it was one of the most successful acts of the Reagan presidency.

## A SCHIZOID SPECTACLE: GEORGE H. W. BUSH

*Time* magazine accorded George Herbert Walker Bush a unique honor: it named him its "Men of the Year" for 1990. There were really two President Bushes, the magazine explained, a strong and visionary leader in international affairs and a directionless fumbler at home. The split in Bush's presidency that *Time* highlighted was as evident in the realm of spectacle as in the realm of policy. The foreign affairs spectacle of the first Bush presidency featured a masterful leader, a powerhouse team, and thrilling gestures. The domestic spectacle featured a confused leader, a colorless team, and gestures of remarkable ineptitude. Together, they created a schizoid spectacle.

Critics could find much to fault in the substance of Bush's foreign policy, but as spectacle, his foreign policy leadership was an unalloyed triumph. The main character in the Bush administration's foreign policy spectacle was experienced, confident, decisive, in charge. Bush seemed bred to foreign policy stewardship in a patrician tradition dating back to Theodore Roosevelt and Henry Stimson. He came across to the public as the master diplomat, successfully cajoling and persuading other world leaders through well-publicized telephone calls; in truth, he moved easily among international elites, obviously in his element. He was an even more triumphant spectacle character when featured in winning tableaux as commander in chief of Operation Desert Storm, which drove occupying Iraqi troops out of Kuwait in 1991.

The foreign policy team made a superb contribution to the global side of the Bush spectacle. Not since the administration of Richard Nixon had a president's skill at diplomacy been so effectively magnified by his top civilian advisers; not since World War II had a commander in chief been blessed with such popular military subordinates. James Baker, Bush's onetime Houston neighbor and longtime political manager, was both courtly and canny as secretary of state. Richard Cheney was a cool, cerebral secretary of defense, with an air of mastery reminiscent of Robert McNamara. Colin Powell, chair of the Joint Chiefs of Staff, radiated dignity and authority as the highest ranking African American in the history of the military and was almost universally admired. General Norman Schwarzkopf was the feisty commander of Desert Storm—an appealing emblem for a military finally restored to glorious health after two decades of licking its Vietnam wounds.

More than anything else, military gestures produced exciting drama in the Bush foreign affairs spectacle. Panama was the prelude to the Persian Gulf War. It featured, in Panamanian leader Manuel Noriega, a doubly immoral adversary—a drug smuggler as well as a dictator. The U.S. military operation to depose Noriega was swift and efficient, and victory was assured once the Panamanian strongman was seized and transported to the United States to face drug-trafficking charges.

The Gulf War victory dwarfed Panama, not only as a significant policy accomplishment but also as spectacle. Bush depicted Iraqi dictator Saddam Hussein as a second Hitler, a figure whose immense record of evil made Noriega look like a small-time thug. To be sure, Operation Desert Storm lacked the satisfying climax of destroying the evil adversary, but as a military display it provided Americans with numerous scenes to cheer. The indisputable favorites were Defense Department videos of laser-guided bombs homing in on Iraqi targets with pinpoint accuracy. In the cinematic terms that President Reagan had made popular, Desert Storm was not the cavalry rescue of Grenada or the capture of the pirate captain in Panama; it was high-tech epic, the return of the American Jedi.

Bush's foreign policy spectacle was successful—perhaps too successful. Once the Soviet Union crumbled and Iraq was militarily humiliated, foreign policy seemed much less relevant to most Americans. According to Walter Dean Burnham, "In 1992 foreign policy issues and public concerns about them played the smallest role in any American presidential election since 1936." As Americans began to focus almost exclusively on the home front, they witnessed a domestic Bush spectacle utterly unlike the foreign affairs version.

The domestic Bush was an uncertain, awkward character, especially in the electorally decisive field of economic policy. Inheriting what he had once derided as Reagan's "voodoo economics," Bush presided over an economic crisis when the policy's magic failed. In the face of this crisis, which was evident by the second year of his administration, Bush drifted, seemingly clueless about how to restore the economy to health. The only economic prescription he ever put forward with any conviction was a cut in the capital gains tax rate that would have most directly benefited wealthy investors. Comfortable dealing with the problems that beset his fellow world leaders, Bush seemed ill at ease with the economic problems plaguing ordinary Americans.

Bush's economic team only magnified his weaknesses. His secretary of the Treasury, Nicholas Brady, and chair of the Council of Economic Advisers, Michael Boskin, were pale, dim figures who barely registered in the public's consciousness. To the extent that anyone did notice them, they seemed to epitomize inaction. A more visible economic team member was the budget director, Richard Darman. But he was portrayed in the media as arrogant and abrasive, epitomizing the antagonism between the Bush White House and Capitol Hill that resulted in domestic policy gridlock.

It was through a series of small gestures, some intended and others inadvertent, that Bush's disengagement from the economic difficulties of ordinary people was demonstrated most dramatically. Touring a grocery store, the president expressed amazement at the electronic scanners that read prices. To those who stood by every week as these scanners recorded their food purchases, here was a president unfamiliar with how families struggled to pay their grocery bills. Visiting a suburban mall on the day after Thanksgiving (the busiest shopping day of the year) in 1991, Bush brought along reporters, who publicized his purchases: athletic socks for himself, Christmas presents for his family. Bush's shopping expedition seemed designed to convey the message that Americans could lift themselves out of recession just by taking a few more trips to the mall. The most telling gesture of disengagement came early in 1992 at a campaign stop in New Hampshire, when Bush blurted out a stage cue from one of his speechwriters: "Message: I care." The message that came through instead was that the president had to be prompted to commiserate with the economic woes of the American people.

Real economic fears and pains denied Bush reelection in 1992. But the fears and pains were made worse by the ineptitude of his domestic spectacle. The president who lacked not only a credible economic plan but also credible gestures that would communicate concern and effort to restore economic health went down to a landslide defeat, with 63 percent of the electorate voting against him. The schizoid spectacle of George Bush, triumphant in its foreign policy performance, disastrous in its domestic policy performance, was over.

## A POSTMODERN SPECTACLE: BILL CLINTON

George H. W. Bush had two disparate spectacles; Bill Clinton had many. Clinton's was a postmodern spectacle. A postmodern spectacle, previously more familiar in popular culture than in presidential politics, features fleeting images and fractured continuity, surfaces without depths, personae rather than personalities. Characters in a postmodern spectacle succeed not by capturing the lasting admiration or trust of their audience but by artfully personifying the changing fashions that fascinate it.

Depictions of Clinton by close observers in the media tended to agree on his shape-shifting presidential performance but to differ about whether it should evoke moral indignation or neutral evaluation. One caustic Clinton watcher, *New York Times* columnist Maureen Dowd, called the president "the man of a thousand faces." Other commentators preferred cool, postmodern terms such as *makeover* and *reinvention,* the same words used to describe the diva of contemporary pop culture, Madonna.

Clinton's presidency had important elements of constancy, including the successful economic course he first charted in 1993 and his underlying attachment to government as a potentially positive force in society. The frequent changes of course during Clinton's two terms owed as much to the formidable political constraints he faced as to the opportunities for spectacle he seized. Moreover, historical precedents for Clinton's "mongrel politics" may be found in the administrations of presidents such as Woodrow Wilson and Richard Nixon, who also were accused of opportunistic borrowing from ideological adversaries in eras when the opposition party set the reigning terms of political discourse. Nonetheless, Clinton's repeated redefinitions of himself and his presidency made these predecessors seem almost static by comparison. Sometimes awkwardly, sometimes nimbly, Clinton pirouetted across the presidential stage as no one before him.

Clinton's first two years in office were largely a failure of spectacle. The promising populist intimacy he displayed in the 1992 campaign quickly gave way to a spectacle of Washington elitism: social life among the rich and famous (including an infamous $200 haircut by a Beverly Hills stylist) and politics among the entrenched and arrogant (the cozy alliance with the Democratic congressional leadership). The new president seemed simultaneously immature (the undisciplined decision delayer aided by a youthful and inexperienced White House staff) and old-fashioned (the big-government liberal with his bureaucratic scheme to reform the health care system). The crushing rebukes that Clinton suffered in 1994—the failure of his health care plan even to reach the floor of either house of Congress and the Republican takeover of both houses in the midterm elections—showed how little he had impressed his audience. Yet a postmodern irony was at work for Clinton—his defeats freed him. Not having to implement a large-scale health care plan, Clinton was able to dance away from the liberal label. Not having to tie himself to his party's congressional leadership in a bid for legislative achievement, he was able to shift his policy stances opportunely to capitalize on the excesses of the new Republican agenda.

In his first two years Clinton lacked an important ingredient of many presidential spectacles: a dramatic foil. Bush had Manuel Noriega and Saddam Hussein, but the post-cold war world was too uninteresting to most Americans to supply foreign leaders ripe for demonization. (That would change after September 11, 2001.) The hidden blessing of the 1994 elections for Clinton was that they provided him with a domestic foil of suitably dramatic proportions: Speaker of the House Newt Gingrich. Gingrich was often compared to Clinton—and the comparison worked mostly in Clinton's favor. Shedding the taint of liberalism, Clinton pronounced himself a nonideological centrist saving the country from Gingrich's conservative extremism. Before, Clinton had talked and shown off too much in public;

now, in comparison to the grandiose garrulousness of Gingrich, he seemed almost reticent—and certainly more mature. Attacked as too soft in his first two years, Clinton could turn the image of compassion into a strength by attacking a foil who proposed to reduce spending for seniors on Medicare and Medicaid and to place the children of welfare mothers in orphanages. Lampooned as spineless in his first two years, Clinton could display his backbone by winning the budget showdown with Gingrich and the Republicans in the winter of 1995–1996.

In a postmodern spectacle, a president can try on a variety of styles without being committed to any one of them. As the 1996 election season commenced (and as Gingrich fled the spotlight after his budget defeat), Clinton executed another nimble pirouette by emulating the patron saint of modern Republicans, Ronald Reagan. Clinton's advisers had him watch Reagan videotapes to study "the Gipper's bearing, his aura of command." His campaign team found a model for 1996 in the 1984 Reagan theme of "Morning in America," in which a sunny president capitalized on peace and prosperity while floating serenely above divisive issues. Like Reagan in 1984, Clinton presented himself in 1996 as the benevolent manager of economic growth, the patriotic commander in chief, and the good father devoted to family values. Unlike Reagan, he added the images of the good son protecting seniors and the good steward protecting the environment. Clinton's postmodern appropriation of Reagan imagery helped to block the Republicans from achieving their goal of a unified party government fulfilling Reagan's ideological dreams.

Clinton's postmodern spectacle shaped the public's impressions of his team. With a man of uncertain character in the White House, strong women in the cabinet drew special attention: Attorney General Janet Reno at the outset of his first term, Secretary of State Madeleine Albright at the outset of his second. But no members of Clinton's cabinet or staff played as important a supporting role in his spectacle as his wife, Hillary, and his vice president, Al Gore. Hillary Rodham Clinton appeared as an updated, postfeminist version of Eleanor Roosevelt, a principled liberal goad pressing against her husband's pragmatic instincts. Like Eleanor, she was a hero to the liberal Democratic faithful and a despised symbol of radicalism to conservative Republican foes. Al Gore's spectacle role was to be the stable and stolid sidekick to the quicksilver president. Even his much-satirized reputation as boring was reassuring when counterpoised to a president who sometimes appeared all too eager to charm and seduce his audience.

A postmodern spectacle is best crafted by postmodern spectacle specialists. When Clinton's presidential image began taking a beating, he turned for help to image makers who previously had worked for Republicans but who were as ideologically unanchored as he was. In 1993 Clinton responded to plunging poll ratings by hiring David Gergen, the White House communications chief during Reagan's first term. But the amiable Gergen was unable to reposition Clinton as a centrist nearly so effectively as Dick Morris, Clinton's image consultant after the 1994 electoral debacle. Morris had worked before for Clinton but also for conservative Republicans such as Senate Majority Leader Trent Lott. As a *Newsweek* story described him, Morris "was a classic mercenary—demonic, brilliant, principle-free." It was Morris's insight, as much as Clinton's, that rhetoric and gesture, supported by the power of the veto, could turn a presidency seemingly moribund after 1994 into a triumphant one in 1996.

The remarkable prosperity the nation enjoyed during Clinton's second term purchased an unusual stretch of calm (some called it lethargy) for his administration—until the Monica Lewinsky storm threatened to wreck it in early 1998. Numerous Americans of all political persuasions were appalled by Clinton's sexual escapades and dishonest explanations in the Lewinsky affair. But for Clinton-haters on the right, long infuriated by the successful spectacles of a character who symbolized (for them) the 1960s culture they despised, the Lewinsky scandal produced a thrill of self-confirmation. See, they proclaimed, his soul is the moral wasteland we always said it was. The unwillingness of most Americans to concur with conservative Republicans that Clinton's moral failures necessitated his ouster from the presidency only made his impeachment

and conviction more urgent for the right. If strong support for Clinton in the polls indicated that the public was following him down the path toward moral hollowness, then removing him became a crusade for the nation's soul, an exorcism of the moral rot jeopardizing the meaning of the Republic.

But the moralistic fulminations of the right were no match for the power of spectacle. It was not spectacle alone that saved the Clinton presidency. Clinton was protected by prosperity and by Americans' preference for his centrist policies over the conservative alternatives. He was aided, too, by the inclination of most Americans to draw a line between public rectitude and private freedom. Nonetheless, Clinton's eventual acquittal by the Senate owed much to spectacle. To be sure, his own spectacle performance in the Year of Lewinsky was hardly his best. Perhaps no role so little suited Clinton as that of repentant sinner. But he was blessed by even worse performances from his adversaries. Just as Newt Gingrich had been necessary to resuscitate Clinton from the political disaster of 1994, so was Kenneth Starr essential to his rescue from the personal disaster of 1998. Starr's self-righteous moralism disturbed most Americans more than Clinton's self-serving narcissism.

In the end, the shallowness of the postmodern spectacle that had characterized the Clinton presidency from the start supplied an ironic benefit in the Lewinsky scandal. Had Clinton possessed a stable, respected character, revelations of secret behavior that violated that character might have startled the public and shrunk its approval of his performance in office. His standing in the polls might have plummeted, as President Reagan's did after the disclosure that his administration was selling arms to terrorists. But because a majority of Americans had long believed, according to the polls, that Clinton was not very honest or trustworthy, his misbehavior in the Lewinsky affair came as less of a shock and was quickly diluted by frequent reminders of his administration's popular achievements and agenda. Postmodern spectacle is not about character, at least not in a traditional sense; it is about delivering what the audience desires at the moment. Personality, political talent, and a keen instinct for survival made Bill Clinton the master of postmodern spectacle.

# SPECTACLE-IN-CHIEF: GEORGE W. BUSH

After reaching the White House in one of the closest and most intensely disputed elections in the history of the presidency, George W. Bush began his administration with a recycled spectacle.

Although he promised the novelty of a "compassionate conservatism" during the campaign, the Bush administration's original agenda mainly followed the familiar priorities of the Republican right. But its conservatism ran deeper than its policy prescriptions. In its characters, its styles, and its gestures, the Bush administration was determined to reach back past the postmodern spectacle of Bill Clinton and restore the faded glories of contemporary conservatism.

One fund of recycled images and themes upon which Bush drew was the Reagan spectacle. As a presidential character, Bush enjoyed many affinities with Reagan. He presented himself as a Reagan-style nonpolitician whose optimism and bonhomie would brighten a harsh and demoralizing political environment. His principal policy prescriptions for the nation also recycled Reaganesque themes and gestures, like Reagan, Bush rapidly pushed through Congress a massive tax cut that favored the wealthy in the guise of an economic stimulus, using "fuzzy math" to promise Americans the pleasure of prosperity without the pain of federal deficits. Like Reagan, Bush promoted a national missile defense system that would use cutting-edge (and still nonexistent) technology to restore the ancient dream of an innocent America invulnerable to the violent quarrels that beset the rest of the world. Even the Bush administration's most politically costly stance in its early months, presidential decisions favoring private interests over environmental protection, was couched in the Reagan-style claim of protecting the pocketbooks of ordinary citizens. Revising a Clinton rule that would have mandated higher efficiency for central air conditioners, Bush's secretary of energy, Spencer Abraham, indicated that his goal was to save low-income consumers from having to pay more to cool their homes or trailers.

Recycled images and themes from his father's administration were equally evident in the early months of Bush's presidency. They were especially useful as emblems of the new president's "compassionate" side. Like his father, "W" trumpeted his conciliatory stance toward congressional opponents. Like his father, he set out to be an "education president." The recycling of paternal gestures also was apparent in Bush's meetings with representatives of the groups that had opposed his election most strongly. Just as the father had met with Jesse Jackson after winning the White House, the son invited the Congressional Black Caucus. Neither Bush expected to win over African American voters through these gestures. Instead, each hoped to signal to moderate whites that he was a "kinder, gentler" conservative who exuded tolerance and good will.

The new Bush administration reached even farther back in time in its bid to dramatize its repudiation of Clinton's postmodern character and style. Two of the new administration's most important figures— Vice President Richard Cheney and Secretary of Defense Donald Rumsfeld—were prominent alumni of the Ford administration. Cheney and Rumsfeld represented Bush's *That '70s Show*, although they no longer sported the long sideburns and wide lapels of Ford's day. Leaping back before the hated 1960s, the Bush administration evoked an even earlier time, when Cheney, echoing the 1950s theme of "our friend, the atom," praised nuclear energy as "the cleanest method of power generation we know."

Bush's first-term presidential team drew upon Republican characters and themes of the past to provide a reassuringly mature, veteran cast in contrast to the youthful self-indulgence associated with the postmodern Clinton. It also drained some of the political danger out of the widespread doubts about Bush's lack of preparation for the presidency. Initially, the most visible team member was the vice president, who played the role of the wise and experienced father to the reformed playboy son, even though Cheney is only five years older than Bush. But Cheney's time in the spotlight was cut short when jokes and cartoons proliferated about the vice president as a puppeteer controlling the puppet in the Oval Office. After Cheney declined in visibility (although not in influence), various members of the Bush cabinet emerged to signal compassion or conservatism as the situation seemed to require. On the compassionate end of the spectrum, the most reassuring (though increasingly ineffectual) figure was Secretary of State Colin Powell, who conveyed the warm image of moderation and multilateralism otherwise absent from the administration's approach to foreign affairs. On the conservative end, the most militant figure was Attorney General John Ashcroft, the dour face of the Christian right's culture wars. The fundamental conservatism of the Bush spectacle was even evident in the first lady. As a demure, traditional wife, who eschews a political role, Laura Bush quietly renounced the feminist activism of Hillary Rodham Clinton.

Perhaps the most revealing spectacle gesture in the early months of the Bush presidency was his August 9, 2001, speech on stem-cell research. Speaking from his Texas ranch in his first televised address to the American people since his inauguration, Bush ended weeks of media speculation by announcing that he would permit federal tax dollars to be used for research on existing stem-cell lines but not for research on lines established after August 9. Balancing the public's hope for miracle cures to an array of severe illnesses with the conservatives' insistence on preserving the life of embryos, Bush's decision was meant to epitomize compassionate conservatism. Yet the heart of the spectacle lay in the presentation of his decision more than in its substance. In a style reminiscent of Reagan at the launch of the Grenada spectacle, Bush's speech countered criticisms of a disengaged presidency by presenting a deeply thoughtful chief executive sacrificing his vacation time to make the gravest of decisions. A president under fire in the media as an intellectual lightweight manipulated by his advisers was presented (by his advisers) as the real decision maker, confronting a policy dilemma worthy of a moral philosopher. To make sure that the public grasped the gesture, the day after the speech presidential communications director Karen Hughes provided the press with a detailed briefing on how Bush had wrestled with the decision. She portrayed the president, in the words of the *New York Times*, as "a soul-searching, intellectually curious leader."

A month after the stem-cell speech, when al Qaeda terrorists killed thousands of Americans in a twisted spectacle of their own by piloting hijacked airliners into the World Trade Center and the Pentagon, Bush shed the ill-fitting guise of moral philosopher for a more comfortable and politically potent role: the warrior president. The recycled spectacle of his first eight months in office, although perpetuated through gestures (such as opposition to gay marriage) that were especially appealing to Bush's evangelical Christian base, was now overshadowed by a more novel spectacle of global reach, as Bush proclaimed a war on terror. Clumsy in his first public responses to the horror of September 11, 2001, Bush quickly hit his stride in what would be remembered as iconic moments of his presidency: his visit with rescue workers at Ground Zero in New York and his impressive speech to Congress on September 20, which struck a delicate balance between a forceful response to terrorism, a compassionate response to tragedy, and a teaching of tolerance toward followers of the Islamic faith. These moments would be etched in the public mind during Bush's campaign for reelection. For example, in narrating Bush's 9/11 heroics near the site of the tragedy, the 2004 Republican convention in New York City was skillfully designed to link Bush inextricably with Americans' determination to defeat the nation's terrorist enemies.

With the swift success of the military campaign against al Qaeda and the Taliban regime that harbored it in Afghanistan, the delicate balance in Bush's initial response to September 11 gave way to a consistently martial tone. Paced by Secretary of Defense Rumsfeld, the Bush administration began to feature a spectacle of muscular globalism. In his State of the Union address in January 2002, the commander in chief previewed an expansion of the war on terror to combat an "axis of evil" composed of North Korea, Iran, and especially Iraq. Bush's dramatic phrase, which made headlines around the world, rhetorically invoked the nation's Axis enemies in World War II and the Soviet "evil empire" of the cold war to amplify the peril posed by adversaries in the Middle East and Asia. In its emphasis on eliminating the regime of Saddam Hussein in Iraq, the phrase gestured toward the spectacular completion by the son of the mission in which the father, it now seemed, had sadly fallen short. The speech began the buildup to war against Iraq a year later, as the Bush administration mustered its political and rhetorical resources to portray Saddam's regime, with its alleged weapons of mass destruction and ties to al Qaeda, as a sinister threat to American security.

Toppling Saddam in spring 2003 proved far easier than bringing security or democracy to Iraq afterward, and the Iraqi insurgency that grew in strength and ferocity in response to the American occupation presented an enormous challenge to the Bush administration's global strategy. Yet if the war on Iraq had turned into a hellish nightmare, one would not know it from the spectacles of the warrior president. In a conflict far more serious and deadly than Reagan's Invasion of Grenada, Bush's spectacle specialists designed even more gripping gestures of a president "standing tall." As Elisabeth Bumiller noted in the *New York Times:* "the Bush administration, going far beyond the foundations in stagecraft set by the Reagan White House, is using the powers of television and technology like never before."

Copiloting an S-3B Viking onto the deck of the aircraft carrier *Abraham Lincoln* on May 1, 2003, President Bush starred in what was instantly recognized as a classic of presidential spectacles; the press quickly dubbed it Bush's *Top Gun* affair, recalling the Tom Cruise movie. The White House used the carrier as its stage to announce that major combat operations in Iraq were over; a banner over the president's head was emblazoned, "Mission Accomplished." Every detail of the event was meticulously planned for how it would look on television and in newspaper photos. The landing at sea highlighted the degree of risk, with the Viking brought to a halt by the last of the four cables that catch planes on the carrier deck. Members of the *Lincoln* crew were garbed in varied but coordinated shirt colors as they surrounded the president (reminiscent of a football halftime ceremony). At the center of this massive stage was President Bush, who

played his part with evident relish. Maureen Dowd described the moment: "He flashed that famous all-American grin as he swaggered around the deck of the aircraft carrier in his olive flight suit, ejection harness between his legs, helmet tucked under his arm, awe-struck crew crowding around."

The spectacle-in-chief reappeared on Thanksgiving Day 2003, when President Bush made a dramatic, surprise visit to Baghdad to succor weary American soldiers. As Elisabeth Bumiller reported, "In one of the most secretive presidential trips in American history, George W. Bush flew to Baghdad under intense security . . . to spend Thanksgiving with United States troops and to thank them for standing up against the 'band of thugs and assassins' they are fighting in Iraq." In a mess hall at Baghdad International Airport, an area sometimes targeted by insurgent mortar fire, the president, clad in an army jacket bearing the patch of the "Old Ironsides" Division, was swarmed by the surprised and delighted troops. In contrast to his aircraft carrier appearance, however, the spectacle this time featured the commander in chief in a humbler mode among young Americans who had experienced combat. Photos depicted the president carrying a glistening roasted turkey on a sumptuous platter to serve the hungry soldiers.

Through these gestures, Bush's spectacle specialists implanted his image as a strong commander in chief, while eliding the grim realities on the ground in Iraq. Adhering to the tradition of civilian control of the military, Bush's predecessors had generally eschewed military garb. But his choice of clothing on the *Abraham Lincoln* and at the Baghdad airport played up his oneness with American armed forces. The copilot's tailhook landing on the carrier and the secret flight into the dangerous Baghdad airport suggested that Bush was willing to share some of the risks to which his decisions as commander in chief exposed American troops. No matter how controversial the war in Iraq might be, the one aspect of it that aroused consensus among Americans was the steadfast courage of the armed forces. Associating himself with the troops through his warrior spectacles, Bush signified that this virtue was his, too.

Subsequent media inquiries unearthed details that potentially called into question this signification. Viewers of Bush's dramatic flight to the *Abraham Lincoln* had witnessed what appeared to be a risky jet landing at sea. Later it was revealed by the press that the aircraft carrier was close to San Diego and could have been reached by helicopter; in fact, the ship had sailed a bit further out into the Pacific so that the California coastline would not be visible on television. (One wonders what the president for whom the carrier had been named would have thought of this stagecraft.) The president also was criticized later on for the "Mission Accomplished" banner; its sentiment turned out to be wildly premature. Bush's gesture in serving a Thanksgiving turkey to American troops in Baghdad proved to involve contrived stagecraft as well. As Mike Alien reported in the *Washington Post:*

In the most widely published image from his Thanksgiving day trip to Baghdad, the beaming president is wearing an Army workout jacket and surrounded by soldiers as he cradles a huge platter laded with a golden-brown turkey. The bird is so perfect that it looks as if it came from a food magazine. But as a small sign of the many ways the White House maximized the impact of the two-and-a-half hour stop at the Baghdad airport, administration officials said that Bush picked up a decoration, not a serving plate. A contractor had roasted and primped the turkey to adorn the buffet line, while the 600 soldiers were served from cafeteria-style steam trays.

Revelations of the contrivances behind Bush's warrior spectacles did not seem to faze the president's supporters. When the premises with which Bush had rallied the nation to go to war proved false and the aftermath of invasion brought embarrassing American blunders and mounting American casualties, the president's popularity declined in the polls. But his image as a warrior president withstood setbacks that likely would have devastated Clinton or perhaps Reagan, Even the ugliest aspects of the war, such as the Abu Ghraib scandal, involving American military police sexually humiliating Iraqi prisoners, did not tarnish Bush except among those who were already opposed to the war. Bush's 9/11 image as America's protector against terrorists and his identification through spectacle with American troops in Iraq were his greatest assets when he faced the voters in 2004. At the hands of the president's campaign managers (some of whom had designed his Iraq spectacles), John Kerry, a decorated war hero in Vietnam, was recreated as a foreign-policy weakling compared to George W. Bush, who had avoided Vietnam but had become a spectacle warrior.

Although the Bush White House featured the president in the heroic guise of commander in chief, it refused to call for the sacrifices that previous wartime presidents had asked of Americans. Rather than requesting greater revenues to fight a war on terror, for example, it introduced a second round of massive tax cuts in 2003. Rather than pursuing national unity, it pushed its conservative Republican agenda even more aggressively. As Stephen Skowronek observes, "Far more remarkable than the fact that the nation rallied to the president's side [after September 11] is the fact that the president's newfound authority as a commander-in-chief in wartime was deployed to further his initial leadership project." The elections of 2004 testified to the effectiveness of the Bush administration's strategy. Reelected primarily as a warrior president, Bush claimed a mandate to remake American politics in conservative terms. If Ronald Reagan's presidency represented the triumph of spectacle, the second term of George W. Bush will test spectacle's capacity to facilitate the revolutionary turn to the right to which Reagan could only aspire.

## CONCLUSION

It is tempting to blame the growth of spectacle on individual presidents, their calculating advisers, and compliant journalists. It is more accurate, however, to attribute the growth of spectacle to larger, structural forces: the extreme personalization of the modern presidency, the excessive expectations of the president that most Americans have, and the voluminous media coverage that fixes on presidents and treats American politics largely as a report of their adventures. Indeed, presidential spectacles can be linked to a culture of consumption in which spectacle is the predominant form that relates the few to the many.

Spectacle, then, is more a structural feature of the contemporary presidency than a strategy of deception adopted by particular presidents. In running for the presidency, then carrying out its tasks, any contemporary chief executive is likely to turn to spectacle. Spectacle has become institutionalized; specialists in the White House routinely devise performances for a vast press corps that is eager to report every colorful detail. Spectacle is expected by the public as the most visible manifestation of presidential leadership. A president who deliberately

eschewed its possibilities would probably encounter the same kind of difficulties as a president who tried to lead by spectacle but failed.

Still, the rise of spectacle in the presidency remains a disturbing development. It is harmful to presidents, promoting gesture over accomplishment and appearance over fact. It is even more harmful to the public because it obfuscates presidential activity, undermines executive accountability, and encourages passivity on the part of citizens. The presentation of leadership as spectacle has little in common with the kind of leadership that American democratic values imply.

---

## DISCUSSION QUESTIONS

1. What examples does Miroff provide to support his view that the presidency as a spectacle "obfuscates presidential activity, undermines executive accountability, and encourages passivity on the part of citizens"?
2. Since the September 11, 2001 attacks, President George W. Bush has been preoccupied with the "war on terrorism." How has Bush invoked symbolic language to build support for this effort?

## 27 *Jennifer Van Bergen*

# THE "UNITARY EXECUTIVE" AND THE THREAT TO DEMOCRATIC GOVERNMENT

*After the 9/11 attacks, the Bush administration claimed sweeping new powers to prosecute the "war on terror." Moving well beyond more traditional wartime assertions of presidential power, the Bush policies are notable for their open-ended and unlimited duration and their rejection of regulation by the legislative and judicial branches of government. In this selection, lawyer and author Jennifer Van Bergen explores President Bush's alarmingly frequent use of presidential signing statements to lay claim to his power as Commander-in-Chief to interpret laws as he chooses, even if it means violating the very laws he signs. Under the invented theory of a "unitary executive," President Bush envisions an executive branch unbridled by the checks and balances that mark the boundaries of constitutional government. Van Bergen then extends her analysis to the more recent case of the Military Commissions Act, enacted in the fall of 2006 before the midterm elections, as an example of the dangers inherent in logic of unilateral presidential power. In light of the executive branch's disregard for traditional notions of due process, she asks us to consider the damage done to the very institutional balance that underlies the American democratic system.*

When President Bush signed the new law [in late December 2005], sponsored by Senator McCain, restricting the use of torture when interrogating detainees, he also issued a Presidential signing statement. That statement asserted that his power as Commander-in-Chief gives him the authority to bypass the very law he had just signed.

This news came fast on the heels of Bush's shocking admission that, since 2002, he has repeatedly authorized the National Security Agency to conduct electronic surveillance without a warrant, in flagrant violation of applicable federal law.

And before that, Bush declared he had the unilateral authority to ignore the Geneva Conventions and to indefinitely detain without due process both immigrants and citizens as enemy combatants.

All these declarations echo the refrain Bush has been asserting from the outset of his presidency. That refrain is simple: Presidential power must be unilateral, and unchecked.

*Source*: Jennifer Van Bergen, "The Unitary Executive: Is The Doctrine Behind the Bush Presidency Consistent with a Democratic State?" *FindLaw.com*, January 9, 2006; Jennifer Van Bergen, "Damage Control," *TomPaine.com*, October 27, 2006.

But the most recent and blatant presidential intrusions on the law and Constitution supply the verse to that refrain. They not only claim unilateral executive power, but also supply the train of the President's thinking, the texture of his motivations, and the root of his intentions.

They make clear, for instance, that the phrase "unitary executive" is a code word for a doctrine that favors nearly unlimited executive power. Bush has used the doctrine in his signing statements to quietly expand presidential authority.

In this article, I will consider the meaning of the unitary executive doctrine within a democratic government that respects the separation of powers. I will ask: Can our government remain true to its nature, yet also embrace this doctrine?

I will also consider what the President and his legal advisers mean by applying the unitary executive doctrine. And I will argue that the doctrine violates basic tenets of our system of checks and balances, quietly crossing longstanding legal and moral boundaries that are essential to a democratic society.

## PRESIDENT BUSH'S AGGRESSIVE USE OF PRESIDENTIAL SIGNING STATEMENTS

Bush has used presidential "signing statements"—statements issued by the President upon signing a bill into law—to expand his power. Each of his signing statements says that he will interpret the law in question "in a manner consistent with his constitutional authority to supervise the unitary executive branch."

Presidential signing statements have gotten very little media attention. They are, however, highly important documents that define how the President interprets the laws he signs. Presidents use such statements to protects the prerogative of their office and ensure control over the executive branch functions.

Presidents also—since Reagan—have used such statements to create a kind of alternative legislative history. Attorney General Ed Meese explained in 1986 that:

To make sure that the President's own understanding of what's in a bill is the same . . . is given consideration at the time of statutory construction later on by a court, we have now arranged with West Publishing Company that the presidential statement on the signing of a bill will accompany the legislative history from Congress so that all can be available to the court for future construction of what that statute really means.

The alternative legislative history would, according to Dr. Christopher S. Kelley, professor of political science at the Miami University at Oxford, Ohio, "contain certain policy or principles that the administration had lost in its negotiations" with Congress.

The Supreme Court has paid close attention to presidential signing statements. Indeed, in two important decisions—the *Chadha* and *Bowsher* decisions—the Court relied in part on president signing statements in interpreting laws. Other federal courts, sources show, have taken note of them too.

President Bush has used presidential signing statements more than any previous president. From President Monroe's administration (1817–25) to the Carter administration (1977–81), the executive branch issued a total of 75 signing statements to protect presidential prerogatives. From Reagan's administration through Clinton's, the total number of signing statements ever issued, by all presidents, rose to a total 322.

In striking contrast to his predecessors, President Bush issued at least 435 signing statements in his first term alone. And, in these statements and in his executive orders, Bush used the term "unitary executive" 95 times. It is important, therefore, to understand what this doctrine means.

## WHAT DOES THE ADMINISTRATION MEAN WHEN IT REFERS TO THE "UNITARY EXECUTIVE"?

Dr. Kelley notes that the unitary executive doctrine arose as the result of the twin circumstances of Vietnam and Watergate. Kelley asserts that "the faith and trust placed into the presidency was broken as a result of the lies of Vietnam and Watergate," which resulted in a congressional assault on presidential prerogatives.

For example, consider the Foreign Intelligence Surveillance Act (FISA) which Bush evaded when authorizing the NSA to tap without warrants—even those issued by the FISA court. FISA was enacted after the fall of Nixon with the precise intention of curbing unchecked executive branch surveillance. (Indeed, Nixon's improper use of domestic surveillance was included in Article 2 paragraph (2) of the impeachment articles against him.)

According to Kelley, these congressional limits on the presidency, in turn, led "some very creative people" in the White House and the Department of Justice's Office of Legal Counsel (OLC) to fight back, in an attempt to foil or blunt these limits. In their view, these laws were legislative attempts to strip the president of his rightful powers. Prominent among those in the movement to preserve presidential power and champion the unitary executive doctrine were the founding members of the Federalist Society, nearly all of whom worked in the Nixon, Ford, and Reagan White Houses.

The unitary executive doctrine arises out of a theory called "departmentalism," or "coordinate construction." According to legal scholars Christopher Yoo, Steven Calabresi, and Anthony Colangelo, the coordinate construction approach "holds that all three branches of the federal government have the power and duty to interpret the Constitution." According to this theory, the president may (and indeed, must) interpret laws, equally as much as the courts.

## THE UNITARY EXECUTIVE VERSUS JUDICIAL SUPREMACY

The coordinate construction theory counters the long-standing notion of "judicial supremacy," articulated by Supreme Court Chief Justice John Marshall in 1803, in the famous case of *Marbury v. Madison*, which held that the Court is the final arbiter of what is and is not the law. Marshall famously wrote there: "It is emphatically the province and duty of the judicial department to say what the law is."

Of course, the President has a duty not to undermine his own office, as University of Miami law professor A. Michael Froomkin notes. And, as Kelley points out, the President is bound by his oath of office and the "Take Care clause" to preserve, protect, and defend the Constitution and to "take care" that the laws are faithfully executed. And those duties require, in turn, that the President interpret what is, and is not constitutional, at least when overseeing the actions of executive agencies.

However, Bush's actions make it clear that he interprets the coordinate construction approach extremely aggressively. In his view, and the view of his Administration, that doctrine gives him license to overrule and bypass Congress or the courts, based on his own interpretations of the Constitution—even where that violates long-established laws and treaties, counters recent legislation that he has himself signed, or (as shown by recent developments in the Padilla case) involves offering a federal court contradictory justifications for a detention.

This is a form of presidential rebellion against Congress and the courts, and possibly a violation of President Bush's oath of office, as well.

After all, can it be possible that that oath means that the President must uphold the Constitution only as he construes it—and not as the federal courts do?

And can it be possible that the oath means that the President need not uphold laws he simply doesn't like—even though they were validly passed by Congress and signed into law by him?

## ANALYZING BUSH'S DISTURBING SIGNING STATEMENT FOR THE McCAIN ANTI-TORTURE BILL

Let's take a close look at Bush's signing statement on the torture bill. It says:

> The executive branch shall construe Title X in Division A of the Act, relating to detainees, in a manner consistent with the constitutional authority of the President to supervise the unitary executive branch and as Commander in Chief and consistent with the constitutional limitations on the judicial power, which will assist in achieving the shared objective of the

Congress and the President, evidenced in Title X, of protecting the American people from further terrorist attacks.

In this signing statement, Bush asserts not only his authority to internally supervise the "unitary executive branch," but also his power as Commander-in-Chief, as the basis for his interpretation of the law—which observers have noted allows Bush to create a loophole to permit the use of torture when he wants.

Clearly, Bush believes he can ignore the intentions of Congress. Not only that but by this statement, he has evinced his intent to do so, if he so chooses.

On top of this, Bush asserts that the law must be consistent with "constitutional limitations on judicial power." But what about presidential power? Does Bush see any constitutional or statutory limitations on that? And does this mean that Bush will ignore the courts, too, if he chooses—as he attempted, recently, to do in the Padilla case?

## THE UNITARY EXECUTIVE DOCTRINE VIOLATES THE SEPARATION OF POWERS

As *Findlaw* columnist Edward Lazarus recently showed, the President does not have unlimited executive authority, not even as Commander-in-Chief of the military. Our government was purposely created with power split between three branches, not concentrated in one.

Separation of powers, then, is not simply a talisman: It is the foundation of our system. James Madison wrote in *The Federalist Papers,* No. 47, that: "The accumulation of all powers, legislative, executive, and judiciary, in the same hands, whether of one, a few, or many, and whether hereditary, self-appointed, or elective, may justly be pronounced the very definition of tyranny."

Another early American, George Nicholas, eloquently articulated the concept of "power divided" in one of his letters:

The most effectual guard which has yet been discovered against the abuse of power, is the division of it. It is our happiness to have a constitution which contains within it a sufficient limitation to the power granted by it, and also a proper division of that power. But no constitution affords any real security to liberty unless it is considered as sacred and preserved inviolate; because that security can only arise from an actual and not from a nominal limitation and division of power.

Yet it seems a nominal limitation and division of power—with real power concentrated solely in the "unitary executive"—is exactly what President Bush seeks. His signing statements make the point quite clearly, and his overt refusal to follow the laws illustrates that point: In Bush's view, there is no actual limitation or division of power; it all resides in the executive.

Thomas Paine wrote in *Common Sense*: "In America, the law is king. For as in absolute governments the King is law, so in free countries the law ought to be king; and there ought to be no other."

The unitary executive doctrine conflicts with Paine's principle—one that is fundamental to our constitutional system. If Bush can ignore or evade laws, then the law is no longer king. Americans need to decide whether we are still a country of laws—and if we are, we need to decide whether a President who has determined to ignore or evade the law has not acted in a manner contrary to his trust as President and subversive of constitutional government.

·   ·   ·

## DAMAGE CONTROL

After President George W. Bush signed the controversial Military Commissions Act [in October 2006], the Justice Department wasted no time in using its new power to deny due process to the detainees swept up in the "war on terror." Now that the bill which Sen. Patrick Leahy called "un-American" has become law, countless hours and dollars will be spent by public interest law organizations trying to undo its damage. In addition to challenges of the provisions that strip *habeas corpus* rights, we can expect constitutional challenges to the military commission procedures and amendments to the War Crimes Act.

The MCA is an unprecedented power grab by the executive branch. Among the Act's worst features, it authorizes the president to detain, without charges, anyone whom he deems an unlawful enemy combatant. This includes U.S. citizens. It eliminates *habeas corpus* review for aliens. It also makes providing "material support" to terrorists punishable by military commission. And the military commissions' procedures allow for coerced testimony, the use of "sanitized classified information"—where the source is not disclosed—and trial for offenses not historically subject to trial by military commissions. (Terrorism is not historically a military offense; it's a crime.) Finally, by amending the War Crimes Act, it allows the president to authorize interrogation techniques that may nonetheless violate the Geneva Conventions and provides future and retroactive "defenses" for those who engage in or authorize those acts.

According to former Justice Department attorney Marty Lederman, who opposed the Act, "the primary impact of the Military Commissions Act is" not to establish military commissions, but "to attempt to eliminate any judicial checks on the Executive's conduct of the conflict against al-Qaida." Conservative law professor John Yoo, a supporter of the Act, writes, "In the struggle for power between the three branches of government, it is not the presidency that 'won.' Instead, it is the judiciary that lost."

As Yoo himself admits, "The new law is, above all, a stinging rebuke to the Supreme Court." Several Supreme Court decisions in the last two years struck down Rumsfeld's previous military commissions and combatant status review tribunals, and granted Guantánamo alien detainees and citizens held in military custody in the U.S. the right to challenge their detentions via *habeas corpus* petitions in U.S. courts. The Bush administration argued against these positions (and indeed, the administration's belief that Guantánamo was not subject to U.S. court jurisdiction was the main reason it chose that as its detention site).

Congress has now, in effect, struck down these Supreme Court decisions that struck down previous executive decisions and actions. What next?

## HABEAS FOR SOME, NOT ALL

The first challenges to the numerous provisions in the MCA will undoubtedly be about the *habeas corpus*-stripping provisions. *Habeas corpus* is the right to have a court determine the legality of one's imprisonment before trial. The U.S. Constitution states that "the privilege of the writ of *habeas corpus* shall not be suspended, unless when in cases of rebellion or invasion, the public safety may require it."

Advocates of the MCA claim that *habeas* has never applied to foreign combatants captured on the battlefield. This claim begs the question: In the "war on terror," how do you know where the battlefield is and how do you know who foreign combatants are? *Habeas* exists exactly for the purpose of challenging wrongful detentions, and in the "war on terror," it has already become abundantly clear that as many as 95 percent of the detentions may be wrongful.

The MCA contains two provisions that strip detainees of their right to *habeas corpus*. One provides that:

> . . . *no court, justice, or judge shall have jurisdiction to hear or consider any claim or cause of action whatsoever*, including any action pending on or filed after the date of the enactment of the Military Commissions Act of 2006 . . . *including challenges to the lawfulness of procedures of military commissions* . . .

The second provision, amending the habeas statute, adds the following:

> No court, justice, or judge shall have jurisdiction to hear or consider an application for a writ of habeas corpus filed by or on behalf of an alien detained by the United States who has been determined by the United States to have been properly detained as an enemy combatant or is awaiting such determination.

It would be surprising if these provisions were not immediately challenged. And those best situated to challenge them are, of course, those who stand to lose the most: the detainees who have already filed *habeas corpus* petitions.

The Justice Department has already asked the D.C. Circuit Court to dismiss 196 of these cases without any determination about the merits of the claims or the guilt or innocence of the petitioners. These cases involve people who have already spent several years in detention without any charges while their *habeas* petitions work their way through the courts.

In essence, the *habeas*-stripping law throws every alien detainee back to legal minus zero. In other words, such detainees cannot challenge their detentions; they must first challenge the law that disallows them from challenging the detentions. These detainees are not back to where they started; they are back to *before* where they started.

What will happen is this: after the government moves to dismiss the cases and the petitioners argue against dismissal (the D.C. Circuit Court has already ordered supplemental briefing in two packets of cases on the issue), the D.C. Circuit will either agree it no longer has jurisdiction (because the MCA stripped it) or it will rule that the MCA *habeas*-stripping provision is unconstitutional and the Constitution allows (or even requires) them to consider the petitioners' claims. If the Circuit court rules in favor of the government, the petitioners will appeal; if the court rules in favor of the petitioners, the government will appeal. Either way, these cases will undoubtedly be consolidated and appealed to the Supreme Court.

Meantime, of course, the detainees remain in detention. Remember, detention centers are not hotels. Consistent abuse, humiliation, beatings, and even torture have been documented at these places. Further, recall that there is credible evidence that a great number of these detainees are not terrorists.

## SECRET EVIDENCE, HEARSAY AND COERCION, OH MY

Other challenges will be about military commission procedures and rules of evidence that have generated controversy because they violate traditional norms of fair trial and due process. The Act permits the admission of hearsay—a general no–no in federal courts, and for good reason, since any witness can simply make up what someone else says and the accused has no way to challenge its validity. Appeals on hearsay would likely be joined with other evidentiary, procedural, and substantive matters, although it is unlikely that hearsay appeals alone would be successful, since the D.C. Circuit Court will probably be deferential to the military commission findings.

Another MCA provision likely to be challenged will almost certainly be the section that allows the use of secret evidence where "disclosure would be detrimental to the national security." Challenges to the use of secret evidence were made in the immigration context long before 9/11. The practice of using secret evidence showed such troubling results that in 1999, Congress nearly passed the Secret Evidence Repeal Act (SERA) "to ensure that no alien is removed, denied a benefit under the Immigration and Nationality Act, or otherwise deprived of liberty, based on evidence that is kept secret from the alien."

In the context of military commissions, where detainees can be sentenced to death, the concern over the use of secret evidence is magnified, and the practice will undoubtedly be challenged at some point by detainees. However, despite these concerns, courts—including the conservative D.C. Circuit Court—have shown a reluctance to second-guess government assertions of the need for secrecy. Thus, it is unlikely that any appeals will be won on this basis alone.

Another troubling provision allows coerced testimony to be admitted into evidence where the military panel decides it is "reliable and possessing sufficient probative value" and "the interests of justice would best be served by admission of the statement into evidence." This clause appears to promote the use of coercion. What it means is that if either the detainee or a witness against him makes statements under coercion (which by some definitions might include torture)—normally inadmissible in court—his admissions can be used against the detainee. How a commission judge could determine the reliability of such testimony or what standard he would use to determine what is "in the interests of justice" are troubling uncertainties. Detainees will almost certainly argue that this provision is unconstitutional, but again challenges on this basis may fall on deaf ears.

Another traditional feature of due process in American courts that the Act removes is the accused's right to "discovery"—or to carry out his or her own investigation. Under the MCA, while the accused is permitted to present evidence in his defense, may cross-examine witnesses, and "shall receive the assistance of counsel" (or may represent himself), he has no right "to conduct his own investigation into the facts using the process of the court." This is also likely to be challenged by detainees.

It is worth remarking that all these provisions will likely be challenged as being in violation of the Supreme Court's 2006 ruling in *Hamdan v. Rumsfeld,* which overturned the administration's previous military commissions, noting that the Code of Military Justice could satisfy due process requirements.

Detainees will also likely challenge the provisions that strip them of the right to claim any protections under the Geneva Conventions. Loyola Law School professor David Glazier notes that: "For several reasons, [the Geneva Conventions] form a logical starting point for any effort to identify potential procedural constraints on the conduct of trials under the law of war."

But, again, federal courts have not widely favored application of Geneva as the basis for individual rights, despite Geneva's requirement that its protections be incorporated into the laws of countries who adopted it.

Finally, the MCA helps to shield U.S. personnel from being held responsible for abuses committed during detentions or interrogations. This is widely considered to be the Bush administration's primary motive in pushing this legislation: To keep Bush administration officials and others from being held accountable for war crimes or other grave violations of the laws of war.

While it does not grant absolute immunity, because it provides for defenses against conviction, the MCA makes it very difficult for a detainee to bring any lawsuit against U.S. personnel or officials for war and other selected crimes committed against him.

The MCA also modified the definitions of war crimes, including torture, narrowing the definitions in such a way as to permit certain forms of interrogation which may constitute torture under international law.

## WHAT'S THE UPSHOT?

Since the MCA was passed in early October, legal scholars have pointed out its weaknesses. It is a poorly drafted law, vague and overbroad to the extent that scholars cannot predict how courts will determine what some provisions mean.

But if courts are stripped from reviewing it at all, if a court may not review poorly drafted and internally contradictory laws, who will determine whether they are lawful or constitutional?

The commission procedures do not meet the requirements set forth by the Supreme Court, by the Military Code of Justice, or by due process. Given that these procedures apply only to detainees who have been designated for trial (not all detainees will necessarily be tried—many may just be held indefinitely without any legal process), one must conclude that the MCA does not give detainees an adequate mechanism—i.e., *habeas corpus*—for challenging their detentions.

What kind of law provides imprisonment without the right of *habeas* or punishment without legitimate appeal? Without those standards, the law is just "victor's justice"—which is no justice at all. The Second World War is often understood to have come about at least in part as a result of the humiliation exacted upon Germans by the victors at the end of the First World War. Victor's justice breeds resentment. It breeds more war.

---

### DISCUSSION QUESTIONS

1. What does Van Bergen mean by the theory of the "unitary" executive? How does it justify the expansion of presidential power? How does it relate to the Military Commissions Act and other actions of the Bush administration?
2. Supporters of President Bush might argue that his expansion of presidential power is necessary in order to confront new dangers and threats such as terrorism. How would you respond to this argument?

**28** *Joseph G. Peschek*

# GEORGE W. BUSH'S IMPERIAL PRESIDENCY

*George W. Bush's presidency has involved far-reaching claims of presidential power both at home and abroad. Some political observers have retrieved the concept of the "imperial presidency"—initially put forward during the crisis of the Nixon presidency in the 1970s—to describe the aims of the Bush administration. In this article, political scientist Joseph G. Peschek explores several dimensions of Bush's imperial presidency. In foreign policy, the overarching context of the "war on terrorism" has enabled President Bush to put forward an aggressive foreign policy doctrine that includes the sanctioning of preventive war. Peschek describes the development of the "Bush Doctrine" as an imperial strategy for American global dominance—military, political, and economic. He explains that the Bush administration's decision to go to war against Iraq in 2003 was driven more by the broader imperial goal of enhancing the strategic position of the United States in the Middle East and beyond than by concerns over Iraq's development of weapons of mass destruction. As for internal governance, Bush's focus on national security and antiterrorism has shaped his approach to such issues as internal surveillance, the rights of criminal defendants, and the power of the president to selectively interpret and implement laws passed by Congress. Bush's assertion of wartime presidential powers served to obscure his highly contestable domestic policy record. But by early 2007, with the mounting possibility of defeat in Iraq, there were signs of growing opposition and resistance to Bush's imperial presidency.*

During the 1970s, scholars and political observers began to speak of an "imperial presidency" in which "the constitutional balance between executive power and presidential accountability is upset in favor of executive power," in the words of historian Arthur Schlesinger Jr. This concern over unchecked executive authority was a response to America's war in Vietnam and to the brazen assertion of executive power by President Richard M. Nixon, who after resigning from office stated, "When the president does it, that means that it is not illegal." In this context, there were calls for limits on presidential power, particularly in the areas of war making, intelligence, and covert operations, and a return to a better constitutional balance between the executive and legislative branches. Thirty years later, many

*Source:* The author has written this article specifically for the seventh edition of *Voices of Dissent.*

observers were struck by the imperial nature of George W. Bush's presidency. In this article, I discuss Bush's imperial presidency at two levels. First, the Bush Doctrine in foreign policy seeks to promote an imperial role for the United States in global politics based on American hegemony, unilateralism, and militarization. Second, the Bush administration has sought to elevate the role of the presidency in the American constitutional system and free it from many traditional constitutional and democratic checks and balances in the context of the "war on terrorism." By the beginning of 2007, there was a sense among many observers that Bush's presidency was in crisis. I begin by describing President Bush's attempt to adjust his strategy in Iraq in the face of rising discontent and opposition from the public and from other political and military leaders. I ask you read this analysis of Bush's imperial presidency, completed early in 2007, in light of subsequent developments.

## CHANGE OF COURSE IN IRAQ?

At the beginning of 2007, as President George W. Bush prepared for his last two years in office, it was clear that foreign policy, especially the war in Iraq, would shape his legacy in ways that were scarcely imaginable during the election campaign of 2000. By the end of 2006, more than three thousand U.S. military personnel had been killed in Iraq. This exceeded the number of Americans who died in the September 11, 2001 terrorist attacks. In the deadliest month for American soldiers in over two years, 111 troops were killed in Iraq during December 2006. The number of U.S. casualties, many of an extremely serious nature, was in the tens of thousands. Of course, these numbers were dwarfed by the devastation suffered by Iraqis. According to the United Nations, 1.6 million Iraqis, or 7 percent of the population, had fled the county since March 2003. Researchers from Johns Hopkins University's Bloomberg School of Public Health, working with teams of Iraqi physicians, published a study in British medical journal *Lancet*. They estimated that about 650,000 Iraqis had died in war-related violence from the U.S. invasion in March 2003 through

July 2006. "I don't consider it a credible report," Bush said at a White House news conference. However, many specialists said that the methodology used by the researchers was appropriate for such a study and had been used effectively to estimate war deaths in other conflicts around the world. Even if the number of Iraqi deaths was far lower, say 100,000, this would be the equivalent of over 1 million Americans killed, since the population of Iraq is less than one-tenth that of the United States.

On November 28, 2006, U.S. involvement in the Iraq war exceeded the duration of U.S. participation in World War II. The execution of Saddam Hussein in late December 2006 brought little relief, as it was widely viewed as a vengeful sectarian killing likely to inflame tensions between Sunni and Shi'ite Muslims. The execution was filmed with a cell phone, revealing that the deposed dictator was taunted with shouts of "Muqtada, Muqtada" from followers of radical Shi'ite cleric Muqtada al-Sadr and his Mahdi militia, which had infiltrated the Iraqi Interior Ministry and the government of Prime Minister Nouri al-Maliki. As Middle East specialist Juan Cole noted, "Instead of promoting national reconciliation, this act of revenge helped Saddam portray himself one last time as a symbol of Sunni Arab resistance, and become one more incitement to sectarian warfare."

On January 10, 2007, in a long-delayed, nationally televised address, Bush laid out his plans for an escalation of U.S. involvement in Iraq, featuring a surge of more than 21,000 American troops to Baghdad and the Sunni stronghold of Anbar province. Despite a widespread consensus that the U.S. mission in Iraq had damaged international antiterrorism efforts, the presidency continued to portray the Iraq war and the struggle against terrorism as inextricably linked. "Tonight in Iraq, the Armed Forces of the United States are engaged in a struggle that will determine the direction of the global war on terror—and our safety here at home. The new strategy I outline tonight will change America's course in Iraq, and help us succeed in the fight against terror," the president asserted.

Bush's surge strategy had been opposed by many senior military commanders, members of Congress, civilian experts, and ordinary citizens.

General John Abazaid, the outgoing commander of the U.S. Central Command, told the Senate Armed Services Committee, "I met with every divisional commander. . . . And I said, in your professional opinion, if we were to bring in more American troops now, does it add considerably to our ability to achieve success in Iraq? And they all said no." After Bush's speech, members of his administration met with growing skepticism and even hostility from congressional Democrats and Republicans alike. Republican Senator Chuck Hagel, a Vietnam veteran, told Secretary of State Condoleezza Rice, "I have to say that I think this speech given last night by this president represents the most dangerous foreign policy blunder for this country since Vietnam." A National Intelligence Estimate (NIE) completed by the U.S. intelligence community in early 2007 characterized the conflict in Iraq as a "civil war." The NIE stressed that the violence in Iraq was internally generated and sustained and was not the result of meddling by outside influences such as Iran. According to the report, it was unlikely that the addition of more U.S. troops would make a significant difference in achieving a political settlement, "given the current winner-take-all attitude and sectarian animosities infecting the political scene."

After Bush's Iraq strategy speech, Scott Reed, a Republican strategist, said, "Republicans are now in an every-man-for themselves mode, bordering on survival." An AP-Ipsos poll conducted during the week of Bush's speech found that just 35 percent of respondents thought it was right for the United States to go to war in Iraq, down from 66 percent two years before. A *Washington Post*–ABC News poll conducted after the president's speech found that 61 percent opposed Bush's force increase, with 52 percent "strongly" opposing the buildup. Americans disapproved of Bush's leadership on Iraq by nearly a 2–1 margin. In a new high for this poll, 57 percent said that the United States was losing the war in Iraq. A *Los Angeles Times*/Bloomberg poll found that half of those surveyed believed that Bush deliberately misled the United States in making his case for invading Iraq. In response to these expressions of nonsupport, Secretary of Defense Robert Gates stated, "Quite honestly I think [Bush]

believes that sometimes the president has to take actions that contemporaneously don't have the broad support of the American people because sometimes he has a longer view."

## PUBLIC OPPOSITION AND THE ELECTIONS OF 2006

During the 2006 congressional election campaign, President Bush stumped for Republicans by touting his party's approach to national security and by tying the war in Iraq to the war on terrorism, as he had done in 2002 and 2004. At a rally in Georgia, Bush said, "The Democrat approach in Iraq comes down to this: The terrorists win and America loses. . . . The Democrat goal is to get out of Iraq. The Republican goal is to win in Iraq. We will not run from thugs and assassins." In a Pennsylvania campaign appearance, Bush stated, "If we were to follow the Democrats' prescriptions and withdraw from Iraq, we would be fulfilling Osama bin Laden's highest aspirations. We should at least be able to agree that the path to victory is not to do exactly what the terrorists want." Four days before the election, Bush reaffirmed his doctrine of preventive war, telling a rally in Missouri, "One of the lessons of September the 11th is that when we see a threat we have got to take that threat seriously before it materializes. It's an essential lesson in this new war. I saw a threat in Saddam Hussein."

This time it did not work. In what President Bush characterized as a "thumping" for his party, the elections resulted in the Democrats taking majorities in the U.S. Senate and House of Representatives. Polls showed that the Iraq war was the foremost single issue on the minds of voters. According to a *New York Times*/CBS News poll conducted shortly before November 7 elections, only 29 percent of Americans approved of the way Bush was managing the war and nearly 70 percent said that Bush did not have a plan to end the war. Just 20 percent said they thought that the United States was winning in Iraq, down from 36 percent in January 2006. According to a Pew Research Center analysis, 59 percent of voters said that they were either "dissatisfied" (30 percent) or "angry" (29 percent) with the president. By more than 2–1, those dissatisfied with Bush supported the Democratic candidate in their district. Among those angry with the president, the margin was more than 15–1. Public concern about the Iraq debacle eroded and neutralized the Republican's traditional edge over the Democrats on national security issues. Exit polls showed that Republicans had a narrow 53–46 percent margin among voters who said terrorism was an extremely important factor in their vote, while Democrats had a large 60–38 percent advantage among those who said Iraq was extremely important.

After the 2006 elections, public dissatisfaction with the Iraq War and Bush's conduct of it intensified. By December, according to a CBS News poll, 43 percent of respondents said that the United States should keep fighting in Iraq, but with new tactics, while 50 percent said that the United States should begin to end its involvement altogether. Only 4 percent said that the United States should keep fighting as it was then doing. Just 21 percent approved of President Bush's handling of the war, the lowest number he had ever received and an 8-point drop from just a month before. Most of that drop took place among Republicans and conservatives. Three-quarters of Americans now disapproved of the way the president was handling Iraq. The poll revealed that opposition to the war was now taking on historic proportions, with 62 percent saying it was "a mistake" to send U.S. troops to Iraq, slightly more than those who told a Gallup Poll in 1973 that it was a mistake to send U.S. forces to Vietnam. Americans generally agreed with the assessment of the Iraq Study Group (ISG), which called the situation in Iraq "grave and deteriorating."

Pessimism about Iraq deepened within the ranks of the military itself. A poll conducted in late 2006 by the *Military Times,* the publisher of weekly newspapers for the armed forces, showed for the first time that more troops disapproved of the president's handling of the war than approved of it. Only 35 percent of military members polled in 2006 said that they approved of the way Bush was handling the war, and 42 percent said they disapproved. In addition, only 41 percent of the military said that the United States should have gone to war in Iraq, down from 65 percent in 2003.

In Iraq itself, a September 2006 poll by the Project on International Policy Attitudes at the University of Maryland found that a large majority of Iraqis—71 percent—said that they would like the Iraqi government to ask for U.S.-led forces to be withdrawn from Iraq within a year or less. Given four options, 37 percent took the position that they would like U.S.-led forces withdrawn "within six months," while another 34 percent opted for "gradually withdraw[ing] U.S.-led forces according to a one-year timeline." Twenty percent favored a two-year timeline and just 9 percent favored "only reduc[ing] U.S.-led forces as the security situation improves in Iraq." Strikingly, support for attacks against U.S.-led forces increased sharply to 61 percent (27 percent "strongly" and 34 percent "somewhat"), representing a 14-point increase from January 2006, when only 47 percent of Iraqis supported attacks.

Bush and his team dismissed the significance of the November congressional elections and public opinion for Iraq policy. On January 14, Vice President Cheney told Fox News Sunday host Chris Wallace, "I don't think any president worth his salt can afford to make decisions of this magnitude according to the polls." Cheney continued:

> And if we have a president who looks at the polls and sees the polls are going south and concludes, "Oh, my goodness, we have to quit," all it will do is validate the Al Qaeda view of the world. It's exactly the wrong thing to do. This president does not make policy based on public opinion polls; he should not. It's absolutely essential here that we get it right.

## BUSH'S IMPERIAL FOREIGN POLICY

During one of his debates with Al Gore during the presidential election campaign of 2000, George W. Bush stated, "If we're an arrogant nation, they'll resent us. If we're a humble nation, they'll welcome us." As I have explained in previous editions of *Voices of Dissent,* in the year after September 11, the Bush administration put together the elements of a far-from-humble foreign policy doctrine based on unilateral action, preemptive military strikes, and prevention of the emergence of any strategic rivals to U.S. supremacy. Bush's grand strategy was formalized in a September 17, 2002 presidential report called *The National Security Strategy of the United States of America*. Maintaining a skeptical view of multilateral action and international treaties, the report argued for preemptive strikes against rogue states and terrorists, even if faced with international opposition, and for the maintenance of American military supremacy. In his introduction to the report, Bush contended that "America will act against such emerging threats before they are fully formed. . . . History will judge harshly those who saw the coming danger but failed to act. In the new world we have entered, the only path to peace and security is the path of action." While many commentators interpreted the national security strategy document as endorsing preemptive military action, it might more accurately be seen as attempting to legitimate the radical concept of "preventive" war, or a decision to attack now to prevent a real or potential adversary from becoming a substantial threat in the future. As Rahul Mahajan, a leader of Peace Action and the National Network to End the War Against Iraq, comments, "Since such a justification could easily be used by any country to attack any other, it's long been understood in international legal circles that preventive war is completely illegitimate."

Such actions are described as "anticipatory" or "preemptive" in the report. They are justified by the nature of new adversaries, who cannot be deterred by conventional measures: "Given the goals of rogue states and terrorists, the United States can no longer rely on a reactive posture as we have in the past." The United States must be prepared to aggressively defend its interests on its own terms. If necessary, it is legitimate for the United States to engage in a defensive first strike against governments that aid or harbor terrorists or pursue the development of weapons of mass destruction. "Traditional concepts of deterrence will not work against a terrorist enemy whose avowed tactics are wanton destruction and the targeting of innocents," the report stated. "America will act against such emerging threats before they are fully formed." The report made clear that the United States will act against its enemies even if

it does not have international support: "While the U.S. will constantly strive to enlist the support of the international community, we will not hesitate to act alone." Additionally, the report placed the United States off-limits to international law, asserting that the jurisdiction of the International Criminal Court "does not extend to Americans and which we do not accept." Underlying the Bush Doctrine is the notion that the United States must remain the unchallenged power in world affairs. "The United States possesses unprecedented—and unequaled—strength and influence in the world," the report began. Supremacy involves maintaining forces that "will be strong enough to dissuade potential adversaries from pursuing a military build-up in hopes of surpassing, or equaling, the power of the United States."

In the Bush Doctrine, military strength is closely linked to an economic model that might be called "market fundamentalism." There is "a single sustainable model for national success: freedom, democracy, and free enterprise," the report contended. "The lessons of history are clear: market economies, not command-and-control economies with the heavy hand of government, are the best way to promote prosperity and reduce poverty." Seeking to "ignite a new era of global economic growth through free markets and free trade," the report advocated specific neoliberal policies such as "pro-growth legal and regulatory policies," "lower marginal tax rates," and "sound fiscal policies to support business activity."

Finally, the Bush report is based on the premise that the United States is the ultimate guarantor of universal values. The report declared that U.S. national security policy "will be based on a distinctly American internationalism that reflects the union of our values and our national interests." Seeking to make the world "not just safer, but better," the report asserted that the values of freedom "are right and true for every person, in every society—and the duty of protecting these values against their enemies is the common calling of freedom-loving people across the globe and across the ages. . . . The United States welcomes our responsibility to lead in this great mission." Hendrik Hertzberg described the perspective of the Bush report as "a vision of what used to be called, when we believed it to be the Soviet ambition, world domination."

This expansive doctrine of unilateral and preemptive military action and the maintenance of American military and economic supremacy was foreshadowed in several earlier presidential statements. On the night of September 11, 2001, Bush declared on national television, "We will make no distinction between the terrorists who committed these acts and those who harbor them." Four days later, Bush made clear that he did not want other countries setting conditions for the new war on terrorism. "At some point we may be the only ones left. That's okay with me. We are America," the president told his advisors. Addressing a joint session of Congress on September 20, 2001, Bush stated, "Every nation, in every region, now has a decision to make. Either you are with us, or you are with the terrorists. From this day forward, any nation that continues to harbor or support terrorism will be regarded by the United States as a hostile regime."

In his January 2002 statement of the union address, Bush widened the war on terrorism when he identified an "axis of evil" involving Iran, Iraq, and North Korea. Maintaining that "our war on terrorism is only beginning," Bush warned the world that "America will do what is necessary to ensure our nation's security. We'll be deliberate, yet time is not on our side. I will not wait on events while dangers gather. I will not stand by as peril draws closer and closer. The United States of America will not permit the world's most dangerous regimes to threaten us with the world's most destructive weapons." In his speech at West Point in June 2002, the president bundled these post-9/11 statements into a proclamation of strategy. Bush called for preemptive attacks on countries that endanger the United States, arguing that American security required "a military ready to strike at a moment's notice in any dark corner of the world." Rejecting as inadequate the Cold War doctrines of containment and deterrence, Bush said the United States must be "ready for preemptive action when necessary to defend our liberty." Speaking with self-described "moral clarity," Bush proclaimed that

"America has no empire to extend or utopia to establish. We wish for others only what we wish for ourselves—safety from violence, the rewards of liberty, and the hope for a better life."

President Bush and other members of his administration deny in public that the United States has imperial ambitions. As a presidential candidate in 2000, George W. Bush argued, "America has never been an empire. . . . We may be the only great power in history that had the chance, and refused." In his "mission accomplished" remarks aboard the U.S.S. *Abraham Lincoln* on May 1, 2003, Bush reiterated, "Other nations in history have fought in foreign lands and remained to occupy and exploit. Americans, following a battle, want nothing more than to return home." For his part, former defense secretary Donald Rumsfeld maintained, "We're not imperialistic. We never have been."

Several well-connected supporters of the administration are not as shy. One of the most articulate supporters of the Bush Doctrine has been neoconservative intellectual Robert Kagan. In 1996, he commented on American dominance, contending that "hegemony must be actively maintained, just as it was actively obtained. . . . Any lessening of that influence will allow others to play a larger part in shaping the world to suit their needs." Four years later, Kagan and William Kristol argued that American hegemony was no danger to the world, "since the United States does not pursue a narrow, selfish definition of its national interest . . . and infuses its foreign policy with an unusually high degree of morality." Targeting the "confusion about our role in the world," they called for stepped-up U.S. commitment to shape the global order, for "[g]iven the dangers we know, and given the certainty that unknown perils await us over the horizon, there can be no respite from our burden of benevolent global hegemony."

Four days after the start of the U.S. attack on Afghanistan in 2001, neoconservative author Max Boot made "The Case for American Empire," in which he famously asserted that "Afghanistan and other troubled lands today cry out for the sort of enlightened foreign administration once provided by self-confident Englishmen in jodhpurs and pith helmets." He went on to recommend, "Once Afghanistan has been dealt with, America should turn its attention to Iraq. . . . Once we have deposed Saddam, we can impose an American-led, international regency on Baghdad, to go along with the one in Kabul. With American credibility and seriousness thus restored, we will enjoy fruitful cooperation from the region's many opportunists, who will show a newfound eagerness to be helpful in our larger task of rolling up the international terror network that threatens us." In May 2003, Boot urged the United States to be prepared to occupy Iraq with troops for years, "possibly decades" and to embrace the practice, if not the term, of imperialism. After all, on the whole, "U.S. imperialism has been the greatest force for good in the world during the past century."

## IRAQ AS TESTING GROUND

What explains the Bush administration's growing focus on "regime change" in Iraq in the year and a half after 9/11? The Bush administration argued that the war with Iraq was necessary to eliminate Saddam Hussein's arsenal of weapons of mass destruction, to diminish the threat of international terrorism, and to promote democracy in Iraq and the region. Little hard evidence was offered in support of the administration's claims about the dangers of Iraq. The Bush administration's claims that Iraq possessed weapons of mass destruction were deflated after the war when no such weapons were found by the Iraq Survey Group, leading to the resignation of chief weapons inspector David Kay in January 2004. While officials spoke of an "intelligence failure" and Kay stated "we were all wrong," it was clear that the buildup to the war had involved a massive propaganda campaign in which the intelligence process was thoroughly politicized. As Sidney Blumenthal contends, "The truth is that much of the intelligence community did not fail, but presented correct assessments and warnings, that were overridden and suppressed. On virtually every single important claim made by the Bush administration in its case for war, there was serious dissension. Discordant views—not from individual analysts but

from several intelligence agencies as a whole—were kept from the public as momentum was built for a congressional vote on the war resolution." Blumenthal's claim was supported by an early 2007 report of the Defense Department's inspector general, which focused on the prewar activities of the Office of Undersecretary of Defense for Policy Douglas Feith, a major neoconservative war hawk. Characterizing the reports issued by Feith's office as "of dubious quality and reliability," the inspector general stated that Feith's team "developed, produced and then disseminated alternative intelligence assessments on the Iraq and Al Qaeda relationship, which included some conclusions that were inconsistent with the consensus of the Intelligence Community, to senior decision-makers."

If the official reasons for the aggressive stance toward Iraq can be refuted, what sort of alternative explanation makes sense? In my view, Iraq represents an opportunity to implement the broad imperial strategy underlying the Bush Doctrine. The Bush administration dismissed options for the containment and deterrence of Iraq because these measures would not allow for the expansion of American power in the region. As Jay Bookman of the *Atlanta Journal-Constitution* wrote, "This war, should it come, is intended to mark the official emergence of the United States as a full-fledged global empire, seizing sole responsibility and authority as planetary policeman. It would be the culmination of a plan 10 years or more in the making, carried out by those who believe the United States must seize the opportunity for global domination, even if it means becoming the 'American imperialists' that our enemies always claimed we were." Writer and activist Tariq Ali made a similar point: "The Iraq war is a demonstration occupation of a country not just for the Arab world or to appease Israel—that's a part of it—but the big game is to show the rest of the world who the United States is and what it's capable of doing."

The conquest of Iraq, were it successful, would also provide an opportunity to realize two more specific U.S. imperial goals: the establishment of new U.S. military bases in the Middle East and the securing of more reliable control over Iraq's vast oil supplies. In January 2003, the U.S. Department of Energy stated that by 2025, imports would account for about 70 percent of U.S. domestic demand, up from 55 percent in 2001. The United States, with only 2 percent of the world's known oil reserves, uses 25 percent of the world's annual output. Estimates from the Energy Department are that Iraq has as much as 220 billion barrels in "probable and possible" reserves, making the estimated total enough to cover U.S. annual oil imports at their current levels for ninety-eight years. However, reference to oil interests alone is an insufficient account of U.S. foreign policy in the Middle East. Oil and other energy and economic interests must be linked to broader U.S. geopolitical and geoeconomic goals to adequately explain the campaign against Iraq. As foreign policy analyst Michael Klare argues, an explanation of the real reason for the Bush administration's campaign to oust Saddam Hussein must include "the pursuit of oil and the preservation of America's status as the paramount world power."

By 2006, it was apparent to many in the U.S. foreign policy establishment that Bush's adventure in Iraq was a disaster of historic proportions from the standpoint of the long-term interests of U.S. global power. In this context, the Iraq Study Group, a bipartisan group authorized by Congress, issued its report in December. The ISG was chaired by former secretary of state James Baker and former representative Lee Hamilton. It was made up of five Democrats and five Republicans, all of whom had held high-level political positions and none of whom had ever expressed unorthodox views on U.S. foreign policy. While the ISG took a dire view of the situation in Iraq, calling it "grave and deteriorating," in many ways its report represented a classic ruling class damage control operation in which fundamental assumptions of the policy were not questioned. As historian and military analyst Andrew J. Bacevich noted, "Their [the ISG] purpose is two fold: first, to minimize Iraq's impact on the prevailing foreign policy consensus with its vast ambitions and penchant for armed intervention abroad; and second, to quell any inclination of ordinary citizens to intrude into matters from which they have long been excluded. The ISG is antidemocratic. Its

implicit message to Americans is this: We'll handle things. Now go back to holiday shopping."

Disavowing any purely military solution, the ISG report's seventy-nine recommendations included downscaling of the U.S. military presence in Iraq and U.S. engagement with Syria and Iran. As such, the ISG maintained a more "realist" position in foreign policy debates with the overreaching and messianic "neoconservatives." But far from holding out an actual exit strategy, the ISG report shared in several ways Bush's imperial strategy for dominating the Middle East and its resources, while differing on the means. While the report recommended that U.S. combat brigades be largely withdrawn from Iraq by early 2008, combat brigades represent less than half of all troops in Iraq. Moreover, the withdrawn troops could be redeployed to U.S. military bases in neighboring countries, creating a "considerable military presence in the region, with our still-significant force in Iraq, and with our air, ground, and naval deployments in Kuwait, Bahrain, and Qatar," in the words of the report. After noting that Iraq "has the world's second-largest known oil reserves," the ISG report states, "The United States should encourage investment in Iraq's oil sector by the international community and by international energy companies." Furthermore, Recommendation 63 advocates that the "United States should assist Iraqi leaders to reorganize the national oil industry as a commercial enterprise, in order to enhance efficiency, transparency and accountability." As *Monthly Review* Editor John Bellamy Foster explains, "In other words, the goal is the privatization of the Iraqi oil industry to an extent that does not currently exist for any major petroleum-exporting country. This will open up the country's oil fields to full exploitation by foreign corporations."

After the ISG presented its report at the White House, President Bush called it a "serious study" and "very instructive." He then proceeded to disavow its very modest and realistic recommendations and insisted that his goal remained "victory" in Iraq. After a strategic review, Bush unveiled his plans for a surge or escalation of U.S. military forces in Iraq. Once again, it appeared that President Bush had sided with hard-line neoconservative foreign policy advocates affiliated with the American Enterprise Institute think tank and allied with hawkish politicians such as Senators John McCain and Joseph Lieberman. By late January 2007, the prospect of a wider Middle East war in the form of a U.S. confrontation with Iran, a nation of 70 million, could not be dismissed. Bush confirmed the existence of a program to apprehend and kill Iranian military and intelligence operatives in Iraq. This followed bellicose threats by Bush against Iran and Syria in several speeches, a U.S. raid on an Iranian consulate in northern Iraq, and the dispatch of a nuclear-armed aircraft carrier battle group to Gulf waters near Iran. Bush's proposed Pentagon budget for fiscal year 2008—over $600 billion—would be the largest in inflation-adjusted dollars since World War II. Despite the growing disaffection from the fiasco in Iraq, it would seem premature to rule out further U.S. imperial ventures in the Middle East.

## EXECUTIVE POWER UNTETHERED

President Bush has described himself as the "decider." Indeed, as Jennifer Van Bergen emphasizes in her article in this chapter, Bush's presidency has involved extraordinary claims by the chief executive to decide on any number of important questions that in the past involved the legislative and judicial branches. Perhaps Bush's understanding of executive power rests on the worldview of a presidential aide who told writer Ron Suskind, "We're an empire now, and when we act, we create our own reality. And while you're studying that reality—judiciously, as you will—we'll act again, creating other new realities, which you can study too, and that's how things will sort out. We're history's actors . . . and you, all of you, will be left to just study what we do."

Expansive claims for presidential power during wartime are not unprecedented in U.S. history, as the actions of Abraham Lincoln during the Civil War and of Franklin D. Roosevelt during World War II make clear. President Bush's legal and political advisors have attempted to develop a doctrine justifying the unleashing of presidential power centering on the concept of the "unitary executive,"

which Jennifer Van Bergen defines as holding that "the executive branch can overrule the courts and Congress on the basis of the president's own interpretations of the Constitution, in effect overturning *Marbury v. Madison* (1803), which established the principle of judicial review, and the constitutional concept of checks and balances." Two weeks after the September 11 attacks, Deputy Assistant Attorney General John Yoo laid out the rationale for unaccountable presidential power: "In the exercise of his plenary power to use military force, the President's decisions are for him alone and are unreviewable."

In line with this doctrine, Bush has used "signing statements" to a greater extent than all previous presidents combined. A signing statement, issued when the president signs a bill into law, describes his interpretation of the bill and declares that some of its provisions may be unconstitutional and thus need not be enforced or obeyed as written. According to the *Boston Globe,* among the laws Bush has claimed the power to disobey are a torture ban and oversight provisions of the USA Patriot Act. As *Globe* reporter Charlie Savage explains, when Bush signed the 2007 military budget bill, he issued a statement challenging sixteen of its provisions, one of which bars the Pentagon from "using any intelligence that was collected illegally, including information about Americans that was gathered in violation of the Fourth Amendment's protections against unreasonable government surveillance." Bush's signed statement instructed the military to view the law in terms of the "president's constitutional authority as commander in chief, including the conduct of intelligence agencies, and to supervise the unitary executive branch."

Many other policies of the Bush administration grow out of the notion of inherent presidential power, including indefinite detention of suspects, the legitimation of torture against detainees, and the use of third country "renditions" in which foreign citizens are apprehended and shipped to countries for "interrogation" on behalf of the U.S. government. Until January 2007, Bush claimed the right to engage in illegal wiretapping in defiance of the 1978 Foreign Intelligence Surveillance Act, which requires court order red warrants for such monitoring. Many accounts point to the office of Vice President Cheney as a forceful advocate of these measures. Under President Ford in the 1970s, Cheney, as chief of staff, resented the modest rollback of presidential power in the post-Watergate era. In 2002, Cheney stated that the presidency "was weaker today as an institution because of the unwise compromises that have been made over the last 30 to 35 years." Along with advancing an imperial foreign policy, a key goal of the Bush presidency has been to assert almost unfettered and unaccountable presidential power in the U.S. system of government.

As I have explained in the previous editions of *Voices of Dissent,* Bush's war on terrorism has served to displace and divert attention from potentially troublesome domestic conditions and policies impacting working Americans. Many employees are seeing sharp declines in health care and pension benefits provided by employers. Despite the series of tax cuts promoted by President Bush and Congressional Republicans as the best way to stimulate the economy, income growth in the Bush years has been sluggish and uneven. In the quarter century from 1979 to 2004, average income rose 27 percent in real terms, according to a *New York Times* analysis, "but the gains were concentrated at the top and offset by losses for the bottom 60 percent of Americans, those making $38,761 in 2004. The bottom 60 percent of Americans, on average, made less than 95 cents in 2004 for each dollar they reported in 1979." Meanwhile, Census Bureau data showed that the portion of national income earned by the top 20 percent of households grew to 50.4 percent in 2005, up from 45.6 in 1985, while the bottom 60 percent of households received 26.6 percent, down from 29.9 percent in 1985. The richest 10 percent of Americans own 70 percent of the nation's wealth.

A Bloomberg/*Los Angeles Times* poll reported in December 2006 found that three-quarters of Americans believe that economic inequality is a major issue. A majority of Republicans—55 percent—agreed. Even Federal Reserve Chair Ben Bernanke warned of the "painful dislocations" associated with capitalism and stated that if "we did not place some limits on the downside risks to individuals affected by economic change, the public at large might become less willing to accept the dynamism that is so essential to economic progress." While Bernanke worries about disillusionment with the "dynamism" of the economy, I would argue that developing a critical perspective on all our major institutions—political and economic—contributes more to a healthy democracy than worshipping at the golden calf of the market. Seeing through the many costs associated with the "imperial presidency" is a vital step in this process.

---

## DISCUSSION QUESTIONS

1. Peschek argues that President Bush's decision to go to war against Iraq reflects a broader "imperial" foreign policy strategy. What evidence does Peschek provide to support this argument and how compelling do you find it?

2. Peschek quotes Secretary of Defense Robert Gates that "sometimes the president has to take actions that contemporaneously don't have the broad support of the American people because sometimes he has a longer view." In your view, how justifiable is this claim of presidential power? As a defense of President Bush's decisions, how compelling do you find it?

3. In what ways has President Bush sought to free presidential power from traditional, constitutional, and democratic checks and balances in the context of the "war on terrorism"? Again how justifiable are these claims of presidential power?

# CHAPTER **8**

# LAW AND THE COURTS

L aw and courts play a central role in settling political conflicts in the United States, a point driven home by the Supreme Court decision that effectively decided the presidential election of 2000. In part, this reflects the dominance of classic liberal thought in America, with its emphasis on resolving disputes through formal procedures. Certainly there is no denying we are a very litigious country, with a presence of lawyers and lawsuits that outstrips most, if not all, of the world's other nations. We also know that a good number of you, political science majors and students in political science courses, are on the road to law school. The articles in this chapter explore connections between law and politics in our legalistic culture and depict courts and judges as *political* actors whose values and practices usually reinforce the structure of power discussed in Part I.

Because we have a written Constitution that declares itself to be the supreme law of the land, who is authorized to interpret that Constitution becomes a crucial question. In our system, courts, especially the Supreme Court, have assumed this power of judicial review. The 1787 Constitution provided for a separate judicial branch of government but left its powers unclear. In *Federalist Paper 78,* Alexander Hamilton, an advocate of a strong central union, argued for a judiciary with the power to declare acts of the other branches of government unconstitutional. Thomas Jefferson, in contrast, feared the antidemocratic nature of Hamilton's argument, especially because the Constitution exempts the Court from direct democratic control. Jefferson argued that all three branches of government, within their assigned spheres of power, have important constitutional roles to play. The Court, he reasoned, is not the sole arbiter of constitutional questions. And government, ultimately, is answerable to the people. Hamilton's position triumphed when the Supreme Court under John Marshall, who was chief justice from 1801 to 1835, asserted the power of judicial review in the historic *Marbury v. Madison* case of 1803.

**29** *Carl Swidorski*

# CORPORATIONS, THE LAW, AND DEMOCRACY

*In this article political scientist Carl Swidorski examines the role of the courts, especially the Supreme Court, in facilitating the development of a capitalist economy and enhancing corporate power. He views law as an arena of political, economic, and social struggles between groups and classes that have taken place throughout U.S. history. Swidorski examines key legal developments related to property rights in the nineteenth century. Next he turns to the transformation of economic doctrines by the Supreme Court to support an emerging corporate-administrative state during and after the New Deal of the 1930s. Swidorski critically examines the important issue of extending First Amendment free speech rights to corporations and the wealthy (see also the next article by Cass Sunstein). He concludes with a discussion of the implications of these developments for politics and democracy in the United States today.*

Stocks are property, yes.
Bonds are property, yes.
Machines, land, buildings, are property, yes.
A job is property,
no, nix, nah nah.
(Carl Sandburg, *The People Yes*)

The more we reflect upon all that occurs in the United States, the more we shall be persuaded that the lawyers . . . form the most powerful . . . counterpoise to the democratic element. . . . The courts of justice are the visible organs by which the legal profession is enabled to control democracy . . .

(Alexis de Tocqueville, *Democracy in America*)

*Source:* Adapted by the author from Carl Swidorski, "Corporations and the Law: Historical Lessons for Contemporary Practice." *New Political Science,* no. 28/29, Winter–Spring 1994, pp. 167–189.

At the beginning of a new century, corporations enjoy a privileged legal position in the United States. Corporations can count on the law to protect their property rights and facilitate further transformations of the political economy to their advantage, such as the contemporary shift to a globalized, capitalist economy. In conflicts between corporate economic rights and individual personal rights, the law generally favors corporate rights. Furthermore, over the past three decades, the Supreme Court has extended rights to corporations that previously had been primarily conceived of as individual political rights. These decisions have serious implications for democratic dialogue and government. As Ralph Nader and Carl Mayer state: "Equality of constitutional rights plus an inequality of legislated and de facto powers leads inevitably to the supremacy of artificial over real persons." This privileged position of corporations is primarily due to the crucial structural role corporations have played and continue to play in the U.S. economy. Ideological factors, such as the "normal" way of thinking about law, interrelate with these structural features. The way the law—the language of the state—"knows" society is an important dimension in understanding this privileged legal status.

Since the ratification of the U.S. Constitution in 1788, the development of the law has been a process of struggle among classes and groups with different interests, values, and visions. The social and economic assumptions underlying the Constitution primarily favored the property owning classes who dominated the writing and initial interpretation of the Constitution. As Supreme Court Justice William Paterson said in *Van Hornes's Lessee v. Dorrance* (1795): "The right of acquiring and possessing property, and having it protected, is one of the natural, inherent and inalienable rights of man," and preserving property "is a primary object of the social compact." But the framers' vision and that of their successors has always been contested. Reflecting on the historical development of the law, therefore, can help us understand broader political and economic developments and assess the possibilities for progressive politics today. The law is both an effect and a cause of other political, economic, and social forces—it helps constitute a society.

Structurally, corporations are the key economic institutions in society. Major decisions about what is produced by whom, when, where, and under what conditions, are largely controlled by corporations. Governments rely on corporations for revenue, job creation, and investment. Planning, to the degree it exists, is dominated by corporate decisions. Thus, governments are highly responsive to the needs and demands of corporations because the perceived success of our economy depends on ensuring a "favorable business climate."

Ideologically, the belief in the "rule of law" and its accompanying concepts of state neutrality, justice, equality before the law, and individual freedom often inhibits people from looking at the law as an arena of political and economic struggle. As Bertell Ollman points out, the law serves as a kind of "bourgeois fairy tale" in which "the struggle over the legitimacy of any social act or relationship is removed from the plane of morality to that of law. Justice is no longer what is fair but what is legal, and politics itself is transformed into the technical wranglings of lawyers and courts." This ideological function of law limits the examination of the role that the law has played in facilitating capitalist development and corporate power. Many scholars refuse to acknowledge the insight of Thomas Gray: ". . . [F]ederal courts have through most of the country's history been the guardians of wealth and property against the excesses of democracy." This ideological attachment to the "rule of law" also has had important effects on the political strategies chosen by liberal reformers and progressives, thus functioning to organize dissent into certain types of activity.

The law is an arena of political, economic, and social struggle that reflects and helps shape those struggles. Overall, the results of the class and group struggles in U.S. history have favored corporate power. It is hard to understand how anyone today could argue otherwise. Yet the process of struggle is important. Working people, women, African Americans, gays and lesbians, and others have used the law to fight for their rights and, at times, win important gains. Nonetheless, the fundamental contradiction between political democracy and economic exploitation remains embodied in the law, and corporate power has more often prevailed than not. As Brooks Adams said early in the twentieth century: "The capitalist . . . regards the constitutional form of government which exists in the United States, as a convenient method of obtaining his own way against a majority."

In this article I focus on the role of the courts, especially the Supreme Court, in facilitating the development of a capitalist economy and enhancing corporate power. First, I examine key legal developments related to property rights in the nineteenth century. I also survey the metamorphosis in property and related jurisprudential accommodations during the late nineteenth and early twentieth centuries. The second part of the article focuses on the transformation of economic doctrines by the Supreme Court to legitimate a consolidating corporate-administrative state during and after the New Deal. Within this context, I examine the attempt to extend property rights concepts to the poor and contrast this with the recrudescence of property protections for corporations and the wealthy beginning in the 1970s. I also look at the trend of extending First Amendment free speech rights to corporations and the wealthy. Finally, I conclude with a discussion of the implications of these developments for politics and democracy.

## COURTS AND PROPERTY RIGHTS BEFORE THE NEW DEAL

There were three important dimensions of the relationship between the law, property rights, and capitalist development during this period. First, in the conflict between slave labor and free labor, legal decisions both protected the system of slavery and, at the same time, fostered the growth of a capitalist economy. Second, in the conflicts between labor and capital, the courts were hostile to the attempt of workers to act collectively. Finally, and most importantly, federal courts, state civil law courts, and legislatures incrementally developed the law to favor the interests of dynamic, entrepreneurial, commercial capital over land-based, vested capital. The courts were the most influential economic policymakers

during this period. It was their responsibility, in the words of Stephen Skowronek, "to nurture, protect, interpret, and invoke the state's prerogatives over economy and society as expressed in law."

Slavery was firmly written into the U.S. Constitution. James Ely states: "No other type of property received such detailed attention from the framers." Slaves were an important form of personal property and a major source of wealth for the antebellum South as well as for those Northern economic interests involved in the trans-Atlantic slave trade, the coastal cotton markets, and the manufacture of textiles. The courts protected this form of property. Individual slaves rarely won freedom in cases in which they contested their condition. The system of slavery itself was never seriously questioned by the federal courts. At the same time, courts recognized the power of states to limit the right of owners to maim and kill their slaves. These regulatory laws were passed not so much out of humanitarian concerns but rather because states recognized the value of slave property for the South's economy, and because states were responding to slave rebellions, sabotage, and other forms of collective actions by African Americans protesting their conditions. In this regard, these slave regulations were similar to much other economic regulation upheld by the courts during this period of time under the broad "police powers" of states to legislate for the health, safety, and welfare of the community.

The second major property rights issue of the period involved the conflict between organized labor and capital. After the Civil War, the courts' general hostility toward labor unions would be graphically demonstrated through their authorization of the widespread use of police and military force against striking and picketing workers, their use of the infamous labor injunction, and their hostility toward social welfare legislation that benefited working Americans. The judiciary used the labor injunction not just to control strikes and demonstrations but to limit the associative and expressive activities of workers and their unions. Over 4,300 injunctions were issued against the labor movement between 1880 and 1930, forbidding a wide variety of associative activities including picketing, striking, holding union meetings, communicating through the mail, saying specific words such as "scab" or "fair," and even supplying food to starving workers and their families. In addition to the use of the injunction, courts struck down social welfare laws such as those establishing minimum wages and maximum hours, requiring safe conditions at work, and forbidding child labor. Between 1900 and 1937, the judiciary ruled unconstitutional over two hundred state social welfare laws or laws regulating business on the grounds that they violated the "due process" or "equal protection" of corporations or individuals with property rights claims. Furthermore, between the 1880s and 1920s courts struck down almost three hundred labor laws aimed at protecting workers.

The third category of significant legal developments during this period was the efforts by the courts and legislatures to promote economic development and stimulate investment by favoring the dynamic use of property. J. Willard Hurst calls it "property in motion or at risk rather than property secure and at rest." State legislatures sold or gave away public lands; subsidized businesses; sponsored internal improvement projects, especially in transportation; and passed a variety of other forms of promotional legislation to stimulate commercial activities. States even went so far as to delegate their own governmental powers of eminent domain to business corporations. The Supreme Court under Chief Justice John Marshall (1801–1835) was especially sympathetic to business and propertied interests. Marshall was very committed to creating a national market and distrusted those state regulations that he feared would interfere with the productive use of economic resources. The contract clause was used to protect the nascent form of corporate organization from excessive state regulation, especially in the banking sector, as well as to limit the ability of states to provide relief to debtors and grant exemptions from taxation. The Marshall Court also relied on a broad interpretation of the national commerce power to encourage the growth of a national market system particularly in transportation. Under Roger Taney (1836–1863), the Supreme Court continued this approach, although it was more inclined to permit states greater latitude in shaping economic

policy that stimulated commercial activities and promoted competition. Also, corporations were constitutionally recognized as "persons" for the first time for the purpose of suing in diversity of citizenship cases in the federal courts.

State courts also played a major role in promoting economic growth through the legal system, instead of the tax system. Private law judges interpreting the common law promoted economic development and carried out a major transformation of the legal system. According to Morton Horwitz, their decisions "enabled emergent entrepreneurial and commercial groups to win a disproportionate share of wealth and power in American society." Judges came to view the ownership of property as conferring the right, and indeed obligation, to develop the property. Eminent domain was one of the most potent legal weapons used to further this process of redistributing "old" property for the benefit of the "new." Land was taken for the purposes of building roads, canals, and railroads. Compensation for these takings was limited because entrepreneurial groups resisted full compensation as a threat to low cost economic development. Another method of encouraging economic growth was changing the common law doctrines on liability to force those injured by economic activity to bear many of the costs of growth. Personal or property damage increasingly became seen as an inevitable cost of doing business, largely to be absorbed by the injured. Finally, the law of contract was transformed, ridding it of medieval concepts of fairness and shifting it to principles compatible with a market economy, such as *caveat emptor* (let the buyer beware).

The courts' role in fostering economic development for the advantage of the more powerful continued after the Civil War. Initially, the Supreme Court upheld broad use of government powers over the economy during the Civil War. Furthermore, courts upheld many state laws regulating the economy during the 1870s and 1880s. However, during the 1870s and 1880s, certain judges and lawyers conducted a vigorous campaign to develop the legal doctrine of laissez-faire constitutionalism to protect corporations from regulatory activity. A key decision was the 1886 *Santa Clara County v. Southern*

*Pacific Railroad* ruling that corporations were "persons" within the meaning of the Fourteenth Amendment, having the same rights as natural persons. After this, the Supreme Court regularly struck down the state and national regulatory regulation that it felt to be unduly restrictive of property rights.

While the legal foundation of the corporate-administrative state was laid between 1900 and 1932, the Court's negative reaction to many of the New Deal programs reflected contradictory nineteenth century visions of free enterprise, competitive capitalism, and "free" labor. However, in 1937 the Court underwent a miraculous change of heart and mind and began to uphold regulatory schemes it had just recently rejected. By 1939, FDR had appointed a majority of the Court, and according to conventional wisdom, the new Roosevelt Court rejected those old economic doctrines that had been selectively used to defeat a great deal of regulatory legislation for over half a century. The Court supposedly washed its hands entirely of economic policy making and slowly took up a new agenda of individual political and civil rights. However, the conventional wisdom is substantially misplaced.

# THE MODERN ROLE OF THE LAW: LEGITIMATING THE NEW CORPORATE-ADMINISTRATIVE STATE

The idealized conception of the modern Supreme Court as the guardian of individual rights and defender of transcendental constitutional values has been problematic even for some mainstream political scientists. To Robert Dahl the Court was a legitimator of the political system not a defender of rights. He argued that the Court had "used the protections of the Fifth, Thirteenth, Fourteenth, and Fifteenth Amendments to preserve the rights and liberties of a relatively privileged group at the expense of the rights and liberties of a submerged group, chiefly slaveholders at the expense of slaves, white people at the expense of colored people, and property holders at the expense of wage earners and other groups." Yet subsequent assessments of the Court by political scientists have tended to stress the

Court's role as "guardian of the Constitution." Even mildly debunking analyses still assume the Court is democratic because it plays a vital legitimizing role in a fundamentally fair, pluralistic political system. However, a more realistic assessment of the role of law and the Supreme Court must place the change in the Court's agenda and doctrines within the context of the changes in the modern capitalist economy, especially the relationship among corporations, government, and organized labor.

After 1937, the Court transformed judicial doctrine to ratify the new social contract of big business, the state, and the unions. Under its terms unions became junior partners in return for recognition and protection of their right to organize, promises of higher wages and better working conditions, and various social programs. Government assumed important responsibilities for rationalizing the market and managing the economy. The new social contract did not challenge capitalism or seriously undermine corporate prerogatives. Instead, it used the expertise of the modern state to coordinate, guide, and supplement the functioning of the capitalist economy. The Court also attempted to manage social conflict by ensuring formal, but limited, representation for "legitimate" affected interests in the administrative agencies of the corporate-administrative state. To the degree racial minorities, women, the poor, consumers, and environmentalists transformed themselves into *organized* interests they became incorporated in varying degrees in the new social compact.

The symbol of the new judicial attitude in economic matters was the famous footnote number four of *U.S. v. Carolene Products* of 1938 that established the "double standard" for due process review. According to this doctrine, the Court would employ different levels of judicial scrutiny to personal or civil rights as opposed to traditional property rights. Legislative regulation of property would be presumed constitutional and subject only to minimal scrutiny to determine if there was a rational basis for the regulation. On the other hand, stricter judicial scrutiny would apply to individual rights under any of three conditions: 1) where fundamental rights were involved; 2) where laws restricted access to the political process; and 3) where governmental action was directed against "discrete and insular" minorities.

To mainstream analysts, the double standard symbolized a Court committed to protecting individual rights and abandoning its historical regard for property rights. However, as Michael McCann makes clear, the "result was nothing less than a significant qualitative transformation in the constitutional status of 'property' itself." Property in a corporate society was no longer perceived as a relatively unfettered domain of freedom or autonomy, but increasingly a set of relationships with the modern administrative state. The Court gradually realized that its dominant purpose was no longer the prevention of unauthorized intrusions on private property, but the assurance of "fair" representation for all organized interests in the corporate-administrative state. The courts adopted an idealized version of democratic elitism. The United States was seen as a pluralistic, liberal society in which all "legitimate" interests were guaranteed representation and the right to pursue their self-interests. The courts' principal functions were protecting individual political liberties to participate in the game of politics and ensuring that the rules of the game were fairly administered.

## LABOR LAW AND CORPORATE CAPITALISM

Labor law offers a good illustration of the legal role in constructing an ideology and an institutional structure to support corporate capitalism. On the one hand, labor law is class-based and justifies hierarchy and domination in the workplace and the community. For example, the preeminent importance of capital mobility and ease of disinvestment is supported by the law. Communities surrounding a plant have few legally protected interests in decisions a company makes affecting that community. Employees do not have a legally recognized interest in the fruits of their labor or the management of a company, much less a right to a job. Management decision about operations and resource allocations, even unauthorized commands, must be obeyed pending completion of grievance procedures. The

workplace, both physically and existentially, belongs to the employer and workers acquire no rights or entitlements there, unless contractually conceded. And even here, companies have maneuverability as evidence by the use of Chapter VI bankruptcy filings to avoid contractual obligations.

On the other hand, labor law reflects the contractions of the modern social contract. It both fosters and constricts worker self-expression. Workers are allowed to organize, and prior to the 1970s, this right was even protected by the National Labor Relations Board (NLRB). But at the same time, labor law tries to guide worker activity into narrow, institutionalized channels in which only "legitimate" conflict is permitted. Forms of worker activity such as wildcat strikes, sit-down strikes, and secondary boycotts are prohibited even under life-threatening conditions. Workers must go through the proper legal procedures to gain recognition as a union or to protest management practices. These administrative requirements moderate social conflict and prevent it from spilling over beyond acceptable boundaries.

Labor law also encourages, yet limits, employee participation in the workplace. Worker participation is facilitated but largely confined to wages and working conditions. The attempts of workers to influence the organization of the work process or decisions about investment, disinvestment, and long-range planning are restricted. The law recognizes a core of managerial prerogatives where decisions are not negotiable. The more important the issue is to employer control the fewer the legal bargaining rights for workers. Finally, labor law enhances the institutional interest of unions at the expense of their own members. In return, unions have accepted a role in preserving industrial peace and performing managerial and disciplinary functions in the workplace.

In sum, labor law reflects the priorities of corporate liberalism. It allows limited opportunities for working people to fight for their rights but increasingly, under this legal model, working people are losing. This legal framework sees conflict as interest-group based, not class-based. It assumes that economic growth is the primary social goal. Permissible conflict by "legitimate" interests is to be directed by the state into acceptable channels and resolved administratively or judicially. Many important societal decisions remain off the public agenda because they are the prerogatives of those who control the corporate-dominated private sphere. The Court has acknowledged this function of labor law in its decision in *First National Maintenance Corporation v. NLRB* of 1981:

> A fundamental aim of the National Labor Relations Act is the establishment and maintenance of industrial peace . . . Central to the achievement of this purpose is the promotion of collective bargaining as a method of defusing and channeling conflict between labor and management . . . In view of an employer's need for unencumbered decision making, bargaining over management decisions that have a substantial impact on the continued availability of employment should be required only if the benefit for labor-management relations and the collective bargaining process, outweighs the burden placed on the conduct of the business.

## FREE SPEECH AND PROPERTY RIGHTS

First Amendment decisions of the last two decades provide a clear example of how the law poses a set of contradictions for those seeking fundamental change in the United States. The "Free Speech Tradition" embodies valuable, hard-won rights for Americans. Yet recent decisions of the Supreme Court show how the First Amendment can be interpreted to limit the rights supposedly contained within it. For example, the Court has shrunk the scope of the public sphere in decisions involving conflicts between freedom of expression and private property. It has refused to equate shopping centers with public streets or parks and allowed mall owners to restrict access to and expression in "private" spaces. The Court also has limited handbilling on a military base crisscrossed by public roads; permitted a city to allow the use of placard space on

public buses for commercial advertising but not for political advertising; and limited press access to jails and pretrial hearings. These decisions suggest that while ownership of or access to property, especially the corporate controlled media, is necessary to effectively exercise one's speech and press rights. The law supports restrictions on such access.

Another series of decisions, dealing with commercial speech, has continued the historical pattern of increasing the constitutional protection of corporations as "persons" with individual rights. Prior to 1975 commercial advertising had not enjoyed full First Amendment protection. However, in *Bigelow v. Virginia* of 1975 the Court decided that commercial speech was protected, finding a public, consumer interest in such speech. A series of other decisions extended these "consumer rights," illustrating the contradictions involved when a liberal, market-based conception of personal liberties is used to interpret the First Amendment. Similar to the way in which the worker's "right to work" was used in the past to legally restrict trade union organizing and enhance corporate power, consumers' "rights to know" have become the basis for the empowerment of corporations and advertising agencies, not consumers. Even more significantly, the Court extended corporations free speech rights and the full protection of the First Amendment in *Consolidated Edison v. Public Service Commission* of 1980. A New York State Public Service Commission regulation prohibiting public utilities from enclosing statements of their views on public issues along with monthly bills was ruled an unconstitutional restriction of a corporation's free speech. Using the same logic, the Court also struck down a ban on utility advertising promoting the use of electricity.

Several related cases further demonstrate the Court's solicitude for expanding speech rights for corporations and the wealthy. In *Miami Herald Publishing Company v. Tornillo* of 1974, Florida's right-of-reply statute, compelling a newspaper to furnish cost-free reply space, was unanimously struck down as an abridgment of the paper's private property rights and its free speech rights to exclude access by third parties. The Court also invalidated a Massachusetts law forbidding corporations from spending corporate funds to influence public referenda (*First National Bank v. Belotti* of 1978). Finally, the 2000 presidential election illustrates the significance of two Court decisions dealing with campaign finance reform and third party access to the nation's voters through media. In 1976, the Court struck down provisions of the Federal Election Campaign Act that placed limits on the amount of money individuals could spend independently to support political candidates as well as limitations on the amount candidates could spend on their own campaigns (*Buckley v. Valeo*). Spending money was seen by the Justices as a form of protected speech, not just speech-related conduct. In 1998, the Court ruled that a decision by a state-operated television station to deny a third party candidate the right to participate in a televised congressional candidate debate did not violate the candidate's First Amendment rights or the public's rights to freedom of information (*Arkansas Educational Television Commission v. Forbes*). According to John Shockley: ". . . [T]he Court has in fact used the First Amendment to protect the influence of the wealthy in American politics, reshaping [the First] Amendment . . . into a means to afford both fundamental and exclusive protection to the wealthy in the political process."

Rather than seeing such decisions as victories for abstract principles of free speech, such as "consumers' rights," we should understand their class dimensions—they benefit the wealthy and corporations over ordinary citizens. These kinds of decisions reveal the structural character of class inequality embedded in U.S. constitutional law. As Michael McCann points out, they parallel "the older judicial activism not only in its substantive and economic character but also in its fundamental, if more subtle, embrace of ideas supporting uniquely capitalist forms of social organization against substantive egalitarian challenge . . . The Court still adheres to the established constitutional tradition of limiting concern for systemic socioeconomic inequalities to an individualistic, exchange-oriented logic of public goods allocation."

## RECENT JUDICIAL TRENDS

Over the past decade, to the disappointment of many conservative legal scholars and judges, the Supreme Court has not issued any major decision that significantly challenges the constitutional principles on which the corporate-administrative state was established after 1937. After all, deregulation, privatization, and the legal changes needed for globalization have been carried out under that system through the legislative and executive branches without the need of any significant judicial involvement. Corporations have learned that they can use their power in legislatures, administrative agencies, political parties, the media, and the universities to accomplish their goals without having to rely on the kind of constitutional doctrines prevalent before 1937. Therefore, the courts have tinkered at the edges of constitutional property doctrine. Recent decisions in the area of federalism, limiting the national government's powers over the states, whether based on grounds of sovereign immunity or of narrower congressional power under the commerce clause and Fourteenth Amendment, may be indirectly beneficial to corporations, but they do not pose a major challenge to the legal foundations of the corporate-administrative state. Occasionally some Justices have hinted at the possibility of significantly changing the post-1937 system, but that is quite unlikely until the economic foundations of that system significantly change.

The judiciary also has been involved during the past two decades in reversing or limiting some of the reforms of the 1960s and 1970s in areas such as individual liberties, affirmative action, freedom of choice, and access to the courts. While many of these decisions have class dimensions and have negative implications for democracy, they also do not directly affect the corporate-administrative system of property that was able to survive, and even flourish, during the period when these liberal reforms were more firmly in place.

However, there is one other area—labor relations—in which the judiciary has played a significant role in protecting corporate power, especially since the Reagan administration. A 2000 report of Human Rights Watch concludes that workers in the U.S. lack the rights to organize, bargain, and strike supposedly guaranteed in the First Amendment's provision of freedom of association and expression, and in internationally recognized human rights norms. The report finds that employers are free to fire, harass, and intimidate with impunity workers trying to organize unions; to refuse to bargain with workers who successfully have stepped over the legal hurdles placed in the way of organizing; and to make the right to strike a travesty by permanently replacing strikers. Furthermore, the report states that millions of workers in the United States are denied coverage of the labor laws that do exist. While some of these principles have been in place since the passage of the Wagner Act in 1935, courts and the National Labor Relations Board have made matters much worse for the labor movement since the Reagan administration. In the process, they have demonstrated the normal, historical tendency of the law to support and facilitate the exercise of corporate power.

## CONCLUSION

So what role does the law play in making anything really different as opposed to supporting the status quo or the kind of reforms that give us more of the same? First, we should not see the law cynically as merely an instrument of class oppression or ideological co-optation. Neither should we see it idealistically as fundamentally autonomous of economic power, and therefore, a principal means to bring about reform. This law can be, and to a degree has been, both a force for maintaining the status quo and an instrument of reform, even sometimes radical reform. However, those forces with the most political-economic power historically have been the most successful in using the law to promote their interests just as they have been in using the media, education, religion, and political parties. The law is one important arena of struggle we should not dismiss. Neither should we be unrealistic about its possibilities. The real issue is about the role law can play in contesting power—a very difficult proposition indeed, given the

tendency of those who have power to hold onto it with all the forces at their disposal.

Second, with this realization, is a major issue of *how* the law can be used to contest power. To the degree that the law can be used within the established political process, judicial strategies for change are less desirable than legislative strategies. The historical record here seems clear. Throughout most of our history, the courts have been one of the most conservative institutions in society. Their patterns of recruitment, socialization, and decision-making all contribute to this. Judges are relatively insulated from public pressures and accountability; are non-representative of the larger population; and are socialized to "know" the law as a non-political, neutral process. Given this, few judges see their role as that of agents of social reform other than through helping adapt the system to necessary economic and political changes.

Too many baby-boomer liberals and legal reformers grew up with an idealized image of the Warren Court as a liberal instrument of change that fostered the Civil Rights movement and tried to bring about other significant changes in U.S. politics until it was frustrated by the Nixon administration. To a minor degree this was true, but it is more mythology than history. The liberal record of the Warren Court contained more blemishes than is often acknowledged; the Warren Court operated within prevailing liberal, individualistic, market-oriented conceptions of society, which largely denied the reality of class or group solutions to social problems; and, to the degree it fostered progressive change, it was facilitating the development of the U.S. post-World War II political economy, just as courts had facilitated capitalist economic development previously. It is more accurate to see the Warren Court as an institution of legitimation and social conflict management than of progressive reform.

Over the last half-century, more reform, even if it was not fundamental, has been brought about through the legislative than the judicial process. For every *Brown v. Board of Education* or *Baker v. Carr* there are many more laws such as the National Labor Relations Act, Civil Rights Act of 1964, and Voting Rights Act of 1965. Quite often, even when progressive legislation is passed, the courts are more likely to interpret the legislation to limit, rather than enhance, the reforms instituted, as indicated by the courts' interpretation of civil rights, labor, and campaign finance reform legislation over the last twenty-five years. Therefore, to the degree people use the law as a vehicle for change, it should de-emphasize, judicial-based strategies.

If legislative legal strategies are more likely to be effective, then how do people participate in changing the law? While not completely dismissing the idea of changing the law by changing people's consciousness, I think language-based strategies are limited. Political activity, both inside and outside established political processes, which leads to laws changing people's material reality, is more important, and in the process is more likely to affect people's consciousness. A law guaranteeing a sustainable income or national health care as a right of citizenship in a modern society can be much more effective in changing people's consciousness than attempts to do so through using language and persuasion to reconstitute their beliefs.

We must remember that a political-economic system dominated by large corporations will tend to have laws reflecting that power and protecting the property interests of those corporations. As Raymond Williams has stated:

> . . . Laws are necessarily the instruments of a particular social order. None can survive without them. But then what is at issue, in any conflict about particular law, is the underlying definition of the desired social order . . . To challenge that order is to challenge those laws.

Challenging that order necessitates challenging capitalism. Many people today do not want to talk about this. They hope to bring about progressive change by avoiding a discussion of the inherent, exploitative characteristics of capitalism. They seem to be hoping for some form of "friendly capitalism." But we need to move beyond capitalism if we are to create a decent, just, and humane world.

---

## DISCUSSION QUESTIONS

1. In what ways does Swidorski's analysis challenge the notion of the neutrality of the law?
2. To what extent does Swidorski see a role for law and the courts in creating social change? Compare his views on this issue with those of Howard Zinn on the Constitution in Article 12.

# 30 *Mark Tushnet*

# DEMOCRACY VERSUS JUDICIAL REVIEW

*Judicial review is the power of courts to decide on the constitutionality of gov-
ernment statutes and actions. In this article legal scholar Mark Tushnet criticizes judicial review and calls for its transformation through an End Judicial
Review Amendment to the Constitution. This amendment would prohibit courts
from reviewing the constitutionality of statues passed by Congress and state
legislatures. It would not apply to the actions of public officials, which would
continue to be subject to review. While calls to curb the powers the courts are a
staple of the political right, Tushnet writes from a left progressive position. He
chastises liberals for their faith in the "false gods" of the Supreme Court and
judicial review. He believes that progressives need to decrease their reliance
on the courts and invest their hopes in the popular outcomes of democratic
political processes. In his article Tushnet anticipates and tries to respond to
progressive concerns that an end to judicial review would lead to regression in
civil liberties, civil rights, and other areas.*

Before the 2004 election, one of George W. Bush's advisers produced a memorable description of liberals as the "reality-based community." Liberals took to wearing the label, offered as a criticism, as a badge of honor.

In one important respect, however, the liberal community is about as faith-based as one can get. Liberals believe in the courts as vehicles for progressive social change-a belief that remains unshaken by the Supreme Court's two-century history and the fact that it has been at best an inconstant defender of progressive values since the 1980s. Liberals were unbelievers for the first half of the twentieth century and then got religion during the short period when liberals dominated the Court. The Supreme Court and judicial review are false gods, and liberals should return to their unbelief.

Suppose that liberals offered a constitutional amendment along these lines: "Except as authorized by Congress, no court of the United States or of any individual state shall have the power to review the constitutionality of statutes enacted by Congress or by state legislatures." Let's call it the End Judicial Review Amendment (EJRA).

I offer this formulation in part simply to focus the discussion, but also as a serious proposal. Progressives and liberals should abandon courts as

*Source:* Mark Tushnet, "Democracy Versus Judicial Review." *Dissent,* Volume 52, Number 2, Spring 2005, pp. 59–63.

a principal resource, for reasons of democratic principle and political strategy.

**Principle:** The basic principle, of course, is that people ought to be able to govern themselves. Judicial review stands in the way of self-government. Constitutionalism- the imposition on the people of restrictions on their own power-does not. The reason is that constitutionalism can be implemented through politics as people listen to arguments about why some policies they might initially prefer are inconsistent with deeper values they hold, values that find expression in the Constitution. As Larry Kramer, dean of Stanford Law School, argues in his recent book *The People Themselves,* the United States has a deep tradition of popular constitutionalism. He suggests it should be retrieved today, and he is right.

This basic democratic principle is supplemented by the basic facts about the U.S. Constitution. It protects fundamental values that it identifies in general terms: "due process of law," "equal protection of the laws," "freedom of speech." These terms are hardly self-defining, and there is inevitable *reasonable* disagreement over what they mean when applied in particular controversies: are hate-speech regulations a violation of freedom of speech or not? The "answer" is that the U.S. Supreme Court says they are. The Canadian Supreme Court, in contrast, says they are not.

Reasonable disagreement about the proper interpretation of the Constitution is usually what informs a Court decision that a statute is unconstitutional. As legal philosopher Jeremy Waldron asks (rightly), why, in cases of reasonable disagreement over interpretation, should the votes of a majority on a Court of nine justices prevail over the votes of a majority of one hundred senators and over four hundred representatives? Contemporary liberals give answers centered on distrust of politics and of the people. These should not be attractive to democrats.

## WHO CHOOSES?

Democrats are committed not only to self-government as a matter of principle but also to the belief that, in the long run and in social conditions approximated in the contemporary United States, the people will make the right choices when presented with arguments about fundamental values. That's a better place to put our faith than in the Supreme Court. Of course, the current political system in the United States is imperfectly democratic. Judicial review *might* be a useful way of addressing some of those imperfections or of offsetting them. But whatever might have been true during the Warren Court era, the prospect of a return to liberalism is slight-not nonexistent, but small enough to make it worthwhile to give up faith in the Supreme Court.

The democratic belief in the people's judgment is confirmed by the important legislative achievements of modern democracy. One T-shirt sold after the 2004 election listed what the Democratic Party has accomplished: "Equal Pay. Equal Rights. 40 Hour Work Week. Social Security. Medicare. Clean Water. Clean Air. Safe Food. Freedom of Speech. Voting Rights." All but the last two were achieved primarily through legislation, and some-the social welfare achievements of the modern state-had little connection to the Supreme Court, except when it obstructed them.

Democratic faith in the people's judgment means that the arguments liberals deploy in court should be just as good in the political arena. We democrats think that we are *right* about fundamental values-that, when put to the choice, the American people will prefer a society in which women have the right to choose to bear or not bear a child; that, when put to the choice, the American people will prefer a society in which gays and lesbians have the same right to express their love that straight people do; and so on through the list of progressive policies. But, if we're *right,* we ought to be able to prevail in everyday politics and elections-maybe not immediately (in part because our reliance on the courts has weakened us politically), but eventually. Progressives should be able to enact statutes that embody our policies (and repeal those that don't) with popular support.

Those are the principled reasons for being suspicious of judicial review on democratic grounds. The proposal needs to be fleshed out a little more before we take up the strategic advantages of advocating the elimination of judicial review.

## DETAILS

The precise form of the EJRA doesn't really matter, and I don't want to worry here about drafting details. (Should the amendment authorize Congress to enforce its provisions? Probably yes, but the answer isn't important for my purposes here.) Some liberals may worry that an EJRA would make authoritarian- or Stalinist or fascistic-excesses much easier. The amendment is modeled on a provision in the constitution of the Netherlands, a country not noted for widespread violations of civil liberties. Reasonably decent democratic societies can avoid illiberal abuses without having to call on the courts. But, as Judge Robert Bork once suggested, such an amendment could enable Congress to override a court decision holding a federal statute unconstitutional by a two-thirds (or even a majority) vote in both houses (with a parallel provision for state legislatures and state laws). I think the proposal to eliminate judicial review is cleaner. The aim-decreasing progressives' reliance on the courts to do what we can't persuade the people to do-can be carried out in many ways.

The EJRA addresses judicial review of statutes, but courts would still have an important role in enforcing the Constitution. Think of the notorious "hitching post" case in which Alabama prison guards allegedly tied a prisoner to a post in the hot sun and gave him no water for most of a day. The proposed amendment wouldn't stop courts from finding this to be a violation of the prisoner's constitutional right to be free from cruel and unusual punishment. The EJRA is directed at statutes, not at the actions of, say, individual guards, police officers, or mayors. Of course, if a state enacted a statute saying, "It's just fine for prison guards to hitch prisoners to posts," the amendment would kick in. However, progressives ought to be quite happy to fight that statute in any legislature in the country.

The proposed amendment wouldn't insulate President Bush's decisions to detain so-called "enemy combatants" at Guantánamo Bay from judicial review, either. Bush claims the constitutional power to do so without authorization from Congress. Under the EJRA, courts would enforce constitutional rights *except* when Congress authorized the president's actions. And, again, we shouldn't be reluctant to take on a legislative fight over whether Congress should authorize torture or lifetime detention without trial. (The model here is the decision by Israel's Supreme Court that its security services didn't have the authority to engage in "aggressive" interrogation techniques. The issue was sent to the Knesset to consider, and it hasn't, and probably won't, enact a statute allowing the use of such techniques. If there, why not here?)

Courts could also interpret statutes to make them consistent with the courts' understandings of the Constitution. They could find that particularly troublesome applications of a statute weren't within the statute's terms. Congress could reinstate the statute in its full scope if it disagreed with the courts' constitutional interpretation.

As that example shows, it's not just courts that would still enforce the Constitution in some contexts. The amendment would let Congress step in when it thought states weren't protecting rights. If some state prohibited early-term abortions, Congress could pass a statute creating a federal right to choose in such situations. Again, that's a political fight progressives should be willing to take on. With judicial review in place, there's actually some question about whether the Supreme Court would allow Congress to enact such a statute. The EJRA would make it clear that the Supreme Court couldn't step in and strike down progressive rights-protecting federal statutes.

The amendment would give Congress another role: The national legislature can expressly authorize judicial review either in respect to a particular statute or to some or even all constitutional claims. All the proposal really does is resolve a long-standing constitutional controversy over how much power Congress already has to eliminate judicial review. The Constitution gives Congress the power to "regulate" the jurisdiction of the lower courts and "make exceptions" to the jurisdiction of the Supreme Court. Some scholars believe that these provisions allow Congress to eliminate judicial review by statute. The proposal would do so directly, and then allow Congress to *create* judicial review when it wanted to.

Why should Congress have that power? Again, for reasons of principle. A democrat can hardly object if the people believe that they should restrain themselves by using the courts. And, once again, reasons matter. Liberals think that there are good arguments for judicial review. But if their reasons are really good, then they should be able to persuade people to put the courts back into the constitutional picture.

Liberal faith in the Supreme Court always had an underside. It was the assumption that people could not be trusted and had to be under the tutelage of the (then-liberal) elites who controlled the Supreme Court. This assumption led to arguments against amending the Constitution *as a matter of principle,* rather than on the grounds that particular amendments are ill-advised. My proposal will have to overcome this anti-amendmentitis, to adapt a label from law professor Kathleen Sullivan. I suspect that the fever will break if, as seems likely, the Arnold Schwarzenegger amendment allowing naturalized citizens to be president is ratified in the next few years.

## OBJECTIONS

Still, the EJRA must be defended on its merits. One obstacle to doing so is liberal nostalgia for the Warren Court. The Warren Court's accomplishments obscured the importance of legislation in providing the foundation for fundamental guarantees of liberty and security. Without understating the social and political importance of decisions such as *Brown v. Board of Education, Roe v. Wade,* and *Lawrence v. Texas,* we should also pay attention to the underside of those landmarks. *Brown* generated a backlash in the South, helped transform many Southern Democrats into Southern Republicans, and-when desegregation litigation moved north and led to busing programs-helped the Goldwater wing of the Republican Party to eliminate the Rockefeller wing. *Roe v. Wade* (and the Warren Court's school prayer decisions) helped to mobilize Christian evangelicals. *Lawrence v. Texas* elevated the issue of gay marriage on the public agenda, producing the anti-gay-marriage constitutional amendments that seem to have played some role in Bush's victory.

In fact, the Warren Court's accomplishments were due in large part to its collaboration with social movements that mobilized support both in the courts *and* in legislatures. A similar collaboration may be emerging between today's Supreme Court and the most mobilized elements in the Republican coalition, especially the religious right. This should give liberals some pause when they consider their immediate goals and, more important here, how they understand the role of the Supreme Court in our political system. My proposed EJRA is likewise premised on the idea that constitutional development is produced as much by mobilized social movements as by the Supreme Court. The question is, who is mobilized?

This question diminishes some of the force of obvious objections to my proposal and its democratic logic. Just look at the cases I've mentioned. Right now, African Americans who benefited from *Brown* get nothing at all from the Supreme Court, and judicial review simply puts legislated programs of affirmative action at risk. Before *Lawrence,* anti-sodomy laws were enforced only sporadically when the sex was consensual. There won't be a flood of new sodomy laws or prosecutions if states know that courts won't strike down the new laws.

That leaves abortion. Where do we stand now? Pro-choice advocates point out how limited access to abortions is today: 87 percent of all U.S. counties are without an abortion provider, medical schools are removing from the curriculum training on performing abortions, twenty-six states have waiting periods, forty-four have parental notification requirements. The list goes on. But why, then, all the fears about overruling *Roe?* Consider the situation with *Roe* already in place. If it's so terrible now, how much worse can it get with *Roe* overruled?

The standard examples of how much worse it can get include statutes with stringent requirements that pregnant young women notify their parents and bans on late-term abortions. But, the constitutional arguments against parental notification statutes and statutes restricting late-term abortions are actually policy arguments. In 2000, the Supreme Court struck down a ban on late-term abortions for two reasons. The more important was that the statute did not allow doctors to use a specific technique even if it was a much safer medical practice. In other words, the ban endangers women while doing little to save fetuses. If that's a good argument in court, it ought to be a good one in politics as well.

Overruling *Roe* means that states can decide to regulate or prohibit abortions. (There is a theory that states would thereby be required to enact restrictive abortion laws, but it is unrealistic to think that the Court would do this.) A fair number of "blue" states would impose few or no regulations beyond what they already have. Some "red" states would undoubtedly go further and perhaps ban early-term abortions. Voters-even in those red states-are then going to have second thoughts about whom they have elected.

This reveals a complex story. It is a mistake to think only of what *today's* legislatures would do without the lid of judicial review. It takes time to amend the Constitution, and progressives would be putting forth candidates in the next series of elections who would be committed both to the EJRA and to the defense of constitutional rights in the legislature. If progressives won enough elections to get the Constitution amended, the legislatures would also be very different from the ones we now have.

## STRATEGY

Claims that liberals trust the people ring hollow today. Liberals can repeat until they are blue in the face that they want gay marriage to be up to state legislatures, but conservative opponents counter-effectively-that liberals hope in their hearts that the courts will go their way if legislatures don't. Liberals say they don't want to impose their values but then run to the courts when they can't get what they want from legislatures. Supporting a constitutional amendment to eliminate judicial review would show that we liberals and progressives really do think that our arguments can ultimately prevail in politics.

The fact that I had to address gay rights and abortion signals one difficulty for progressives. There is a widespread feeling that we don't have fundamental commitments, but only obligations to interest groups. That's not true. Our positions on choice and gay rights flow from the same commitment to human dignity and freedom that under girds our desire to enact health care legislation. Nonetheless, the image of an interest-group-dominated left has real, and bad, political effects. Getting rid of the albatross of judicial review-indeed, even *advocating* its end-would help to change that image.

My proposal would force conservatives to put up or shut up. They would have to say whether they object to judicial activism, which the proposed amendment would prohibit, or whether they are just as opportunistic as they say progressives are and oppose judicial activism only when it reaches conclusions they don't like.

In the Winter 2005 issue of this magazine, the editors printed an excerpt from a letter Thomas Jefferson wrote in 1798. His political opponents had enacted the Alien and Sedition Acts and seemed to be in firm control of the national government. Jefferson counseled "a little patience." The "reign of witches," he wrote, would "pass over," and the people would restore the government to "its true principles." He ended, "If the game runs sometimes against us at home, we must have patience until luck turns, and then we shall have an opportunity of winning back the principles we have lost. For this is a game where principles are the stake."

Jefferson was a smart man and, for his times, a real democrat. He did not place his hopes in the Supreme Court. The game he thought he and his allies could win was the game of electoral politics. Two years later, they did. Maybe there's a lesson in that for today's progressives.

---

## DISCUSSION QUESTIONS

1. Explain specifically how Tushnet's proposed End Judicial Review Amendment (EJRA) would work. What responsibilities would courts continue to exercise?
2. Describe the main objections to the EJRA. How does Tushnet respond to these objections? In particular, what does he say about the prospects for legal abortion if the EJRA were to pass?

**31** *Patricia J. Williams*

# THIS DANGEROUS PATRIOT'S GAME

*In the aftermath of the September 11 bombings of the World Trade Center and the Pentagon, political leaders enacted a series of sweeping laws, which restricted traditional constitutional liberties in the name of enhanced security. Columnist and Columbia University law professor Patricia Williams offers her assessment of the cost and benefits of this darkened legal landscape in this probing selection. For Williams, the devastation of September 11 left in its wake many profound, long-term tests for America. These challenges stem from the need to balance our response to the threat of terrorism with the need to pre-serve the rights of citizens. From her perspective, the balance has tipped dra-matically away from civil rights and freedoms, toward "the 'comfort' and convenience of high-tech totalitarianism." As a result, today we face "one of the more dramatic Constitutional crises in United States history." She explores this crisis as it impinges on three areas of constitutional protection: freedom of the press, freedom from unreasonable searches and seizures, and the right to due process of law (including the right to adequate counsel, the right to a speedy public and impartial trial, and the right against self-incrimination). In each area, of course, defenders of the shrinkage of civil liberties justify it in the name of fighting "terrorism," assuring us that only those justly suspected of being a terrorist, or aiding terrorists, need have any fear. But given the elastic nature of the term "terrorist" and the nation's history of abusing rights during the panic of wartime, Williams fears expansive use of executive and judicial power may go largely unchecked. As she explains, "A war against terrorism is a war of the mind, so broadly defined that the enemy becomes anybody who makes us afraid." She reminds us that rights exist as a ritualized legal process intended to ensure that "we don't allow the grief of great tragedies to blind us with mob fury, inflamed judgments and uninformed reasoning." An erosion of the tempering impact of legal rights strikes Williams as dangerous—indeed, perhaps a danger as great as terrorism itself.*

*Source:* Patricia J. Williams, "This Dangerous Patriot's Game." *The Observer* (U.K.), 2 December 2001.

Things fall apart, as Chinua Achebe put it, in times of great despair. The American nightmare that began with the bombing of the World Trade Center and the Pentagon, has, like an earthquake, been followed by jolt after jolt of disruption and fear. In the intervening three months, yet another airplane crashed, this time into a residential section of New York City. Anthrax contamination succeeded in closing, for varying lengths of time, all three branches of government. From the tabloids to *The New York Times,* major media outlets have had their centers of operation evacuated repeatedly. The United States Postal Service is tied in knots. Hundreds of anthrax hoaxes have stretched law enforcement beyond all capacity. Soldiers guard all our public buildings.

Around four thousand Americans have died in planes, collapsing buildings or of anthrax toxin since that morning in September; tens of thousands more have lost their jobs. Some 5000 Arab residents between the ages of 18 and 33 have been summoned for interrogation by the FBI. And twenty million resident aliens live suddenly subject to the exceedingly broad terms of a new martial law. Even while we try to follow the president's advice to pick ourselves up in time for the Christmas shopping season, punchdrunk and giddily committed to soldiering on as before, we know that the economic and emotional devastation of these events has only begun to register.

As the enormity of the destruction settles in and becomes less dreamlike, more waking catastrophe, American society begins to face those long-term tests that inevitably come after the shock and horror of so much loss. We face the test of keeping the unity that visited us in that first moment of sheer chaos. We face the test of maintaining our dignity and civility in a time of fear and disorder. Above all, we face the test of preserving the rights and freedoms in our Constitution and its Bill of Rights.

Few in the United States question the necessity for unusual civil measures in keeping with the current state of emergency. But a number of the Bush administration's new laws, orders and policies are deservedly controversial: the disregard for international treaties and conventions; strict controls on media reports about the war; secret surveillance and searches of citizens' computers; widespread ethnic profiling; indefinite detention of non-citizens; offers of expedited American citizenship to those who provide evidence about terrorists; and military tribunals with the power to try enemies in secret, without application of the usual laws of evidence, without right of appeal, yet with the ability to impose the death penalty. Opportunity for legislative or other public discussion of these measures has been largely eclipsed by the rapidity with which most of them have been pushed into effect. This speed, one must accede, is in large part an exigency of war. It is perhaps also because Mr. Bush has always preferred operating in a rather starkly corporate style. In any event, the president has attempted to enlarge the power of the executive to an unprecedented extent, while limiting both Congressional input as well as the check of the judiciary.

Overall, we face one of the more dramatic Constitutional crises in United States history. First, while national security mandates some fair degree of restraint, blanket control of information is in tension with the Constitution's expectation that freedom of a diverse and opinionated press will moderate the tyrannical tendencies of power. We need to have some inkling of what is happening on the battlefield in our name. On the domestic front, moreover, the First Amendment's protection of free speech, is eroded if even peaceful dissent becomes casually categorized as dangerous or unpatriotic, as it has sometimes been in recent weeks. This concern is heightened by the fact that the war has been framed as one against "terror"—against unruly if deadly emotionalism—rather than as a war against specific bodies, specific land, specific resources.

A war against terrorism is a war of the mind, so broadly defined that the enemy becomes anybody who makes us afraid. Indeed what is conspicuous about American public discourse right now is how hard it is to talk about facts rather than fear.

In a struggle that is coloured by a degree of social panic, we must be very careful not to allow human rights to be cast as an indulgence. There is always a certain hypnosis to the language of war—the poetry of the Pentagon a friend calls it—in which war means peace, and peace-mongering invites war. In this somewhat inverted system of reference, the bleeding heart does not beat within the corpus of law but rather in the bosom of those whose craven sympathies amount to naive and treacherous self-delusion. Everywhere one hears what, if taken literally, amounts to a death knell for the American dream: rights must be tossed out the window because "the constitution is not a suicide pact."

But accepting rational reasons to be afraid, the unalloyed ideology of efficiency has not only chilled free expression, but left us poised at the gateway of an even more fearsome world in which the "comfort" and convenience of high-tech totalitarianism gleam temptingly; a world in which our Americanness endures only with hands up so that our fingerprints can be scanned, and our nationalized-identity scrutinised for signs of suspicious behaviour.

This brings me to the second aspect of our Constitutional crisis—that is, the encroachment of our historical freedom from unreasonable searches and seizures. The establishment of the new Office of Homeland Security and the passage of the so-called USA Patriot Act has brought into being an unprecedented merger between the functions of intelligence agencies and law enforcement. What this means might be clearer if we used the more straightforward term for intelligence—that is, spying. Law enforcement agents can now spy on us, "destabilizing" citizens not just non-citizens.

They can gather information with few checks or balances from the judiciary. Morton Halperin, a defense expert who worked with the National Security Council under Henry Kissinger, was quoted, in *The New Yorker* magazine, worrying that if a government intelligence agency thinks you're under the control of a foreign government, "they can wiretap you and never tell you, search your house and never tell you, break into your home, copy your hard drive, and never tell you that they've done it." Moreover, says Halperin, upon whose own phone Kissinger placed a tap, "Historically, the government has often believed that anyone who is protesting government policy is doing it at the behest of a foreign government and opened counterintelligence investigations of them."

This expansion of domestic spying highlights the distinction between punishing what has already occurred and preventing what might happen in the future. In a very rough sense, agencies like the F.B.I. have been concerned with catching criminals who have already done their dirty work, while agencies like the CIA have been involved in predicting or manipulating future outcomes—activities of prior restraint, in other words, from which the Constitution generally protects citizens.

The third and most distressing area of Constitutional concern has been Mr. Bush's issuance of an executive order setting up military tribunals that would deprive even long-time resident aliens of the right to due process of law. The elements of the new order are as straightforward as trains running on time. The President would have the military try non-citizens suspected of terrorism in closed tribunals rather than courts. No requirement of public charges, adequacy of counsel, usual rules of evidence, nor proof beyond a reasonable doubt. The cases would be presented before unspecified judges, with rulings based on the accusations of unidentified witnesses. The tribunals would have the power to execute anyone so convicted, with no right of appeal. According to polls conducted by National Public Radio, *The Washington Post,* and ABC News, approximately 65 percent of Americans wholeheartedly endorse such measures.

"Foreign terrorists who commit war crimes against the United States, in my judgment, are not entitled to and do not deserve the protections of the American Constitution," says Attorney General John Ashcroft in defense of tribunals. There are a number of aspects of that statement that ought to worry us. The reasoning is alarmingly circular in Ashcroft's characterization of suspects who have not yet been convicted as "terrorists." It presumes guilt before adjudication. Our system of innocent-until-proven-guilty is hardly foolproof, but does provide an essential, base-line bulwark against the furious thirst for quick vengeance, the carelessly deadly mistake—albeit in the name of self-protection.

It is worrisome, too, when the highest prosecutor in the land declares that war criminals do not "deserve" basic constitutional protections. We confer due process not because putative criminals are "deserving" recipients of rights-as-reward. Rights are not "earned" in this way. What makes rights rights is that they ritualize the importance of solid, impartial and public consensus before we take life or liberty from anyone, particularly those whom we fear. We ritualize this process to make sure we don't allow the grief of great tragedies to blind us with mob fury, inflamed judgments and uninformed reasoning. In any event, Bush's new order bypasses not only the American Constitution but the laws of most other democratic nations. It exceeds the accepted conventions of most military courts. (I say all this provisionally, given that the Bush administration is urging the enactment of similar anti-terrorism measures in Britain, Russia, and that troublesome holdout, the European Union).

As time has passed since the order was published, a number of popular defenses of tribunals have emerged: we should trust our president, we should have faith in our government, we are in a new world facing new kinds of enemies who have access to new weapons of mass destruction. Assuming all this, we must wonder if this administration also questions whether citizens who are thought to have committed heinous crimes "deserve" the protections of American citizenship. The terrorist who mailed "aerosolised" anthrax spores to various Senate offices is, according to the FBI, probably a lone American microbiologist. Although we have not yet rounded up thousands of microbiologists for questioning by the FBI, I wonder if the government will be hauling them before tribunals—for if this is a war without national borders, the panicked logic of secret trials will surely expand domestically rather than contract. A friend observes wryly that if reasoning behind the order is that the perpetrators of mass death must be summarily executed, then there are some CEOs in the tobacco industry who ought to be trembling in their boots. Another friend who works with questions of reproductive choice notes more grimly that that is exactly the reasoning used by those who assault and murder abortion doctors.

"There are situations when you do need to presume guilt over innocence," one citizen from Chattanooga told *The New York Times*. The conservative

talk show host Mike Reagan leads the pack in such boundlessly-presumed guilt by warning that you might think the guy living next door is the most wonderful person in the world, you see him playing with his children, but in fact "he might be part of a sleeper cell that wants to blow you away." We forget, perhaps, that J. Edgar Hoover justified sabotaging Martin Luther King and the "dangerous suspects" of that era with similar sentiment.

In addition to the paranoia generated, the importance of the right to adequate counsel has been degraded. Attorney General Ashcroft's stated policies include allowing federal officials to listen in on conversations between suspected terrorists and their lawyers. And President Bush's military tribunals would not recognize the right of defendants to choose their own lawyers. Again, there has been very little public opposition to such measures. Rather, one hears many glib, racialized references to O.J. Simpson—who, last anyone heard, was still a citizen: "You wouldn't want Osama Bin Laden to have O.J.'s lawyer, or they'd end up playing golf together in Florida."

The tribunals also challenge the right to a speedy, public and impartial trial. More than 1000 immigrants have been arrested and held, approximately 800 with no disclosure of identities or location or charges against them. This is "frighteningly close to the practice of disappearing people in Latin America," according to Kate Martin, the director of the Center for National Security Studies.

Finally, there has been an ominous amount of public vilification of the constitutional right against self-incrimination. Such a right is, in essence, a proscription against the literal arm-twisting and leg pulling that might otherwise be necessary to physically compel someone to testify when they do not want to. It is perhaps a rather too-subtly-worded limitation of the use of torture.

While not yet the direct subject of official sanction, torture has suddenly gained remarkable legitimacy. Callers to radio programs say that we don't always have the "luxury of following all the rules"; that given recent events, people are "more understanding" of the necessity for a little behind-the-scenes roughing up. The unanimity of international conventions against torture notwithstanding, one hears authoritative voices—for example, Robert Litt, a former Justice Department official—arguing that while torture is not "authorized," perhaps it could be used in "emergencies," as long as the person who tortures then presents himself to "take the consequences."

Harvard Law School Professor Alan Dershowitz has suggested the use of "torture warrants" limited, he insists, to cases where time is of the essence. Most alarming of all, a recent CNN poll revealed that 45 percent of Americans would not object to torturing someone if it would provide information about terrorism. While fully acknowledging the stakes of this new war, I worry that this attitude of lawless righteousness is one that has been practiced in oppressed communities for years. It is a habit that has produced cynicism, riots and bloodshed. The always-urgently-felt convenience of torture has left us with civic calamities ranging from Abner Louima—a Haitian immigrant whom two New York City police officers beat and sodomized with a broom handle because they mistook him for someone involved in a barroom brawl—to Jacobo Timerman in Argentina to Alexander Solzhenitsyn in the Soviet Union—all victims of physical force and mental manipulation, all people who refused to speak or didn't speak the words their inquisitors wanted to hear, but who were 'known' to know something. In such times and places, the devastation has been profound. People know nothing so they suspect everything. Deaths are never just accidental. Every human catastrophe is also a mystery and mysteries create ghosts, hauntings, "blowback," and ultimately new forms of terror. The problem with this kind of 'preventive' measure is that we are not mindreaders. Even with sodium pentathol, whose use some have suggested recently, we don't and we can't know every last thought of those who refuse to speak.

Torture is an investment in the right to be all-knowing, in the certitude of what appears "obvious." It is the essence of totalitarianism. Those who justify it with confident proclamations of "I have nothing to hide, why should they," overlap substantially with the class of those who have never been the persistent object of suspect profiling, never been harrassed, never been stigmatized or generalized or feared just for the way they look.

The human mind is endlessly inventive. People create enemies as much as fear real ones. We are familiar with stories of the intimate and wrongheaded projections heaped upon the maid who is accused of taking something that the lady of the house simply misplaced. Stoked by trauma, tragedy and dread, the creativity of our paranoia is in overdrive right now. We must take a deep collective breath and be wary of persecuting those who conform to our fears instead of prosecuting enemies who were and will be smart enough to play against such prejudices.

In grief, sometimes we merge with the world, all boundary erased in deference to the commonality of the human condition. But traumatic loss can also mean—sometimes—that you want to hurt anyone in your path. Anyone who is lighthearted, you want to crush. Anyone who laughs is discordant. Anyone who has a healthy spouse or child is your enemy, is undeserving, is frivolous and in need of muting.

When I served as a prosecutor years ago, I was very aware of this propensity among victims, the absolute need to rage at God or whoever is near—for that is what great sorrow feels like when the senses are overwhelmed. You lose words and thus want to reinscribe the hell of which you cannot speak. It is unfair that the rest of the world should not suffer as you have.

This is precisely why we have always had rules in trials about burdens of proof, standards of evidence, the ability to confront and cross-examine witnesses. The fiercely evocative howls of the widow, the orphan, the innocently wronged—these are the forces by which many a lynch mob has been rallied, how many a posse has been motivated to bypass due process, how many a holy crusade has been launched. It is easy to suspend the hard work of moral thought in the name of Ultimate Justice, or even Enduring Freedom, when one is blindly griefstricken. "If you didn't do it then your brother did," is the underlying force of blood feuds since time began. "If you're not with us, you're against us," is the dangerous modern corollary to this rage.

I have many friends for whom the dominant emotion is anger. Mine is fear, and not only of the conflagration smouldering throughout the Middle East. I fear no less the risks closer to home: this is how urban riots occur, this is how the Japanese were interned during World War II, this is why hundreds of "Arab-looking" Americans have been attacked and harassed in the last weeks alone.

I hear much about how my sort of gabbling amounts to nothing but blaming the victim. But it is hardly a matter of condoning to point out that we cannot afford to substitute some statistical probability or hunch for actual evidence. We face a wrenching global crisis now, of almost unimaginable proportion, but we should take the risks of precipitous action no less seriously than when the grief with which we were stricken drove us to see evil embodied in witches, in Jews, in blacks or heathens or hippies.

Perhaps our leaders have, as they assure us, more intelligence about these matters than we the people can know at this time. I spend a lot of time praying that they are imbued with greater wisdom. But the stakes are very, very high. We cannot take an evil act and use it to justify making an entire people, an entire nation or an entire culture the corpus of "evil."

Give the government the power to assassinate terrorists, comes the call on chat shows. Spare us a the circus of long public trials, say the letters to the editor.

I used to think that the most important human rights work facing Americans would be a national reconsideration of the death penalty. I could not have imagined that we would so willingly discard even the right of habeus corpus. I desperately hope we are a wiser people than to unloose the power to kill based on undisclosed "information" with no accountability.

We have faced horrendous war crimes in the world before. World War II presented lessons we should not forget, and Nuremburg should be our model. The United States and its allies must seriously consider the option of a world court. Our greatest work is always keeping our heads when our hearts are broken. Our best resistance to terror is the summoning of those principles so suited to keep us from descending into infinite bouts of vengeance and revenge with those who wonder, like Milton's Stygian Counsel.

Will he, so wise, let loose at once his ire,
Belike through impotence, or unaware,
To give his Enemies their wish, and end
Them in his anger, whom his anger saves
To punish endless. . . .

---

## DISCUSSION QUESTIONS

1. Williams writes, "A war against terrorism is a war of the mind . . ." Explain. in what way(s) might the constitutional CRISES engendered by the patriot act affect the minds of americans?
2. The essay poses a distinction between a criminal justice system based on reason, as represented in rules of procedure, and a system rooted in collective fear, prejudice, and hatred. What are the differences? Is collective fear a threat to individual rights? To democracy?
3. Williams warns us against the temptations of "the 'comfort' and convenience of high-tech totalitarianism." What are some contemporary examples of the technology of surveillance and control? How might these technologies collide with the basic values embodied in the First Amendment to the United States Constitution? The Fourth Amendment? The Fifth and Sixth Amendments?

# 32 R. Claire Snyder

# NEO-PATRIARCHY AND THE ANTI-HOMOSEXUAL AGENDA

*By 2004 same-sex marriage had perhaps equaled abortion as a contentious and divisive social issue in American politics. Even as lesbians and gay men wed legally in Massachusetts, a constitutional amendment to ban homosexual marriage was becoming a kind of political litmus test among conservatives. In this article political scientist R. Claire Snyder explores and criticizes opposition to same-sex marriage. In many ways the liberal principle of legal equality would seem to support the case for gay marriage. However an overlapping coalition of religious and political conservatives, "pro-family" activists, and political theorists have developed an antigay agenda powered by a rhetoric that "resonates with many of our most cherished cultural narratives and personal fantasies." Snyder, author of* Gay Marriage and Democracy: Equality for All *finds that these arguments are "based on an idealized, inegalitarian heterosexual family with rigid gender roles." She argues that the antihomosexual agenda threatens valuable aspects of the liberal democratic tradition, including the separation of church and state, legal equality, and personal freedom. In this way Snyder demonstrates that the stakes in the battle debate over sexual orientation and marriage involve the core values of democracy itself.*

Since the late 1990s a series of court decisions has raised the possibility that the civil right to marriage might soon be accorded to all citizens, not just to heterosexuals. Most significantly, in 2003 the Massachusetts Supreme Court ruled that denying same-sex couples access to civil marriage violates the state's constitution, which "forbids the creation of "second class citizens," and on May 17, 2004,

Massachusetts began issuing marriage licenses to same-sex couples who reside in the state. In direct opposition to legal equality for lesbian and gay couples, conservative forces have mobilized across the country in "defense" of heterosexual-only marriage. The Massachusetts decision fuelled calls for the passage of the Federal Marriage Amendment, originally introduced in 2001, which states

*Source:* Revised and updated by the author from R. Claire Snyder, "Neo-Patriarchy and the Anti-Homosexual Agenda." *Fundamental Differences: Feminists Talk Back to Social Conservatives,* Cynthia Burack and Jyl J. Josephson, eds., Lanham, MD: Rowman and Littlefield, 2003, pp. 157–171.

"Marriage in the United States shall consist only of the union of a man and a woman. Neither this Constitution, nor the constitution of any State, shall be construed to require that marriage or the legal incidents thereof be conferred upon any union other than the union of a man and a woman." The Amendment would make permanent the 1996 Defense of Marriage Act (DOMA)—"no State shall be required to give effect to a law of any other State with respect to a same-sex 'marriage'"—which might be found to violate the Constitution's "full faith and credit clause." Even without the Amendment, however, DOMA prohibits the extension of federal benefits to legally married same-sex couples, thus denying those married in Massachusetts full equality before the law.

In their attempt to prevent the logical extension of liberal principles to lesbian and gay citizens, anti-homosexual activists have made common cause with a number of other reactionary movements that want to undo the progress of feminism and reestablish the patriarchal nuclear family as the dominant family form. This essay examines the interconnected arguments advanced by a number of conservative constituencies committed to the politics of neo-patriarchy, including the religious particularism of the Christian Right, the homophobic anti-feminism of Concerned Women for America, the "family values" of James Dobson, the Fatherhood movement spearheaded by David Blankenhorn, and the conservative democratic theory of William Galston. While the details of these arguments differ, all have a similar form and use the same authorities, and all are both homophobic and anti-feminist. Thus, all undermine the principles of liberal democracy, despite rhetorical assertions to the contrary.

## LESBIAN/GAY CIVIL RIGHTS AND THE LOGIC OF LIBERALISM

Legal equality constitutes one of the most important founding principles of liberal democracy in the United States. While the equal rights of the Declaration of Independence were largely aspirational at the time they were written, over the course of the twentieth century, American society has become increasingly imbued with a liberal public philosophy

that values individual choice, civil rights, legal equality, and a "neutral state" that leaves individuals free to pursue their own vision of the good life in civil society and the private sphere without interference from the government.

The revolutionary principle of legal equality has been successfully used to justify progressive change. African-Americans utilized this principle during the Civil Rights Movement in their struggle to end segregation. While violently opposed by the Right at the time, the principle of color-blind law has been largely accepted by contemporary conservatives. The struggle for gender-blind law has also been largely successful. Although feminists lost the battle for the Equal Rights Amendment (ERA) during the 1970s, since that time the principle of legal equality for women has been implemented through the Courts, which are charged with following the logic of liberalism as they apply the principles of the Constitution to new areas. While progress has not been inevitable or without setbacks, overall the level of legal equality within American society has advanced over time.

Despite the compelling logic of philosophical liberalism, the American Right actively opposed the extension of legal equality in every instance. The Old Right was explicitly racist and violently fought to stop the extension of civil rights to African-Americans. By 1965, however, Gallup polls "showed that 52 percent of Americans identified civil rights as the 'most important problem' confronting the nation, and an astonishing 75 percent of respondents favored federal voting rights legislation.'" With explicit racism on the decline, in 1965 right-wing leaders began developing a more marketable message, "mainstreaming the ideological positions of the Old Right and developing winnable policies" that "highlighted a protest theme" against a wide range of cultural changes inaugurated by the new social movements of the 1960s. This "New Right" successfully created a coalition between cultural conservatives, including Christian fundamentalists, and anti-government, fiscal conservatives (*aka* neo-liberals).

Feminism constituted precisely the enemy the New Right needed to consolidate its base. Anti-feminism "provided a link with fundamentalist churches," focused "the reaction against the changes in child rearing, sexual behavior, divorce, and the use of drugs that had taken place in the 1960s and 1970s," and "mobilized a group, traditional home-makers, that had lost status over the two previous decades and was feeling the psychological effects of the loss." The conservative mobilization against feminism solidified the New Right during the 1970s and played a "very important" role in its success: the election of Ronald Reagan in 1980 and the rightward shift of American politics.

The women's movement and the lesbian/gay civil rights movement were linked theoretically and through common struggle, and the Right used this connection to its advantage. For example, Phyllis Schlafly's Eagle Forum argued that "militant homo-sexuals from all over America have made the ERA issue a hot priority. Why? To be able finally to get homosexual marriage licenses, to adopt children and raise them to emulate their homosexual 'parents,' and to obtain pension and medical benefits for odd-couple 'spouses.' . . . Vote *NO on 6!* The Pro-Gay E.R.A." In its rise to power, the New Right successfully manipulated homophobia to increase opposition to gender equality and explicitly condemned all attempts to accord lesbians and gay men the equal protection of the law.

While the Christian Right continues to pose a serious threat to civil rights and has achieved unprecedented levels of power since 1980, the logic of liberalism in American society is hard to deny. While public opinion polls vary, support for same-sex marriage is particularly strong among young people who have come to age during an era of nearly hegemonic liberalism. A UCLA survey of first-year college students revealed that 58 percent of first year college students now "think gay and lesbian couples should have the right to 'equal marital status,' i.e., civil marriage." Remarkably, of that 58 percent, half consider themselves conservative or "middle-of-the-road" in their political views. A poll of first year students at Ithaca College shows that "79 percent of Ithaca College freshmen agreed that same-sex marriage should be legal, compared to 59.3 percent nationwide." In the New Jersey poll an overwhelming 71 percent of those between 18 and 29 support the legalization of same-sex marriage,

and in the New Hampshire poll, 70 percent of 17 to 29 year olds do. While the media widely publicized a Gallup poll conducted after the *Lawrence v. Texas* ruling striking down anti-homosexual sodomy laws that revealed some decline in support for same-sex unions, the decline was not evident among the young (18–29), 61 percent of whom "say they support legalizing same-sex 'marriage.'" Nevertheless, a coalition of religious, secular, and academic activists and organizations continue to oppose, and organize around their opposition to, the rights of gays and lesbians to marry or form civil unions.

## RELIGIOUS PARTICULARISM AND THE ANTI-HOMOSEXUAL AGENDA

The Christian Right opposes legal equality for les-bians and gay men when it comes to marriage because it defines marriage as a sacred religious institution, and its particular version of Christianity views homosexuality as a particularly grave sin. According to the Family Research Council (FRC) marriage is "the *work of heaven and every major religion* and culture throughout world history." Concerned Women for America (CWA) proclaims "we believe that marriage is *a covenant established by God* wherein one man and one woman, united for life, are licensed by the state for the purpose of founding and maintaining a family." Focus on the Family (FOF) opposes even "civil unions" because they "would essentially legalize homosexual marriage and therefore undermine the *sanctity* of marriage." Indeed because of this religious worldview, all three groups have made opposition to same-sex marriage a centerpiece of their political agenda.

The Christian Right's vision of heterosexual marriage directly relates to its understanding of gender differences, which it bases on its particular interpretation of the Christian Bible. More specifi-cally, this reading focuses on the second creation story in Genesis, in which God created Eve out of Adam's rib to be his helper and declared that the man and his wife would become "one flesh" (Genesis 18:21–24), rather than on the first story in which "God created man in His image, in the image of God He created him; *male and female He created them*" (Genesis 1:26–27, emphasis added).

Additionally, instead of reading the latter version as establishing gender equality at the origin, or even androgyny, as some religious scholars do, the Christian Right interprets it to mean "God's purpose for man was that there should be two sexes, male and female. Every person is either a 'he' or a 'she.' God did not divide mankind into three or four or five sexes." The Christian Right bolsters its interpretation with a few New Testament verses stating that woman is the "weaker vessel" (1 Peter 3:7), that man is "joined to his wife, and the two become one flesh" (Eph. 5:31–32), and that the "husband is the head of the wife" (1 Cor. 11:4; Eph. 5:23).

For the Christian Right, the Bible not only proclaims a natural gender hierarchy but also condemns homosexuality as a sin. It bases its interpretation on two sentences in Leviticus that proclaim "do not lie with a male as one lies with a woman; it is an abhorrence" (Leviticus 18:22) and "if a man lies with a male as one lies with a woman, the two of them have done an abhorrent thing; they shall be put to death" (Leviticus 20:13), completely ignoring the fact that the Ten Commandments did not include a prohibition on homosexuality. The Christian Right also stresses an interpretation of the Sodom and Gomorrah story (Genesis 18:16–19:29) that depicts the city's destruction as God's punishment for homosexuality, an interpretation that is highly contested by religious scholars. Finally, right-wing Christians justify their condemnation of lesbian and gay sexuality on three passages in Paul's writings—two words and two sentences total (I Corinthians 6:9–10, I Timothy 1:8–10, and Romans 1:26–27). They cannot base it on what Jesus said because he never even mentioned homosexuality. Although the meanings of all these passages have been debated at length by religious scholars, and no consensus exists as to their meanings, nevertheless, conservative Christians insist that God's will is as clear as it is specific: man and woman are naturally different, designed by God for heterosexual marriage and the establishment of the patriarchal family.

As far as their own religious rites are concerned, Christian Right churches certainly have the religious liberty to define marriage any way they see fit. However, when the faithful of the Christian Right ask the U.S. government and the governments of the states to restrict the right to civil marriage because of their particular interpretation of revealed religion, they violate the separation of church and state mandated by the First Amendment. Not all religions share the Christian Right's definition of marriage. For example, Reform Judaism not only favors civil marriage for gays and lesbians but also allows for religious unions, and many Muslims practice polygamy. In fact, even within Christianity, no clear consensus exists on the question of same-sex marriage. Nevertheless, despite the diversity of beliefs within America's religiously pluralistic society, the Christian Right group Alliance for Marriage has introduced a Federal Marriage Amendment that declares "Marriage in the United States shall consist only of the union of a man and a woman." Clearly this Amendment asks the federal government to establish one particular religious definition of marriage as the law of the land, thus violating the separation of church and state.

## THAT '70S ARGUMENT: THE ANXIETY OF RIGHT-WING WOMEN

The Christian Right group Concerned Women for America, which claims to be the largest women's group in the country, consistently asserts that the struggle of lesbians and gay men for the right to marry is not an attempt to participate in the institution of marriage but rather an attempt to "undermine marriage" and destroy the family. In strictly logical terms this makes no sense. Aren't lesbians and gays actually *reinforcing* the legitimacy of marriage as an institution through their struggle for the right to marry? Indeed many within the LGBT community have criticized this struggle for doing precisely that and not much more. While same-sex marriage would not undermine the institution of marriage in general, it would undermine the *traditional patriarchal heterosexual vision of marriage* in particular, which is precisely what the Christian Right desperately wants to re-establish.

Concerned Women for America wants heterosexual marriage to maintain its privileged status in American society and to continue to function as the justification for special rights. This line of argumentation plays on a number of anxieties expressed by the first generation of New Right women who mobilized in opposition to the ERA and abortion rights during the 1970s. Status was a key concern for those women. "At the beginning of the contemporary women's movement, in 1968, women of all classes found themselves in something like the same boat." Most were homemakers and/or low-level employees. However, over the course of the next two decades "homemakers suffered a tremendous loss in social prestige" as "high-status women" began choosing careers over homemaking. Consequently, conservative homemakers—who, after all, had done the *right thing* for their time—now found themselves facing "status degradation," and they resented it. Twenty-five years later, the special status of heterosexual marriage is being threatened by lesbians and gays, and many right-wing women again feel diminished.

Opposed to government-sponsored family support, Christian Right women favor laws that force individual men to take responsibility for the children they father and for the mothers who bear those children. The '70s generation feared that the changes inaugurated by feminism—the ERA, reproductive freedom, no-fault divorce, and the loosening of sexual mores—would make it easier for men to get out of their familial commitments. As opposed to liberal feminist women who wanted the right to compete equally with men, many anti-feminist women did not have the educational level or job skills that would allow them to pursue satisfying careers if forced to work outside the home. They feared that the ERA would eliminate the traditional legal requirement for husbands to support their wives financially. Phyllis Schlafly told homemakers that the ERA would say "Boys, supporting your wives isn't your responsibility anymore." At the same time, the rise of "no-fault" divorce laws during this period further threatened the economic security of traditional "housewives." As Schlafly put it, "even though love may go out the window, the obligation should remain. ERA would eliminate that obligation." To this day, Christian Right women condemn no-fault divorce, which "allows one person to decide when a relationship can be severed," often catapulting women into poverty. While higher wages for women, safe and affordable childcare,

and universal health insurance constitute a progressive solution to the problems caused by the fragility of marriage and callousness of deadbeat dads, right-wing women demand the return of a traditional patriarchal vision of marriage, ignoring the reality of social change.

In the 1970s, conservative women worried that if sex became widely available outside of marriage, they would have difficulty keeping their husbands interested in them. Kristen Luker's interviews with the first generation of "pro-life" women revealed the following insight:

> If women plan to find their primary role in marriage and the family, then they face a need to create a "moral cartel" when it comes to sex. . . . If many women are willing to sleep with men outside of marriage, then the regular sexual activity that comes with marriage is much less valuable an incentive to marry. . . . [For] traditional women, their primary resource for marriage is the promise of a stable home, with everything it implies: children, regular sex, a "haven in a heartless world."

For the first generation of Christian Right women, the sexual liberation of many feminist women threatened to destabilize the marital bargain that many traditional women relied upon. Given the option, their husbands might abandon them for more exciting women.

Do today's Christian Right women fear that if given the choice their husbands might choose other men? Perhaps. After all, anti-gay activist Dr. Paul Cameron tells them that "the evidence is that men do a better job on men, and women on women, if all you are looking for is orgasm." If you want "the most satisfying orgasm you can get," he explains, "then homosexuality seems too powerful to resist. . . . It's pure sexuality. It's almost like pure heroin. It's such a rush." In opposition, "marital sex tends toward the boring" and generally "doesn't deliver the kind of sheer sexual pleasure that homosexual sex does." Although the American Psychological Association expelled Cameron for ethics violations in 1983, he still serves as an oft-quoted right-wing "expert" on homosexuality. In light of his comments, it would be understandable if Christian Right women feel anxious about their ability to keep their husbands interested in heterosexual marriage.

Fundamentally different, men and women come together to reproduce and remain coupled in order to rear their children. Because homosexuality severs the connection between sex and reproduction, CWA sees homosexual relationships as necessarily fleeting, as driven by sexual gratification alone. For example, Beverly LaHaye insists that "homosexual relationships are not only the antithesis to family, but also threaten its very core. It is *the compulsive desire for sexual gratification without lasting commitment,* the high rate of promiscuity, and the self-defined morality among homosexuals that sap the vitality of the family structure, making it something less than it was, is, and should be." Clearly the desire of many gay and lesbian couples to marry and to raise children belies this argument. Nevertheless, Christian Right groups like CWA purposely depict the struggle for lesbian/gay civil rights in a reductive and patently distorted way in order to manipulate the anxieties of traditional women, secure their own special interests and advance their larger political agenda.

## NEO-PATRIARCHY AND THE FATHERHOOD MOVEMENT

Joining the opposition to same-sex marriage are advocates of the fatherhood movement who seek to restore traditional gender roles and reestablish the patriarchal family as the dominant family form in America. Because no evidence exists that same-sex couples are less functional than heterosexual ones, or that their children are more likely to suffer negative effects, allowing same-sex couples to marry and have children would clearly undermine the myth that the patriarchal heterosexual family is the superior family form. Consequently, the fatherhood activists repeatedly assert that children need both a masculine father and a feminine mother in order to develop properly.

The fatherhood movement blames feminism and single mothers for the social problems caused by men and teenaged boys. While the packaging of their arguments varies slightly, advocates of this school of thought generally make a similar claim:

Refusing to respect natural gender differences, feminists have pathologized masculinity and futilely attempted to change the behavior of men and boys. They have undermined the rightful authority of men as the head of the household, attempted to change the natural division of labor that exists between mothers and fathers, and propagated the idea that a woman can fulfill the role traditionally played by a man, thus rendering fathers superfluous to family life. Consequently, men have lost interest in fulfilling their traditional family responsibilities, and boys have no one to teach them how to become responsible men. Detached from the civilizing influence of the traditional patriarchal family, males increasingly cause a wide array of social problems, and everybody suffers.

Focus on the Family president James Dobson makes this argument from a Christian Right perspective. In *Bringing Up Boys,* he argues that traditional gender roles are natural and cannot be changed. He points to the continued power of men in society as evidence of their natural, "biochemical and anatomical," dominance. Dobson strongly opposes attempts to change the gender socialization of children and explicitly links this "unisex" idea to "the powerful gay and lesbian agenda," whose propagandists are teaching a revolutionary view of sexuality called "gender feminism," which insists that sex assignment is irrelevant. While Dobson sees this as dangerous for both sexes, it is particularly harmful for boys: "Protect the masculinity of your boys, who will be under increasing political pressure in years to come."

Dobson believes that a breakdown of traditional gender roles within the family fosters homosexuality in children. The prevention of homosexuality among boys requires the involvement of a properly masculine heterosexual father, especially during the early years. Dobson relies on the work of Dr. Joseph Nicolosi, a leading proponent of the Christian Right's "ex-gay" movement, who urges parents to monitor their children for signs of "prehomosexuality," so professionals can step in before it is too late. While "feminine behavior in boyhood" is clearly a sign, so is "nonmasculinity" defined as not fitting in with male peers. "The father," Nicolosi asserts, "plays an essential role in a boy's normal development as a man. The truth is, Dad is more important than Mom." In order to ensure heterosexuality, the father "needs to mirror and affirm his son's maleness. He can play rough-and-tumble games with his son, in ways that are decidedly different from the games he would play with a little girl. He can help his son learn to throw and catch a ball. . . . He can even take his son with him into the shower, where the boy cannot help but notice that Dad has a penis, just like his, only bigger."

Based solely on the work of Nicolosi, Dobson concludes, "if you as a parent have an effeminate boy or a masculinized girl, I urge you to get a copy [of Nicolosi's book] and then seek immediate professional help." Beware, however, of "secular" mental health professionals who will most certainly "take the wrong approach—telling your child that he is homosexual and needs to accept that fact." Instead, Dobson recommends a referral from either Exodus International, the leading organization of the ex-gay ministries, or the National Association for Research and Therapy of Homosexuality, "formed to oppose the 1973 decision by the American Psychological Association to no longer classify homosexuality as an emotional or mental disorder."

Dobson's emphasis on the important role played by fathers bolsters the arguments of the "fatherhood movement," which emerged during the 1990s. One of the first organizations to spearhead this movement was the Promise Keepers (PK), founded by Bill McCartney in 1990 as a "Christ-centered ministry dedicated to uniting men through vital relationships to become godly influences in their world." This organization wants to restore fathers to their rightful place at the head of the patriarchal family.

Institute for American Values president David Blankenhorn advances a similar agenda using secular arguments. His book *Fatherless America* (1995) and the follow-up volume *The Fatherhood Movement* (1999)—co-edited with Wade Horn (George W. Bush's Secretary of Health and Human Services) and Mitchell Pearlstein—blames the "declining child well-being in our society," not on growing levels of poverty, deteriorating public services, lack of safe and affordable childcare, the lower income of women, child abuse, racism or misogyny, but rather on fatherlessness. Fatherlessness, he tells us,

is "the engine driving our most urgent social problems, from crime to adolescent pregnancy to child sexual abuse to domestic violence against women." While some conservatives argue that "the best anti-poverty program for children is a stable, intact family," Blankenhorn demands more: "a married father on the premises."

Like those on the Christian Right, Blankenhorn insists that children need not just two involved parents but more specifically *a male father and a female mother enacting traditional gender roles.* Citing two anthropologists, Blankenhorn claims that "gendered parental roles derive precisely from children's needs." During childhood "the needs of the child compel mothers and fathers to specialize in their labor and to adopt gender-based parental roles." Consequently, men and women should stick with traditional roles, Blankenhorn insists, even if this conflicts with their "narcissistic claims" to personal autonomy.

Like Dobson, Blankenhorn condemns attempts to equalize the roles of mothers and fathers in childrearing, and derides what he calls the new "like-a-mother father." While Blankenhorn barely mentions lesbians and gay men in his analysis, his argument clearly justifies an opposition to same-sex marriage. Obviously, his insistence that proper childhood development requires heterosexual parents who enact traditional gender roles implies that, in his view, homosexual couples cannot raise healthy children. In addition, however, Blankenhorn specifically advocates laws to prohibit unmarried women from accessing sperm banks. Perhaps he shares the fear of CWA that gender equality would mean that "lesbian women would be considered no different from men," especially once they get access to male seed. If that were to happen, where would that leave men?

## "SEEDBEDS OF VIRTUE": WHAT LESSONS DOES THE PATRIARCHAL FAMILY TEACH?

Building directly on the body of literature outlined above, a growing number of right-wing activists, respectable scholars, and well-known political theorists have begun connecting the neo-patriarchal movement to the survival and revitalization of

American democracy. This approach claims, in short, that liberal democracy requires virtuous citizens, and virtue is best learned at home in a traditional family with two married parents. The Institute for American Values sponsored a conference on this topic that resulted in the publication of *Seedbeds of Virtue: Sources of Competence, Character, and Citizenship in American Society* that Blankenhorn edited with Mary Ann Glendon who so strongly opposes same-sex unions that she helped draft both the Federal Marriage Amendment and a similar amendment to the Massachusetts constitution.

While many conservative thinkers support the "seedbeds of virtue" approach to justifying the patriarchal heterosexual family—many in exactly the same terms as the fatherhood movement—I will concentrate on the arguments advanced by political theorist William Galston, who served as Deputy Assistant to the President for Domestic Policy under Bill Clinton, a *Democratic* president. While Galston's defense of the family does not explicitly specify the patriarchal heterosexual family form in particular, one can only infer that he endorses that vision for several reasons. First, he makes arguments similar to those of the neo-patriarchalists *without any caveats*. Second, he explicitly praises Mary Ann Glendon and Jean Bethke Elshtain for having "already said nearly every thing that needs saying on [the subject of the family]." While Glendon works politically in opposition to same-sex marriage, Elshtain's scholarship specifically proposes "a normative vision of the family—mothers, fathers, and children" and claims that this particular family form "is not only *not* at odds with democratic civil society but is in fact, now more than ever, a prerequisite for that society to function." Third, Galston himself signs *A Call to Civil Society: Why Democracy Needs Moral Truths* that says the number one priority for American democracy should be "to increase the likelihood that more children will grow up with their two married parents."

In addition, the lack of explicit references to homosexuality should not be interpreted as a lack of homophobia. As Jean Hardisty has discovered, since the mid-1980s, Christian Right organizations have tended to "highlight the religious principles undergirding their anti-homosexual politics only when they are targeting other Christians. When organizing in the wider political arena, they frame their anti-gay organizing as a struggle for secular ends, such as 'defense of the family.'" Thus you get James Dobson in Christian Right circles, David Blankenhorn in secular circles, and William Galston in academic circles. Despite variations on the theme, one thing remains constant: the normative vision presented by these conservatives gives lesbians and gay men absolutely no place in family life, and, by extension, no place in democratic society.

Working from a firm foundation in the history of political thought, Galston argues that liberal democracy requires individuals who have the virtues necessary for life in a free society. The claim is simple: "that the operation of liberal institutions is affected in important ways by the character of citizens (and leaders), and that at some point, the attenuation of individual virtue will create pathologies with which liberal political contrivances, however technically perfect their design, simply cannot cope." Cataloguing the wide array of virtues necessary for liberal democracy, Galston only implies that the traditional family best teaches these virtues to youngsters; he never argues it explicitly.

An examination of how the particular virtues cited by Galston relate to the traditional family produces three different arguments. First, many of the virtues Galston emphasizes, while originally acquired in a family, do not require a patriarchal heterosexual family form in particular. For example, important virtues like civility, the work ethic, delayed gratification, adaptability, discernment, and "the ability to work within constraints on action imposed by social diversity and constitutional institutions" could certainly be instilled in children by any functional family, including one headed by same-sex parents. Galston makes no argument for the superiority of heterosexuals in fostering these characteristics in children, and such an argument is not supported by empirical evidence.

Second, the traditional patriarchal family could actually undermine a number of important virtues extolled by Galston. For example, he argues that a liberal society is characterized by two key features—individualism and diversity. While children certainly need to learn independence, how does the traditional patriarchal family, in which wives are dependent upon their husbands' leadership and economic support, teach the virtue of independence to future *female* citizens? Galston must be focusing on boys only. Additionally, Galston cites "loyalty" as a central virtue for liberal democracy, defining it as "the developed capacity to understand, to accept, and to act on the core principles of one's society." This "is particularly important in liberal communities," he argues, because they "tend to be organized around abstract principles rather than shared ethnicity, nationality, or history." But if one of the fundamental principles of liberal democracy is legal equality for all citizens, again we must ask: What lessons does a child learn about equality growing up in a patriarchal nuclear family in which *men lead and women submit?* While the traditional family may provide certain benefits to children, it is unclear how it teaches them the universal principle of equality for all citizens, when this family form models gender inequality.

Third, a number of the democratic virtues Galston emphasizes could be undermined by the normative vision of the Christian Right. For example, Galston emphasizes "the willingness to *listen seriously to a range of views*" and the "willingness to set forth one's own views intelligibly and candidly as the basis of a *politics of persuasion rather than manipulation or coercion.*" This directly relates to the virtue of *tolerance.* While Galston stresses that tolerance does not mean a belief that all lifestyles are "equally good," it does mean that "the pursuit of the better course should be (and in some cases can only be) the consequence of *education or persuasion rather than coercion.*" While open-mindedness, tolerance, and non-coercion certainly constitute important virtues for any democratic society, they are not hallmarks of the Christian Right, especially when it comes to its anti-homosexual agenda.

## CONCLUSION

The fight against the extension of civil rights to lesbians and gay men forms a central component of the larger battle against women's equality. While the rhetoric deployed by conservatives resonates with many of our most cherished cultural narratives and personal fantasies, their overarching agenda actually undermines our most precious political values, including the separation of church and state, legal equality and personal liberty. While liberal democracy has its limitations, its virtue is that it maximizes the freedom of all by allowing individuals to organize their personal lives as they see fit. While a liberal state may respond to the will of its citizens by providing a default set of legal entanglements that make it easier for individuals to establish families (i.e., civil marriage), it may not legitimately deny equal protection of the laws to particular groups of citizens, no matter how unpopular they are. The conservative arguments against same-sex marriage, whether religious, secular, or academic, are all similarly structured and based on an idealized, inegalitarian heterosexual family with rigid gender roles. Justified by references to the well-being of children, these arguments are unsustainable when subjected to close scrutiny.

---

## DISCUSSION QUESTIONS

1. Snyder argues that the founding principles of liberal democracy lend support to the struggle for equality of lesbians and gay men? How compelling do you find her argument?
2. Identify the leading arguments against homosexual equality and gay marriage. What are Snyder's arguments against each of these positions? Do you agree that these antigay perspectives serve to uphold rigid gender roles or "neo-patriarchy"?

# PART III

# POLITICS AND VISION

Politics is everywhere. Although you may not think of yourself as a political person, you are surrounded by, bombarded by, and inescapably influenced by politics. There is no shelter from the storm.

We firmly believe that as citizens you have an enormous stake in the direction American politics takes in the twenty-first century. We further assume that you do not automatically agree that the direction we are heading is the direction we ought to take. If our assumption is correct, and your views are not cast in stone, you may want to question critically the possible future options open to us. Given the structural context we have sketched in Part I, and the discussion of political institutions in Part II, it follows that we think conventional political leaders lack the creative vision necessary to move us beyond status quo conceptions of "problems" and "solutions." In our judgment, we face a potentially stifling lack of national political imagination.

In Part III, we offer you chapters that attempt to spark your interest in and imagination on two fronts. First we look at some particularly important policy challenges involving issues of class and inequality, gender, race, and U.S. foreign policy. Our selection of these issues does not pretend to be exhaustive, but we do think that these articles will give you a clearer sense of how an alternative critical perspective looks at difficult political questions.

After exploring these issues, we conclude with a chapter that amounts to a call for action. Government, corporate, and media elites routinely defend their behavior by saying they act with peoples' best interests at heart. In their minds, this may well be true, for they often equate their class interests and political interests with a broader public interest. We are quite skeptical of this equation. Nevertheless, there is a sense in which we are all indirectly responsible for the actions of political and economic elites, at least to the extent that we remain silent in the face of actions we find morally wrong.

We are implicated in behavior we oppose if we have the freedom to oppose that behavior, but we choose not to. This is especially true for those of us who have gone to college and presumably have had the time and resources to develop the skills to think critically in an academic environment where alternative information should be readily available. The final chapter of our anthology thus encourages you to take responsibility in a political world that too often fosters apathy and disengagement.

# CHAPTER 9

# POLITICAL CHALLENGES AT HOME AND ABROAD

We live in a changing world. Our values, ideologies, politics, society, economics, and the larger world outside America are being challenged and transformed, often in directions we only dimly understand. In the final chapter, we stress that the shape of the future partly depends on choices we make and interpretations we reach. In this chapter we wish to indicate, without any attempt to be comprehensive, some of the major policy challenges facing Americans in the twenty-first century. By now it should be clear that we do not believe these challenges can be resolved on a humane and democratic basis unless we make far-reaching economic, political, and social changes. Confronted with crises, many of us react by withdrawing from politics or by hoping to muddle through. But opinion polls and other evidence convince us that millions of Americans have a sober-minded desire to comprehend and grapple with the dangers and opportunities we face. Each of the four readings in this chapter prepares us for the critical choices ahead.

# 33 *Paul Krugman*

# THE TAX-CUT CON

*The belief that Americans are taxed too heavily—that economic salvation can be achieved in no small measure by cutting taxes—has been an article of faith in American politics for the past 25 years. To economist and* New York Times *columnist Paul Krugman, the tax cutting fervor has all the markings of a crusade, with advocates displaying a stridency that is "relentless, even fanatical." In this article Krugman explores the dynamics of the tax cut crusade, focusing on the two wings of the movement—"supply-siders" and "starve-the-beasters"— the latter aided by their "lucky-ducky" argument. He traces the history of tax cut mania from its debut in the Reagan administration of the 1980s through its "second wind" in the presidency of George W. Bush. Krugman critiques various claims of the conservative tax cut movement, particularly their charge that U.S. citizens pay taxes that are wildly high, and he exposes much of their analysis and reasoning as an economic "con". He concludes that "If taxes stay as low as they are now, government as we know it cannot be maintained"—a prospect that greatly pleases the tax cut crowd, who are guiding the nation into the early part of the twenty-first century by recreating levels of economic inequality not seen since the nineteenth. The resulting implications of this anti-tax crusade are dire for the American political economy as we risk sinking into a planned fiscal crisis that will de-legitimize the very idea of the government pursuing most public purposes. To stave off such a fate, Americans must move beyond the superficially attractive idea of tax cuts and ask themselves "what kind of a country we want to be."*

## THE CARTOON AND THE REALITY

Bruce Tinsley's comic strip, "Mallard Fillmore," is, he says, "for the average person out there: the forgotten American taxpayer who's sick of the liberal media." In June, that forgotten taxpayer made an appearance in the strip, attacking his TV set with a baseball bat and yelling: "I can't afford to send my kids to college, or even take 'em out of their substandard public school, because the federal, state and local governments take more than 50 percent of my income in taxes. And then the guy on the news asks with a straight face whether or not we can 'afford' tax cuts."

*Source:* Paul Krugman, "The Tax-Cut Con." *The New York Times Magazine*, September 14, 2003, pp. 54–62.

But that's just a cartoon. Meanwhile, Bob Riley has to face the reality.

Riley knows all about substandard public schools. He's the governor of Alabama, which ranks near the bottom of the nation in both spending per pupil and educational achievement. The state has also neglected other public services—for example, 28,000 inmates are held in a prison system built for 12,000. And thanks in part to a lack of health care, it has the second-highest infant mortality in the nation.

When he was a member of Congress, Riley, a Republican, was a staunch supporter of tax cuts. Faced with a fiscal crisis in his state, however, he seems to have had an epiphany. He decided that it was impossible to balance Alabama's budget without a significant tax increase. And that, apparently, led him to reconsider everything. "The largest tax increase in state history just to maintain the status quo?" he asked. "I don't think so." Instead, Riley proposed a wholesale restructuring of the state's tax system: reducing taxes on the poor and middle class while raising them on corporations and the rich and increasing overall tax receipts enough to pay for a big increase in education spending. You might call it a New Deal for Alabama.

Nobody likes paying taxes, and no doubt some Americans are as angry about their taxes as Tinsley's imaginary character. But most Americans also care a lot about the things taxes pay for. All politicians say they're for public education; almost all of them also say they support a strong national defense, maintaining Social Security and, if anything, expanding the coverage of Medicare. When the "guy on the news" asks whether we can afford a tax cut, he's asking whether, after yet another tax cut goes through, there will be enough money to pay for those things. And the answer is no.

But it's very difficult to get that answer across in modern American politics, which has been dominated for 25 years by a crusade against taxes.

I don't use the word "crusade" lightly. The advocates of tax cuts are relentless, even fanatical. An indication of the movement's fervor—and of its political power—came during the Iraq war. War is expensive and is almost always accompanied by tax increases. But not in 2003. "Nothing is more important in the face of a war," declared Tom DeLay, the House majority leader, "than cutting taxes." And sure enough, taxes were cut, not just in a time of war but also in the face of record budget deficits. Nor will it be easy to reverse those tax cuts: the tax-cut movement has convinced many Americans—like Tinsley—that everybody still pays far too much in taxes.

A result of the tax-cut crusade is that there is now a fundamental mismatch between the benefits Americans expect to receive from the government and the revenues government collects. This mismatch is already having profound effects at the state and local levels: teachers and policemen are being laid off and children are being denied health insurance. The federal government can mask its problems for a while, by running huge budget deficits, but it, too, will eventually have to decide whether to cut services or raise taxes. And we are not talking about minor policy adjustments. If taxes stay as low as they are now, government as we know it cannot be maintained. In particular, Social Security will have to become far less generous; Medicare will no longer be able to guarantee comprehensive medical care to older Americans; Medicaid will no longer provide basic medical care to the poor.

How did we reach this point? What are the origins of the antitax crusade? And where is it taking us? To answer these questions, we will have to look both at who the antitax crusaders are and at the evidence on what tax cuts do to the budget and the economy. But first, let's set the stage y taking a look at the current state of taxation in America.

## HOW HIGH ARE OUR TAXES?

The reason Tinsley's comic strip about the angry taxpayer caught my eye was, of course, that the numbers were all wrong. Very few Americans pay as much as 50 percent of their income in taxes; on average, families near the middle of the income distribution pay only about half that percentage in federal, state and local taxes combined.

In fact, though most Americans feel that they pay too much in taxes, they get off quite lightly compared with the citizens of other advanced countries.

*The Tax & Spend Paradox*

Furthermore, for most Americans tax rates probably haven't risen for a generation. And a few Americans—namely those with high incomes—face much lower taxes than they did a generation ago.

To assess trends in the overall level of taxes and to compare taxation across countries, economists usually look first at the ratio of taxes to gross domestic product, the total value of output produced in the country. In the United States, all taxes—federal, state and local—reached a peak of 29.6 percent of G.D.P. in 2000. That number was, however, swollen by taxes on capital gains during the stock-market bubble. By 2002, the tax take was down to 26.3 percent of G.D.P., and all indications are that it will be lower still this year and next.

This is a low number compared with almost every other advanced country. In 1999, Canada collected 38.2 percent of G.D.P. in taxes, France collected 45.8 percent and Sweden, 52.2 percent.

Still, aren't taxes much higher than they used to be? Not if we're looking back over the past 30 years. As a share of G.D.P., federal taxes are currently at their lowest point since the Eisenhower administration. State and local taxes rose substantially between 1960 and the early 1970's, but have been roughly stable since then. Aside from the capital gains taxes paid during the bubble years, the share of income Americans pay in taxes has been flat since Richard Nixon was president.

Of course, overall levels of taxation don't necessarily tell you how heavily particular individuals and families are taxed. As it turns out, however, middle-income Americans, like the country as a whole, haven't seen much change in their overall taxes over the past 30 years. On average, families in the middle of the income distribution find themselves paying about 26 percent of their income in taxes today. This number hasn't changed significantly since 1989, and though hard data are lacking, it probably hasn't changed much since 1970.

Meanwhile, wealthy Americans have seen a sharp drop in their tax burden. The top tax rate—the income-tax rate on the highest bracket—is now 35 percent, half what it was in the 1970's. With the exception of a brief period between 1988 and 1993, that's the lowest rate since 1932. Other taxes that, directly or indirectly, bear mainly on the very affluent have also been cut sharply. The effective tax rate on corporate profits has been cut in half since the 1960's. The 2001 tax cut phases out the inheritance tax, which is overwhelmingly a tax on the very wealthy: in 1999, only 2 percent of estates paid any tax, and half the tax was paid by only 3,300 estates worth more than $5 million. The 2003 tax act sharply cuts taxes on dividend income, another boon to the very well off. By the time the Bush tax cuts have taken full effect, people with really high incomes will face their lowest average tax rate since the Hoover administration.

So here's the picture: Americans pay low taxes by international standards. Most people's taxes haven't gone up in the past generation; the wealthy have had their taxes cut to levels not seen since before the New Deal. Even before the latest round of tax cuts, when compared with citizens of other advanced nations or compared with Americans a generation ago, we had nothing to complain about—and those with high incomes now have a lot to celebrate. Yet a significant number of Americans rage against taxes, and the party that controls all three branches of the federal government has made tax cuts its supreme priority. Why?

## SUPPLY-SIDERS, STARVE-THE-BEASTERS AND LUCKY DUCKIES

It is often hard to pin down what antitax crusaders are trying to achieve. The reason is not, or not only, that they are disingenuous about their motives—though as we will see, disingenuity has become a hallmark of the movement in recent years. Rather, the fuzziness comes from the fact that today's antitax movement moves back and forth between two doctrines. Both doctrines favor the same thing: big tax cuts for people with high incomes. But they favor it for different reasons.

One of those doctrines has become famous under the name "supply-side economics." It's the view that the government can cut taxes without severe cuts in public spending. The other doctrine is often referred to as "starving the beast," a phrase coined by David Stockman, Ronald Reagan's budget director. It's the view that taxes should be cut precisely in order to force severe cuts in public spending. Supply-side economics is the friendly, attractive face of the tax-cut movement. But starve-the-beast is where the power lies.

The starting point of supply-side economics is an assertion that no economist would dispute: taxes reduce the incentive to work, save and invest. A businessman who knows that 70 cents of every extra dollar he makes will go to the I.R.S. is less willing to make the effort to earn that extra dollar than if he knows that the I.R.S. will take only 35 cents. So reducing tax rates will, other things being the same, spur the economy.

This much isn't controversial. But the government must pay its bills. So the standard view of economists is that if you want to reduce the burden of taxes, you must explain what government programs you want to cut as part of the deal. There's no free lunch.

What the supply-siders argued, however, was that there was a free lunch. Cutting marginal rates, they insisted, would lead to such a large increase in gross domestic product that it wouldn't be necessary to come up with offsetting spending cuts. What supply-side economists say, in other words, is, "Don't worry, be happy and cut taxes." And when they say cut taxes, they mean taxes on the affluent: reducing the top marginal rate means that the biggest tax cuts go to people in the highest tax brackets.

The other camp in the tax-cut crusade actually welcomes the revenue losses from tax cuts. Its most visible spokesman today is Grover Norquist, president of Americans for Tax Reform, who once told National Public Radio: "I don't want to abolish government. I simply want to reduce it to the size where I can drag it into the bathroom and drown it in the bathtub." And the way to get it down to that size is to starve it of revenue. "The goal is reducing the size and scope of government by draining its lifeblood," Norquist told *U.S. News & World Report.*

What does "reducing the size and scope of government" mean? Tax-cut proponents are usually vague about the details. But the Heritage Foundation, ideological headquarters for the movement, has

made it pretty clear. Edwin Feulner, the foundation's president, uses "New Deal" and "Great Society" as terms of abuse, implying that he and his organization want to do away with the institutions Franklin Roosevelt and Lyndon Johnson created. That means Social Security, Medicare, Medicaid—most of what gives citizens of the United States a safety net against economic misfortune.

The starve-the-beast doctrine is now firmly within the conservative mainstream. George W. Bush himself seemed to endorse the doctrine as the budget surplus evaporated: in August 2001 he called the disappearing surplus "incredibly positive news" because it would put Congress in a "fiscal straitjacket."

Like supply-siders, starve-the-beasters favor tax cuts mainly for people with high incomes. That is partly because, like supply-siders, they emphasize the incentive effects of cutting the top marginal rate; they just don't believe that those incentive effects are big enough that tax cuts pay for themselves. But they have another reason for cutting taxes mainly on the rich, which has become known as the "lucky ducky" argument.

Here's how the argument runs: to starve the beast, you must not only deny funds to the government; you must make voters hate the government. There's a danger that working-class families might see government as their friend: because their incomes are low, they don't pay much in taxes, while they benefit from public spending. So in starving the beast, you must take care not to cut taxes on these "lucky duckies." (Yes, that's what *The Wall Street Journal* called them in a famous editorial.) In fact, if possible, you must raise taxes on working-class Americans in order, as *The Journal* said, to get their "blood boiling with tax rage."

So the tax-cut crusade has two faces. Smiling supply-siders say that tax cuts are all gain, no pain; scowling starve-the-beasters believe that inflicting pain is not just necessary but also desirable. Is the alliance between these two groups a marriage of convenience? Not exactly. It would be more accurate to say that the starve-the-beasters hired the supply-siders—indeed, created them—because they found their naïve optimism useful.

A look at who the supply-siders are and how they came to prominence tells the story.

The supply-side movement likes to present itself as a school of economic thought like Keynesianism or monetarism—that is, as a set of scholarly ideas that made their way, as such ideas do, into political discussion. But the reality is quite different. Supply-side economics was a political doctrine from Day 1; it emerged in the pages of political magazines, not professional economics journals.

That is not to deny that many professional economists favor tax cuts. But they almost always turn out to be starve-the-beasters, not supply-siders. And they often secretly—or sometimes not so secretly—hold supply-siders in contempt. N. Gregory Mankiw, now chairman of George W. Bush's Council of Economic Advisers, is definitely a friend to tax cuts; but in the first edition of his economic-principles textbook, he described Ronald Reagan's supply-side advisers as "charlatans and cranks."

It is not that the professionals refuse to consider supply-side ideas; rather, they have looked at them and found them wanting. A conspicuous example came earlier this year when the Congressional Budget Office tried to evaluate the growth effects of the Bush administration's proposed tax cuts. The budget office's new head, Douglas Holtz-Eakin, is a conservative economist who was handpicked for his job by the administration. But his conclusion was that unless the revenue losses from the proposed tax cuts were offset by spending cuts, the resulting deficits would be a drag on growth, quite likely to outweigh any supply-side effects.

But if the professionals regard the supply-siders with disdain, who employs these people? The answer is that since the 1970's almost all of the prominent supply-siders have been aides to conservative politicians, writers at conservative publications like *National Review,* fellows at conservative policy centers like Heritage or economists at private companies with strong Republican connections. Loosely speaking, that is, supply-siders work for the vast right-wing conspiracy. What gives supply-side economics influence is its connection with a powerful network of institutions that want to shrink the government and see tax cuts as a way to achieve that goal. Supply-side economics is a feel-good cover story for a political movement with a much harder-nosed agenda.

This isn't just speculation. Irving Kristol, in his role as co-editor of *The Public Interest,* was arguably the single most important proponent of supply-side economics. But years later, he suggested that he himself wasn't all that persuaded by the doctrine: "I was not certain of its economic merits but quickly saw its political possibilities." Writing in 1995, he explained that his real aim was to shrink the government and that tax cuts were a means to that end: "The task, as I saw it, was to create a new majority, which evidently would mean a conservative majority, which came to mean, in turn, a Republican majority—so political effectiveness was the priority, not the accounting deficiencies of government."

In effect, what Kristol said in 1995 was that he and his associates set out to deceive the American public. They sold tax cuts on the pretense that they would be painless, when they themselves believed that it would be necessary to slash public spending in order to make room for those cuts.

But one supposes that the response would be that the end justified the means—that the tax cuts did benefit all Americans because they led to faster economic growth. Did they?

## FROM REAGANOMICS TO CLINTONOMICS

Ronald Reagan put supply-side theory into practice with his 1981 tax cut. The tax cuts were modest for middle-class families but very large for the well-off. Between 1979 and 1983, according to Congressional Budget Office estimates, the average federal tax rate on the top 1 percent of families fell from 37 to 27.7 percent.

So did the tax cuts promote economic growth? You might think that all we have to do is look at how the economy performed. But it's not that simple, because different observers read different things from Reagan's economic record.

Here's how tax-cut advocates look at it: after a deep slump between 1979 and 1982, the U.S. economy began growing rapidly. Between 1982 and

1989 (the first year of the first George Bush's presidency), the economy grew at an average annual rate of 4.2 percent. That's a lot better than the growth rate of the economy in the late 1970's, and supply-siders claim that these "Seven Fat Years" (the title of a book by Robert L. Bartley, the longtime editor of *The Wall Street Journal's* editorial page) prove the success of Reagan's 1981 tax cut.

But skeptics say that rapid growth after 1982 proves nothing: a severe recession is usually followed by a period of fast growth, as unemployed workers and factories are brought back on line. The test of tax cuts as a spur to economic growth is whether they produced more than an ordinary business cycle recovery. Once the economy was back to full employment, was it bigger than you would otherwise have expected? And there Reagan fails the test: between 1979, when the big slump began, and 1989, when the economy finally achieved more or less full employment again, the growth rate was 3 percent, the same as the growth rate between the two previous business cycle peaks in 1973 and 1979. Or to put it another way, by the late 1980's the U.S. economy was about where you would have expected it to be, given the trend in the 1970's. Nothing in the data suggests a supply-side revolution.

Does this mean that the Reagan tax cuts had no effect? Of course not. Those tax cuts, combined with increased military spending, provided a good old-fashioned Keynesian boost to demand. And this boost was one factor in the rapid recovery from recession that developed at the end of 1982, though probably not as important as the rapid expansion of the money supply that began in the summer of that year. But the supposed supply-side effects are invisible in the data.

While the Reagan tax cuts didn't produce any visible supply-side gains, they did lead to large budget deficits. From the point of view of most economists, this was a bad thing. But for starve-the-beast tax-cutters, deficits are potentially a good thing, because they force the government to shrink. So did Reagan's deficits shrink the beast?

A casual glance at the data might suggest not: federal spending as a share of gross domestic product was actually slightly higher at the end of the 1980's than it was at the end of the 1970's. But that number includes both defense spending and "entitlements," mainly Social Security and Medicare, whose growth is automatic unless Congress votes to cut benefits. What's left is a grab bag known as domestic discretionary spending, including everything from courts and national parks to environmental cleanups and education. And domestic discretionary spending fell from 4.5 percent of G.D.P. in 1981 to 3.2 percent in 1988.

But that's probably about as far as any president can shrink domestic discretionary spending. And because Reagan couldn't shrink the belly of the beast, entitlements, he couldn't find enough domestic spending cuts to offset his military spending increases and tax cuts. The federal budget went into persistent, alarming, deficit. In response to these deficits, George Bush the elder went back on his "read my lips" pledge and raised taxes. Bill Clinton raised them further. And thereby hangs a tale.

For Clinton did exactly the opposite of what supply-side economics said you should do: he raised the marginal rate on high-income taxpayers. In 1989, the top 1 percent of families paid, on average, only 28.9 percent of their income in federal taxes; by 1995, that share was up to 36.1 percent.

Conservatives confidently awaited a disaster—but it failed to materialize. In fact, the economy grew at a reasonable pace through Clinton's first term, while the deficit and the unemployment rate went steadily down. And then the news got even better: unemployment fell to its lowest level in decades without causing inflation, while productivity growth accelerated to rates not seen since the 1960's. And the budget deficit turned into an impressive surplus.

Tax-cut advocates had claimed the Reagan years as proof of their doctrine's correctness; as we have seen, those claims wilt under close examination. But the Clinton years posed a much greater challenge: here was a president who sharply raised the marginal tax rate on high-income taxpayers, the very rate that the tax-cut movement cares most about. And instead of presiding over an economic disaster, he presided over an economic miracle.

Let's be clear: very few economists think that Clinton's policies were primarily responsible for that miracle. For the most part, the Clinton-era surge probably reflected the maturing of information technology: businesses finally figured out how to make effective use of computers, and the resulting surge in productivity drove the economy forward. But the fact that America's best growth in a generation took place after the government did exactly the opposite of what tax-cutters advocate was a body blow to their doctrine.

They tried to make the best of the situation. The good economy of the late 1990's, ardent tax-cutters insisted, was caused by the 1981 tax cut. Early in 2000, Lawrence Kudlow and Stephen Moore, prominent supply-siders, published an article titled "It's the Reagan Economy, Stupid."

But anyone who thought about the lags involved found this implausible—indeed, hilarious. If the tax-cut movement attributed the booming economy of 1999 to a tax cut Reagan pushed through 18 years earlier, why didn't they attribute the economic boom of 1983 and 1984—Reagan's "morning in America"—to whatever Lyndon Johnson was doing in 1965 and 1966?

By the end of the 1990's, in other words, supply-side economics had become something of a laughingstock, and the whole case for tax cuts as a route to economic growth was looking pretty shaky. But the tax-cut crusade was nonetheless, it turned out, poised for its biggest political victories yet. How did that happen?

## Second Wind: The Bush Tax Cuts

As the economic success of the United States under Bill Clinton became impossible to deny, there was a gradual shift in the sales strategy for tax cuts. The supposed economic benefits of tax cuts received less emphasis; the populist rationale—you, personally, pay too much in taxes—was played up.

I began this article with an example of this campaign's success: the creator of Mallard Fillmore apparently believes that typical families pay twice as much in taxes as they in fact do. But the most striking example of what skillful marketing can accomplish is the campaign for repeal of the estate tax.

As demonstrated, the estate tax is a tax on the very, very well off. Yet advocates of repeal began portraying it as a terrible burden on the little guy. They renamed it the "death tax" and put out reports decrying its impact on struggling farmers and businessmen—reports that never provided real-world examples because actual cases of family farms or small businesses broken up to pay estate taxes are almost impossible to find. This campaign succeeded in creating a public perception that the estate tax falls broadly on the population. Earlier this year, a poll found that 49 percent of Americans believed that most families had to pay the estate tax, while only 33 percent gave the right answer that only a few families had to pay.

Still, while an insistent marketing campaign has convinced many Americans that they are overtaxed, it hasn't succeeded in making the issue a top priority with the public. Polls consistently show that voters regard safeguarding Social Security and Medicare more much more important than tax cuts.

Nonetheless, George W. Bush has pushed through tax cuts in each year of his presidency. Why did he push for these tax cuts, and how did he get them through?

You might think that you could turn to the administration's own pronouncements to learn why it has been so determined to cut taxes. But even if you try to take the administration at its word, there's a problem: the public rationale for tax cuts has shifted repeatedly over the past three years.

During the 2000 campaign and the initial selling of the 2001 tax cut, the Bush team insisted that the federal government was running an excessive budget surplus, which should be returned to taxpayers. By the summer of 2001, as it became clear that the projected budget surpluses would not materialize, the administration shifted to touting the tax cuts as a form of demand-side economic stimulus: by putting more money in consumers' pockets, the tax cuts would stimulate spending and help pull the economy out of recession. By 2003, the rationale had changed again: the administration argued that reducing taxes on dividend income, the core of its plan, would improve incentives and hence long-run growth—that is, it had turned to a supply-side argument.

These shifting rationales had one thing in common: none of them were credible. It was obvious to independent observers even in 2001 that the budget projections used to justify that year's tax cut exaggerated future revenues and understated future costs. It was similarly obvious that the 2001 tax cut was poorly designed as a demand stimulus. And we have already seen that the supply-side rationale for the 2003 tax cut was tested and found wanting by the Congressional Budget Office.

So what were the Bush tax cuts really about? The best answer seems to be that they were about securing a key part of the Republican base. Wealthy campaign contributors have a lot to gain from lower taxes, and since they aren't very likely to depend on Medicare, Social Security or Medicaid, they won't suffer if the beast gets starved. Equally important was the support of the party's intelligentsia, nurtured by policy centers like Heritage and professionally committed to the tax-cut crusade. The original Bush tax-cut proposal was devised in late 1999 not to win votes in the national election but to fend off a primary challenge from the supply-sider Steve Forbes, the presumptive favorite of that part of the base.

This brings us to the next question: how have these cuts been sold?

At this point, one must be blunt: the selling of the tax cuts has depended heavily on chicanery. The administration has used accounting trickery to hide the true budget impact of its proposals, and it has used misleading presentations to conceal the extent to which its tax cuts are tilted toward families with very high income.

The most important tool of accounting trickery, though not the only one, is the use of "sunset clauses" to understate the long-term budget impact of tax cuts. To keep the official 10-year cost of the 2001 tax cut down, the administration's Congressional allies wrote the law so that tax rates revert to their 2000 levels in 2011. But, of course, nobody expects the sunset to occur: when 2011 rolls around, Congress will be under immense pressure to extend the tax cuts.

The same strategy was used to hide the cost of the 2003 tax cut. Thanks to sunset clauses, its headline cost over the next decade was only $350 billion, but if the sunsets are canceled—as the president proposed in a speech early this month—the cost will be at least $800 billion.

Meanwhile, the administration has carried out a very successful campaign to portray these tax cuts as mainly aimed at middle-class families. This campaign is similar in spirit to the selling of estate-tax repeal as a populist measure, but considerably more sophisticated.

The reality is that the core measures of both the 2001 and 2003 tax cuts mainly benefit the very affluent. The centerpieces of the 2001 act were a reduction in the top income-tax rate and elimination of the estate tax—the first, by definition, benefiting only people with high incomes; the second benefiting only heirs to large estates. The core of the 2003 tax cut was a reduction in the tax rate on dividend income. This benefit, too, is concentrated on very high-income families.

According to estimates by the Tax Policy Center—a liberal-oriented institution, but one with a reputation for scrupulous accuracy—the 2001 tax cut, once fully phased in, will deliver 42 percent of its benefits to the top 1 percent of the income distribution. (Roughly speaking, that means families earning more than $330,000 per year.) The 2003 tax cut delivers a somewhat smaller share to the top 1 percent, 29.1 percent, but within that concentrates its benefits on the really, really rich. Families with incomes over $1 million a year—a mere 0.13 percent of the population—will receive 17.3 percent of this year's tax cut, more than the total received by the bottom 70 percent of American families. Indeed, the 2003 tax cut has already proved a major boon to some of America's wealthiest people: corporations in which executives or a single family hold a large fraction of stocks are suddenly paying much bigger dividends, which are now taxed at only 15 percent no matter how high the income of their recipient.

It might seem impossible to put a populist gloss on tax cuts this skewed toward the rich, but the administration has been remarkably successful in doing just that.

One technique involves exploiting the public's lack of statistical sophistication. In the selling of the 2003 tax cut, the catch phrase used by administration spokesmen was "92 million Americans will receive an average tax cut of $1,083." That sounded, and was intended to sound, as if every American family would get $1,083. Needless to say, that wasn't true.

Yet the catch phrase wasn't technically a lie: the Tax Policy Center estimates that 89 million people will receive tax cuts this year and that the total tax cut will be $99 billion or about $1,100 for each of those 89 million people. But this calculation carefully leaves out the 50 million taxpayers who received no tax cut at all. And even among those who did get a tax cut, most got a lot less than $1,000, a number inflated by the very big tax cuts received by a few wealthy people. About half of American families received a tax cut of less than $100; the great majority, a tax cut of less than $500.

But the most original, you might say brilliant, aspect of the Bush administration's approach to tax cuts has involved the way the tax cuts themselves are structured.

David Stockman famously admitted that Reagan's middle-class tax cuts were a "Trojan horse" that allowed him to smuggle in what he really wanted, a cut in the top marginal rate. The Bush administration similarly follows a Trojan horse strategy, but an even cleverer one. The core measures in Bush's tax cuts benefit only the wealthy, but there are additional features that provide significant benefits to some—but only some—middle-class families. For example, the 2001 tax cut included a $400 child credit and also created a new 10 percent tax bracket, the so-called cutout. These measures had the effect of creating a "sweet spot" that could be exploited for political purposes. If a couple had multiple children, if the children were all still under 18 and if the couple's income was just high enough to allow it to take full advantage of the child credit, it could get a tax cut of as much as 4 percent of pretax income. Hence the couple with two children and an income of $40,000, receiving a tax cut of $1,600, who played such a large role in the administration's rhetoric. But while most couples have children, at any given time only a small minority of families contains two or more children under 18—and many of these families have income too low to take full advantage of the child tax credit. So that "typical" family wasn't typical at all.

Last year, the actual tax break for families in the middle of the income distribution averaged $469, not $1,600.

So that's the story of the tax-cut offensive under the Bush administration: through a combination of hardball politics, deceptive budget arithmetic and systematic misrepresentation of who benefits, Bush's team has achieved a major reduction of taxes, especially for people with very high incomes.

But where does that leave the country?

## A Planned Crisis

Right now, much of the public discussion of the Bush tax cuts focuses on their short-run impact. Critics say that the 2.7 million jobs lost since March 2001 prove that the administration's policies have failed, while the administration says that things would have been even worse without the tax cuts and that a solid recovery is just around the corner. But this is the wrong debate. Even in the short run, the right question to ask isn't whether the tax cuts were better than nothing; they probably were. The right question is whether some other economic-stimulus plan could have achieved better results at a lower budget cost. And it is hard to deny that, on a jobs-per-dollar basis, the Bush tax cuts have been extremely ineffective. According to the Congressional Budget Office, half of this year's $400 billion budget deficit is due to Bush tax cuts. Now $200 billion is a lot of money; it is equivalent to the salaries of four million average workers. Even the administration doesn't claim its policies have created four million jobs. Surely some other policy—aid to state and local governments, tax breaks for the poor and middle class rather than the rich, maybe even W.P.A.-style public works—would have been more successful at getting the country back to work.

Meanwhile, the tax cuts are designed to remain in place even after the economy has recovered. Where will they leave us?

Here's the basic fact: partly, though not entirely, as a result of the tax cuts of the last three years, the government of the United States faces a fundamental fiscal shortfall. That is, the revenue it collects falls well short of the sums it needs to pay for existing programs. Even the U.S. government must, eventually, pay its bills, so something will have to give.

The numbers tell the tale. This year and next, the federal government will run budget deficits of more than $400 billion. Deficits may fall a bit, at least as a share of gross domestic product, when the economy recovers. But the relief will be modest and temporary. As Peter Fisher, under secretary of the treasury for domestic finance, puts it, the federal government is "a gigantic insurance company with a sideline business in defense and homeland security." And about a decade from now, this insurance company's policyholders will begin making a lot of claims. As the baby boomers retire, spending on Social Security benefits and Medicare will steadily rise, as will spending on Medicaid (because of rising medical costs). Eventually, unless there are sharp cuts in benefits, these three programs alone will consume a larger share of G.D.P. than the federal government currently collects in taxes.

Alan Auerbach, William Gale and Peter Orszag, fiscal experts at the Brookings Institution, have estimated the size of the "fiscal gap"—the increase in revenues or reduction in spending that would be needed to make the nation's finances sustainable in the long run. If you define the long run as 75 years, this gap turns out to be 4.5 percent of G.D.P. Or to put it another way, the gap is equal to 30 percent of what the federal government spends on all domestic programs. Of that gap, about 60 percent is the result of the Bush tax cuts. We would have faced a serious fiscal problem even if those tax cuts had never happened. But we face a much nastier problem now that they are in place. And more broadly, the tax-cut crusade will make it very hard for any future politicians to raise taxes.

So how will this gap be closed? The crucial point is that it cannot be closed without either fundamentally redefining the role of government or sharply raising taxes. Politicians will, of course, promise to eliminate wasteful spending. But take out Social Security, Medicare, defense, Medicaid, government pensions, homeland security, interest on the public debt and veterans' benefits—none of them what people who complain about waste usually have in mind—and you are left with spending equal

to about 3 percent of gross domestic product. And most of that goes for courts, highways, education and other useful things. Any savings from elimination of waste and fraud will amount to little more than a rounding-off error.

So let's put a few things back on the table. Let's assume that interest on the public debt will be paid, that spending on defense and homeland security will not be compromised and that the regular operations of government will continue to be financed. What we are left with, then, are the New Deal and Great Society programs: Social Security, Medicare, Medicaid and unemployment insurance. And to close the fiscal gap, spending on these programs would have to be cut by around 40 percent.

It's impossible to know how such spending cuts might unfold, but cuts of that magnitude would require drastic changes in the system. It goes almost without saying that the age at which Americans become eligible for retirement benefits would rise, that Social Security payments would fall sharply compared with average incomes, that Medicare patients would be forced to pay much more of their expenses out of pocket—or do without. And that would be only a start.

All this sounds politically impossible. In fact, politicians of both parties have been scrambling to expand, not reduce, Medicare benefits by adding prescription drug coverage. It's hard to imagine a situation under which the entitlement programs would be rolled back sufficiently to close the fiscal gap.

Yet closing the fiscal gap by raising taxes would mean rolling back all of the Bush tax cuts, and then some. And that also sounds politically impossible.

For the time being, there is a third alternative: borrow the difference between what we insist on spending and what we're willing to collect in taxes. That works as long as lenders believe that someday, somehow, we're going to get our fiscal act together. But this can't go on indefinitely. Eventually—I think within a decade, though not everyone agrees—the bond market will tell us that we have to make a choice.

In short, everything is going according to plan.

For the looming fiscal crisis doesn't represent a defeat for the leaders of the tax-cut crusade or a miscalculation on their part. Some supporters of President Bush may have really believed that his tax cuts were consistent with his promises to protect Social Security and expand Medicare; some people may still believe that the wondrous supply-side effects of tax cuts will make the budget deficit disappear. But for starve-the-beast tax-cutters, the coming crunch is exactly what they had in mind.

## WHAT KIND OF COUNTRY?

The astonishing political success of the antitax crusade has, more or less deliberately, set the United States up for a fiscal crisis. How we respond to that crisis will determine what kind of country we become.

If Grover Norquist is right—and he has been right about a lot—the coming crisis will allow conservatives to move the nation a long way back toward the kind of limited government we had before Franklin Roosevelt. Lack of revenue, he says, will make it possible for conservative politicians—in the name of fiscal necessity—to dismantle immensely popular government programs that would otherwise have been untouchable. In Norquist's vision, America a couple of decades from now will be a place in which elderly people make up a disproportionate share of the poor, as they did before Social Security. It will also be a country in which even middle-class elderly Americans are, in many cases, unable to afford expensive medical procedures or prescription drugs and in which poor Americans generally go without even basic health care. And it may well be a place in which only those who can afford expensive private schools can give their children a decent education.

But as Governor Riley of Alabama reminds us, that's a choice, not a necessity. The tax-cut crusade has created a situation in which something must give. But what gives—whether we decide that the New Deal and the Great Society must go or that taxes aren't such a bad thing after all—is up to us. The American people must decide what kind of a country we want to be.

---

## DISCUSSION QUESTIONS

1. Krugman contends that for the past 25 years American politics has been dominated by a crusade against taxes. In what ways has this crusade been a con game? From Krugman's perspective, why haven't the real goals of tax cutting conservatives been at the forefront of their political sales pitch?

2. Compare and contrast the perspectives of supply-siders and starve-the-beasters. How have their budget and tax perspectives evolved from the Reagan presidency of the 1980s through the current administration of George W. Bush?

3. Why does Krugman believe that conservative tax cut policy will lead to a fiscal crisis of huge proportions? What are the political and economic implications of such a crisis?

4. This article concludes with the statement that "The American people must decide what kind of a country we want to be." This sounds pretty dramatic. Why does Krugman think the stakes for tax policy are so high?

## 34 Barbara Ehrenreich

# DOING IT FOR OURSELVES: CAN FEMINISM SURVIVE CLASS POLARIZATION?

*Barbara Ehrenreich is a popular and prolific writer, feminist and social critic who often writes about the intersection of gender and class. In this article she contends that class polarization in America over the past three decades has created divisions among previously united feminists, with those in the top 20 to 30 percent of income earners (professional women) having significantly different lifestyles and consumption patterns than those in the bottom 40 percent (working class women). "Frequent-flying female executives" find themselves with little or nothing in common with "airport cleaning women." This class polarization has dampened the egalitarianism of the early feminist movement, dramatically weakening "the sense of shared conditions" that was vital to sisterhood. Ehrenreich examines the impact of class polarization on three core feminist issues—welfare, health care, and housework—finding that in each instance class differences now trump feminist solidarity. Only the issues of sexual harassment and violence against women have survived growing female class inequality. The solution to this gender-class dilemma does not lie in a retreat into conservative abandonment of the feminist project. Rather, Ehrenreich suggests that feminists reclaim the original radical feminist vision of the abolition of all forms of hierarchy, be they based on race, gender, or class. The problem, most fundamentally, from Ehrenreich's perspective is class inequality—among women, and between women and men. Challenging that class inequity should be the first priority of those seeking to fashion public policy for women and to revitalize the feministmovement.*

Here's a scene from feminist ancient history: It's 1972 and about twenty of us are gathered in somebody's living room for our weekly "women's support group" meeting. We're all associated, in one way or another, with a small public college catering mostly to "nontraditional" students, meaning those who are older, poorer and more likely to be black or Latina than typical college students in this suburban area. Almost every level of the college hierarchy is represented—students of all ages, clerical workers,

---

*Source:* Barbara Ehrenreich, "Doing It for Ourselves: Can Feminism Survive Class Polarization?" *In These Times,* Volume 23, Number 26, November 28, 1999, pp. 10–12.

junior faculty members and even one or two full professors. There are acknowledged differences among us—race and sexual preference, for example— which we examine eagerly and a little anxiously. But we are comfortable together, and excited to have a chance to discuss everything from the administration's sexist policies to our personal struggles with husbands and lovers. Whatever may divide us, we are all women, and we understand this to be one of the great defining qualities of our lives and politics.

Could a group so diverse happily converse today? Please let me know if you can offer a present day parallel, but I tend to suspect the answer is "very seldom" or "not at all." Perhaps the biggest social and economic trend of the past three decades has been class polarization—the expanding inequality in income and wealth. As United for a Fair Economy's excellent book, *Shifting Fortunes: The Perils of the Growing American Wealth Gap,* points out, the most glaring polarization has occurred between those at the very top of the income distribution— the upper 1 to 5 percent—and those who occupy the bottom 30 to 40 percent. Less striking, but more ominous for the future of feminism, is the growing gap between those in the top 40 percent and those in the bottom 40. One chart in *Shifting Fortunes* shows that the networth of households in the bottom 40 percent declined by nearly 80 percent between 1983 and 1995. Except for the top 1 percent, the top 40 percent lost ground too—but much less. Today's college teacher, if she is not an adjunct, occupies that relatively lucky top 40 group, while today's clerical worker is in the rapidly sinking bottom 40. Could they still gather comfortably in each other's living rooms to discuss common issues? Do they still have common issues to discuss?

Numbers hardly begin to tell the story. The '80s brought sharp changes in lifestyle and consumption habits between the lower 40 percent—which is roughly what we call the "working class"—and the upper 20 to 30, which is populated by professors, administrators, executives, doctors, lawyers and other "professionals." "Mass markets" became "segmented markets," with different consumer trends signaling differences in status. In 1972, a junior faculty member's living room looked much like that of

a departmental secretary—only, in most cases, messier. Today, the secretary is likely to accessorize her home at Kmart; the professor at Pottery Barn. Three decades ago, we all enjoyed sugary, refined-flour treats at our meetings (not to mention Maxwell House coffee and cigarettes!) Today, the upper-middle class grinds its own beans, insists on whole grains, organic snacks, and vehemently eschews hot dogs and meatloaf. In the '70s, conspicuous, or even just overly enthusiastic, consumption was considered gauche—and not only by leftists and feminists. Today, professors, including quite liberal ones, are likely to have made a deep emotional investment in their houses, their furniture and their pewter ware. It shows how tasteful they are, meaning—when we cut through the garbage about aesthetics—how distinct they are from the "lower" classes.

In the case of women, there is an additional factor compounding the division wrought by class polarization: In the '60s, only about 30 percent of American women worked outside their homes; today, the proportion is reversed, with more than 70 percent of women in the work force. This represents a great advance, since women who earn their own way are of course more able to avoid male domination in their personal lives. But women's influx into the work force also means that fewer and fewer women share the common occupational experience once defined by the word "housewife." I don't want to exaggerate this commonality as it existed in the '60s and '70s; obviously the stay-at-home wife of an executive led a very different life from that of the stay-at-home wife of a blue-collar man. But they did perform similar daily tasks— housecleaning, childcare, shopping, cooking. Today, in contrast, the majority of women fan out every morning to face vastly different work experiences, from manual labor to positions of power. Like men, women are now spread throughout the occupational hierarchy (though not at the very top), where they encounter each other daily as unequals—bosses vs. clerical workers, givers of orders vs. those who are ordered around, etc.

Class was always an issue. Even before polarization set in, some of us lived on the statistical hilltops, others deep in the valleys. But today we are distributed on what looks less like a mountain range and more like a cliff-face. Gender, race and sexual preference still define compelling commonalities, but the sense of a shared condition necessarily weakens as we separate into frequent-flying female executives on the one hand and airport cleaning women on the other. Can feminism or, for that matter, any cross-class social movement, survive as class polarization spreads Americans further and further apart?

For all the ardent egalitarianism of the early movement, feminism had the unforeseen consequence of heightening the class differences between women. It was educated, middle-class women who most successfully used feminist ideology and solidarity to advance themselves professionally. Feminism has played a role in working-class women's struggles too—for example, in the union organizing drives of university clerical workers—but probably its greatest single economic effect was to open up the formerly male-dominated professions to women. Between the '70s and the '90s, the percentage of female students in business, medical and law schools shot up from less than 10 percent to more than 40 percent.

There have been, however, no comparable gains for young women who cannot afford higher degrees, and most of these women remain in the same low-paid occupations that have been "women's work" for decades. All in all, feminism has had little impact on the status or pay of traditional female occupations like clerical, retail, health care and light assembly line work. While middle-class women gained MBAs, working-class women won the right not to be called "honey"—and not a whole lot more than that.

Secondly, since people tend to marry within their own class, the gains made by women in the professions added to the growing economic gap between the working class and the professional-managerial class. Working-class families gained too, as wives went to work. But, as I argued in *Fear of Falling: The Inner Life of the Middle Class,* the most striking gains have accrued to couples consisting of two well-paid professionals or managers. The doctor/lawyer household zoomed well ahead of the truck driver/typist combination.

So how well has feminism managed to maintain its stance as the ground shifts beneath its feet? Here are some brief observations of the impact of class polarization on a few issues once central to the feminist project:

# WELFARE

This has to be the most tragic case. In the '70s, feminists hewed to the slogan, "Every woman is just one man away from welfare." This was an exaggeration of course; even then, there were plenty of self-supporting and independently wealthy women. But it was true enough to resonate with the large numbers of women who worked outside their homes part time or not at all. We recognized our commonality as homemakers and mothers as we considered this kind of work to be important enough to be paid for—even when there was no husband on the scene. Welfare, in other words, was potentially every woman's concern.

Flash forward to 1996, when Clinton signed the odious Republican welfare reform bill, and you find only the weakest and most tokenistic protests from groups bearing the label "feminist." The core problem, as those of us who were pro-welfare advocates found, was that many middle- and upper-middle class women could no longer see why a woman should be subsidized to raise her children. "Well, I work and raise my kids—why shouldn't they?" was a common response, as if poor women could command wages that would enable them to purchase reliable childcare. As for that other classic feminist slogan—"every mother is a working mother"—no one seems to remember it anymore.

# HEALTH CARE

Our bodies, after all, are what we have most in common as women, and the women's health movement of the '70s and early '80s probably brought together as diverse a constituency—at least in terms of class—as any other component of feminism. We worked to legalize abortion and to stop the involuntary sterilization of poor women of color, to challenge the sexism of medical care faced by all women consumers and to expand low-income women's access to care.

In many ways, we were successful: Abortion is legal, if not always accessible; the kinds of health information once available only in underground publications like the original *Our Bodies, Ourselves* can now be found in *Mademoiselle;* the medical profession is no longer an all-male bastion of patriarchy. We were not so successful, however, in increasing low-income women's access to health care—in fact, the number of the uninsured is far larger than it used to be, and poor women still get second-class health care when they get any at all. Yet the only women's health issue that seems to generate any kind of broad, cross-class participation today is breast cancer, at least if wearing a pink ribbon counts as "participation."

Even the nature of medical care is increasingly different for women of different classes. While lower-income women worry about paying for abortions or their children's care, many in the upper-middle class are far more concerned with such medical luxuries as high-tech infertility treatments and cosmetic surgery. Young college women get bulimia; less affluent young women are more likely to suffer from toxemia of pregnancy, which is basically a consequence of malnutrition.

## HOUSEWORK

In the '70s, housework was a hot feminist issue and a major theme of consciousness-raising groups. After all, whatever else women did, we did housework; it was the nearly universal female occupation. We debated Pat Mainardi's famous essay on "The Politics of Housework," which focused on the private struggles to get men to pick up their own socks. We argued bitterly about the "wages for housework" movement's proposal that women working at home should be paid by the state. We studied the Cuban legal code, with its intriguing provision that males do their share or face jail time.

Thirty years later, the feminist silence on the issue of housework is nearly absolute. Not, I think, because men are at last doing their share, but because so many women of the upper-middle class now pay other women to do their housework for them. Bring up the subject among affluent feminists

today, and you get a guilty silence, followed by defensive patter about how well they pay and treat their cleaning women.

In fact, the $15 an hour commonly earned by freelance maids is not so generous at all, when you consider that it has to cover cleaning equipment, transportation to various cleaning sites throughout the day, as well as any benefits, like health insurance, the cleaning person might choose to purchase for herself. The fast-growing corporate cleaning services like Merry Maids and The Maids International are far worse, offering (at least in the northeastern urban area I looked into) their workers between $5 (yes, that's below the minimum wage) and $7 an hour.

In a particularly bitter irony, many of the women employed by the corporate cleaning services are former welfare recipients bumped off the rolls by the welfare reform bill so feebly resisted by organized feminists. One could conclude, if one was in a very bad mood, that it is not in the interests of affluent feminists to see the wages of working class women improve. As for the prospects of "sisterhood" between affluent women and the women who scrub their toilets—forget about it, even at a "generous" $15 an hour.

The issues that have most successfully weathered class polarization are sexual harassment and male violence against women. These may be the last concerns that potentially unite all women; and they are of course crucial. But there is a danger in letting these issues virtually define feminism, as seems to be the case in some campus women's centers today: Poor and working-class women (and men) face forms of harassment and violence on the job that are not sexual or even clearly gender-related. Being reamed out repeatedly by an obnoxious supervisor of either sex can lead to depression and stress-related disorders. Being forced to work long hours of overtime, or under ergonomically or chemically hazardous conditions, can make a person physically sick. Yet feminism has yet to recognize such routine workplaces experiences as forms of "violence against women."

When posing the question—"can feminism survive class polarization?"—to middle-class feminist acquaintances, I sometimes get the response: "Well, you're right—we have to confront our classism." But the problem is not classism, the problem is class itself: the existence of grave inequalities among women, as well as between women and men.

We should recall that the original radical—and, yes, utopian—feminist vision was of a society without hierarchies of any kind. This of course means equality among the races and the genders, but class is different: There can be no such thing as "equality among the classes." The abolition of hierarchy demands not only racial and gender equality, but the abolition of class. For a start, let's put that outrageous aim back into the long-range feminist agenda and mention it as loudly and often as we can.

In the shorter term, there's plenty to do, and the burden necessarily falls on the more privileged among us: to support working-class women's workplace struggles, to advocate for expanded social services (like childcare and health care) for all women, to push for greater educational access for low-income women and so on and so forth. I'm not

telling you anything new here, sisters—you know what to do.

But there's something else, too, in the spirit of another ancient slogan that is usually either forgotten or misinterpreted today: "The personal is the political." Those of us who are fortunate enough to have assets and income beyond our immediate needs need to take a hard look at how we're spending our money. New furniture—and please, I don't want to hear about how tastefully funky or antique-y it is—or a donation to a homeless shelter? A chic outfit or a check written to an organization fighting sweatshop conditions in the garment industry? A maid or a contribution to a clinic serving low-income women?

I know it sounds scary, but it will be a lot less so if we can make sharing stylish again and excess consumption look as ugly as it actually is. Better yet, give some of your time and your energy too. But if all you can do is write a check, that's fine: Since Congress will never redistribute the wealth (downward, anyway), we may just have to do it ourselves.

---

## DISCUSSION QUESTIONS

1. According to Ehrenreich, in what ways have class differences among women complicated feminism since its revival in the 1970s?
2. How would you interpret Ehrenreich's comment that "the problem is not classism, the problem is class itself"?

**35** *Brian Gilmore*

# BLACK AMERICA AND THE DILEMMA OF PATRIOTISM

*Poet and attorney Brian Gilmore explores with sensitivity his complex reactions as a black American to the September 11 attacks. While he is obviously appalled and saddened by the attacks, Gilmore is concerned about the implications for black America of the call to unconditionally "stand by the man" and support the "war on terrorism" launched by President George W. Bush. Reflecting on statements made by the novelist Richard Wright during World War II, Gilmore explains that calls for Americans to close ranks during wartime have often served to remove the problems and grievances of black Americans from the political agenda. In the tradition of scholar and activist W. E. B. Du Bois, Gilmore explores black American "double consciousness" in a way that enables all Americans to comprehend the complexities of national identity. He helps us understand how a ritual like flying the flag has distinct meanings in different communities.*

"I pledge my loyalty and allegiance, without mental reservation or evasions, to America. I shall through my writing seek to rally the Negro people to stand shoulder to shoulder with the Administration in a solid national front to wage war until victory is won."

—*Richard Wright (December 16, 1941)*

On the morning of September 11, I was driving down R Street in Washington on my way to a local foundation where I was working as a writer when I saw a huge cloud of smoke off in the distance. I had already heard that two hijacked planes had crashed into the twin towers of the World Trade Center in New York City. When I saw the huge cloud of smoke rising into the sky, I kind of figured it wasn't someone's house on fire. No more than a minute later, the radio reported that a plane had hit the Pentagon. I immediately pulled over and went inside the Washington Legal Clinic for the Homeless, where

*Source:* Brian Gilmore, "Stand by the Man: Black America and the Dilemma of Patriotisms." *The Progressive,* Volume 66, Number 1, January 2002, pp. 24–27.

I once worked. Everyone there was distraught. Some people began crying. Others were speechless. Then the newscaster announced that the towers had collapsed with possibly thousands of people trapped inside. I told my former co-workers I was leaving.

"Where are you headed?"

"The racetrack," I answered.

My answer was knee-jerk but honest. I wasn't at all surprised at what happened that day because I have always suspected that there are people and nations and factions that do not like America. Oftentimes, Black America does not like America, but, for the most part, many of us remain quiet. We go along for the ride because it is what we are accustomed to doing. Our interests are tied to America. And if you want to know the most poignant truth of all: We really have no choice in the matter. Where are we to go? We are, though some of us forget sometimes, American, perhaps more so than anyone else.

But that is, of course, part of why I was headed to the racetrack. I wanted to pretend that the bombing hadn't happened. I also knew that all of us—every black American—would be called upon (like every other American) from that day forth until we were instructed otherwise, to stand by our man—Uncle Sam. Support the war unconditionally. One shouldn't even question the approach to solving the problem (as if there is only one way to fight this battle). Any other conduct during the war would be deemed un-American.

For black Americans, it has always been that way, no matter our position in society. We would be asked to do what we had always done without any promise of future benefit: to prove our unconditional love and loyalty for America. Drop any grievances or problems we have with our American condition for the time being, or maybe for a generation or so. I didn't want to deal with the bombings, and I definitely didn't want to deal with the culture of violence that the bombings had spawned.

I preferred simply to go look at the horses.

Days after the bombing, with all of those thoughts of my American self still bearing down on me, I read Richard Wright's statement on World War II that appears above. I found it in Michel Fabre's celebrated biography of Wright, *The Unfinished*

*Quest of Richard Wright* (University of Illinois, 1993). I had been in search of statements by authors, black authors in particular, following Pearl Harbor. I wanted to know what they had to say as that attack became part of us. This was war, and that was war back in 1941, and I knew they found themselves in a difficult spot. Before that war, Roosevelt had expressed some interest in being a friend of Black America, but he hadn't really gone that far. Most people even forget that Black America had planned a March on Washington in 1941 that was canceled at the last minute. The argument by black Americans that fighting against tyranny will make democracy for blacks more possible in America was strong even before the Japanese bombed Pearl Harbor; afterwards, it was overwhelming.

Before the September 11 attack, Black America was even more frustrated. The election and subsequent decision by the Supreme Court that propelled George W. Bush into office still burned in the souls of many black folks. In fact, I can't remember a day that went by in the last year that at least one of my black American friends or acquaintances didn't bring up the vote count irregularities among blacks in Florida and how they couldn't wait to vote Bush out of office in 2004.

Even more painfully, our issues, the issues that at least were on the table during the Clinton years (despite his failure to address them), weren't even being discussed anymore. The country was talking tax cuts; we were asking about job cuts. The country was talking education reform; we were asking about just getting an education for our children. Then there were the bigger fish that Clinton turned and ran from for eight years: reparations, racial profiling, police brutality, reforming "drug war" sentencing guidelines, black men disproportionately going to jail.

But when those planes plunged into the World Trade Center and the Pentagon on that blue, blue morning of September 11, 2001, not only was the black agenda taken off the table for the foreseeable future, the table itself was taken down.

That is why Richard Wright's statement struck a chord in me. I finally began to think clearly for the first time about the September 11 bombing. I began to put the attack into some sort of context without being "upset" or "angry" or full of guilt about my initial reaction of wanting to go to the racetrack. I finally knew where I was at that moment, right after I read that quote. I was where the average black American always seems to be in America—in that tragic Duboisian state of double consciousness.

What did the average African American say about the attack and what we should do? This is what I was hearing:

It was an awful thing.
Evil.
Kill the bastards.
Crush them.
Bomb them.
Kill them all.
Profile them Arabs.
Deport them all.

(Note: It was especially vexing to hear black people come on the radio following the bombing and basically call for racial profiling of Arab Americans and deportation. I assure you, this view was rampant. On one radio program based in Washington, D.C., caller after caller, black Americans, stated that "profiling" of Arab Americans was, in fact, needed and had to be done for the good of the nation.)

But that is just one side of the black American experience. Here is the other that I began to hear:

Don't we bomb people all the time?
And look how they treated us for so long.
Slavery.
Lynchings.
Second-class citizenship.
Segregation.
Not to mention the same old bullshit we still got to put up with in daily life.
We are arguing over an apology for slavery.
How can we forget any of it?
We the ones who are going to be over there fighting, too.
And after this war, what then? The same?
Two peoples always, it seems.

I could not get it out of my head that Wright had felt a need to make a statement in support of World War II. For one thing, he was a pacifist. And prior to

December 7, 1941, he was badgering America about the need for social justice and equality for the Negro society. He was against any involvement in the war; he was more interested in addressing America's racial policies. Months before the war, on June 6, 1941, at a League of American Writers council meeting, Wright delivered a speech entitled "Not My People's War" that basically stated World War II was not a war black people should participate in because of how they are treated in society. Even after America's entry into that war, Wright remained focused on the improvement of conditions for America's black citizens.

Though he eventually volunteered to contribute to the war effort through writing, Wright's ambivalence was obvious. He supported the war for essentially the same naive reasons Frederick Douglass asked black people to fight with the Union in the Civil War: It was a chance for freedom and democracy. How could they continue to hold us down if we fought beside them against the true oppressors?

But though I was sure something drastic had to be done against terrorism, I couldn't support America's call for war against Afghanistan. I was against terrorism and violence, for sure, with every bone in my body. I abhorred the actions of the suicide bombers, which were so sick and so terribly destructive. Yet, I was sure that bombing a country that is hopelessly stuck in the medieval age would not solve anything. I was sure that as America began dropping bombs, we would become even more unsafe. I was more concerned about civil defense than revenge. I also could not get all that history out of my head about America and its black American people.

But still I wondered: Why wasn't I deeply depressed? This was a tragedy of epic proportions. The loss of human life was unfathomable. We were all attacked that day, too. Black America as well. Osama bin Laden issued a *fatwa* (holy war decree) years ago, and he said all Americans should be killed. Not white Americans, but all Americans. That meant me and my wife and my daughter and the rest of my family and Americans of every race and ethnicity.

This wasn't the Iranian hostage crisis of 1979 and '80, when the captors, in a clever show of political solidarity, released the black American hostages from the U.S. Embassy. Whoever was responsible for the crashes of September 11 didn't give a damn who you were as a person; this was an attack on America. If the bombers of September 11, 2001, were acting upon bin Laden's *fatwa,* or whoever's order, black America was also a target.

A very good family friend, a schoolteacher, Lizzie Jones, a black American woman who was like a second mother to me, lost one of her best friends in one of the suicide crashes. Her friend was a schoolteacher. They had known each other for more than thirty years and had talked right before the bombing. Her friend was taking a student on a study trip sponsored by *National Geographic.* She told Ms. Jones she would be back on Saturday, and that she would tell her all about it. Her friend did not come back. She is gone. I saw Ms. Jones on television on the news speaking to her lost friend in spiritual phrases. I felt nauseous.

I am afraid for my daughter. She does not need to live in a world that is full of violence, death, and chaos. My sincere hope is that all of us now understand the real horror of mass violence of this magnitude. I know I do. No way should anyone suffer as we did on September 11, 2001. The frantic phone calls looking for friends and family members, the e-mails seeking out answers, the devastation, the catastrophic grief.

Chilean writer Ariel Dorfman refers to America now as "Unique No More." Dorfman says this is so because America has finally experienced what "so many other human beings" in "faraway zones, have suffered." Yes, we have felt it.

I am pretty sure that Richard Wright anguished over writing all the other words he wrote supporting entry into World War II. But he felt America in 1941 was still his country. America is my country, too, but it is much more complex than that. I don't mean just the place where I was born, but a place that is unequivocally my land and the land of my people without the enormous contradictions that create a strange dialogue, which can be summed up like this:

"But we ended slavery."

"But you allowed it to be legal for hundreds of years."

"We conquered Jim Crow and segregation."

"But it was legal for most of the twentieth century, and we had to almost burn the country down to get you to do it."

Today, I marvel at my friends who talk of their families coming to America from India or Nicaragua or my law school classmates who speak about their grandfather or grandmother's journey to America from Italy or Ireland or Greece in search of a better life in America. It is a magical story I don't have. That's why black Americans can never be whole in America, no matter how hard we try. How can we? We don't even have a past that can be defined, and the part that we know, the story that is passed to us regarding our country's relationship to us, is a complete tragedy. America is my country, yet my country, it seems, has never wanted me.

They were blowing their car horn. They were drunk. I was in Georgetown, and several young, white youths were hanging out of the windows of the car with a sign that read: "Honk, If You Love America." It was cute in a way to see such brash patriotism. Drivers began honking in response to the sign. This was September 16, and everyone was still in immense pain. The young drunks were trying to make themselves feel better and everyone else at the same time. I didn't honk my horn. I was in the Georgetown traffic jam, frozen and unable to do anything. I began looking around and realized that no one really would notice because so many cars were honking. Most of the people I saw honking their horns were white. I didn't see any black people around. I didn't honk. It was a disturbing moment for me because I wasn't standing by my man in one of his toughest times. I realized again (as I have been reminded many times since) that though I was and am an American, I didn't have what most Americans feel—that unique sense of belonging. The tragedy was a part of me but it was mostly about the victims, the injured, the dead. I knew I wasn't alone, either.

On the radio in the days after the bombing, I heard many black Americans state that they felt bad for the victims, they felt violated, and they felt that America had to do something, but then some would add at the end of their comments statements about not feeling that deep sense of patriotism that most Americans feel. The kind of emotion that pushes you to put your hand over your heart, take your hat off when the National Anthem is played. The "God Bless America" brand of patriotism. They were Americans, but not quite as American as white Americans. They cried for the victims but not necessarily for America.

In the days following the bombing, I was asked several times with strange looks: "Where is your flag?" I told some people I didn't have a flag. I told others that I simply could not lie to myself. It never dawned on me that I should fly a flag. I felt terrible for the victims. Awful. If the flag was for the victims, it should be flown, but I didn't fly a flag because I remembered the victims in other ways. For me, simply to resign myself to flying the flag was not enough. It was superficial, and it took the focus away from those who had died.

I spent much of my time in the days following the bombing riding through the city, looking at flags. I wanted to see who was flying them, and who wasn't. It would tell me something about America. I rode to upper Northwest first. This is the area of Washington where the affluent live, and I saw the American flag waving on nearly every street. On some streets you could tell that the neighbors probably had talked to each other because nearly every house had a flag out front. There was a pride there that was impressive. Cars had flags, too. It made the streets look like there was going to be a July 4 parade.

Then I rode to my old neighborhood, where I grew up. The families there are less affluent, but they are doing fairly well, at least most of them. They've always wanted to be American. Black Americans live there mostly, some middle class, some working class, but the neighborhood has only small pockets of despair and is usually quiet except on hot summer nights. There were American flags flying up here, too, but not as many as in upper Northwest. My mother, who still lives there, had a tiny flag on her front door. You could barely see it. She said someone gave it to her.

Finally, I rode through the most economically depressed areas of Washington: The Hood—Northwest below Howard university, but above downtown—streets where crack and herion continued to be sold and used as the tragedy unfolded. Drunks were laid out in the gutter, children ran the streets late at nights, addicts came up to my car trying to sell stolen items. There was hardly a flag in sight.

---

## DISCUSSION QUESTIONS

1. Why does Gilmore believe that the war on terrorism might in some ways undercut the interests and agenda of black America?
2. Compare Gilmore's reaction to September 11 with Richard Wright's comments about World War II that open this selection. What is it about the black experience in America that leads Gilmore to feel ambivalence about the call to rally around the flag?

## 36 *Chalmers Johnson*

# SORROWS OF EMPIRE

*The period since 9/11 has seen the development of an expansive and aggressive Bush Doctrine that includes an emphasis on the need for preemptive or preventive war, market fundamentalist policies, and the U.S. as the ultimate guarantor of universal values. Among the many questions raised by the trajectory of U.S. policy under George W. Bush are the following two: What is distinctive about the Bush administration's militarism and unilateralism? What are the political, ideological, and economic roots of the turn in U.S. foreign policy under George W. Bush? In the last few years, a stream of books and articles have appeared that explore critically the nature of U.S. imperialism, militarism, and hegemony early in the twenty-first century, especially in the context of the "war on terrorism." One of the most contributions has been made by Chalmers Johnson, a longtime foreign policy expert and specialist on Asia who served as a consultant to the CIA in the 1960s and 1970s. In this adaptation from his 2004 book* Sorrows of Empire, *Johnson weighs the consequences or "sorrows" of the imperial policies that America's political elites have embraced, focusing on endless war, the loss of Constitutional liberties, and financial ruin. As you read this selection, which was written in 2003, ponder two points. First, Johnson identifies a fourth "sorrow" that he does not discuss in this piece—"the replacement of truth by propaganda, disinformation, and the glorification of war, power, and the military legions." Do you see strong evidence of this "sorrow" in American public life? Second, do developments in the several years since Johnson wrote this analysis justify his concerns about the costs of American empire?*

Although tyranny, because it needs no consent, may successfully rule over foreign peoples, it can stay in power only if it destroys first of all the national institutions of its own people.

Hannah Arendt, *The Origins of Totalitarianism*

---

*Source:* Chalmers Johnson, "Sorrows of Empire." *Foreign Policy in Focus* (Silver City, NM: Interhemispheric Resource Center, November 2003). This essay is an excerpt from Johnson's *The Sorrows of Empire: Militarism, Secrecy, and the End of the Republic,* New York: Metropolitan Books, 2004.

The United States has been inching toward imperialism and militarism for many years. Disguising the direction they were taking, American leaders cloaked their foreign policy in euphemisms such as "lone superpower," "indispensable nation," "reluctant sheriff," "humanitarian intervention," and "globalization." However, with the advent of the George Bush administration in 2001, these pretenses gave way to assertions of the Second Coming of the Roman Empire. "American imperialism used to be a fiction of the far-left imagination," writes the English journalist Madeleine Bunting, "now it is an uncomfortable fact of life."

On March 19, 2003, the Bush administration took the imperial step of invading Iraq, a sovereign nation one-twelfth the size of the U.S. in terms of population and virtually undefended in the face of the awesome array of weapons employed against it. The U.S. undertook its second war with Iraq with no legal justification and worldwide protests against its actions and motives, thereby bringing to an end the system of international order that existed throughout the cold war and that traces its roots back to seventeenth century doctrines of sovereignty, non-intervention in the affairs of other states, and the illegitimacy of aggressive war.

From the moment the United States assumed the permanent military domination of the world, it was on its own—feared, hated, corrupt and corrupting, maintaining "order" through state terrorism and bribery, and given to megalomaniacal rhetoric and sophistries while virtually inviting the rest of the world to combine against it. The U.S. had mounted the Napoleonic tiger and could not get off. During the Watergate scandal of the early 1970s, the president's chief of staff, H. R. Haldeman, once reproved White House counsel, John Dean, for speaking too frankly to Congress about the felonies President Nixon had ordered. "John," he said, "once the toothpaste is out of the tube, it's hard to get it back in." This homely metaphor by a former advertising executive who was to spend 18 months in prison for his own role in Watergate fairly accurately describes the situation of the United States.

The sorrows of empire are the inescapable consequences of the national policies American elites chose after September 11, 2001. Militarism and imperialism always bring with them sorrows. The ubiquitous symbol of the Christian religion, the cross, is perhaps the world's most famous reminder of the sorrows that accompanied the Roman Empire—it represents the most atrocious death the Roman proconsuls could devise in order to keep subordinate peoples in line. From Cato to Cicero, the slogan of Roman leaders was "Let them hate us so long as they fear us."

Four sorrows, it seems to me, are certain to be visited on the United States. Their cumulative effect guarantees that the U.S. will cease to resemble the country outlined in the Constitution of 1787. First, there will be a state of perpetual war, leading to more terrorism against Americans wherever they may be and a spreading reliance on nuclear weapons among smaller nations as they try to ward off the imperial juggernaut. Second is a loss of democracy and Constitutional rights as the presidency eclipses Congress and is itself transformed from a co-equal "executive branch" of government into a military junta. Third is the replacement of truth by propaganda, disinformation, and the glorification of war, power, and the military legions. Lastly, there is bankruptcy, as the United States pours its economic resources into ever more grandiose military projects and shortchanges the education, health, and safety of its citizens. All I have space for here is to touch briefly on three of these: endless war, the loss of Constitutional liberties, and financial ruin.

Allegedly in response to the attacks of al Qaeda on September 11, 2001, President Bush declared that the United States would dominate the world through absolute military superiority and wage preventive war against any possible competitor. He began to enunciate this doctrine in his June 1, 2002, speech to the cadets of the U.S. Military Academy at West Point, and spelled it out in his "National Security Strategy of the United States" of September 20, 2002.

At West Point, the president said that the United States had a unilateral right to overthrow any government in the world that it deemed a threat to American security. He argued that the United States must be prepared to wage the "war on terror" against as many as sixty countries if weapons of mass destruction are to be kept out of terrorists' hands. "We must take that battle to the enemy, disrupt his plans and confront the worst threats before they emerge." Americans must be "ready for preemptive action when necessary to defend our liberty and to defend our lives. . . . In the world we have entered, the only path to safety is the path of action. And this nation will act." Although Bush did not name every single one, his hit-list of sixty possible target countries was an escalation over Vice President Dick Cheney, who in November 2001, said that there were only "forty or fifty" countries that United States wanted to attack after eliminating the al Qaeda terrorists in Afghanistan.

At West Point, the president justified his proposed massive military effort in terms of alleged universal values: "We will defend the peace against threats from terrorists and tyrants. We will preserve the peace by building good relations among the great powers. And we will extend the peace by encouraging free and open societies on every continent." He added an assertion that is demonstrably untrue but that in the mouth of the president of the United States on an official occasion amounted to the announcement of a crusade: "Moral truth is the same in every culture, in every time, in every place."

In his *National Security Strategy,* he expanded on these goals to include "America must stand firmly for the non-negotiable demands of human dignity; the rule of law; limits on the absolute power of the state; free speech; freedom of worship; equal justice; respect for women; religious and ethnic tolerance; and respect for private property." In the preamble to the strategy, he (or Condoleezza Rice, the probable actual author) wrote that there is "a single sustainable model for national success"—America's—that is "right and true for every person in every society. . . . The United States must defend liberty and justice because these principles are right and true for all people everywhere."

The paradoxical effect of this grand strategy is that it may prove more radically disruptive of world order than anything the terrorists of September 11, 2001, could have hoped to achieve on their own. Through its actions, the United States seems determined to bring about precisely the threats that it says it is trying to prevent. Its apparent acceptance of a "clash of civilizations"—wars to establish a moral truth that is the same in every culture—sounds remarkably like a *jihad,* even to its basis in Christian fundamentalism. Bush seems to equate himself with Jesus Christ in his repeated statements (notably on September 20, 2001) that those who are not with us are against us, which duplicates Matthew chapter 12, verse 30, "He that is not with me is against me."

Implementation of the *National Security Strategy* will be considerably more problematic than its promulgation and contains numerous unintended consequences. By mid-2003, the United States armed forces were already seriously overstretched, and the U.S. government was going deeply into debt to finance its war machine. The American budget dedicated to international affairs allocates 93% to the military and only 7% to the State Department, and does not have much flexibility left for further military adventures. The Pentagon has deployed a quarter of a million troops against Iraq, several thousand soldiers are engaged in daily skirmishes in Afghanistan, countless Navy and Air Force crews are manning strategic weapons in the waters off North Korea, a few thousand Marines have been dispatched to the southern Philippines to fight a century-old Islamic separatist movement, several hundred "advisers" are participating in the early stages of a Vietnam-like insurgency in Colombia and elsewhere in the Andean nations, and the U.S. currently maintains a military presence in 140 of the 189 member countries of the United Nations, including significant deployments in twenty-five. The U.S. has military treaties or binding security arrangements with at least thirty-six countries.

Aside from the financial cost, there is another constraint. The American people are totally unwilling to accept large numbers of American casualties. In order to produce the "no-contact" or "painless dentistry" approach to warfare, the Pentagon has committed itself to a massive and very expensive effort to computerize battle. It has spent lavishly on smart bombs, battlefield sensors, computer-guided munitions, and extremely high performance aircraft and ships. The main reason for all this gadgetry is to keep troops out of the line of fire.

Unfortunately, as the conflicts in both Afghanistan and Iraq have demonstrated, ground troops follow in the wake of massive aerial bombing and missile attacks. The first Iraq War produced four classes of casualties—killed in action, wounded in action, killed in accidents (including "friendly fire"), and injuries and illnesses that appeared only after the end of hostilities. During 1990 and 1991, some 696,778 individuals served in the Persian Gulf as elements of Operation Desert Shield and Operation Desert Storm. Of these 148 were killed in battle, 467 were wounded in action, and 145 were killed in accidents, producing a total of 760 casualties, quite a low number given the scale of the operations.

However, as of May 2002, the Veterans Administration (VA) reported that an additional 8,306 soldiers had died and 159,705 were injured or ill as a result of service-connected "exposures" suffered during the war. Even more alarmingly, the VA revealed that 206,861 veterans, almost a third of General Schwarzkopf's entire army, had filed claims for medical care, compensation, and pension benefits based on injuries and illnesses caused by combat in 1991. After reviewing the cases, the agency has classified 168,011 applicants as "disabled veterans." In light of these deaths and disabilities, the casualty rate for the first Gulf War is actually a staggering 29.3%.

A significant probable factor in these deaths and disabilities is depleted uranium (or DU) ammunition, although this is a hotly contested proposition. Some researchers, often paid for by the Pentagon, argue that depleted uranium could not possibly be the cause of these war-related maladies and that a more likely explanation is dust and debris from the blowing up of Saddam Hussein's chemical and biological weapons factories in 1991, or perhaps a "cocktail" of particles from DU ammunition, the destruction of nerve gas bunkers, and polluted air from burning oil fields. But the evidence—including abnormal clusters of childhood cancers and birth defects in Iraq and also in the areas of Kosovo where the U.S. used depleted-uranium weapons in the 1999 air war—points primarily toward DU. Moreover, simply by insisting on employing such weaponry, the American military is deliberately flouting a 1996 United Nations resolution that classifies DU ammunition as an illegal weapon of mass destruction.

DU, or Uranium-238, is a waste product of power-generating nuclear-reactors. It is used in projectiles like tank shells and cruise missiles because it is 1.7 times denser than lead, burns as it flies, and penetrates armor easily, but it breaks up and vaporizes on impact—which makes it potentially very deadly. Each shell fired by an American tank includes between three and ten pounds of DU. Such warheads are essentially "dirty bombs," not very radioactive individually but nonetheless suspected of being capable in quantity of causing serious illnesses and birth defects.

In 1991, U.S. forces fired a staggering 944,000 DU rounds in Kuwait and Iraq. The Pentagon admits that it left behind at a bare minimum 320 metric tons of DU on the battlefield. One study of Gulf War veterans showed that their children had a higher possibility of being born with severe deformities, including missing eyes, blood infections, respiratory problems, and fused fingers.

Aside from the damage done to our own troops and civilians by depleted uranium, the United States military remains committed to the most devastating forms of terror bombing, often without even a pretense of precision targeting of militarily significant installations. This aspect of current American military thinking can be found in the writing of Harlan Ullman, a high-ranking Pentagon official and protégé of General Colin Powell, who advocates that the United States attack its enemies in the same way it defeated Japan in World War II. He writes, "Super tools and weapons—information age equivalents of the atomic bomb—have to be invented. As the atomic bombs dropped on Hiroshima and Nagasaki finally convinced the Japanese Emperor and High Command that even suicidal resistance was futile, these tools must be directed toward a similar outcome." Ullman is the author of the idea is that the U.S. should "deter and overpower an adversary through the adversary's perception and fear of his vulnerability and our own invincibility." He calls this "rapid dominance" or "shock and awe." He once suggested that it might be a good idea to use electromagnetic waves to attack peoples' neurological systems and scare them to death.

The United States government has other ways to implement its new world strategy without getting its hands dirty, including what it and its Israeli allies call "targeted killings." During February, 2003, the Bush administration sought the Israeli government's counsel on how to create a legal justification for the assassination of terrorism suspects. In his 2003 State of the Union speech, President Bush said that terrorism suspects who were not caught and brought to trial have been "otherwise dealt with" and observed that "more than 3,000 suspected terrorists have been arrested in many countries, and many others have met a different fate. Let's put it this way: they are no longer a problem to the United States and our friends and allies."

High-tech warfare invites the kind of creative judo the terrorists of al Qaeda utilized on September 11. Employing domestic American airliners as their weapons of mass destruction, they took a deadly toll of innocent American bystanders. The U.S. worries that they might acquire or be given fissionable material by a "rogue state," but the much more likely source is via theft from the huge nuclear stockpiles of the United States and Russia. The weapons-grade anthrax used in the September 2001 terrorist attacks in the United States almost certainly came from the Pentagon's own biological stockpile, not from some poverty stricken Third World country. The U.S. government has probably solved the case but is too embarrassed by it actually to apprehend those responsible and bring them publicly before a court of justice. Meanwhile, the emphasis on using a professional military with its array of "people-zappers" will only strengthen the identification between the United States and tyranny.

If the likelihood of perpetual war hangs over the world, the situation domestically in the United States is no better. Militarism and imperialism threaten democratic government at home just as seriously as they menace the independence and sovereignty of other countries. Whether George Bush and his zealots can ever bring about a "regime change" in Iraq or any other country is an open question, but there is no doubt that they already have done so within the United States. In keeping with the Roman pretensions of his administration, Bush often speaks as if he were a modern Caligula (the Roman emperor who reigned from 37 to 41 AD and who wanted to appoint his horse to the Senate). In the second presidential debate on October 11, 2000, Bush said,

"If this were a dictatorship, it'd be a heck of a lot easier, just so long as I'm the dictator." A little more than a year later, he replied to a question by the *Washington Post* journalist Bob Woodward, "I'm the commander—see, I don't need to explain—I do not need to explain why I say things. That's the interesting thing about being president. Maybe somebody needs to explain to me why they say something, but I don't feel like I owe anybody an explanation."

Bush and his administration have worked zealously to expand the powers of the presidency at the expense of the other branches of government. Article 1, Section 8, of the Constitution says explicitly that "The Congress shall have the power to declare war." It prohibits the president from making that decision. The most influential author of the Constitution, James Madison, wrote in 1793, "In no part of the Constitution is more wisdom to be found than in the clause which confides the question of war or peace to the legislature, and not the executive department. . . . The trust and the temptation would be too great for any one man." Yet, after September 11, 2001, President Bush unilaterally declared that the nation was "at war" against terrorism, and a White House spokesman later noted that the president "considers any opposition to his policies to be no less than an act of treason."

During October 3 to 10, 2002, Congress's "week of shame," both houses voted to give the president open-ended authority to wage war against Iraq. It permitted the president to use any means, including military force and nuclear weapons, in a preventive strike against Iraq as soon and as long as he—and he alone—determined it to be "appropriate." The vote was 296 to 33 in the House and 77 to 23 in the Senate. There was no debate; the members were too politically cowed to address the issue directly. Thus, for example, Sen. Pete Domenici (R-New Mexico) spoke on the hundredth anniversary of the 4-H Club; Sen. Jim Bunning (R-Kentucky) talked about the Future Farmers of America in his state; and Sen. Barbara Boxer (D-California) gave Congress a brief history of the city of Mountain View, California.

Equally serious, the Bush administration arrogated to itself the power unilaterally to judge whether an American citizen or a foreigner is part of a terrorist organization and can therefore be stripped of all Constitutional rights or rights under international law. President Bush's government has imprisoned 664 individuals from forty-two countries, including teenage children, at a concentration camp in Guantánmo, Cuba, where they are beyond the reach of the Constitution. It has also designated them "illegal combatants," a concept unknown in international law, to place them beyond the Geneva Conventions on the treatment of prisoners of war. None of them has been charged with anything: they are merely captives.

The key cases here concern two native-born American citizens—Yasir Esam Hamdi and Jose Padilla. Hamdi, age 22, was born in Baton Rouge, Louisiana, but raised in Saudi Arabia. The Pentagon claimed he was captured fighting for the Taliban in Afghanistan, although in a more detailed submission it acknowledged that he surrendered to the Northern Alliance forces, the warlords whom the U.S. had paid to fight on its side, before he engaged in any form of combat. Padilla is a Brooklyn-born American of Puerto Rican ancestry. He was arrested by federal agents on May 8, 2002, at O'Hare Airport, Chicago, after he arrived on a flight from Pakistan. He was held for a month without any charges being filed or contact with an attorney or the outside world. On the eve of his appearance in federal court in New York, he was hastily transferred to a military prison in Charleston, South Carolina; and President Bush designated him "a bad guy" and an "enemy combatant." No charges were brought against him, and attempts to force the government to make its case via writs of *habeas corpus* were routinely turned down on grounds that the courts have no jurisdiction over a military prisoner.

A year and a half after September 11, 2001, at least two articles of the Bill of Rights were dead letters—the fourth prohibiting unwarranted searches and seizures and the sixth guaranteeing a jury of peers, the assistance of an attorney in offering a defense, the right to confront one's accusers, protection against self-incrimination, and, most critically, the requirement that the government spell out its charges and make them public. The second half of Thomas Jefferson's old warning—"When the

government fears the people, there is liberty; when the people fear the government, there is tyranny"— clearly applies.

The final sorrow of empire is financial ruin. It is different from the other three in that bankruptcy may not be as fatal to the American Constitution as endless war, loss of liberty, and habitual official lying; but it is the only sorrow that will certainly lead to a crisis. The U.S. proved to be ready *militarily* for an Iraq war, maybe even a North Korea war, and perhaps an Iran war, but it is unprepared economically for even one of them, much less all three in short succession.

The permanent military domination of the world is an expensive business. During fiscal year 2003, the U.S.'s military appropriations bill, signed on October 23, 2002, came to $354.8 billion. For fiscal year 2004, the Department of Defense asked Congress for a 4.2% increase, to $380 billion. When the budget was presented, sycophantic Congressmen spent most of their time asking the defense secretary if he was sure he did not need even more money and suggesting big weapons projects that could be built in their districts. They seemed to say that no matter how much the U.S. spends on "defense," it will not be enough. The next largest military spender is Russia, but its military budget is only 14% of the U.S.'s total. To equal current U.S. expenditures, the military budgets of the next twenty-seven highest spenders would have to be added together. The American amounts do not include the intelligence budgets, most of which are controlled by the Pentagon, nor do they include expenditures for the Iraq war or the Pentagon's request for a special $10 billion account to combat terrorism.

Estimates of the likely cost of the war vary widely. In 2002, President Bush's first chief economic adviser, Lawrence Lindsey, guessed that attacking Iraq—an economy somewhat smaller than that of Louisiana's—would require around $140 billion, but this figure already looks too small. In March 2003, the Bush administration said it would need an additional amount somewhere between $60 billion and $95 billion just to cover the build-up of troops in and around Iraq, the ships and planes carrying them, their munitions and other supplies, and the fuel they will consume. These figures did not include the costs of the postwar occupation and reconstruction of the country. A high-level Council on Foreign Relations study concluded that President Bush has failed "to fully describe to Congress and the American people the magnitude of the resources that will be required to meet the post-conflict needs" of Iraq.

The first Gulf war cost about $61 billion. However, American allies such as Saudi Arabia, Kuwait, the United Arab Emirates, Germany, Japan, and South Korea chipped in some $54.1 billion, about 80% of the total, leaving the U.S.'s financial contribution a minuscule $7 billion. Japan alone contributed $13 billion. Nothing like that will happen again. Virtually the entire world is agreed that if the lone superpower wants to go off in personal pursuit of a preventive war, it can pick up its own tab. The problem is that the U.S. is becoming quite short on cash. The budget for 2003 forecasts a $304 billion federal deficit, excluding the costs of the Iraq war and shortfalls in the budgets of programs that are guaranteed, backed, or sponsored by the U.S. government. Virtually all of the U.S. states face severe fiscal shortages and are pleading with the federal government for bailouts, particularly to pay for congressionally mandated anti-terrorism and civil defense programs. The Congressional Budget Office projects federal deficits over the next five years of over $1 trillion, on top of an already existing government debt in February 2003 of $6.4 trillion.

In my judgment, American imperialism and militarism are so far advanced and obstacles to its further growth have been so completely neutralized that the decline of the U.S. has already begun. The country is following the path already taken by its erstwhile adversary in the cold war, the former Soviet Union. The U.S.'s refusal to dismantle its own empire of military bases when the menace of the Soviet Union disappeared, combined with its inappropriate response to the blowback of September 11, 2001, makes this decline virtually inevitable.

There is only one development that could conceivably stop this cancerous process, and that is for the people to retake control of Congress, reform it and the election laws to make it a genuine assembly of democratic representatives, and cut off the supply of money to the Pentagon and the Central Intelligence Agency. That was, after all, the way the Vietnam War was finally brought to a halt.

John le Carré, the novelist most famous for his books on the role of intelligence services in the cold war, writes, "America has entered one of its periods of historical madness, but this is the worst I can remember: worse than McCarthyism, worse than the Bay of Pigs and in the long term potentially more disastrous than the Vietnam War." His view is somewhat more optimistic than mine. If it is just a period of madness, like musth in elephants, we might get over it. The U.S. still has a strong civil society that could, at least in theory, overcome the entrenched interests of the armed forces and the military-industrial complex. I fear, however, that the U.S. has indeed crossed the Rubicon and that there is no way to restore Constitutional government short of a revolutionary rehabilitation of American democracy. Without root and branch reform, Nemesis awaits. She is the goddess of revenge, the punisher of pride and arrogance, and the United States is on course for a rendezvous with her.

---

## DISCUSSION QUESTIONS

1. According to Johnson, how have specific policies of the Bush administration furthered the sorrows of empire?
2. How would assess Johnson's discussion of the prospects for reversing the sorrows of empire as laid out in the last three paragraphs? How deeply rooted in U.S. politics, society, and culture are these imperial patterns?

# CHAPTER 10

# VISIONS OF A NEW DEMOCRACY

Y our actions, and inactions, have an impact on the world. The status quo, the political norm, is either challenged or left unchallenged by what you do with your life. In this way no one, not even the most ardent hater of things "political," is politically neutral.

Though in different ways, the readings in this final chapter all have at their core a belief that you can and should be politically involved in the United States through careful reflection and sustained action. Citizenship demands that we attempt to "do the right thing," even in the face of a political culture that too often seems mired in lethargy and disengagement. Obviously unanimity does not exist on what constitutes the "right thing." Political and economic elites may say that political participation is a good thing, for example, while actually being suspicious of the impact of citizen involvement on societal stability. And, of course, ordinary citizens themselves disagree on many issues. The point is that there is a place for *you* in debating, and perhaps changing, the priorities of the nation you live in. Discussion and debate over the ends of public life, the give-and-take, is what politics is all about.

## 37 *Martin Luther King, Jr.*

# LETTER FROM BIRMINGHAM JAIL

*"Letter from Birmingham Jail" is a classic statement of the civil rights move-ment. Written on scraps of paper found in his jail cell, this 1963 essay by the Reverend Dr. Martin Luther King, Jr., crystallizes many of the themes that served as catalysts to the movement for racial equality he helped lead. The let-ter was written in response to a statement issued by eight white Alabama cler-gymen who criticized King and other demonstrators for causing violence with their protests against segregation. King's searing moral response in support of nonviolent civil disobedience makes a powerful and impassioned call for democracy and human freedom. Among the many compelling points he makes, King criticizes political moderates—in this case the "white moderate" who, in King's words, "is more devoted to 'order' than to justice." To people who follow the doctrinaire belief that the truth always lies in the middle, his position may be surprising. He suggests that we should question the wisdom of assuming that gradual change and piecemeal reforms are the best way to approach a problem.*

April 16, 1963

My Dear Fellow Clergymen:

While confined here in the Birmingham city jail, I came across your recent statement calling my present activities "unwise and untimely." Seldom do I pause to answer criticism of my work and ideas. If I sought to answer all the criticisms that cross my desk, my secretaries would have little time for anything other than such correspondence in the course of the day, and I would have no time for constructive work. But since I feel that you are men of genuine good will and that your criticisms are sincerely set forth, I want to try to answer your statement in what I hope will be patient and reason-able terms.

I think I should indicate why I am here in Birm-ingham, since you have been influenced by the view which argues against "outsiders coming in." I have the honor of serving as president of the Southern Christian Leadership Conference, an organization operating in every southern state, with headquarters in Atlanta, Georgia. We have some eighty-five affili-ated organizations across the South, and one of them is the Alabama Christian Movement for Human Rights. Frequently we share staff, educational and financial resources with our affiliates. Several months ago the affiliate here in Birmingham asked us to be on call to engage in a nonviolent direct-action program if such were deemed necessary. We readily consented, and when the hour came we lived up to our promise. So I, along with several members of my staff, am here because I was invited here. I am here because I have organizational ties here.

But more basically, I am in Birmingham because injustice is here. Just as the prophets of the eighth century B.C. left their villages and carried their "thus saith the Lord" far beyond the boundaries of their home towns, and just as the Apostle Paul left his village of Tarsus and carried the gospel of Jesus Christ to the far corners of the Greco-Roman world, so am I compelled to carry the gospel of freedom beyond my own home town. Like Paul, I must constantly respond to the Macedonian call for aid.

Moreover, I am cognizant of the interrelatedness of all communities and states. I cannot sit idly by in Atlanta and not be concerned about what happens in Birmingham. Injustice anywhere is a threat to justice everywhere. We are caught in an inescapable network of mutuality, tied in a single garment of destiny. Whatever affects one directly, affects all indirectly. Never again can we afford to live with the narrow, provincial "outside agitator" idea. Anyone who lives inside the United States can never be considered an outsider anywhere within its bounds.

You deplore the demonstrations taking place in Birmingham. But your statement, I am sorry to say, fails to express a similar concern for the conditions that brought about the demonstrations. I am sure that none of you would want to rest content with the superficial kind of social analysis that deals merely with effects and does not grapple with underlying causes. It is unfortunate that demonstrations are taking place in Birmingham, but it is even more unfortunate that the city's white power structure left the Negro community with no alternative.

In any nonviolent campaign there are four basic steps: collection of the facts to determine whether injustices exist; negotiation; self-purification; and direct action. We have gone through all these steps in Birmingham. There can be no gain

saying the fact that racial injustice engulfs this community. Birmingham is probably the most thoroughly segregated city in the United States. Its ugly record of brutality is widely known. Negroes have experienced grossly unjust treatment in the courts. There have been more unsolved bombings of Negro homes and churches in Birmingham than in any other city in the nation. These are the hard, brutal facts of the case. On the basis of these conditions, Negro leaders sought to negotiate with the city fathers. But the latter consistently refused to engage in good-faith negotiation. . . .

You may well ask: "Why direct action? Why sit-ins, marches and so forth? Isn't negotiation a better path?" You are quite right in calling for negotiation. Indeed, this is the very purpose of direct action. Nonviolent direct action seeks to create such a crisis and foster such a tension that a community which has constantly refused to negotiate is forced to confront the issue. It seeks so to dramatize the issue that it can no longer be ignored. My citing the creation of tension as part of the work of the nonviolent resister may sound rather shocking. But I must confess that I am not afraid of the word "tension." I have earnestly opposed violent tension, but there is a type of constructive, nonviolent tension which is necessary for growth. Just as Socrates felt that it was necessary to create a tension in the mind so that individuals could rise from the bondage of myths and half-truths to the unfettered realm of creative analysis and objective appraisal, so must we see the need for nonviolent gadflies to create the kind of tension in society that will help men rise from the dark depths of prejudice and racism to the majestic heights of understanding and brotherhood.

The purpose of our direct-action program is to create a situation so crisis-packed that it will inevitably open the door to negotiation. I therefore concur with you in your call for negotiation. Too long has our beloved Southland been bogged down in a tragic effort to live in monologue rather than dialogue.

. . . My friends, I must say to you that we have not made a single gain in civil rights without determined legal and nonviolent pressure. Lamentably, it is an historical fact that privileged groups seldom give up their privileges voluntarily. Individuals may see the moral light and voluntarily give up their unjust posture; but, as Reinhold Niebuhr has reminded us, groups tend to be more immoral than individuals.

We know through painful experience that freedom is never voluntarily given by the oppressor; it must be demanded by the oppressed. Frankly, I have yet to engage in a direct-action campaign that was "well timed" in the view of those who have not suffered unduly from the disease of segregation. For years now I have heard the word "Wait!" It rings in the ear of every Negro with piercing familiarity. This "Wait" has almost always meant "Never." We must come to see, with one of our distinguished jurists, that "justice too long delayed is justice denied."

We have waited for more than 340 years for our constitutional and God-given rights. The nations of Asia and Africa are moving with jetlike speed toward gaining political independence, but we still creep at horse-and-buggy pace toward gaining a cup of coffee at a lunch counter. Perhaps it is easy for those who have never felt the stinging darts of segregation to say, "Wait." But when you have seen vicious mobs lynch your mothers and fathers at will and drown your sisters and brothers at whim; when you have seen hate-filled policemen curse, kick and even kill your black brothers and sisters; when you see the vast majority of your twenty million Negro brothers smothering in an airtight cage of poverty in the midst of an affluent society; when you suddenly find your tongue twisted and your speech stammering as you seek to explain to your six-year-old daughter why she can't go to the public amusement park that has just been advertised on television, and see tears welling up in her eyes when she is told that Funtown is closed to colored children, and see ominous clouds of inferiority beginning to form in her little mental sky, and see her beginning to distort her personality by developing an unconscious bitterness toward white people; when you have to concoct an answer for a five-year-old son who is asking: "Daddy, why do white people treat colored people so mean?"; when you take a cross-country drive and find it necessary to sleep night after night in the uncomfortable corners of your automobile because no motel will accept you; when you are humiliated day in and day out by nagging signs reading "white" and "colored"; when your first name becomes "nigger," your middle name becomes "boy" (however old you are) and your last name becomes "John," and your wife and mother are never given the respected title "Mrs."; when you are harried by day and haunted by night by the fact that you are a Negro, living constantly at tiptoe stance, never quite knowing what to expect next, and are plagued with inner fears and outer resentments; when you are forever fighting a degenerating sense of "nobodiness"—then you will understand why we find it difficult to wait. There comes a time when the cup of endurance runs over, and men are no longer willing to be plunged into the abyss of despair. I hope, sirs, you can understand our legitimate and unavoidable impatience.

You express a great deal of anxiety over our willingness to break laws. This is certainly a legitimate concern. Since we so diligently urge people to obey the Supreme Court's decision of 1954 outlawing segregation in the public schools, at first glance it may seem rather paradoxical for us consciously to break laws. One may well ask: "How can you advocate breaking some laws and obeying others?" The answer lies in the fact that there are two types of laws: just and unjust. I would be the first to advocate obeying just laws. One has not only a legal but a moral responsibility to obey just laws. Conversely, one has a moral responsibility to disobey unjust laws. I would agree with St. Augustine that "an unjust law is no law at all."

Now, what is the difference between the two? How does one determine whether a law is just or unjust? A just law is a man-made code that squares with the moral law or the law of God. An unjust law is a code that is out of harmony with the moral law. To put it in the terms of St. Thomas Aquinas: An unjust law is a human law that is not rooted in eternal law and natural law. Any law that uplifts human personality is just. Any law that degrades human personality is unjust. All segregation statutes are unjust because segregation distorts the soul and damages the personality. It gives the segregator a false sense of superiority and the segregated a false sense of inferiority. Segregation, to use the terminology of the Jewish philosopher Martin Buber, substitutes an "I-it" relationship for an "I-thou" relationship and ends up relegating persons to the status of things. Hence segregation is not only politically, economically and sociologically unsound, it is morally wrong and sinful. Paul Tillich has said that sin is separation. Is not segregation an existential expression of man's tragic separation, his awful estrangement, his terrible sinfulness? Thus it is that I can urge men to obey the 1954 decision of the Supreme Court for it is morally right; and I can urge them to disobey segregation ordinances, for they are morally wrong.

Let us consider a more concrete example of just and unjust laws. An unjust law is a code that a numerical or power majority group compels a minority group to obey but does not make binding on itself. This is *difference* made legal. By the same token, a just law is a code that a majority compels a minority to follow and that it is willing to follow itself. This is *sameness* made legal.

Let me give another explanation. A law is unjust if it is inflicted on a minority that, as a result of being denied the right to vote, had no part in enacting or devising the law. Who can say that the legislature of Alabama which set up that state's segregation laws was democratically elected? Throughout Alabama all sorts of devious methods are used to prevent Negroes from becoming registered voters, and there are some counties in which, even though Negroes constitute a majority of the population, not a single Negro is registered. Can any law enacted under such circumstances be considered democratically structured?

Sometimes a law is just on its face and unjust in its application. For instance, I have been arrested on a charge of parading without a permit. Now, there is nothing wrong in having an ordinance which requires a permit for a parade. But such an ordinance becomes unjust when it is used to maintain segregation and to deny citizens the First Amendment privilege of peaceful assembly and protest.

I hope you are able to see the distinction I am trying to point out. In no sense do I advocate evading or defying the law, as would the rabid segregationist.

That would lead to anarchy. One who breaks an unjust law must do so openly, lovingly, and with a willingness to accept the penalty. I submit that an individual who breaks a law that conscience tells him is unjust, and who willingly accepts the penalty of imprisonment in order to arouse the conscience of the community over its injustice, is in reality expressing the highest respect for law.

Of course, there is nothing new about this kind of civil disobedience. It was evidenced sublimely in the refusal of Shadrach, Meshach and Abednego to obey the laws of Nebuchadnezzar, on the ground that a higher moral law was at stake. It was practiced superbly by the early Christians, who were willing to face hungry lions and the excruciating pain of chopping blocks rather than submit to certain unjust laws of the Roman Empire. To a degree, academic freedom is a reality today because Socrates practiced civil disobedience. In our own nation, the Boston Tea Party represented a massive act of civil disobedience.

We should never forget that everything Adolf Hitler did in Germany was "legal" and everything the Hungarian freedom fighters did in Hungary was "illegal." It was "illegal" to aid and comfort a Jew in Hitler's Germany. Even so, I am sure that, had I lived in Germany at the time, I would have aided and comforted my Jewish brothers. If today I lived in a Communist country where certain principles dear to the Christian faith are suppressed, I would openly advocate disobeying that country's antireligious laws.

I must make two honest confessions to you, my Christian and Jewish brothers. First, I must confess that over the past few years I have been gravely disappointed with the white moderate. I have almost reached the regrettable conclusion that the Negro's great stumbling block in his stride toward freedom is not the White Citizen's Counciler or the Ku Klux Klanner, but the white moderate, who is more devoted to "order" than to justice; who prefers a negative peace which is the absence of tension to a positive peace which is the presence of justice; who constantly says: "I agree with you in the goal you seek, but I cannot agree with your methods of direct action"; who paternalistically believes he can set the timetable for another man's freedom; who lives by a mythical concept of time and who constantly advises the Negro to wait for a "more convenient season." Shallow understanding from people of good will is more frustrating than absolute misunderstanding from people of ill will. Lukewarm acceptance is much more bewildering than outright rejection.

I had hoped that the white moderate would understand that law and order exist for the purpose of establishing justice and that when they fail in this purpose they become the dangerously structured dams that block the flow of social progress. I had hoped that the white moderate would understand that the present tension in the South is a necessary phase of the transition from an obnoxious negative peace, in which the Negro passively accepted his unjust plight, to a substantive and positive peace, in which all men will respect the dignity and worth of human personality. Actually, we who engage in nonviolent direct action are not the creators of tension. We merely bring to the surface the hidden tension that is already alive. We bring it out in the open, where it can be seen and dealt with. Like a boil that can never be cured so long as it is covered up but must be opened with all its ugliness to the natural medicines of air and light, injustice must be exposed, with all the tension its exposure creates, to the light of human conscience and the air of national opinion before it can be cured.

In your statement you assert that our actions, even though peaceful, must be condemned because they precipitate violence. But is this a logical assertion? Isn't this like condemning a robbed man because his possession of money precipitated the evil act of robbery? Isn't this like condemning Socrates because his unswerving commitment to truth and his philosophical inquiries precipitated the act by the misguided populace in which they made him drink hemlock? Isn't this like condemning Jesus because his unique God-consciousness and never-ceasing devotion to God's will precipitated the evil act of crucifixion? We must come to see that, as the federal courts have consistently affirmed, it is wrong to urge an individual to cease his efforts to gain his basic constitutional rights because the quest may precipitate violence. Society must protect the robbed and punish the robber.

I had also hoped that the white moderate would reject the myth concerning time in relation to the struggle for freedom. I have just received a letter from a white brother in Texas. He writes: "All Christians know that the colored people will receive equal rights eventually, but it is possible that you are in too great a religious hurry. It has taken Christianity almost two thousand years to accomplish what it has. The teachings of Christ take time to come to earth." Such an attitude stems from a tragic misconception of time, from the strangely irrational notion that there is something in the very flow of time that will inevitably cure all ills. Actually, time itself is neutral; it can be used either destructively or constructively. More and more I feel that the people of ill will have used time much more effectively than have the people of good will. We will have to repent in this generation not merely for the hateful words and actions of the bad people but for the appalling silence of the good people. Human progress never rolls in on wheels of inevitability; it comes through the tireless efforts of men willing to be co-workers with God, and without this hard work, time itself becomes an ally of the forces of social stagnation. We must use time creatively, in the knowledge that the time is always ripe to do right. Now is the time to make real the promise of democracy and transform our pending national elegy into a creative psalm of brotherhood. Now is the time to lift our national policy from the quicksand of racial injustice to the solid rock of human dignity.

You speak of our activity in Birmingham as extreme. At first I was rather disappointed that fellow clergymen would see my nonviolent efforts as those of an extremist. I began thinking about the fact that I stand in the middle of two opposing forces in the Negro community. One is a force of complacency, made up in part of Negroes who, as a result of long years of oppression, are so drained of self-respect and a sense of "somebodiness" that they have adjusted to segregation; and in part of a few middle-class Negroes who, because of a degree of academic and economic security and because in some ways they profit by segregation, have become insensitive to the problems of the masses. The other force is one of bitterness and hatred, and it comes perilously close to advocating violence. It is expressed in the various black nationalist groups that are springing up across the nation, the largest and best-known being Elijah Muhammad's Muslim movement. Nourished by the Negro's frustration over the continued existence of racial discrimination, this movement is made up of people who have lost faith in America, who have absolutely repudiated Christianity, and who have concluded that the white man is an incorrigible "devil."

I have tried to stand between these two forces, saying that we need emulate neither the "do-nothingism" of the complacent nor the hatred and despair of the black nationalist. For there is the more excellent way of love and nonviolent protest. I am grateful to God that, through the influence of the Negro church, the way of nonviolence became an integral part of our struggle.

If this philosophy had not emerged, by now many streets of the South would, I am convinced, be flowing with blood. And I am further convinced that if our white brothers dismiss as "rabble-rousers" and "outside agitators" those of us who employ nonviolent direct action, and if they refuse to support our nonviolent efforts, millions of Negroes will, out of frustration and despair, seek solace and security in black-nationalist ideologies—a development that would inevitably lead to a frightening racial nightmare.

Oppressed people cannot remain oppressed forever. The yearning for freedom eventually manifests itself, and that is what has happened to the American Negro. Something within has reminded him of his birthright of freedom, and something without has reminded him that it can be gained. Consciously or unconsciously he has been caught up by the *Zeitgeist,* and with his black brothers of Africa and his brown and yellow brothers of Asia, South America and the Caribbean, the United States Negro is moving with a sense of great urgency toward the promised land of racial justice. If one recognizes this vital urge that has engulfed the Negro community, one should readily understand why public demonstrations are taking place. The Negro has many pent-up resentments and latent frustrations, and he must release them. So let him march; let him make prayer

pilgrimages to the city hall; let him go on freedom rides—and try to understand why he must do so. If his repressed emotions are not released in nonviolent ways, they will seek expression through violence; this is not a threat but a fact of history. So I have not said to my people: "Get rid of your discontent." Rather, I have tried to say that this normal and healthy discontent can be channeled into the creative outlet of nonviolent direct action. And now this approach is being termed extremist.

But though I was initially disappointed at being categorized as an extremist, as I continued to think about the matter I gradually gained a measure of satisfaction from the label. Was not Jesus an extremist for love: "Love your enemies, bless them that curse you, do good to them that hate you, and pray for them which despitefully use you, and persecute you." Was not Amos an extremist for justice: "Let justice roll down like waters and righteousness like an ever-flowing stream." Was not Paul an extremist for the Christian gospel: "I bear in my body the marks of the Lord Jesus." Was not Martin Luther an extremist: "Here I stand: I cannot do otherwise, so help me God." And John Bunyan: "I will stay in jail to the end of my days before I make a butchery of my conscience." And Abraham Lincoln: "This nation cannot survive half slave and half free." And Thomas Jefferson: "We hold these truths to be self-evident, that all men are created equal. . . ." So the question is not whether we will be extremists, but what kind of extremists we will be. Will we be extremists for hate or for love? Will we be extremists for the preservation of injustice or for the extension of justice? In that dramatic scene on Calvary's hill three men were crucified. We must never forget that all three were crucified for the same crime—the crime of extremism. Two were extremists for immorality, and thus fell below their environment. The other, Jesus Christ, was an extremist for love, truth and goodness, and thereby rose above his environment. Perhaps the South, the nation and the world are in dire need of creative extremists.

I had hoped that the white moderate would see this need. . . .

Before closing I feel impelled to mention one other point in your statement that has troubled me profoundly. You warmly commended the Birmingham police force for keeping "order" and "preventing violence." I doubt that you would have so warmly commended the police force if you had seen its dogs sinking their teeth into unarmed, nonviolent Negroes. I doubt that you would so quickly commend the policemen if you were to observe their ugly and inhumane treatment of Negroes here in the city jail; if you were to watch them push and curse old Negro women and young Negro girls; if you were to see them slap and kick old Negro men and young boys; if you were to observe them, as they did on two occasions, refuse to give us food because we wanted to sing our grace together. I cannot join you in your praise of the Birmingham police department.

It is true that the police have exercised a degree of discipline in handling the demonstrators. In this sense they have conducted themselves rather "nonviolently" in public. But for what purpose? To preserve the evil system of segregation. Over the past few years I have consistently preached that nonviolence demands that the means we use must be as pure as the ends we seek. I have tried to make clear that it is wrong to use immoral means to attain moral ends. But now I must affirm that it is just as wrong, or perhaps even more so, to use moral means to preserve immoral ends. Perhaps Mr. Connor and his policemen have been rather nonviolent in public, as was Chief Pritchett in Albany, Georgia, but they have used the moral means of nonviolence to maintain the immoral end of racial injustice. As T. S. Eliot has said: "The last temptation is the greatest treason: To do the right deed for the wrong reason."

I wish you had commended the Negro sitinners and demonstrators of Birmingham for their sublime courage, their willingness to suffer and their amazing discipline in the midst of great provocation. One day the South will recognize its real heroes. They will be the James Merediths, with the noble sense of purpose that enables them to face jeering and hostile mobs, and with the agonizing loneliness that characterizes the life of the pioneer. They will be old, oppressed, battered Negro women, symbolized in a seventy-two-year-old woman in Montgomery, Alabama, who rose up with a sense of dignity and with her people decided not to ride segregated buses, and who responded with ungrammatical profundity to one who inquired about her weariness: "My feets is tired, but my soul is at rest." They will be the young high school and college students, the young ministers of the gospel and a host of their elders, courageously and nonviolently sitting in at lunch counters and willingly going to jail for conscience' sake. One day the South will know that when these disinherited children of God sat down at lunch counters, they were in reality standing up for what is best in the American dream and for the most sacred values in our Judaeo-Christian heritage, thereby bringing our nation back to those great wells of democracy which were dug deep by the founding fathers in their formulation of the Constitution and the Declaration of Independence.

•  •  •

Yours for the cause of Peace and Brotherhood, Martin Luther King, Jr.

---

## DISCUSSION QUESTIONS

1. Explain why Martin Luther King may have come to the conclusion that the white moderate's devotion to order has been "the Negro's great stumbling block" rather than the persecutions of the White Citizen's Counciler or the Ku Klux Klan.
2. In what way does King criticize the white moderate? What does he mean by the statement "justice too long delayed is justice denied"?
3. Why would King object to the pluralist understanding of American politics as explained in the introduction to this reader? How is the kind of action that King calls for viewed in our society today?

# 38 *Naomi Klein*

# RECLAIMING THE COMMONS

*One of the most striking developments in U.S. and world politics in recent years has been the growth of a diverse and broad-based movement against corporate domination of the global economy. Misleadingly labeled the "antiglobalization" movement, this new wave of activism reached mass awareness with the protests in Seattle at the meeting of the World Trade Organization in 1999. One of the most articulate thinkers of the movement is the Canadian author and activist Naomi Klein, whose book* No Logo *(2000) found an international audience. In this article Klein clarifies the nature and goals of the movement, which opposes the privatization and commodification of everyday life rather than globalization as such. She explains that activists have targeted "free-market" trade agreements as a way of resisting "McGovernment"—the "happy meal" of cutting taxes, privatizing services, slashing regulations, busting unions, and removing any obstacles to the unfettered reign of the market which is the hidden agenda of the free trade agenda. Far from seeing democracy and the freemarket as synonymous, Klein asserts that the dominant form of corporate globalization amounts to "a crisis in representative democracy." For her the spirit of the oppositional campaigns and movements is one of the "reclaiming the commons"—acting to create a public sphere in which grassroots democracy can flourish and resist the boundless drive of the corporate project.*

What is 'the anti-globalization movement'? I put the phrase in quote-marks because I immediately have two doubts about it. Is it really a movement? If it is a movement, is it anti-globalization? Let me start with the first issue. We can easily convince ourselves it is a movement by talking it into existence at a forum like this—I spend far too much time at them—acting as if we can see it, hold it in our hands. Of course, we have seen it—and we know it's come back in Quebec, and on the U.S.–Mexican border during the Summit of the Americas and the discussion for a hemispheric Free Trade Area. But then we leave rooms like this, go home, watch some TV, do a little shopping and any sense that it exists disappears, and we feel like maybe we're going nuts. Seattle—was that a movement or a collective hallucination? To most of us here, Seattle meant a kind of coming-out party for a global resistance movement,

*Source:* Naomi Klein, "Reclaiming the Commons." *New Left Review,* 9, May–June 2001, pp. 81–89.

or the 'globalization of hope,' as someone described it during the World Social Forum at Porto Alegre. But to everyone else Seattle still means limitless frothy coffee, Asian-fusion cuisine, e-commerce billionaires and sappy Meg Ryan movies. Or perhaps it is both, and one Seattle bred the other Seattle—and now they awkwardly coexist.

This movement we sometimes conjure into being goes by many names: anti-corporate, anti-capitalist, anti-free trade, anti-imperialist. Many say that it started in Seattle. Others maintain it began five hundred years ago—when colonialists first told indigenous peoples that they were going to have to do things differently if they were to 'develop' or be eligible for 'trade.' Others again say it began on 1 January 1994 when the Zapatistas launched their uprising with the words *Ya Basta!* on the night NAFTA became law in Mexico. It all depends on whom you ask. But I think it is more accurate to picture a movement of many movements—coalitions of coalitions. Thousands of groups today are all working against forces whose common thread is what might broadly be described as the privatization of every aspect of life, and the transformation of every activity and value into a commodity. We often speak of the privatization of education, of healthcare, of natural resources. But the process is much vaster. It includes the way powerful ideas are turned into advertising slogans and public streets into shopping malls; new generations being target-marketed at birth; schools being invaded by ads; basic human necessities like water being sold as commodities; basic labour rights being rolled back; genes are patented and designer babies loom; seeds are genetically altered and bought; politicians are bought and altered.

At the same time there are oppositional threads, taking form in many different campaigns and movements. The spirit they share is a radical reclaiming of the commons. As our communal spaces—town squares, streets, schools, farms, plants—are displaced by the ballooning marketplace, a spirit of resistance is taking hold around the world. People are reclaiming bits of nature and of culture, and saying 'this is going to be public space.' American students are kicking ads out of the classrooms. European environmentalists and ravers are throwing parties at busy intersections. Landless Thai peasants are planting organic vegetables on over-irrigated golf courses. Bolivian workers are reversing the privatization of their water supply. Outfits like Napster have been creating a kind of commons on the internet where kids can swap music with each other, rather than buying it from multinational record companies. Billboards have been liberated and independent media networks set up. Protests are multiplying. In Porto Alegre, during the World Social Forum, José Bové, often caricatured as only a hammer of McDonald's, travelled with local activists from the Movimento Sem Terra to a nearby Monsanto test site, where they destroyed three hectares of genetically modified soya beans. But the protest did not stop there. The MST has occupied the land and members are now planting their own organic crops on it, vowing to turn the farm into a model of sustainable agriculture. In short, activists aren't waiting for the revolution, they are acting right now, where they live, where they study, where they work, where they farm.

But some formal proposals are also emerging whose aim is to turn such radical reclamations of the commons into law. When NAFTA and the like were cooked up, there was much talk of adding on 'side agreements' to the free trade agenda, that were supposed to encompass the environment, labour and human rights. Now the fight-back is about taking them out. José Bové—along with the Via Campesina, a global association of small farmers—has launched a campaign to remove food safety and agricultural products from all trade agreements, under the slogan 'The World is Not for Sale.' They want to draw a line around the commons. Maude Barlow, director of the Council of Canadians, which has more members than most political parties in Canada, has argued that water isn't a private good and shouldn't be in any trade agreement. There is a lot of support for this idea, especially in Europe since the recent food scares. Typically these anti-privatization campaigns get under way on their own. But they also periodically converge—that's what happened in Seattle, Prague, Washington, Davos, Porto Alegre and Quebec.

# BEYOND THE BORDERS

What this means is that the discourse has shifted. During the battles against NAFTA, there emerged the first signs of a coalition between organized labour, environmentalists, farmers and consumer groups within the countries concerned. In Canada most of us felt we were fighting to keep something distinctive about our nation from 'Americaniza- tion.' In the United States, the talk was very protec- tionist: workers were worried that Mexicans would 'steal' away 'our' jobs and drive down 'our' envi- ronmental standards. All the while, the voices of Mexicans opposed to the deal were virtually off the public radar—yet these were the strongest voices of all. But only a few years later, the debate over trade has been transformed. The fight against globaliza- tion has morphed into a struggle against corporati- zation and, for some, against capitalism itself. It has also become a fight for democracy. Maude Barlow spearheaded the campaign against NAFTA in Canada twelve years ago. Since NAFTA became law, she's been working with organizers and activists from other countries, and anarchists suspi- cious of the state in her own country. She was once seen as very much the face of a Canadian national- ism. Today she has moved away from that dis- course. 'I've changed,' she says, 'I used to see this fight as saving a nation. Now I see it as saving democracy.' This is a cause that transcends nation- ality and state borders. The real news out of Seattle is that organizers around the world are beginning to see their local and national struggles—for better funded public schools, against union-busting and casualization, for family farms, and against the widening gap between rich and poor—through a global lens. That is the most significant shift we have seen in years.

How did this happen? Who or what convened this new international people's movement? Who sent out the memos? Who built these complex coali- tions? It is tempting to pretend that someone did dream up a master plan for mobilization at Seattle. But I think it was much more a matter of large-scale coincidence. A lot of smaller groups organized to get themselves there and then found to their surprise

just how broad and diverse a coalition they had become part of. Still, if there is one force we can thank for bringing this front into being, it is the multinational corporations. As one of the organizers of Reclaim the Streets has remarked, we should be grateful to the CEOs for helping us see the problems more quickly. Thanks to the sheer imperialist ambi- tion of the corporate project at this moment in his- tory—the boundless drive for profit, liberated by trade deregulation, and the wave of mergers and buy-outs, liberated by weakened anti-trust laws— multinationals have grown so blindingly rich, so vast in their holdings, so global in their reach, that they have created our coalitions for us.

Around the world, activists are piggy-backing on the ready-made infrastructures supplied by global corporations. This can mean cross-border unionization, but also cross-sector organizing— among workers, environmentalists, consumers, even prisoners, who may all have different relationships to one multinational. So you can build a single cam- paign or coalition around a single brand like Gen- eral Electric. Thanks to Monsanto, farmers in India are working with environmentalists and consumers around the world to develop direct-action strategies that cut off genetically modified foods in the fields and in the supermarkets. Thanks to Shell Oil and Chevron, human rights activists in Nigeria, demo- crats in Europe, environmentalists in North America have united in a fight against the unsustainability of the oil industry. Thanks to the catering giant Sodexho-Marriott's decision to invest in Correc- tions Corporation of America, university students are able to protest against the exploding U.S. for- profit prison industry simply by boycotting the food in their campus cafeteria. Other targets include pharmaceutical companies who are trying to inhibit the production and distribution of low-cost AIDS drugs, and fast-food chains. Recently, students and farm workers in Florida have joined forces around Taco Bell. In the St. Petersburg area, field hands— many of them immigrants from Mexico—are paid an average $7,500 a year to pick tomatoes and onions. Due to a loophole in the law, they have no bargaining power: the farm bosses refuse even to talk with them about wages. When they started to look into who bought what they pick, they found that Taco Bell was the largest purchaser of the local tomatoes. So they launched the campaign *Yo No Quiero Taco Bell* together with students, to boycott Taco Bell on university campuses.

It is Nike, of course, that has most helped to pioneer this new brand of activist synergy. Students facing a corporate take-over of their campuses by the Nike swoosh have linked up with workers making its branded campus apparel, as well as with parents concerned at the commercialization of youth and church groups campaigning against child labour—all united by their different relationships to a common global enemy. Exposing the underbelly of high-gloss consumer brands has provided the early narratives of this movement, a sort of call-and-response to the very different narratives these companies tell every day about themselves through advertising and public relations. Citigroup offers another prime target, as North America's largest financial institution, with innumerable holdings, which deals with some of the worst corporate malefactors around. The campaign against it handily knits together dozens of issues—from clear-cut logging in California to oil-and-pipeline schemes in Chad and Cameroon. These projects are only a start. But they are creating a new sort of activist: 'Nike is a gateway drug,' in the words of Oregon student activist Sarah Jacobson.

By focusing on corporations, organizers can demonstrate graphically how so many issues of social, ecological and economic justice are interconnected. No activist I've met believes that the world economy can be changed one corporation at a time, but the campaigns have opened a door into the arcane world of international trade and finance. Where they are leading is to the central institutions that write the rules of global commerce: the WTO, the IMF, the FTAA, and for some the market itself. Here too the unifying threat is privatization—the loss of the commons. The next round of WTO negotiations is designed to extend the reach of commodification still further. Through side agreements like GATS (General Agreement on Trade and Services) and TRIPS (Trade-Related Aspects of Intellectual Property Rights), the aim is to get still tougher

protection of property rights on seeds and drug patents, and to marketize services like health care, education and water-supply.

The biggest challenge facing us is to distil all of this into a message that is widely accessible. Many campaigners understand the connexions binding together the various issues almost intuitively—much as Subcomandante Marcos says, 'Zapatismo isn't an ideology, it's an intuition.' But to outsiders, the mere scope of modern protests can be a bit mystifying. If you eavesdrop on the movement from the outside, which is what most people do, you are liable to hear what seems to be a cacophony of disjointed slogans, a jumbled laundry list of disparate grievances without clear goals. At the Democratic National Convention in Los Angeles last year, I remember being outside the Staples Centre during the Rage Against the Machine concert, just before I almost got shot, and thinking there were slogans for everything everywhere, to the point of absurdity.

## MAINSTREAM FAILURES

This kind of impression is reinforced by the decentralized, non-hierarchical structure of the movement, which always disconcerts the traditional media. Well-organized press conferences are rare, there is no charismatic leadership, protests tend to pile on top of each other. Rather than forming a pyramid, as most movements do, with leaders up on top and followers down below, it looks more like an elaborate web. In part, this web-like structure is the result of internet-based organizing. But it is also a response to the very political realities that sparked the protests in the first place: the utter failure of traditional party politics. All over the world, citizens have worked to elect social democratic and workers' parties, only to watch them plead impotence in the face of market forces and IMF dictates. In these conditions, modern activists are not so naive as to believe change will come from electoral politics. That's why they are more interested in challenging the structures that make democracy toothless, like the IMF's structural adjustment policies, the WTO's ability to override national sovereignty, corrupt campaign financing, and so on. This is not just making a virtue of necessity. It responds at the ideological level to an understanding that globalization is in essence a crisis in representative democracy. What has caused this crisis? One of the basic reasons for it is the way power and decision-making has been handed along to points ever further away from citizens: from local to provincial, from provincial to national, from national to international institutions, that lack all transparency or accountability. What is the solution? To articulate an alternative, participatory democracy.

If you think about the nature of the complaints raised against the World Trade Organization, it is that governments around the world have embraced an economic model that involves much more than opening borders to goods and services. This is why it is not useful to use the language of anti-globalization. Most people do not really know what globalization is, and the term makes the movement extremely vulnerable to stock dismissals like: 'If you are against trade and globalization why do you drink coffee?' Whereas in reality the movement is a rejection of what is being bundled along with trade and so-called globalization—against the set of transformative political policies that every country in the world has been told they must accept in order to make themselves hospitable to investment. I call this package 'McGovernment.' This happy meal of cutting taxes, privatizing services, liberalizing regulations, busting unions—what is this diet in aid of? To remove anything standing in the way of the market. Let the free market roll, and every other problem will apparently be solved in the trickle down. This isn't about trade. It's about using trade to enforce the McGovernment recipe.

So the question we are asking today, in the run up to the FTAA, is not: are you for or against trade? The question is: do we have the right to negotiate the terms of our relationship to foreign capital and investment? Can we decide how we want to protect ourselves from the dangers inherent in deregulated markets—or do we have to contract out those decisions? These problems will become much more acute once we are in a recession, because during the economic boom so much has been destroyed of

what was left of our social safety net. During a period of low unemployment, people did not worry much about that. They are likely to be much more concerned in the very near future. The most controversial issues facing the WTO are these questions about self-determination. For example, does Canada have the right to ban a harmful gasoline additive without being sued by a foreign chemical company? Not according to the WTO's ruling in favour of the Ethyl Corporation. Does Mexico have the right to deny a permit for a hazardous toxic-waste disposal site? Not according to Metalclad, the U.S. company now suing the Mexican government for $16.7 million damages under NAFTA. Does France have the right to ban hormone-treated beef from entering the country? Not according to the United States, which retaliated by banning French imports like Roquefort cheese—prompting a cheese-maker called Bové to dismantle a McDonald's; Americans thought he just didn't like hamburgers. Does Argentina have to cut its public sector to qualify for foreign loans? Yes, according to the IMF—sparking general strikes against the social consequences. It's the same issue everywhere: trading away democracy in exchange for foreign capital.

On smaller scales, the same struggles for self-determination and sustainability are being waged against World Bank dams, clear-cut logging, cash-crop factory farming, and resource extraction on contested indigenous lands. Most people in these movements are not against trade or industrial development. What they are fighting for is the right of local communities to have a say in how their resources are used, to make sure that the people who live on the land benefit directly from its development. These campaigns are a response not to trade but to a trade-off that is now five hundred years old: the sacrifice of democratic control and self-determination to foreign investment and the panacea of economic growth. The challenge they now face is to shift a discourse around the vague notion of globalization into a specific debate about democracy. In a period of 'unprecedented prosperity,' people were told they had no choice but to slash public spending, revoke labour laws, rescind environmental protections—deemed illegal trade barriers—defund schools, not build affordable housing. All this was necessary to make us trade-ready, investment-friendly, world-competitive. Imagine what joys await us during a recession.

We need to be able to show that globalization—this version of globalization—has been built on the back of local human welfare. Too often, these connexions between global and local are not made. Instead we sometimes seem to have two activist solitudes. On the one hand, there are the international anti-globalization activists who may be enjoying a triumphant mood, but seem to be fighting far-away issues, unconnected to people's day-to-day struggles. They are often seen as elitists: white middle-class kids with dreadlocks. On the other hand, there are community activists fighting daily struggles for survival, or for the preservation of the most elementary public services, who are often feeling burnt-out and demoralized. They are saying: what in the hell are you guys so excited about?

The only clear way forward is for these two forces to merge. What is now the anti-globalization movement must turn into thousands of local movements, fighting the way neoliberal politics are playing out on the ground: homelessness, wage stagnation, rent escalation, police violence, prison explosion, criminalization of migrant workers, and on and on. These are also struggles about all kinds of prosaic issues: the right to decide where the local garbage goes, to have good public schools, to be supplied with clean water. At the same time, the local movements fighting privatization and deregulation on the ground need to link their campaigns into one large global movement, which can show where their particular issues fit into an international economic agenda being enforced around the world.

If that connexion isn't made, people will continue to be demoralized. What we need is to formulate a political framework that can both take on corporate power and control, and empower local organizing and self-determination. That has to be a framework that encourages, celebrates and fiercely protects the right to diversity: cultural diversity, ecological diversity, agricultural diversity—and yes, political diversity as well: different ways of doing politics. Communities must have the right to plan and manage their schools, their services, their natural settings, according to their own lights. Of course, this is only possible within a framework of national and international standards—of public education, fossil-fuel emissions, and so on. But the goal should not be better far-away rules and rulers, it should be close-up democracy on the ground.

The Zapatistas have a phrase for this. They call it 'one world with many worlds in it.' Some have criticized this as a New Age non-answer. They want a plan. 'We know what the market wants to do with those spaces, what do *you* want to do? Where's your scheme?' I think we shouldn't be afraid to say: 'That's not up to us.' We need to have some trust in people's ability to rule themselves, to make the decisions that are best for them. We need to show some humility where now there is so much arrogance and paternalism. To believe in human diversity and local democracy is anything but wishy-washy. Everything in McGovernment conspires against them. Neoliberal economics is biased at every level towards centralization, consolidation, homogenization. It is a war waged on diversity. Against it, we need a movement of radical change, committed to a single world with many worlds in it, that stands for 'the one no and the many yesses.'

---

## DISCUSSION QUESTIONS

1. How does Klein characterize the "corporate agenda" in the age of globalization? Why does she think that this agenda is a threat to democracy in any meaningful sense?
2. Contemporary political discourse often speaks of "free market democracy" as an ideal that all countries strive to attain. Why would the movements that Klein discusses take issue with this easy equation of democracy and free markets?

## 39 *Steven Hill*

# TEN STEPS TO IMPROVE OUR DEMOCRACY

*The presidential elections of both 2000 and 2004 made many Americans aware of the political importance of such seemingly technical matters as ballot design, the counting process, and registration rolls. In this article longtime election reform advocate Steven Hill puts forward ten measures that would improve the quality of elections and American democracy more generally. These range from establishing better national election standards and public interest voting machines to making both registration and voting easier. Hill supports abolition of the Electoral College and reform of the campaign finance system, as do several other authors in this book. Hill aims to stimulate awareness of the gap between democratic ideals and realities in America, a country that takes pride in serving as a global model for democracy. While political reform has a tendency to be acknowledged and then placed on the back burner, Hill asks us not to rest satisfied with the status quo and to make a practical program for political and electoral reform an essential component of democratic and progressive projects today.*

The U.S. electoral system is our nation's crazy aunt in the attic. Every few years she pops out and creates a scene, and everyone swears that something must be done. But as soon as election day passes, we're happy to ignore her again—at least until the next time she frustrates the will of the people.

Under a fair, equitable, and democratic system of voting, Al Gore would have been elected president in 2000, and George W. Bush would still be whacking weeds in Crawford. In 2004, even though Bush won the popular vote by some 3 million ballots, the election was still tarnished. Florida replayed its 2000 debacle with attempts to purge African-American voters from the rolls, and voters who requested absentee ballots but never received them were barred from voting in person. There were hundreds of complaints of voting irregularities in Ohio, with voters in some black precincts waiting in lines at polling places for seven hours because of voting-machine shortages. Some voters were required to show identification, even though the demand was illegal. Approximately 92,000 ballots failed to record a vote for president, most of them on the same type of discredited punch-card systems that malfunctioned in Florida in 2000. Ohio election officials may have improperly disqualified thousands of the 155,000 provisional ballots cast. Bush won the state—and thus the presidency—by 118,000 votes.

*Source:* Steven Hill, "10 Steps to Better Elections." *Sierra*, Volume 90, Number 3, May 2005, pp. 46–53.

Although the United States prides itself as a beacon of democracy to the rest of the world, for the second time in a row our presidential election appeared bumbling, if not outright fraudulent. Sergio Aguayo, an election observer and political scientist at the Colegio de Mexico in Mexico City, told Business Week that the partisan way our election was run "looks an awful lot like the old Mexican PRI," referring to the notoriously corrupt ruling party that dominated Mexican politics for seven decades. President Jimmy Carter, whose Carter Center monitors elections around the world, said that in Florida, "some basic international requirements for a fair election are missing."

When elections are unfair, the environment loses. While polls show that large majorities of the American public favor strong environmental protections, those aspirations are routinely frustrated by a flawed voting system. In San Diego last November, environmental write-in candidate Donna Frye won the most votes for mayor, but lost on a technicality when the clear intent of some 5,000 write-in voters was ignored. (The decision is being appealed; see "Profile," page 22.) In Washington State, after Republican gubernatorial candidate Dino Rossi claimed victory, it took a hand recount to find that more than 700 absentee votes had been ignored. When all the votes were counted, Sierra Club-endorsed Democrat Christine Gregoire was declared the victor by 129 votes. And as long as the winner-take-all system remains intact, the Green Party is doomed to retain the role of spoiler instead of electoral leader for environmental issues.

We don't have to quietly accept the status quo. Here are ten ways we could dramatically improve our electoral system. None is officially endorsed by the Sierra Club, but all are worthy of bipartisan consideration. Some could be implemented at county or state levels, and some are more readily achievable than others. All have the same end: to expand the franchise, and make sure that every vote is counted.

1. HAVE NONPARTISAN OFFICIALS ADMINISTER ELECTIONS. We should have learned this lesson in the 2000 presidential election, when the co-chair of Bush's Florida campaign,

Katherine Harris, also ran the election as Florida's secretary of state. For the 2004 election, it was as though Harris had cloned herself: The secretaries of state overseeing elections in the battleground states of Missouri, Ohio, and Michigan were all co-chairs of their states' Bush reelection campaigns. In Missouri, Secretary of State Matt Blunt was also running for governor, and so oversaw his own race. In the days leading up to the election in Ohio, Secretary of State Kenneth Blackwell sought to rule out (largely Democratic) voter registrations submitted on paper of the wrong weight, and to strictly limit the counting of provisional ballots. During the election, African-American precincts and other strongholds of support for John Kerry were allocated far fewer voting machines than the Republican suburbs. In the subsequent recount, Blackwell allowed different counties to handle the process according to the whim of local officials. In Florida, a highly partisan Republican secretary of state once again ran the election, as did a partisan Democrat in New Mexico.

Without nonpartisan election managers, the outcomes of elections will always be open to conflict-of-interest questions. In addition, many current election officials are ignorant of the technology of voting equipment, or even how to run elections. Election administrators should be well-trained professional civil servants who know how to make electoral processes transparent and secure.

2. ESTABLISH NATIONAL STANDARDS FOR FAIR ELECTIONS. The United States leaves the administration of elections to local officials in more than 3,000 counties. This creates different standards and practices for recounts and use of absentee and provisional ballots, as well as wide discrepancies in the quality of voting equipment. Most established democracies use national election commissions to set uniform standards, to develop secure and reliable voting equipment, and to work with state and local election officials to ensure pre- and post-election accountability. The U.S. Election

Assistance Commission, established by the Help America Vote Act of 2002, is a pale version of such an entity, and needs to be strengthened. A robust elections commission, for example, would crack down on the revolving door between state election regulators and officials and the voting equipment industry (see below).

3. DEVELOP "PUBLIC INTEREST" VOTING EQUIPMENT. The voting-equipment industry is dominated by three companies: Sequoia Voting Systems, Election Systems and Software (ES&S), and Diebold Election Systems. These companies develop their own private software and hardware that is then certified by state authorities, although the rigor of the certification procedures varies widely from state to state. Laxness is encouraged by the revolving door between state officials and the industry. New Hampshire senator John Sununu (R) and former California secretary of state Bill Jones (R) have acted as private consultants on behalf of Diebold and Sequoia, respectively. Chuck Hagel resigned as chair of Election Systems and Software's parent company, and eight months later was elected Republican senator from Nebraska, with his own former company's machines counting the votes. And Katherine Harris's predecessor as secretary of state in Florida, Sandra Mortham (R), was hired by ES&S to peddle its voting machines in the state. In Ohio, according to the *Los Angeles Times,* one vendor competing for $100 million in contracts treated election officials to free meals, limousine rides, and concert tickets. Other vendors have spent thousands of dollars on conferences for election officials, footing the bill for hospitality suites, banquets, lobster bakes, and pool parties.

Even more unsettling, the voting-machine companies openly favor the Republican Party. The executives and founders of the big three vendors have poured hundreds of thousands of dollars into party coffers in the past few years. Ciber Labs, one of the federal testing laboratories, has donated tens of thousands of dollars to the Republican National Committee and to GOP candidates. Walden O'Dell, Diebold's CEO, is a big Bush fundraiser who attended strategy powwows at the president's Crawford, Texas, ranch; he famously told Republicans in a fundraising letter that he was "committed to helping Ohio deliver its electoral votes to the president," even as his company was seeking multimillion-dollar contracts to provide computerized voting equipment in that state.

In Hocking County, Ohio, three days before the statewide recount for the 2004 presidential election was to begin in mid-December, deputy elections director Sherole Eaton went public with a troubling incident: An employee of Triad Systems, the company that owns and runs the voting equipment in 41 Ohio counties (and is another Republican donor), came into the office, modified the computer tabulator, and advised voting officials how to manipulate the machinery so that "the count would come out perfect and we wouldn't have to do a full hand recount of the county." This prompted Representative John Conyers (D-Mich.) to request an FBI investigation into illegal election tampering.

At the very least, advocates of fair elections should demand a voter-verified paper trail so that any recounts would have a chance of uncovering errors or fraud. We have such an audit trail for ATM transactions; are our votes less important? Better still would be to develop "public interest" voting equipment. Instead of the nuts and bolts of our democracy being in the hands of private companies, software code would be owned and managed by a government elections commission working in conjunction with the private sector, subject to the rules and disclosures of open government. And that voting equipment then would be deployed to rich and poor neighborhoods alike to ensure that every voter is using the same, best equipment. Publicly developed voting systems are already in place in Belgium, Brazil, and Argentina. India, which is the world's largest democracy and has twice as many voters as the United States, recently held nationwide elections, with voters from New Delhi to the Himalayas, illiterate voters and polyglot communities alike, all voting on the same computerized equipment developed by the government.

4. REGISTER EVERY CITIZEN. The United States has some 60 million potential voters who are disenfranchised because they are not registered. In most of the world's established democracies, every citizen who turns 18 is automatically registered to vote. This is known as universal voter registration. Were it implemented in the United States, it would prevent shameful shenanigans such as the Republican-paid registrars in Nevada who simply threw away the cards of those registering Democratic, and the Republican challenges to minority voters at the polls in Ohio.

Under the Help America Vote Act, all states need to establish statewide voter databases by 2006. Additional state or federal regulations could require these databases to be melded with U.S. Census Bureau databases so that anyone turning 18 is automatically registered to vote.

5. MAKE VOTING EASIER. Voting on the first Tuesday in November in the middle of a busy workweek is not a requirement of the U.S. Constitution. It's just a tradition dating from the 1840s, when President James Polk changed the date to make it easier for farmers to vote. Most other democracies vote on the weekend or make Election Day a holiday. Puerto Rico typically does so, and has a higher voter turnout than all 50 states. The commission established in the wake of the 2000 meltdown, co-chaired by Presidents Jimmy Carter and Gerald Ford, recommended that election day be a holiday, but Congress ignored their proposal.

Again, states and local governments need not wait for the feds. In odd-numbered years when only local races are on the ballot, local jurisdictions can hold elections on any day they wish. And in non-presidential election years, states can do the same, or even make Election Day a state holiday.

6. GIVE THIRD PARTIES A CHANCE. Our current plurality (that is, "highest vote-getter wins") method of electing political representatives hobbles our choices by casting third-party candidates as potential spoilers. Last year's furious battles over Ralph Nader's candidacy demonstrated that our system is not designed to accommodate more than two choices, yet important policy areas can be completely ignored by major-party candidates. This situation can be easily redressed through instant-runoff elections. In this system, voters rank candidates in terms of preference. If no candidate achieves a majority, the least popular candidate is axed, and the votes of his or her supporters go to their second choices. The method is repeated until one candidate has support from a majority of voters. Instant runoff (also known as "ranked choice") voting was successfully employed in San Francisco last November for local races, and will soon be implemented in Burlington, Vermont; Ferndale, Michigan; and Berkeley, California. With cross-partisan support, including Senator John McCain (R-Ariz.) and Democratic National Committee chair Howard Dean, legislative bills for instant runoff voting were introduced in 22 states in 2003–4, and several more are poised to address the issue this year.

7. RETHINK REDISTRICTING. Electing one district representative at a time requires periodic redrawing of lines to account for shifts in population. In many states, redistricting is a blatantly political exercise in which the ruling party manipulates the lines so as to guarantee its continued supremacy. In California, for example, Democratic congressional incumbents paid the political consultant drawing the district lines—who happened to be the brother of one of the incumbents—$20,000 apiece to manipulate the lines to give them all safe seats. Districts are traditionally redrawn every ten years, following the U.S. census. But House Majority Leader Tom Delay's brazen mid-decade redistricting in Texas—which added five Republicans to the state's delegation—raised the abuse of partisan-controlled redistricting to a new level.

America is increasingly balkanized into red and blue enclaves; Democrats dominate cities and coastlines, and Republicans rule rural areas. When combined with partisan redistricting, this has produced a travesty of choiceless elections. In 2004, 98 percent of U.S. House incumbents kept their seats; 83 percent of all 435 races were won by landslides and 95 percent by uncompetitive margins of ten points or higher. State legislative elections were even less competitive, with 40 percent of more than 7,000 seats uncontested. One solution is to have the district lines drawn by independent, nonpartisan commissions driven by criteria like keeping districts compact, respecting geographic boundaries, and enhancing competition. While this removes the blatant conflict of interest in having incumbents draw their own district lines, the track records of such "public interest" redistricting efforts in states like Washington, Iowa, Arizona, and New Jersey have not been encouraging. Most races remain noncompetitive, because regional partisan demographics trump the well-meaning efforts of the redistricting commissions.

But single-member districts are not the only way to elect representatives. Larger, multi-member districts can accommodate systems like choice voting, a ranked-ballot proportional representation system already used in local elections in Cambridge, Massachusetts, and national elections in Ireland and Australia. A state with 20 congressional seats, for example, could be divided up into 4 super-districts of 5 seats each. Voters in those districts would indicate their candidates in order of preference, ranking as many (or few) as they wished. The threshold of victory would be set to allow for only 5 winners—thus, any candidate winning 17 percent on the first round would be elected. Any further votes for that candidate would have the voters' second choices counted, and so on until five candidates pass the threshold.

An alternative system, used in more than 100 localities as well as by many corporate boards, is cumulative voting, whereby voters (also in multi-seat districts) cast as many votes as there are contested seats. Voters can give all their votes to one candidate, or split them as they see fit. Like choice voting, cumulative voting tends to foster competition, more choice for voters, better opportunities for pro-environment candidates, and a decrease in regional partisan balkanization. (A plan for a choice-voting scheme for California can be viewed at fairvote.org/pr/super/2004/california.htm.)

8. ABOLISH THE ELECTORAL COLLEGE. The Electoral College method of electing the president is an 18th-century horse-and-buggy anachronism that enables campaigns to almost completely ignore most states. It allows a shift of a handful of votes in one or two states like Ohio or Florida to decide the presidency (and therefore increases the incentives for committing fraud in those states). Senator Dianne Feinstein (D-Calif.) and Representative Jesse Jackson Jr. (D-Ill.) have both introduced constitutional amendments to abolish the electoral college and institute direct election of the president. Representative Jackson's includes a requirement that the president win with a majority of the nationwide popular vote. (If that majority were not achieved, a runoff election using a method like instant runoff voting would be required.)

Democrats already have ample reason to support such a move: After all, the Electoral College system denied Al Gore the presidency in 2000, even though he had the most votes. And in 2004, if a mere 60,000 swing voters in Ohio had changed their minds and voted for John Kerry, he would have won the presidency while losing the national popular vote by 3 million ballots. That would have made believers in direct national elections out of many Republicans.

9. MAKE VOTING A RIGHT. As American voters discovered in 2000, we have no legal right to vote directly for president. In Bush v. Gore, the Supreme Court reaffirmed that, under the Constitution, voting for president is reserved for state legislatures, who decide whether they wish to delegate it to the voters. A constitutional amendment spelling out our right to vote could guarantee the franchise to all citizens. It would

also guard against practices that can disenfranchise groups such as minority voters, prisoners, District of Columbia voters, and those using provisional ballots. Already, every returning member of the Congressional Black Caucus has signed on to Representative Jackson's legislation to provide such a constitutional right.

10. MINIMIZE MONEY'S ROLE. With political campaigns largely financed by private sources, the views of those with the most money are disproportionately heard. Public financing of elections could open up an increasingly brain-dead political debate, and widen the narrowing spectrum of political ideas. One promising new approach is mandating free airtime for candidates. Broadcast media is the greatest expense of any candidate's campaign, yet providing free airtime would cost the taxpayers nothing.

AS THE SUPREME COURT STATED over a century ago, the right to vote is "a fundamental political right, because it preserves all other rights." But it's still a right we must fight for. These ten reforms could revitalize American representative democracy in the 21st century. They will not be easy to achieve, because the party in power has little incentive to change the system that has served it so well. Cities, counties, and states will be the laboratories for new approaches, and a number of organizations are already highlighting reform packages, among them Common Cause and the Center for Voting and Democracy.

Shortly after last November's contentious presidential election in the United States, Ukraine held an equally charged contest. When the ruling party stole the election through massive fraud, tens of thousands of Ukrainians poured into the streets for weeks on end until the results were overturned. Whether we're Democrats, Republicans, Greens, or other, we need that same fighting spirit to rescue our own democracy.

---

### DISCUSSION QUESTIONS

1. Hill hopes that political reforms would lead to greater political participation and involvement by ordinary citizens? Which of his proposed reforms would be most likely to achieve this desired effect?
2. In what ways are the basic values of fairness and transparency violated by existing election practices? Which of Hill's proposed reforms would be most likely to realize these basic values?
3. Apply your skills as a political analyst to Hill's reform agenda. Think about the potential opposition to several of his proposals. What sort of strategy might prove effective in overcoming the opposition and building greater support for change?

**40** *Jared Bernstein*

# ALL TOGETHER NOW: COMMON SENSE FOR A FAIR ECONOMY

*The Introduction to Voices of Dissent was framed by a quote from the quintessential American revolutionary, Thomas Paine. "A long habit of not thinking a thing wrong, gives it the superficial appearance of being right" was his call to arms in his 1776 pamphlet Common Sense. In this, the final article of our book, culminating a chapter titled "Visions of a New Democracy," we offer you a selection from a book animated by the spirit captured in a different quote from Paine's famous pamphlet: "We have it in our power to begin the world again." Paine believed that. The American revolution depended on such a belief. And in this final article, Jared Bernstein, an economist with the Economic Policy Institute, offers his vision for a new democracy that springs from a conviction that beginning the world again is necessary and possible if we move forward with a common sense commitment to basic fairness for all. Bernstein's proposition is straightforward: our political culture is steeped in the ideology of individualism—a core value that has hardened into an extreme version of hyperindividualism that he captures in the acronym YOYO, meaning "You're on your own." Although the roots of YOYO reach back at least to 1900, the policy thrust of YOYO lies beneath virtually every conservative initiative of the past 25 years. The conservative mantra boils down to the assumption that everything public is bad, everything private is good. Government is to be feared and attacked; private business is to be praised and expanded. Against the chorus of YOYO supporters demonizing the common good, Bernstein articulates an alternative vision he calls WITT—the philosophy that "We're in this together." The WITT philosophy is collaborative in nature, using the federal government to help us achieve important public purposes. For Bernstein argues that without a renewed sense that "We're in this together," our most vexing problems—from globalization, to health care, to environmental degradation—will remain unsolved while the vast majority of our citizens watch their fortunes languish amid rising inequality. Democratic citizenship requires more from us, and the spirit of WITT is, in fact, the spirit of a fairer, healthy democracy.*

---

*Source:* Jared Bernstein, "Ready or Not, You're on Your Own." *All Together Now: Common Sense for a Fair Economy,* San Francisco: Berrett-Koehler, 2006.

# Ready or Not, You're on Your Own

I once heard an allegory about mealtime in heaven and hell. It turns out that in both places, meals are served at a huge round table with lots of delicious food in the center. The food is out of reach, but everyone's got really long forks.

In hell, everyone starves because, while people can reach the food with their forks, the forks are much longer than their arms, so nobody can turn a fork around and eat what's on the end of it.

In heaven, faced with the same problem, people eat well. How?

By feeding each other.

Protecting the rights of individuals has always been a core American value. Yet in recent years the emphasis on individualism has been pushed to the point where, like the diners in hell, we're starving. This political and social philosophy is hurting our nation, endangering our future and that of our children, and, paradoxically, making it harder for individuals to get a fair shot at the American dream.

This extreme individualism dominates the way we talk about the most important aspects of our economic lives, those that reside in the intersection of our living standards, our government, and the future opportunities for ourselves and our children. The message, sometimes implicit but often explicit, is, *You're on your own*. Its acronym, YOYO, provides useful shorthand to summarize this destructive approach to governing.

The concept of YOYO, as used in this book, isn't all that complicated. It's the prevailing vision of how our country should be governed. As such, it embodies a set of values, and at the core of the YOYO value system is hyper-individualism: the notion that whatever the challenges we face as a nation, the best way to solve them is for people to fend for themselves. Over the past few decades, this harmful vision has generated a set of policies with that hyper individualistic gene throughout their DNA.

The YOYO crowd—the politicians, lobbyists, and economists actively promoting this vision—has stepped up its efforts to advance its policies in recent years, but hyper-individualism is not a new phenomenon. I document archaeological evidence of YOYO thinking and policies from the early 1900s, along with their fingerprint: a sharp increase in the inequality of income, wealth, and opportunity. The most recent incarnation can be found in the ideas generated by the administration of George W. Bush, but the YOYO infrastructure—the personnel with a vested interest in the continued dominance of these policies—will not leave the building with Bush. Unless, that is, we recognize the damage being done and make some major changes.

One central goal of the YOYO movement is to continue and even accelerate the trend toward shifting economic risks from the government and the nation's corporations onto individuals and their families. You can see this intention beneath the surface of almost every recent conservative initiative: Social Security privatization, personal accounts for health care (the so-called Health Savings Accounts), attacks on labor market regulations, and the perpetual crusade to slash the government's revenue through regressive tax cuts—a strategy explicitly tagged as "starving the beast"—and block the government from playing a useful role in our economic lives. You can even see this go-it-alone principle in our stance toward our supposed international allies.

While this fast-moving reassignment of economic risk would be bad news in any period, it's particularly harmful today. As the new century unfolds, we face prodigious economic challenges, many of which have helped to generate both greater inequalities and a higher degree of economic insecurity in our lives. But the dominant vision has failed to develop a hopeful, positive narrative about how these challenges can be met in such a way as to uplift the majority.

Instead, messages such as "It's your money" (the mantra of the first George W. Bush campaign in 2000), and frames such as "the ownership society," stress an ever shrinking role for government and much more individual risk taking. Yet global competition, rising health costs, longer life spans with weaker pensions, less secure employment, and unprecedented inequalities of opportunity and wealth are calling for a much broader, more inclusive approach to helping all of us meet these challenges, one that taps government as well as market solutions.

To cite one potent example, 46 million people lack health coverage, and the share of our economy devoted to health care is headed for unsustainable levels. We urgently need to begin planning a viable alternative, such as a system of universal coverage as exists in every other advanced economy. In every case, these countries insure their citizens, control health costs better than we do, and have better overall health outcomes. Yet our leaders want to solve the problem with an individualistic, market-based system of private accounts designed to cut costs by shifting risk from the insurer to the patient, unleashing more of the very market forces that got us into this mess in the first place.

As I stress throughout, those crafting such policies are trapped in the YOYO paradigm, one where common-sense solutions, even those embraced by the rest of the advanced world, are out of bounds. This book has but a few central messages, but this is one of them: we simply can no longer afford to be led by people wearing ideological blinders. We must seriously investigate a new way of thinking if we are to successfully craft an equitable approach to growth, risk, and the distribution of opportunity and income.

For decades in the post-WWII era, the income of the typical family rose in lockstep with the economy's performance. As the bakers of the economic pie—the workforce—grew more productive, they benefited commensurately from their work: between the mid-1940s and the mid-1970s, both productivity and real median family income doubled.

Since the mid-1970s, however, family income has grown at one third the rate of productivity, even though families are working harder and longer than ever. Recently, the problem has grown more severe. In late 2003, we finally pulled out of the longest "jobless recovery" on record, going back to the 1930s. Our economy expanded, but we were losing jobs. Moreover, despite solid overall growth since the recession of 2001, the typical family's income has consistently fallen and poverty has gone up. The gap between the growth in productivity, which has been quite stellar, and the very flat pace at which the living standards of most families are improving has never been wider. This is a characteristic of YOYO economics: the economy does fine; the people in the economy do not.

How has this occurred, and what role do the people and politics of YOYO play? While the whole story might be made more interesting by a right-wing conspiracy, the rise of YOYO isn't one. Though conservatives have introduced recent YOYO initiatives like Social Security privatization and private accounts for health care and unemployment, this is not a story of good Democrats and bad Republicans. It is the story of the ascendancy of a largely bipartisan vision that promotes individualist market-based solutions over solutions that recognize there are big problems that markets cannot effectively solve.

We cannot, for example, constantly cut the federal government's revenue stream without undermining its ability to meet pressing social needs. We know that more resources will be needed to meet the challenges of prospering in a global economy, keeping up with technological changes, funding health care and pension systems, helping individuals balance work and family life, improving the skills of our workforce, and reducing social and economic inequality. Yet discussion of this reality is off the table.

## WE'RE IN THIS TOGETHER

We need an alternative vision, one that applauds individual freedom but emphasizes that such freedom is best realized with a more collaborative approach to meeting the challenges we face. The message is simple: *We're in this together*. Here, the acronym is *WITT*.

Though this alternative agenda uses the scope and breadth of the federal government to achieve its ends, this book is not a call for more government in the sense of devoting a larger share of our economy to government spending. In fact, there is surprisingly little relationship between the ideological agenda of those in charge and the share of the economy devoted to the federal government. To the contrary, some of the biggest spenders of federal funds have been purveyors of hyper-individualism (with G. W. Bush at the top of the list). But, regardless of what you feel the government's role should be in the economy and society, an objective look at the magnitude of the challenges we face shows we must restore the balance between individual and collective action. We simply cannot effectively address globalization, health care, pensions, economic insecurity, and fiscal train wrecks by cutting taxes, turning things over to the market, and telling our citizens they're on their own, like the gold prospectors of the 1800s, to strike it rich or bust.

*All Together Now* aims to set us on a new path. At the heart of the WITT agenda is the belief that we can wield the tools of government to build a more just society, one that preserves individualist values while ensuring that the prosperity we generate is equitably shared. Importantly, under the WITT agenda, this outcome occurs not through redistributionist Robin Hood schemes, but through creating an economic architecture that reconnects our strong, flexible economy to the living standards of all, not just to the residents of the penthouse. As the pie grows, all the bakers get bigger slices.

Where YOYO economics explains why we cannot shape our participation in the global economy to meet our own needs, or provide health coverage for the millions who lack that basic right, or raise the living standards of working families when the economy is growing, WITT policies target these challenges head on.

As YOYOism rolls on, the amplitude of our national discomfort, the vague sense that something is fundamentally wrong in how we conduct our national and international affairs is climbing. In poll after poll, solid majorities view our country as headed in the wrong direction, and there are signs that the YOYO infrastructure is not impenetrable. Though the administration may ultimately get its way, some members of Congress have unexpectedly been resisting White House demands for billions more in tax cuts for the wealthy. In a totally uncharacteristic reversal, the Bush administration was forced to reinstate the prevailing wage rule it suspended in the wake of Hurricane Katrina. In the off-year 2005 elections, a few closely watched races revealed that simply pledging to cut taxes wasn't enough. In a couple of important cases, candidates and initiatives that delivered more WITTisms than YOYOism prevailed. The climate of a few years ago has changed, and resistance is no longer futile.

A growing chorus is calling for a more balanced role of government in our lives. In the words of Iowa governor Tom Vilsack, "Government is nothing more nor less than the instrument whereby our people come together to undertake collectively the responsibilities we cannot discharge alone." If enough of us add our voices, we can reject messages like "It's your money" and "You're on your own" as divisive and counterproductive.

We can move the pendulum away from a politics that excessively focuses on individuals—the YOYO agenda toward an approach wherein we work together to craft solutions to the challenges we face. Embedded in these solutions is a healthy respect for markets and individuals. But that respect is not excessive. It does not lead us to stand idly by while the economy expands year after year as poverty rises and the real incomes of working families stagnate. Neither does it impel us to shy away from our goal: building a society where the fruits of economic growth are broadly shared with those who create that growth each day of their working lives.

## A RETURN TO COMMON SENSE

The subtitle of this book invokes *Common Sense,* the most famous work of the American revolutionary Thomas Paine. What's the connection?

It's partly, of course, the issue of whom our government represents. Paine was ready to throw off the yoke of British tyranny well before most of the nation's founders were. In this spirit, part of what follows is a common-sense critique of the United States' current situation. Hyper-individualism has held sway numerous times in our history, and a characteristic of these periods is the extent to which they favor the chosen few over the majority.

But what makes Paine so relevant today was his ability to see outside the box. While the majority of the colonists were unhappy with the Crown, most were unable to envision ending their relationship with England and seriously consider independence. *Common Sense,* which starts right off with a vitriolic personal attack on King George III, offered the colonists a radically different view of their options. Paine told the colonists that their humanity was a gift from God, not from the king. Thus, they had a responsibility to themselves and their children to construct a system of government that would free them from the constraints of the Crown to pursue their "natural rights." We can see this philosophy clearly embedded in the Declaration of Independence, where the right to life, liberty, and the pursuit of happiness was enshrined as a God-given, self-evident right of humanity.

We have drifted too far from Paine's vision. Many of us share a sense of deep discomfort and insecurity about the direction our country is taking. But there do not seem to be any signposts pointing to a better way. Why not?

It's easy to blame the lack of leadership, and there's something to that. The quality of many of our leaders does seem particularly suspect these days. Opportunists can always be found in politics, but their influence is often countered by those truly motivated to promote the public good (which is not to say that such people agree on how to do so, of course). Right now, the ratio of opportunists to idealists may be unusually high.

But the problem cuts deeper. The emphasis on individualism will always be a core American value, but it has been stressed to the breaking point. As the YOYO influence has spread, assisted by the muscular application of contemporary economics (as discussed in chapter 2), the YOYOs have implemented a philosophy of hyperindividualism that disdains using the tools of government to seek solutions. More than anything else, this policy has led to our current predicament. Under the banner of "You're on your own," we have lost a sense of common ownership of our government, an institution that many of us now distrust as feckless at best and corrupt at worst.

This abandonment of our faith in government to help meet the challenges we face—social, economic, and international—has been costly. We have shut off our critical faculties that under normal circumstances would lead us to be deeply angered by much of what's going on. Despite the events of September 11, 2001, we are less prepared for a national disaster now than we were a few years ago. Our citizens are dying in an underfunded war launched on false pretenses, and our actions have helped to unleash powerful forces that are both lethal and destabilizing. A majority of our representatives are addicted to tax cuts with no regard for their future impact. Short-sighted vested interests are at the table, constructing self-enriching energy policies instead of incentives to conserve; polluters are editing the science out of environmental protection acts.

These are front-page stories. Yet in the absence of a broadly shared vision in which we see that each one of these calamities poses a deep threat to our common fate, it's not clear how we should react. We have a vague sense that something important is off-kilter, but since the YOYOs have taken government solutions off the table, we have no means of crafting a suitable response. When the answer for every problem is a market-based solution—a private account, leavened with a tax cut for the wealthiest—we are trapped.

Clearly, we need to escape from that restrictive, cynical vision. Pursuing our collective, rather than strictly personal, interests will help. The plan I offer is straightforward: diagnose the point at which we got off course and chart the way forward.

## DISCUSSION QUESTIONS

1. Discuss the core vision of the YOYO and WITT positions. How do these positions connect with the analysis of liberal individualism offered by Bellah and his associates in Article 6? Is Bernstein against individualism?

2. Compare and contrast Bernstein's YOYO philosophy to the three aspects of the tax cut crusaders Krugman discusses in Article 33—supply-siders, starve-the-beasters and lucky duckies. Why does Bernstein think the YOYO perspective will not suffice in the future?

3. Which message—You're on your own" or "We're in the together"—makes the most political sense to you, and why? Based on his essay in Article 37, would Martin Luther King agree with you?

# RESOURCES FOR FURTHER STUDY

## MEDIA

**AlterNet**
77 Federal Street
San Francisco, CA 94107
Tel: +1-415-284-1420
http://www.alternet.org

**Common Dreams News Center**
P.O. Box 443
Portland, ME 04112-0443
Tel: +1-207-775-0488
http://www.commondreams.org

**FAIR Fairness and Accuracy in Reporting**
112 West 27th Street
New York, NY 10001
Tel: +1-212-633-6700
http://www.fair.org

**Free Press**
100 Main Street
P.O. Box 28
Northampton, MA 01061
Tel: +1-413-585-1533
http://www.freepress.net

**Independent Media Center (Washington Office)**
P.O. Box 21372
Washington, DC 20009
Tel: +1-202-452-5936
http://www.indymedia.org

**Media Access Project**
1625 K Street, N.W.
Washington, DC 20006
Tel: +1-202-232-4300
http://www.mediaaccess.org

**Progressive Media Project**
409 E. Main Street
Madison, WI 53703
Tel: +1-608-257-4626
http://www.progressive.org/
    mediaproj.htm

**Z Net**
18 Millfield Street
Woods Hole, MA 02543
Tel: +1-508-548-9063
http://www.zmag.org

## RESEARCH, POLICY, AND ADVOCACY

**Center on Budget and Policy Priorities**
820 First Street, N.E., Suite 510
Washington, DC 20002
Tel: +1-202-408-1080
http://www.cbpp.org

**Center for Defense Information**
1779 Massachusetts Avenue, N.W.
Washington, DC 20036
Tel: +1-202-332-0600
http://www.cdi.org

**Center for Responsive Politics**
1101 14th Street, N.W., Suite 1030
Washington, DC 20005-5635
Tel: +1-202-857-0044
http://www.opensecrets.org

**Center for Voting and Democracy**
6930 Carroll Avenue, Suite 601
Takoma Park, MD 20912
Tel: +1-301-270-4616
http://www.fairvote.org

**Children's Defense Fund**
25 E Street, N.W.
Washington, DC 20001
Tel: +1-202-628-8787
http://www.
    childrensdefense.org

**Citizens for Tax Justice**
1311 L Street, N.W., Suite 400
Washington, DC 20005
Tel: +1-202-626-3780
http://www.ctj.org

**Economic Policy Institute**
1660 L Street, N.W., Suite 1200
Washington, DC 20036
Tel: +1-202-775-8810
http://www.epinet.org

**Foreign Policy In Focus**
Interhemispheric Resource
    Center
P.O. Box 2178
Silver City, NM 88062
Tel: +1-505-388-0208
http://www.fpif.org

**Institute for Policy Studies
(IPS)**
733 15th Street, N.W., Suite 1020
Washington, DC 20005
Tel: +1-202-234-9382
http://www.ips-dc.org

**Physicians for a National
Health Program**
29 E. Madison Street 602
Chicago, IL 60602
Tel: +1-312-782-6007
http://www.pnhp.org/

**Public Campaign**
1320 19th Street, N.W., Suite
    M-1
Washington, DC 20036
Tel: +1-202-293-0222
http://www. publiccampaign.org

**Public Citizen (Includes:
Buyers Up, Congress Watch,
Critical Mass Energy
Project, Global Trade
Watch,Health Research
Group, Litigation Group)**

1600 20th Street, N.W.
Washington, DC 20009
Tel: +1-202-588-1000
http://www.citizen.org

**United for a Fair Economy**
37 Temple Pl., 2nd Floor
Boston, MA 02111
Tel: +1-617-423-2148
http://www.faireconomy.org

**U.S. PIRG (Public Interest
Research Groups)**
218 D Street, S.E.
Washington, DC 20003
Tel: +1-202-546-9707
http://www.uspirg.org

# PUBLICATIONS

## *Magazines*

**Defense Monitor (CDI)**
1779 Massachusetts Avenue,
    N.W.
Washington, DC 20036
Tel: +1-202-862-0700
http://www.cdi.org/dm/

**Dollars and Sense**
740 Cambridge Street
Cambridge, MA 02141
Tel: +1-617-876-2434
http://www.dollarsandsense.org

**Extra! (FAIR)**
112 West 27th Street
New York, NY 10001
Tel: +1-212-633-6700
http://www.fair.org/extra/

**In These Times**
2040 N. Milwaukee Avenue
Chicago, IL 60647
Tel: +1-773-772-0100
http://www.inthesetimes.com

**Left Business Observer**
38 Green Street, Floor 4
New York, NY 10013-2502
Tel: +1-212-219-0010
http://www.
        leftbusinessobserver.com

**Ms.**
20 Exchange Place, 22nd floor
New York, NY 10005
Tel: +1-212-509-2092
http://www.msmagazine.com

**Mother Jones**
731 Market Street, 6th Floor
San Francisco, CA 94103
Tel: +1-415-665-6637
http://www.motherjones.com

**Multinational Monitor**
P.O. Box 19405
Washington, DC 20036
Tel: +1-202-387-8030
http://www.
        multinationalmonitor.org

**Nation**
33 Irving Place
New York, NY 10003
Tel: +1-212-209-5400
http://www.thenation.com

**The Progressive**
409 East Main Street
Madison, WI 53703
Tel: +1-608-257-4626
http://www.progressive.org

**Utne Reader**
1624 Harmon Place #330
Minneapolis, MN 55403
Tel: +1-612-338-5040
http://www.utne.com

**Z Magazine**
18 Millfield Street
Woods Hole, MA 02543
Tel: +1-508-548-9063
http://www.zmag.org

## *Journals*

**Boston Review**
E53-407 MIT
Cambridge, MA 02139
Tel: +1-617-253-3642
http://bostonreview.net

**Dissent**
310 Riverside Drive,
   Suite 1201
New York, NY 10025
Tel: +1-212-316-3120
http://www.dissentmagazine.org

**Monthly Review**
122 West 27th Street, 10th floor
New York, NY 10001
Tel: +1-212-691-2555
http://www.monthlyreview.org

**New Left Review**
6 Meard Street
London W1F 0EG
United Kingdom
Tel: +44-20-7734-8830x30
http://www.newleftreview.net/

**Tom Paine.com**
Institute For America's Future
1025 Connecticut Avenue, N.W.,
   Suite 205
Washington, DC 20036
Tel:
http://www.tompaine.com

# POLITICAL PARTIES

**Green Parties of North America**
The Greens/Green Party USA
P.O. Box 1134
Lawrence, MA 01842
Tel: +1-978-682-4353
http://www.greens.org/na.html

**Labor Party (U.S.)**
P.O. Box 53177
Washington, DC 20009-3177
Tel: +1-202-234-5190
http://www.thelaborparty.org

**Northeast Action**
621 Farmington Avenue
Hartford, CT 06105
Tel: +1-860-231-2414
http://www.neaction.org

**Vermont Progressive Party**
P.O. Box 281
Montpelier, VT 05601
Tel: +1-802-229-0800
http://www.progressiveparty.org

**Working Families Party**
88 Third Avenue
Brooklyn, NY 11217
Tel: +1-718-222-3796
http://www.
   workingfamiliesparty.org

# RELATED ORGANIZATIONS

## *AIDS*

**ACT UP/New York**
332 Bleecker Street, G5
New York, NY 10014
Tel: +1-212-966-4873
http://www.actupny.org

**Community HIV/AIDS Mobilization Project (CHAMP)**
80A 4th Avenue
Brooklyn, NY 11217
Tel: +1-212-437-0254
http://www.aidsinfonyc.org/
   champ

**Health Global Access Project (GAP)**
584 Castro Street, #416
San Francisco, CA 94114
Tel: +1-415-863-4676
http://www.healthgap.org

## Civil Rights

**Rainbow/PUSH Coalition**
930 E. 50th Street
Chicago, IL 60615-2702
Tel: +1-773-373-3366
http://www.rainbowpush.org

**NAACP**
4805 Mt. Hope Drive
Baltimore, MD 21215
Tel: +1-877-NAACP-98
http://www.naacp.org

**Human Rights Campaign**
1640 Rhode Island Avenue,
N.W.
Washington, DC 20036-3278
Tel: +1-202-628-4160
http://www.hrc.org

## Environmental Organizations

**Friends of the Earth**
1717 Massachusetts Avenue,
N.W. 600
Washington, DC 20036-2002
Tel: +1-877-843-8687
http://www.foe.org

**Greenpeace**
702 H. Street, Suite 300
Washington, DC 20001
Tel: +1-202-462-1177
http://www.greenpeaceusa.org

## Labor

**AFL-CIO**
815 16th Street N.W.
Washington, DC 20006
Tel: +1-202-637-5000
http://www.aflcio.org

**Harvard Trade Union
Program**
Harvard Law School
125 Mt. Auburn Street, 3rd Floor
Cambridge, MA 02138
Tel: +1-617-495-9265
http://www.law.harvard.edu/
program

**National Labor Committee
for Worker and Human
Rights**
540 West 48th Street, 3rd Floor
New York, NY 10036
Tel: +1-212-242-3002
http://www.nlcnet.org

## Women's Organizations

**NOW (National Organiza-
tion for Women)**
733 15th Street, N.W.,
2nd Floor
Washington, DC 20005
Tel: +1-202-628-8669
http://www.now.org

# APPENDIX

## THE DECLARATION OF INDEPENDENCE
### In Congress, July 4, 1776

### The unanimous Declaration of the Thirteen United States of America

When in the Course of human events, it becomes necessary for one people to dissolve the political bands which have connected them with another, and to assume among the Powers of the earth, the separate and equal station to which the Laws of Nature and of Nature's God entitle them, a decent respect to the opinions of mankind requires that they should declare the causes which impel them to the separation.

We hold these truths to be self-evident, that all men are created equal, that they are endowed by their Creator with certain unalienable Rights, that among these are Life, Liberty and the pursuit of Happiness. That to secure these rights, Governments are instituted among Men, deriving their just powers from the consent of the governed. That whenever any Form of Government becomes destructive of these ends, it is the Right of the People to alter or to abolish it, and to institute new Government, laying its foundation on such principles and organizing its powers in such form, as to them shall seem most likely to effect their Safety and Happiness. Prudence, indeed, will dictate that Governments long established should not be changed for light and transient causes; and accordingly all experience hath shown, that mankind are more disposed to suffer, while evils are sufferable, than to right themselves by abolishing the forms to which they are accustomed. But when a long train of abuses and usurpations, pursuing invariably the same Object evinces a design to reduce them under absolute Despotism, it is their right, it is their duty, to throw off such Government, and to provide new Guards for their future security. Such has been the patient sufferance of these Colonies; and such is now the necessity which constrains them to alter their former Systems of Government. The history of the present King of Great Britain is a history of repeated injuries and usurpations, all having in direct object the establishment of an absolute Tyranny over these States. To prove this, let Facts be submitted to a candid world.

He has refused his Assent to Laws, the most wholesome and necessary for the public good.

He has forbidden his Governors to pass Laws of immediate and pressing importance, unless suspended in their operation till his Assent should be obtained; and when so suspended, he has utterly neglected to attend to them.

He has refused to pass other Laws for the accommodation of large districts of people, unless those people would relinquish the right of Representation in the Legislature, a right inestimable to them and formidable to tyrants only.

He has called together legislative bodies at places unusual, uncomfortable, and distant from the depository of their Public Records, for the sole purpose of fatiguing them into compliance with his measures.

He has dissolved Representative Houses repeatedly, for opposing with manly firmness his invasions on the rights of the people.

He has refused for a long time, after such dissolutions, to cause others to be elected; whereby the Legislative Powers, incapable of Annihilation, have returned to the People at large for their exercise; the State remaining in the meantime exposed to all the dangers of invasion from without, and convulsions within.

He has endeavoured to prevent the population of these States; for that purpose obstructing the Laws for Naturalization of Foreigners; refusing to pass others to encourage their migrations hither, and raising the conditions of new Appropriations of Lands.

He has obstructed the Administration of Justice, by refusing his Assent to Laws for establishing Judiciary Powers.

He has made Judges dependent on his Will alone, for the tenure of their offices, and the amount and payment of their salaries.

He has erected a multitude of New Offices, and sent hither swarms of Officers to harass our people; and eat out their substance.

He has kept among us, in times of peace, Standing Armies without the Consent of our legislatures.

He has affected to render the Military independent of and superior to the Civil Power.

He has combined with others to subject us to a jurisdiction foreign to our constitution, and unacknowledged by our laws; giving his Assent to their acts of pretended Legislation.

For quartering large bodies of armed troops among us.

For protecting them, by a mock Trial, from Punishment for any Murders which they should commit on the inhabitants of these States.

For cutting off our Trade with all parts of the world.

For imposing taxes on us without our Consent.

For depriving us in many cases, of the benefits of Trial of Jury.

For transporting us beyond Seas to be tried for pretended offences.

For abolishing the free System of English Laws in a neighboring Province, establishing therein an Arbitrary government, and enlarging its Boundaries so as to render it at once an example and fit instrument for introducing the same absolute rule into these Colonies.

For taking away our Charters, abolishing our most valuable Laws, and altering fundamentally the Forms of our Governments.

For suspending our own Legislatures, and declaring themselves invested with Power to legislate for us in all cases whatsoever.

He has abdicated Government here, by declaring us out of his Protection and waging War against us.

He has plundered our seas, ravaged our Coasts, burnt our towns, and destroyed the lives of our people.

He is at this time transporting large armies of foreign mercenaries to compleat the works of death, desolation and tyranny, already begun with circumstances of Cruelty & perfidy scarcely paralleled in the most barbarous ages, and totally unworthy the Head of a civilized nation.

He has constrained our fellow Citizens taken Captive on the high Seas to bear Arms against their Country, to become the executioners of their friends and Brethren, or to fall themselves by their Hands.

He has excited domestic insurrections amongst us, and has endeavoured to bring on the inhabitants of our frontiers, the merciless Indian Savages, whose known rule of warfare, is an undistinguished destruction of all ages, sexes and conditions.

In every stage of these Oppressions We have Petitioned for Redress in the most humble terms: Our repeated Petitions have been answered only by repeated injury. A Prince, whose character is thus marked by every act which may define a Tyrant, is unfit to be the ruler of a free people.

Nor have We been wanting in attentions to our British brethren. We have warned them from time to time of attempts by their legislature to extend an unwarrantable jurisdiction over us. We have reminded them of the circumstances of our emigration and settlement here. We have appealed to their native justice and magnanimity, and we have conjured them by the ties of our common kindred to disavow these usurpations which, would inevitably interrupt our connections and correspondence. They too have been deaf to the voice of justice and of consanguinity. We must, therefore, acquiesce in the necessity, which denounces our Separation, and hold them, as we hold the rest of mankind, Enemies in War, in Peace Friends.

We, therefore, the Representatives of the United States of America, in General Congress, Assembled, appealing to the Supreme Judge of the world for the rectitude of our intentions, do, in the Name, and by authority of the good People of these Colonies, solemnly publish and declare, that these United Colonies are, and of Right ought to be Free and Independent States; that they are Absolved from all Allegiance to the British Crown, and that all political connection between them and the State of Great Britain, is and ought to be totally dissolved; and that as Free and Independent States, they have full power to levy War, conclude Peace, contract Alliances, establish Commerce, and to do all other Acts and Things which Independent States may of right do. And for the support of this Declaration, with a firm reliance on the Protection of Divine Providence, we mutually pledge to each other our Lives, our Fortunes and our sacred Honor.

# THE CONSTITUTION OF THE UNITED STATES

WE THE PEOPLE OF THE UNITED STATES, IN ORDER TO FORM A MORE PERFECT UNION, ESTABLISH JUSTICE, INSURE DOMESTIC TRANQUILITY, PROVIDE FOR THE COMMON DEFENSE, PROMOTE THE GENERAL WELFARE, AND SECURE THE BLESSINGS OF LIBERTY TO OURSELVES AND OUR POSTERITY, DO ORDAIN AND ESTABLISH THIS CONSTITUTION FOR THE UNITED STATES OF AMERICA.

## ARTICLE I

**Section 1.**    All legislative Powers herein granted shall be vested in a Congress of the United States, which shall consist of a Senate and House of Representatives.

**Section 2.**    The House of Representatives shall be composed of members chosen every second Year by the People of the several States, and the Electors in each State shall have the Qualifications requisite for Electors of the most numerous Branch of the State Legislature.

No person shall be a representative who shall not have attained to the Age of twenty five Years, and been seven Years a Citizen of the United States, and who shall not, when elected, be an Inhabitant of that State in which he shall be chosen.

Representatives and direct Taxes shall be apportioned among the several States which may be included within this union, according to their respective Numbers, which shall be determined by adding to the whole Number of free Persons, including those bound to Service for a Term of Years, and excluding Indians not taxed, three fifths of all other Persons. The actual Enumeration shall be made within three Years after the first Meeting of the Congress of the United States, and within every subsequent Term of ten Years, in such Manner as they shall by Law direct. The Number of Representatives shall not exceed one for every thirty Thousand, but each State shall have at Least one Representative; and until such enumeration shall be made, the State of New Hampshire shall be entitled to chuse three, Massachusetts eight, Rhode-Island and Providence Plantations one, Connecticut five, New York six, New Jersey four, Pennsylvania eight, Delaware one, Maryland six, Virginia ten, North Carolina five, South Carolina five, and Georgia three.

When vacancies happen in the Representation from any State, the Executive Authority thereof shall issue Writs of Election to fill such Vacancies.

The House of Representatives shall chuse their speaker and other Officers; and shall have the sole Power of Impeachment.

**Section 3.**    The Senate of the United States shall be composed of two Senators from each State, chosen by the Legislature thereof, for six Years; and each Senator shall have one Vote.

Immediately after they shall be assembled in Consequence of the first Election, they shall be divided as equally as may be into three Classes. The Seats of the Senators of the first Class shall be vacated at the Expiration of the second Year, of the second Class at the Expiration of the fourth Year, and of the third Class at the Expiration of the sixth Year, so that one third may be chosen every second Year; and if Vacancies happen by Resignation, or otherwise, during the Recess of the Legislature of any State, the Executive thereof may take temporary Appointments until the next Meeting of the Legislature, which shall then fill such Vacancies.

No Person shall be a Senator who shall not have attained to the Age of thirty Years, and been nine Years a Citizen of the United States, and who shall not, when elected, be an Inhabitant of that State for which he shall be chosen.

The Vice President of the United States shall be President of the Senate, but shall have no Vote, unless they be equally divided.

The Senate shall chuse their other Officers, and also a President pro tempore, in the Absence of the Vice President, or when he shall exercise the Office of the President of the United States.

The Senate shall have the sole Power to try all Impeachments. When sitting for that Purpose, they shall be on Oath of Affirmation. When the President of the United States is tried, the Chief Justice shall preside: And no Person shall be convicted without the Concurrence of two thirds of the Members present.

Judgment in Cases of Impeachment shall not extend further than to removal from Office, and disqualification to hold and enjoy any Office of honor, Trust or Profit under the United States: but the Party convicted shall nevertheless be liable and subject to Indictment, Trial, Judgment and Punishment, according to law.

**Section 4.**    The Times, Places and Manner of holding Elections for Senators and Representatives, shall be prescribed in each State by the Legislature thereof; but the Congress may at any time by Law make or alter such regulations, except as to the Places of chusing Senators.

The Congress shall assemble at least once in every Year, and such Meeting shall be on the first Monday in December, unless they shall by Law appoint a different Day.

**Section 5.**    Each House shall be the Judge of the Elections, Returns and Qualifications of its own Members, and a Majority of each shall constitute a Quorum to do Business; but a smaller Number may adjourn from day to day, and may be authorized to compel the Attendance of absent Members, in such Manner, and under such Penalties as each House may provide

Each House may determine the Rules for its Proceedings, punish its Members for disorderly Behaviour, and, with the Concurrence of two thirds, expel a Member.

Each House shall keep a Journal of its Proceedings, and from time to time publish the same, excepting such Parts as may in their Judgment require Secrecy; and the Yeas and Nays of the Members of either House on any question shall, at the Desire of one fifth of those Present, be entered on the Journal.

Neither House, during the Session of Congress, shall, without the Consent of the other, adjourn for more than three days, nor to any other Place than that in which the two Houses shall be sitting.

**Section 6.**    The Senators and Representatives shall receive a Compensation for their Services, to be ascertained by Law, and paid out of the Treasury of the United States. They shall in all Cases, except Treason, Felony and Breach of the Peace, be privileged from Arrest during their Attendance at the Session of their respective Houses, and in going to and returning from the same; and for any Speech or Debate in either House, they shall not be questioned in any other Place.

No Senator or Representative shall, during the Time for which he was elected, be appointed to any civil Office under the Authority of the United States, which shall have been created, or the Emoluments whereof shall have been encreased during such time; and no Person holding any Office under the United States, shall be a Member of either House during his Continuance in Office.

**Section 7.**    All Bills for raising Revenue shall originate in the House of Representatives; but the Senate may propose or concur with Amendments as on other Bills.

Every Bill which shall have passed the House of Representatives and the Senate, shall, before it become a Law, be presented to the President of the United States; If he approve he shall sign it, but if not he shall return it, with his Objections to that House in which it shall have originated, who shall enter the Objections at large on their Journal, and proceed to reconsider it. If after such Reconsideration two thirds of that House shall agree to pass the Bill, it shall be sent, together with the Objections, to the other House, by which it shall likewise be reconsidered, and if approved by two thirds of that House, it shall become a Law. But in all such Cases the Votes of both Houses shall be determined by Yeas and Nays, and the Names of the Persons voting for and against the Bill shall be entered on the Journal of each House respectively. If any Bill shall not be returned by the president within ten Days (Sundays excepted) after it shall have been presented to him, the Same shall be a Law, in like Manner as if he had signed it, unless the Congress by their Adjournment prevent its Return, in which Case it shall not be a Law.

Every Order, Resolution, or Vote to which the Concurrence of the Senate and House of Representatives may be necessary (except on a question of Adjournment) shall be presented to the President of the United States; and before the Same shall take Effect, shall be approved by him, or being disapproved by him, shall be repassed by two thirds of the Senate and House of Representatives, according to the Rules and Limitations prescribed in the Case of a Bill.

**Section 8.** The Congress shall have Power To lay and collect Taxes, Duties, Imposts and Excises, to pay the Debts and provide for the common Defence and general Welfare of the United States; but all Duties, Imposts and Excises shall be uniform throughout the United States;

To borrow Money on the credit of the United States;

To regulate Commerce with foreign Nations, and among the several States, and with the Indian Tribes;

To establish an uniform Rule of Naturalization, and uniform Laws on the subject of Bankruptcies throughout the United States;

To coin Money, regulate the Value thereof, and of foreign Coin, and fix the Standard of Weights and Measures;

To provide for the Punishment of counterfeiting the Securities and current Coin of the United States;

To establish Post Offices and post Roads;

To promote the Progress of Science and useful Arts, by securing for limited Times to Authors and Inventors the exclusive Right to their respective Writings and Discoveries;

To constitute Tribunals inferior to the supreme Court;

To define and punish Piracies and Felonies committed on the high Seas, and Offences against the Law of Nations;

To declare War, grant Letters of Marque and Reprisal, and make Rules concerning Captures on Land and Water;

To raise and support Armies, but no Appropriation of Money to that Use shall be for a longer Term than two Years;

To provide and maintain a Navy;

To make Rules for the Government and Regulation of the land and naval Forces;

To provide for calling forth the Militia to execute the Laws of the Union, suppress Insurrections and repel Invasions;

To provide for organizing, arming, and disciplining, the Militia, and for governing such Part of them as may be employed in the Service of the United States, reserving to the States respectively, the Appointment of the Officers, and the Authority of training the Militia according to the discipline prescribed by Congress;

To exercise exclusive Legislation in all Cases whatsoever, over such District (not exceeding ten Miles square) as may, by Cession of particular States, and the Acceptance of Congress, become the Seat of the Government of the United States, and to exercise like Authority over all Places purchased by the Consent of the Legislature of the State in which the Same shall be for the Erection of Forts, Magazines, Arsenals, dock-Yards, and other needful Buildings; and

To make all Laws which shall be necessary and proper for carrying into Execution the foregoing Powers, and all other Powers vested by this Constitution in the Government of the United States, or in any Department or Officer thereof.

**Section 9.** The Migration or Importation of such Persons as any of the States now existing shall think proper to admit, shall not be prohibited by the Congress prior to the Year one thousand eight hundred and eight, but a Tax or duty may be imposed on such Importation, not exceeding ten dollars for each Person.

The Privilege of the Writ of Habeas Corpus shall not be suspended, unless when in Cases of Rebellion or Invasion the public Safety may require it.

No Bill of Attainder or ex post facto Law shall be passed.

No Capitation, or other direct, Tax shall be laid, unless in Proportion to the Census or Enumeration herein before directed to be taken.

No Tax or Duty shall be laid on Articles exported from any State.

No Preference shall be given by any Regulation of Commerce or Revenue to the Ports of one State over those of another: nor shall Vessels bound to, or from, one State be obliged to enter, clear, or pay Duties in another.

No money shall be drawn from the Treasury, but in Consequence of Appropriations made by Law; and a regular Statement and Account of the Receipts and Expenditures of all public Money shall be published from time to time.

No Title of Nobility shall be granted by the United States: And no Person holding any office of Profit or Trust under them, shall, without the Consent of the Congress, accept of any present, Emolument, Office, or Title, of any kind whatever, from any King, Prince, or foreign States.

**Section 10.**   No State shall enter into any Treaty, Alliance, or Confederation; grant Letters of Marque and Treaty; Alliance, or Confederation; grant Letters of Marque and Reprisal; coin Money; emit Bills of Credit; make any Thing but gold and silver Coin a Tender in Payment of Debts; pass any Bill of Attainder, ex post facto Law, or Law impairing the Obligation of Contracts, or grant any Title of Nobility.

No State shall, without the Consent of the Congress, lay any Imposts or Duties on Imports or Exports, except what may be absolutely necessary for executing its inspection Laws: and the net Produce of all Duties and Imposts, laid by any State on Imports and Exports, shall be for the Use of the Treasury of the United States; and all such Laws shall be subject to Revision and Control of the Congress.

No State shall, without the Consent of Congress, lay any Duty of Tonnage, keep Troops, or Ships of War in time of Peace, enter into any Agreement or Compact with another State, or with a foreign Power, or engage in War, unless actually invaded, or in such imminent Danger as will not admit of delay.

## ARTICLE II

**Section 1.**   The executive Power shall be vested in a President of the United States of America. He shall hold his Office during the Term of four Years, and, together with the Vice President, chosen for the same term, be elected, as follows

Each State shall appoint, in such Manner as the Legislature thereof may direct, a Number of Electors, equal to the whole Number of Senators and Representatives to which the State may be entitled in the Congress: but no Senator or Representative, or Person holding an office of Trust or Profit under the United States, shall be appointed an Elector.

The Electors shall meet in their respective States, and vote by Ballot for two Persons, of whom one at least shall not be an Inhabitant of the same State with themselves. And they shall make a List of all the Persons voted for, and of the Number of Votes for each; which List they shall sign and certify, and transmit sealed to the Seat of the Government of the United States, directed to the President of the Senate. The President of the Senate shall, in the Presence of the Senate and House of Representatives, open all the Certificates, and the Votes shall then be counted. The Person having the greatest Number of Votes shall be the President, if such Number be a Majority of the whole Number of Electors appointed; and if there be more than one who have such Majority, and have an equal Number of Votes, then the House of Representatives shall immediately chuse by Ballot one of them for President: and if no Person have a Majority, then from the five highest on the List the said House shall in like Manner chuse the President. But in chusing the President, the Votes shall be taken by States, the Representation from each State having one Vote; A quorum for this Purpose shall consist of a Member or Members from two thirds of the States, and a Majority of all the States shall be necessary to a Choice. In every Case, after the Choice of the President, the Person having the greatest Number of Votes of the Electors shall be the Vice President. But if there should remain two or more who have equal Votes, the Senate shall chuse from them by Ballot the Vice President.

The Congress may determine the Time of chusing the Electors and the Day on which they shall give their Votes; which Day shall be the same throughout the United States.

No Person except a natural born Citizen, or a Citizen of the United States, at the time of the Adoption of this Constitution, shall be eligible to the Office of President; neither shall any person be eligible to that Office who shall not have attained to the Age of thirty five Years, and been fourteen Years a Resident within the United States.

In case of the Removal of the President from Office, or of his Death, Resignation, or Inability to discharge the Powers and Duties of the said Office, the Same shall devolve on the Vice President, and the Congress may by Law provide for the Case of Removal, Death, Resignation or Inability, both of the President and Vice President, declaring what Officer shall then act as President, and such Officer shall act accordingly, until the Disability be removed, or a President shall be elected.

The President shall, at stated Times, receive for his Services a Compensation, which shall neither be encreased nor diminished during the Period for which he shall have been elected, and he shall not receive within that Period any other Emolument from the United States, or any of them.

Before he enter on the Execution of his Office, he shall take the following Oath or Affirmation:- "I do solemnly swear (or affirm) that I will faithfully execute the Office of President of the United States, and will to the best of my Ability, preserve, protect and defend the Constitution of the United States."

**Section 2.** The President shall be Commander in Chief of the Army and Navy of the United States, and of the Militia of the several States, when called into the actual Service of the United States; he may require the Opinion, in writing, of the principal Officer in each of the executive Departments, upon any Subject relating to the Duties of their respective Offices, and he shall have power to grant Reprieves and Pardons for Offences against the United States, except in Cases of Impeachment.

He shall have Power, by and with the Advice and Consent of the Senate, to make Treaties, provided two thirds of the Senators present concur; and he shall nominate, and by and with the Advice and Consent of the Senate, shall appoint Ambassadors, other public Ministers and Consuls, Judges of the supreme Court, and all other Officers of the United States, whose Appointments are not herein otherwise provided for, and which shall be established by Law; but the Congress may by Law vest the Appointment of such inferior officers, as they think proper, in the President alone, in the Courts of Law, or in the Heads of Departments.

The President shall have Power to fill up all Vacancies that may happen during the Recess of the Senate, by granting Commissions which shall expire at the end of their next Session.

**Section 3.** He shall from time to time give to the Congress Information of the State of the Union, and recommend to their Consideration such Measures as he shall judge necessary and expedient; he may, on extraordinary Occasions, convene both Houses, or either of them, and in Case of Disagreement between them, with Respect to the Time of Adjournment, he may adjourn them to such Time as he shall think proper; he shall receive Ambassadors and other public Ministers; he shall take Care that the Laws be faithfully executed, and shall Commission all of the officers of the United States.

**Section 4.** The President, Vice President and all civil Officers of the United States, shall be removed from Office on Impeachment for, and Conviction of, Treason, Bribery, or other High Crimes and Misdemeanors.

## ARTICLE III

**Section 1.** The judicial Power of the United States, shall be vested in one supreme Court, and in such inferior Courts as the Congress may from time to time ordain and establish. The Judges, both of the supreme and inferior Courts, shall hold their offices during good Behaviour, and shall, at stated Times, receive for their Services, a Compensation, which shall not be diminished during their Continuance in Office.

**Section 2.** The judicial Power shall extend to all Cases, in Law and Equity, arising under this Constitution, the Laws of the United States, and Treaties made, or which shall be made, under their Authority; to all Cases affecting Ambassadors, other public Ministers and Consuls; to all Cases of admiralty and maritime Jurisdiction; to Controversies to which the United States shall be a party; to

Controversies between two or more States; between a State and Citizens of another State; between Citizens of different States; between Citizens of the same State claiming Lands under Grants of different States, and between a State, or the Citizens thereof, and foreign States, Citizens or Subjects.

In all Cases affecting Ambassadors, other public Ministers and Consols, and those in which a State shall be Party, the supreme Court shall have original Jurisdiction. In all the other Cases before mentioned, the supreme Court shall have appellate Jurisdiction, both as to Law and Fact, with such Exceptions, and under such Regulations as the Congress shall make.

The Trial of all Crimes, except in Cases of Impeachment, shall be by Jury; and such Trial shall be held in the State where the said Crimes shall have been committed; but when not committed within any State, the Trial shall be at such Place or Places as the Congress may by Law have directed.

**Section 3.**   Treason against the United States, shall consist only in levying War against them, or in adhering to their Enemies, giving them Aid and Comfort. No Person shall be convicted of Treason unless on the Testimony of two Witnesses to the same overt Act, or on Confession in open Court.

The Congress shall have Power to declare the Punishment of Treason, but no Attainder of Treason shall work Corruption of Blood, or Forfeiture except during the Life of the Person attainted.

## ARTICLE IV

**Section 1.**   Full Faith and Credit shall be given in each State to the public Acts, Records, and judicial Proceedings of every State. And the Congress may by general Laws prescribe the Manner in which such Acts, Records, and Proceedings shall be proved, and the Effect thereof.

**Section 2.**   The Citizens of each State shall be entitled to all Privileges and Immunities of Citizens in the several States.

A Person charged in any State with Treason, Felony, or other Crime, who shall flee from Justice, and be found in another State, shall on Demand of the executive Authority of the State from which he fled, be delivered up, to be removed to the State having Jurisdiction of the Crime.

No Person held to Service or Labour in one State, under the Laws thereof, escaping into another, shall, in Consequence of any Law or Regulation therein, be discharged from such Service or Labour, but shall be delivered up on Claim of the Party to whom such Service or Labour may be due.

**Section 3.**   New States may be admitted by the Congress into this Union; but no new State shall be formed or erected within the Jurisdiction of any other State; nor any State be formed by the Junction of two or more States, or Parts of States, without the Consent of the Legislatures of the States concerned as well as of the Congress.

The Congress shall have Power to dispose of and make all needful Rules and Regulations respecting the Territory or other Property belonging to the United States; and nothing in this Constitution shall be so construed as to Prejudice any Claims of the United States, or of any particular State.

**Section 4.**   The United States shall guarantee to every State in this Union a Republican Form of Government, and shall protect each of them against Invasion; and on Application of the Legislature, or of the Executive (when the Legislature cannot be convened) against domestic Violence.

## ARTICLE V

The Congress, whenever two thirds of both Houses shall deem it necessary, shall propose Amendments to this Constitution, or, on the Application of the Legislatures of two thirds of the several States, shall call a Convention for proposing Amendments, which, in either Case, shall be valid to all Intents and Purposes, as Part of this Constitution, when ratified by the Legislatures of three fourths of the several States, or by Conventions in three fourths thereof, as the one or the other Mode of Ratification may be proposed by the Congress; Provided that no Amendment which may be made prior to the Year One thousand eight hundred and eight shall in any Manner affect the first and fourth Clauses in the Ninth Section of the first Article; and that no State, without its Consent, shall be deprived of its equal Suffrage in the Senate.

## ARTICLE VI

All Debts contracted and Engagements entered into, before the Adoption of this Constitution, shall be as valid against the United States under this Constitution, as under the Confederation.

This Constitution, and the Laws of the United States which shall be made in Pursuance thereof; and all Treaties made, or which shall be made, under the Authority of the United States, shall be the supreme Law of the Land; and the Judges in every State shall be bound thereby, any Thing in the Constitution of Laws of any State to the Contrary notwithstanding.

The Senators and Representatives before mentioned, and the Members of the several State Legislatures, and all executive and judicial Officers, both of the United States and of the several States, shall be bound by Oath or Affirmation, to support this Constitution; but no religious Test shall ever be required as a Qualification to any Office or public Trust under the United States.

## ARTICLE VII

The Ratification of the Conventions of nine States shall be sufficient for the Establishment of this Constitution between the States so ratifying the Same.

Done in Convention by the Unanimous Consent of the States present the Seventeenth Day of September in the Year of our Lord one thousand seven hundred and Eighty seven and of the Independence of the United States of America the Twelfth. In witness whereof We have hereunto subscribed our Names.

[The first 10 Amendments were ratified December 5, 1791, and form what is known as the Bill of Rights.]

## AMENDMENT 1

Congress shall make no law respecting an establishment of religion, or prohibiting the free exercise thereof; or abridging the freedom of speech, or of the press; or the right of the people peaceably to assemble, and to petition the Government for a redress of grievances.

## AMENDMENT 2

A well regulated Militia, being necessary to the security of a free State, the right of the people to keep and bear Arms, shall not be infringed.

## AMENDMENT 3

No Soldier shall, in time of peace be quartered in any house, without the consent of the Owner, nor in time of war, but in a manner to be prescribed by Law.

## AMENDMENT 4

The right of the people to be secure in their persons, houses, papers, and effects, against unreasonable searches and seizures, shall not be violated, and no Warrants shall issue, but upon probable cause, supported by Oath or affirmation, and particularly describing the place to be searched and the persons or things to be seized.

## AMENDMENT 5

No person shall be held to answer for a capital, or otherwise infamous crime, unless on a presentment or indictment of a Grand Jury, except in cases arising in the land or naval forces, or in the Militia, when in actual service in time of War or public danger; nor shall any person be subject for the same offence to be twice put in jeopardy of life or limb; nor shall be compelled in any criminal case to be a witness against himself, nor be deprived of life, liberty, or property, without due process of law; nor shall private property be taken for public use, without just compensation.

## AMENDMENT 6

In all criminal prosecutions, the accused shall enjoy the right to a speedy and public trial, by an impartial jury of the State and district wherein the crime shall have been committed, which district shall have been previously ascertained by law, and to be informed of the nature and cause of the accusation; to be confronted with the witnesses against him; to have compulsory process for obtaining witnesses in his favor, and to have the Assistance of Counsel for his defense.

## AMENDMENT 7

In Suits at common law, where the value in controversy shall exceed twenty dollars, the right of trial by jury shall be preserved, and no fact tried by a jury, shall be otherwise reexamined in any Court of the United States, than according to the rules of the common law.

## AMENDMENT 8

Excessive bail shall not be required, nor excessive fines imposed, nor cruel and unusual punishments inflicted.

## AMENDMENT 9

The enumeration in the Constitution, of certain rights, shall not be construed to deny or disparage others retained by the people.

## AMENDMENT 10

The powers not delegated to the United States by the Constitution, nor prohibited by it to the States, are reserved to the States respectively, or to the people.

## AMENDMENT 11
### [Ratified February 7, 1795]

The Judicial power of the United States shall not be construed to extend to any suit in law or equity, commenced or prosecuted against one of the United States by Citizens of another State, or by Citizens or Subjects of any Foreign State.

## AMENDMENT 12
### [Ratified July 27, 1804]

The Electors shall meet in their respective states and vote by ballot for President and Vice-President, one of whom, at least, shall not be an inhabitant of the same state with themselves; they shall name in their ballots the person voted for as President, and in distinct ballots the person voted for as Vice-President, and they shall make distinct lists of all persons voted for as President, and of all persons voted for as Vice-President, and of the number of votes for each, which lists they shall sign and certify, and transmit sealed to the seat of the government of the United States, directed to the President of the Senate; The President of the Senate shall, in the presence of the Senate and House of Representatives, open all the certificates and the votes shall then be counted; The person having the greatest number of votes for President, shall be the President, if such number be a majority of the whole number of Electors appointed; and if no person have such majority, then from the persons having the highest numbers not exceeding three in the list of those voted for as President, the House of Representatives shall choose immediately by ballot, the President. But in choosing the President, the votes shall be taken by states, the representation from each state having one vote; a quorum for this purpose shall consist of a member or members from two-thirds of the states, and a majority of all the states shall be necessary to a choice. And if the House of Representatives shall not choose a President whenever the right of choice shall devolve upon them, before the fourth day of March next following, the Vice-President shall act as President, as in the case of the death or other constitutional disability of the President. The person having the greatest number of votes as Vice-President, shall be the Vice-President, if such number be a majority of the whole number of Electors appointed, and if no person have a majority, then from the two highest numbers on the list, the Senate shall choose the Vice-President; a quorum for the purpose shall consist of two-thirds of the whole number of Senators, and a majority of the whole number shall be necessary to a choice. But no person constitutionally ineligible to the office of President shall be eligible to that of Vice-President of the United States.

## AMENDMENT 13
### [Ratified December 6, 1865]
**Section 1.**    Neither slavery nor involuntary servitude, except as a punishment for crime whereof the party shall have been duly convicted, shall exist within the United States, or any place subject to their jurisdiction.

**Section 2.**    Congress shall have the power to enforce this article by appropriate legislation.

## AMENDMENT 14
### [Ratified July 9, 1868]
**Section 1.**    All persons born or naturalized in the United States, and subject to the jurisdiction thereof, are citizens of the United States and of the State wherein they reside. No State shall make or enforce any law which shall abridge the privileges or immunities of citizens of the United States; nor shall any State deprive any person of life, liberty, or property, without due process of law; nor deny to any person within its jurisdiction the equal protection of the laws.

**Section 2.**    Representatives shall be appointed among the several States according to their respective numbers, counting the whole number of persons in each State, excluding Indians not taxed. But when the right to vote at any election for the choice of electors for President and Vice President of the United States, Representatives in Congress, the Executive and Judicial Officers of a State, or the members of the Legislature thereof, is denied to any of the male inhabitants of such State, being twenty-one years of age, and citizens of the United States, or in any way abridged, except for participation in rebellion, or other crime, the basis of representation therein shall be reduced in the proportion which the number of such male citizens shall bear to the whole number of male citizens twenty-one years of age in such State.

**Section 3.**    No person shall be a Senator or Representative in Congress, or elector of President and Vice President, or hold any office, civil or military, under the United States, or under any State, who, having previously taken an oath, as a member of Congress, or as an officer of the United States, or as a member of any State legislature, or as an executive or judicial officer of any State, to support the Constitution of the United States shall have engaged in insurrection or rebellion against the same, or given aid or comfort to the enemies thereof. But Congress may by a vote of two-thirds of each House, remove such disability.

**Section 4.**    The validity of the public debt of the United States, authorized by law, including debts incurred for payment of pensions and bounties for services in suppressing insurrection or rebellion, shall not be questioned. But neither the United States nor any State shall assume or pay any debt or obligation incurred in aid of insurrection or rebellion against the United States, or any claim for the loss or emancipation of any slave; but all such debts, obligations and claims shall be held illegal and void.

**Section 5.**    The Congress shall have power to enforce, by appropriate legislation, the provisions of this article.

## AMENDMENT 15
### [Ratified February 3, 1870]
**Section 1.**    The right of citizens of the United States to vote shall not be denied or abridged by the United States or by any State on account of race, color, or previous condition of servitude.

**Section 2.**    The Congress shall have power to enforce this article by appropriate legislation.

## AMENDMENT 16
### [Ratified February 3, 1913]
The Congress shall have power to lay and collect taxes on incomes, from whatever source derived, without apportionment among the several States, and without regard to any census or enumeration.

## AMENDMENT 17
### [Ratified April 8, 1913]
The Senate of the United States shall be composed of two Senators from each State, elected by the people thereof for six years; and each Senator shall have one vote. The electors in each state shall have the qualification requisite for electors of the most numerous branch of the State legislatures.

When vacancies happen in the representation of any State in the Senate, the executive authority of such State shall issue writs of election to fill such vacancies; *Provided,* That the legislature of any State may empower the executive thereof to make temporary appointments until the people fill the vacancies by election as the legislature may direct.

This amendment shall not be so construed as to affect the election or term of any Senator chosen before it becomes valid as part of the Constitution.

## AMENDMENT 18
### [Ratified January 16, 1919]
**Section 1.**    After one year from the ratification of this article the manufacture, sale, or transportation of intoxicating liquors within, the importation thereof into, or the exportation thereof from the United States and all territory subject to the jurisdiction thereof for beverage purposes is hereby prohibited.

**Section 2.**    The Congress and the several States shall have concurrent power to enforce this article by appropriate legislation.

**Section 3.**    This article shall be inoperative unless it shall have been ratified as an amendment to the Constitution by the legislatures of the several States, as provided in the Constitution, within seven years from the date of the submission hereof to the State by the Congress.

## AMENDMENT 19
### [Ratified August 18, 1920]
The right of citizens of the United States to vote shall not be denied or abridged by the United States or by any State on account of sex. Congress shall have the power to enforce this article by appropriate legislation.

## AMENDMENT 20
### [Ratified January 23, 1933]
**Section 1.**    The terms of the President and Vice President shall end at noon on the 20th day of January, and the terms of Senators and Representatives at noon on the 3rd day of January, of the years in which such terms would have ended if this article had not been ratified; and the terms of their successors shall then begin.

**Section 2.**    The Congress shall assemble at least once in every year, and such meeting shall begin at noon on the 3d day of January, unless they shall by law appoint a different day.

**Section 3.**    If, at the time fixed for the beginning of the term of the President, the President elect shall have died, the Vice President elect shall become President. If a President shall not have been chosen before the time fixed for the beginning of his term, or if the President elect shall have failed to qualify, then the Vice President elect shall act as President until a President shall have qualified; and the Congress may by law provide for the case wherein neither a President elect nor a Vice President elect shall have qualified, declaring who shall then act as President, or the manner in which